Introduction to
ESTATE
PLANNING

The Irwin Series in Financial Planning and Insurance
Consulting Editor   Jerry S. Rosenbloom   University of Pennsylvania

Introduction to
ESTATE
PLANNING

Second Edition

Chris J. Prestopino, M.B.A. (Tax), Ph.D.
Professor of Finance
California State University–Chico

1989

Homewood, IL 60430
Boston, MA 02116

To my students, whose interest, involvement, and encouragement have been an ongoing inspiration

A professional edition of this book is available through Dow Jones-Irwin.

© RICHARD D. IRWIN, INC., 1987 and 1989

Acquisitions editor: Lawrence E. Alexander
Project editor: Waivah Clement
Production manager: Bette Ittersagen
Compositor: Compset Inc.
Typeface: 11/13 Times Roman
Printer: Arcata Graphics/Kingsport

Library of Congress Cataloging-in-Publication Data

Prestopino, Chris J.
    Introduction to estate planning.

    Bibliography: p.
    Includes index.
        1. Estate planning—United States.   I. Title.
KF750.P74   1989   346.7305′2   88–11909
ISBN 0-256-06955-7 (pbk.)   347.30652

Printed in the United States of America

1 2 3 4 5 6 7 8 9 0 K 5 4 3 2 1 0 9 8

Preface

My interest in writing *Introduction to Estate Planning* began in 1974, after my first unsuccessful search for a textbook. For the next eight years, each time I taught estate planning in the undergraduate or graduate business curriculum, I had to settle on a book not designed primarily for the student. My options always seemed to be limited to three types of publications: simple primers intended exclusively for the lay reader; technical references, often encyclopedic in structure and content, best suited to supplement the knowledge of the informed professional; and complex treatises written for the third-year law student.

Introduction to Estate Planning, first published in 1987, offers a new alternative, one having both a different format and a different intended reader. It is a textbook, designed primarily to be used in an academic program. Its concepts are introduced logically rather than encyclopedically; as the reader's knowledge grows, more advanced principles are covered. The text has been thoroughly classroom tested.

Introduction to Estate Planning also has a different intended reader. It is principally designed to be read by the professional or student pursuing a career in financial services or law in which estate planning is but one of several principal areas of practice. Applicable careers include financial planning, insurance sales, accounting, banking, trust management, paralegal work, investment brokerage and management, and real estate. And although the text does not have quite the depth required of an advanced law school course in estate planning, it can furnish the third-year law student with a succinct but technical overview of the subject's main concepts and techniques.

The book is divided into three parts. The first two sections present the basic language and the legal constraints in planning, including the underlying tax and nontax law which serve as the basis for planning. The third and largest part surveys the major estate planning strategies used by practitioners. This sequential approach aids learning because estate planning techniques presuppose a familiarity with many fundamental legal concepts. It also minimizes repetition; concepts need be repeated and redefined far less frequently.

Introduction to Estate Planning presents a concise, integrated overview of the subject. Its exposition is designed to highlight the essence of a concept without confusing the reader with every technical qualification and reference, a problem which has impaired the readability of many books in the field. For example, the text explicitly refers only to those case names and code section numbers that have attained the status of common industry jargon. Nonetheless, the book's content is comprehensive. For example, it is quantitatively oriented, frequently demonstrating the numerical consequences of planning (and failure to plan) on family wealth. Few writers in the field today regularly integrate quantitative analysis into their exposition.

Many pedagogical devices are used to aid comprehension. For example, each chapter contains an outline, end-of-chapter questions and problems, and an extensive list of recommended readings. Numerous specific examples are included in each chapter to clarify more difficult concepts. Appendixes include a glossary, tax and valuation tables, as well as a number of relevant sections of the Internal Revenue Code. And to stress the typical reader's perspective as consultant in the estate planning process, the text uses the terms *client* and *planner* frequently. A manual is available to instructors who adopt the book.

The revised edition has been thoroughly updated to reflect the changes brought about by the Tax Reform Act of 1986 and the Revenue Act of 1987. Other major changes and additions include an analysis of the living trust and a lengthier introduction to the will in Chapter 3; a description of the Generation-Skipping Transfer Tax in Chapter 7; a revision and relocation of the material on the interest-free loan, short-term trust, and spousal remainder trust to an appendix in Chapter 14; a discussion of the delegation of health care decisions using the living will and the durable power of attorney for health care in Chapter 17; more numerical problems; the inclusion of greater technical detail, mostly in footnotes, enabling me to present greater depth yet still keep the basic material concisely worded; an extensive glossary; and a thoroughly revised and expanded instructor's manual.

Introduction to Estate Planning can be used in a two- or three-hour quarter or semester introductory college undergraduate or graduate course. Or it can be read in conjunction with a certificate-type course offered to the financial services industry. It can also be read independently by anyone seeking a moderately technical overview, including the practitioner in financial services, the law student, the attorney in general practice, and the determined lay reader.

I wish to thank the following people who have helped in making this book possible: Martin Anderson, Michael Anderson, John Bost, Larry Cox, W.W. Dotterweich, Keith Fevurly, Marilyn Gallaty, Jerry Kasner, Stephanie Lomeli, Robert Matson, Michael O'Neill, Dennis Schlais, Haney Scott, and Richard Wellman.

Chris J. Prestopino

Contents

Part 1
Overview and Conceptual Background   1

1   **Introduction**   3

What Estate Planning Is About.   Developing an Estate Plan:
Acquiring Client Facts and Objectives.   *Reviewing the Facts and
Preparing the Plan.* *Implementing the Plan.* *Following Up.* The
Estate Planning Team: *The Attorney.* *The Accountant.* *The Life
Underwriter.* *The Trust Officer.* *The Financial Planner.*
Organization of the Book.   Appendix 1A   Sample Client Fact-
Finding Questionnaire.

2   **Survey of the Basic Concepts of Estate Planning**   23

Concepts Dealing with Estates.   Concepts Dealing with Transfers
of Property.   Beneficiaries.   Wills, Trusts, and Probate.   Life
Insurance.   Taxation.   Property Interests: *Basic Interests in
Property.* *Classification of Property by Physical Characteristics.
Concurrent Ownership.* *Legal versus Beneficial Interests:
Introduction to the Trust.* *Power of Appointment.* *Present versus
Future and Vested versus Contingent Interests.* Important
Concepts Covered in This Chapter.

Part 2
The Constraints in Planning   45

3   **Introduction to Property Transfers I: The Documents**   47
     of Transfer

Overview.   Joint Tenancy Arrangements.   Property Disposal by
Contract: *Life Insurance.* *Pension and Profit Sharing Plans.*

The Will: *Who May Execute a Will? Statutory Format Requirements for Wills. The Simple Will. Analysis of the Simple Will.* The Trust: *The Living Trust. The Trust-Will.* Appendix 3A The Rule against Perpetuities. Appendix 3B The California Statutory Wills.

4 **Introduction to Property Transfers II: The Transfer Process** 96

Overview. State Laws on Intestate Succession: *Degrees of Consanguinity. Per Stirpes versus Per Capita. Intestacy in UPC States. Intestacy in Non-UPC States.* Legal Rights of Omitted and Adopted Children. Legal Rights of Omitted, Divorced, and Disinherited Spouses. Principles of Probate Administration: *Substantial Formal Supervision: The Non-UPC Model. Estate Administration in UPC States: A Study in Flexibility.* Appendix 4A Summary Probate Proceedings in California: One Non-UPC State's Alternatives to Formal Probate.

5 **Introduction to Federal Unified Wealth Transfer Taxation** 129

Overview. Brief History. The Unified Transfer Tax Framework. The Unified Rate Schedule. The Unified Credit. The Marital Deduction. The $10,000 Annual Exclusion for Lifetime Gifts. Wealth Transfers Are Unified and Taxed Cumulatively. The Complete Unified Tax Framework: Some Examples. Appendix 5A Form 709: United States Gift Tax Return. Appendix 5B Form 706: United States Estate Tax Return.

6 **The Federal Estate Tax** 185

Overview. One: Components of the Gross Estate: *Interests Owned at Death. Transfers with Retained Interest or Control. Certain Transfers within Three Years of Death. Part-Sale, Part-Gift Transfers.* Two: Estate Tax Deductions. *2056:The Marital Deduction.* Three: Estate Tax Credits: *Credits for State Death Taxes. Credit for Gift Tax. Credit for Tax on Prior Transfers. Credit for Foreign Death Taxes.*

7 **The Federal Gift Tax: The Federal Generation-Skipping** 217
Transfer Tax

The Federal Gift Tax: *Requirements for a Valid Gift. Types of Taxable Gifts. Deductible Gifts. The Gift Tax Annual Exclusion. Gift Splitting. Powers of Appointment. Life Insurance. Gifts of Property in Joint Ownership. Disclaimers.* The Federal Generation-Skipping Transfer Tax: *Nature of the Generation-Skipping Transfer Tax. Exceptions to GSTT Taxation.*

8 Introduction to the Federal Income Tax   **235**

Income Taxation of Individuals: *Gross Income. Deductions from Gross Income. Standard Deduction or Total Itemized Deductions. Personal Exemptions. Taxable Income. Credits. The Kiddie Tax. Sale or Exchange of Property.* Federal Income Taxation of Estates and Trusts: *Estates. Trusts.* The Corporate Income Tax. Appendix 8A Form 1040: U.S. Individual Income Tax Return. Appendix 8B Form 1041: U.S. Fiduciary Income Tax Return.

Part 3
The Techniques of Planning   271

9 Introduction to Part 3: The Goals of Estate Planning   **273**

Overview and Caution. Nonfinancial Goals: *Care of Future Dependents. Privacy in the Property Transfer Process. Speed in the Property Transfer Process.* Financial Goals: *Nontax Financial Goals. Tax-Saving Goals.*

10 The Decision to Avoid Probate   **294**

Overview. The Benefits and Drawbacks of Probate. *The Benefits of Probate. The Drawbacks of Probate.* One Alternative to Probate: Joint Tenancy: *Advantages of Joint Tenancy. Disadvantages of Joint Tenancy.* The Other Alternative to Probate: The Living Trust: *Advantages of the Living Trust. Disadvantages of the Living Trust.* A Quantitative Comparison of the Costs of Probate versus the Living Trust. Which Alternative Is Best? *Probate. Joint Tenancy. Living Trust.*

11 Marital Deduction and Bypass Planning I   **320**

Overview. Planning Option 1: 100 Percent Marital Deduction: *Advantages. Disadvantages. Three Impracticable Alternatives.* Planning Option 2: The Credit Shelter Bypass: *The Bypass Trust.* Planning Option 3: Bypass with Estate Equalization: *Factors Influencing Deferral versus Equalization.*

12 Marital Deduction and Bypass Planning II   **338**

Overview. Planning Options 4: Full Marital Deduction with Disclaimer into Bypass: *Disadvantages.* Planning Software. The Marital Trust. A Case Study in Marital Deduction and Bypass

Planning: *Option 1: 100 Percent Marital Deduction. Option 2: Credit Shelter Bypass. Option 3: Bypass with Estate Equalization. Option 4: 100 Percent Marital Deduction with Disclaimer into Bypass. Other Factors.*

13 Lifetime Transfers I: Overview and Survey of Gift Planning   356

Overview.   Tax Considerations in Making Gifts: *Tax Advantages of Gifting. Tax Disadvantages of Gifting. Types of Assets to Give: Basis Considerations. Postgift Appreciation. Administration Problems. Other Asset Choice Considerations.* Gifts to the Spouse: Techniques and Considerations: *Interspousal Gifts to Save Death Taxes. Interspousal Gifts to Save Income Taxes.* Gifts to Minor Children: Techniques and Considerations: *Gifts under Guardianship. Custodial Gift. Gifts to an Irrevocable Trust.*

14 Lifetime Transfers II: Other Intrafamily Transfers;   387
Charitable Transfers

Overview.   Completed Transfers for Consideration: *Ordinary Sale. Bargain Sale. Installment Sale. Private Annuity. Sale of a Remainder Interest and Joint Purchase.* Incomplete Intrafamily Transfers: *Gift-Leaseback. Grantor Income Trust.* Planning for Charitable Transfers: *Introduction. Gifts of Split Interests.* Appendix 14A: Defective Incomplete Transfers.

15 Liquidity Planning   422

Overview.   Summary of Cash Needs.   Sale of Assets during Lifetime.   Life Insurance: *Introduction. Types of Insurance. Taxation of Life Insurance. Life Insurance Planning.* Flower Bonds.   Liquidity Planning Devices Unique to Business Owners: *Sale of the Business.* 6166:*FET in Installments. Section 303 Redemption.* 2032A:*Special Use Valuation.* Other Liquidity Sources: *Employee Benefits. Postmortem Liquidity Planning Techniques.*

16 Planning for Closely Held Business Interests   449

Overview.   Planning in General for Closely Held Business Interests: *Minimizing Decline in Value Resulting from Withdrawal from the Firm. Transferring the Business Interest. The Need for Early Planning.* Business Buyout Agreement: *Determining the Selling Price. Funding. Income Tax Effects.* The Corporate Recapitalization.   The Partnership Capital Freeze.

17 Miscellaneous Lifetime Planning   474

Overview.   Will and Trust Planning: *Planning for the Care of
Family Members: An Introduction.   Planning for the Care of the
Client's Minor Children.   Executor.   Allocation of Death Taxes.
Survival Clauses.   Selection of the Trustee.   Determining the Age
of Outright Distribution from a Trust.   Restrictions against
Assignment.   Perpetuities Savings Clause.   Powers of the Trustee.*
Planning for the Client's Incapacity: *Planning for the Care of the
Incapacitated Clients' Property   Planning for the Care of the
Incapacitated Client.*   Appendix 17A   Durable Power of Attorney
for Health Care.   Appendix 17B   Living Will Declaration.
Appendix 17C   Directive to Physicians.

18 Postmortem Tax Planning   520

Overview.   Tax Returns after Death.   Planning Devices Primarily
Designed to Save Income Taxes: *Expense Elections Available to
the Executor.   Selection of Estate Taxable Year.   Distribution
Planning.*   Planning Devices Primarily Designed to Save Death
Taxes: *Alternative Valuation Date.   Disclaimers.   QTIP
Election.   Other Postmortem Death Tax-Saving Devices.*
Appendix A   Tax and Valuation Tables.   Appendix B   Internal
Revenue Code: Selected Edited Sections.

Index   588

PART 1

Overview and Conceptual Background

1

Introduction

WHAT ESTATE PLANNING IS ABOUT

Estate planning is the study of the principles of planning for the use, conservation, and transfer of an individual's wealth.[1] Its concepts are based on the premise that people don't live forever; sooner or later, death will bring about a fundamental shift in the possession and ownership of family wealth. Estate planning seeks to arrange future wealth transfers to maximize financial well-being, for both the client and the client's survivors. Thus, in a nutshell, estate planning is the study of financial planning in anticipation of death.

Planning for future wealth transfers usually requires the preparation of contracts, such as life insurance policies, and other documents, including wills, trusts, deeds, and powers of attorney. These documents implement the plan by arranging, in writing, the future financial affairs of the individual.

---

[1]Some definitions of estate planning also include, as an additional estate planning activity, the *accumulation* of wealth. That would unrealistically broaden the subject's scope to include the field of investment management. Investment management is another specialty of great scope, one usually left to be covered in textbooks devoted to investment analysis. Practitioners specializing exclusively in estate planning give little or no advice on investment management.

Learning how to plan wealth transfers with these documents requires an understanding of many legally related subjects, including the law of property, wills, trusts, future interests, estate administration, intestacy, insurance, income taxation, gift taxation, and death taxation.

How can the reader benefit from a knowledge of such an extensive subject? Foremost, as a planner, the reader can help avoid the adverse consequences of inadequate planning. Here are a few common examples of what can happen without proper planning.

EXAMPLE 1–1 Joanne died last week. She is survived by her husband and their two young daughters. Because Joanne did not write a will, the law of her state requires that two thirds of her $300,000 estate must *pass to her daughters*, who will each receive the property outright from their guardian-father on their 18th birthdays. The other one third passes to Joanne's husband, who is rather shocked that he is not inheriting it all.

EXAMPLE 1–2 Both Marge and Henry, parents of five-year-old twins, were killed in an auto accident last month. Who will be chosen by the court to be the twin's *guardians* remains uncertain, since the parents left no written evidence of any preference.

EXAMPLE 1–3 Maggie died last month at age 80. Six weeks prior to her death, she gave 1,600 shares of ABC common stock to her children, who sold it last week, incurring an *income tax* of over $22,000. No one told Maggie that had she instead given the stock to the children at her death, they could have sold it at little or no income tax cost.

EXAMPLE 1–4 Before Christine's death two years ago, her family lawyer drafted a *simple will,* leaving all of the family wealth to her husband, Evan. Today, as outright owner of all of the family wealth, Evan realizes that, at his death, his estate will incur sizable *transfer costs,* much of which could have been eliminated had Christine's will incorporated a more sophisticated estate planning device known as the bypass.

EXAMPLE 1–5 Facts similar to Example 1–4, above, except that instead of receiving the property by will, Evan received it as survivor under several *joint tenancy* arrangements. Today, Evan anticipates the same transfer cost problem at his death.

EXAMPLE 1–6 Leslie is the founder of a highly successful *business,* a real estate sales firm. She died last year, having done no estate planning. Her children are struggling with several problems, including how to generate sufficient liquidity to pay the death taxes, and whether or not to sell the business. Further, they worry that no one will buy the business for an amount anywhere near its predeath value.

EXAMPLE 1–7 Elmer had a *stroke* three months ago; since then he has been unable to communicate with anyone. He has a fairly large estate, and his family now realizes that they should have encouraged Elmer to consult an estate planner years ago, at a time when Elmer's knowledge and personal objectives could have been incorporated into an effective estate plan.

EXAMPLE 1–8 At the advice of a friend, Marty executed a revocable living trust by simply filling in the blanks on a *form document* photocopied from a page of his friend's copy of a popular "how to" book. Marty may never realize that since title to most of his property is held in joint tenancy form, the trust is almost totally worthless.

These and many other problems occur every day because of the failure to engage in effective estate planning. Estate planning is a technical, rapidly changing subject about which laypeople have numerous misconceptions. And because it anticipates death, many who need it would prefer not to focus on it. Thus, estate planning requires the helpful encouragement of professionals.

How these professionals develop an estate plan is described next.

DEVELOPING AN ESTATE PLAN

Developing an estate plan culminates in the creation of a set of documents and related recommendations which skillfully allow for the best use, conservation, and transfer of the client's wealth. It requires several steps: acquiring client facts and objectives, reviewing the facts and preparing the plan, implementing the plan, and following up.

Acquiring Client Facts and Objectives

To be able to make good recommendations, the planner must first acquire sufficient information about the client and the client's family. Necessary information includes the client's financial and personal situation and the client's objectives.

The client's financial situation and objectives. To understand the client's financial situation, the planner will require several types of statements. First, he or she will need a current balance sheet, showing the fair market value of all assets and liabilities. Regarding each asset, information will be needed about the form in which title is held, date of acquisition, and current adjusted tax basis.

> EXAMPLE 1–9 Relying on the client's oral comment that she owned a parcel of investment property as an individual, an inexperienced planner didn't take the trouble to *examine the actual deed*. Two years after executing a will which left all property to her husband, the client died, at which time the planner discovered that the parcel was held in joint tenancy with the client's niece, who became the sole, outright owner of the parcel.

In addition to a description of assets and liabilities, the planner will need an income statement, describing sources of income and major categories of expenses.

The planner will also need other facts, such as information about significant gifts or inheritances received or expected to be received, and a listing of all of the client's financial and other advisers, including accountant, lawyer, investment broker, life underwriter, realtor, physician, and religious adviser. Further, the planner will need a description of the client's and the spouse's financial objectives, a self-appraisal of their ability to manage their finances, and the location of any wills.

The client's personal situation and objectives. The planner must also acquire personal nonfinancial information, including the names of all of the members of the family, their ages, their health, and their station in life (occupations, etc.).

The planner will also need an understanding of the client's personal objectives, especially with regard to dispositive preferences for the spouse and the children before and at the client's death, and any interests in donating to charities.

Many planners, often with the help of financial institutions, develop customized questionnaires and checklists to help them acquire this information as efficiently as possible. An example of a questionnaire can be found in Appendix 1A at the end of this chapter.[2]

Reviewing the Facts and Preparing the Plan

After acquiring the necessary facts, the planner will review the facts and prepare a plan that incorporates preliminary recommendations. The most common recommendations fall in two areas: financial planning for property transfers, and personal planning for the client's incapacity and death.

Financial planning for property transfers. The major purpose of an estate plan is to efficiently distribute the client's wealth to the proper persons in the proper amount at the proper time. To do this, the planner will need to keep in mind the following considerations, which relate to more specific estate planning goals:

- Deciding whether or not to *avoid probate* as a means of transferring property at the death of the client.
- Examining alternatives to reduce and possibly eliminate *transfer taxes* at the death of the client and the client's spouse.
- Considering *lifetime transfers,* partly to reduce transfer costs and partly to shift taxable income to a lower-tax-bracket family member.
- Arranging to provide the *liquidity* to cover cash outlays at the client's disability or death.
- Devising a strategy to unwind the client's *business affairs* in a manner that can maintain the greatest income and value for the survivors.

Personal planning for incapacity and death. The major areas in personal planning for client incapacity and death include arranging for someone to care for the client and the client's property at the onset of incompetence, and arranging for someone to care for the client's children if both parents die before the children reach adulthood.

---

[2]In addition to acquiring a checklist, the planner should routinely examine existing documents, such as the will and evidence of title to property. Too often, checklist information is inaccurate. Example 1–9 illustrates one problem.

Since this text is primarily devoted to an explanation of these and other objectives and planning techniques, further discussion will not be undertaken here.

Implementing the Plan

After the planner and the client meet to discuss and agree on specifics, the planner can implement the plan. Transfer documents will be drafted by the attorney and executed by the client.[3] A life underwriter may be needed to secure the appropriate insurance contracts. If a trust managed by a corporate trustee is included in the plan, a bank trust officer will usually be contacted for authorization and advice.

Following Up

The last and indispensable part of the estate planning process is following up. Laws change. The client's personal situation and objectives change. By keeping up-to-date, the planner can periodically recommend any necessary revisions to the plan. Events which may require plan revision include marriage, divorce, birth of a child, new legislation, and new court decisions.

> EXAMPLE 1–10 In 1981, Congress made many significant changes in the law of federal transfer taxation. One major change involved the taxation of property passing at death to the surviving spouse. Up to then, many planners used a provision in their clients' wills and trusts that had the effect of passing to the spouse the maximum amount possible without resulting in a tax. Prior to the new law, this amount usually turned out to be about one half of the client's estate. However, under the new law, the maximum amount would usually turn out to be the client's entire estate. Concerned that many clients with such a provision currently in their estate plans might not want to leave their entire estate to their spouse, Congress included a transition rule which continued to apply the *old* tax law to any client who died with-

---

[3]To "execute" a document is to complete it, that is, to do what is necessary to render it valid. For example, as we shall see in Chapter 3, execution of a will normally requires, among other things, the client's signing the will in the presence of witnesses, who also sign, attesting to the authenticity of the client's signature.

out revising the plan. Thus, to take advantage of the new, more beneficial tax provisions, transfer documents had to be revised, and most planners contacted all of their affected clients.

For these and many other reasons, periodic follow-up has become a way of life for estate planners.

THE ESTATE PLANNING TEAM

Often, estate planning cannot be conducted by only one professional; the job can require the diverse knowledge and skills of a number of practitioners, including attorneys, accountants, life underwriters, trust officers, and financial planners. Some in the industry call these individuals the *estate planning team*. How each member of that team can uniquely contribute to the overall plan is described next.

The Attorney

As the only professional legally permitted to draft documents and render legal advice, the attorney is the indispensable team member in the estate planning process. Document preparation requires the ability to make fine legal distinctions. Years later, these documents will usually become the final authority and will usually be taken literally. Thus, by putting an estate plan into print, the attorney places his or her professional reputation on the line for many to see, criticize, and, sometimes, second guess.

Most attorneys accept even greater responsibility by *coordinating* the actions of the other members of the estate planning team. This is especially common among lawyers specializing in estate planning and taxation.

Often, the attorney's role will not end at the client's death. He or she may be hired to *probate* the client's estate; that is, to complete the process involving the legal transfer of certain of the client's assets to surviving beneficiaries. In addition, the attorney may engage in postmortem tax planning, a job which, as we shall see in Chapter 18, entails choosing certain tax options available after the client's death.

The Accountant

By preparing the client's financial statements and tax returns, the accountant is often the professional having the earliest and greatest financial contact with the client.[4] The accountant is often able to spot specific financial problems requiring attention, especially with regard to the client's business interests. And after the client's death, the accountant may be called on to complete any necessary income tax and death tax returns.

The Life Underwriter

The life underwriter's crucial role is to provide insurance contracts to meet liquidity requirements expected to arise at the client's disability or death. The efficient use of life insurance requires an understanding of estate planning partly because proper planning can minimize both transfer costs and personal strain.

As an active solicitor, the life underwriter is often the first professional to recommend estate planning to the client, and may have the opportunity to select the other members of the client's estate planning team.

The Trust Officer

As a skilled professional executor and trustee, the trust officer performs *fiduciary* services for clients and estates.[5] As *executor* of the client's estate, the trust officer is responsible for managing those assets which are being transferred through the probate process. Similarly, as *trustee* of a trust created by a client, the trust officer is responsible for managing those assets placed in the trust. Thus, the trust officer can be particularly helpful in the planning stage by offering advice in the area of management and distribution of assets.

---

[4]Typically, these forms are so financially revealing to accountants that financial planners have described them as the client's "personal annual business report."

[5]A fiduciary is a person having a legal duty to act for the benefit of another. See Chapter 2 for a further discussion.

The Financial Planner

As the newest member of the estate planning team, the financial planner is a professional potentially capable of creating a complete integrated financial plan, one that includes recommendations concerning insurance, investments, retirement planning, and income tax planning, as well as estate planning.

Next, let's turn to a description of the organization of the text.

ORGANIZATION OF THE BOOK

This book is divided into three parts. *Part 1* includes this introductory chapter and Chapter 2, which introduces the major elementary concepts that will be used throughout the text.

Chapter 2 defines and describes the elementary concepts of estate planning, including such terms as *fee simple, life estate, remainder, probate, trust, irrevocable,* and *insured.*

Part 2 provides the more detailed background knowledge needed to understand the techniques of estate planning. It introduces the constraints in planning, that is, the basic principles of tax and property law on which all planning rests.

Part 2 begins with Chapter 3, which explores the rudimentary contents of the will and the trust, the two major documents of property transfer. Sample forms are included to give the reader an early awareness of the focus of planning.

Chapter 4 explains how property is actually transferred. The probate process is featured and includes a discussion of supervised probate, probate alternatives in states adopting the Uniform Probate Code, and some examples of summary probate.

Chapter 5 introduces federal wealth transfer taxation by describing the computation of both the gift tax and the estate tax, and compares and contrasts their methodology.

Continuing the material on wealth transfer taxation, Chapter 6 contains a robust examination of the federal estate tax, exploring three major topics: components of the gross estate, estate tax deductions, and estate tax credits. In the same spirit, Chapter 7 covers the major principles of the federal gift tax and the generation-skipping transfer tax.

Chapter 8 concludes Part 2 with an introduction to the federal income tax, emphasizing the sale, gift, and exchange of property and the income taxation of estates, trusts, and their beneficiaries.

Part 3 utilizes the material in Parts 1 and 2 to survey the actual techniques used in planning. It begins with Chapter 9 by surveying the principal goals of estate planning. Examples include minimizing the costs of the property transfer process, shifting taxable income to a lower-bracket taxpayer, and reducing the taxable estate.

Chapter 10 examines the controversial decision to avoid probate. We will contrast probate with its alternatives, including the very popular revocable living trust.

Chapters 11 and 12 focus on planning for those transfers at death that can defer or completely eliminate the client's death taxes. We will see that the major transfer strategies incorporate the estate tax marital deduction and the bypass.

Chapters 13 and 14 explore various aspects of planning for lifetime transfers. Chapter 13 surveys gift planning and shows that although gifting can save both income and transfer taxes, its harsh requirement of a complete relinquishment of control over the gifted assets forces many clients to consider instead property transfers which are not so total. Chapter 14 surveys incomplete lifetime transfers, ones in which the client retains some control over the gift property. It also highlights lifetime transfers that are less than total because the client will receive some consideration in exchange. The chapter also covers charitable transfers.

The death of a client owning significant wealth can trigger sizable cash outlays, such as for death taxes. Chapter 15 surveys common methods of providing the client's estate with adequate liquidity to fund these outlays. Topics include sale of assets before death, life insurance, and flower bonds.

Chapter 16 explores the principles of planning for closely held business interests. Frequently, their owners have special estate planning problems, including maintaining sufficient income after withdrawing from the business and transferring to their chosen beneficiaries the maximum value attributable to that business. In addition to an extended discussion of these problems, the chapter covers several specific techniques, including sale of the business during lifetime and the business buyout.

Chapter 17 surveys other miscellaneous techniques that estate planners routinely employ, including providing for minor children, selecting a trustee, and planning for the client's incapacity.

Finally, Chapter 18 examines the principles of postmortem tax planning, a topic which illustrates that income tax and death tax planning are still possible even after a client's death. Major topics include expense elections, QTIP planning, and disclaimers.

Chapter 2 will next survey the major elementary concepts that will be used throughout the text.

RECOMMENDED READING

ASTRACHAN, JOHN M. "Why People Don't Make Wills." *Trusts & Estates* 118 (1979), p. 45.

BARR, KATHERINE. "General Practitioners Beware: The Duty to Refer an Estate Planning Client to a Specialist." *Cumberland Law Review* 14 (1984), pp. 103–34.

CRUMBLEY, D. LARRY, AND EDWARD E. MILAM. "Personalizing the Estate Planning Process." *Trusts & Estates* 116 (1977), p. 8.

EBER, VICTOR. "The Personal Audit: The First Step in Life-Time Financial and Estate Planning." *Estate Planning* 1 (1973), p. 30.

HERTING, CLAIREEN L. "How to Build and Maintain a Successful Personal Financial Planning Practice." *Estate Planning,* November 1986, pp. 254–56.

JOHNSTON, GERALD. "An Ethical Analysis of Common Estate Planning Practices— Is Good Business Bad Ethics?" *Ohio State Law Journal* 45 (1984), pp. 57–141.

————. "Estate Planners' Accountability in the Representation of Agricultural Clients" *Kansas Law Review* 34 (1986), pp. 611–50.

LUTON, JAMES. "Accountant's Role in Estate Planning." *Estate Planning* 5 (1978), p. 40.

McCARTER, CHARLES. "Cost-Efficient Estate Planning." *Journal of the Kansas Bar Association,* Spring 1984, pp. 51–57.

OBEGI, JOSEPH C. "Handling Conflict of Interest Problems in Estate Planning." *Community Property Journal* 13 (1987), pp. 47–72.

PEDRICK, WILLARD H. "When Does the Estate Planning Team Huddle?" *University of Miami Institute on Estate Planning* 5 (1971), p. 1900.

TATE, MERCER D. "Strategies for Establishing a Fair Rate of Compensation for Planning a Client's Estate." *Estate Planning,* July 1986, pp. 194–97.

QUESTIONS AND PROBLEMS

1. At a dinner party, the wife of one of your clients asks you what estate planning entails. Define it, and name the legally related subjects that it embraces.

2. A man comes into your office to inquire about your services. You find out that he owns a closely held business and has a wife and two young children. He has never written a will. Explain briefly how failure to plan could lead to adverse consequences.

3. Fill in the questionnaire in Appendix 1A with information about yourself, a client, or a friend. Which items would you expect would usually be most difficult to acquire?

4. Outline the steps required in developing an estate plan.

5. Explain the unique contribution made by each member of the estate planning team.

Sample Client Fact-Finding Questionnaire*

Date: _____

CONFIDENTIAL ESTATE PLANNING QUESTIONNAIRE

Family and Financial Information

The following questionnaire is designed to expedite our efforts to plan your estate. Whether you are a new or an established client, we have found this questionnaire extremely helpful and therefore ask your indulgence in completing it fully. Those questions that are irrelevant to your family or financial situation may simply be ignored. Please feel free to attach additional pages where space is insufficient or to provide other information you feel is relevant.

A. Husband
   1. Name _____
   2. Other names used _____
   3. Address _____ County _____
      City _____ State _____
   4. Telephone (Home) _____ (Business) _____
   5. Employer _____

---

*Reprinted with permission of its author, Robert M. Grant.

APPENDIX 1A *(continued)*

    6. Birthdate _____

    7. Citizenship _____

B. Wife

    1. Name _____

    2. Other or former names _____

    3. Date and place of marriage _____

    4. Telephone (Business) _____

    5. Employer _____

    6. Birthdate _____

    7. Citizenship _____

    8. Beginning dates and states (or countries) of residence since current marriage, and approximate net worth at each time.

Beginning Date	State	Approximate Net Worth
_____	_____	_____
_____	_____	_____
_____	_____	_____
_____	_____	_____

    9. Have either you or your spouse been married before? _____ (If yes, give for each prior marriage: *(a)* the prior spouse's name; *(b)* whether marriage was terminated by death or divorce; and *(c)* the date and place of termination.)

_____

_____

_____

C. Children and Grandchildren

    1. Children of present marriage (living and deceased).

Name	Current Residence	Birth Date	Check if Adopted
_____	_____	_____	_____
_____	_____	_____	_____
_____	_____	_____	_____
_____	_____	_____	_____

APPENDIX 1A *(continued)*

2. Children of Husband's prior marriage to _____

Name	Current Residence	Birth Date	Check if Adopted
_____	_____	_____	_____
_____	_____	_____	_____
_____	_____	_____	_____
_____	_____	_____	_____

3. Children of Wife's prior marriage to _____

Name	Current Residence	Birth Date	Check if Adopted
_____	_____	_____	_____
_____	_____	_____	_____
_____	_____	_____	_____
_____	_____	_____	_____

4. Grandchildren

Name	Parent	Birth Date	Check if Adopted
_____	_____	_____	_____
_____	_____	_____	_____
_____	_____	_____	_____
_____	_____	_____	_____

D. Gifts

Have you or your spouse filed federal or state gift tax returns? _____ If yes, please provide a copy of the most recent returns.

E. Will

Do you or your spouse currently have a will? Husband _____ Wife _____
If yes, please provide a copy.

APPENDIX 1A *(continued)*

Assets Owned by Husband and/or Wife—in General

	How Title Is Held	Estimated Fair Market Value (Where appropriate, indicate whether husband's separate property [HSP], wife's separate property [WSP], or community property [CP].)
1. Jewelry, Clothing, Household Furniture and Furnishings, Personal Automobiles, Boats, Paintings, Books and Other Tangible Articles of a Personal Nature and Special Collections		
_____	_____	_____
_____	_____	_____
_____	_____	_____
2. Cash or Equivalents (Checking and savings accounts, money market accounts or funds)		
_____	_____	_____
_____	_____	_____
_____	_____	_____
_____	_____	_____
_____	_____	_____

	How Title Is Held	Estimated Fair Market Value (Where appropriate, indicate whether husband's separate property [HSP], wife's separate property [WSP], or community property [CP].)

APPENDIX 1A *(continued)*

3. Real Estate—Principal Residence, Vacation, and Investment

_____ _____ _____

_____ _____ _____

_____ _____ _____

_____ _____ _____

4. Publicly Traded Stocks and Bonds

_____ _____ _____

_____ _____ _____

_____ _____ _____

_____ _____ _____

_____ _____ _____

_____ _____ _____

5. Interest in Closely Held Corporations, Proprietorships, and Limited or General Partnerships

_____ _____ _____

_____ _____ _____

_____ _____ _____

_____ _____ _____

6. Promissory Notes Receivable

_____ _____ _____

_____ _____ _____

_____ _____ _____

APPENDIX 1A *(continued)*

7. Other Assets (annuities, patents, and copyrights, etc.)

_____ _____ _____

_____ _____ _____

_____ _____ _____

_____ _____ _____

_____ _____ _____

_____ _____ _____

Liabilities of Husband and/or Wife

Amount of Present Liability (Where
appropriate, indicate whether husband's separate liability [HSL], wife's
separate liability [WSL], or community liability [CL].)

1. Mortgages on Real Property

_____ _____

_____ _____

_____ _____

_____ _____

2. Notes, Loans, Support Obligations,
and Other Liabilities

_____ _____

_____ _____

_____ _____

_____ _____

APPENDIX 1A (*continued*)

Life Insurance

Company/ Policy Number	Face Amount	Cash Surrender Value	Insured	Owner	Beneficiary
_____	_____	_____	_____	_____	_____
_____	_____	_____	_____	_____	_____
_____	_____	_____	_____	_____	_____
_____	_____	_____	_____	_____	_____
_____	_____	_____	_____	_____	_____

Employee Benefit Plans

Employment Benefit—Describe type of plan (Pension, profit sharing, IRA, Keogh) and company	Employee	Approximate Value	Beneficiary
_____	_____	_____	_____
_____	_____	_____	_____
_____	_____	_____	_____

APPENDIX 1A (concluded)

Interest in Estates or Trusts

Do you or your spouse have an interest in an estate or trust as a beneficiary, trustee, holder of a power of appointment, or trustor? If yes, please provide a copy of each trust and an estimate of the current fair market value of the assets thereof.

Yes _____ No _____

Name of Estate or Trust	Fiduciary	Value of Interest
_____	_____	_____
_____	_____	_____
_____	_____	_____

Expectancies

Do you or your spouse expect to receive anything from another person's will? _____

From Whom	Value of Interest
_____	_____
_____	_____
_____	_____

2

Survey of the Basic Concepts of Estate Planning

This chapter will introduce many of the elementary concepts commonly used in estate planning. They will be mentioned throughout the text, and the reader is advised to study them carefully. Along with many others, these terms are defined in the Glossary at the back of this book. The terminology can be subdivided into several classes, including those dealing with estates, transfers of property, beneficiaries, wills, trusts and probate, life insurance, taxation, and types of property interests.

CONCEPTS DEALING WITH ESTATES

An *estate* is a quantity of wealth or property. *Property* represents things or objects over which we may lawfully exercise the right to use, control, and dispose. More simply, property is anything that can be owned.

Ordinarily, for a person or for a family, an estate represents the total amount of property owned. However, the word *estate* is often used in several other contexts in estate planning to mean some type of smaller amount. First, in certain situations, estate means the *net* value of property owned, calculated by subtracting the amount of the estates owner's liabilities from the value of the property. Second, estate can be limited to the *probate estate*, which constitutes all of the property that passes to others by means of the probate process, on the death of the individual owner. Third, estate could be limited to the *gross estate* and *taxable estate,* two concepts which include only property subject to death taxation. Later it will be shown that the probate estate and the tax-related estate will probably be very different in size and composition.

CONCEPTS DEALING WITH TRANSFERS OF PROPERTY

A *transfer* or *assignment* of property can mean any type of passing of property in which the *transferor* gives up some kind of interest to the *transferee.* The interest transferred can be purely legal, purely beneficial, or a combination of legal and beneficial. Where only title is passed, the interest given up can be purely *legal.* We shall see later that this is all that the typical trustee receives. Title alone gives trustees the ability to manage property but not to enjoy it. On the other hand, where the transferee receives something that carries an economic benefit, but not title, the interest transferred can be purely *beneficial.* Examples of beneficial interest in property include the temporary or permanent right to possess, consume, and pledge the property. Finally, an interest given up by the transferor can be both legal and beneficial, whereby the transferee receives both title and economic benefit. An *outright* transfer is said to occur when one transferee receives both legal and all beneficial interests, subject to no restrictions or conditions.

Most commonly, property is transferred by sale, by gift, or by a combination of both sale and gift. A *sale* is a transfer of property under which the transferor receives an amount of *consideration* that is regarded equivalent to the value of the property transferred. By contrast, a *gift* is a transfer of property for which a transferor receives nothing in exchange. The two most common methods of making gift transfers are *outright* and *in trust.* Transfers in trust will be discussed later in the chapter.

Technically speaking, when a person transfers property in exchange for other property whose value is less than the amount transferred, but greater than zero, a *bargain sale* has occurred. A bargain sale, therefore, involves a transfer that is part sale, part gift. The notion of the bargain sale causes most estate planning practitioners to define a gift somewhat more broadly. While the above definition of a gift is technically correct, estate planners also consider a bargain sale to be a type of gift, even though some property is received in exchange. Federal tax law treats the actual amount of the gift as the difference between the respective values of the consideration exchanged. Thus, in this text, a transfer will be considered either a gift or a sale, with a *gift* defined as a transfer for any amount that is less than full consideration.

A transfer of property can be *inter vivos,* made while the transferor is alive, or it can be made at death. Transfers at death are typically made pursuant to either a valid document, also called in the trade an *instrument,* prepared by the owner before death (e.g., will, trust, title by joint tenancy, and insurance beneficiary designation) or pursuant to a state law, in the event that no such document exists.

BENEFICIARIES

A *beneficiary,* or *donee,* is a person who is receiving or will receive a gift of a beneficial interest in property from a transferor, who is also known as a *donor.* Although in the most general sense, donee and beneficiary are synonymous, in certain contexts one or the other term is used more commonly. For example, the recipient of an inter vivos gift directly from the donor is usually called a donee. On the other hand, the recipient of a gift under a will or a trust, whether inter vivos or testamentary (see following section) is usually called a beneficiary.

WILLS, TRUSTS, AND PROBATE

In estate planning, a person who has died is called a *decedent.*[1] When a person dies, property owned by the decedent must be transferred. Each state in the nation takes special interest in ensuring that each piece of property owned by the decedent will be transferred to the proper parties. This is done in two basic ways. First, state law looks to any valid documents prepared by the decedent (wills, trusts, joint tenancy arrangements, life insurance policies, etc.) to determine proper disposition. A *will* is a written document disposing of a person's probate property at death. The will is said to make *testamentary* transfers. It is *executed* at the

---

[1]The word *deceased* is a word of limited application in estate planning, one perhaps more commonly used in connection with funerals. In estate planning contexts, the deceased is usually called the decedent.

time it is properly signed by the *testator*. A *trust* is a legal arrangement that divides legal and beneficial interests among two or more people. The trust will be described in greater detail later in the chapter.

Second, if no such documents are found which dispose of a decedent's property, the decedent is said have died *intestate* with regard to that property.[2] If a valid will is found, the decedent is said to have died *testate* with regard to that property.

Probate is a legal process that focuses on the will and the probate estate, that is, property which will be disposed of by, and *only* by, either the will or by the state laws of intestate succession. Essentially, in probate, the governmental unit, often the court, determines the validity of the will, if any, and authorizes distribution of the probate estate to creditors and beneficiaries. The court appoints a *personal representative* to act as *fiduciary,* to represent and manage the probate estate. If the court appoints the person nominated in the will to be personal representative, that person is called the *executor*.[3] Otherwise, the personal representative appointed by the court is called the *administrator*.

Beneficiaries of a decedent's probate property are called heirs, devisees, or legatees. An *heir* is a beneficiary who will receive property that passes by intestacy.[4] A *devisee* is a beneficiary, under a will, of a gift of real property. A devisee is said to receive a *devise*. A *legatee* is a beneficiary, under a will, of a gift of personal property. A legatee is said to receive a *legacy,* also known as a *bequest*. For simplicity, this text will usually refer to a testamentary gift of any property, real or personal, as a bequest.

The term *issue* refers to a person's descendants, or offspring, including, children, grandchildren, great-grandchildren and the like. Degrees of blood relationship will be further examined in Chapter 4.

---

[2]More common, though less consistent, usage holds that any person dying without any valid will has died intestate. However, if all of the decedent's property is disposed of by alternative dispositive devises (e.g., trusts), a will may not be necessary and the absence of a will may not actually result in a probate "intestacy."

[3]In some states, a female personal representative is called an executrix. Other states have eliminated this word from their probate vocabulary. This text will use the term executor to refer to either sex.

[4]In some states, however, an heir is also a person receiving property by will.

Most bequests are either specific, general, or residuary. A *specific bequest* is a gift of a particular item of property which is capable of being identified and distinguished from all other property in the testator's estate. For example, the bequest "I leave all my household furnishings to . . ." and "I leave my high school ring to . . ." are specific bequests because they specify particular, identifiable property.

A *general bequest* is a gift payable out of the general assets of the estate, but not one that specifies one or more particular items. For example, the bequest "I leave $500 to . . ." is a general bequest because it can be paid from more than one asset.

A *residuary bequest* is a gift of that part of the testator's estate not otherwise disposed of by the will. For example, the bequest "I leave the rest of my estate to . . ." is a residuary bequest. The *residue* is the remainder of an estate.

LIFE INSURANCE

A *life insurance* policy is a contract in which the insurance company agrees to pay a cash lump-sum amount (the *face value* or *policy proceeds*) to the person named in the policy to receive it (the *beneficiary*) upon the death of the subject of the insurance (the *insured*). One other important party in the life insurance contract is the *owner,* who typically possesses both legal and beneficial interests in the policy. As legal owner, the policy owner has title to the policy. As beneficial owner, the policy owner has the right to benefit from the policy. Beneficial rights include the right to receive policy dividends, the right to change the beneficiary, and the right to surrender the policy. These rights can have economic value, even before the death of the insured. Whether or not a life insurance policy has economic value prior to the insured's death depends upon the type of policy, as we shall see next.

A *term life insurance* policy has no value prior to the death of the insured because the premium charged, which increases over time along with increasing risk of death, simply buys pure protection: If the insured dies during the policy term, the company will pay the face value; otherwise, it will pay nothing.

In contrast to a term policy, a *cash value* policy accumulates economic value because the insurer charges a constant premium that is considerably higher than mortality costs require during the earlier years. Part of this overpayment accumulates as a *cash sur-*

render value which, prior to the death of the insured, can be enjoyed by the owner, basically in one of two ways. First, at any time the owner can surrender the policy and receive this value in cash. Second, the owner can make a policy loan and borrow up to the amount of this value.

Because life insurance policies can have value prior to the insured's death, and because the insured's death usually triggers the payment of a substantial amount of cash, life insurance can make a significant contribution to estate planning. For example, life insurance proceeds can be used to provide needed cash to pay the death taxes on the death of a closely held business owner. However, to use life insurance properly, the planner must be aware of the impact of taxes, a subject to be introduced briefly next and explained in considerable detail in Chapters 5 through 8.

TAXATION

In estate planning, the two principal types of taxing authority are the individual states and the federal government. The three major types of taxes are gift tax, death tax, and income tax.

A *gift tax* is a tax on a lifetime transfer of property for less than full consideration.

A *death tax* is essentially a tax levied on certain property owned or transferred by the decedent at death. Death taxes have two forms, an estate tax and an inheritance tax. An *estate tax* is considered to be a tax on the decedent's right to transfer property, while an *inheritance tax* is considered to be a tax on the right of a beneficiary to receive property from a decedent. Either way, their net effect is essentially the same: they are both death taxes because each is based on a certain amount of property owned by the decedent at death. The federal death tax is an estate tax and is called the federal estate tax. At the state level, some states impose an estate tax and others have an inheritance tax. However, California, Nevada, and Florida, in effect, impose no death tax.[5]

An *income tax* is essentially a tax levied on income earned by a taxpayer during a given year. Income tax laws usually distinguish

---

[5]We shall see, however, that these states impose a "pickup tax," which is in fact a death tax but which does not result in a larger combined state and federal death tax burden. For details, see Chapter 6.

four different taxpaying entities: individuals, corporations, estates, and trusts. Principles of taxation can differ substantially for each, as we shall see. Essentially, each entity is required annually to submit a unique tax form which reports certain items, including income, deductions, credits, and the net tax due, calculated by using tax tables applicable to that entity. Married individuals may file a *joint income tax return,* in which they report their combined income, deductions, and other information on one form. Since income tax rates are *progressive,* that is, they increase as taxable income increases, the joint return usually results in lower total taxes than if the spouses file individually.

PROPERTY INTERESTS

Estate planning seeks to efficiently preserve and transfer an individual's wealth or property. This section will describe the legal forms in which property can be owned. Essentially, ownership can be classified in the following ways: extent of interests in property (e.g., fee simple); physical characteristic of property (e.g., real versus personal); number of owners and type of ownership (e.g., individual versus interest in common); legal versus beneficial interests; present versus future interests (e.g., a remainder interest); and vested versus contingent (future) interests.

Basic Interests in Property

The three basic interests in property are fee simple, life estate, and estate for years.

Fee simple. A fee simple interest, often called simply a *fee,* represents the greatest interest that a person can have over property, and corresponds to the layperson's usual notion of full ownership. Common powers include the right to possess, use, pledge, transfer, and often destroy the property. You probably own a fee in this textbook. Under traditional property law, fee simple interests are associated only with land, but in this text the concept fee simple will be used to describe either type of property, real or personal, because over the years common usage has come to regard fee simple as the nearly absolute dominion and control enjoyable over most property, whether real or personal. A fee simple interest is, therefore, subject to the highest dollar valuation of any interest in property.

Life estate.　A life estate in property, like a fee simple, is a powerful form of ownership, but is different in that the interest ceases upon someone's death. Ordinarily, the *measuring life* is that of the owner of the interest. However, it could be any other person.

> EXAMPLE 2–1 Doctor Bud assigns his interest in a house to his widowed mother for hcr to use and enjoy until her death. Mother has received a life estate in the house. Her own life is the measuring life.

A life estate for the life of someone other than the owner of the interest is simply called an estate *for the life of another.*

> EXAMPLE 2–2 Facts are similar to Example 2–1, except that Mother's interest will instead cease upon the death of Bud. Mother still has a life estate in the house, but now Bud, not she, is the measuring life. She has an estate for the life of another.

Ordinarily, the owner of a life estate enjoys, for the length of a measuring life, a complete ownership, one that is nearly equivalent to a fee. However, life estates are sometimes created so that the recipient enjoys an interest in only a portion of the property.

> EXAMPLE 2–3 Aunt Jane, owner of dividend-paying common stock, gives to her niece Barbie the right to receive those dividends for as long as Barbie lives. Barbie is said to have received a life estate in the income of the stock. Under the customary arrangements, Barbie does not have many rights in the stock itself. For example, she does not have the right to possess or sell the stock or to use it as collateral against a loan. The stock will be held by someone else, usually either the original owner or, more commonly, a trustee under a trust arrangement.

Trusts will be used in many contexts in almost every chapter of this text and will be described further within the next few pages.

Interest for years.　Often a person transfers property to another person, giving the transferee the right to possess it for a fixed period. This is an "interest for years."

> EXAMPLE 2–4 Professor Jackson lets his student Byron, a graduating senior, use one of his bicycles for three months. Byron has received an interest in the bicycle "for years."

> EXAMPLE 2–5 Mary is presently enjoying a life estate, for her lifc, in the income from certain common stock. Today Mary transfers to Mark her interest for the next two years. Technically, if Mary does

not survive the full two years, Mark's interest will be cut off upon Mary's death; Mary cannot transfer any greater interest than she actually owns, and Mark's interest is limited to that which Mary can legally give. Thus, Mark has an income interest in the stock, ending at the sooner of either two years or Mary's death.

A more common example of an interest for years is a *leasehold,* which entitles the lessee to possess and use the property (e.g., a house or computer) for a specified time, usually in exchange for a fixed series of payments. Leasehold interest can be a valuable part of a lessor's wealth if the fixed payments are below current market rates, and if the lessee is permitted to "sublet" the property.

EXAMPLE 2–6 For the past two years, Freda has owned a four-year leasehold interest in a commercial building, and has been obligated to pay $15,000 per year for the entire period. If the rent for comparable buildings is expected to be $25,000 per year for the next two years, and assuming a discount rate of 10 percent, the value of Freda's leasehold is the present value of $10,000 for two years, discounted at 10 percent, or $17,355. Freda could possible sell her interest for that amount.

Classification of Property by Physical Characteristics

Property may also be classified as real or personal. *Real property* includes fee simple or life estate interests in land and any improvements. Hence, a fee or a life estate in a house would constitute real property. Curiously, an interest for years (a leasehold) in real estate is considered personal property. Accordingly, *personal property* is defined as all property except fees and life estates in land and its improvements.

Personal property may be classified as tangible or intangible. In some cases, this distinction is not entirely clear. Tangible property has several common definitions. Some say it is capable of being "apprehended by the senses, which is accessible, identifiable." For our purposes, however, we shall use the U.S. Supreme Court's definition, in a tax case, that *tangible personal property* is personal property which has value of its own. Conversely, *intangible personal property* is not in itself valuable, but derives its value from that which it represents. For example, a building is tangible property, while the common stock certificates of the corporation owning the building are intangible. Included also in intangibles would be a *chose in action,* which is a claim or debt recoverable in a lawsuit. A chose in action can constitute a part of an individual's wealth for two reasons. First, it represents money owed. Second, the owner is usually permitted by law to sell this claim to another, who can then act on it in the seller's name. the buyer would be entitled to keep any recovery.

EXAMPLE 2–7 Another driver negligently wrecks George's new car. Since he can potentially recover money damages in a court of law, George has a chose in action, which can be assigned. For example, if George decides to ask for reimbursement from his own insurance company, the company will pay only if George assigns his right to sue (subrogates) to the insurer, who will probably pursue the claim in George's name.

Concurrent Ownership

Property may be owned individually, in which case one person owns and uses it, or it may be owned concurrently, by two or more persons. Common forms of *concurrent ownership* are joint interests, interests in common, interests by the entirety, and community property interests.

Joint Interests.   When two or more persons own an equal undivided interest in and right to possess property that, upon death of one owner, automatically passes to the surviving owner(s), they are said to have a *joint interest*, or *joint tenancy*.

EXAMPLE 2–8 John and Mary owned a house as joint tenants. At John's death earlier, Mary automatically became complete owner of the house, as an individual.

Under joint tenancy, ownership passes to the surviving cotenants automatically at a cotenant's death by what is called *operation of law* and does not depend on physical transfer of title. However, some authorities, such as banks, require formal document revision in order to transact further business.

The automatic right of survivorship inherent in joint tenancy ordinarily prevails over other means of transfer at death, including the will and the trust instrument.

> EXAMPLE 2–9 Continuing Example 2–8, if, prior to his death, John had executed a will that left the house to his son, Mary would still receive the house by automatic right of survivorship. The joint tenancy designation supersedes the will.

However, in certain jurisdictions, agreements can be executed between joint owners to nullify a joint tenancy designation.

> EXAMPLE 2–10 Continuing Examples 2–8 and 2–9, if John and Mary were to execute a written agreement stating that it is their intention that the house, presently in joint tenancy, is in fact intended to be held by them as community property, or as tenants in common (see description below), many jurisdictions will honor the agreement, and the house may not pass to Mary by automatic right of survivorship.

Whether or not such documents will be recognized will hinge, in part, upon whether all joint owners are included in the agreement.

Joint interests are most commonly created among family members, who often wish to transfer property, at their death, to coowning relatives.

Interests in common. Like joint interests, *interests in common* are held by two or more persons, each having an equal undivided right to possess property. Unlike joint interests, however, interests in common may be owned in unequal percentages, and when one owner dies the remaining owners do not automatically succeed in ownership. Instead, the decedent's interest passes through his or her estate, by will, by some other document, or by the laws of intestate distribution.

> EXAMPLE 2–11 Jack owns a 16 percent real estate interest in common with two other individuals. Upon Jack's earlier death, his interest will not pass to the other cotenants, but to his wife, who is named to receive it in his will.

In contrast with joint interests, interests in common are more frequently created between nonrelated parties, as a means of enjoying common ownership without losing the right of disposition at death.

Interests by the entirety. An *interest by the entirety* is much like a joint tenancy; however, it can be created only between husband and wife. And unlike joint tenancy, neither spouse may transfer the property without the consent of the other. A number of states do not recognize interests by the entirety.

Community property interests.[6] In the eight states[7] recognizing it, *community property* is any property that has been acquired by either of the spouses during their marriage, but not by gift, devise, bequest or inheritance, or, often, by the income therefrom.[8] Community property is considered to be owned equally by both spouses, and those ownership interests are created at the moment the property is acquired.

In contrast, all property in community property states that is not community property (that is, all property acquired by a person not during marriage, and property acquired during a marriage by gift, devise, bequest or inheritance, or, often, income earned on property so acquired) is called *separate property.*[9] Separate property is considered entirely owned by the acquiring spouse. In states without community-property provisions, of course, separate property is the only recognized type of property, in this context. In those states, it would simply be called "property owned by an individual."

---

[6]Students who are residents of noncommunity property states can omit this section without loss of continuity.

[7]Arizona, California, Idaho, Louisiana, Nevada, New Mexico, Texas, and Washington. In addition, Wisconsin has recently adopted a form of community property known as "marital property," based on the Uniform Martial Property Act (UMPA). For a UMPA bibliography, see the Wenig article cited at the end of the chapter.

[8]Three community property states, Texas, Idaho, and Louisiana, treat income earned from separate property during the marriage as community property.

[9]Idaho and California also have a concept called *quasi-community property,* which is defined as property that would have been community property if acquired in the community property state. For example, common stock acquired with salary income by New York residents during their marriage would be considered quasi-community property if they moved to California. Essentially, California quasi-community property is treated as separate property of the acquiring spouse until divorce or death. If the parties divorce, the property is divided in a manner similar to community property. Treatment at death depends on which spouse dies first. If the acquiring spouse dies first, the surviving spouse is entitled to one half of the property. On the other hand, the nonacquiring spouse's rights to the property cease at his or her earlier death.

EXAMPLE 2–12 Pat and Mary live in a community property state. When they married two years ago, Pat owned a sports car, which Mary also uses. Pat works as a shoe salesman and Mary is a bank teller. Last year Mary's father gave her 100 shares of XYZ stock, which pays a quarterly dividend. Mary used the last dividend check to buy a 10-speed bicycle. Pat bought a bicycle from money saved from his July paycheck. The stock and Mary's bicycle are Mary's separate property.[10] The car is Pat's separate property. All of the other assets, including both salaries, are community property, since their source is nongift, noninheritance property acquired during the marriage.

Community property laws represent certain state governments' attempt to impose greater fairness in property ownership between married couples, According to old common law, the husband became the owner of all property that he acquired. Typically earning all or most of the outside income while the wife performed the nonincome-producing household chores, husbands usually acquired virtually all of the family wealth. By common law, a wife was entitled to own none of this property until her husband's death, at which time she received a life estate in one third of her husband's real property. Called a "dower" interest, it has been modified by many states, but not so radically as in those states incorporating community property laws, which implicitly assume that during their lives the husband and wife should immediately share the property acquired by their joint efforts during their marriage.

Summarizing, the major distinction between community property states and "common law states," as they are called, hinges on when the nonacquiring spouse attains beneficial interest in the property. In common law states the nonacquiring spouse is technically not entitled to ownership, dominion, or control over any of the property acquired by the other spouse during the latter's lifetime; such rights will eventually arise in different degrees, but usually only upon divorce or at death of the acquiring spouse. In contrast, the nonacquiring spouse in community property states attains legal and beneficial interest in any community property the moment the other spouse acquires it.

---

[10]In Texas, Idaho, and Louisiana, the bicycle would be community property.

As different types of co-ownership of property, joint tenancy (JT) and community property (CP) have several major similarities and differences, which are summarized in the outline below.

1. *Major similarities*:
   a. Ownership by more than one person.
   b. The owners have equal ownership rights and equal rights to use the entire property. Their interests are undivided.
   c. Any owner may demand a division of the property into separate, equal shares.
2. *Major differences*:
   a. CP exists only between spouses. JT can exist between any two or more persons.
   b. CP rights arise automatically, by operation of law, under state statute. Hence, they are created immediately upon acquisition of the property. JT rights usually arise at the time of the agreement between the parties and are not governmentally imposed.
   c. JT includes automatic right of succession to ownership (right of survivorship) by surviving joint owners. This right takes priority over any will.[11] In contrast, CP includes no automatic succession to ownership of the decedent's share by the surviving spouse.[12] Therefore, at death, a spouse can transfer his or her share of CP, by will, to someone other than the spouse. However, as we shall see in Chapter 4, intestacy will ordinarily result in succession by the surviving spouse, under typical state laws of intestate succession.
   d. Property held in JT will not be subject to the probate process. In contrast, the decedent's share of CP will be

---

[11]However, as we have said, some states, such as New York, recognize an agreement between the spouses declaring that specified property is held in joint tenancy "for convenience only." In addition, the American Bar Association is considering a "Blockbuster Will," which would override the effect of joint tenancy, life insurance, and other beneficiary designations.

[12]However, Idaho, Nevada, and Washington statutes sanction the designation, "community property with right of survivorship," which, upon the death of the first spouse, results in the passing of the property to the surviving spouse, free of probate administration.

subject to probate or possibly to a form of summary probate as described in Appendix 4A.

Legal versus Beneficial Interests: Introduction to the Trust

Ordinarily, the owner of an interest in property has some right to possess and enjoy the property. Occasionally, however, as implied earlier, these interests are divided so that one party has only "bare legal title," responsible solely for preserving and managing property for the benefit of another who is entitled to enjoy the property in specified ways. The former holds *legal interest* while the latter holds *beneficial interest,* or equitable interest, in the property. The trust is the most common legal arrangement employing this division of rights.

There are three major parties to a trust: a trustor, trustee, and beneficiary. The *trustor*, also called *grantor, creator* or *settlor,* is the person who creates the trust and whose property usually winds up in it. The property in a trust is called the *principal* or the *corpus*. The *trustee* is the person, persons or firm named by the trustor to administer the trust. The trustee holds legal interest to the trust property. The trust beneficiary is the person or persons who are named to enjoy beneficial interest in the trust. A trust can be a *living* or *inter vivos trust,* to take effect during the life of the trustor, or it can be a *testamentary trust,* to take effect at the trustor's death. A testamentary trust is created in a will. An example of a testamentary trust can be found in Chapter 3, Exhibit 3–3.

> EXAMPLE 2–13 Trustor Craig transfers 1,000 shares of ABC stock in trust to Uncle Tom as trustee, with the dividend income payable to Craig's son Chet for 11 years. Tom receives legal title and is responsible for managing the property during this period. He may not use it for his own benefit, and he is required to pay all dividend income received to Chet, the beneficiary. Chet has a beneficial interest, that is, an estate for years in the income of the trust.

Clients may wish to create trusts for two principal reasons: to avoid making outright transfers to family members and to reduce taxes. First, clients may be reluctant to make outright transfers to a spouse or the children if there is concern that the property may be dissipated, invested unwisely, or transferred to undesired beneficiaries. Second, tax saving also encourages trust creation. We shall see later in the the text that trusts can be uniquely capable of facilitating the reduction of income and transfer taxes, often in the only manner satisfactory to clients.

Power of Appointment

In arranging property transfers into trust or otherwise, clients can add considerable flexibility to their estate plans by granting a power of appointment. A power of appointment is a power to name someone to receive a beneficial interest in property. The grantor of the power is called the donor. The person receiving the power is called the *holder* or donee. The parties whom the holder may appoint by *exercising* the power are called the *permissible appointees,* and the parties whom the holder actually appoints are called the *appointees.* In addition, the persons who receive the property if the holder permits the power to *lapse* (i.e., does not exercise the power within the permitted period) are called the *takers in default.* Summarizing in an example, if A transfers to B a power of appointment over A's 100 shares of IBM stock, permitting B to appoint C, D, or E, and B eventually appoints D to receive the stock, then A is the donor; B is the holder (of the power); C, D, and E are the permissible appointees; and D is the appointee (of the stock). There are no takers in default because the holder did not permit the power to lapse.

In Chapter 6, we shall see that death taxes play an important role in the use of powers of appointment, so much so that we commonly classify two types of powers in the same way that they are implicitly classified in the Internal Revenue Code. Under the Code, a power of appointment is either considered a general power of appointment or a nongeneral power of appointment. Defining these terms will be deferred until Chapter 6. The next example shows a common use of the power of appointment.

> EXAMPLE 2–14 Charles died recently, and his will places some of his property in trust for the benefit of his children. A bank is named trustee and is given a nongeneral power of appointment over the corpus. The bank has, among other things, discretion to distribute corpus to the children in accordance with their needs "for their proper support, health, and education." This year, the trust has distributed $6,000 to one son and $4,000 to a daughter to pay their college tuition.

Present versus Future and Vested versus Contingent Interests

A beneficial interest in property may be classified as a present interest or a future interest, depending on whether or not the owner has the immediate right to possess or enjoy the property.[13] An owner of a *present interest* has an immediate right to possess or enjoy the property, while an owner of a *future interest* does not, because the latter's right to possess or enjoy the property is delayed, either by a specific period of time or until the happening of a future event.

The most common types of future interests are reversions and remainders. A *reversion* is a future interest in property that is retained by the transferor after the transferor transfers to another some interest in the property. The reversion will become a present interest of the transferor, or the transferor's estate, at the termination of all of the interests that were transferred.

> EXAMPLE 2–15 Jerry transfers property to Eva for her life. Jerry has implicitly retained a reversion, also called reversionary interest. It will become Jerry's (or his estate's) present interest at Eva's death.

A *remainder* is a type of future interest held by someone other than the transferor; it will become a present interest when all other interests created at the same time have ended.

> EXAMPLE 2–16 George transfers property to Sally for her life, then to John or his estate. John's future interest in the property is a remainder. It is not a *reversion* because John was not the tranferor.

A *vested* remainder is a remainder that is nonforfeitable; i.e., it is a remainder whose possession and enjoyment are delayed *only by time* and are not dependent on the happening of any future event.

> EXAMPLE 2–17 With regard to the transfer by George in Example 2–16, John's remainder is vested: Nothing prevents him or his estate from receiving possession, except the passage of time. Morbidly but accurately speaking, Sally will die; it is only a matter of time.

---

[13]We shall see later that this distinction is of great importance in connection with the $10,000 annual exclusion for gifts.

A *contingent remainder* is a remainder that is not vested; that is, it is a remainder whose possession and enjoyment are dependent on the happening of a future event, other than the passage of time.

> EXAMPLE 2–18 Catherine transfers property to Flo for her life, then outright in fee simple to Jason, if alive, otherwise to Chris, if alive. Jason and Chris each have a contingent remainder interest in the property. Both interests are dependent on each of them living long enough. From today's perspective, each may or may not survive the required period; either Jason's or Chris's or both of their interests will be cut off by the happening of an event: their own prior death.

A vested remainder is usually enforceable in court, while a contingent remainder is usually not. Both, however, may be subject to transfer taxation.

A few more examples, presented in the context of common transfer devices, should help to clarify these distinctions.

> EXAMPLE 2–19 Gary's will leaves a parcel of real estate in trust, with income payable to his wife Joan for her life. At Joan's death, the trust will terminate and the property will pass outright in fee to Gary's son Max, if still alive, otherwise to the Salvation Army. At Gary's death, assuming that Joan and Max are still alive, Joan will receive a present interest called a life estate in the income, and Max and the Salvation Army will each receive a future interest, called a contingent remainder in the corpus. Max and the Salvation Army share something in common: Either interest may never become a present interest since an event may occur that would defeat either one. Max's interest will cease if he predeceases Joan. The Salvation Army's interest will cease if Max survives Joan. Both are contingent remainders because, for each, possession is dependent upon the happening of a future event other than the mere passage of time.[14]

> EXAMPLE 2–20 Sam's will leaves property in trust, with income to his wife June for her life. Then the trust will terminate and the corpus will pass to Sam's son Kurt or his estate. At Sam's death, Kurt will receive a vested remainder in the property. Although initially a future interest, we are certain that it will become a present interest; it cannot

---

[14]In addition, if the trust is revocable, all future interests are contingent on one other "event": Gary's not amending or revoking the trust sometime before his death.

be defeated. Only the passage of time keeps Kurt's interest from being immediately a present interest. Of course, Kurt may not be alive to enjoy the property, but the beneficiaries of his estate will.

We have seen that the transfer of property into a trust results in a division into two interests, with the trustee receiving the legal interest and the beneficiaries receiving the beneficial interests. In addition, transfers into trust typically result in a second type of division of interests when the beneficial interests are split among two or more beneficiaries. Ordinarily, one group of beneficiaries, called the *income beneficiaries,* receive a life estate or estate for years in the trust income, while the other group, called the *remaindermen,* receive the remainder at the termination of all other interests. There are many reasons for splitting beneficial interests into life estate or estate for years and remainder, and we will have much to say about them in later chapters. At present, the reader should simply be aware of the interest-splitting nature of the trust, and should recognize that at the time of the transfer into the trust the life estate and estate for years are usually present interests, while the remainder is a future interest, which may be vested or contingent.

The next chapter will apply many of the concepts introduced in this chapter to describe the provisions of the major documents utilized in the property transfer process.

IMPORTANT CONCEPTS COVERED IN THIS CHAPTER

Estate	Consideration	Testate
Property	Gift	Probate
Probate estate	Inter vivos	Personal representative
Gross estate	Instrument	Fiduciary
Taxable estate	Beneficiary	Executor
Transfer	Donor	Administrator
Assignment	Decedent	Heir
Transferor	Will	Devisee
Transferee	Testamentary	Legatee
Legal interest	Executed	Legacy
Beneficial interest	Testator	Bequest
Outright transfer	Trust	Issue
Sale	Intestate	Specific bequest

General bequest
Residuary bequest
Residue
Life insurance
Insured
Term life insurance
Cash value life
  insurance
Cash surrender value
Gift tax
Death tax
Estate tax
Inheritance tax
Income tax
Joint income tax return
Progressive tax rates
Fee simple
Life estate
Measuring life
Interest for years

Leasehold
Real property
Personal property
Tangible personal
  property
Intangible personal
  property
Chose in action
Concurrent ownership
Joint interest
Interest in common
Interest by the entirety
Community property
Separate property
Trust
Trustor
Grantor
Creator
Settlor
Trust principal

Corpus
Trustee
Trust beneficiary
Living trust
Testamentary trust
Power of appointment
Holder
Permissible appointee
Appointee
Exercise (a power)
Lapse (of a power)
Taker in default
Present interest
Future interest
Reversion
Remainder
Vested remainder
Contingent remainder
Income beneficiary
Remainderman

RECOMMENDED READING

ABNEY, DAVID L. "Impact of California Community Property Presumptions on Joint Tenancy," *Community Property Journal* 13 (January 1987), pp. 40–45.

BERGIN, THOMAS F., AND PAUL G. HASKELL. *Prefaces to Estates in Land and Future Interests.* 2nd ed. New York: Foundation Press, 1984.

HILKER, ANNE K. "Planning for the Married Couple Moving into or out of Community Property States" *Estate Planning,* July 1987, pp. 212–16.

RAABE, WILLIAM A., AND RICK J. TAYLOR. "Wisconsin's Uniform Marital Property Act: Community Property Moves East." *Community Property Journal* 12 (Spring 1985), pp. 83–117.

STEPHENSON, GILBERT T., AND NORMAN A. WIGGINS. *Trusts and Estates,* 5th ed. New York: Appleton-Century-Crofts, 1973.

WENIG, MARY M. "UMPA Bibliography" *Community Property Journal,* July 1986, pp. 92–97.

QUESTIONS AND PROBLEMS

1. Describe four different meanings of the concept "estate."
2. (*a*) Contrast a legal interest with a beneficial interest. (*b*) Why might a person want to transfer such interests in the same property to different individuals, rather than outright to one person?
3. Contrast a sale with a gift.
4. One of your clients shows you the following clipping from a trade journal:

   "John Smith, a prominent local resident, died on Thursday. His generosity was legend. Last year, he made several large *outright inter vivos gifts* to his alma mater and to another charitable *donee*. In addition, in a lengthy handwritten *will executed* last year, the *decedent* made several large *general bequests* and *specific devises* to the local orphans' fund, including a *transfer* into a *testamentary trust*. Finally, as *holder* of a *power of appointment* over several parcels of land on the outskirts of town, Smith *exercised* the power in favor of several trustee-*appointees,* one of whom is a grandson of the *donor.* Interestingly, no *residuary bequest* was included in the will, which means that the *testator* died *intestate* with regard to a considerable portion of his *estate*. Smith nominated as *executor* of his *probate* estate several of his surviving *issue.*"

   Explain to your client the meaning of each highlighted word.
5. Contrast the insured, the owner, and the beneficiary of a life insurance policy.
6. (*a*) Why is a fee simple interest greater than a life estate or an estate for years? (*b*) Can you think of any sense in which all three interests can be considered nearly equal?
7. Compare and contrast joint interests with interests in common.
8. Define community property and separate property.
9. Compare and contrast community property with joint interests.

10. Cindy and Dennis were married in 1980. At that time, they each owned a car and some furnishings. Since then Dennis has been working full-time and Cindy has been an unemployed mother and homemaker. In 1982, Dennis was given 100 shares of IBM stock. In 1983, Cindy inherited her father's computer. This year, Dennis put one half of a year's salary as down payment on a house for his family. Making your own assumptions when necessary, identify the community property and the separate property.

11. Continuing Problem 10, suppose Dennis paid the down payment on the house with dividend income from the IBM stock, but the house payments were made from Dennis' salary. Is the house community property, separate property, or part community and part separate property?

12. Contrast a present interest with a future interest.

13. (a) If Walsh named Paul today to be the sole beneficiary under her will, does Paul today have a present or future interest? (b) If future, is it vested or contingent? (c) If contingent, when will it vest, if ever? Explain each answer carefully.

PART 2

The Constraints in Planning

3

Introduction to Property Transfers I: The Documents of Transfer

OVERVIEW

Estate planning seeks to facilitate the transfer of the client's wealth as efficiently as possible. Efficiency in estate planning usually requires the preparation of one or more formal documents, ones which will be accepted by those authorities that ultimately authorize and make the transfers. For example, the proper preparation and execution of a will is essential to the efficient disposal of any probate property. The will must be drafted correctly to ensure proper disposition, and it must be signed and witnessed according to law so that many officials, including the probate judge, the court clerk, the county recorder, and the bank officer will stand willing to participate in the title transfer process.

This chapter is the first of two which introduce the principles of property transfer. It will explore the documents used in the process of transferring wealth. Specifically, it will examine the creation of four common property transfer devices: joint tenancy, property disposition by contract, the will, and the trust. Appendixes at the end of the chapter will cover the rule against perpetuities and will describe a type of will whose provisions are created entirely by statute. The next chapter will examine the actual process of transfer of the property disposed of by these documents, with emphasis on the probate process. And, because probate also administers the decedent's intestate property, the next chapter will also survey the law of intestate succession.

Property transfers are regulated by state, not federal, law. State laws in this area vary greatly, making generalization difficult. However, a sizable minority of the states have many property distribution laws in common because they have adopted all or a significant part of the Uniform Probate Code (UPC). The UPC was introduced in 1966, partly in answer to the criticism that probate procedures in the United States were too costly, too time-consuming, and too complicated. Idaho was the first state to adopt it in 1972, and since then a total of 20 states have adopted it in whole or in large part.[1] In presenting the material in this and the next chapter, we will often refer to the laws of those states which have adopted the UPC, especially in three major areas: will execution, intestate succession, and probate administration.

JOINT TENANCY ARRANGEMENTS

The acquisition of title in joint tenancy is ordinarily a simple matter, requiring the completion of one or two preprinted forms. An attorney need not be present.[2] Title to real property is usually completed in the realtor's or title company's office. Similarly, written title in joint ownership of personal property, when it can easily be created, is completed in the office of the professional who helps to acquire it. Examples include title to securities by the investment broker, to a car by the motor vehicle bureau, and to a bank account by the bank. Again, an attorney need not be present to simply create the title.

---

[1]Alabama, Alaska, Arizona, Colorado, Florida, Hawaii, Idaho, Maine, Maryland, Michigan, Minnesota, Montana, Nebraska, New Mexico, New Jersey, North Dakota, Oregon, Pennsylvania, Wisconsin, and Utah.

[2]Later in the text, particularly in Chapter 10, the reader will learn several significant disadvantages to taking title in joint tenancy. Thus, the decision as to whether or not to take title in joint tenancy can be far from clear and may require the advice of an attorney. However, the focus of the present material is on how title in joint tenancy is taken, not whether it should be taken.

PROPERTY DISPOSAL BY CONTRACT

There are a number of significant ways in which property can be transferred pursuant to a contract. Life insurance and pension and profit sharing plans are common examples.

Life Insurance

Wealth derived from life insurance comes in two forms, the policy proceeds and the policy itself. Different means are undertaken in arranging the transfer of each.

Planning the transfer of the *proceeds* of a life insurance policy is arranged during the application process, when the chosen beneficiary is designated in the written application. The beneficiary's name will then be printed on the policy itself, when issued. Anytime thereafter, the beneficiary designation can easily be changed by the owners by giving written notice to the company.

Arranging the transfer of the life insurance *policy itself* is also simple, requiring the completion of a short assignment form provided by the insurance company.

Pension and Profit Sharing Plans

Pension and profit sharing plans are contracts between the employee-client and the employer. Ordinarily, the employer initially requests that the employee fill out a simple written form designating the beneficiary, the party who will be entitled to any benefits paid after the employee's death. Thus, the actual process of title designation for most retirement plans is both simple and straightforward.

The document preparation process for the will and the trust are not simple. Unlike joint tenancy and written contracts, the will and the trust are capable of disposing of nearly all of the client's estate, as well as providing for the care of the testator's minor children. Thus, the will and the trust will contain more provisions usually affecting all of the testator's surviving family. Further, unlike insurance and retirement contracts, which are drafted by the insurer or the employer rather than the client, the responsibility for drafting the will and the trust falls on the individual client. The following material presents an overview of the common provisions of the will and the trust.

THE WILL

Individuals often die leaving no formal directions as to how to dispose of their probate property or who should care for their minor children. In such cases, the state seeks to make these decisions equitably and sensibly, using statutory guidelines and examining the family situation. Too often, however, state actions appear to conflict with the apparent wishes of a decedent, as recollected by the survivors. Too often, the state does not write a good will for an intestate decedent. Individuals can avoid an undesired outcome by expressing these wishes while still alive, preferably in a legally acceptable manner, as a direction and guide for those who will survive. The will is the most common formal document serving this purpose.

Who May Execute a Will

A will is a written document disposing of a person's probate property at death.[3] In most states, any individual 18 or older who is of sound mind may dispose of his or her property by will. The implications of this are twofold. First, individuals under the age of 18 cannot usually transfer property by will unless they are emancipated minors. Their probate property will pass, at death, in accordance with the laws of intestate succession. This usually means that their parents will inherit it. Second, a will can be denied probate if it can be established that the testator, at date of execution of the will, lacked testamentary capacity ("sound mind") or was subject to undue influence or to fraud.[4] These three concepts are discussed next.[5]

---

[3]In a few states, wills can be oral, but laws usually greatly restrict the scope of their ability to dispose of wealth. Often, a limit is placed on the value that can be disposed of, such as $2,000. In addition, the testator is often required to be a member of the armed forces. Practically speaking, all wills prepared in the estate planning process are written.

[4]A will can also be contested on the basis of a *mistake*. Examples include (*a*) the testator leaves her estate to only one son, mistakenly believing that the other is wealthy; (*b*) the testator mistakenly leaves out an intended clause; and (*c*) the will mistakenly includes an unintended clause.

[5]Ordinarily, a finding of lack of testamentary capacity will invalidate the entire will, while a finding of undue influence or fraud will invalidate only those provisions that relate to the misconduct.

Testamentary capacity. Testamentary capacity concerns the testator's mental ability to validly execute a will. Ordinarily, a testator has testamentary capacity if he or she possesses each of these three attributes:

1. Sufficient mental capacity to understand the nature of the act being undertaken (writing a will).
2. Sufficient mental capacity to understand and recollect the nature and situation of his or her property.
3. Sufficient mental capacity to remember and understand his or her relationship to the persons who have natural claims on his or her bounty and whose interests are affected by the provisions of the will.

Essentially, then, testators must know that they are executing a will, they must be aware of what they own, and they must be cognizant of their heirs. On its face, this test is quite severe; strictly construed, it would prevent many older testators from executing a valid will. However, probate courts have not usually been so strict, and at various times they have admitted to probate wills executed by individuals who have been blind, alcoholic, and judicially declared mentally incompetent, or even insane. Nonetheless, in other situations, failure to meet one or more of these conditions has resulted in a finding of insufficient testamentary capacity.[6] The outcome usually hinges on whether or not, at or about the specific time the will was executed, the three-prong test was met.[7]

Undue influence. A will executed by a testator who was subject to undue influence will also be denied probate. Undue influence is influence of another which has the effect of impeding the testator's free will. Examples include threats, the use of force (duress), and the use of overpersuasion and psychological domination, as when "Snake Oil Sam," the smooth-talking newcomer, makes

---

[6]Appellate courts do not like setting a will aside, and will reverse most jury set-aside decisions.

[7]Some attorneys like to videotape the will execution of a testator who may have questionable capacity, believing that the testator's capacity will become more apparent. On the other hand, others believe that videotaping can enhance the success of a contest, reasoning that often testators can look terrible on the screen (especially if they are shown lying in a hospital bed), and that the taping constitutes additional evidence that even the attorney wasn't confident of the testator's capacity.

a romantic play for the 92-year-old widow, "encouraging" her to disinherit her children and leave her entire estate to him.

Fraud. Fraud involves deception through false information, as, for example, when niece tells great uncle that she is penniless when, in fact, she is wealthy.

Statutory Format Requirements for Wills

Most states, including those that have adopted the Uniform Probate Code, recognize at least two types of wills, the *witnessed will* and the *holographic will*.

Witnessed will. Although state laws vary, a witnessed or "attested" will must usually meet the following requirements:

1. Must be *in writing* (handwritten, typed, etc.)
2. In the presence of *two witnesses* (three in a few states) the testator must sign the will. However in some states, someone else may sign for the testator, at the testator's direction and in the testator's presence. In such case, the testator must acknowledge that he or she has authorized the signature.
3. The witnesses *must sign* their names to the will, understanding that the instrument they sign is the testator's will. The main purpose of requiring witnesses is to prevent forgery and coercion of the testator.

Beneficiaries should not be witnesses to a will because that could imperil their right to receive some or all of their bequest. In most states, a bequest to a witness is a void, unless the witness is an heir. In such a case the witness can take no more than his or her intestate share. In some other states, if challenged, an "interested witness" may take under a will only if he or she is able to rebut a statutory presumption that the devise was procured by duress, menace, fraud, or undue influence. Although inability to rebut this presumption will not totally invalidate the will, it will invalidate the bequest to that witness.

Holographic will. If a will does not meet all of the requirements for a witnessed will, in many states it can still often be admitted to probate if it meets the requirements for a holographic will. Typical state requirements for a holographic will are:

1. Signature is in the testator's handwriting.
2. All of the "material provisions" of the will are in the testator's handwriting.

Holographic wills are recognized in about two fifths of the states.

Contrasting witnessed and holographic wills.   The differences between the two sets of formal requirements are twofold: First, the witnessed will requires the performance of certain activities in connection with two witnesses. In contrast, the holographic will may, but need not, be witnessed. Second, the holographic will requires that all material provisions of the will be in the testator's handwriting. In contrast, the witnessed will requires that only the testator's signature be handwritten, and even this may be unnecessary when a proper authorization is arranged.

The Simple Will

Wills can be quite complex, but this chapter will focus on a relatively simple will. In fact, that's just what the profession calls its most common uncomplicated will. A *simple will* is a will prepared for a family having a small estate, one for whom death tax planning is not a significant concern.[8] Thus, the simple will contains no tax provisions but usually includes all of the following provisions: nominating both an executor and a guardian for minor children, waiving the probate bond, and, in most cases, disposing of most or all of the testator's property to the spouse, if alive, otherwise to the children, who are called contingent beneficiaries. The simple will is introduced at this point in the text not to emphasize estate planning devices for the small family estate. They will be discussed in the chapters in Part 3. Instead it is presented to simply demonstrate, by example, the essential nature of that probate property transfer document which we call the will.

-----

[8]As we shall see later, numerically, a small estate is considered less than about $600,000. A medium-size estate ranges between $600,000 and $1,200,000, while a larger estate is considered to exceed $1,200,000.

An example of a simple will is presented in Exhibit 3–1.[9] The reader is encouraged to study it carefully, so that the analysis that follows will have maximum impact.

EXHIBIT 3–1 Simple Will

WILL OF JOHN CARTER JONES

I, John Carter Jones, declare this to be my will and revoke all prior wills and codicils.

First: Family and Guardian

My wife, Jane ("my wife"), and our two children, Tom and Mary, comprise my immediate family. All reside with me at 1234 Maple Street, Anytown, Mystate. This will applies to all my children, including any hereafter born or adopted, and to their issue.

If my wife does not survive me, I appoint Ralph P. Smith guardian of the person and estate of each minor child of mine. If for any reason Ralph P. Smith does not act as guardian, I appoint James I. Thompson as guardian of the person and estate.

Second: Executor

A. *Designation*   I appoint my wife executor. If for any reason she does not act as executor, I appoint Roger C. Riley my executor. If for any reason neither my wife nor Roger C. Riley acts as executor, I appoint First National Bank of Anytown my executor.

B. *Bond waiver*   My executor shall not be required to give bond, surety, or other security.

C. *Taxes from residue*   My executor shall pay from the residue of my estate all death taxes imposed because of my death and interest and penalties on those taxes, whether on property passing under this will or otherwise.

---

[9]Will clauses derived, with permission, from two articles in *Estate Planning* magazine (published by Warren, Gorham & Lamont): (*a*) Lynn B. Squires and Robert S. Mucklestone, "Drafting a Truly 'Simple Will' that Can Effectively Communicate to Both Client and Court," *Estate Planning,* March 1983, pp. 80–84; (*b*) Leon Feldman, "'Simple Will' Can be Simplified Further to Produce a More Concise but Effective Document," *Estate Planning,* September 1983, pp. 290–93.

EXHIBIT 3–1 *(continued)*

Third: Disposition of Property

A. *Home and tangible personal property* If my wife survives me by 30 days, I give her all of my interest in:

1. The residence property which we occupy as a home at my death, and all rights associated with it.

2. All tangible personal property, for example, vehicles, boats, furniture, furnishings, books, art objects, sporting equipment, jewelry, and clothing.

If my wife does not survive me by 30 days, I give tangible personal property (except vehicles and boats) in equal shares to my children who survive me by 30 days, but my executor shall consider their personal preferences in making that division. My executor may sell any of that property and distribute the proceeds to equalize the shares. My executor shall be discharged for tangible personal property so given to any minor child if the child or adult having the child's custody gives a written receipt to my executor.

B. *Residue* If my wife survives me by four months, I give her the residue of my estate. If my wife does not survive me by four months, I give the residue in equal shares: one to each of my children who survives me by four months and one to the descendants per stirpes who survive me by four months of each of my children who does not so survive me.

If neither my wife nor any of my descendants survives me by four months, I give the residue of my estate according to Mystate's laws of descent and distribution, one half as if I had died with no will on the last day of that four-month period and one half as if it were my wife's estate and she had died with no will on that last day.

Fourth: Powers of Executor

My executor shall have power, without court order, to settle my estate as this will provides and to do all my executor thinks necessary or desirable to administer my estate, including power to:

1. Distribute principal and income on an interim basis to those entitled to it.

2. Sell, lease, exchange, mortgage, pledge, or assign all or part of my estate's property, whether or not necessary to pay debts, taxes, or administration expenses.

3. Invest and reinvest property not specifically given.

4. Continue to operate any business or business properties in which I have an interest at my death and, in so doing, delegate powers.

EXHIBIT 3–1 *(concluded)*

I have initialed all pages of this will and have signed it on March 19, 1999, at Anytown, Mystate.

_____
(Signature)

Statement of Witnesses

Each of the undersigned declares under penalty of perjury under Mystate law, on March 19, 1999, that the following is true:

· A. I am over 21 and competent to witness this will.

B. The testator in my presence and in the presence of the other undersigned witness

    1. Declared the foregoing document to be his will.

    2. Asked me to act as a witness to his will and to make this statement.

    3. Signed his will.

C. I believe that the testator is of sound mind and did not act under duress, fraud, or undue influence in so declaring and signing.

D. In the presence of the testator and of the other witness I sign as witness to this will.

_____
(Signature)

_____
(Address)

_____
(Signature)

_____
(Address)

Analysis of the Simple Will. Let's analyze the major provisions of this will, section by section.

Will of John C. Jones. In this introductory paragraph, the testator explicitly "declares" it to be his will, primarily to satisfy the law's requirement that a testator have an intent to make a will.

A *codicil* is a separate written document that amends or revokes a prior will. It is executed if, sometime later, the testator wishes to change or add to the will. As a separate document, it also must meet all of the legal requirements imposed on the witnessed will, including subscription by witnesses.

Revoking all prior wills and codicils eliminates the danger that provisions in prior wills which are not inconsistent with the present will have to be construed together with the current will. Without a revocation clause, needless litigation can arise over whether or not the provisions in two or more wills are inconsistent.[10]

First: Family and guardian.   Naming all members of the immediate family can assist a personal representative in finding relatives and locating assets.

Including afterborn children in the will can prevent a child born after the execution of the will and not provided for in it from being left to inherit under the laws of the intestate succession, a consequence that often conflicts with the testator's intent.

As we shall see in Chapter 17, a minor orphan child who has survived both parents is required by law to have a guardian of both the person and the estate of that child. The guardian of the person is responsible for a minor child's care, custody, control, and education, while a guardian of the child's estate is responsible for managing the minor child's property. A testator's nominations carry great weight and will usually be respected, but the probate judge has the power to appoint other persons as guardians. Nominating an alternate guardian increases the likelihood that the testator's preferences will be observed.

Second: Executor.   Similar to nomination of a guardian, nomination of the executor and an alternate executor can be helpful to the probate court in its selection process.

Often, the executor is required to give a bond, which commercially insures the estate against a breach of trust by the executor. However, the will can waive this requirement, one which the testator may consider unnecessary for two reasons: first, because it results in additional expense to the estate, and second, because it may be largely unnecessary if a highly trusted party, such as a spouse, is being nominated.

Declaring that all death taxes be paid from the residue of the estate may be the fairest plan, and one that can minimize admin-

---

[10]In one state supreme court case, a decedent-testator had written two "last" wills within three weeks' time. The first simply left "a tract of land" to a friend. The second contained no revocation clause and left "all my effects" to siblings Y and Z. The court permitted a new trial to determine whether the first will should be construed along with the second, reasoning that they were not necessarily inconsistent because the testator could have used the word "effects" to mean only personal property. Wolfe's will 185NC563, (1923).

istrative delay. On the one hand, it relieves recipients of nonresidue property from having to share in this burden.[11] On the other, it relieves the executor from the responsibility of seeking reimbursement from individuals who may have received only relatively illiquid assets, such as a painting or a piano. And reimbursement for death taxes can be difficult to obtain from individuals not at all connected with the probate process, such as those succeeding to ownership as former joint tenants with the decedent, and beneficiaries of a life insurance policy on the life of the decedent.

Third: Disposition of property. Inclusion of a survival requirement, such as 30 days or four months, reduces the likelihood that the death of both spouses in a common accident will result in subjecting some of the family property to two successive probates. This *survival clause,* as it is called, helps in situations not covered by the Uniform Simultaneous Death Act (USDA).

Enacted by every state, the USDA provides that when transfer of title to property depends on the order of deaths and when no sufficient evidence exists that two people died other than simultaneously, the property of each is disposed of as if each had survived the other.[12] Thus, in the case of a married couple, the husband's estate would pass to his heirs and the wife's estate will pass to her heirs.[13] This statute is of limited value, however, because it will not avoid double probate when the order of deaths can in fact be established. For example, if it *can* be established that one spouse survived the other, even only by seconds, then the USDA will not apply and, absent a survival clause, the upshot will be a double probate of the property owned by the first spouse to die. Perhaps worse, the property will probably ultimately pass to that spouse's in-laws, rather than the surviving relatives. By requiring a survival

---

[11]However, in some circumstances, fairness would dictate apportioning the taxes among all beneficiaries. See Chapter 17.

[12]The Uniform Probate Code, in Section 2–104, is a bit more liberal, providing that the property of each is disposed of as if each had survived the other if it cannot be established that the other person survived *by 120 hours*.

[13]Similarly, with regard to *insurance* on the life of a decedent, the USDA states that in the event of an apparent simultaneous death of the insured and the beneficiary, the policy proceeds are to be distributed as if the insured survived the beneficiary. Thus, the proceeds will be paid to the contingent beneficiary.

period as a precondition to receiving property, a survival requirement, such as the one in this simple will, can better protect the estate from these two unfortunate consequences. For a further discussion of survival clauses, see Chapter 17.

Disposing of estate property by differentiating the residence and the tangible personal property from the residue can speed up probate distribution and can defer the payment of estate income taxes.

Distribution by *per stirpes,* or right of representation, is a method of allocating a gift of the decedent's property to the descendants of a predeceased heir of a person named in the will and is covered in some detail in Chapter 4.

The "laws of descent and distribution," also described in Chapter 4, are different for each state. They spell out the priority of succession rights of the decedent's spouse and kin, in the event of intestacy. In this will, the testator has chosen to divide his property in half, with one half going by intestate succession to his relatives and the other half going by intestate succession to his wife's relatives, in the event that his wife and descendants all fail to survive him by four months.

Fourth: Powers of executor. Explicitly granting powers to the executor can eliminate the need to secure permission of the probate court to undertake certain administrative actions. Ordinarily, testators would like their executors to act without such unnecessary delay.

Statement of witness. Every state imposes formal requirements regarding the role of witnesses in the execution of a will. The sentences included in this section of the will offer additional evidence of the testator's capacity to execute a will. They also maximize the likelihood of compliance with these formal requirements by explicitly stating them, which the witnesses acknowledge by signing.

Next, we'll examine the trust, the other major planning document of transfer.

THE TRUST

As described in Chapter 2, the principal parties to a trust are the trustor, the trustee, and the beneficiary. A trust is created by the trustor and divides and transfers interests in property between two or more people, none of whom is able to exercise complete control over it. Any interests or control over the trust that are not given to the beneficiaries are either retained by the trustor, granted to the trustee, or exercisable by both.

A trust can take effect during the lifetime of the trustor, or it can take effect at the trustor's death. As we have seen, the former is called a *living* (or inter vivos) *trust,* while the latter is called a *testamentary trust,* that is, a trust created in a will.

At any given point in time, a trust is revocable and amendable, in which case the trustor is capable of voiding or amending it, or it is irrevocable, that is, not voidable or amendable. A living trust usually contains specific language stating whether it is revocable or irrevocable.[14] A revocable living trust usually, but not always, becomes irrevocable at the death of the trustor(s). Like the contents of most wills, the provisions of a testamentary trust can be amended or revoked before the testator's death by codicil, revocation or destruction of the trust-will. At the testator's death, a testamentary trust takes effect and becomes by nature irrevocable, since the only person capable of amending or voiding it, the trustor, will, of course, be unavailable.

A trust usually contains two different legal types of property, principal and income. The *principal* of a trust is its invested wealth, and its size will fluctuate as additions are made to it and as charges are made against it. Additions to principal accrue from such things as asset appreciation and stock dividends. Charges against principal are made for such things as costs of investing the principal (commissions, legal fees, etc.), and transfer taxes.

In contrast with trust principal, the *income* of a trust is the return in money or property derived from use of the trust principal.[15] Examples of income include cash dividends, rent, and interest. Trust income also has charges against it, most of which usually reflect expenses incurred in managing the trust property, such as insurance premiums, and some or all of the trustee's fee. Any trust income not distributed to beneficiaries is said to be *accumulated* in the trust and kept allocable to income, not principal.

---

[14]In most states, unless specified as revocable, a trust is irrevocable.

[15]In Chapter 8, we shall call this income "fiduciary accounting income," or FAI.

The accounting distinction between principal and income is particularly important because, as we'll see next, most trusts contain provisions that will bestow rights to principal and income to different beneficiaries. And in Chapter 8, we'll see that the distinction between principal and income will influence trust income taxation.

The beneficiaries of an irrevocable trust are usually either *income beneficiaries* (i.e., those having certain rights to the income) or they are *principal beneficiaries* (for example, a remainderman). These two types of beneficiaries may have conflicting or "adverse" interests, since distributions to one of them may have the effect of reducing future distributions to the other.

There are other ways of classifying trusts, especially in connection with tax planning. The chapters in Part 3 of this text, for example, will introduce many tax-saving trusts, including the bypass trust, the Crummey trust, and the QTIP trust. First, however, the reader must be exposed to the law of estate, gift, and income taxation to understand how and why taxes can be saved. The purpose of focusing on trusts in the present chapter is, however, considerably more basic: to enable the reader to learn the essential structure of documents creating the trust. To do this as plainly as possible, the following material will highlight two trust instruments: an uncomplicated living trust and a trust-will.

The Living Trust

The living trust is created by a document of agreement between trustor and trustee. Let us now compare and contrast the characteristics of that document with its common legal alternative, the will.

Similarities. The will and the document creating the living trust are similar in three important ways. First, both are capable of disposing of property at the client's later death. Second, both direct that a fiduciary be responsible for managing certain property for a period of time. Third, as we saw a bit earlier, both can be made amendable and revocable. The will can nearly always be amended by a codicil, or revoked by its destruction or by execution of a later will that explicitly revokes the prior will.[16] The trust can either be made revocable, or is inherently revocable. In most states, a trust must provide in its instrument that it is revocable, otherwise it becomes irrevocable upon execution. In the other states, a trust is revocable unless otherwise specified.

Differences. The will and the document creating the living trust are also different in several important ways. First, a living trust cannot dispose of property not owned by the trustee. Thus, with regard to property transfers, the living trust and the will are mutually exclusive; property owned by a trustee is not subject to probate, while probate property can only have been owned by a decedent, not a trustee. Second, with regard to choosing a fiduciary, a living trust instrument *appoints* a trustee while a will *nominates* an executor. Ordinarily, since the trustor is alive when the trustee is appointed, the trustor has complete control over the appointment. On the other hand, the probate judge appoints the executor after the testator's death. Thus, the testator can never be absolutely certain that the nomination will be successful. The judge may appoint someone else for any number of reasons, including the nominee's inability to serve due to death, disability, or incompetence. Third, while the formal execution requirements for writing a will are quite strict, the requirements for properly executing a trust are simple to meet. In most cases, the trust document is simply dated and signed by the trustor and the trustee. Witnesses are not required.

Exhibit 3–2 presents an uncomplicated living trust. Please read it in its entirety. An analysis follows.

EXHIBIT 3–2 Living Trust

JOHN C. JONES

Revocable Living Trust

Dated March 19, 1999

TRUST AGREEMENT made March 19, 1999, between John C. Jones, as trustor, resident of Common County, Mystate, and Harold Reliable, resident of Common County, Mystate, as trustee.

---

[16]One exception is the joint and mutual will.

EXHIBIT 3–2 (continued)

1. Trust property. The trustor hereby transfers to the trustee the property described on Schedule A attached hereto and made a part hereof. The trustee agrees to hold such property and any other property which it may receive during the trustor's lifetime or thereafter, in trust, under the terms and conditions provided therein.

2. Successor trustee. If Harold Reliable for any reason ceases to act as trustee, First National Bank of Anytown shall become trustee.

3. Power to amend or revoke. The trustor reserves the right at any time to amend or revoke this trust, in whole or in part, by an instrument in writing signed by him and delivered during his lifetime to the trustee.

4. Operation of trust during trustor's lifetime. During the trustor's lifetime, the trustee shall administer and distribute the trust as follows:

a. Trust income. The trustee shall pay the net income of this trust to the trustor at convenient intervals but at least quarter-anually.

b. Trust principal. The trustee shall pay to the trustor from time to time such amounts of the principal of this trust as the trustor shall direct in writing or as the trustee deems necessary or advisable for the trustor's support and comfort.

5. Operation of trust after trustor's death. Upon the death of the trustor, the trust estate shall be held, administered, and distributed as follows:

a. Wife survives by four months. If the trustor's wife survives trustor by four months, the trustee shall distribute the entire trust estate to her and the trust shall terminate.

b. Wife does not survive by four months. If the trustor's wife does not survive the trustor by four months and if no then-living child of the trustor is under age 21, then the trustee shall divide the trust into as many equal shares as there are children of the trustor's then living and children of the trustor's then deceased with descendants then living. Each share set aside for a child then deceased with descendants then living shall be further divided into shares for such descendants, by right of representation. The trust estate shall be held, administered, and distributed in the manner described in subsections 5(b.)(2)(a) and (b), below.

If neither the trustor's wife nor any of the trustor's descendants survives the trustor by four months, the trustee shall distribute the entire trust estate according to Mystate's laws of descent and distribution, one half as if the trustor had died with no will on the last day

EXHIBIT 3–2 *(continued)*

of the four-month period and one half as if it were the trustor's wife's estate and she had died with no will on the last day.

If the trustor's wife does not survive the trustor by four months and if any then-living child of the trustor is under age 21, then the trust estate shall be held, administered, and distributed as follows:

(1) *Any child under age 21.* So long as any of the trustor's children are living who are under twenty-one (21), the trustee shall pay to or apply for the benefit of all of the trustor's children as much of the net income and principal as the trustee in the trustee's discretion deems necessary for their proper support, health, and education, after taking into consideration, to the extent that the trustee considers advisable, the value of the trust assets, the relative needs, both present and future, of each of the beneficiaries, and their other income and resources made known to the trustee and reasonably available to meet beneficiary needs. The trustee may make distributions under this provision that benefit one or more beneficiaries to the absolute exclusion of others. Any net income not distributed shall be accumulated and added to principal.

(2) *Youngest child reaches age 21.* When the youngest of the trustor's then-living children reaches the age of 21, the trustee shall divide the trust into as many equal shares as there are children of the trustor's then living and children of the trustor's then deceased with descendants then living. Each share set aside for a child then deceased with descendants then living shall be further divided into shares for such descendants, by right of representation. Each such share shall be distributed, or retained in trust, as hereafter provided.

(a) Each share set aside for a descendant shall be distributed to that descendant free of trust if that descendant has then reached age twenty-one (21).

(b) Each share set aside for a descendant who has not then reached age twenty-one (21) shall be retained in trust. The trustee shall pay to or for the benefit of that descendant as much of the income and principal of the trust as the trustee, in the trustee's discretion, considers appropriate for that descendant's support, health, and education. When that descendant reaches age 21, that descendant's share shall be distributed to that descendant, free of trust. If that descendant dies before receiving distribution of that descendant's entire share, the undistributed balance of that descendant's share shall be distributed, free of trust, to that descendant's then-living issue, by right of representation, or if there are none, to the trustor's then-living issue, by right of representation.

EXHIBIT 3–2 *(continued)*

(3) *If wife and issue are deceased.* If at any time before full distribution of the trust estate, the trustor's and all the trustor's issue are deceased and no other disposition of property is directed by this will, the trust remaining shall be distributed according to Mystate's laws of descent and distribution, one half as if the trustor had died with no will and one half as if it were the trustor's wife's estate and she had died with no will.

6. Restriction against assignment, etc. No interest in the principal or income of this trust shall be anticipated, assigned, encumbered, or subject to any creditor's claim or to legal process before its actual receipt by the beneficiary.

7. Perpetuities saving. Any trust created by this will that has not terminated sooner shall terminate twenty-one (21) years after the death of the last survivor of the class composed of my wife and those of my issue living at my death.

8. Powers of trustee. To carry out the purposes of this trust the trustee is vested with the following powers with respect to the trust estate and any part of it, in addition to those powers now or hereafter conferred by law:

a. To continue to hold any property, including shares of the trustee's own stock, and to operate at the risk of the trust estate any business that the trustee receives or acquires under the trust as long as the trustee deems advisable.

b. To manage, control, grant options on, sell (for cash or on deferred payments), convey, exchange, partition, divide, improve, and repair trust property.

c. To lease trust property for terms within or beyond the term of the trust and for any purpose, including exploration for and removal of gas, oil, and other minerals and to enter into community oil leases, pooling, and unitization agreements.

d. To borrow money, and to encumber or hypothecate trust property by mortgage, deed of trust, pledge, or otherwise.

e. To invest and reinvest the trust estate in every kind of property, real, personal, or mixed, and every kind of investment, specifically including, but not by way of limitation, corporate obligations of every kind, stocks, preferred or common, shares of investment trusts, investment companies and mutual funds, and mortgage participations, which men of prudence, discretion, and intelligence acquire for their own account, and any common trust fund administered by the trustee.

f. In any case in which the trustee is required, pursuant to the provisions of the trust, to divide any trust property into parts or

---

EXHIBIT 3–2 *(concluded)*

shares for the purpose of distribution, or otherwise, the trustee is authorized, in the trustee's absolute discretion, to make the division and distribution in kind, including undivided interests in any property, or partly in kind and partly in money, and for this purpose to make such sales of the trust property as the trustee may deem necessary on such terms and conditions as the trustee shall see fit.

IN WITNESS THEREOF this instrument has been executed as of the date set forth on the first page of this instrument.

_____
(Signature of Trustor)

_____
(Signature of Trustee)

Analysis of the living trust. Let's examine the major provisions of this living trust instrument, section by section.

Trust Agreement. A trust is, in effect, a contract or agreement between two parties, the trustor and the trustee. Both sides agree to perform certain tasks: among other things, the trustor agrees to deliver property described in Schedule A (not shown) to the trustee, and the trustee agrees to hold, administer, and distribute the trust property in the manner prescribed.

1. Trust property. The agreement specifies that additional assets may be put in trust in the future, even after the trustor's death. For example, a decedent's will can be directed to "pour over" probate property into a trust after the trustor-testator's death.[17]

2. Successor trustor. Since the trust states the trustee's name in the opening paragraph, this section need only name a successor trustee. Naming a bank or other corporate trustee virtually ensures that a competent trustee will be available to serve for the life of the trust.

3. Power to amend or revoke. This trust can be amended or revoked by a written document, signed by the trustor and delivered to the trustee. An amendment is similar to a codicil to a will, without the strict formal execution requirements.

4. Operation of trust during trustor's lifetime. During the trustor's lifetime, the trustee is required to pay to the trustor all income

---

[17]For a further discussion of the *pour over will,* see Chapter 10.

at least quarterly and any principal as requested. The phrase "or as the trustee deems necessary or advisable . . ." is included to cover the possibility that the trustor can become mentally incompetent.

The reader will notice that the wording assumes that the trustor and the trustee are different parties. However, many living trusts name the trustor to be trustee. In such case, this paragraph would still be used, but would be meaningful only if the client became incompetent, thus requiring the appointment of a different, successor trustee.

5. Operation of trust after trustor's death. This section is substantially longer than the Disposition of Property section in the simple will. It provides for several alternative outcomes depending upon who survives. First, the trust terminates if the trustor's spouse survives the trustor by four months, and all trust property passes outright to her. Second, if the trustor's spouse fails to survive the trustor by four months and if no living child is under age 21, the trust is immediately divided into shares and is administered in a manner (described below) quite similar to the way it is administered for a living child when under 21. Third, if the trustor is survived neither by a spouse nor any descendants, the trust terminates and the trust property passes by intestate succession, with one half to the trustor's relatives and the other half to the trustor's spouse's relatives.[18] Finally, if the trustor's spouse does not survive by four months but one or more of the trustor's living children is under 21, the trust does not terminate. Instead, the trustee is instructed to use trust principal and income to provide for the children's support, education, and other legitimate needs. Then, when the youngest child reaches 21, the trust is divided into equal shares, one for each child then living, and one for each child not living but having living descendants. These descendants, an example of which is any living child of the decedent's deceased children, will share equally in the share of the child-ancestor.[19] Each share is then distributed outright to each descendant when he or she reaches age 21.

The above disposition, via trustee, has much to recommend it

---

[18]The laws of intestate succession are covered in Chapter. 4.

[19]The wording implicitly directs a distribution *per stirpes,* a concept fully explained in Chapter 4.

over the will's provisions making outright gifts to the minor children, via a property guardian. A description of these advantages, however, will be deferred to the material in Part 3 of the text.

6. *Restriction against assignment.* This is an example of a *spendthrift clause*. Many states allow trust beneficiaries to transfer their interests in the trust property. For example, beneficiaries can often mortgage trust property, sell a future interest in it, and devise it. A spendthrift clause restricts such transfers. However, it only protects trust property while held by the trustee, not after it has been transferred outright to the beneficiary. For more information on the spendthrift clause, refer to Chapter 17.

7. *Perpetuities saving.* This clause is included to prevent a contingent gift from being ruled invalid because it vests too long after the death of the decedent. A further description of the common-law rule against perpetuities will be found in Appendix 3A.

8. *Powers of trustee.* Since the trustee may manage estate property for a considerably longer period than the executor, powers explicitly granted to the trustee are usually more detailed than those explicitly granted to the executor. In addition to these powers, both executor and trustee automatically have other implicit powers, ones derived from both statutory law and case law. For example, trustees have the power to defend against claims brought against the trust property, whether or not that power is explicitly granted in the document.

This completes the analysis of the living trust. The third and final document, covered next, combines the disposition characteristics of a will with the many benefits of a trust that takes effect at the client's death.

The Trust-Will

At this point we discuss the trust-will, the third principal document of property disposition commonly prepared by attorneys in the estate planning process. In essence, a trust-will is actually one type of *will*: it serves to dispose of the testator-trustor's probate property at death. But instead of transferring all property to individuals, it disposes of some or all of the probate property to the trustee of the trust described in the document. The trust usually is directed to take effect at the testator's death. As a will it must conform to all of the formal legal requirements for the execution of wills. And as a will the trust-will contains all of those essential provisions found in any will—such as the one that nominates a guardian of the person and estate of the testator's minor children, the one that nominates one or more executors, and the provisions that make outright gifts of certain property. Finally, as a will the trust-will includes the entire section dealing with witnesses.

In addition to containing all of the provisions customarily found in the nontrust-will, the trust-will, like the living trust, must include other clauses that relate to the trust itself. Thus, it will include provisions for distributing probate property into the trust, for naming one or more trustees, for indicating who will be the trust beneficiaries, for specifying how much income and principal they will receive and when they will receive it, and for describing the trustee's duties and powers in connection with managing the trust property. All but the first clause just mentioned are also included in the living trust.

It should be noted that as a will the trust-will is not an "agreement" between testator and future trustee. In fact, the potential trustee may not even be aware that he or she will be performing this task, and may not even be born at execution date of the trust-will.

Exhibit 3–3 presents a relatively uncomplicated trust-will.

EXHIBIT 3–3   Trust-Will

WILL OF JOHN CARTER JONES

I, John Carter Jones, declare this to be my will and revoke all prior wills and codicils.

First: Family and Guardian

My wife, Jane ("my wife"), and our two children, Tom and Mary, comprise my immediate family. All reside with me at 1234 Maple Street, Anytown, Mystate. This will applies to all my children, including any hereafter born or adopted, and to their issue.

If my wife does not survive me, I appoint Ralph P. Smith guardian of the person and estate of each minor child of mine. If for any reason Ralph P. Smith does not act as guardian, I appoint James I. Thompson as guardian of the person and estate.

Second: Executor and Trustee

A. *Designation of executor*   I appoint my wife executor. If for any reason she does not act as executor, I appoint Roger C. Riley my executor. If for any reason neither my wife nor Roger C. Riley

---

EXHIBIT 3–3 *(continued)*

---

acts as executor, I appoint First National Bank of Anytown, NT&SA, my executor.

B. *Designation of trustee* I appoint Roger C. Riley as the trustee of all trusts provided for under this will. If for any reason he does not act as trustee, I appoint First National Bank of Anytown as trustee.

C. *Bond waiver* Neither my executor nor my trustee shall be required to give bond, surety, or other security.

D. *Taxes from residue* My executor shall pay from the residue of my estate all death taxes imposed because of my death and interest and penalties on those taxes, whether on property passing under this will or otherwise.

Third: Disposition of Property

A. *Tangible personal property* If my wife survives me by 30 days, I give her all of my interest in all tangible personal property, for example, vehicles, boats, furniture, furnishings, books, art objects, sporting equipment, jewelry, and clothing.

If my wife does not survive me by 30 days, I give my tangible personal property (except vehicles and boats) in equal shares to my children who survive me by 30 days, but my executor shall consider their personal preferences in making that division. My executor may sell any of that property and distribute the proceeds to equalize the shares. My executor shall be discharged for tangible personal property so given to any minor child if the child or adult having the child's custody gives a written receipt to my executor.

B. *Residue* If my wife survives me by four months, I give her the residue of my estate. If my wife does not survive me by four months, I give the residue in equal shares: one to each of my children who survives me by four months and one to the descendants *per stirpes* who survive me by four months of each of my children who does not so survive me.

If neither my wife nor any of my descendants survives me by four months, I give the residue of my estate according to Mystate's laws of descent and distribution, one half as if I had died with no will on the last day of that four-month period and one half as if it were my wife's estate and she had died with no will on that last day.

If my wife does not survive me and if any then-living child of mine is under age 21, then the residue of my estate shall not vest in my descendants as provided above; rather, such property shall be distributed to my trustee, to he held, administered, and distributed as follows:

EXHIBIT 3–3 *(continued)*

---

1. *Any child under age 21*   So long as any of my children is living who is under age twenty-one (21) the trustee shall pay to or apply for the benefit of all of my children, as much of the net income and principal as the trustee in the trustee's discretion deems necessary for their proper support, health, and education, after taking into consideration, to the extent that the trustee considers advisable, the value of the trust assets, the relative needs, both present and future, of each of the beneficiaries, and their other income and resources made known to the trustee and reasonably available to meet beneficiary needs. The trustee may make distributions under this provision that benefit one or more beneficiaries to the absolute exclusion of others. Any net income not distributed shall be accumulated and added to principal.

2. *Youngest child reaches age 21*   When the youngest of my then-living children reaches the age of 21, the trustee shall divide the trust into as many equal shares as there are children of mine then living and children of mine then deceased with descendants then living. Each share set aside for a child of mine then deceased with descendants then living shall be further divided into shares for such descendants, by right of representation. Each such share shall be distributed, or retained in trust, as hereafter provided.

a. Each share set aside for a descendant shall be distributed to that descendant free of trust if that descendant has then reached age twenty-one (21).

b. Each share set aside for a descendant who has not then reached age twenty-one (21) shall be retained in trust. The trustee shall pay to or for the benefit of that descendant as much of the income and principal of the trust as the trustee, in the trustee's discretion, considers appropriate for that descendant's support, health, and education. When that descendant reaches age 21, that descendant's share shall be distributed to that descendant, free of trust. If that descendant dies before receiving distribution of that descendant's entire share, the undistributed balance of that descendant's share shall be distributed, free of trust, to that descendant's then-living issue, by right of representation, or if there are none, to my then-living issue, by right of representation.[20]

3. *If wife and issue are deceased*   If at any time before full distribution of the trust estate, my wife and all my issue are deceased and no other disposition of property is directed by this will, the trust estate remaining shall be distributed according to Mystate's

---

[20]The terms *descendants* and *issue* are synonymous.

EXHIBIT 3–3 *(continued)*

---

laws of descent and distribution, one half as if I had died with no will and one half as if it were my wife's estate and she had died with no will.

    4. *Restriction against assignment, etc.* No interest in the principal or income of this trust shall be anticipated, assigned, encumbered, or subject to any creditor's claim or to legal process before its actual receipt by the beneficiary.

    5. *Perpetuities saving* Any trust created by this will that has not terminated sooner shall terminate twenty-one (21) years after the death of the last survivor of the class composed of my wife and those of my issue living at my death.

Fourth: Powers of Executor

My executor shall have power, without court order, to settle my estate as this will provides and to do all my executor thinks necessary or desirable to administer my estate, including power to:

    1. Distribute principal and income on an interim basis to those entitled to it.

    2. Sell, lease, exchange, mortgage, pledge, or assign all or part of my estate's property, whether or not necessary to pay debts, taxes, or administration expenses.

    3. Invest and reinvest property not specifically given.

    4. Continue to operate any business or business properties in which I have an interest at my death and, in so doing, delegate powers.

Fifth: Powers of Trustee

To carry out the purposes of any trust created under this paragraph third, and subject to any limitations stated elsewhere in this will, the trustee is vested with the following powers with respect to the trust estate and any part of it, in addition to those powers now or hereafter conferred by law:

    1. To continue to hold any property, including shares of the trustee's own stock, and to operate at the risk of the trust estate any business that the trustee receives or acquires under the trust as long as the trustee deems advisable.

    2. To manage, control, grant options on, sell (for cash or on deferred payments), convey, exchange, partition, divide, improve, and repair trust property.

    3. To lease trust property for terms within or beyond the term of the trust and for any purpose, including exploration for and removal of gas, oil, and other minerals and to enter into community oil leases, pooling, and unitization agreements.

EXHIBIT 3–3 *(concluded)*

4. To borrow money, and to encumber or hypothecate trust property by mortgage, deed of trust, pledge, or otherwise.

5. To invest and reinvest the trust estate in every kind of property, real, personal, or mixed, and every kind of investment, specifically including, but not by way of limitation, corporate obligations of every kind, stocks, preferred or common, shares of investment trusts, investment companies and mutual funds, and mortgage participations, which men of prudence, discretion, and intelligence acquire for their own account, and any common trust fund administered by the trustee.

6. In any case in which the trustee is required, pursuant to the provisions of the trust, to divide any trust property into parts or shares for the purpose of distribution, or otherwise, the trustee is authorized, in the trustee's absolute discretion, to make the division and distribution in kind, including undivided interests in any property, or partly in kind and partly in money, and for this purpose to make such sales of the trust property as the trustee may deem necessary on such terms and conditions as the trustee shall see fit.

I have initialed all pages of this will and have signed it on March 19, 1999, at Anytown, Mystate.

_____
(Signature)

Statement of Witnesses

Each of the undersigned declares under penalty of perjury under Mystate law, on March 19, 1999, that the following is true:

A. I am over age 21 and competent to witness this will.

B. The testator in my presence and in the presence of the other undersigned witness

    1. Declared the foregoing document to be his will.

    2. Asked me to act as a witness to his will and to make this statement.

    3. Signed his will.

C. I believe that the testator is of sound mind and did not act under duress, fraud, or undue influence in so declaring and signing.

D. In the presence of the testator and of the other witness I sign as witness to this will.

_____
(Signature)

_____
(Address)

_____
(Signature)

_____
(Address)

Further comparison of these documents will be deferred to the material in Part 3 of the text, with particular emphasis in Chapters 10, 11 and 12.

This chapter has introduced the documents used in the transfer of an estate, with particular emphasis on the simple will, the living trust, and the trust-will. The next chapter focuses on the actual process of transfer of the property disposed of by these documents, with particular emphasis on the probate process and its handling of intestate succession.

RECOMMENDED READING

BUCKLEY, WILLIAM R. "Videotaped Wills: More than a Testator's Curtain Call." *Trusts & Estates,* October 1987, pp. 48–49.

CHARROW, VEDA R. "Write a Will that Can be Understood." *California Lawyer,* November 1981, pp. 45–62.

DUBOVICH, DEBRA L. "The Blockbuster Will: Effectuating the Testator's Intent to Change Will. Substitute Beneficiaries." *Valparaiso University Law Review* 21 (1987), pp. 719–40. The type of will discussed would override joint tenancy and life insurance beneficiary designations.

EARLY, CHARLES E., and ROBERT L. FREEDMAN. "Some Boiler Plate Pitfalls." *Probate Notes* 9 (1983), pp. 111–28.

EFFLAND, RICHARD W. "Will Construction under the Uniform Probate Code." *Oregon Law Review* 63, no. 3 (1984), pp. 337–80.

FIELDMAN, LEON. "'Simple Will' Can Be Simplified Further to Produce a More Concise but Effective Document." *Estate Planning,* September 1983, pp. 290–93.

HASKELL, PAUL G. *Preface to Wills, Trusts and Administration.* New York: Foundation Press, 1987.

HEATON, J. ANDREW. "The Intestate Claims of Heirs Excluded by Will: Should 'Negative Wills' Be Enforced?" *University of Chicago Law Review* 52 (1985), pp. 177–93.

LANGBEIN, JOHN H., and LAWRENCE W. WAGGONER. "Reformation of Wills on The Ground of Mistake: Change of Direction in American Law?" *University of Pennsylvania Law Review* 130 (January 1982), pp. 521–90.

LEVIN, LEONARD. "Legal Ramifications of Unethical Estate Planning Practices." *Trusts & Estates,* October 1985, pp. 47–56.

MUCKLESTONE, ROBERT S., and LYNN B. SQUIRES. "Drafting a Truly 'Simple Will' that Can Effectively Communicate to Both Client and Court." *Estate Planning,* March 1983, pp. 80–84.

NASH, JODI G. "A Videowill: Safe and Sure." *Estate Planning* 70 (October 1984), pp. 87–89.

WALSH, KAREN J. "The Statute of Frauds' Lifetime and Testamentary Provisions: Safeguarding Decedents Estates." *Fordham Law Review* 50 (1981), pp. 239–70.

WHITMAN, ROBERT, and DAVID HOOPES. "The Confidential Relationship in Will Contests." *Trusts and Estates,* February 1985, pp. 53–55.

WONG, WILLIAM. "Iron Curtain Statutes, Communist China, and the Right to Devise."*UCLA Law Review* 32 (1985). pp. 643–89.

QUESTIONS AND PROBLEMS

1. (*a*) Name the major documents used in the estate planning process to transfer wealth. (*b*) Do they all require the same effort in their preparation? Why or why not?

2. Describe the four major reasons why a will might not be admitted to probate.

3. Name and describe the two different types of wills recognized by many states.

4. Can a valid will meet the typical requirements for both the witnessed will and the holographic will? Why or why not?

5. (*a*) What is a simple will? (*b*) List its major sections.

6. (*a*) What is a codicil? (*b*) Why is it mentioned in the typical will?

7. (*a*) Why does the will nominate two types of guardians? (*b*) Must the probate judge follow the testator's nominations?

8. The lawyer for one of your clients advises against waiving the executor's bond? Can you think of any reason why? (Hint: consider whom a court might appoint as executor.)

9. What is the purpose of the clause directing that all death taxes be paid from the residue?

10. Why does the disposition section in a will often contain a survival clause?

11. Describe the contents of the "statement of witnesses" section of a will.

12. (*a*) Distinguish between a living trust and a trust-will. (*b*) Are all testamentary trusts established in wills?

13. List the sections of a trust-will that are common to all wit-

nessed wills and the sections that are found only in trust-wills.

14. (a) Describe in general how the living trust included in Exhibit 3–2 disposes of the testator's property. (b) Which parties stand to receive a contingent future interest? (c) When, if ever, will each become vested future interests?

15. Finnegan, a widower, died last week. He is survived by the following family members (current ages in parentheses): Two children, Joe (26) and Gary (17). Joe has four children, Jackie (5), John (3), Carol (2), and Bob (1). Finnegan is also survived by two other grandchildren, Floyd (4) and Fred (3), who are the sons of Finnegan's deceased daughter, Kerri. Kerri's husband, Kurt (23) is still alive. Joe has come to your office requesting some information. Assuming that Finnegan's $1 million estate will be distributed in accordance with the trust-will contained in Exhibit 3–3, who will receive how much, and when will they receive it? Assume that none of the living persons named above dies prematurely.

The Rule against Perpetuities

The rule against perpetuities (the Rule) originated in English common law.[1] It acts to prevent a transferor from controlling the disposition of property for an unreasonably long period after making the transfer. The classic, concise statement of the Rule, with this author's emphasis added, is:

> No *interest* is good unless is must *vest,* if at all, not later than 21 years after some *life in being* at the creation of the interest.

In simpler though a bit less exact language, the Rule has the effect of invalidating a future contingent interest which does not vest within 21 years after the death of certain people alive at the time the interest took effect. This will require some explanation.

In estate planning, an interest in property can take effect during the transferor's lifetime, or it can take effect at the transferor's death. A transfer into an irrevocable living trust is an example of the creation of a property interest that will take effect during the transferor's lifetime, while a transfer into the typical revocable living trust and a transfer by will are examples of transfers that take effect at the tranferor's death. Thus, to satisfy the requirements of the Rule, the interest must *vest,* if at all, within 21 years after the death of someone alive at the moment of transfer into an irrevocable trust or at the moment of the transferor's death, for interests created by will or by revocable living trust.

---

[1] The statutes of all states except Wisconsin, North Dakota, and South Dakota contain some variation of this rule.

Interests that vest immediately when they take effect will automatically meet the requirements of the Rule. Thus, a transfer in a will "to John, for his life, then to Mary or her estate" creates vested interests for both John and Mary at the testator's death. Nothing (except perhaps the passage of time) will prevent them from receiving possession of the property. Therefore, the Rule need only be used to determine the validity of contingent future interests, that is, interests that are *not vested* when created.

The requirement that the interest must vest "if at all" means that a contingent future interest will not violate the Rule merely because it failed to vest because the happening of the contingency did not work favorably for the named party. Thus, the transfer "to Jane if she survives Margo" gives Jane a contingent future interest that must vest or fail to vest within the permitted time. Failure to vest will not violate the Rule, so long as that failure (along with vesting) must occur within the required period. Thus, Jane will or will not survive Margo. What is required is that the interest must either vest or fail to vest within the required period. If we can't be sure that either of these will happen, then the interest violates the Rule.

To qualify under the Rule, an interest must vest or fail to vest "not later than 21 years after some life in being at the creation of the interest." The "life in being" concept is difficult to explain precisely. For our purposes, however, we can say that the persons permitted to be lives in being are usually those mentioned or implied in the transfer document itself. Thus, for the transfer "to Carrie for her life, then to Carrie's living children," Carrie would be the sole measuring life. She is alive at the creation of the children's interest, and the length of her life span will determine the devolution of the property. Taking a second example, the provision that a trust will terminate no later than "21 years after the death of the last survivor of the class composed of my wife and those of my issue living at my death" explicitly creates the measuring lives to be used in the test. This "perpetuities saving clause," included in the trust-will in Exhibit 3–3, is a clause that can further protect an interest from vesting too remotely. It will be discussed further, shortly.

The requirement of vesting within "21 years" after the death of a life in being was originally included to enable the transferor to control the disposition of property for his or her life, for the lives of the children, and for the period of the grandchildren's minority, but no longer. For those individuals, all interests created which are contingent solely upon *parent survival* will usually vest within the required period. The children's interest will vest by the time of the death of the transferor, and the grandchildren's interest will all vest within 21 years of the death of the last surviving child. All of their interests will vest within the required period. On the other hand, a great-grandchild's interest will typically (but not always) vest *after* the 21-year period, and thus will usually fail.

A violation of the Rule will cause that particular interest to be void. The interest will then revert to the transferor or the transferor's successors.

Let's consider some examples. In each case, assume that T has died leaving a will containing the following disposition of property:

EXAMPLE 3A–1 "To my wife, Mary, for her life, then to Bill or his estate." Both Mary's and Bill's interest vested immediately when they took effect (at T's death) because at that point nothing except the passage of time will delay their possession or enjoyment. Therefore, neither interest is at any time contingent, that is, depending on the happening of a future event, other than the passage of time. Applying the Rule, their interests "must vest . . . not later than . . ." Thus, both interests are valid under the Rule.

EXAMPLE 3A–2 "To my husband, Bert, for his life, then to my son James, if still living, otherwise to Ron or his estate." Bert's vested interest is valid under the rule, for the same reason that Mary's was, in the preceding example. Both James and Ron have contingent interests in the property. Thus, we must ask whether they must vest within the specified time. Bert is a "life in being" at the time of T's death. Both James's and Ron's interests will vest, if at all (either one or the other will never vest, depending on whether or not James survives T) at the death of Bert which is within "21 years after some life in being." Bert is the life in being, and both interests will vest or will fail to vest at his death, which literally is within 21 years after his death. Therefore, both James's and Ron's interests are valid under the Rule.

EXAMPLE 3A–3 "To my wife Sarah, for her life, then to my son Greg, for his life, then equally to Greg's living children when the youngest child reaches age 25." Assume that Greg is presently an infant. Are Greg's children's interests valid under the Rule? Greg was the "life in being" at the creation of the interest. Must all of the children's interest vest, if at all, within 21 years after Greg's death? The answer is no, since there is a possibility that they may not. Greg could die before a child reaches age four, and thus that child's interest would not vest, if at all, "not later than 21 years after" Greg's death. Therefore, all of the grandchildren's interests are void, and T or his successors would receive a reversionary interest in them.

EXAMPLE 3A–4 ". . . then to my great, great, great-grandchildren. . . ." Assuming that T is survived only by children and grandchildren, it is possible that the great, great, great-grandchildren's contingent interest will vest after 21 years after the death of all grandchildren, who are the only apparent lives in being at T's death. Thus, their interests are void.

Here are two general rules of thumb when applying the Rule to transfers of interests to surviving issue:

1. Transferors usually can create valid contingent interests for their *grandchildren,* as long as all of the interests must vest by the time their grandchildren reach age 21.
2. Transferors usually can create valid interests for their *great-grandchildren* only if they outlive all of their children.

Today, not all dispositions in violation of the Rule are invalid. Two types of safeguards designed to overcome the Rule are available to transferors. First, most states have enacted *statutes* that limit application of the Rule, or even invalidate it entirely. For example, many states have enacted a "wait and see" statute which, in effect, will find an interest void only if the interest turns out *in fact* not to vest within the required period. In addition, some states have a type of wait-and-see statute which states that any interest which actually vests within a certain period of time (e.g., 60 years) after its creation cannot be declared void, even if it violates the Rule.[2] Another statutory safeguard is the application of the "*cy pres*" rule to enable the courts to correct violations of the rule, if at all possible, so that the transferor's intentions can be respected.[3]

A second type of safeguard against a perpetuities violation involves the lawyer's insertion in the document of the earlier mentioned *perpetuities saving clause,* similar to the one in the *trust-will* in Exhibit 3–3. Such a provision, however, may act to prevent the client from making an otherwise valid transfer, perhaps simply because the attorney chose not to test the interest against the Rule. In fact, none of the above safeguards is as effective as the thoughtful analysis and planning of an expert.

Yet, one must have sympathy for the lawyers who use this clause. The Rule often requires complex analysis to test a given interest, and it can even puzzle experts. One state supreme court called it "a dangerous instrumentality in the hands of most members of the bar." It held that

---

[2]In 1986 the National Conference of Commissioners on Uniform State Laws approved the Uniform Statutory Rule Against Perpetuities, recommending that it be enacted in all states. It includes a wait-and-see period of 90 years after creation. For a discussion of the proposal, see the Young article cited at the end of this Appendix.

[3]*Cy pres,* French for "as near as possible," is a principle, used primarily in the context of charitable bequests, which permits the substitution of one beneficiary for another when the original charitable purpose is impossible, illegal, or impracticable. For example, over a century ago one testator left property in trust to fight for the cause of abolition. After the 13th Amendment freed the slaves, a court applied *cy pres* to permit the trust to continue by assisting freed slaves.

even though an attorney sued by a client for malpractice did in fact violate the Rule, he was innocent because he did not fail to use ordinary skill commonly exercised by lawyers![4]

The purpose of this appendix has been to present an overview of the rule against perpetuities, without exploring the complexities occasionally encountered by attorneys. This author believes that all members of the estate planning team should acquire a general understanding of the Rule, primarily because it constitutes a material constraint on the temporal boundaries of intelligent planning.

RECOMMENDED READING

BECKER, DAVID M. "Understanding the Rule against Perpetuities in Relation to the Lawyer's Role—To Construe or Construct." *San Diego Law Review* 20 (1983), pp. 733–61.

DUKEMINIER, JESSE. "A Modern Guide to Perpetuities." *California Law Review* 74 (December 1986), pp. 1867–1913.

————. "Perpetuities: The Measuring Lives." *Columbia Law Review* 85 (1985), pp. 1648–1713.

LEACH, W. BARTON. "Perpetuities in a Nutshell." *Harvard Law Review* 51 (1938), p. 638.

————. "Perpetuities: The Nutshell Revisited." *Harvard Law Review* 78 (1965), pp. 973–92.

WAGGONER, LAWRENCE W. "Perpetuities: A Perspective on Wait-and-See." *Columbia Law Review* 85 (December 1985).

YOUNG, RAYMOND H. "Uniform Statutory Rule Against Perpetuities." *Probate Notes* 12 (1987), pp. 244–46.

---

[4] *Lucas v. Hamm,* 56 Cal. 2d 583.

QUESTIONS

1. What is the purpose of the Rule against perpetuities?
2. Helen's will leaves one half of her wealth outright to Vinnie and the other half in trust for Johnny, with all income payable annually to Johnny and, at the earlier of Johnny's death or his reaching age 21, corpus to Johnny or his estate. Does this will violate the Rule? Why or why not?
3. Holly's will leaves all of her property in trust, with income to her living children for life, then income to her then-living grandchildren for their lives, and then remainder over to her great-grandchildren. Who will get Holly's property?
4. How is the Rule frequently avoided today?
5. ("Off the wall" question.) How did our subject matter arise in the 1981 movie, "Body Heat," starring William Hurt and Kathleen Turner? Explain. Did the movie make any pertinent legal mistakes?

The California Statutory Wills

This appendix has been written to illustrate a new type of will, one whose provisions are entirely created by statute. The California Statutory Will, drafted by practicing lawyers and adopted in 1982, comes in two different formats and is designed to encourage citizens to execute a will, rather than do nothing, and subsequently die intestate.[1]

Sections 6200–6248 of the Probate Code completely delineate the format of these novel witnessed wills. The statute specifies the precise language to be used, and it even outlines the location of blank spaces at points where the testator is given discretion over the terms. The statute incorporates a nontrust will form, shown in Exhibit 3B–1, and a will form with a trust, shown in Exhibit 3B–2. Statutory wills are available in pre-printed format in many California stationery stores, law offices, and also from the California State Bar.

To execute a statutory will, the testator follows the printed instructions and fills in the blank spaces. This type of will is far less flexible than other wills, since additional provisions cannot be included. However, most commentators consider it superior to intestacy.

The statutory wills are called "California Statutory Will" and "California Statutory Will with Trust." An analysis of each follows.

---

[1]Statutory wills have also been enacted in Maine and Wisconsin.

Statutory Nontrust Will (Exhibit 3B–1)

Instructions. A set of 11 boldface statements on the first page prefaces the statutory will. Essentially, it offers advice to the testator regarding will preparation. It states, among other things, that:

  a. A lawyer may be needed.
  b. The will does not dispose of property that has been disposed of by will substitutes.
  c. The will isn't designed to reduce taxes.
  d. The will can't be changed.
  e. The format of the will is written into the Probate Code.
  f. Beneficiaries should not be witnesses to the will.
  g. The will should be kept in a safe place.
  h. Adopted children and natural children are treated equally.
  i. A new will should be executed after marriage or divorce.
  j. Testators with children under 21 might wish to use the statutory will with trust.

Let's examine some of these statements more carefully. *First,* a lawyer might be needed to make clear to the testator the limitations of the statutory will, a subject to be covered in some detail below. Also, a lawyer can be helpful in ensuring correct draftmanship.[2]

Second, that the statutory will is not designed to reduce taxes will become clear as the reader works through the rest of the text. Tax planning is too complex to be simply incorporated in a "fill in the blanks" dispositive instrument.

Third, the printed wording of this will can't be changed. Any changes in wording and the like will, at best, be disregarded or, at worst, result in denial of probate. After executing this will, the testator may amend it by codicil. As indicated earlier, a codicil must satisfy all of the formal requirements imposed upon the will that it changes. Thus, a codicil to a witnessed will (e.g., the California Statutory Will) must meet all of the requirements of the witnessed will (written, two witnesses, etc.), and a codicil to a holographic will must meet all of the requirements of the holographic will (signature and all material provisions in testator's handwriting). Keep in mind that inasmuch as additions to or deletions from the statutory will, at best, will be disregarded, codicil clauses containing additions or deletions will also, at best, be disregarded. Thus a codicil can only amend or revoke, but not add to or delete, portions of a statutory will. For example, a codicil to a statutory will can change the name of the

---

[2]Actually, clients consulting a lawyer to help them draft a statutory will would be well-advised to pay the few additional dollars to obtain a professionally drafted will, one which can invariably reflect their family situation and needs more precisely.

EXHIBIT 3B–1

CALIFORNIA STATUTORY WILL

NOTICE to the person who signs this will:

1. It may be in your best interest to consult with a California lawyer because this Statutory Will has serious legal effects on your family and property.

2. This will does not dispose of property which passes on your death to any person by operation of law or by any contract. For example, the will does not dispose of joint tenancy assets or your spouse's share of community property, and it will not normally apply to proceeds of life insurance on your life or your retirement plan benefits.

3. This will is not designed to reduce death taxes or any other taxes. You should discuss the tax results of your decisions with a competent tax advisor.

4. You cannot change, delete, or add words to the face of this California Statutory Will. If you do, the change or the deleted or added words will be disregarded and this will may be given effect as if the change, deletion, or addition had not been made. You may revoke this California Statutory Will and you may amend it by codicil.

5. If there is anything in this will that you do not understand, you should ask a lawyer to explain it to you.

6. The full text of this California Statutory Will, the definitions and rules of construction, the property disposition clauses, and the mandatory clauses follow the end of this will and are contained in the Probate Code of California.

7. The witnesses to this will should not be people who may receive property under this will. You should carefully read and follow the witnessing procedure described at the end of this will. All of the witnesses must watch you sign this will.

8. You should keep this will in your safe-deposit box or other safe place.

9. This will treats most adopted children as if they are natural children.

10. If you marry or divorce after you sign this will, you should make and sign a new will.

11. If you have children under 21 years of age, you may wish to use the California Statutory Will With Trust or another type of will.

ADDITIONAL INFORMATION, contained in California Probate Code Sections 6220, 6221, 6223, and 6226:

1. Any person of sound mind over the age of 18 may complete a California Statutory Will.
2. In order to complete a valid California Statutory Will,
   (a) the testator (the person making the will) must:
      (1) fill in all the appropriate blanks.
      (2) sign the will.
   (b) two or more witnesses must:
      (1) observe the testator's signing of the will.
      (2) sign their names on the will in the presence of the testator.

3. The testator must select only *one* "Property Disposition" clause under Section 2.3 of a California Statutory Will. If more than one clause or no clause is selected, the testator's property will be distributed as if the testator did not make a will. This means that the testator's property will go to certain family members, starting with those most closely related, in the order specified in Sections 6400-6414 of the Probate Code.
4. Dissolution (divorce) or annulment of marriage revokes any gift or disposition of property made in this will by the testator to his or her former spouse. It also revokes any appointment of the former spouse as executor or guardian.

Note: This will form is based on California law and is designed for California residents.

CALIFORNIA STATUTORY WILL OF

_____

(Insert Your Name)

Article 1. Declaration

This is my will and I revoke any prior wills and codicils.

Article 2. Disposition of My Property

2.1. PERSONAL AND HOUSEHOLD ITEMS.
I give all my furniture, furnishings, household items, personal automobiles and personal items to my spouse, if living; otherwise they shall be divided equally among my children who survive me.

2.2. CASH GIFT TO A PERSON OR CHARITY.
I make the following cash gift to the person or charity in the amount stated in words and figures in the box which I have completed and signed. If I fail to sign in the box, no gift is made. If the person mentioned does not survive me, or the charity designated does not accept the gift, then no gift is made. No death tax shall be paid from this gift.

FULL NAME OF PERSON OR CHARITY TO RECEIVE CASH GIFT (Name only one. Please print.).

AMOUNT OF GIFT $ _____
AMOUNT WRITTEN OUT:

_____ Dollars

Signature of Testator

2.3. ALL OTHER ASSETS (MY "RESIDUARY ESTATE").
I adopt only one Property Disposition Clause in this paragraph 2.3 by writing my signature in the box next to the title of the Property Disposition Clause I wish to adopt. I sign in only one box. I write the words "not used" in the remaining boxes. If I sign in more than one box or if I fail to sign in any box, the property will be distributed as if I did not make a will.

PROPERTY DISPOSITION CLAUSES (Select one.)

(a) TO MY SPOUSE IF LIVING; IF NOT LIVING, THEN TO MY CHILDREN AND THE DESCENDANTS OF ANY DECEASED CHILD. . . . .

(b) TO MY CHILDREN AND THE DESCENDANTS OF ANY DECEASED CHILD. I LEAVE NOTHING TO MY SPOUSE. IF LIVING. . . . .

(c) TO BE DISTRIBUTED AS IF I DID NOT HAVE A WILL. . . . .

Article 3. Nominations of Executor and Guardian

3.1. EXECUTOR (Name at least one.)
I nominate the person or institution named in the first box of this paragraph 3.1 to serve as executor of this will. If that person or institution does not serve, then I nominate the others to serve in the order I list them in the other boxes.

FIRST EXECUTOR.

SECOND EXECUTOR.

THIRD EXECUTOR.

EXHIBIT 3B–1 *(continued)*

3.2. GUARDIAN (If you have a child under 18 years of age, you should name at least one guardian of the child's person and at least one guardian of the child's property. The guardian of the child's person and the guardian of the child's property may, but need not, be the same. An individual can serve as guardian of either the person or the property, or as guardian of both. An institution can serve only as guardian of the property.)

If a guardian is needed for any child of mine, then I nominate the individual named in the first box of this paragraph 3.2 to serve as guardian of the person of that child, and I nominate the individual or institution named in the second box of this paragraph 3.2 to serve as guardian of the property of that child. If that person or institution does not serve, then I nominate the others to serve in the order I list them in the other boxes.

FIRST GUARDIAN OF THE PERSON.

FIRST GUARDIAN OF THE PROPERTY.

SECOND GUARDIAN OF THE PERSON.

SECOND GUARDIAN OF THE PROPERTY.

THIRD GUARDIAN OF THE PERSON.

THIRD GUARDIAN OF THE PROPERTY.

3.3. BOND.
My signature in this box means that a bond is not required for any individual named in this will as executor or guardian. If I do not sign in this box, then a bond is required for each of those persons as set forth in the Probate Code. (The bond provides a fund to pay those who do not receive the share of your estate to which they are entitled, including your creditors, because of improper performance of duties by the executor or guardian. Bond premiums are paid out of your estate.)

Notice to Testator: The witnesses shall do the following:
    (1) Observe the testator's signing.
    (2) Sign their names in the presence of the testator and each other.

I sign my name to this California Statutory Will on _____ at

                                      Date

_____, _____.   _____
        City   State   Signature of Testator

STATEMENT OF WITNESSES
(You must use two adult witnesses and three would be preferable.)

Each of us declares under penalty of perjury under the laws of California that the testator signed this California statutory will in our presence, all of us being present at the same time, and we now, at the testator's request, in the testator's presence, and in the presence of each other, sign below as witnesses, declaring that the testator appears to be of sound mind and under no duress, fraud, or undue influence.

Signature _____

Print Name Here: _____

Residence Address: _____

_____

Signature _____

Print Name Here: _____

Residence Address: _____

_____

Signature _____

Print Name Here: _____

Residence Address: _____

_____

EXHIBIT 3B–1 *(concluded)*

Definitions, Rules of Construction and Text
of the California Statutory Will

Definitions and Rules of Construction

Unless the provision or context clearly requires otherwise, these definitions and rules of construction govern the construction of this California Statutory Will.

(a) "Testator" means a person choosing to adopt a California statutory will.

(b) "Spouse" means the testator's husband or wife at the time the testator signs a California statutory will.

(c) "Executor" means both the person so designated in a California statutory will and any other person acting at any time as the executor or administrator under a California statutory will.

(d) "Trustee" means both the person so designated in a California statutory will and any other person acting at any time as the trustee under a California statutory will.

(e) "Descendants" means children, grandchildren, and their lineal descendants of all generations, with the relationship of parent and child at each generation being determined by the definitions of child and parent in Sections 26 and 54. A reference to "descendants" in the plural includes a single descendant where the context so requires.

(f) A reference in a California statutory will to the "Uniform Gifts to Minors Act of any state" includes both the Uniform Gifts to Minors Act of any state and the Uniform Transfers to Minors Act of any state.

(g) Masculine pronouns include the feminine, and plural and singular words include each other, where appropriate.

(h) If a California statutory will states that a person shall perform an act, the person is required to perform that act. If a California statutory will states that a person may do an act, the person's decision to do or not to do the act shall be made in the exercise of the person's fiduciary powers.

(i) Whenever a distribution under a California statutory will is to be made to a person's descendants, the property shall be divided into as many equal shares as there are then living descendants of the nearest degree of living descendants and deceased descendants of that same degree who leave descendants then living; and each living descendant of the nearest degree shall receive one share and the share of each deceased descendant of that same degree shall be divided among his or her descendants in the same manner.

(j) "Person" includes individuals and institutions.

Property Disposition Clauses

1. The following is the full text of paragraph 2.1 of this California Statutory Will:

   If my spouse survives me, I give my spouse all my books, jewelry, clothing, personal automobiles, household furnishings and effects, and other tangible articles of a household or personal use. If my spouse does not survive me, the executor shall distribute those items among my children who survive me, and shall distribute those items in as nearly equal shares as feasible in the executor's discretion. If none of my children survive me, the items described in this paragraph shall become part of the residuary estate.

2. The following are the full texts of the property disposition clauses referred to in paragraph 2.3 of this California Statutory Will:
   (a) TO MY SPOUSE IF LIVING; IF NOT LIVING, THEN TO MY CHILDREN AND THE DESCENDANTS OF ANY DECEASED CHILD.

If my spouse survives me, then I give all my residuary estate to my spouse. If my spouse does not survive me, then I give all my residuary estate to my descendants who survive me.
(b) TO MY CHILDREN AND THE DESCENDANTS OF ANY DECEASED CHILD. I LEAVE NOTHING TO MY SPOUSE, IF LIVING.

I give all my residuary estate to my descendants who survive me. I leave nothing to my spouse, even if my spouse survives me.
(c) TO BE DISTRIBUTED AS IF I DID NOT HAVE A WILL.

The executor shall distribute my residuary estate to my heirs at law, their identities and respective shares to be determined according to the laws of the State of California in effect on the date of my death relating to intestate succession.

Mandatory Clauses

The mandatory clauses of this California Statutory Will are as follows:

(a) INTESTATE DISPOSITION. If the testator has not made an effective disposition of the residuary estate, the executor shall distribute it to the testator's heirs at law, their identities and respective shares to be determined according to the laws of the State of California in effect on the date of the testator's death relating to intestate succession.

(b) POWERS OF EXECUTOR.

(1) In addition to any powers now or hereafter conferred upon executors by law, including all powers granted under the Independent Administration of Estates Act, the executor shall have the power to: (A) sell estate assets at public or private sale, for cash or on credit terms, (B) lease estate assets without restriction as to duration, and (C) invest any surplus moneys of the estate in real or personal property, as the executor deems advisable.

(2) The executor may distribute estate assets otherwise distributable to a minor beneficiary to (A) the guardian of the minor's person or estate, (B) any adult person with whom the minor resides and who has the care, custody, or control of the minor, or (C) a custodian, serving on behalf of the minor under the Uniform Gifts to Minors Act of any state or the Uniform Transfers to Minors Act of any state.

The executor is free of liability and is discharged from any further accountability for distributing assets in compliance with the provisions of this paragraph.

(3) On any distribution of assets from the estate, the executor shall have the discretion to partition, allot, and distribute the assets (A) in kind, including undivided interests in an asset or in any part of it, or (B) partly in cash and partly in kind, or (C) entirely in cash. If a distribution is being made to more than one beneficiary, the executor shall have the discretion to distribute assets among them on a pro rata or non-pro rata basis, with the assets valued as of the date of distribution.

(c) POWERS OF GUARDIAN. A guardian of the person nominated in the California statutory will shall have the same authority with respect to the person of the ward as a parent having legal custody of a child would have. A guardian of the estate nominated in a California statutory will shall have all of the powers conferred by law. All powers granted to guardians in this paragraph may be exercised without court authorization.

person who will receive the cash gift under Section 2.2, or it can change the amount of the gift, but it cannot name someone to receive a second cash gift.

Fourth, beneficiaries should not be witnesses to the will for the reasons mentioned in Chapter 3. Under §6112, if challenged, an "interested witness" may take under a will only if he or she is able to rebut a statutory presumption that the devise was procured by duress, menace, fraud, or undue influence.

Fifth, with regard to adopted children, we will see in several examples in Chapter 4 the implications of §6408 and §6408.5, which state that adopted children are treated similar to natural children, and that the natural parents of a child adopted by another have no rights to inherit by intestate succession from their natural child.

Sixth, regarding marriage and divorce, again, an example in Chapter 4 will illustrate the effect of §6560-62, which states that marriage will usually partially revoke a will which was written prior to the marriage, which did not provide for the spouse, and in which the omission appears unintentional.

In most cases, these and other succession statutes prevent an undesired disposition. However, their result is not always ideal, and as a precaution, the statutory will instructions recommend that a person execute a new will after marriage or after a dissolution of marriage.

Finally, the instructions state that the statutory will form with trust may be preferred to the nontrust form if the testator has children under age 21, because the trust version can eliminate the need for a guardianship of the minor's property, similar to the trust-will illustrated in Chapter 3.

Provisions of the California Statutory Will. We are now ready to examine the actual provisions of the California Statutory Will.

Except for all signatures, insertions by the testator in the blank spaces in the California Statutory Will may either be handwritten or typed. The testator writes his or her name at the top of page 2.

Section 2.1 disposes of all tangible items typically found in and around the household, including all autos, to the surviving spouse. The testator has no discretion over any part of this section, which gives the assets to the surviving spouse, if alive, and if not alive, to the testator's children. Section 2.2 permits the testator to make one (and only one) testamentary cash gift to a person or to a charity. The provision will be ignored if either:

a. It is left blank.
b. The person predeceases the decedent.
c. The charity refuses the gift.
d. The testator fails to sign his or her name in the space provided.

EXHIBIT 3B–2

CALIFORNIA STATUTORY WILL
WITH TRUST

NOTICE to the person who signs this will:

1. This form contains a trust for your descendants. If you do not want to create a trust, do not use this form.

2. It may be in your best interest to consult with a California lawyer because this Statutory Will has serious legal effects on your family and property.

3. This will does not dispose of property which passes on your death to any person by operation of law or by any contract. For example, the will does not dispose of joint tenancy assets or your spouse's share of community property, and it will not normally apply to proceeds of life insurance on your life or your retirement plan benefits.

4. This will is not designed to reduce death taxes or any other taxes. You should discuss the tax results of your decisions with a competent tax advisor.

5. You cannot change, delete, or add words to the face of this California Statutory Will. If you do, the change or the deleted or added words will be disregarded and this will may be given effect as if the change, deletion, or addition had not been made. You may revoke this California Statutory Will and you may amend it by codicil.

6. If there is anything in this will that you do not understand, you should ask a lawyer to explain it to you.

7. The full text of this California Statutory Will, the definitions and rules of construction, the property disposition clauses, and the mandatory clauses follow the end of this will and are contained in the Probate Code of California.

8. The witnesses to this will should not be people who may receive property under this will. You should carefully read and follow the witnessing procedure described at the end of this will. All of the witnesses must watch you sign this will.

9. You should keep this will in your safe-deposit box or other safe place.

10. This will treats most adopted children as if they are natural children.

11. If you marry or divorce after you sign this will, you should make and sign a new will.

ADDITIONAL INFORMATION, contained in California Probate Code Sections 6220, 6221, 6223, and 6226:

1. Any person of sound mind over the age of 18 may complete a California Statutory Will.
2. In order to complete a valid California Statutory Will,
   (a) the testator (the person making the will) must:
      (1) fill in all the appropriate blanks.
      (2) sign the will.
   (b) two or more witnesses must:
      (1) observe the testator's signing of the will.
      (2) sign their names on the will in the presence of the testator.

3. The testator must select only *one* "Property Disposition" clause under Section 2.3 of a California Statutory Will. If more than one clause or no clause is selected, the testator's property will be distributed as if the testator did not make a will. This means that the testator's property will go to certain family members, starting with those most closely related, in the order specified in Sections 6400-6414 of the Probate Code.
4. Dissolution (divorce) or annulment of marriage revokes any gift or disposition of property made in this will by the testator to his or her former spouse. It also revokes any appointment of the former spouse as executor, guardian or trustee.

Note: This will form is based on California law and is designed for California residents.

Published in the Public Interest by The State Bar of California.

EXHIBIT 3B–2 *(continued)*

CALIFORNIA STATUTORY WILL WITH TRUST OF

Article 1. Declaration

This is my will and I revoke any prior wills and codicils.

Article 2. Disposition of My Property

2.1. PERSONAL AND HOUSEHOLD ITEMS.
I give all my furniture, furnishings, household items, personal automobiles, and personal items to my spouse, if living; otherwise they shall be divided equally among my children who survive me.

2.2. CASH GIFT TO A PERSON OR CHARITY.
I make the following cash gift to the person or charity in the amount stated in words and figures in the box which I have completed and signed. If I fail to sign in the box, no gift is made. If the person mentioned does not survive me, or the charity designated does not accept the gift, then no gift is made. No death tax shall be paid from this gift.

> FULL NAME OF PERSON OR CHARITY TO RECEIVE CASH GIFT (Name only one. Please print.).
> _____
>
> AMOUNT OF GIFT $ _____
> AMOUNT WRITTEN OUT:
> _____ Dollars
>
> Signature of Testator

2.3. ALL OTHER ASSETS (MY "RESIDUARY ESTATE").
I adopt only one Property Disposition Clause in this paragraph 2.3 by writing my signature in the box next to the title of the Property Disposition Clause I wish to adopt. I sign in only one box. I write the words "not used" in the remaining boxes. If I sign in more than one box or if I fail to sign in any box, the property will be distributed as if I did not make a will.

PROPERTY DISPOSITION CLAUSES (Select one.)

(a) TO MY SPOUSE IF LIVING; IF NOT LIVING, THEN IN ONE TRUST TO PROVIDE FOR THE SUPPORT AND EDUCATION OF MY CHILDREN AND THE DESCENDANTS OF ANY DECEASED CHILD UNTIL I HAVE NO LIVING CHILD UNDER 21 YEARS OF AGE. . . . .

(b) TO MY CHILDREN AND THE DESCENDANTS OF ANY DECEASED CHILD IN ONE TRUST TO PROVIDE FOR THEIR SUPPORT AND EDUCATION UNTIL I HAVE NO LIVING CHILD UNDER 21 YEARS OF AGE. I LEAVE NOTHING TO MY SPOUSE, IF LIVING. . . . .

Article 3. Nominations of Executor, Trustee, and Guardian

3.1. EXECUTOR (Name at least one.)
I nominate the person or institution named in the first box of this paragraph 3.1 to serve as executor of this will. If that person or institution does not serve, then I nominate the others to serve in the order I list them in the other boxes.

FIRST EXECUTOR.

SECOND EXECUTOR.

THIRD EXECUTOR.

EXHIBIT 3B–2 *(continued)*

3.2. TRUSTEE (Name at least one.)

Because it is possible that after I die my property may be put into a trust, I nominate the person or institution named in the first box of this paragraph 3.2 to serve as trustee of that trust. If that person or institution does not serve, then I nominate the others to serve in the order I list them in the other boxes.

FIRST TRUSTEE.

SECOND TRUSTEE.

THIRD TRUSTEE.

3.3. GUARDIAN (If you have a child under 18 years of age, you should name at least one guardian of the child's person and at least one guardian of the child's property. The guardian of the child's person and the guardian of the child's property may, but need not, be the same. An individual can serve as guardian of either the person or the property, or as guardian of both. An institution can serve only as guardian of the property.)

If a guardian is needed for any child of mine, then I nominate the individual named in the first box of this paragraph 3.3 to serve as guardian of the person of that child, and I nominate the individual or institution named in the second box of this paragraph 3.3 to serve as guardian of the property of that child. If that person or institution does not serve, then I nominate the others to serve in the order I list them in the other boxes.

FIRST GUARDIAN OF THE PERSON.

FIRST GUARDIAN OF THE PROPERTY.

SECOND GUARDIAN OF THE PERSON.

SECOND GUARDIAN OF THE PROPERTY.

THIRD GUARDIAN OF THE PERSON.

THIRD GUARDIAN OF THE PROPERTY.

3.4. BOND.

My signature in this box means that a bond is not required for any individual named in this will as executor, trustee, or guardian. If I do not sign in this box, then a bond is required for each of those persons as set forth in the Probate Code. (The bond provides a fund to pay those who do not receive the share of your estate to which they are entitled, including your creditors, because of improper performance of duties by the executor, trustee, or guardian. Bond premiums are paid out of your estate.)

Notice to Testator: The witnesses shall do the following:

(1) Observe the testator's signing.

(2) Sign their names in the presence of the testator and each other.

I sign my name to this California Statutory Will With Trust on _____ at

Date

_____ , _____ . _____

City   State   Signature of Testator

STATEMENT OF WITNESSES

(You must use two adult witnesses, and three witnesses would be preferable.)

Each of us declares under penalty of perjury under the laws of California that the testator signed this California statutory will with trust in our presence, all of us being present at the same time, and we now, at the testator's request, in the testator's presence, and in the presence of each other, sign below as witnesses, declaring that the testator appears to be of sound mind and under no duress, fraud, or undue influence.

Signature _____

Print Name Here: _____

Residence Address: _____

Signature _____

Print Name Here: _____

Residence Address: _____

Signature _____

Print Name Here: _____

Residence Address: _____

EXHIBIT 3B–2 *(concluded)*

Definitions, Rules of Construction and Text
of the California Statutory Will With Trust

Definitions and Rules of Construction

Unless the provision or context clearly requires otherwise, these definitions and rules of construction govern the construction of this California Statutory Will With Trust.

(a) "Testator" means a person choosing to adopt a California statutory will.

(b) "Spouse" means the testator's husband or wife at the time the testator signs a California statutory will.

(c) "Executor" means both the person so designated in a California statutory will and any other person acting at any time as the executor or administrator under a California statutory will.

(d) "Trustee" means both the person so designated in a California statutory will and any other person acting at any time as the trustee under a California statutory will.

(e) "Descendants" means children, grandchildren, and their lineal descendants of all generations, with the relationship of parent and child at each generation being determined by the definitions of child and parent in Sections 26 and 54. A reference to "descendants" in the plural includes a single descendant where the context so requires.

(f) A reference in a California statutory will to the "Uniform Gifts to Minors Act of any state" includes both the Uniform Gifts to Minors Act of any state and the Uniform Transfers to Minors Act of any state.

(g) Masculine pronouns include the feminine, and plural and singular words include each other, where appropriate.

(h) If a California statutory will states that a person shall perform an act, the person is required to perform that act. If a California statutory will states that a person may do an act, the person's decision to do or not to do the act shall be made in the exercise of the person's fiduciary powers.

(i) Whenever a distribution under a California statutory will is to be made to a person's descendants, the property shall be divided into as many equal shares as there are then living descendants of the nearest degree of living descendants and deceased descendants of that same degree who leave descendants then living; and each living descendant of the nearest degree shall receive one share and the share of each deceased descendant of that same degree shall be divided among his or her descendants in the same manner.

(j) "Person" includes individuals and institutions.

Property Disposition Clauses

1. The following is the full text of paragraph 2.1 of this California Statutory Will With Trust:

If my spouse survives me, I give my spouse all my books, jewelry, clothing, personal automobiles, household furnishings and effects, and other tangible articles of a household or personal use. If my spouse does not survive me, the executor shall distribute those items among my children who survive me, and shall distribute those items in as nearly equal shares as feasible in the executor's discretion. If none of my children survive me, the items described in this paragraph shall become part of the residuary estate.

2. The following are the full texts of the property disposition clauses referred to in paragraph 2.3 of this California Statutory Will With Trust:

(a) TO MY SPOUSE IF LIVING; IF NOT LIVING, THEN IN ONE TRUST TO PROVIDE FOR THE SUPPORT AND EDUCATION OF MY CHILDREN AND THE DESCENDANTS OF ANY DECEASED CHILD UNTIL I HAVE NO LIVING CHILD UNDER 21 YEARS OF AGE.

(1) If my spouse survives me, then I give all my residuary estate to my spouse.

(2) If my spouse does not survive me and if any child of mine under 21 years of age survives me, then I give all my residuary estate to the trustee, in trust, on the following terms:

(A) As long as any child of mine under 21 years is living, the trustee shall distribute from time to time to or for the benefit of any one or more of my children and the descendants of any deceased child (the beneficiaries) of any age as much, or all, of the (i) principal or (ii) net income of the trust, or (iii) both, as the trustee deems necessary for their health, support, maintenance, and education. Any undistributed income shall be accumulated and added to the principal. "Education" includes, but is not limited to, college, graduate, postgraduate, and vocational studies, and reasonably related living expenses. Consistent with the trustee's fiduciary duties, the trustee may distribute trust income or principal in equal or unequal shares and to any one or more of the beneficiaries to the exclusion of other beneficiaries. In deciding on distributions, the trustee may take into account, so far as known to the trustee, the beneficiaries' other income, outside resources, or sources of support, including the capacity for gainful employment of a beneficiary who has completed his or her education.

(B) The trust shall terminate when there is no living child of mine under 21 years of age. The trustee shall distribute any remaining principal and accumulated net income of the trust to my descendants who are then living.

(3) If my spouse does not survive me and if no child of mine under 21 years of age survives me, then I give all my residuary estate to my descendants who survive me.

(b) TO MY CHILDREN AND THE DESCENDANTS OF ANY DECEASED CHILD IN ONE TRUST TO PROVIDE FOR THEIR SUPPORT AND EDUCATION UNTIL I HAVE NO LIVING CHILD UNDER 21 YEARS OF AGE. I LEAVE NOTHING TO MY SPOUSE, IF LIVING.

(1) I give all my residuary estate to the trustee, in trust, on the following terms:

(A) As long as any child of mine under 21 years of age is living, the trustee shall distribute from time to time to or for the benefit of any one or more of my children and the descendants of any deceased child (the beneficiaries) of any age as much or all, of the (i) principal, or (ii) net income of the trust, or (iii) both, as the trustee deems necessary for their health, support, maintenance, and education. Any undistributed income shall be accumulated and added to the principal. "Education" includes, but is not limited

to, college, graduate, postgraduate, and vocational studies, and reasonably related living expenses. Consistent with the trustee's fiduciary duties, the trustee may distribute trust income or principal in equal or unequal shares and to any one or more of the beneficiaries to the exclusion of other beneficiaries. In deciding on distributions, the trustee may take into account, so far as known to the trustee, the beneficiaries' other income, outside resources, or sources of support, including the capacity for gainful employment of a beneficiary who has completed his or her education.

(B) The trust shall terminate when there is no living child of mine under 21 years of age. The trustee shall distribute any remaining principal and accumulated net income of the trust to my descendants who are then living.

(2) If no child of mine under 21 years of age survives me, then I give all my residuary estate to my descendants who survive me.

(3) I leave nothing to my spouse, even if my spouse survives me.

Mandatory Clauses

The mandatory clauses of this California Statutory Will With Trust are as follows:

(a) INTESTATE DISPOSITION. If the testator has not made an effective disposition of the residuary estate, the executor shall distribute it to the testator's heirs at law, their identities and respective shares to be determined according to the laws of the State of California in effect on the date of the testator's death relating to intestate succession.

(b) POWERS OF EXECUTOR.

(1) In addition to any powers now or hereafter conferred upon executors by law, including all powers granted under the Independent Administration of Estates Act, the executor shall have the power to: (A) sell estate assets at public or private sale, for cash or on credit terms, (B) lease estate assets without restriction as to duration, and (C) invest any surplus moneys of the estate in real or personal property, as the executor deems advisable.

(2) The executor may distribute estate assets otherwise distributable to a minor beneficiary to (A) the guardian of the minor's person or estate, (B) any adult person with whom the minor resides and who has the care, custody, or control of the minor, or (C) a custodian, serving on behalf of the minor under the Uniform Gifts to Minors Act of any state or the Uniform Transfers to Minors Act of any state.

The executor is free of liability and is discharged from any further accountability for distributing assets in compliance with the provisions of this paragraph.

(3) On any distribution of assets from the estate, the executor shall have the discretion to partition, allot, and distribute the assets (A) in kind, including undivided interests in an asset or in any part of it, or (B) partly in cash and partly in kind, or (C) entirely in cash. If a distribution is being made to more than one beneficiary, the executor shall have the discretion to distribute assets among them on a pro rata or non-pro rata basis, with the assets valued as of the date of distribution.

(c) POWERS OF GUARDIAN. A guardian of the person nominated in the California statutory will shall have the same authority with respect to the person of the ward as a parent having legal custody of a child would have. A guardian of the estate nominated in a California statutory will shall have all of the powers conferred by law. All powers granted to guardians in this paragraph may be exercised without court authorization.

(d) INEFFECTIVE DISPOSITION. If, at the termination of any trust created in the California statutory will with trust, there is no effective disposition of the remaining trust assets, then the trustee shall distribute those assets to the testator's then living heirs at law, their identities and respective shares to be determined as though the testator had died on the date of the trust's termination and according to the laws of the State of California then in effect relating to intestate succession.

(e) POWERS OF TRUSTEE.

(1) In addition to any powers now or hereafter conferred upon trustees by law, the trustee shall have all the powers listed in Section 1120.2. The trustee may exercise those powers without court authorization.

(2) In addition to the powers granted in the foregoing paragraph, the trustee may

(A) Hire and pay from the trust the fees of investment advisors, accountants, tax advisors, agents, attorneys, and other assistants for the administration of the trust and for the management of any trust asset and for any litigation affecting the trust.

(B) On any distribution of assets from the trust, the trustee shall have the discretion to partition, allot, and distribute the assets (i) in kind, including undivided interests in an asset or in any part of it, or (ii) partly in cash and partly in kind, or (iii) entirely in cash. If a distribution is being made to more than one beneficiary, the trustee shall have the discretion to distribute assets among them on a pro rata or non-pro rata basis, with the assets valued as of the date of distribution.

(C) The trustee may, upon termination of the trust, distribute assets to a custodian for a minor beneficiary under the Uniform Gifts to Minors Act of any state or the Uniform Transfers to Minors Act of any state.

(3) The trustee is free of liability and is discharged from any further accountability for distributing assets in compliance with the provisions of this paragraph.

(f) TRUST ADMINISTRATIVE PROVISIONS. The following provisions shall apply to any trust created by a California statutory will with trust:

(1) The interests of trust beneficiaries are not transferable by voluntary or involuntary assignment or by operation of law and shall be free from the claims of creditors and from attachment, execution, bankruptcy, or other legal process to the fullest extent permissible by law.

(2) The trustee is entitled to reasonable compensation for ordinary and extraordinary services, and for all services in connection with the complete or partial termination of any trust created by this will.

(3) All persons who have any interest in a trust under a California statutory will with trust are bound by all discretionary determinations the trustee makes in good faith under the authority granted in the California statutory will with trust.

Section 2.3 disposes of the residue. Here, the testator must choose one of three options:

    a. To the spouse if alive; if spouse is dead, then to the decedent's issue.
    b. Nothing to the spouse; instead, all to the decedent's issue.
    c. Distribution as if the decedent died intestate.

The testator selects a provision by signing his or her name in one of the boxes and writing "not used" in the other two boxes. Failure to sign the name in any box or signing it in more than one box will result in disposition of the residuary estate by intestacy.

Section 3.1 provides for nomination of an executor and two alternates. The testator simply writes in each box the names of the persons selected.

Section 3.2 provides for the nomination of a guardian of the person and of the estate of all minor children (under 18 years of age). Again, three choices, including two alternates, may be made for each.

Section 3.3 provides a box, which if signed waives the statutory bond requirement for any individual executor or guardian named in the will. The waiver will not apply if the box is unsigned, or even if it is signed if the court appoints an executor who was not nominated in the will.

Next, the testator fills in the date, city, state, and his or her signature. This must be done under the watchful presence of at least two witnesses, who then sign and print their names and write their residence addresses.

Statutory Will with Trust (Exhibit 3B–2)

The second version, California Statutory Will with Trust, has the same format as the nontrust statutory will, with two exceptions, to be examined next.

First, Section 2.3 has two, not three options. The first option disposes of the residuary estate to the spouse, if living; if the spouse is not living, the residuary estate is passed outright to decedent's children, provided that no child is under 21 years of age. If one or more children are under 21, the property passes instead to a trust, which terminates when the youngest child reaches age 21, at which time the property passes outright to all descendants.

The second option, under Section 2.3, is essentially similar to the first with regard to the creation of a trust, except that a surviving spouse will receive nothing. And, as the fine print on page 4 of the will form indicates, the trustee is given discretion to pay out income and principal to any child for "health, support, maintenance, and education."

The second difference between the two statutory will forms involves, of course, the selection of a trustee. In the trust-will the testator is permitted to name a trustee and two alternate trustees.

Limitations of the California Statutory Wills. Transfer of property at death pursuant to a California statutory will is universally believed to be preferable to the consequences of intestacy. It should be kept in mind, however, that clients would be well advised to obtain a professionally drafted will, which is usually a far superior planning device. Drawbacks of the statutory will are described next.

First, as mentioned in each will, and described earlier, the statutory will is not designed to save taxes, and its printed words cannot be changed, deleted, or added to.

Second, the statutory will is extremely inflexible, not allowing for much choice with regard to disposition of property. Some examples, outlined next, include the handling of cash gifts and the residuary estate.

1. Only one nonresiduary cash gift may be made. Further, that cash gift, if elected, may be made to only one person or charity. If the testator wishes to make more than one cash gift, a different type of will must be chosen.
2. The entire residuary estate must pass outright to the spouse, or outright or in trust to the testator's issue, or to the testator's intestate heirs. This prevents a partial disposition to both spouse and issue, or a transfer in trust for the benefit of the spouse. It also prevents disposition of any residuary probate assets to anyone other than these parties.

Finally, no other provisions may be added to the statutory will.

This appendix has been written to illustrate the statutory framework underlying wills in a particular state. The next chapter will introduce probate and other procedures used by most states to effect property transfers.

RECOMMENDED READING

KIRK, ROBERT P. "The New Holographic Will in California: Has It Outlived Its Usefulness?" *California Western Law Review* 20 (1984), pp. 258–78.

QUESTIONS

1. (*a*) Why were the California statutory wills created? (*b*) Can they totally replace the professionally drafted will?
2. What are the principal limitations of the California Statutory Wills?

4

Introduction to Property Transfers II:
The Transfer Process

<hr>

OVERVIEW

This is the second of two chapters that introduce the principles of property transfer. Chapter 3 examined the documents employed in the planning of property transfers. Documents covered included joint tenancy arrangements, property dispositions by contract, the will, and the trust. This chapter will look at the actual process of transfer of the property disposed of by these documents, emphasizing transfers taking effect at death.[1]

When a person dies, steps must be taken to transfer ownership of his or her property interests to the proper beneficiaries. Recognized agents try to undertake these transfers as well as possible, hopefully in accordance with the deceased's prior wishes. The documents covered in Chapter 3 are the legal embodiments of those wishes and are used as the basis for transferring the property.

Historically, each of the 50 states and the District of Columbia has assumed a significant role in the estate distribution process. Each has chosen to protect the decedent's property in two basic ways. First, each state has enacted succession or intestacy laws

<hr>

[1]The most common planning document disposing of property *during lifetime* is the living trust. It directs the trustee to make the distributions, if any. The procedure is uncomplicated and usually unsupervised by the state.

that specify *who is to receive* property in the event that the decedent left no formal transfer documents. Succession laws are designed to reflect the probable disposition preferences of decedents. The second way in which the states have sought to protect the decedent's property is by developing probate administration procedures designed to ensure that the intended beneficiaries, including creditors and taxing authorities, *will actually receive* their legal share of the estate property.

Transfers at death are subject to far greater state supervision for property that is held in title in a manner which does not itself indicate a method of transfer. Several examples will be cited shortly. On the other hand, title to property left in a manner which itself provides for transfer will not ordinarily be subject to much, if any, state supervision. As an example of the latter, title in *joint tenancy* with right of survivorship means, as we have seen, automatic survivorship by the surviving cotenants, by operation of law. The state does not "oversee" this title transfer, which legally occurs automatically and instantly.[2]

In contrast with title held in joint tenancy, title that had been held by a decedent either as an *individual,* as a *tenant in common,* or as a spouse owning an interest in *community property,* in themselves indicate no procedure for title transfer, so the states have established a process to transfer title by reference to an independent, acceptably drafted document. The state-administered process of transferring such title is called *probate*. The transfer document to which the probate process refers is called, of course, the will.

At this point, the reader might be asking where *trusts* fit into this transfer scheme. The answer is that it depends on the type of document creating the trust. Property that at the decedent's death is being held in a revocable or irrevocable *living trust* does not legally belong to the decedent. Title is actually held by the trustee. Since probate is concerned only with transfer of property held in the decedent's name, property already held by a trustee is not subject to probate. If, in accordance with the underlying trust document, the decedent's death triggers a transfer out of trust, the

---

[2]An additional step is necessary to clear title, since the decedent's name will need to be removed from the actual document. This is usually processed quickly by those authorities keeping record of the title when the survivors appear before them with a copy of the death certificate.

transfer process is uncomplicated and unsupervised. The trustee simply makes the distribution, free of probate. On the other hand, property owned by the decedent to be transferred *at death* into, rather than out of, a trust will be subject to probate, because the decedent still held title to the property at death. We have seen in Chapter 3 that disposition to a testamentary trust is actually made in a type of will called the trust-will. Thus, the property of which it disposes is subject to probate.

Are transfers of property disposed of by contract, including *life insurance proceeds* on the life of the decedent and *retirement benefits,* subject to probate? They are not, again because title to those assets is not actually held by the decedent. Instead, title is held by the insurance company and the pension fund, respectively, which have agreed to directly transfer title to the beneficiary at the death of the decedent. Thus, when the transfer is made, state supervision under the probate process is not required, because the decedent's estate is not a party to the transfers. Thus, the process of transferring these assets can also be less complicated and less supervised; the insurance company or pension fund simply delivers a check to the beneficiary.

Often, individuals will die owning property not disposed of by any formal transfer documents.[3] As we have said, the state's laws covering intestate succession will determine proper distribution. Intestate distribution is carried out in the probate process. In fact, one would think that probating an intestate decedent's property is even more necessary to ensure proper selection of beneficiaries, as well as to ensure actual distribution to them.

By way of summary, Figure 4–1 pictorially represents the probate and nonprobate interests of a decedent at the moment of death. The right side contains the nonprobate property, including interests in living trusts that are revocable by the decedent, jointly owned property, life insurance policies on the decedent's life other than those payable to the decedent's estate,[4] and certain other nonprobate interests. The left side contains probate assets, including

---

[3]One study found that, in general, 40 percent of all adults die intestate.

[4]Proceeds payable to the decedent's (probate) estate must, by definition, be a probate asset, since the probate estate will own the proceeds until they are distributed to heirs, legatees, and devisees.

FIGURE 4–1 Pictorial Representation of Probate and Nonprobate Interests of a Decedent at Moment of Death

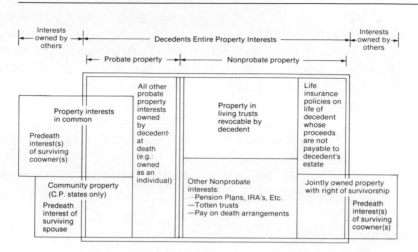

the decedent's one half interest in community property, the decedent's interests in property held in common with others, and the catchall—all other probate property owned by the decedent. Of course, interests held *by others* in common, jointly, and as community property are not part of the decedent's probate or nonprobate estate.

The logic of Figure 4–1 suggests a relatively straightforward *procedure* to determine the assets of a decedent that will be subject to probate. First, list all of the decedent's property interests owned immediately prior to death, including all insurance policies, whether on the decedent's life or on the life of anyone else. Then delete from the list the nonprobate assets, including property in living trusts revocable by the decedent, jointly held property, life insurance policies whose proceeds are payable to a nonestate beneficiary, and miscellaneous nonprobate interests. The remainder of the decedent's property interests will be subject to probate.

So far, we have seen how the decedent's probate property is determined. The next logical step is to decide who will receive this property. To do this, one first looks to the will, a document thoroughly examined in the last chapter. If there is no will, the state laws of intestate succession are applied. Details of these succession laws are covered next.

STATE LAWS ON INTESTATE SUCCESSION

So far, we have seen that a decedent who dies without leaving a valid will is said to die intestate, and all property owned by the decedent in a form other than joint tenancy will pass under the state's laws of intestate succession. Further, a person receiving property under these laws is called an heir and is said to inherit the property.[5] In determining who should inherit, state laws typically give priority first to the decedent's spouse, then to the children, and then to the decedent's other blood relatives, with higher priority given to closer relations. A more detailed description of a commonly used order of intestate succession will be examined shortly. But first, let's explore two important underlying concepts in the area of inheritance.

Degrees of Consanguinity

Let's examine a family tree. Figure 4–2 depicts *degrees of consanguinity,* or blood relationship, between a decedent and the decedent's relatives. As we have said, descendants (issue) of the decedent include children, grandchildren, great-grandchildren, and so on. Ascendants (ancestors) include parents, grandparents, and the like. Descendants and ascendants of a decedent are said to be in the decedent's *lineal,* or vertical, line, meaning that the decedent was an ancestor or descendant of each of them. The other relationships shown are *collateral,* meaning that they share with the decedent a common ancestor, but they are neither ascendants nor descendants of the decedent. Collaterals are not in the decedent's lineal or vertical line. For example, a nephew of a decedent is not her ascendant or her issue, but shares a common ascendant with the decedent, namely the decedent's parent.[6]

The most common method of measuring degree of affinity to the decedent is the civil law procedure of counting blocks along degree lines. For example, the decedent's uncle is three steps from the decedent, because we first count upward to the common ancestor and then collaterally, or diagonally, down to the box where the

---

[5]Note that attorneys in most states employ a more narrow use of the terms *heir* and *inherit* than does the general public. This text will conform to the expert's usage.

[6]Try saying that fast three times!

FIGURE 4–2   Degrees of Consanguinity

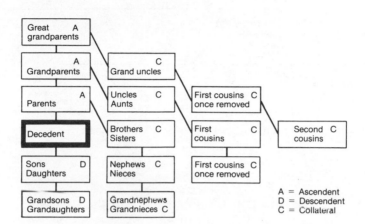

uncle is located. Figure 4–2 can be helpful in searching for the decedent's nearest surviving relative, especially in some states that have not adopted the succession rules of the Uniform Probate Code, which will be described shortly.

Per Stirpes versus Per Capita

If an intestate decedent's only heirs are one living son and two grandchildren who are the daughters of a predeceased daughter, how much will each of the three inherit? Will they inherit one third each, or will the son be entitled to a larger proportion because he is a closer relative? To answer questions like this, we much distinguish between a per stirpes and a per capita distribution. A *per stirpes* distribution requires that certain issue of a decedent, as a group, inherit the share of an estate that their immediate ancestor would have inherited if he or she had been living.[7] Per stirpes, or right of representation, as it is also called, is distinguished from the second method of division, called *per capita,* which means share and share alike.

For a better understanding of the difference between per stirpes and per capita, consider the following description of a fairly complicated family tree, which is also illustrated in Figure 4–3. Crossmarks in the diagram indicate those issue who have predeceased

---

[7]Per stirpes is Latin for "by the roots"; per capita, "by the head."

FIGURE 4-3 Example Illustrating Distribution by Right of Representation (per stirpes)

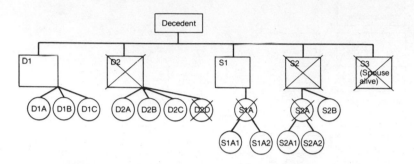

the decedent. Assume that the decedent had the following issue: Two daughters, D1 and D2, and three sons, S1, S2, and S3. Only D1 and S1 survived the decedent. D1 has three children, D1A, D1B, and D1C, all alive, but has no other issue. D2 is survived by three children, D2A, D2B, D2C, all living. A fourth child, D2D, predeceased the decedent. D2 has no other issue. S1 originally had one child, S1A, who is deceased, but is survived by two of his own children, whom we shall call S1A1 and S1A2. S1 has no other issue. S2 had two children, S2A and S2B. S2A is deceased, but is survived by two children, S2A1 and S2A2. S2B is alive. S2 has no other issue. S3 predeceased the decedent and leaves a spouse but no issue.

A *per stirpes distribution* to children and other issue of the decedent would divide the estate into as many shares as the decedent had of the following, at death: (*a*) predeceased children having living issue and (*b*) surviving children. Although the decedent had five children, S3 is not a predeceased child having living issue. S3's spouse will therefore receive nothing. So the estate will be divided into four equal shares. Each living child, D1 and S1, will receive a one quarter share, and thus nothing will pass to their issue. For the same reason, D1A, D1B, D1C, S1A, S1A1, and S1A2 all will not inherit from the decedent. However, the next level of surviving issue shares equally in any deceased child's share. Thus, D2's living children, D2A, D2B, and D2C, will share equally in D2's one-fourth share. Further, with regard to the one-quarter share of the estate that goes to S2's issue, S2A1 and S2A2 will share equally in the share that S2A would have received had S2A been alive at the decedent's death. Thus, S2B will receive one half of the S2 quarterly share and S2A1 and S2A2 each will receive one quarter of the quarterly share.

Summarizing, a per stirpes distribution of the decedent's estate will be divided as follows: D1:$\frac{1}{4}$; D2A, D2B, and D2C: $\frac{1}{12}$ each ($\frac{1}{4} \times \frac{1}{3}$); S1:$\frac{1}{4}$; S2B:$\frac{1}{8}$ ($\frac{1}{4} \times \frac{1}{2}$); S2A1 and S2A2:$\frac{1}{16}$ each ($\frac{1}{4} \times \frac{1}{2} \times \frac{1}{2}$).

A *per capita distribution,* where the estate is divided on a share-and-share-alike basis, is similar to per stirpes in that the very same issue will receive portions of the estate. However, it is different from per stirpes because the proportions will be different. Under the per capita rule, each person will receive an *equal amount,* regardless of degree of blood relationship. Hence, since there are eight recipients, each will receive one eighth of the estate. Most state laws on intestate succession, including the UPC, require a per stirpes distribution, when applicable.[8]

Intestacy in UPC States

We are now ready to look at the rules of intestate succession used by those states which have adopted the Uniform Probate Code. The Code's principal intestate sections are reproduced in Exhibit 4–1. In general, §2-101 prefaces the next four sections, which specify actual succession. The intestate share of the surviving spouse is determined by referring to §2-102 for common law states, or to §2-102A for community property states. The intestate share of heirs other than the surviving spouse is determined by referring to §2-103. Section 2-104 covers survival situations. Finally, if there are no "takers" under the above sections, §2-105 requires a procedure called "escheat." A more specific analysis follows.

EXHIBIT 4–1   Intestate Succession under the Uniform Probate Code

---

2-101   Intestate Estate

Any part of the estate of a decedent not effectively disposed of by his will passes to his heirs as prescribed in the following sections of this Code.

---

[8]Answering the question posed at the beginning of this section, under per stirpes distribution, the son would inherit one half and the granddaughters would inherit one quarter each. Under per capita distribution, all three would inherit one third each.

EXHIBIT 4–1 *(continued)*

2-102   Share of the Spouse (Common Law States)

The intestate share of the surviving spouse is:
1. if there is no surviving issue or parent of the decedent, the entire intestate estate.
2. if there is no surviving issue but the decedent is survived by a parent or parents, the first ($50,000), plus one half of the balance of the intestate estate.
3. if there are surviving issue all of whom are issue of the surviving spouse also, the first ($50,000), plus one half of the balance of the intestate estate.
4. if there are surviving issue one or more of whom are not issue of the surviving spouse, one half of the intestate estate.

2-102A   Share of the Spouse (Community Property States)

The intestate share of the surviving spouse is as follows:
1. As to separate property
   (i) if there is no surviving issue or parent of the decedent, the entire intestate estate.
   (ii) if there is no surviving issue but the decedent is survived by a parent or parents, the first ($50,000), plus one half of the balance of the intestate estate.
   (iii) if there are surviving issue all of whom are issue of the surviving spouse also, the first ($50,000), plus one half of the balance of the intestate estate.
   (iv) if there are surviving issue one or more of whom are not issue of the surviving spouse, one half of the intestate estate.
2. As to community property
   (i) the one half of the community property that belongs to the decedent passes to the (surviving spouse).

2-103   Shares of Heirs Other than Surviving Spouse

The part of the intestate estate not passing to the surviving spouse under Section 2-102, or the entire intestate estate if there is no surviving spouse, passes as follows:
1. to the issue of the decedent; if they are all of the same degree of kinship to the decedent they take equally, but if of unequal degree, then those of more remote degree take by representation.
2. if there is no surviving issue, to his parent or parents equally.

EXHIBIT 4–1 *(concluded)*

---

3. if there is no surviving issue or parent, to the issue of the parents or either of them by representation.

4. if there is no surviving issue, parent, or issue of a parent, but the decedent is survived by one or more grandparents or issue of grandparents, half of the estate passes to the paternal grandparents if both survive, or to the surviving paternal grandparent, or to the issue of the paternal grandparents if both are deceased, the issue taking equally if they are all of the same degree of kinship to the decedent; but if of unequal degree those of more remote degree take by representation, and the other half passes to the maternal relatives in the same manner; but if there be no surviving grandparent or issue of grandparent on either the paternal or the maternal side, the entire estate passes to the relatives on the other side in the same manner as the half.

2-104   Requirement that Heir Survive Decedent for 120 Hours

Any person who fails to survive the decedent by 120 hours is deemed to have predeceased the decedent for purposes of . . . intestate succession. . . .

2-105   No Taker

If there is no taker under the provisions of this Article, the intestate estate passes to the state.

Intestate share to surviving spouse.   In common law states, under §2-102, the surviving spouse is entitled to all of the decedent's intestate estate if the decedent leaves no parent or issue. Alternatively, the spouse takes the first $50,000 plus one half of the rest in the event that the decedent leaves one or more parents but no issue, or that the decedent leaves issue, regardless of whether the decedent leaves any parents. Finally, as a limitation to the above, if the issue that the decedent leaves are not the issue of the surviving spouse, the spouse's share is cut to just one half.

Under §2-102A, the surviving spouse's intestate share in community property states is identical to that for common law states, except for an additional provision for the distribution of the community property. Thus, that spouse takes the same share of the decedent's separate property as he or she would take in a common law state. In addition, the surviving spouse is entitled to the decedent's entire half of the community property.

Intestate share to others.   According to §2-103, other relatives of the decedent are divided into a hierarchical list of classes, corresponding to the degree of blood relationship to the decedent. Thus, to determine which class is entitled to succession of an intestate decedent's property, one would move down the list, stopping at the first class containing at least one living member. Distribution would be made only to members within that class. A summary of this prioritized list follows:

1. Surviving issue, per stirpes.
2. Parents.
3. Issue of parents, per stirpes.
4. Paternal and maternal grandparents and their issue, one half to each side, per stirpes.

Under Section 2-104, any heir must survive the decedent by 120 hours to take by intestate succession. This state-imposed survival requirement has the effect of avoiding double probate in some common accident situations.

Finally, under §2-105, if none of the above relatives survive, then the decedent's intestate property passes to the state, under the doctrine of *escheat*. In English feudal law, escheat meant that the feudal lord received a reversion in the property, either because the tenant died without issue or because the tenant committed a felony. In American law, escheat has come to mean a reversion of the decedent's property to the state because no individual is "competent" to inherit. In some states, there will be no escheat unless the decedent is not survived by *any* kin, no matter how remote the relationship. The UPC, on the other hand, limits inheritance to the closer relatives, under the (arguable) premise that more remote "laughing heirs" would be receiving a windfall not ever intended by the decedent.[9]

The examples listed next should help to illustrate these principles. In each case, assume that D is a decedent who died a resident

---

[9]Query whether the decedent really would have preferred leaving property to the state rather than to distant relatives.

of a common law UPC state and owned $100,000 in property. Relevant UPC sections are cited parenthetically.

> EXAMPLE 4–1 D is survived only by spouse and a cousin. Spouse will inherit all. [2-102(1)]
>
> EXAMPLE 4–2 D is survived by spouse and their five children, one of whom has a daughter. Spouse inherits $50,000 plus one half of the remainder, or a total of $75,000. Each of the five children inherits an equal share of the rest, or $5,000. D's granddaughter inherits nothing. [2-102(3) and 2-103(1)]
>
> EXAMPLE 4–3 Facts similar to Example 4-2, above, except that spouse survived decedent by only 5 hours. Spouse will not inherit. Each of the five children will inherit one-fifth of the total, or $20,000. D's granddaughter still inherits nothing. [2-104 and 2-103(1)].
>
> EXAMPLE 4–4 D is survived by parents and two children. The children take all. [2-103(1)]
>
> EXAMPLE 4–5 D is survived by spouse, a parent, and a sister. Spouse inherits $75,000 and parents inherit $25,000. Sister receives nothing. [2-102(2) and 2-103(2)]
>
> EXAMPLE 4–6 D is survived by a sister and two nephews, the sons of D's deceased brother. Based on the required per stirpes distribution, sister inherits $50,000, and each of the nephews takes $25,000. [2-103(3)]
>
> EXAMPLE 4–7 D's closest surviving relative is a second cousin. All property will escheat to the state. [2-105]

Each of the above dispositions of the decedent's separate property would still be correct if the decedent had been a resident of a community property state. But in addition, all of the decedent's one half of the community property, if any, would pass to the surviving spouse.

Intestacy in Non-UPC States

The intestate succession laws in non-UPC states vary considerably, but all have a common thread: they are all more or less determined by degrees of affinity. For example, if an intestate decedent is survived by children but no spouse, the children usually take all. If the decedent leaves a spouse and children, the spouse and the children will usually share the property, with the spouse receiving from one third to one half. If the decedent is survived by a spouse but no children, the spouse usually receives all. If, in addition to the spouse, the decedent's parents are still alive, then in some states the spouse gets all, and in others the spouse shares with the parents.

Since state intestate succession laws do vary, the reader is urged to make an independent investigation of the succession laws in his or her own state.

LEGAL RIGHTS OF OMITTED AND ADOPTED CHILDREN

Occasionally, a parent will die leaving a will that was executed prior to the birth of a child. Will that *after-born child* receive anything? Most often, yes. In most states, including UPC states, an after-born child is entitled to take the share he or she would receive had the decedent died without a will, unless any one of the following is true: (*a*) the omission was intentional; (*b*) the will left substantially all of the estate to the other parent; or (*c*) the testator made some other provision for the child. An after-born child is one of two common examples of an *omitted child,* which is defined as any child or issue of any deceased child who was not provided for in the will. The second common example of an omitted child is one not named in the will, although alive at its execution. While some states still permit this latter type of omitted child to take an intestate share, others, including UPC states, do not.

With regard to *adopted children,* many states, including those that have incorporated the UPC, treat adopted children similar to natural children, so that an adopted child can inherit from the *adoptive parents* (and their blood relatives), and the adoptive parents (and their blood relatives) can inherit from the adopted child. Conversely, most states give the *natural parents* of a child adopted by another no rights to inherit by intestate succession from their natural child. Similarly, adopted children usually have no succession rights to the interests of their natural parents, unless there is a stepparent adoption, as illustrated in Example 4–9.

EXAMPLE 4–8 Sam and Sue placed their infant child, Gloria, up for adoption. Sometime later, Gloria was adopted by Kevin and Kay. If Sam later dies intestate, in many states, Gloria cannot inherit any of Sam's property. If Kay then dies intestate, Gloria will inherit equally with Kay's natural children. If Gloria subsequently dies intestate,

Kevin and Kay's issue can inherit, but neither Sue, her issue, nor Sam's issue will inherit. Of course, any of these individuals may receive property if they are named in a given decedent's will.

EXAMPLE 4–9 Mike was six years old when his father, Frank, died. His natural mother, Edith, subsequently married Archie, who adopted Mike. In many states, Mike will be able to inherit from both Edith, his natural parent, and from Archie, his stepparent.

LEGAL RIGHTS OF OMITTED, DIVORCED, AND DISINHERITED SPOUSES

An *omitted spouse* whom the testator marries *after* executing a will is usually treated in the same manner as an omitted child. The spouse takes an intestate share, unless the omission was intentional or unless the spouse was otherwise provided for. And, as in the case of omitted children alive at the execution of the will, an omitted spouse whom the testator married *before* executing the will may or may not take an intestate share, depending upon the state.[10]

EXAMPLE 4–10 Prior to Claude and Betty's engagement, Claude prepared his only will. Then the couple married, and Claude subsequently died. Assuming no other relevant contract exists, if Claude's will does not provide for Betty and the omission appears unintentional, the will can be admitted to probate and in many states Betty will receive her intestate share of Claude's property. In those states, if the will has provided for Betty, she will receive just the amount devised to her, which could range between nothing and the entire estate.

Omitted heir situations have a peculiar consequence: They result in the application of the intestacy laws to a decedent who actually died testate, with a valid will.[11]

In most states, a *dissolution of marriage* will ordinarily revoke a will executed before the dissolution with regard to the surviving

---

[10]In UPC states, that spouse would not take an intestate share.

[11]Another example of the need for intestacy proceedings when a valid will exists would be the situation in which a will did not dispose of all of a decedent's property, as when it fails to contain a residuary clause. The result is sometimes called "partial intestacy."

ex-spouse's share.[12] In effect, the surviving ex-spouse is treated as having predeceased the testator.

Can one spouse totally "disinherit" the other?

EXAMPLE 4–11 Mean Max, former owner of a very successful business, died last month leaving his entire $3-million estate to his brother. Max's wife, Helen, who was a homemaker owning no property of her own, was left penniless.

The above story is fiction, not fact. All states have laws designed to prevent this consequence.[13] States handle this problem by enforcing one or more of the following concepts: community property, dower and curtesy, and the spousal right of election.

As we have seen, *community property states* protect spouses by automatically and immediately attributing to each spouse ownership of one half of certain property acquired during the marriage. Thus many, perhaps most, spouses in community property states each own a nearly equal amount of property.[14]

Some common law states frustrate spousal disinheritance with *dower and curtesy laws,* which were briefly mentioned in Chapter 6. Originating in English common law, a *dower* represents a surviving wife's life interest in a portion of the real property owned by her deceased husband. A *curtesy* represents a surviving husband's life interest in a portion of the real property owned by his deceased wife. In the few states still recognizing dower and curtesy rights, the surviving spouse would be able to exercise that right against the deceased spouse's property.

Most common law states have enacted legislation replacing dower and curtesy with a spousal *right of election*, which essen-

---

[12]However, a divorce in itself will not usually have the effect of invalidating an existing provision designating the ex-spouse as a beneficiary under a life insurance policy or a retirement plan.

[13]For an interesting discussion of agreements executed between spouses before and during marriage which have the effect of altering property rights between them, see the Johnstone article cited at the end of the chapter.

[14]However, recently married spouses will own little community property. Some protection may be available under the Retirement Equity Act of 1984, which provides that a person married for at least one year to an employee who is a participant in a retirement plan has a vested one-half interest in the plan.

tially gives a surviving spouse the right to a choice. Either the spouse can "take under the will", that is, accept the provisions of the deceased spouse's will, if any, or the spouse can "take against the will", that is, elect to receive a statutorily specified minimum share, which in most states is that share the spouse would have inherited had the other spouse died intestate.

Thus, all states have laws that will usually prevent the death of one spouse from impoverishing the surviving spouse.

Next, we direct our study to the probate process.

PRINCIPLES OF PROBATE ADMINISTRATION

The principles underlying probate administration of an American decedent's estate originated in Old England, where public officials and the Church of England commonly took control of it, and then distributed it to the heirs and devisees.[15] The word *probate* stems from the Latin word *to prove,* meaning to certify the validity of a will. Attorneys occasionally use probate in this more restrictive sense. More commonly though, it is used generally to mean the entire process of administration of a decedent's estate.

Probate has been said to have three main *purposes*. First, it protects creditors by mandating that valid debts of the decedent be paid. Second, it implements the dispositive wishes of the testator by supervising the distribution of estate assets to beneficiaries. And third, probate serves to clear title to property; that is, it enables survivors to receive property in a form that is marketable.

Presenting a comprehensive overview of the principles of probate administration in the United States is almost an impossible task, one that can easily lead either to overgeneralization or hopeless detail. Each state has its own set of rules, many of which are unique. However, there are some similarities, which will be described next.

With regard to the states in general, nearly all have at least one set of *formal probate* procedures characterized by the following:

1. Formal appearance in *court,* before a judge.
2. Presentation of at least two formal *petitions,* and at least two

---

[15]Or supervised those individuals taking control.

court *hearings,* for which written *notice* has been given to all interested parties.[16]

3. Review and approval, by the court, of one or two formal financial *accountings*.

4. Issuance, by the court, of a signed written *order* as a precondition to the performance of the personal representative's major administrative responsibilities.

These traditional formal requirements are said to reflect the strong interest each state has in protecting creditors and beneficiaries from mistakes in estate administration.

In addition to providing these elaborate procedures, one group of 20 states offers estates the option of other, *less formal* settlement devices. These states have recently adopted all or most of the provisions of the Uniform Probate Code. Flexibility under the UPC enables the estate's interested parties to choose whether to be extensively supervised by court in the usual manner, to be supervised only with regard to certain specific acts, or to be totally unsupervised by the judicial process. Most other states do not offer such flexibility. Instead, many of their estates, by and large, must follow the traditional formal procedures.

This section will examine both the traditional approach and the flexible approach to estate administration, partly to show that their underlying philosophies are very different, and partly to give the reader an indication of the current trend in probate reform. Actually, this reform has influenced all states to some degree, including those offering much less flexibility. The traditionalist states are deregulating, but in a more fragmentary manner, as we shall see. We begin with a description of the traditional formal method of estate administration.

Substantial Formal Supervision: The Non–UPC Model

A somewhat detailed study of the formal probate procedures imposed by a typical non-UPC state such as California can give the reader a reasonable grasp of the major requirements of formal probate in nearly all states (including those which have adopted the

---

[16]Interested parties are those who could be influenced by the probate process. They include beneficiaries, creditors, and fiduciaries nominated in the will, including executors, guardians, and trustees.

UPC). Details will vary a bit, but the major characteristics are nearly universal.[17] Sections of the California Probate Code are cited parenthetically.

The formal probate process. Formal probate is required to begin just after death. Within 30 days after a California resident's death, anyone having custody of a will of the decedent is required to deliver it to the clerk of the superior court of the county where the decedent resided (§320).

The petition. Any executor nominated in a will is required to petition the court for probate of the will within 30 days from the date of knowledge of the nomination (§324). In addition, any person "interested in the estate" may make a similar petition (§323). Upon filing the petition, the county clerk must schedule a hearing on the petition within 45 days (§327). Ordinarily, the person nominated in the will to be executor files the petition, requesting (1) probate of the will, (2) letters testamentary, and (3) authorization to administer under the Independent Administration of Estates Act. Each request will be described briefly.

1. *Probate of the will:* If, after the hearing, the will is "admitted to probate," that will is thereby considered to be the only valid will and, except in the most unusual circumstances, net probate assets will eventually be distributed in accordance with its terms.

2. *Letters testamentary:* Also known as "Letters," this document states the court's formal authorization of the person named to be personal representative for the estate. Letters testamentary empowers the personal representative to deal legally with third parties.

3. *Independent Administration of Estates Act:* This is a part of the California Probate Code which simplifies formal probate administration. Essentially, it eliminates court approval for many minor actions undertaken by the personal representative. However, some actions are not exempt and require either express court approval or written notice. Provisions of the act will be described shortly.

---

[17]For example, there is at least one significant difference with regard to the disclosure requirements of an appointed personal representative between UPC states and non-UPC states. Further, formal UPC procedures are elective, while those in many non-UPC states are mandatory.

In addition to making these requests, the petition also makes several representations, including facts about the bond and the heirs and beneficiaries. A *bond* is required unless the will waives it or unless all potential beneficiaries agree to waive it (§541b). As indicated earlier, the bond protects the estate against mistakes and misappropriations of the personal representative. Ordinarily, the bond amount will be set equal to the total value of the personal probate property plus one year's estimated income from all of the probate property. The bond premium is charged to the estate (§541a). The petition must also state that the requirements for a bond, if any, have been met. As a second representation, the petition for probate is required to describe all heirs and beneficiaries named in the will.

Two other forms are ordinarily filed with the county clerk at the time of filing the petition for probate. First, a *Proof of Subscribing Witness* is submitted, in which one witness to the will offered for probate declares that he or she signed the attached will, that the decedent was of sound mind and was over age 18 at the time of the signing, and that he or she had no knowledge that the will was signed under duress, menace, fraud, or undue influence. If a witness can't be found, or if all witnesses have died, proof can be offered by handwriting analysis.[18]

The second form, which is ordinarily filed along with the probate petition, is the *Notice of Death and of Petition to Administer Estate*. This form contains essentially the same information as an announcement notice that is required to be published (three times prior to the hearing) in a newspaper of general circulation in the city in which the decedent resides. The filed notice and the published notice are intended to announce the following to the public:

1. That a petition for probate has been filed.
2. That a hearing will be held.
3. That interested parties may attend the hearing to object to the granting of the petition.

---

[18]Most states recognize a "self-proved" will, that is, a will containing a formal affidavit by witnesses stating that all formalities were complied with. At a minimum, this eliminates the need for witnesses to later testify in probate. And in some states, such an affidavit creates a conclusive presumption that all formalities were complied with, making the will incontestable on grounds of faulty execution.

4. That creditors must file claims against the estate within four months after the issuance of Letters.
5. That anyone may examine the probate file kept by the county clerk.
6. That the petitioner is requesting authority to administer the estate under the Independent Administration of Estates Act.

Copies of the filed notice must be mailed to all heirs and potential beneficiaries at least 10 days prior to the date of the hearing.

The hearing. The "hearing" for any particular probate estate may last only a few seconds. The judge gives anyone in the court the opportunity to object, but objections are rarely raised. Grounds for objection include the allegation that there exists a more recently executed will, or that even though the will in question is the only or most recent one, it was not validly executed due to mistakes in drafting, to the testator's lack of capacity, or to undue influence, fraud, or mistake. If the judge feels that the objection appears valid, he or she will order further proceedings to settle the dispute which, if not quickly resolved, can turn into what is called a *will contest.* On the other hand, if the petition for probate is granted, the judge signs an *Order for Probate,* which first states the court's findings that:

1. All notices have been filed.
2. The decedent died on the specified date.
3. The will in question is admitted to probate.

Then, the Order usually mandates that:

1. The named personal representative is appointed.
2. Letters will be issued.
3. The personal representative is given authority to administer the estate under the Independent Administration of Estates Act.
4. A bond is or is not required.

Upon issuance of the Order for Probate, the executor secures his or her Letters from the probate clerk. As we have noted, Letters testamentary is the formal document of court authorization of the appointment of the personal representative.

This completes the first state of formal dealings between the personal representative and the court.

After the hearing. After Letters are issued, the personal representative, usually in conjunction with his or her chosen probate attorney, undertakes a marshaling of estate assets and expected claims. Within three months of appointment, the personal representative must file with the probate clerk a formal document called *Inventory and Appraisement.* This form lists all probate assets at their fair market value. The personal representative is permitted to determine the value of most cash items (bank deposits, etc.), but other assets must be appraised by a "probate referee," who is a governmentally appointed person located in that county.

The Inventory and Appraisement is said to perform several important functions, First, it delineates those assets for which the personal representative is responsible. Second, as a public document available for public inspection at the county clerk's office, it describes the contents of the probate estate to all interested parties, including potential heirs, legatees, devisees, and creditors. Third, it provides information to the court to determine, among other things, the proper bond amount, the amount of the family allowance, and—if and when property should be sold—the minimum bid that the court will accept. Finally, it may influence the taxing authorities with regard to valuation of assets included in the death tax returns.[19]

During the "creditor's period," which lasts for four months after the date Letters are issued, each creditor is expected to file with the court or personal representative a document called a *creditor's claim.* Failure to file within this period will bar later collection, unless an exception is allowed (§700). Exceptions include:

1. The creditor has been out of the state and hasn't received notice.
2. Taxes are owed (taxing authorities are not subject to the creditor's period).
3. It is a claim for which the decedent was insured (§707).

Availability of a shortened creditor's period is said to be a major advantage to formal probate for estates that may have problems with creditors.

---

[19]Some California attorneys, however, believe that the IRS doesn't place a high regard on appraisals by probate referees, and that use of such values on federal tax returns can result in a tax penalty.

During estate administration, the personal representative is responsible for handling the financial affairs of the estate. Common responsibilities include:

1. Paying customary monthly estate bills (rent, utilities, insurance premiums).
2. Accumulating liquid assets so that large bills can eventually be paid (e.g., taxes and legal fees).
3. Protecting estate assets from exposure to loss by insuring and safeguarding them.

If the court authorizes the personal representative to act under the *Independent Administration of Estates Act* (the Act), the need for court approval is greatly lessened (§591.1-9). Except for the following, most minor administrative acts by the personal representative will be permitted without notice or express court approval:

1. Actions still needing express court approval:
   a. Allowance for personal representative's commission and attorney's fees.
   b. Settlement of accountings.
   c. Distribution of the estate to beneficiaries.
   d. Discharge of the personal representative.
2. Actions that can be undertaken by "advice of proposed action" (below), but without express court approval:
   a. Selling personal or real property.
   b. Leasing of certain real property.
   c. Entering in contracts not performable within two years.
   d. Operating a business for longer than six months.
   e. Investing funds in other than bank accounts and short-term governments.
   f. Borrowing money.
   g. Executing a mortgage or deed of trust.
   h. Deciding on the validity of certain claims.

An "advice of proposed action" is a written statement of the intended action and is filed with the probate clerk. It serves to put the probate court and others on notice as to the action described. Summarizing, unless the action is specified above, it will ordinarily be permitted under the Independent Administration of Estates Act without court notice or permission.

Distribution of estate assets. The net estate will be distributed to the beneficiaries only after all matured debts and taxes[20] have been paid. However, a partial distribution to beneficiaries may be made upon court approval of a *Petition for Preliminary Distribution*. Ordinarily, this petition is filed only after the end of the creditor's period. Further, the court must be satisfied that the estate is "but little indebted" and that such distribution can be made without loss to creditors or beneficiaries. No more than 50 percent of the estate can be distributed in a preliminary distribution (§1000–1004).

"Final distribution" is made upon approval of a petition, at a hearing, after the court determines that all current debts and taxes have been paid. At the same time, the judge normally approves a final estate accounting and attorney's fees and discharges the personal representative (§1020-1028)[21]

The entire formal probate procedure takes from 6 to 24 months, in most cases.

Attorney's fees for California probate work are determined by statute, in the absence of a different agreement by the parties.[22] Statutory probate fees are summarized in Table 4–1. These fees are based on the *gross* probate estate, not net of liabilities. In this regard, California is not typical. In most states, probate fees must be "reasonable"; specific amounts or percentages are not statutorily mandated.

Summarizing: Formal probate in most non-UPC states requires at least four document filings (petition for probate, notice of death, inventory and appraisement, and final distribution). It also requires at least two formal court hearings (prior to admission of will to probate and appointment of Letters, and prior to final distribution), one newspaper publication of notice, and at least one and possible two accountings (inventory and appraisement, and final accounting).

We next turn to the second major type of state probate supervision, the flexible approach under the Uniform Probate Code. A

---

[20]Except the federal estate tax.

[21]The account may be avoided by waiver of all of the beneficiaries (§933).

[22]Some law firms refuse to negotiate with executors, insisting on receiving California's Statutory Fee.

TABLE 4–1 California Statutory Probate Fees

Probate Estate	Rate
First $15,000	4%
Next $85,000	3
Next $900,000	2
Next $9,000,000	1
Next $15 million	.5
Over $25 million	Reasonable amount to be determined by the court.

For example, single fee on a $500,000 probate estate = ($15,000)(0.04) + ($85,000)(0.03) + ($400,000)(0.02) = $11,150.

SOURCE: California Probate Code §901,910.

discussion of one non-UPC state's less comprehensive attempt at simplifying probate procedures can be found in Appendix 4A.

Estate Administration in UPC States: A Study in Flexibility

Except for their ability to utilize summary probate procedures for smaller estates and for property passing outright to the surviving spouse, personal representatives in California and other states must use formal probate. In contrast, probate procedures in UPC states are much more liberal, allowing interested parties to largely select the degree of supervision they desire.[23] The basic choices are three: completely court-supervised administration, totally unsupervised (informal) administration, or a combination of unsupervised and supervised administration.[24] They are described next.

Complete court-supervised administration. UPC states may require an estate to be subject to "supervised administration," which is essentially the same as California's formal continuing court-supervision model (described in the last section) and also found in nearly all other states. UPC-supervised administration is a bit less regulated, however, because the personal representative is given

---

[23]For a list of the states having adopted the UPC, see footnote 1, Chapter 3.

[24]The UPC also provides a simple summary procedure for estates worth less than $5,000. It is basically similar to that of California's affidavit-of-right procedure, described in Appendix 4A. Thus, very small estates will often be able to be settled without any administration.

greater freedom to act independently. Usually, there will be no court involvement between the time Letters are issued and the time the personal representative petitions the court for closing of the estate. In contrast, probate administration in non-UPC states, as we have seen, involves frequent court supervision over the major transactions of the personal representative.

Most personal representatives of estates in UPC jurisdictions choose not to be subject to supervised administration. Occasionally, an interested party will request it because he or she feels that close supervision is necessary to ensure a just distribution.

Informal and formal administration. In addition to supervised administration, which is pretty much a court-supervised process, UPC jurisdictions allow two other types of procedures, called informal and formal administration.

Informal administration procedures usually require no court appearances and very little notice. The application for informal appointment is the simplest way for a personal representative to be appointed. The prospective personal representative files an application with a court registrar, whose role is administrative rather than judicial. Once appointed, the personal representative has all the powers needed to perform the job, including the power to deal with creditors and distributees in confidence. The personal representative is required to give notice of the appointment to all heirs and devisees by ordinary mail within 30 days of appointment. Within three months, the personal representative must prepare an inventory of the estate and mail it to all parties requesting it. The inventory can be entirely valued by the personal representative, unless an interested party objects.

Under informal administration, the procedure to give notice to creditors is available. The personal representative will usually want to give formal newspaper notice, in the manner similar to the procedure for formal probate in non-UPC states, in order to limit the creditor's claim period to four months from date of first publication. Without notice to creditors, the limitations period usually runs to three years after the date of the decedent's death.

The personal representative can apply to the registrar for an informal closing of the estate anytime after six months after appointment. Six months after closing, the personal representative will be discharged from all liability, except due to fraud and other major offenses. Distributees of estate property will continue to be liable until the later of three years after date of the decedent's death or one year after the date of the distribution.

Formal administration procedures under the UPC include the petition for "formal testacy" (proving the will), petition for formal appointment of the personal representative, and petition for formal closing. Each is undertaken in a manner similar to that for supervised administration and requires giving proper notice to interested parties, filing a petition with the court, and appearing at a court hearing.

The UPC's unique method of settling disputes has been described as an "in and out" method. During informal proceedings, a dissatisfied interested party can petition the court for a formal resolution of a controversy, whereupon probate will continue "in" court. Once the dispute is settled, administration can resume in informal proceedings, "out" of court.

In addition to the right to petition the court, interested parties have other protective remedies, including the right to request that the personal representative obtain a bond, the right to request a restraining order on the personal representative, and the right to demand notice, that is, to receive a copy of any filings or orders in connection with the estate.

We can now see the relationship between informal and formal proceedings under the UPC. At each significant step in the probate process, the interested parties can elect a different degree of supervision. For example, the probate process may begin with an application for informal appointment of the personal representative. Then a controversy may arise, which will require court resolution. Finally, the personal representative may feel compelled to file a formal petition for closing. Only in an unusual case will an interested party early on petition for complete supervised administration, making the informal process unavailable. The underlying premise throughout is the desire to avoid judicial supervision when at all possible.

From this brief presentation, it should be clear why many states have chosen to adopt the UPC scheme of probate administration. To a more modest degree, the movement toward reduced state regulation has spread to other states, too; this is due partly to the influence of the UPC. As illustrated in Appendix 4A, traditional states have moved to reduce court supervision by adopting summary procedures, set-asides, and procedures to reduce the personal representative's court-reporting requirements. The overall effect of all state deregulation has been to reduce court congestion considerably.

The next chapter will require a change of focus from the qualitative to the quantitative. It will be the first of four chapters to introduce the principles of taxation.

RECOMMENDED READING

(ANONYMOUS.) "Inheritance Problems of Frozen Embryos (The Child *En Ventre Sa Frigidaire*). *Probate Law Journal* 7 (1986), pp. 119–43.

(ANONYMOUS.) "Social Changes Outpace the Laws of Inheritance." *Trusts and Estates,* April 1986, p. 22ff. (Interview with a New York County surrogate court law assistant discussing the impact of unwed couples and multiple marriages on succession laws.)

CICERO, JILL M. "How to Handle Efficiently the Myriad Details Required to Settle an Estate."*Estate Planning,* July 1987, pp. 208–11.

DECKER, ANDREW. "The Billion-Dollar Picasso Estate." *ARTnews,* December 1986, pp. 81–99.

DUNHAM, ALLISON. "The Method, Process and Frequency of Wealth Transmission at Death."*University of Chicago Law Review* 30 (1963), pp. 241–85.

FALSEY, MARIE. "Spousal Disinheritance: The New York Solution—A Critique of Forced Share Legislation." *Western New England Law Review* 7 (1985), pp. 881–908.

FELLOWS, MARY L. "The Slayer Rule: Not Solely a Matter of Equity."*Iowa Law Review,* 71 (1986), pp. 489–555.

FRIEDMAN, LAWRENCE M. "The Law of the Living, the Law of the Dead: Property, Succession,and Society." *Wisconsin Law Review,* Spring 1966, pp. 340–78.

HARRIS, MARLYS. "The War of the Wills." *Money,* July 1985, pp. 150–63. (Regarding the controversy over the estate of Darryl F. Zanuck.)

HASKELL, PAUL G. *Preface to Wills, Trusts and Administration.* New York: *Foundation Press,* 1987.

JOHNSTONE, WILLIAM S., AND SUSAN S. WESTERMAN. "Estate Planning for Spouses and Prospective Spouses—Drafting and Enforcing Pre and Post Marital Agreements." *Estate Planning 1986,* California Continuing Education of the Bar, 1986.

MASON, PETER I., AND MARK W. WEISBARD. "The Pitfalls of Will Contest Litigation." *John Marshall Law Review* 16 (1983), pp. 499–522.

NOMMAY, TINA. "One Way to Insure Inheritance Is Murder, or Is It?" *Valparaiso University Law Review* 21 (1987) pp. 763–96. (Review of state statutes prohibiting a killer from inheriting or receiving a legacy, etc., from the victim, and a proposal for change.)

STEIN, ROBERT A. "Probate Administration Study: Some Emerging Conclusions." *Real Property, Probate and Trust Journal* 9 (Winter 1974), pp. 596–610.

STEIN, ROBERT A., and IAN G. FIERSTEIN. "The Demography of Probate Administration." *Baltimore Law Review* 15 (1985), pp. 54–107. (A detailed survey of probate administration practices in the states of California, Florida, Maryland, Massachusetts, and Texas, based on data gathered in 1976.)

SUGAYAN, CATALINA. Abandoning Ad Valorem Estate Administration Charges." *Probate Law Journal* 7 (1985), pp. 33–60.

TUCKER, JAMES B. "If a Will Is Contested." *California State Bar Journal,* September/October 1975, pp. 382–412.

WELLMAN, RICHARD V. "The New Uniform Probate Code." *American Bar Association Journal* 56 (July 1970), pp. 636–40.

————. *Palmer's Trusts and Succession.* 4th ed. St. Paul, Minn.: West Publishing, 1983, chap. 1.

————. "Recent Developments in the Struggle for Probate Reform." *Michigan Law Review* 79 (January 1981), pp. 501–49.

————. "Solving the Probate Mess." *Graduate Woman,* January/February 1980, pp. 15–17.

QUESTIONS AND PROBLEMS

1. True or false: A decedent's intestate property does not go through the probate process. Explain.

2. Harry, who is single, owns a house, some furniture, a car and a one half interest in some common stock. The car is in joint tenancy with his mother. The house is in trust, and the trust document says "for Harry's use for life, then to cousin Joe." With regard to the stock, Harry is an equal tenant in common with Sam. Harry's will says: "I leave my car, my stock, and my house to Betty." It has no other dispositive provisions.

   a. Assuming that Mother and Joe are Harry's only living relatives, who will receive what if Harry dies today?

   b. What will be included in Harry's probate estate? His nonprobate estate? His testate estate? His intestate estate?

   c. Who will be an heir? A legatee? A devisee?

   d. In your state (or under the UPC, if state law is unavailable), will your answers to the above questions change if Harry was also survived by a son? Why or why not?

3. Describe your state's laws covering inheritance by intestate succession. They are usually found in a chapter of the state's probate or estates and trusts code. If unavailable, describe the UPC rules.

4. Mary and John are married residents of your state and own the following property: As joint tenants, they own their home and a car. They own 1,000 shares of General Electric stock as tenants in common (assume community property if you are in a community property state). As individuals, Mary owns $80,000 in a money market fund, and John owns an apartment house. How will this property be distributed, in accordance with your state's laws on intestate succession (if unavailable, use UPC rules), if Mary dies without a will, leaving only the following surviving relatives:

   a. Only John.

   b. John and one child.

   c. John and three children.

   d. John, Mary's mother, and three children.

  e. John and Mary's mother.

  f. John and Mary's sister.

  g. John, Mary's mother, and Mary's fifth cousin.

  h. John and Mary's fifth cousin.

  i. Mary's fifth cousin.

  j. John, two living children, and three granddaughters (the daughters of a predeceased child).

  k. There are no surviving relatives.

  How would your answers to the above questions change if Mary died with a valid will containing a residuary clause?

5. Assume that Mary and John own the property stated in Question 4 above, that Mary and John are childless, and that Mary's and John's sole surviving relatives are their parents. In your state, or under the UPC, who will inherit Mary's money market fund account if John and Mary both die intestate and, alternatively,

  a. John predeceased Mary

  b. John, in fact, predeceased Mary by 10 minutes, but there is no evidence of this.

  c. John survived Mary by six hours.

  d. John survived Mary by six days.

6. Frank and Joan, husband and wife, had two living children, C1 and C2, four years ago when Frank executed his only will. The will leaves one half of his property each to C1 and Joan. A year later, C3 was born. Today, Frank tells you that he would like to leave all his property to Joan when he dies. Advise Frank, being sure to tell him who would get his property if he died now. Apply your state law or, if unavailable, the UPC.

7. Ten years ago, George, who was single, executed his first and only will, leaving everything to his mother. Two years later, George married Karla. Today, George is in your office telling you that he would still like his mother to receive all his property at his death. Based on your state law, or the UPC if unavailable, advise George.

8. Who is closer to you, your first cousin or your niece? Why?

9. List the purposes of the form "petition for probate."

10. Find, cut out, and bring to class a newspaper-published

"notice of death." It need not be current. What is its purpose?

11. You have been asked to attend a hearing for probate. What is its purpose?

12. A client of yours shows you an "inventory and appraisement." What are its uses?

13. What is the purpose of the creditor's claim? Who files it?

14. Ordinarily, what must the personal representative accomplish before a judge will permit final distribution under supervised probate?

15. Summarize the minimum legal procedures which are involved in supervised probate in most states.

16. Why is probate in UPC states considered so flexible?

17. Describe the informal probate administration procedures under the UPC.

18. Fifteen years ago, your client's uncle wrote a will leaving his entire estate to your client. Five years ago, he wrote a second will leaving his entire estate to your client's brother. In each case, he asked you to safeguard the original. You believe that he made no copies. Uncle died last week. What do your ethics tell you to do?

Summary Probate Proceedings in California: One Non-UPC State's Alternatives to Formal Probate

As we have seen, formal probate typically requires at least four document filings, two formal court hearings, one newspaper publication of notice, and at least one and possibly two accountings. Although these procedures were allegedly designed to protect estate assets and ensure their proper distribution, many are considered unnecessary in rather simple estate situations. Over the years, non-UPC states have also simplified probate procedures for less complicated estates.

This appendix will summarize the progress of probate simplification in California. Presently, California has two major types of "summary probate," as it is called, neither of which require newspaper notice, and both of which require not more than one petition and hearing. The two types, discussed next, are the affidavit of right and the summary distribution to the surviving spouse.

AFFIDAVIT OF RIGHT[1]

The affidavit of right is a procedure that acknowledges a valid will (or the application of the laws of intestacy) and permits a settlement of the decedent's affairs more rapidly than formal probate. This action speeds up the transfer of property to the named heir. Essentially, an affidavit, signed by the heir, is presented to the person or institution holding the property or title to it. That party is then required to turn ownership of the property over to the heir. The affidavit of right for *personal property* can only be

---

[1]California Probate Code §13,500–13,660.

used if the decedent's total estate does not exceed $60,000, an amount that does not include joint tenancy property, life estate interests, a motor vehicle or mobile home, $5,000 in salary, and any property subject to the summary distribution which is described below. The affidavit of right for *real property* can only be used if the decedent owned no more than $10,000 in California real property. A court-certified affidavit is issued by the county clerk to the county recorder.

SUMMARY DISTRIBUTION TO THE SURVIVING SPOUSE[2]

Married spouses in California frequently own separate or community property which at death will wind up passing outright to the surviving spouse, either because the spouse was named in the will or by the operation of the laws of intestate succession. In two important ways, California probate law has simplified the administration requirements of such property.

Spousal Set-Aside

First, the surviving spouse may elect to have separate or community property "set aside," that is, pass to him or her without formal probate administration.

Summary Distribution Petition

Second, the surviving spouse can also elect, under a summary distribution, one court hearing for the purpose of obtaining written confirmation by the court that such property has in fact passed to him or her. This may be helpful to clear title and to distinctly isolate that property which is not subject to formal probate administration. Essentially, at the hearing the judge confirms that the property is, in fact, either community or separate property and that it should, in fact, pass to the surviving spouse. The judge will sign an order confirming these findings. A summary distribution petition may be filed regardless of the amount or type of other property owned by the decedent at death, and therefore formal probate may be required for other assets. Further, an affidavit of right and a summary distribution petition may both be used in the same estate, provided that all of the requirements are met.

Attorney fees for summary distribution legal work are not set by statute, but in practice these fees are substantially less than those for formal probate. One third of the statutory fee is an amount commonly charged. Even less is charged for a spousal set-aside without the petition for summary distribution.

---

[2]California Probate Code §13,100–13,209.

5

Introduction to Federal Unified Wealth Transfer Taxation

OVERVIEW

This chapter is the first of four covering taxation and will introduce the federal taxation of wealth transfers. Since individual wealth can be transferred during lifetime and at death, we must examine the tax effects on each type of transfer. The chapter will show how the gift and estate tax systems are similar (or "unified") and how they differ.[1]

BRIEF HISTORY

Congress first created a wealth transfer tax during the Civil War, with the enactment of an inheritance tax. It was repealed shortly after the war. In 1916, Congress passed an estate tax, with rates ranging between 1 and 10 percent. As a tax only on transfers at death, it was relatively easy to circumvent through the use of life-time gifts which, at death, had the effect of reducing the size of a person's taxable estate. In 1924, Congress plugged this loophole somewhat by enacting a gift tax, which was repealed in 1926 and reenacted in 1932. However, with regard to tax *rate* planning, life-

---

[1]Federal tax law also has a "generation-skipping transfer tax," which will be introduced in Chapter 7.

time-gift strategies were still worthwhile pursuing up to 1977—because up to then gift tax *rates* were substantially lower than estate tax rates. With the passage of the Tax Reform Act of 1976, a single "unified" rate schedule was adopted, thereby taxing cumulative lifetime gifts at rates essentially the same as if these gifts had not been made (i.e., taxed as if the planner died owning all of the property). With regard to gift *planning in general,* we shall see later in the text that there remain several excellent tax reasons for making lifetime gifts.

THE UNIFIED TRANSFER TAX FRAMEWORK

An overview model for federal gift taxation is presented in Table 5–1.

The scheme is simpler for a one-gift, individual donor who has made no prior taxable gifts, and can be summarized by the following steps: Subtract the annual exclusion ($10,000) from the amount of the gift and calculate a tentative tax on that amount. The net tax is equal to the tentative tax reduced by the current unified credit. Appendix 5B includes a copy of the Federal Gift Tax Return, Form 709, which should help to illustrate the gift tax scheme. The *donor* is responsible for filing the return and paying the tax.

An overview model for federal estate (death) taxation is presented in Table 5–2. The scheme for calculating the net federal estate tax can be described as follows: Deductions are subtracted from the gross estate to arrive at the taxable estate. Then, lifetime taxable gifts are added to determine the estate tax base, on which

---

TABLE 5–1 Federal Gift Tax (Form 709)

Current year's gross gifts	$xxx,xxx		
Less: Annual exclusion(s) and deductions	xxx,xxx		
Equals: Current taxable gifts		$xxx,xxx	
Plus: Total prior taxable gifts		xx,xxx	
Equals: Total taxable gifts			$xxx,xxx
Calculate: Tentative tax on total taxable gifts			xx,xxx
Less: Tentative tax on total prior taxable gifts			x,xxx
Leaves: Tentative tax on current gifts			x,xxx
Less: Unused unified credit			xx,xxx
Equals: Net current gift tax			$ xx,xxx

TABLE 5–2 Federal Estate Tax (Form 706)

Gross estate	$xxx,xxx	
Less: Total deductions	$xxx,xxx	
Leaves: Taxable estate	xxx,xxx	
Plus: Adjusted taxable gifts	xx,xxx	
Equals: Estate tax base		$xxx,xxx
Calculate: Tentative estate tax		xxx,xxx
Less: Gift taxes payable on adjusted taxable gifts		xxx,xxx
Less: Unified credit		xxx,xxx
Less: Other credits		xx,xxx
Equals: Net estate tax		$xxx,xxx

a tentative tax is calculated, using the unified rates found in the tax table. Finally, various credits are subtracted, including the unified credit, to arrive at the net estate tax. Appendix 5C includes a copy of the Federal Estate Tax Return, Form 706, which should help to illustrate the estate tax structure. The *executor* is responsible for filing the return and paying the tax.

Obviously, gift and estate taxation is somewhat complicated and will need careful explanation. These tax models have been presented at the outset not to overwhelm, but simply to provide the reader with the overall scheme to refer to while reading this and the next two chapters. Each of the major components will be introduced sequentially, with illustrations.

For the moment, the reader should simply be aware of several important similarities between federal gift taxation and estate taxation. First, certain *lifetime gifts* are added to the total taxable amount. These are represented by "total prior taxable gifts" in Table 5–1 and by "adjusted taxable gifts" in Table 5–2. Second, *deductions* are subtracted before arriving at the taxable amount. Third, the *tentative tax* on the total taxable amount is calculated for both the gift tax and the estate tax from the same unified transfer tax rate schedule, which will be introduced shortly. Fourth, although certain prior gifts are included in the taxable amount in calculating the tax, an amount of *gift tax on prior gifts* is subtracted before calculating the net tax to prevent double taxation. These are represented by "tentative tax on total prior taxable gifts" in Table 5–1 and by "adjusted taxable gifts" in Table 5–2. Finally, one or more *credits,* including a "unified credit," are subtracted from the tentative tax in arriving at the net tax.

THE UNIFIED RATE SCHEDULE

Table 4 in Appendix A at the end of the text depicts the Federal Unified Tax Rate Schedule. As a result of the Economic Recovery Act of 1981 (ERTA), revised by the Tax Reform Act of 1984 (TRA 84) and the Revenue Act of 1987, rates on amounts over $2.5 million have been decreasing periodically. Hence, the schedule is divided into six parts. The first part shows rates for *all* transfer years after 1976 for taxable amounts up to $2.5 million. The next five parts represent transition rates on taxable amounts over $2.5 million, which apply for transfers during the years 1977–81, 1982, 1983, 1984–1992, and 1993 and thereafter.[2]

A few examples will demonstrate the application of the unified rates.

EXAMPLE 5–1 The *tentative tax* on the amount $600,000 in 1990 is $192,800. This represents the sum of $155,800 plus $37,000, which is 37 percent of $100,000, the excess of $600,000 over $500,000. Since the same rate table applies to all years for amounts up to $2.5 million, $192,800 would be the tentative tax on the amount $600,000 for all years after 1977.

EXAMPLE 5–2 The *tentative tax* on the amount $3,250,000 in 1992 is $1,428,300. This represents the sum of $1,290,800 plus $137,500, which is 55 percent of $250,000, the excess of $3,250,000 over $3,000,000.

Federal unified transfer tax rates are progressive, with marginal rates ranging from 18 percent, to 55 percent for all amounts in excess of $3 million (prior to 1993).[3]

---

[2]The Revenue Act of 1987 delayed until 1993 the reduction of the 53 and 55 percent rates to 50 percent for taxable amounts exceeding $2.5 million. In addition, the act phased out the transfer tax benefits of the graduated rates and the unified credit for estates with a tax base exceeding $10 million. This phaseout is implemented with the imposition of an additional 5 percent estate tax on amounts in the tax base exceeding $10 million.

[3]The *marginal rate* is the rate levied on the next dollar of taxable amount. An "average rate," on the other hand, is the result obtained by dividing the total tax by the total taxable amount.

THE UNIFIED CREDIT

In federal estate and gift tax law, a *credit* is a dollar-for-dollar reduction in the *tentative tax*. It is to be distinguished from a *deduction,* which is a dollar-for-dollar reduction in the *amount taxable* and provides only a fractional reduction in the tentative tax, with the fraction determined by the particular estate's marginal tax rate. In the next two chapters, we will study several credits, but the most significant one, the unified credit, will be introduced now.

Prior to 1977, estate and gift tax law permitted a deduction of $30,000 on the gift-tax return for total lifetime gifts and $60,000 on the estate-tax return for decedent's estates. These had the effect of eliminating taxation of small amounts of lifetime gifts and small estates.[4] Thus, for example, in the estate tax area prior to 1977, the first $60,000 of taxable estate was tax free. Then Congress passed the Tax Reform Act of 1976 (TRA 76), which eliminated these deductions and substituted a single "unified" credit, applicable to either estates or taxable gifts after 1976. The unified credit has been phased in since 1977 in increasing amounts, as shown in Table 5 of Appendix A. The third column in that table shows the "exemption equivalent" of that year's unified credit, representing the amount of the deduction needed to produce the same net tax effect as that produced by the matching credit.

> EXAMPLE 5–3 After the unified credit is subtracted, the *net tax* on the amount $600,000 in 1983 is $113,500, which is the tentative tax of $192,800, reduced by the 1983 unified credit of $79,300.

> EXAMPLE 5–4 Facts similar to Example 5–3 above, except the relevant year is 1996, or for that matter, any year after 1986. After the unified credit is subtracted, the net tax on the amount $600,000 is zero, which is the tentative tax of $192,800, reduced by the post-1986 unified credit of $192,800. Thus, $600,000 is that year's "exemption equivalent"; starting in 1987, the first $600,000 in taxable amount is tax free.

---

[4]Technically, the $30,000 deduction was called an exemption. In addition, a $3,000 gift exclusion per donor per donee per year was allowed until 1982, when it was raised to $10,000. More on this shortly.

THE MARITAL DEDUCTION

Since 1982, virtually all transfers to a spouse, whether made during lifetime or at death, have been tax free; the amount of the transfer is treated as a deduction from the total gross estate or gross gift.[5] The "unlimited marital deduction," as it is called, will be examined in greater detail in the next two chapters.

Wealth transfer taxes incorporate other significant deductions and credits, but their examination will also be deferred.

THE $10,000 ANNUAL EXCLUSION FOR LIFETIME GIFTS

The first $10,000 of total post-1981 gifts by any donor to each donee in a given year is treated as a deduction.[6] Technically, it is called the annual exclusion.

> EXAMPLE 5–5 In 1982, Dad gave $21,000 cash amounts to both son Bob and Uncle Bill. Assuming that Dad made no other gifts in that year, he would file only one gift tax return, and his "total taxable gifts" for 1982 would equal $22,000, which is twice the amount of each "net gift," or 2 × ($21,000 − $10,000).

> EXAMPLE 5–6 Mary gave husband Karl $200,000 in 1983. Assuming that it was her only gift in 1983, Mary's "total taxable gifts" for 1983 equals zero, which is $200,000, the amount of the gross gift, reduced by $200,000, the amount of the marital deduction. In this case, the annual exclusion is not really needed to reduce the tax to zero.

In Chapter 7, the reader will learn that spouses can "split" a lifetime gift, enabling a gift of property owned entirely by one spouse to be treated as if each spouse made one half of the gift, thus qualifying for two annual exclusions.

---

[5]For a brief description of the maximum amount of the estate and gift tax marital deduction prior to 1982, see the footnotes in the marital deduction sections of the next two chapters.

[6]As stated earlier, for gifts prior to 1982, the amount was $3,000.

WEALTH TRANSFERS ARE UNIFIED AND TAXED CUMULATIVELY

In wealth transfer taxation, succeeding transfers are unified, in part because they are taxed cumulatively. Under the *cumulative gift doctrine,* all lifetime gifts are accumulated; that is, prior taxable gifts are added to current taxable transfers to determine the transfer tax base. This often causes the current gifts to be taxed at the higher marginal rates. In the example below, for simplicity, assume no annual exclusion for gifts.

EXAMPLE 5–7 If Carla gives Katie $500,000 cash all at once, Carla's tentative gift tax will be $155,800. Instead, if Carla gives Katie $250,000 in one year, her total tentative tax will *still* be $155,800, as shown in the following table:

	First Gift	Second Gift
Total current taxable gifts	$250,000	$250,000
Plus: Total prior taxable gifts	—0—	250,000
Equals: Total taxable gifts	250,000	500,000
Tentative tax on total gifts	70,800	155,800
Less: Tentative tax on prior gifts	—0—	70,800
Equals: Tentative tax on current gifts	70,000	85,000
Total cumulative tentative tax	$ 70,800	$155,800

Prior taxable gifts are similarly accumulated on the estate tax return, as we shall see later.

As we have seen, TRA 76 created what has been called a unified transfer tax, one which has combined gift and estate taxation into a single tax structure having one rate schedule. However, TRA 76 did not achieve complete unification. It did not produce a tax system that would make a planner indifferent, from a transfer tax point of view, between recommending lifetime and deathtime gifts. We shall see in later chapters, particularly Chapters 9 and 13, how our current transfer tax system is still quite imperfect and how the planner can employ numerous strategies to capitalize on these imperfections.

Before considering an example of the complete unified transfer tax scheme, we must cover three important technical points.

First, regarding taxable gifts, in calculating the gift tax one includes in the item called "total taxable gifts" all taxable gifts made *since 1932,* the year of enactment of the gift tax. On the other hand, as we have said, in calculating the (FET) estate tax base one includes in the item called "adjusted taxable gifts" only *post-1976* taxable gifts. Further, recall that the annual exclusion for gifts made prior to 1982 was $3,000, not $10,000. Finally, an additional $30,000 "lifetime exemption" was allowed and accumulated for gifts made after 1931 and before 1977.

Second, in the *gift* tax model, the "unused unified credit" is the amount of the current unified credit reduced by the unified credit amount already used up in prior years. It is based on the premise that once the amount of the (lifetime) unified credit is fully used up, each additional dollar of taxable gift is fully taxable.

Third, as we have said, gift tax rates changed in 1977, when they became equal to estate tax rates. We have already examined the unified rates for transfers after 1977. Gift tax rates for the period prior to 1977 were exactly three quarters of pre-1977 estate tax rates. Pre-1977 estate tax and gift tax rates are illustrated in Tables 7 and 8, respectively, of Appendix A at the end of the text.

THE COMPLETE UNIFIED TAX FRAMEWORK: SOME EXAMPLES

We are ready to apply the overall scheme of the gift and estate tax to a series of connected examples.

EXAMPLE 5–9 Dan, a widower, gave his son Tom $260,000 cash in 1973. In 1978, Joe, a widower, gave his son Tom an apartment house worth $260,000. In 1982, Pete, a widower, gave his son Tom a parcel of land worth $260,000. Assuming that each person has not made prior taxable gifts, Dan's, Joe's, and Pete's net gift-tax liabilities are calculated in the following table:

	Dan 1973	Joe 1978	Pete 1982
Current gross gift	$260,000	$260,000	$260,000
Less: Annual exclusion	3,000	3,000	10,000
Less: Lifetime exemption	30,000	n.a.	n.a.
Current taxable gift	227,000	257,000	250,000
Plus: Total prior taxable gifts	—0—	—0—	—0—
Total taxable gifts	227,000	257,000	250,000
Tentative tax on total gifts	44,100	73,180	70,800
Less: Tentative tax on prior gifts	—0—	—0—	—0—

	Dan 1973	Joe 1978	Pete 1982
Tentative tax on current gift	$ 44,100	$ 73,180	$ 70,800
Less: Unused unified credit	n.a.	34,000	62,800
Net gift tax	$ 44,100	$ 39,180	$ 8,000

n.a. = Not applicable.

Note several points: First, since there were no prior gifts, there is no tentative tax on prior gifts. Second, two different rate tables and two different annual exclusion amounts were used for calculating the tentative tax, depending on the year of the gift. Third, the lifetime exemption applies only to pre-1977 gifts, and the unified credit applies only to gifts made after 1976.

Now let's change the facts a bit to illustrate the impact of the cumulative gift doctrine.

EXAMPLE 5–10 Continuing Example 5–9, suppose that Dan, Joe, and Pete are really one and the same person named Steve, who, by himself, made those three gifts successively to the same person, his son Tom, in the indicated years. Steve's three gift tax liabilities are calculated in the following table:

	1973 Gift	1978 Gift	1982 Gift
Current gross gift	$260,000	$260,000	$260,000
Less: Annual exclusion	3,000	3,000	10,000
Less: Lifetime exemption	30,000	n.a.	n.a.
Current taxable gift	227,000	257,000	250,000
Plus: Total prior taxable gifts	—0—	227,000	484,000
Total Taxable gifts	227,000	484,000	734,000
Tentative tax on total gifts	44,100	150,360	242,380
Less: Tentative tax on prior gifts	—0—	63,440	150,360
Tentative tax on current gift	44,100	86,920	92,020
Less: Unused unified credit	n.a.	34,000	28,800
Net gift tax	$ 44,100	$ 52,920	$ 63,220

n.a. = Not applicable.

Again note several points: First, the tentative 1978 tax of $63,440 on prior gifts is not equal to the actual tentative tax of $44,100 on the 1973 prior gift. For any given year, tentative tax calculations are always made using that *current* year's tax rates.

This has prompted some commentators to call the $63,440 a "theoretical tax." Second, as mentioned above, the unused unified credit is equal to the amount of the full unified credit in the year of the gift, less the amount of the unified credit used in prior years. Therefore, the 1982 unused unified credit equals $62,800 minus $34,000, or $28,800.

> EXAMPLE 5–11 Continuing Example 5–10, assume that Steve dies in 1991. Let's calculate Steve's estate tax, assuming no deductions and no credits except the unified credit. Assume further that after making the three gifts and paying the gift taxes, Steve's gross estate has been reduced to $1 million at date of death.

Gross estate	$1,000,000
Less: Deductions	—0—
Taxable estate	1,000,000
Plus: Adjusted taxable gifts	507,000
Equals: Estate tax base	1,507,000
Tentative estate tax	558,950
Less: Gift taxes payable on adjusted (post-1976) taxable gifts	116,140
Less: Unified credit*	192,800
Less: Other credits	—0—
Net estate tax	250,010
Total transfer taxes	$ 410,250

> *Students often ask, "If only the unused unified credit is subtracted from the tentative tax on the gift tax return, why is the *full* unified credit subtracted on the estate tax return?" The reason is that the tentative estate tax is reduced not by the entire tentative gift tax on lifetime gifts, but only by the *net* gift tax, which is lower than the tentative tax on lifetime gifts by the amount of the unified credit taken during lifetime. For a more extensive explanation, with a numerical example, see Appendix 5A.

Referring to the preceding example, notice first that the line "adjusted taxable gifts" does not include the 1973 gift since it was not made after 1976. Second, the $116,140 in gift tax payable does not include the gift tax of $44,100 on the 1973 gift, for the same reason.

The next two chapters cover the estate tax and the gift tax, respectively, with regard to other important characteristics, mostly nonquantitative in nature.

RECOMMENDED READING

ARMSTRONG, ARTHUR A., and RONALD R. ST. JOHN. "Estate Planning Overview: Federal Estate and Gift Taxes, Past, Present and Future." *Taxes,* (October 1986), pp. 634–53.

DODGE, JOSEPH M. "The Taxation of Wealth and Wealth Transfers: Where do We Go after ERTA?" *Rutger's Law Review* 34 (1982), pp. 739–75.

Estate and Gift Tax Reporter. Chicago: Commerce Clearing House.

Federal Tax Estate and Gift Taxes. Englewood Cliffs, N.J.: Prentice-Hall.

TAGGART, JOHN Y. "The New Estate and Gift Tax Regime." *Buffalo Law Review* 31 (1982), pp. 797–882.

QUESTIONS AND PROBLEMS

1. Outline the history of federal wealth transfer taxation.

2. Why would the imposition of a transfer tax at death without an accompanying gift tax be largely ineffective?

3. Outline the basic computational scheme of the federal gift tax and the federal estate tax.

4. Describe the five computational steps that the gift tax and estate tax calculations have in common.

5. Calculate the tentative tax, the net tax, the marginal tax rate, and the average tax rate on the taxable amount $600,000 for both 1989 and 1993. Assume the transfers are made by different parties and that there are no other taxable gifts and no credits, except the unified credit.

6. Redo Question 5 for the taxable amount $3,250,000.

7. Let's assume that for a given estate the amount to be taxed in 1991, before deductions, is $2 million.
   a. Calculate the *net* tax in two ways. First assume $100,000 in total deductions and no credits. Second, assume no deductions and $100,000 in total credits.
   b. Why are your results different?
   c. Which is preferred, a deduction or a credit of a given amount? Why? (Actually, there are no situations where a taxpayer has the choice.)

8. (a) Describe briefly the chronological progression of the amounts of the unified credit. (b) What is the exemption equivalent?

9. Describe the unlimited marital deduction.

10. During his lifetime, Dad gave his wife and his daughter $42,000 cash each outright in both 1981 and 1982. Calculate Dad's "total current taxable gifts" for each year. Assume no gift splitting, and assume that the unlimited marital deduction applies in both years.

11. This is a comprehensive transfer tax problem in which you will calculate each gift tax and an estate tax. In 1975, Mary, a widow, owned $1.2 million in wealth (assume for simplicity that it is all cash in a mattress). In that year, she gave

$36,000 to each of her two sons. In 1983, Mary gave $400,000 to one son. Assume that Mary dies in 1991. Hints: Be sure that your 1975 calculations reflect pre-1977 law, including different tax tables, the lifetime exemption, a lower annual exclusion, and no unified credit.

(Answers: gift taxes of $3,060 and $44,020; FET of $138,057. Author's suggestion: The answers to this question constitute the foundation for several aspects of gift planning and are referred to in Chapter 9, Problem 12. You may care to save your notes.)

Answer to Question: "Why not Subtract only the *Unused* Unified Credit in Calculating the Federal Estate Tax"?

This Appendix has been written to explain why the full unified credit, rather than just the gift tax return's unused unified credit is subtracted on the federal estate tax return.

Consider a highly abstract example, which, for ease of comprehension, makes the following assumptions:

- the tax rate on all transfers is a flat 50 percent;
- the unified credit is $30;
- there is no annual exclusion;
- there are no deductions.

Marie's total wealth consists of $200 in cash. If our basic federal unified transfer tax scheme is working properly and consistently, this wealth should incur a total tax of $70, regardless when she makes her transfers, during lifetime or at death. Proof:

Total transfer taxes = $200 times .50, less $30 = $70

Now suppose Marie makes post–1976 lifetime gifts of $40 and $20 in two different years. Her gift tax returns are shown thus:

	First Gift	**Second Gift**
Current taxable gifts	$40	$20
Plus: Prior taxable gifts	0	40
Equals: Total taxable gifts	40	60
Tentative tax on total gifts	20	30
Less: Tentative tax on prior gifts	0	20*
Equals: Tentative tax on current gifts	20	10
Less: Unused unified credit	20	10
Leaves: Net gift tax	$ 0	$ 0

Next, assume that Marie dies. Her gross estate will be $140, which is the amount of her original wealth, $200, reduced by $60, the amount of the lifetime gifts. Marie's FET, assuming that the full unified credit is taken, will be $70, as shown below:

Gross estate	$140
Plus: Adjusted taxable gifts	60
Equals: Estate tax base	200
Tentative estate tax	100
Less: Gift tax paid on adjusted taxable gifts	0*
Less: Unified credit	30
Leaves: FET	$ 70

Thus, total lifetime plus deathtime transfer taxes are $70, as they should be. The average tax rate is 35% (= $70/$200). Had we mistakenly subtracted only the "unused" unified credit on the FET return (which, because of the gifts, would have been reduced to $0 at death), total transfer taxes would have been $100, resulting in an average tax rate of 50%. The upshot would have been the total failure to utilize the unified credit.

The critical reason that the full unified credit is subtracted on the estate tax return is that the tentative estate tax is reduced not by the entire *tentative* gift tax on lifetime gifts, (as we did on the second gift tax return, above), but only by the *net* gift tax on lifetime gifts, which is lower than the tentative tax on lifetime gifts by the amount of the unified credit taken during lifetime. (These items are marked with asterisks above). Since we haven't yet gotten on the FET return the benefit of the already used portion of the unified credit, we must take it now, by subtracting the entire unified credit.

The estate tax return subtracts the gift taxes paid on lifetime gifts from the tentative estate tax only because it reflects a *prepayment of the transfer tax;* not to do so would result in double tax payment for the gifts. The gift tax return, on the other hand, subtracts the tentative gift tax on prior gifts for a totally different reason: it subtracts it to consistently implement the law's intent to push current gifts into a (potentially) *higher tax bracket.* And since the gift tax return subtracts the full tentative gift tax on prior gifts, it must deduct only the unused unified credit; to subtract the full unified credit on the gift tax return would doublecount the benefit of the unified credit.

It would have been simpler to understand the unified scheme if the gift tax were calculated like the estate tax: by figuring a tentative tax on *all* taxable gifts—current and prior—and then subtracting from it the entire unified credit, as well as any gift tax paid on prior gifts. Such a scheme would truly make the two transfer taxes appear more similar. But although the gift tax and the estate tax appear to produce inconsistent results, their effect on net transfer taxes, as we have seen from the above, is the same.

APPENDIX 5B

Form **709**	United States Gift (and Generation-Skipping Transfer) Tax Return	
(Rev. January 1987)	(Section 6019 of the Internal Revenue Code) (For gifts made after December 31, 1981, and before January 1, 1989)	OMB No. 1545-0020
Department of the Treasury Internal Revenue Service	**Calendar year 19** _____ ▶ For Privacy Act Notice, see the Instructions for Form 1040.	Expires 12-31-89

Part 1.—General Information

1 Donor's first name and middle initial	2 Donor's last name	3 Social security number
4 Address (number and street)		5 Domicile
6 City, state, and ZIP code		7 Citizenship

		Yes	No
8	If the donor died during the year, check here ▶ ☐ and enter date of death _____, 19 _____		
9	If you received an extension of time to file this Form 709, check here ▶ ☐ and attach the Form 4868, 2688, 2350, or extension letter.		
10	If you (the donor) filed a previous Form 709 (or 709-A), has your address changed since the last Form 709 (or 709-A) was filed? . .		
11	Gifts by husband or wife to third parties.—Do you consent to have the gifts (including generation-skipping transfers) made by you and by your spouse to third parties during the calendar year considered as made one-half by each of you? (See instructions.)		

(If the answer is "Yes," the following information must be furnished and your spouse is to sign the consent shown below. If the answer is "No," skip lines 12–17 and go to Schedule A.)

12 Name of consenting spouse	13 Social security number

14	Were you married to one another during the entire calendar year? (See instructions.)	
15	If the answer to 14 is "No," check whether ☐ married ☐ divorced or ☐ widowed, and give date (see instructions) ▶	
16	Will a gift tax return for this calendar year be filed by your spouse?	

17 **Consent of Spouse**—I consent to have the gifts (and generation-skipping transfers) made by me and by my spouse to third parties during the calendar year considered as made one-half by each of us. We are both aware of the joint and several liability for tax created by the execution of this consent.

Consenting spouse's signature ▶   Date ▶

Part 2.—Tax Computation

1	Enter the amount from Schedule A, line 15	1
2	Enter the amount from Schedule B, line 3	2
3	Total taxable gifts (add lines 1 and 2)	3
4	Tax computed on amount on line 3 (see Table A for the current year in separate instructions)	4
5	Tax computed on amount on line 2 (see Table A for the current year in separate instructions)	5
6	Balance (subtract line 5 from line 4)	6
7	Enter the unified credit from Table B (see instructions)	7
8	Enter the unified credit against tax allowable for all prior periods (from Sch. B, line 1, col. (c))	8
9	Balance (subtract line 8 from line 7)	9
10	Enter 20% of the amount allowed as a specific exemption for gifts made after September 8, 1976, and before January 1, 1977 (see instructions)	10
11	Balance (subtract line 10 from line 9)	11
12	Unified credit (enter the smaller of line 6 or line 11)	12
13	Credit for foreign gift taxes (see instructions)	13
14	Total credits (add lines 12 and 13).	14
15	Balance (subtract line 14 from line 6) (do not enter less than zero)	15
16	Generation-skipping transfer taxes (from Schedule C, Part 4, col. H, total) . . .	16
17	Total taxes (add lines 15 and 16)	17
18	Gift and generation-skipping transfer taxes prepaid with extension of time to file	18
19	If line 18 is less than line 17, enter BALANCE DUE (see instructions)	19
20	If line 18 is greater than line 17, enter AMOUNT TO BE REFUNDED	20

Please attach the necessary supplemental documents; see instructions.

Under penalties of perjury, I declare that I have examined this return, including any accompanying schedules and statements, and to the best of my knowledge and belief it is true, correct, and complete. Declaration of preparer (other than donor) is based on all information of which preparer has any knowledge.

Donor's signature ▶   Date ▶

Preparer's signature (other than donor) ▶   Date ▶

Preparer's address (other than donor) ▶

For Paperwork Reduction Act Notice, see page 1 of the separate instructions to this form.   Form **709** (Rev. 1-87)

Please attach check or money order here

APPENDIX 5B (*continued*)

Form 709 (Rev. 1-87)   Page **2**

SCHEDULE A	**Computation of Taxable Gifts**

Part 1.—Gifts Subject Only to Gift Tax. *Gifts less political organization, medical, and educational exclusions—see instructions*

A Item number	B Donee's name and address and description of gift. If the gift was made by means of a trust, enter trust's identifying number below and attach a copy of the trust instrument. If the gift was securities, enter the CUSIP number(s), if available.	C Donor's adjusted basis of gift	D Date of gift	E Value at date of gift
1				

Part 2.—Gifts Subject to Both Gift Tax and Generation-Skipping Transfer Tax. **You must list the gifts in chronological order.**
Gifts less political organization, medical, and educational exclusions—see instructions

A Item number	B Donee's name and address and description of gift. If the gift was made by means of a trust, enter trust's identifying number below and attach a copy of the trust instrument. If the gift was securities, enter the CUSIP number(s), if available.	C Donor's adjusted basis of gift	D Date of gift	E Value at date of gift
1				

Part 3.—Gift Tax Reconciliation

1	Total value of gifts of donor (add column E of Parts 1 and 2) (see instructions)	1	
2	One-half of items _____ attributable to spouse (see instructions)	2	
3	Balance (subtract line 2 from line 1)	3	
4	Gifts of spouse to be included (from Schedule A, Part 3, line 2 of spouse's return—see instructions)	4	
	If any of the gifts included on this line are also subject to the generation-skipping transfer tax, check here ► ☐ and enter those gifts also on Schedule C, Part 1.		
5	Total gifts (add lines 3 and 4)	5	
6	Total annual exclusions for gifts listed on Schedule A (including line 4, above) (see instructions)	6	
7	Total included amount of gifts (subtract line 6 from line 5)	7	

Deductions (see instructions)

8	Gifts of interests to spouse for which a marital deduction will be claimed, based on items _____ of Schedule A	8		
9	Exclusions attributable to gifts on line 8	9		
10	Marital deduction—subtract line 9 from line 8	10		
11	Charitable deduction, based on items _____ to _____ less exclusions	11		
12	Total deductions—add lines 10 and 11		12	
13	Subtract line 12 from line 7		13	
14	Generation-skipping transfer taxes payable with this Form 709 (from Schedule C, Part 4, col. H, Total)		14	
15	Taxable gifts (add lines 13 and 14). Enter here and on line 1 of the Tax Computation		15	

(If more space is needed, attach additional sheets of same size.)

APPENDIX 5B *(continued)*

Form 709 (Rev. 1-87)   Page **3**

| SCHEDULE A | Computation of Taxable Gifts (continued) |

16 Terminable Interest (QTIP) Marital Deduction. (See instructions.)

☐ ◄ Check here if you elected, under the rules of section 2523(f), to include gifts of qualified terminable interest property on line 8, above. Enter the item numbers (from Schedule A) of the gifts for which you made this election ► -

| SCHEDULE B | Gifts From Prior Periods |

Did you (the donor) file gift tax returns for prior periods? (If "Yes," see instructions for completing Schedule B below.)   ☐ Yes   ☐ No

A Calendar year or calendar quarter (see instructions)	B Internal Revenue office where prior return was filed	C Amount of unified credit against gift tax for periods after December 31, 1976	D Amount of specific exemption for prior periods ending before January 1, 1977	E Amount of taxable gifts

1 Totals for prior periods (without adjustment for reduced specific exemption) | **1** |

2 Amount, if any, by which total specific exemption, line 1, column (D), is more than $30,000 . . . . | **2** |

3 Total amount of taxable gifts for prior periods (add amount, column (E), line 1, and amount, if any, on line 2).
   (Enter here and on line 2 of the Tax Computation on page 1.) . . . . | **3** |

| SCHEDULE C | Computation of Generation-Skipping Transfer Tax |

Part 1.—Generation-Skipping Transfers

A Item No. (from Schedule A, Part 2, col. A)	B Value (from Schedule A, Part 2, col. E)	C Split Gifts (enter ½ of col. B) (see instructions)	D Subtract col. C from col. B	E Annual Exclusion Claimed	F Subtract col. E from col. D	G Grandchild Exclusion Claimed	H Net Transfer (subtract col. G from col. F)
1							
2							
3							
4							
5							
6							
7							
8							

If you elected gift splitting and your spouse was required to file a separate Form 709 (see the instructions for Split Gifts), you must enter all of the gifts shown on Schedule A, Part 2, of your spouse's Form 709 here.	Split gifts from spouse's Form 709 (enter number)	Value included from spouse's Form 709					
In column C, enter the item number of each gift in the order it appears in column A of your spouse's Schedule A, Part 2. We have preprinted the prefix "S-" to distinguish your spouse's item numbers from your own when you complete column A of Schedule C, Part 4.	S- S- S- S- S- S- S- S-						
In column D, for each gift, enter the amount reported in column C, Schedule C, Part 1, of your spouse's Form 709.	Total grandchild exclusions claimed on this return. Must equal total of column D, Schedule C, Part 2						

(If more space is needed, attach additional sheets of same size.)

APPENDIX 5B *(concluded)*

Form 709 (Rev. 1-87)   Page **4**

SCHEDULE C	Computation of Generation-Skipping Transfer Tax (continued)				

Part 2.—Grandchild Exclusion Reconciliation

Name of Grandchild	A Maximum Allowable Exclusion	B Total of Exclusions Claimed on Previous Returns	C Exclusion Available for This Return (subtract col. B from col. A)	D Exclusion Claimed on this Return	E Exclusion Available for Future Returns (subtract col. D from col. C)
	$2,000,000				
	$2,000,000				
	$2,000,000				
	$2,000,000				
	$2,000,000				
	$2,000,000				
	$2,000,000				
	$2,000,000				

Total grandchild exclusions claimed on this return. Must equal total of column G, Part 1

Part 3.—GST Exemption Reconciliation (Code section 2631)

1	Maximum allowable exemption	1	$1,000,000
2	Total exemption used for periods before filing this return	2	
3	Exemption available for this return (subtract line 2 from line 1)	3	
4	Exemption claimed on this return (from Part 4, col. C total, below)	4	
5	Exemption elected for transfers not shown on Part 4, below. You must attach a Notice of Allocation. (See instructions.)	5	
6	Add lines 4 and 5	6	
7	Exemption available for future transfers (subtract line 6 from line 3)	7	

Part 4.—Tax Computation

A Gift No. (from Schedule C, Part 1)	B Net transfer (from Schedule C, Part 1, col. H)	C GST Exemption Allocated	D Divide col. C by col. B	E Inclusion Ratio (subtract col. D from 1.000)	F Maximum Gift Tax Rate (see instructions)	G Applicable Rate (multiply col. E by col. F)	H Generation-Skipping Transfer Tax (multiply col. B by col. G)
1							
2							
3							
4							
5							
6							
7							
8							

Total exemption claimed. Enter here and on line 4, Part 3, above. May not exceed line 3, Part 3, above		**Total generation-skipping transfer tax.** Enter here, on line 14 of Schedule A, Part 3, and on line 16 of the Tax Computation on page 1	

(If more space is needed, attach additional sheets of same size.)

☆ U.S. Government Printing Office: 1987—181-447/40091

APPENDIX 5C

Form **706**	**United States Estate (and Generation-Skipping Transfer) Tax Return**	
(Rev. November 1987) Department of the Treasury Internal Revenue Service	Estate of a citizen or resident of the United States (see separate instructions). To be filed for decedents dying after December 31, 1981, and before January 1, 1990. For Paperwork Reduction Act Notice, see page 1 of the instructions.	OMB No. 1545-0015 Expires 5-31-90

Part 1.—Decedent, Executor, and Representative

1a Decedent's first name and middle initial (and maiden name, if any)	**1b** Decedent's last name	**2** Decedent's social security no.
3a Domicile at time of death	**3b** Year domicile established **4** Date of birth	**5** Date of death
6a Name of executor (see instructions)	**6b** Executor's address (number and street including apartment number or rural route; city, town, or post office; state; and ZIP code)	
6c Executor's social security number (see instructions)		
7a Name and location of court where will was probated or estate administered		**7b** Case number

8 If decedent died testate, check here ▶ ☐ and attach a certified copy of the will. **9** If Form 4768 is attached, check here ▶ ☐

Authorization to receive confidential tax information under Regulations section 601.502(c)(3)(ii), to act as the estate's representative before the Internal Revenue Service, and to make written or oral presentations on behalf of the estate if return prepared by an attorney, accountant, or enrolled agent for the executor:

10a Name of representative (print or type)	**10b** State	**10c** Address (number and street, city, state, and ZIP code)

I declare that I am the attorney/accountant/enrolled agent (strike out the words that do not apply) for the executor and prepared this return for the executor. I am not under suspension or disbarment from practice before the Internal Revenue Service and am qualified to practice in the state shown above.

Signature	Date	Telephone Number

Part 2.—Tax Computation

1	Total gross estate (from Recapitulation, page 3, item 10)	1	
2	Total allowable deductions (from Recapitulation, page 3, item 21)	2	
3	Taxable estate (subtract line 2 from line 1)	3	
4	Adjusted taxable gifts (total taxable gifts (within the meaning of section 2503) made by the decedent after December 31, 1976, other than gifts that are includible in decedent's gross estate (section 2001(b))). . .	4	
5	Add lines 3 and 4	5	
6	Tentative tax on the amount on line 5 from Table A in the instructions	6	
7	Total gift tax payable with respect to gifts made by the decedent after December 31, 1976. Include gift taxes paid by the decedent's spouse for split gifts (section 2513) only if the decedent was the donor of these gifts and they are includible in the decedent's gross estate (see instructions)	7	
8	Gross estate tax (subtract line 7 from line 6)	8	
9	Unified credit against estate tax from Table B in the instructions	9	
10	Adjustment to unified credit. (This adjustment may not exceed $6,000. See instructions.)	10	
11	Allowable unified credit (subtract line 10 from line 9)	11	
12	Subtract line 11 from line 8 (but do not enter less than zero)	12	
13	Credit for state death taxes. Do not enter more than line 12. Compute credit by using amount on line 3 less $60,000. See Table C in the instructions and **attach credit evidence** (see instructions)	13	
14	Subtract line 13 from line 12	14	
15	Credit for Federal gift taxes on pre-1977 gifts (section 2012)(attach computation)	15	
16	Credit for foreign death taxes (from Schedule(s) P). (Attach Form(s) 706CE)	16	
17	Credit for tax on prior transfers (from Schedule Q)	17	
18	Total (add lines 15, 16, and 17)	18	
19	Net estate tax (subtract line 18 from line 14)	19	
20	Generation-skipping transfer taxes (from Schedule R, Part 2, line 12)	20	
21	Section 4981A increased estate taxes (attach Schedule S (Form 706)) (see instructions). . . .	21	
22	Total transfer taxes (add lines 19, 20, and 21)	22	
23	Prior payments. Explain in an attached statement	23	
24	United States Treasury bonds redeemed in payment of estate tax . . .	24	
25	Balance (add lines 23 and 24)	25	
26	Balance due (subtract line 25 from line 22)	26	

Under penalties of perjury, I declare that I have examined this return, including accompanying schedules and statements, and to the best of my knowledge and belief, it is true, correct, and complete. Declaration of preparer other than the executor is based on all information of which preparer has any knowledge.

Signature(s) of executor(s) _____ Date _____

_____ Date _____

Signature of preparer other than executor _____ Address (and ZIP code) _____ Date _____

For sale by the Superintendent of Documents, U.S. Government Printing Office Washington, D.C. 20402

APPENDIX 5C *(continued)*

Form 706 (Rev. 11-87)

Estate of:

Part 3.—Elections by the Executor

Please check the "Yes" or "No" box for each question.	Yes	No
1 Do you elect alternate valuation?		
2 Do you elect special use valuation? . . . . If "Yes," complete and attach Schedule A–1		
3 Do you elect to pay the taxes in installments as described in section 6166? . . . . If "Yes," you must attach the additional information described in the instructions.		
4 Do you elect to postpone the part of the taxes attributable to a reversionary or remainder interest as described in section 6163?		
5 Do you elect to have part or all of the estate tax liability assumed by an Employee Stock Ownership Plan (ESOP) as described in section 2210? If "Yes," enter the amount of tax assumed by the ESOP here ▶ $_____ and attach the supplemental statements described in the instructions.		

Part 4.—General Information Note: *Please attach the necessary supplemental documents.* **You must attach the death certificate.**

1   Death certificate number and issuing authority (attach a copy of the death certificate to this return).

2   Decedent's business or occupation. If retired check here ▶ ☐ and state decedent's former business or occupation.

3   Marital status of the decedent at time of death:
   ☐ Married
   ☐ Widow or widower—Name and date of death of deceased spouse ▶ _____

   ☐ Single
   ☐ Legally separated
   ☐ Divorced—Date divorce decree became final ▶

4a Surviving spouse's name	4b Social security number	4c Amount received (see instructions)

5   Individuals (other than the surviving spouse), trusts, or other estates who receive benefits from the estate (do not include charitable beneficiaries shown in Schedule O) (see instructions). For Privacy Act Notice (applicable to individual beneficiaries only), see the Instructions for Form 1040.

Name of individual, trust or estate receiving $5,000 or more	Identifying number	Relationship to decedent	Amount (see instructions)

All unascertainable beneficiaries and those who receive less than $5,000   . . . . ▶

Total   . . . .

(Continued on next page)   **Page 2**

APPENDIX 5C *(continued)*

Form 706 (Rev. 11-87)

Part 4.—General Information *(continued)*

Please check the "Yes" or "No" box for each question.	Yes	No
6 Does the gross estate contain any section 2044 property (see instructions)?		
7a Have Federal gift tax returns ever been filed?		
If "Yes," please attach copies of the returns, if available, and furnish the following information:		
7b Period(s) covered **7c** Internal Revenue office(s) where filed		

If you answer "Yes" to any of questions 8–16, you must attach additional information as described in the instructions.

	Yes	No
8a Was there any insurance on the decedent's life that is not included on the return as part of the gross estate?		
b Did the decedent own any insurance on the life of another that is not included in the gross estate?		
9 Did the decedent at the time of death own any property as a joint tenant with right of survivorship in which (1) one or more of the other joint tenants was someone other than the decedent's spouse and (2) less than the full value of the property is included on the return as part of the gross estate? If "Yes," you must complete and attach Schedule E		
10 Did the decedent, at the time of death, own any interest in a partnership or unincorporated business or any stock in an inactive or closely held corporation?		
11 Did the decedent make any transfer described in sections 2035, 2036, 2037 or 2038 (see the instructions for Schedule G)? If "Yes," you must complete and attach Schedule G		
12 Were there in existence at the time of the decedent's death:		
a Any trusts created by the decedent during his or her lifetime?		
b Any trusts not created by the decedent under which the decedent possessed any power, beneficial interest, or trusteeship?		
13 Did the decedent ever possess, exercise, or release any general power of appointment? If "Yes," you must complete and attach Schedule H.		
14 Was the marital deduction computed under the transitional rule of Public Law 97-34, section 403(e)(3) (Economic Recovery Tax Act of 1981)?		
If "Yes," attach a separate computation of the marital deduction, enter the amount on item 18 of the Recapitulation, and note on item 18 "computation attached."		
15 Was the decedent, immediately before death, receiving an annuity described in the "General" paragraph of the instructions for Schedule I? If "Yes," you must complete and attach Schedule I.		
16 Did the decedent have a total "excess retirement accumulation" (as defined in section 4981A(d)) in qualified employer plan(s) and individual retirement plan(s)?		
If "Yes," you must attach Schedule S (Form 706) (see instructions).		

Part 5.—Recapitulation

Item number	Gross estate	Alternate value	Value at date of death
1	Schedule A—Real Estate		
2	Schedule B—Stocks and Bonds		
3	Schedule C—Mortgages, Notes, and Cash		
4	Schedule D—Insurance on the Decedent's Life (attach Form(s) 712)		
5	Schedule E—Jointly Owned Property (attach Form(s) 712 for life insurance)		
6	Schedule F—Other Miscellaneous Property (attach Form(s) 712 for life insurance) . .		
7	Schedule G—Transfers During Decedent's Life (attach Form(s) 712 for life insurance) .		
8	Schedule H—Powers of Appointment		
9	Schedule I—Annuities		
10	Total gross estate (add items 1 through 9). Enter here and on line 1 of the Tax Computation.		

Item number	Deductions	Amount
11	Schedule J—Funeral Expenses and Expenses Incurred in Administering Property Subject to Claims	
12	Schedule K—Debts of the Decedent	
13	Schedule K—Mortgages and Liens	
14	Total of items 11 through 13	
15	Allowable amount of deductions from item 14 (see the instructions for item 15 of the Recapitulation)	
16	Schedule L—Net Losses During Administration	
17	Schedule L—Expenses Incurred in Administering Property Not Subject to Claims	
18	Schedule M—Bequests, etc., to Surviving Spouse	
19	Schedule N—ESOP Deduction	
20	Schedule O—Charitable, Public, and Similar Gifts and Bequests	
21	Total allowable deductions (add items 15 through 20). Enter here and on line 2 of the Tax Computation	

Page 3

APPENDIX 5C *(continued)*

Form 706 (Rev. 11-87)

Estate of:

SCHEDULE A—Real Estate

(For jointly owned property that must be disclosed on Schedule E, see the Instructions for Schedule E.)

(Real estate that is part of a sole proprietorship should be shown on Schedule F. Real estate that is included in the gross estate under sections 2035, 2036, 2037, or 2038 should be shown on Schedule G. Real estate that is included in the gross estate under section 2041 should be shown on Schedule H.)

(If you elect section 2032A valuation, you must complete Schedule A and Schedule A-1.)

Item number	Description	Alternate valuation date	Alternate value	Value at date of death
1				
	Total from continuation schedule(s) (or additional sheet(s)) attached to this schedule			
	TOTAL. (Also enter on Part 5, Recapitulation, page 3, at item 1.)			

(If more space is needed, attach the continuation schedule from the end of this package or additional sheets of the same size.)

Schedule A—Page 4

APPENDIX 5C *(continued)*

Form 706 (Rev. 11-87)

Instructions for Schedule A.— Real Estate

If the total gross estate contains any real estate, you must complete Schedule A and file it with the return.

On Schedule A list real estate the decedent owned or had contracted to purchase. Number each parcel in the left-hand column.

Describe the real estate in enough detail so that IRS can easily locate it for inspection and valuation. For each parcel of real estate report the area and, if the parcel is improved, describe the improvements. For city or town property, report the street and number, ward, subdivision, block and lot, etc. For rural property, report the township, range, landmarks, etc.

If any item of real estate is subject to a mortgage for which the decedent's estate is liable, that is, if the indebtedness may be charged against other property of the estate that is not subject to that mortgage or if the decedent was personally liable for that mortgage, you must report the full value of the property in the value column.

Enter the amount of the mortgage under "Description" on this schedule. The unpaid amount of the mortgage may be deducted on Schedule K. If the decedent's estate is NOT liable for the amount of the mortgage, report only the value of the equity of redemption (or value of the property less the indebtedness) in the value column as part of the gross estate. Do not enter any amount less than zero. Do not deduct the amount of indebtedness on Schedule K.

Also list on Schedule A real property the decedent contracted to purchase. Report the full value of the property and not the equity in the value column. Deduct the unpaid part of the purchase price on Schedule K.

Report the value of real estate without reducing it for homestead or other exemption, or the value of dower, curtesy, or a statutory estate created instead of dower or curtesy.

Explain how the reported values were determined and attach copies of any appraisals.

Schedule A Examples

In this example the alternate valuation is not adopted; the date of death is January 1, 1988.

Item number	Description	Alternate valuation date	Alternate value	Value at date of death
1	House and lot, 1921 William Street NW., Washington, D.C. (lot 6, square 481). Rent of $2,700 due at end of each quarter, February 1, May 1, August 1, and November 1. Value based on appraisal, copy of which is attached.			108,000
	Rent due on item 1 for quarter ending November 1, 1987, hut not collected at date of death			2,700
	Rent accrued on item 1 for November and December 1987			1,800
2	House and lot, 304 Jefferson Street, Alexandria, Va. (lot 18, square 40). Rent of $300 payable monthly. Value based on appraisal, copy of which is attached			36,000
	Rent due on item 2 for December 1987, but not collected at date of death			300

In this example alternate valuation is adopted; the date of death is January 1, 1988.

Item number	Description	Alternate valuation date	Alternate value	Value at date of death
1	House and lot, 1921 William Street NW., Washington, D.C. (lot 6, square 481). Rent of $2,700 due at end of each quarter, February 1, May 1, August 1, and November 1. Value based on appraisal, copy of which is attached. Not disposed of within 6 months following death	7/1/88	90,000	108,000
	Rent due on item 1 for quarter ending November 1, 1987, but not collected until February 1, 1988	2/1/88	2,700	2,700
	Rent accrued on item 1 for November and December 1987, collected on February 1, 1988	2/1/88	1,800	1,800
2	House and lot, 304 Jefferson Street, Alexandria, Va. (lot 18, square 40). Rent of $300 payable monthly. Value based on appraisal, copy of which is attached. Property exchanged for farm on May 1, 1988	5/1/88	30,000	36,000
	Rent due on item 2 for December 1987, but not collected until February 1, 1988	2/1/88	300	300

Schedule A—Page 5

APPENDIX 5C *(continued)*

Form 706 (Rev. 11-87)

| Decedent's Social Security Number |

Estate of:

SCHEDULE A-1—Section 2032A Valuation

Part 1.—Type of Election:

☐ **Protective election (regulations section 20.2032A-8(b)).**—Complete Part 2, line 1, and column A of lines 3 and 4. (See instructions.)

☐ **Regular election.**—Complete all of Part 2 (including line 11, if applicable) and Part 3. (See instructions.)

Part 2.—Notice of Election (regulations section 20.2032A-8(a)(3))

Note: *All real property entered on lines 2 and 3 must also be entered on Schedules A, E, F, G, or H, as applicable.*

1 Qualified use—check one ▶ ☐ Farm used for farming *or*
      ▶ ☐ Trade or business other than farming

2 Real property used in a qualified use, passing to qualified heirs, and to be specially valued on this Form 706.

A Schedule and item number from Form 706	B Full value (without section 2032A(b)(3)(B) adjustment)	C Adjusted value (with section 2032A(b)(3)(B) adjustment)	D Value based on qualified use (without section 2032A(b)(3)(B) adjustment)

Totals . . . .

Attach a legal description of all property listed on line 2.

Attach copies of appraisals showing the column B values for all property listed on line 2.

3 Real property used in a qualified use, passing to qualified heirs, but not specially valued on this Form 706.

A Schedule and item number from Form 706	B Full value (without section 2032A(b)(3)(B) adjustment)	C Adjusted value (with section 2032A(b)(3)(B) adjustment)	D Value based on qualified use (without section 2032A(b)(3)(B) adjustment)

Totals . . . .

If you checked "Regular election" you must attach copies of appraisals showing the column B values for all property listed on line 3.

(Continued on next page)

Schedule A-1—Page 6

APPENDIX 5C *(continued)*

Form 706 (Rev. 11-87)

4 Personal property used in a qualified use and passing to qualified heirs.

A Schedule and item number from Form 706	B Adjusted value (with section 2032A(b)(3)(B) adjustment)	A (continued) Schedule and item number from Form 706	B (continued) Adjusted value (with section 2032A(b)(3)(B) adjustment)
		"Subtotal" from Col. B, below left	

Subtotal . . . .   Total Adjusted Value . . . .

5 Enter the value of the total gross estate as adjusted under section 2032A(b)(3)(A). ▶ _____

6 Attach a description of the method used to determine the special value based on qualified use.

7 Did the decedent and/or a member of his or her family own all property listed on line 2 for at least 5 years of the 8 years immediately preceding the date of the decedent's death? . . . . □ Yes □ No

8 Were there any periods during the 8-year period preceding the date of the decedent's death during which the decedent or a member of his or her family:

  a Did not own the property listed on line 2 above? . . . .

  b Did not use the property listed on line 2 above in a qualified use? . . . .

  c Did not materially participate in the operation of the farm or other business within the meaning of section 2032A(e)(6)? . .

	Yes	No

If "Yes" to any of the above, you must attach a statement listing the periods. If applicable, describe whether the exceptions of sections 2032A(b)(4) or (5) are met.

9 Attach affidavits describing the activities constituting material participation and the identity and relationship to the decedent of the material participants.

10 Persons holding interests. Enter the requested information for each party who received any interest in the specially valued property.

	Name	Address
A		
B		
C		
D		
E		
F		
G		
H		

	Identifying number	Relationship to decedent	Fair market value	Special use value
A				
B				
C				
D				
E				
F				
G				
H				

You must attach a computation of the GST tax savings attributable to direct skips for each person listed above who is a skip person. (See Instructions.)

11 Woodlands election.—Check here ▶ □ if you wish to make a woodlands election as described in section 2032A(e)(13). Enter the Schedule and item numbers from Form 706 of the property for which you are making this election ▶ ....

You must attach a statement explaining why you are entitled to make this election. The IRS may issue regulations that require more information to substantiate this election. You will be notified by IRS if you must supply further information.

Schedule A-1—Page 7

APPENDIX 5C *(continued)*

Form 706 (Rev. 11-87)

Part 3.—Agreement to Special Valuation Under Section 2032A

Estate of:	Date of Death	Decedent's Social Security Number

We (list all qualified heirs and other persons having an interest in the property required to sign this agreement)

_____

being all the qualified heirs and _____

being all other parties having interests in the property which is qualified real property and which is valued under section 2032A of the Internal Revenue Code, do hereby approve of the election made by _____ ,
Executor/Administrator of the estate of _____ ,
pursuant to section 2032A to value said property on the basis of the qualified use to which the property is devoted and do hereby enter into this agreement pursuant to section 2032A(d).

The undersigned agree and consent to the application of subsection (c) of section 2032A of the Code with respect to all the property described on line 2 of Part 2 of Schedule A-1 of Form 706, attached to this agreement. More specifically, the undersigned heirs expressly agree and consent to personal liability under subsection (c) of 2032A for the additional estate and GST taxes imposed by that subsection with respect to their respective interests in the above-described property in the event of certain early dispositions of the property or early cessation of the qualified use of the property. It is understood that if a qualified heir disposes of any interest in qualified real property to any member of his or her family, such member may thereafter be treated as the qualified heir with respect to such interest upon filing a Form 706-A and a new agreement.

The undersigned interested parties who are not qualified heirs consent to the collection of any additional estate and GST taxes imposed under section 2032A(c) of the Code from the specially valued property.

If there is a disposition (other than to a member of his or her family) of any interest which passes or has passed to him or her or if there is a cessation of the qualified use of any specially valued property which passes or passed to him or her, each of the undersigned heirs agrees to file a **Form 706-A**, United States Additional Estate (and Generation-Skipping Transfer) Tax Return, and pay any additional estate and GST taxes due within 6 months of the disposition or cessation.

It is understood by all interested parties that this agreement is a condition precedent to the election of special use valuation under section 2032A of the Code and must be executed by every interested party even though that person may not have received the estate (or GST) tax benefits or be in possession of such property.

Each of the undersigned understands that by making this election, a lien will be created and recorded pursuant to section 6324B of the Code on the property referred to in this agreement for the adjusted tax differences with respect to the estate as defined in section 2032A(c)(2)(C).

As the interested parties, the undersigned designate the following individual as their agent for all dealings with the Internal Revenue Service concerning the continued qualification of the specially valued property under section 2032A of the Code and on all issues regarding the special lien under section 6324B. The agent is authorized to act for the parties with respect to all dealings with the Service on matters affecting the qualified real property described earlier. This authority includes the following:

- To receive confidential information on all matters relating to continued qualification under section 2032A of the specially valued real property and on all matters relating to the special lien arising under section 6324B.
- To furnish the Service with any requested information concerning the property.
- To notify the Service of any disposition or cessation of qualified use of any part of the property.
- To receive, but not to endorse and collect, checks in payment of any refund of Internal Revenue taxes, penalties, or interest.
- To execute waivers (including offers of waivers) of restrictions on assessment or collection of deficiencies in tax and waivers of notice of disallowance of a claim for credit or refund.
- To execute closing agreements under section 7121.
- Other acts (specify) ▶ _____

By signing this agreement, the agent agrees to provide the Service with any requested information concerning this property and to notify the Service of any disposition or cessation of the qualified use of any part of this property.

Name of Agent	Signature	Address

The property to which this agreement relates is listed in Form 706, United States Estate (and Generation-Skipping Transfer) Tax Return, and in the Notice of Election, along with its fair market value according to section 2031 of the Code and its special use value according to section 2032A. The name, address, social security number, and interest (including the value) of each of the undersigned in this property are as set forth in the attached Notice of Election.

IN WITNESS WHEREOF, the undersigned have hereunto set their hands at _____ ,
this_____ day of _____ .
Qualified Heirs _____

Other Interested Parties _____

Schedule A-1—Page 8

APPENDIX 5C *(continued)*

Form 706 (Rev. 11-87)

Instructions for Schedule A-1.—Section 2032A Valuation

The election to value certain farm and closely held business property at its special use value is made by checking "Yes" to line 2 of Elections by the Executor. Schedule A-1 is used to report the additional information that must be submitted to support this election. In order to make a valid election, you must complete Schedule A-1 and attach all of the required statements and appraisals.

For definitions and additional information concerning special use valuation, see section 2032A and the related regulations.

Part 1.—Type of Election

Estate and GST Tax Elections.—If you make an estate tax special use value election, you must also make a GST tax special use value election. You may not make a GST tax special use value election unless you also make an estate tax special use value election.

You must value each specific property interest at the same value for GST tax purposes that you value it at for estate tax purposes.

Protective Election.—To make the protective election described in the separate instructions for line 2 of Elections by the Executor, you must check this box, enter the decedent's name and social security number in the spaces provided at the top of Schedule A-1, and complete line 1 and column A of lines 3 and 4 of Part 2. You need not complete columns B–D of lines 3 and 4. You need not complete any other line entries on Schedule A-1. Completing Schedule A-1 as described above constitutes a Notice of Protective Election as described in Regulations section 20.2032A-8(b).

Part 2.—Notice of Election

Line 10.—Because the special use valuation election creates a potential tax liability for the recapture tax of section 2032A(c), you must list each person who receives an interest in the specially valued property on Schedule A-1. If there are more than 8 persons who receive interests, use an additional sheet that follows the format of line 10. In the columns "Fair market value" and "Special use value," you should enter the total respective values of all the specially valued property interests received by each person.

GST Tax Savings.—In order to compute the additional GST tax due upon disposition (or cessation of qualified use) of the property, each "skip person" (as defined in the instructions for Schedule R) who receives an interest in the specially valued property must know the total GST tax savings with respect to all of the interests in specially valued property received. This GST tax savings is the difference between the total GST tax that was imposed with respect to all of the interests in specially valued property received by the skip person valued at their special use value and the total GST tax that would have been imposed on the same interests received by the skip person had they been valued at their fair market value.

Because the GST tax depends on the executor's allocation of the GST exemption and the grandchild exclusion, the skip person who receives the interests is unable to compute this GST tax savings.

For each skip person who receives an interest in specially valued property, you must attach worksheets showing the total GST tax savings attributable to all of that person's interests in specially valued property.

How To Compute the GST Tax Savings.—Before computing each skip person's GST tax savings, you must complete Schedules R and R-1 for the entire estate (using the special use values).

For each skip person, you must complete two Schedules R (Parts 2 and 3 only) as worksheets, one showing the interests in specially valued property received by the skip person at their special use value and one showing the same interests at their fair market value.

If the skip person received interests in specially valued property that were shown on Schedule R-1, show these interests on the Schedule R, Parts 2 and 3 worksheets, as appropriate. Do not use Schedule R-1 as a worksheet.

Completing the Special Use Value Worksheets.—On lines 2–6 and 8, enter "-0-".

Completing the Fair Market Value Worksheets.—*Lines 2 and 3, fixed taxes and other charges.*—If valuing the interests at their fair market value (instead of special use value) causes any of these taxes and charges to increase, enter the increased amount (only) on these lines and attach an explanation of the increase. Otherwise, enter "-0-".

Line 6—Grandchild exclusion.—If part of the skip person's grandchild exclusion available for Form 706 (shown on Schedule R, Part 1A, column D) was not claimed on the Schedules R and R-1 that you are actually filing with this Form 706, you must enter the unused grandchild exclusion on line 6 and attach a computation of the total grandchild exclusion claimed on the Form 706 to support your entry. If you do not claim the entire available exclusion, it will be allocated by the IRS, upon disposition or cessation, to the property interests in the order you listed them.

If interests are shown on both Parts 2 and 3 worksheets, you should divide the previously unclaimed grandchild exclusion between the Parts as required to offset the transfers.

If all of the skip person's grandchild exclusion available for Form 706 was already claimed on the Schedules R and R-1 that you are filing with this Form 706, enter "-0-" on line 6 of Parts 2 and 3.

Line 8—GST exemption.—If you completed line 10 of Schedule R, Part 1B, enter on line 8 the amount shown for the skip person on the *line 10 special use allocation schedule* you attached to Schedule R. If you did not complete line 10 of Schedule R, Part 1B, enter "-0-" on line 8.

Total GST Tax Savings.—For each skip person, subtract the special use value worksheet, Part 2, line 12 tax amount from the fair market value worksheet, Part 2, line 12 tax amount. This difference is the skip person's total GST tax savings.

Part 3.—Agreement to Special Valuation Under Section 2032A

The agreement to special valuation by persons with an interest in property is required under section 2032A(a)(1)(B) and (d)(2) and must be executed by all parties who have any interest in the property being valued based on its qualified use as of the date of the decedent's death.

An interest in property is an interest that, as of the date of the decedent's death, can be asserted under applicable local law so as to affect the disposition of the specially valued property by the estate. Any person in being at the death of the decedent who has any such interest in the property, whether present or future, or vested or contingent, must enter into the agreement. Included are owners of remainder and executory interests; the holders of general or special powers of appointment; beneficiaries of a gift over in default of exercise of any such power; joint tenants and holders of similar undivided interests when the decedent held only a joint or undivided interest in the property or when only an undivided interest is specially valued; and trustees of trusts and representatives of other entities holding title to, or holding any interests in, the property. An heir who has the power under local law to caveat (challenge) a will and thereby affect disposition of the property is not, however, considered to be a person with an interest in property under section 2032A solely by reason of that right. Likewise, creditors of an estate are not such persons solely by reason of their status as creditors.

If any person required to enter into the agreement either desires that an agent act for him or her or cannot legally bind himself or herself due to infancy or other incompetency, or due to death before the election under section 2032A is timely exercised, a representative authorized by local law to bind the person in an agreement of this nature is permitted to sign the agreement on his or her behalf.

The Internal Revenue Service will contact the agent designated in the agreement on all matters relating to continued qualification under section 2032A of the specially valued real property and on all matters relating to the special lien arising under section 6324B. It is the duty of the agent as attorney-in-fact for the parties with interests in the specially valued property to furnish the IRS with any requested information and to notify the IRS of any disposition or cessation of qualified use of any part of the property.

Schedule A-1—Page 9

APPENDIX 5C *(continued)*

Form 706 (Rev. 11-87)

Estate of:

SCHEDULE B—Stocks and Bonds
(For jointly owned property that must be disclosed on Schedule E, see the Instructions for Schedule E.)

Item number	Description including face amount of bonds or number of shares and par value where needed for identification. Give CUSIP number if available.	Unit value	Alternate valuation date	Alternate value	Value at date of death
1					
	Total from continuation schedules(s) (or additional sheet(s)) attached to this schedule . . .				
	TOTAL. (Also enter on Part 5, Recapitulation, page 3, at item 2.)				

(If more space is needed, attach the continuation schedule from the end of this package or additional sheets of the same size.)
(The instructions to Schedule B are in the separate instructions.)

Schedule B—Page 10

APPENDIX 5C *(continued)*

Form 706 (Rev. 11-87)

Estate of:

SCHEDULE C—Mortgages, Notes, and Cash

(For jointly owned property that must be disclosed on Schedule E, see the Instructions for Schedule E.)

Item number	Description	Alternate valuation date	Alternate value	Value at date of death
1				

Total from continuation schedules(s) (or additional sheet(s)) attached to this schedule . . .

TOTAL. (Also enter on Part 5, Recapitulation, page 3, at item 3.) . . . .

(If more space is needed, attach the continuation schedule from the end of this package or additional sheets of the same size.)

197-904 O - 87 - 2

Schedule C—Page 11

APPENDIX 5C *(continued)*

Form 706 (Rev 11-87)

Instructions for Schedule C.— Mortgages, Notes, and Cash

If the total gross estate contains any mortgages, notes, or cash, you must complete Schedule C and file it with the return.

On Schedule C list mortgages and notes *payable to* the decedent at the time of death. (Mortgages and notes *payable by* the decedent should be listed (if deductible) on Schedule K.) Also list on Schedule C cash the decedent had at the date of death.

Group the items in the following categories and list the categories in the following order:

1. Mortgages.—List: (1) the face value and unpaid balance; (2) date of mortgage; (3) date of maturity; (4) name of maker; (5) property mortgaged; and (6) interest dates and rate of interest. For example: bond and mortgage of $10,000, unpaid balance $4,000; dated January 1, 1979; John Doe to Richard Roe; premises 22 Clinton Street, Newark, N.J.; due January 1, 1989, interest payable at 6% a year January 1 and July 1.

2. Promissory notes.—Describe in the same way as mortgages.

3. Contract by the decedent to sell land.—List: (1) the name of the purchaser; (2) date of contract; (3) description of property; (4) sale price; (5) initial payment; (6) amounts of installment payment; (7) unpaid balance of principal; and (8) interest rate.

4. Cash in possession.—List separately from bank deposits.

5. Cash in banks, savings and loan associations, and other types of financial organizations.—List: (1) the name and address of each financial organization; (2) amount in each account; (3) serial number; and (4) nature of account, indicating whether checking, savings, time deposit, etc. If you obtain statements from the financial organizations, keep them for Internal Revenue Service inspection.

APPENDIX 5C *(continued)*

Form 706 (Rev. 11-87)

Estate of:

SCHEDULE D—Insurance on the Decedent's Life
You must attach a Form 712 for each policy.

Item number	Description	Alternate valuation date	Alternate value	Value at date of death
1				

Total from continuation schedules(s) (or additional sheet(s)) attached to this schedule . . . .

TOTAL. (Also enter on Part 5, Recapitulation, page 3, at item 4.) . . . .

(If more space is needed, attach the continuation schedule from the end of this package or additional sheets of the same size.)

Schedule D—Page 13

APPENDIX 5C *(continued)*

Form 706 (Rev 11-87)

Instructions for Schedule D.— Insurance on the Decedent's Life

If there was any insurance on the decedent's life, whether or not included in the gross estate, you must complete Schedule D and file it with the return.

Insurance you must include on Schedule D.—Under section 2042 you must include in the gross estate:

- Insurance on the decedent's life receivable by or for the benefit of the estate; and
- Insurance on the decedent's life receivable by beneficiaries other than the estate, as described below.

The term "insurance" refers to life insurance of every description, including death benefits paid by fraternal beneficiary societies operating under the lodge system, and death benefits paid under no fault automobile insurance policies if the no fault insurer was unconditionally bound to pay the benefit in the event of the insured's death.

Insurance in favor of the estate.—Include on Schedule D the full amount of the proceeds of insurance on the life of the decedent receivable by the executor or otherwise payable to or for the benefit of the estate. Insurance in favor of the estate includes insurance used to pay the estate tax, and any other taxes, debts, or charges which are enforceable against the estate. The manner in which the policy is drawn is immaterial as long as there is an obligation, legally binding on the beneficiary, to use the proceeds to pay taxes, debts, or charges. You must include the full amount even though the premiums or other consideration may have been paid by a person other than the decedent.

Insurance receivable by beneficiaries other than the estate.—Include on Schedule D the proceeds of all insurance on the life of the decedent not receivable by or for the benefit of the decedent's estate if the decedent possessed at death any of the incidents of ownership, exercisable either alone or in conjunction with any person.

Incidents of ownership in a policy include:

- The right of the insured or estate to its economic benefits;
- The power to change the beneficiary;
- The power to surrender or cancel the policy;
- The power to assign the policy or to revoke an assignment;
- The power to pledge the policy for a loan;
- The power to obtain from the insurer a loan against the surrender value of the policy;
- A reversionary interest if the value of the reversionary interest was more than 5% of the value of the policy immediately before the decedent died. (An interest in an insurance policy is considered a reversionary interest if, for example, the proceeds become payable to the insured's estate or payable as the insured directs if the beneficiary dies before the insured.)

Life insurance not includible in the gross estate under section 2042 may be includible under some other section of the Code. For example, a life insurance policy could be transferred by the decedent in such a way that it would be includible in the gross estate under sections 2036, 2037, or 2038. (See the instructions to Schedule G for a description of these sections.)

Completing the Schedule

You must list **every policy** of insurance on the life of the decedent, whether or not it is included in the gross estate.

Under "Description" list:

- Name of the insurance company
- Number of the policy

For every policy of life insurance listed on the schedule, you must request a statement on **Form 712,** Life Insurance Statement, from the company which issued the policy. Attach the Form 712 to the back of Schedule D.

If the policy proceeds are paid in one sum, enter the net proceeds received (from Form 712, line 24) in the value (and alternate value) columns of Schedule D. If the policy proceeds are not paid in one sum, enter the value of the proceeds as of the date of the decedent's death (from Form 712, line 25).

If part or all of the policy proceeds are not included in the gross estate, you must explain why they were not included.

APPENDIX 5C *(continued)*

Form 706 (Rev. 11-87)

Estate of:

SCHEDULE E—Jointly Owned Property
(If you elect section 2032A valuation, you must complete Schedule E and Schedule A-1.)

PART 1.— Qualified Joint Interests—Interests Held by the Decedent and His or Her Spouse as the Only Joint Tenants (Section 2040(b)(2))

Item number	Description For securities, give CUSIP number, if available.	Alternate valuation date	Alternate value	Value at date of death
	Total from continuation schedule(s) (or additional sheet(s)) attached to this schedule.			
1a	Totals. **1a**			
1b	Amounts included in gross estate (one-half of line 1a) **1b**			

PART 2.—All Other Joint Interests

2a   State the name and address of each surviving co-tenant. If there are more than three surviving co-tenants, list the additional co-tenants on an attached sheet.

Name	Address (number and street, city, state, and ZIP code)
A.	
B.	
C.	

Item number	Enter letter for co-tenant	Description (including alternate valuation date if any) For securities, give CUSIP number, if available.	Percentage includible	Includible alternate value	Includible value at date of death
		Total from continuation schedule(s) (or additional sheet(s)) attached to this schedule			
2b		Total other joint interests **2b**			

Total includible joint interests (add lines 1b and 2b). Also enter on Part 5, Recapitulation, page 3, at item 5

(If more space is needed, attach the continuation schedule from the end of this package or additional sheets of the same size.)

Schedule E—Page 15

APPENDIX 5C *(continued)*

Form 706 (Rev. 11-87)

Instructions for Schedule E.— Jointly Owned Property

You must complete Schedule E and file it with the return if the decedent owned any joint property at the time of death, whether or not the decedent's interest is includible in the gross estate.

All property of whatever kind or character, whether real estate, personal property, or bank accounts, in which the decedent held at the time of death an interest either as a joint tenant with right to survivorship or as a tenant by the entirety must be entered on this schedule.

Property that the decedent held as a tenant in common should not be listed on this schedule, but the value of the interest should be reported on Schedule A if real estate, or if personal property on the appropriate schedule. Similarly, community property held by the decedent and spouse should be reported on the appropriate Schedules A through I. The decedent's interest in a partnership should not be included on this schedule, but should be reported on Schedule F, "Other Miscellaneous Property."

Part 1.—Qualified joint interests held by decedent and spouse. —Under section 2040(b)(2), a joint interest is a qualified joint interest if the decedent and the surviving spouse held the interest as:

- Tenants by the entirety; or
- Joint tenants with right of survivorship if the decedent and the decedent's spouse are the *only* joint tenants.

Interests which meet either of the two requirements above should be entered in Part 1. Joint interests that do not meet either of the two requirements above should be entered in Part 2.

Under "Description," describe the property as required in the instructions for Schedules A, B, C, and F for the type of property involved. For example, jointly held stocks and bonds should be described using the rules given in the instructions to Schedule B.

Under "Alternate value" and "Value at date of death," enter the *full value* of the property.

Part 2.—Other joint interests.—All joint interests that were not entered in Part 1 must be entered in Part 2.

For each item of property, enter the appropriate letter A, B, C, etc., from line 2a to indicate the name and address of the surviving co-tenant.

Under "Description," describe the property as required in the instructions for Schedules A, B, C, and F for the type of property involved.

In the "Percentage includible" column, enter the percentage of the total value of the property that you intend to include in the gross estate.

Generally, you must include the full value of the jointly owned property in the gross estate. However, the full value should not be included if you can show that a part of the property originally belonged to the other tenant or tenants and was never received or acquired by the other tenant or tenants from the decedent for less than an adequate and full consideration in money or money's worth, or unless you can show that any part of the property was acquired with consideration originally belonging to the surviving joint tenant or tenants. In this case, you may exclude from the value of the property an amount proportionate to the consideration furnished by the other tenant or tenants. Relinquishing or promising to relinquish dower, curtesy, or statutory estate created instead of dower or curtesy, or other marital rights in the decedent's property or estate is not consideration in money or money's worth. See the Schedule A instructions for the value to show for real property that is subject to a mortgage.

If the property was acquired by the decedent and another person or persons by gift, bequest, devise, or inheritance as joint tenants and their interests are not otherwise specified by law, include only that part of the value of the property that is figured by dividing the full value of the property by the number of joint tenants.

If you believe that less than the full value of the entire property is includible in the gross estate for tax purposes, you must establish the right to include the smaller value by attaching proof of the extent, origin, and nature of the decedent's interest and the interest(s) of the decedent's co-tenant or co-tenants.

In the "Includible alternate value" and "Includible value at date of death" columns, you should enter only the values that you believe are includible in the gross estate.

APPENDIX 5C *(continued)*

Form 706 (Rev. 11-87)

Estate of:

SCHEDULE F—Other Miscellaneous Property Not Reportable Under Any Other Schedule
(For jointly owned property that must be disclosed on Schedule E, see the Instructions for Schedule E.)
(If you elect section 2032A valuation, you must complete Schedule F and Schedule A-1.)

		Yes	No
1	Did the decedent at the time of death own any articles of artistic or collectible value in excess of $3,000 or any collections whose artistic or collectible value combined at date of death exceeded $10,000?		
	If "Yes," full details must be submitted on this schedule.		
2	Has the decedent's estate, spouse, or any other person, received (or will receive) any bonus or award as a result of the decedent's employment or death?		
	If "Yes," full details must be submitted on this schedule.		
3	Did the decedent at the time of death have, or have access to, a safe deposit box?		
	If "Yes," state location, and if held in joint names of decedent and another, state name and relationship of joint depositor.		

If any of the contents of the safe deposit box are omitted from the schedules in this return, explain fully why omitted.

Item number	Description For securities, give CUSIP number, if available.	Alternate valuation date	Alternate value	Value at date of death
1				
	Total from continuation schedule(s) (or additional sheet(s)) attached to this schedule . . .			
	TOTAL. (Also enter on Part 5, Recapitulation, page 3, at item 6.)			

(If more space is needed, attach the continuation schedule from the end of this package or additional sheets of the same size.)

Schedule F—Page 17

APPENDIX 5C *(continued)*

Form 706 (Rev. 11-87)

Instructions for Schedule F.— Other Miscellaneous Property

You must complete Schedule F and file it with the return.

On Schedule F list all items that must be included in the gross estate that are not reported on any other schedule, including:

- Debts due the decedent (other than notes and mortgages included on Schedule C)
- Interests in business
- Insurance on the life of another (obtain and attach **Form 712**, Life Insurance Statement, for each policy)
  Note for single premium or paid-up policies: *In certain situations, for example where the surrender value of the policy exceeds its replacement cost, the true economic value of the policy will be greater than the amount shown on line 56 of Form 712. In these situations you should report the full economic value of the policy on Schedule F. See Rev. Rul. 78-137, 1978-1 C.B. 280 for details.*
- Section 2044 property
- Claims (including the value of the decedent's interest in a claim for refund of income taxes or the amount of the refund actually received)
- Rights
- Royalties
- Leaseholds
- Judgments
- Reversionary or remainder interests

- Shares in trust funds (attach a copy of the trust instrument)
- Household goods and personal effects, including wearing apparel
- Farm products and growing crops
- Livestock
- Farm machinery
- Automobiles

If the decedent owned any interest in a partnership or unincorporated business, attach a statement of assets and liabilities for the valuation date and for the 5 years before the valuation date. Also attach statements of the net earnings for the same 5 years. You must account for goodwill in the valuation. In general, furnish the same information and follow the methods used to value close corporations. See the instructions for Schedule B.

If real estate is owned by the sole proprietorship, it should be reported on Schedule F and not on Schedule A. Describe the real estate with the same detail required for Schedule A.

Line 1.—If the decedent owned at the date of death articles with artistic or intrinsic value (for example, jewelry, furs, silverware, books, statuary, vases, oriental rugs, coin or stamp collections), check the "Yes" box on line 1 and provide full details. If any one article is valued at more than $3,000, or any collection of similar articles is valued at more than $10,000, attach an appraisal by an expert under oath and the required statement regarding the appraiser's qualifications (see Regulations section 20.2031-6(b)).

APPENDIX 5C *(continued)*

Form 706 (Rev. 11-87)

Estate of:

SCHEDULE G—Transfers During Decedent's Life

(If you elect section 2032A valuation, you must complete Schedule G and Schedule A-1.)

Item number	Description For securities, give CUSIP number, if available.	Alternate valuation date	Alternate value	Value at date of death
A.	Gift tax paid by the decedent or the estate for all gifts made by the decedent or his or her spouse within 3 years before the decedent's death (section 2035(c))	X X X X X		
B.	Transfers includible under sections 2035(a), 2036, 2037, or 2038:			
1				

Total from continuation schedule(s) (or additional sheet(s)) attached to this schedule . . . . .

TOTAL. (Also enter on Part 5, Recapitulation, page 3, at item 7.) . . . .

SCHEDULE H—Powers of Appointment

(If you elect section 2032A valuation, you must complete Schedule H and Schedule A-1.)

Item number	Description	Alternate valuation date	Alternate value	Value at date of death
1				

Total from continuation schedule(s) (or additional sheet(s)) attached to this schedule . . .

TOTAL. (Also enter on Part 5, Recapitulation, page 3, at item 8.) . . . .

(If more space is needed, attach the continuation schedule from the end of this package or additional sheets of the same size.)
(The instructions to Schedule H are in the separate instructions.)   **Schedules G and H—Page 19**

APPENDIX 5C *(continued)*

Instructions for Schedule G.— Transfers During Decedent's Life

You must complete Schedule G and file it with the return if the decedent made any of the transfers described below in (1) through (5) or if you answered "Yes" on lines 11 or 12a of Part 4, General Information.

Five types of transfers should be reported on this schedule:

(1) Certain gift taxes.—Section 2035(c). Enter at item A of the Schedule the total value of the gift taxes that were paid by the decedent or the estate on gifts made by the decedent or the decedent's spouse within 3 years before death.

The date of the gift, not the date of payment of the gift tax, determines whether a gift tax paid is included in the gross estate under this rule. Therefore, you should carefully examine the **Forms 709,** United States Gift (and Generation-Skipping Transfer) Tax Return, filed by the decedent and the decedent's spouse to determine what part of the total gift taxes reported on them was attributable to gifts made within 3 years before death. For example, if the decedent died on July 10, 1988, you should examine gift tax returns for 1988, 1987, 1986, and 1985. However, the gift taxes on the 1985 return(s) that are attributable to gifts made before July 10, 1985, are not included in the gross estate.

Attach an explanation of how you computed the includible gift taxes if you do not include in the gross estate the entire gift taxes shown on any Form 709 filed within 3 years of death. Also attach copies of any pertinent gift tax returns filed by the decedent's spouse within 3 years of death.

(2) Other transfers within 3 years before death.—Section 2035(a). These transfers include *only* the following:

- Any transfer by the decedent of a life insurance policy within 3 years before death.
- Any transfer within 3 years before death of a retained section 2036 life estate, section 2037 reversionary interest or section 2038 power to revoke, etc., if the property subject to the life estate, interest, or power would have been included in the gross estate had the decedent continued to possess the life estate, interest, or power until death.

These transfers are reported on Schedule G regardless of whether a gift tax return was required to be filed for them when they were made. However, the amount includible and the information required to be shown for the transfers are determined:

- For insurance on the life of the decedent using the instructions to Schedule D. (Attach Form(s) 712.)
- For insurance on the life of another using the instructions to Schedule F. (Attach Form(s) 712.)
- For sections 2036, 2037, and 2038 transfers, using paragraphs (3), (4), and (5) of these instructions.

(3) Transfers with retained life estate (section 2036).—These are transfers in which the decedent retained the income from the transferred property or the right to designate the person or persons who will possess or enjoy the transferred property, or the income from the transferred property if the transfer was made:

(a) between March 4, 1931, and June 6, 1932, inclusive, and the decedent alone retained the right to so designate for life, or for any period which did not in fact end before the decedent's death; or

(b) after June 6, 1932, and the decedent retained the right to so designate, either alone or with any person, for life, for any period that must be ascertained by reference to the decedent's death, or for any period which did not in fact end before the decedent's death.

Transfers with a retained life estate also include transfers of stock in a "controlled corporation" after June 22, 1976, if the decedent retained or acquired voting rights in the stock. If the decedent retained direct or indirect voting rights in a controlled corporation, the decedent is considered to have retained enjoyment of the transferred property. A corporation is a "controlled corporation" if the decedent owned (actually or constructively) or had the right (either alone or with any other person) to vote at least 20% of the total combined voting power of all classes of stock. See section 2036(b). If these voting rights ceased or were relinquished within 3 years before the decedent's death, the corporate interests are included in the gross estate as if the decedent had actually retained the voting rights until death.

(4) Transfers taking effect at death (section 2037).—These are transfers made on or after September 8, 1916, that took effect at the decedent's death. A transfer that takes effect at the decedent's death is one under which possession or enjoyment can be obtained only by surviving the decedent. A transfer is not treated as one that takes effect at the decedent's death unless the decedent retained a reversionary interest in the property which immediately before the decedent's death had a value of more than 5% of the value of the transferred property. If the transfer was made before October 8, 1949, the reversionary interest must have arisen by the express terms of the instrument of transfer.

(5) Revocable Transfers (section 2038).—These are transfers in which the enjoyment of the transferred property was subject at decedent's death to any change through the exercise of a power to alter, amend, revoke, or terminate, as follows:

- If the transfer was made before 4:01 p.m., eastern standard time, June 2, 1924, and the power was reserved at the time of the transfer and was exercisable by the decedent alone or with a person who had no substantial adverse interest in the transferred property.
- If the transfer was made on or after 4:01 p.m., eastern standard time, June 2, 1924, and before June 23, 1936, and the power was reserved at the time of the transfer and was exercisable by the decedent alone or with any person (regardless of whether that person had a substantial adverse interest in the transferred property), or
- If the transfer was made after June 22, 1936, regardless of whether the power was reserved at the time of the transfer or later created or conferred, regardless of the source from which the power was acquired, regardless of whether the power was exercisable by the decedent alone or with any person, and regardless of whether that person had a substantial adverse interest in the transferred property.
- If the decedent relinquished within 3 years before death any of the includible powers described above, you should determine the gross estate as if the decedent had actually retained the power(s) until death.

For more detailed information on which transfers are includible in the gross estate, see the Estate Tax Regulations.

How To Complete Schedule G

All transfers (other than outright transfers not in trust and bona fide sales) made by the decedent at any time during life must be reported with the Schedule regardless of whether you believe the transfers are subject to tax. If the decedent made any transfers not described in the instructions above, the transfers should not be shown on Schedule G. Instead, attach a statement describing these transfers: list the date of the transfer, the amount or value, and the type of transfer.

Complete the schedule for each transfer that is included in the gross estate under sections 2035(a), 2036, 2037, and 2038 as described above.

In the "Item number" column, number each transfer consecutively beginning with 1.

In the "Description" column, list the name of the transferee, and the date of the transfer and give a complete description of the property. Transfers included in the gross estate should be valued on the date of the decedent's death or, if the alternate valuation is adopted, according to section 2032.

If only part of the property transferred meets the terms of sections 2035(a), 2036, 2037, or 2038, then only a corresponding part of the value of the property should be included in the value of the gross estate. If the transferee makes additions or improvements to the property, the increased value of the property at the valuation date should not be included on Schedule G. However, if only a part of the value of the property is included, enter the value of the whole under the column headed "Description" and explain what part was included.

Attachments.—If a transfer, by trust or otherwise, was made by a written instrument, attach a copy of the instrument to the Schedule. If of public record, the copy should be certified; if not of record, the copy should be verified.

Schedule G—Page 20

APPENDIX 5C *(continued)*

Form 706 (Rev. 11-87)

Estate of:

SCHEDULE I—Annuities

Note: *The total combined exclusion for lump sum distributions and "Annuities Under Approved Plans" is $100,000 for the estates of certain decedents dying after December 31, 1982. No exclusion is generally allowed for the estates of decedents dying after December 31, 1984 (see instructions).*

A Are you excluding from the decedent's gross estate the value of a lump-sum distribution described in section 2039(f)(2)?
If "Yes," you must attach the information required by the instructions.

Item number	Description Show the entire value of the annuity before any exclusions.	Alternate valuation date	Includible alternate value	Includible value at date of death
1				
	Total from continuation schedule(s) (or additional sheet(s)) attached to this schedule . . .			
	TOTAL. (Also enter on Part 5, Recapitulation, page 3, at item 9.)			

(If more space is needed, attach the continuation schedule from the end of this package or additional sheets of the same size.)
(The instructions to Schedule I are in the separate instructions.) **Schedule I—Page 21**

APPENDIX 5C *(continued)*

Form 706 (Rev. 11-87)

Estate of:

SCHEDULE J—Funeral Expenses and Expenses Incurred in Administering Property Subject to Claims

Note: *Do not list on this schedule expenses of administering property not subject to claims. For those expenses, see the Instructions for Schedule L.*

If executors' commissions, attorney fees, etc., are claimed and allowed as a deduction for estate tax purposes, they are not allowable as a deduction in computing the taxable income of the estate for Federal income tax purposes. They are allowable as an income tax deduction on Form 1041 if a waiver is filed to waive the deduction on Form 706 (see the Form 1041 instructions).

Item number	Description	Expense amount	Total Amount
	A. Funeral expenses:		
1			
	Total funeral expenses		. . . .
	B. Administration expenses:		
1	Executors' commissions—amount estimated/agreed upon/paid. (Strike out the words that do not apply.)		. . . .
2	Attorney fees—amount estimated/agreed upon/paid. (Strike out the words that do not apply.)		. . . .
3	Accountant fees—amount estimated/agreed upon/paid. (Strike out the words that do not apply.)		. . . .
4	Miscellaneous expenses:	Expense amount	
	Total miscellaneous expenses from continuation schedule(s) (or additional sheet(s)) attached to this schedule		
	Total miscellaneous expenses		

TOTAL. (Also enter on Part 5, Recapitulation, page 3, at item 11.) . . . .

(If more space is needed, attach the continuation schedule from the end of this package or additional sheets of the same size.) **Schedule J—Page 22**

APPENDIX 5C *(continued)*

Form 706 (Rev. 11-87)

Instructions for Schedule J.—
Funeral Expenses and Expenses Incurred in Administering Property Subject to Claims

General.— You must complete and file Schedule J if you claim a deduction on item 11 of the Recapitulation.

On Schedule J itemize funeral expenses and expenses incurred in administering property subject to claims. List the names and addresses of persons to whom the expenses are payable and describe the nature of the expense. **Do not list expenses incurred in administering property not subject to claims on this schedule. List them on Schedule L instead.**

Funeral Expenses.—Itemize funeral expenses on line A. Deduct from the expenses any amounts that were reimbursed, such as death benefits payable by the Social Security Administration and the Veterans' Administration.

Executors' Commissions.—When you file the return, you may deduct commissions which have actually been paid to you or which you expect will be paid. You may not deduct commissions if none will be collected. If the amount of the commissions has not been fixed by decree of the proper court, the deduction will be allowed on the final examination of the return, provided that:

- The District Director is reasonably satisfied that the commissions claimed will be paid;
- The amount entered as a deduction is within the amount allowable by the laws of the jurisdiction where the estate is being administered;
- It is in accordance with the usually accepted practice in that jurisdiction for estates of similar size and character.

If you have not been paid the commissions claimed at the time of the final examination of the return, you must support the amount you deducted with an affidavit or statement signed under the penalties of perjury that the amount has been agreed upon and will be paid.

You may not deduct a bequest or devise made to you instead of commissions. If, however, the decedent fixed by will the compensation payable to you for services to be rendered in the administration of the estate, you may deduct this amount to the extent it is not more than the compensation allowable by the local law or practice.

Do not deduct on this schedule amounts paid as trustees' commissions whether received by you acting in the capacity of a trustee or by a separate trustee. If such amounts were paid in administering property not subject to claims, deduct them on Schedule L.

Note: *Executors' commissions are taxable income to the executors. Therefore, be sure to include them as income on your individual income tax return.*

Attorney Fees.—Enter the amount of attorney fees that have actually been paid or which you reasonably expect to be paid. If on the final examination of the return the fees claimed have not been awarded by the proper court and paid, the deduction will be allowed provided the District Director is reasonably satisfied that the amount claimed will be paid and that it does not exceed a reasonable payment for the services performed, taking into account the size and character of the estate and the local law and practice. If the fees claimed have not been paid at the time of final examination of the return, the amount deducted must be supported by an affidavit, or statement signed under the penalties of perjury, by the executor or the attorney stating that the amount has been agreed upon and will be paid.

Do not deduct attorney fees incidental to litigation incurred by the beneficiaries. These expenses are charged against the beneficiaries personally and are not administration expenses authorized by the Code.

Schedule J—Page 23

APPENDIX 5C *(continued)*

Form 706 (Rev. 11-87)

Estate of:

SCHEDULE K—Debts of the Decedent, and Mortgages and Liens

Item number	Debts of the Decedent—Creditor and nature of claim, and allowable death taxes	Amount unpaid to date	Amount in contest	Amount claimed as a deduction
1				

Total from continuation schedule(s) (or additional sheet(s)) attached to this schedule . . . .

TOTAL. (Also enter on Part 5, Recapitulation, page 3, at item 12.) . . . .

Item number	Mortgages and Liens—Description	Amount
1		

Total from continuation schedule(s) (or additional sheet(s)) attached to this schedule . . . .

TOTAL. (Also enter on Part 5, Recapitulation, page 3, at item 13.) . . . .

(If more space is needed, attach the continuation schedule from the end of this package or additional sheets of the same size.)
(The instructions to Schedule K are in the separate instructions.)

Schedule K —Page 24

APPENDIX 5C *(continued)*

Form 706 (Rev. 11-87)

Estate of:

SCHEDULE L—Net Losses During Administration and Expenses Incurred in Administering Property Not Subject to Claims

Item number	Net losses during administration (**Note:** *Do not deduct losses claimed on a Federal income tax return.*)	Amount
1		

Total from continuation schedule(s) (or additional sheet(s)) attached to this schedule . . . .

TOTAL. (Also enter on Part 5, Recapitulation, page 3, at item 16.) . . . .

Item number	Expenses incurred in administering property not subject to claims (Indicate whether estimated, agreed upon, or paid.)	Amount
1		

Total from continuation schedule(s) (or additional sheet(s)) attached to this schedule . . . .

TOTAL. (Also enter on Part 5, Recapitulation, page 3, at item 17.) . . . .

(If more space is needed, attach the continuation schedule from the end of this package or additional sheets of the same size.)

(The instructions to Schedule L are in the separate instructions.)

Schedule L —Page 25

APPENDIX 5C *(continued)*

Form 706 (Rev. 11-87)

Estate of:

SCHEDULE M—Bequests, etc., to Surviving Spouse

		Yes	No
1	Did any property pass to the surviving spouse as a result of a qualified disclaimer?		

If "Yes," attach a copy of the written disclaimer required by section 2518(b).

2 **Terminable Interest (QTIP) Marital Deduction.**—Check here ▶ ☐ if you elect to claim a marital deduction for qualified terminable interest property (QTIP) under section 2056(b)(7). **You must complete Part 2 of Schedule M.**

Part 1.—Property Interests Which Are Not Subject to a QTIP Election

Item number	Description of property interests passing to surviving spouse	Value
1		
	Total from continuation schedule(s) (or additional sheet(s)) attached to this schedule	
	Total value of property interests not subject to a QTIP election (enter here and on line 1 of Part 3)	

(If more space is needed, attach the continuation schedule from the end of this package or additional sheets of the same size.)
(The instructions to Schedule M are in the separate instructions.)　　　　　　　　　　**Schedule M—Page 26**

APPENDIX 5C *(continued)*

Form 706 (Rev. 11-87)

Part 2.—Property Interests Which Are Subject to a QTIP Election

Item number	Description of property interests passing to surviving spouse (Describe portion of trust for which allocation is made.)	Value
1		

Total from continuation schedule(s) (or additional sheet(s)) attached to this schedule . . . .

A. Total value of property interests subject to a QTIP election . . . . | **A** |

Part 3.—Reconciliation

1 Enter the total from part 1 . . . . | **1** |

2 Total interests passing to surviving spouse (add lines A and 1, above) . . . . | **2** |

3a Federal estate taxes (including section 4981A taxes) payable out of property interests listed on Parts 1 and 2 | **3a** |

  b Other death taxes payable out of property interests listed on Parts 1 and 2 . . . . | **3b** |

  c Federal and state GST taxes payable out of property interests listed on Parts 1 and 2 . . . . . | **3c** |

  d Add items a, b, and c . . . . | **3d** |

4 Net value of property interests listed on Schedule M (subtract 3d from 2). Also enter on Part 5, Recapitulation, page 3, at item 18 | **4** |

(If more space is needed, attach the continuation schedule from the end of this package or additional sheets of the same size.)

Schedule M—Page 27

APPENDIX 5C *(continued)*

Form 706 (Rev. 11-87)

Estate of:

SCHEDULE N —ESOP Deduction (Under Section 2057)

		Yes	No
A Did the decedent directly own on the date of death all of the employer securities for which a deduction is being claimed?			
B Are all of the securities, after their sale, allocated to the participants or held for future allocation as described in the instructions? . . .			

1	Total qualified sales of employer securities to plans or cooperatives		**1**	
2	Total 401(a) distributions (see instructions)	**2**		
3	Total transfers pursuant to options (see instructions)	**3**		
4	Add lines 2 and 3		**4**	
5	Subtract line 4 from line 1		**5**	
6	Multiply line 5 by 50%. Enter the amount here and on Part 5, Recapitulation, page 3, at item 19.		**6**	

You must attach the required statement by the employer or cooperative officer. (See instructions.)

SCHEDULE O—Charitable, Public, and Similar Gifts and Bequests

		Yes	No
1a	If the transfer was made by will, has any action been instituted to have interpreted or to contest the will or any provision thereof affecting the charitable deductions claimed in this schedule?		
	If "Yes," full details must be submitted with this schedule.		
b	According to the information and belief of the person or persons filing the return, is any such action designed or contemplated?. . .		
	If "Yes," full details must be submitted with this schedule.		
2	Did any property pass to charity as the result of a qualified disclaimer?		
	If "Yes," attach a copy of the written disclaimer required by section 2518(b).		

Item number	Name and address of beneficiary	Character of institution	Amount
1			

Total from continuation schedule(s) (or additional sheet(s)) attached to this schedule. . . . .

3	Total		**3**	
4 **a**	Federal estate tax (including section 4981A taxes) payable out of property interests listed above.	**4a**		
b	Other death taxes payable out of property interests listed above	**4b**		
c	Federal and state GST taxes payable out of property interests listed above	**4c**		
d	Add items a, b, and c		**4d**	
5	Net value of property interests listed above (subtract 4d from 3). Also enter on Part 5, Recapitulation, page 3, at item 20 .		**5**	

(If more space is needed, attach the continuation schedule from the end of this package or additional sheets of the same size.)

(The instructions to Schedules N and O are in the separate instructions.)

Schedules N and O—Page 28

APPENDIX 5C *(continued)*

Form 706 (Rev. 11-87)

Estate of:

SCHEDULE P—Credit for Foreign Death Taxes

List all foreign countries to which death taxes have been paid and for which a credit is claimed on this return.

If a credit is claimed for death taxes paid to more than one foreign country, compute the credit for taxes paid to one country on this sheet and attach a separate copy of Schedule P for each of the other countries.

The credit computed on this sheet is for ....
(Name of death tax or taxes)

.... imposed in ....
(Name of country)

Credit is computed under the ....
(Insert title of treaty or "statute")

Citizenship (nationality) of decedent at time of death

(All amounts and values must be entered in United States money)

1	Total of estate, inheritance, legacy, and succession taxes imposed in the country named above attributable to property situated in that country, subjected to these taxes, and included in the gross estate (as defined by statute)	
2	Value of the gross estate (adjusted, if necessary, according to the instructions for item 2)	
3	Value of property situated in that country, subjected to death taxes imposed in that country, and included in the gross estate (adjusted, if necessary, according to the instructions for item 3)	
4	Tax imposed by section 2001 reduced by the total credits claimed under sections 2010, 2011, and 2012 (see instructions)	
5	Amount of Federal estate tax attributable to property specified at item 3. (Divide item 3 by item 2 and multiply the result by item 4.)	
6	Credit for death taxes imposed in the country named above (the smaller of item 1 or item 5). Also enter on line 16 of the Tax Computation.	

SCHEDULE Q—Credit for Tax on Prior Transfers

	Name of transferor	Social security number	IRS office where estate tax return was filed	Date of death
A				
B				
C				

Check here ▶ ☐ if section 2013(f) (special valuation of farm, etc., real property) adjustments to the computation of the credit were made (see instructions).

	Item	Transferor			Total A, B, & C
		A	B	C	
1	Transferee's tax as apportioned (from worksheet, (line 7 + line 8) x line 35 for each column) . . .				
2	Transferor's tax (from each column of worksheet, line 20)				
3	Maximum amount before percentage requirement (for each column, enter amount from line 1 or 2, whichever is smaller)				
4	Percentage allowed (each column) (see instructions).	%	%	%	
5	Credit allowable (line 3 x line 4 for each column)				
6	TOTAL credit allowable (add columns A, B, and C of line 5). Enter here and on line 17 of the Tax Computation.				

(The instructions to Schedules P and Q are in the separate instructions.)

Schedules P and Q—Page 29

APPENDIX 5C *(continued)*

Form 706 (Rev. 11-87)

Schedule R.—Generation-Skipping Transfer Tax

Part 1.—Reconciliations and Section 2652(a)(3) (Special QTIP) Election

A. Grandchild Exclusion Reconciliation (Section 1433(b)(3) of the Tax Reform Act of 1986)

A Name of grandchild	B Maximum allowable exclusion	C Total grandchild exclusions claimed on gift tax returns	D Grandchild exclusion available for this Form 706
	$2,000,000		
	2,000,000		
	2,000,000		
	2,000,000		
	2,000,000		
	2,000,000		
	2,000,000		
	2,000,000		
	2,000,000		
	2,000,000		
	2,000,000		
	2,000,000		

B. GST Exemption Reconciliation (Section 2631) and Section 2652(a)(3) Election

Check box ▶ ☐ if you are making a section 2652(a)(3) (special QTIP) election (see instructions)

1	Maximum allowable GST exemption	**1**	$1,000,000
2	Total GST exemption allocated by the decedent against decedent's lifetime transfers	**2**	
3	Total GST exemption allocated by the executor, using Form 709, against decedent's lifetime transfers	**3**	
4	GST exemption allocated on line 8 of Schedule R, Part 2	**4**	
5	GST exemption allocated on line 8 of Schedule R, Part 3	**5**	
6	Total GST exemption allocated on line(s) 6 of Schedule(s) R-1	**6**	
7	Total GST exemption allocated to intervivos transfers and direct skips (add lines 2–6)	**7**	
8	GST exemption available to allocate to trusts and section 2032A interests (subtract line 7 from line 1)	**8**	

9 Allocation of GST exemption to trusts (as defined for GST tax purposes):

A Name of trust	B Trust's EIN (if any)	C GST exemption allocated on lines 2–6, above (see instructions)	D Additional GST exemption allocated (see instructions)	E Trust's inclusion ratio (optional—see instructions)

9D Total. May not exceed line 8, above . . . . **9D** | |

10 GST exemption available to allocate to section 2032A interests received by individual beneficiaries (subtract line 9D from line 8). You must attach special use allocation schedule (see instructions) . . **10**

(The instructions to Schedule R are in the separate instructions.)

Schedule R—Page 30

APPENDIX 5C *(continued)*

Form 706 (Rev. 11-87)

Estate of:

Part 2.—Direct Skips Where the Property Interests Transferred Bear the GST Tax on the Direct Skips

Name of skip person	Description of property interest transferred	Estate tax value

1	Total estate tax values of all property interests listed above	1	
2	Estate taxes, state death taxes, and other charges borne by the property interests listed above	2	
3	GST taxes borne by the property interests listed above but imposed on direct skips other than those shown on this Part 2. (See instructions.)	3	
4	Total fixed taxes and other charges. (Add lines 2 and 3.)	4	
5	Subtract line 4 from line 1	5	
6	Total grandchild exclusion(s) claimed against property interests listed above	6	
7	Total tentative maximum direct skips. (Subtract line 6 from line 5.)	7	
8	GST exemption allocated	8	
9	Subtract line 8 from line 7	9	
10	GST tax due: a. If decedent died in 1986 or 1987, divide line 9 by 2.818182 } b. If decedent died in 1988 or thereafter, divide line 9 by 3.000* }	10	
11	Enter the amount on line 10 of Schedule R, Part 3	11	
12	**Total GST taxes payable by the estate.** (Add lines 10 and 11.) Enter here and on line 20 of the Tax Computation on page 1	12	

*At the time this Form 706 was sent to print, legislation was pending that would freeze the GST tax rate for decedents dying in 1988 and later at the rate shown for decedents dying in 1987.

Schedule R—Page 31

APPENDIX 5C *(continued)*

Form 706 (Rev. 11-87)

Estate of:

Part 3.—Direct Skips Where the Property Interests Transferred Do Not Bear the GST Tax on the Direct Skips

Name of skip person	Description of property interest transferred	Estate tax value

1 Total estate tax values of all property interests listed above **1**

2 Estate taxes, state death taxes, and other charges borne by the property interests listed above **2**

3 GST taxes borne by the property interests listed above but imposed on direct skips other than those shown on this Part 3. (See instructions.) **3**

4 Total fixed taxes and other charges. (Add lines 2 and 3.) **4**

5 Subtract line 4 from line 1 . . . . **5**

6 Total grandchild exclusion(s) claimed against property interests listed above **6**

7 Total tentative maximum direct skips. (Subtract line 6 from line 5.) **7**

8 GST exemption allocated **8**

9 Subtract line 8 from line 7 . . . . **9**

10 GST tax due:

   a. If decedent died in 1986 or 1987, multiply line 9 by .55

   b. If decedent died in 1988 or thereafter, multiply line 9 by .50*

     Enter here and on Schedule R, Part 2, line 11 . . . . **10**

*At the time this Form 706 was sent to print, legislation was pending that would freeze the GST tax rate for decedents dying in 1988 and later at the rate shown for decedents dying in 1987.

Schedule R—Page 32

APPENDIX 5C *(continued)*

SCHEDULE R-1 (Form 706)	**Generation-Skipping Transfer Tax**	
(November 1987) Department of the Treasury Internal Revenue Service	**Direct Skips From a Trust** **Payment Voucher**	OMB No. 1545-0015 Expires 5-31-90

Executor: File one copy with Form 706 and send two copies to the fiduciary. Do not pay the tax shown. See the separate instructions.
Fiduciary: See instructions on reverse side. Pay the tax shown on line 8.

Name of Trust		Trust's EIN
Name and title of fiduciary	Name of decedent	
Address of fiduciary (number and street)	Decedent's SSN	Service Center where Form 706 was filed
City, state, and ZIP code	Name of executor	
Address of executor (number and street)	City, state, and ZIP code	
Date of decedent's death	Filing due date of Schedule R, Form 706 (with extensions)	

Part 1.—Computation of the GST Tax on the Direct Skip

Description of property interests subject to the direct skip	Estate tax value

1 Total estate tax value of all property interests listed above	1	
2 Estate taxes, state death taxes, and other charges borne by the property interests listed above	2	
3 Subtract line 2 from line 1.	3	
4 Total grandchild exclusion(s) claimed against property interests listed above.	4	
5 Tentative maximum direct skip from trust. (Subtract line 4 from line 3.)	5	
6 GST exemption allocated	6	
7 Subtract line 6 from line 5	7	
8 GST tax due from fiduciary (See instructions if property will not bear the GST tax.):		
a If decedent died in 1986 or 1987, divide line 7 by 2.818182		
b If decedent died in 1988 or thereafter, divide line 7 by 3.000*	8	

Under penalties of perjury, I declare that I have examined this return, including accompanying schedules and statements, and to the best of my knowledge and belief, it is true, correct, and complete.

Signature(s) of executor(s)	Date
Signature of fiduciary or officer representing fiduciary	Date

*At the time this Form 706 was sent to print, legislation was pending that would freeze the GST tax rate for decedents dying in 1988 and later at the rate shown for decedents dying in 1987.

Schedule R-1 (Form 706)–Page 33

APPENDIX 5C *(continued)*

Instructions for Fiduciary

Purpose of Schedule R-1

Code section 2603(a)(2) provides that the Generation-Skipping Transfer (GST) tax imposed on a direct skip from a trust is to be paid by the trustee. Schedule R-1 (Form 706) serves as a payment voucher for the trustee to remit the GST tax to the IRS. See the instructions for Form 706 as to when a direct skip is from a trust.

How To Pay the GST Tax

The executor will compute the GST tax, complete Schedule R-1, and give you two copies. You should pay the GST tax using one copy and retain the other copy for your records.

The GST tax due is the amount shown on line 8. Make your check or money order for this amount payable to "Internal Revenue Service," write "GST tax" and the trust's EIN on it, and send it and one copy of the completed Schedule R-1 to the IRS Service Center where the Form 706 was filed, as shown on the front of the Schedule R-1.

When To Pay the GST Tax

The GST tax is due and payable the latest of: 9 months after the decedent's date of death (entered by the executor on Schedule R-1); May 2, 1988, or 90 days after the IRS publishes in the Federal Register Temporary Regulations under section 2662 establishing GST tax due dates. Interest will be charged on any GST taxes unpaid as of that date. However, you have an automatic extension of time to file Schedule R-1 and pay the GST tax due until 2 months after the due date (with extensions) for filing the decedent's Schedule R, Form 706. This Schedule R, Form 706 due date is entered by the executor on Schedule R-1. Thus, while interest will be due on unpaid GST taxes, no penalties will be charged if you file Schedule R-1 by this extended due date.

Signature

You, as fiduciary, must sign the Schedule R-1 in the space provided.

Schedule R-1 (Form 706)—Page 34

APPENDIX 5C *(continued)*

Form 706 (Rev. 11-87)   (Make copies of this schedule before completing it if you will need more than one schedule.)

Estate of:

CONTINUATION SCHEDULE

Continuation of Schedule _____
(Enter letter of schedule you are continuing.)

Item number	Description For securities, give CUSIP number, if available.	Unit value (Sch B or E only)	Alternate valuation date	Alternate value	Value at date of death or amount deductible
1					

TOTAL. (Carry forward to main schedule.) . . . .

See instructions on back.

Continuation Schedule—Page 35

APPENDIX 5C *(concluded)*

Instructions for Continuation Schedule

The Continuation Schedule on page 35 provides a uniform format for listing additional assets from Schedules A, B, C, D, E, F, G, H, and I and additional deductions from Schedules J, K, L, M, and O. Use the Continuation Schedule when you need to list more assets or deductions than you have room for on one of the main schedules.

Use a separate Continuation Schedule for each main schedule you are continuing. For each schedule of Form 706, you may use as many Continuation Schedules as needed to list all the assets or deductions to be reported. Do not combine assets or deductions from different schedules on one Continuation Schedule. Since there is only one Continuation Schedule in this package, you should make copies of the schedule before completing it if you expect to need more than one.

Enter the letter of the schedule you are continuing in the space provided at the top of the Continuation Schedule. Complete the rest of the Continuation Schedule as explained in the instructions for the schedule you are continuing. Use the *Unit value* column only if you are continuing Schedules B or E. For all other schedules, you may use the space under the *Unit value* column to continue your description.

To continue Schedule E, Part II, you should enter the *Percentage includible* in the *Alternate valuation date* column of the Continuation Schedule.

To continue Schedule K, you should use the *Alternate valuation date* and *Alternate value* columns of the Continuation Schedule as *Amount unpaid to date* and *Amount in contest* columns, respectively.

To continue Schedules J, L, and M, you should use the *Alternate valuation date* and *Alternate value* columns of the Continuation Schedule to continue your description of the deductions. You should enter the amount of each deduction in the *amount deductible* column of the Continuation Schedule. Use a separate Continuation Schedule for each part of Schedule M. Do not combine QTIP and non-QTIP property on the same Continuation Schedule.

To continue Schedule O, you should use the space under the *Alternate valuation date* and *Alternate value* columns of the Continuation Schedule to provide the *Character of institution* information required on Schedule O. You should enter the amount of each deduction in the *amount deductible* column of the Continuation Schedule.

Carry the total from the Continuation Schedule(s) forward to the appropriate line of the main schedule.

—6——

The Federal Estate Tax

OVERVIEW

A comprehensive outline of the Federal Estate Tax (FET) is shown in Table 6–1.

Basically, as outlined in the previous chapter, the unified transfer tax rate schedule forms the basis to calculate a tentative tax.[1] This tax is on the sum of the decedent's property interests (gross estate) plus certain gifts (post-1976 taxable gifts) and reduced by allowed deductions. Credits are subtracted from the tentative tax to arrive at the net tax liability.[2]

This chapter is divided into three major parts. Each part will examine one of the three principal items found on the estate tax return: components of the gross estate, allowable deductions, and allowable credits. All Code sections (e.g., §2033) included in this chapter refer to those found in the Internal Revenue Code. Many of these sections are included in Appendix B at the end of the book.

---

[1]See Table 4 of Appendix A at the end of the book.

[2]In general, a federal estate tax return must be filed for decedents dying with a total gross estate plus adjusted taxable gifts equaling or exceeding the amount of the exemption equivalent of the unified credit for the year of death. For example, the estate of a decedent who died in 1985 having a gross estate of $355,000 and adjusted taxable gifts of $100,000 must file a return because their sum exceeds $400,000. Unfortunately, filing is required even though no FET will be due, as in the case where the entire estate is left to a surviving spouse.

TABLE 6–1 Federal Estate Tax (Form 706)

Gross estate		$xxx,xxx
Less deductions:		
Expenses and indebtedness	$xxx	
Losses during administration	xxx	
Charitable bequests	xxx	
Marital deduction	xxx	xx,xxx
Leaves: Taxable estate		xxx,xxx
Plus: Adjusted taxable gifts		xx,xxx
Equals: Tax base		xxx,xxx
Tentative tax on tax base		xxx,xxx
Less credits, etc.:		
Gift tax payable on post-1976 taxable gifts	xxx	
Unified credit	xxx	
Credit for state death tax paid	xxx	
Credit for tax on prior transfers	xxx	
Credit for foreign death taxes	xxx	
Credit for gift taxes on pre-1977 gifts		
included in the gross estate	xxx	xx,xxx
Leaves: Net estate tax (FET)		$xxx,xxx

While studying this chapter, the student is urged to look over Form 706, Federal Estate Tax Return, shown in Appendix 5C, and those relevant sections of the Internal Revenue Code, to strengthen comprehension in this complex area.

ONE: COMPONENTS OF THE GROSS ESTATE

There is no short definition of the term *gross estate*. One might think that it would consist solely of property in which the decedent had a clear beneficial interest at death. However, in developing the rules, Congress has added other items which, in its judgment, must be included to prevent substantial FET avoidance through planning. For example, as we shall see below, included in a decedent's gross estate will be all gift taxes paid on gifts made within three years of death.

Another example involves retained interests. In the past, property owners attempted to reduce FET by making gifts with "strings attached," retaining some power to control beneficial enjoyment. Specifically, a Mom and Dad might have wanted to transfer the family residence to their adult son with the agreement that the parents could continue to live there. Recognizing that such strings-attached transfers meant that the property owner had retained a substantial beneficial interest, Congress enacted Code Sections 2036, 2037, and 2038, thereby including such property in the transferor's gross estate at death.

Analysis of the components of the gross estate will be divided into three parts. First, we'll examine those sections covering interests owned at death (§2033–4, 2039–42). Second, we will focus on those sections which include in the gross estate certain transfers made with retained interests or with control over beneficial enjoyment (§2036, 2037, and 2038). And third, we'll cover certain other transferred interests, including those which the decedent relinquished within three years of death (§2035). Again, in studying the components of the gross estate, it would be well to remember that many peculiar items have been included over the years solely to prevent what Congress has seen to be substantial FET avoidance.

Interests Owned at Death

§2033: Property owned by the decedent.   Section 2033 includes in the gross estate all property in which the decedent had a beneficial interest at death. Common examples are fee simple interests, such as ownership interests typically held in assets such as a house, furniture, personal effects, business interests, investments, and even intangible property such as patent rights. However, many interests that are less encompassing than fee simple interests are also included. In principle, if the property had some value and the decedent had some beneficial interest in it at death, it is probably includable. A few not-so-obvious examples follow:

EXAMPLE 2033–1   Decedent died on June 18 owning 100 shares of XYZ stock, worth $10,000. On May 26, a *dividend* of $1.50 per share was declared, payable to stockholders of record on June 14, with payment on June 22. Includable in the gross estate will be $10,150, representing the value of the stock plus the dividends. At death, decedent was entitled by right to receive the dividend.

EXAMPLE 2033–2   Same facts as Example 2033–1, except that the holder-of-record date was June 24. The value of the dividends is not includable in the decedent's gross estate because at date of death, decedent was not legally entitled to the dividend.

EXAMPLE 2033–3 Prior to his death in 1985, decedent had the right to receive his parent's 1984 Cadillac automobile when his Dad retired in 1988. This was an arm's length agreement, negotiated for valuable consideration. (Decedent, in exchange, gave Dad 10 shares of XYZ stock in 1984). The gross estate will include the value of the *remainder interest* in the car. Its value will be the present discounted value of the car's estimated worth in 1988.

EXAMPLE 2033–4 At her death, decedent owned *state municipal water district bonds*. Although income from such bonds is exempt from federal income tax, the value of the bonds is not exempt from FET and is includable in her gross estate.

EXAMPLE 2033–5 At his death, decedent shared with his wife an ownership in $100,000 of *community property*. His gross estate will include $50,000, representing his one-half interest in the property.

EXAMPLE 2033–6 At her death, decedent had been receiving a monthly pension income from an insurance company, to be paid for as long as she lived (a straight-line annuity). Decedent's gross estate will not include the value of the annuity because her interest terminated at her death. *Life estates for the life of the decedent* are not includable in a decedent's gross estate. In contrast, the present value of a *joint and survivor annuity,* one that continues to be payable in whole or in part to another after the decedent's death, is includable in the decedent's gross estate.[3]

EXAMPLE 2033–7 At his death, decedent had a right to receive a monthly income for as long as the decedent's wife was alive. Decedent's wife is still alive. The gross estate will include the present actuarial value of the remaining income, based on wife's life expectancy. The value of a *life estate for the life of another* is includable in the decedent's gross estate.

EXAMPLE 2033–8 Same facts as Example 2033–7, except that wife predeceased decedent. Decedent's gross estate will not include any amount in connection with the income since decedent's *interest terminated* prior to his death.

EXAMPLE 2033–9 When she died, Carol was a named beneficiary in her father's will. Father is still alive. Carol's gross estate will not

---

[3]Code Section 2039, which includes survivorship annuities in the decedent's gross estate, more directly deals with this type of fact situation. Section 2039 will be covered shortly.

include the value of this bequest. Although her estate may one day receive some of Dad's property, her estate's right to it is contingent upon her father's not changing the terms of his will. *Contingent future interests* normally are not includable in the decedent's gross estate.

EXAMPLE 2033–10 Prior to his death, Jim created an irrevocable trust, with income to his daughter Jodi for her life, then corpus to Jim or to his estate if he dies first. Jim's gross estate will include the value of his *reversionary interest,* which will depend upon Jodi's age at Jim's death.

The above examples illustrate the broad scope of §2033. The gross estate also embraces other types of interests which are defined in several other Code sections, described below.[4]

§2034: Dower and curtesy interests. As mentioned in Chapter 4, a dower represents a surviving wife's life interest in a portion of the real property owned by her deceased husband, and a curtesy represents a surviving husband's life interest in a portion of the real property owned by his deceased wife. The extent of these statutory interests varies from state to state. Some states grant surviving spouses dower and curtesy interests in a percentage of the deceased spouse's real and personal property. As we have seen, one purpose of these laws is to prevent a decedent from entirely disinheriting the surviving spouse, especially when the decedent, as breadwinner, acquired and owned most or all of the family estate.[5] §2034 includes the surviving spouse's dower or curtesy interest in the gross estate of the first spouse to die.[6]

§2039: Survivorship annuities. An annuity is a series of one

---

[4]As you read them, you'll probably notice some conceptual overlap with §2033. That is, you might suspect that §2033, which covers all beneficial interests owned at death, is so all-encompassing as to make the other sections superfluous. You're partly correct. Congress created these additional sections to provide more specific detail in its requirements for overall includability in the gross estate.

[5]As mentioned in Chapter 4, community property states do not have dower or curtesy laws, since community property laws perform essentially the same function: to enable spouses to share in property rights.

[6]The net estate tax effect of dower and curtesy interests and community property is the same. Dower and curtesy interests are included in the gross estate but are fully deducted, under the marital deduction, as interests passing to the surviving spouse. In community property states, the surviving spouse's interest in community property is excluded from the decedent's gross estate. Whether deducted or excluded, these interests are not taxed at the first spouse's death.

or more periodic payments, usually received by the annuitant monthly or annually. Annuities are commonly used in retirement planning, often in conjunction with pension and insurance contracts. Ordinarily, an employee, upon retirement, will begin receiving a monthly annuity, possibly for as long as the retiree lives or, perhaps more commonly, for as long as the retiree and the retiree's spouse live. §2039 includes in the decedent's gross estate the date of death value of an annuity "receivable by any beneficiary by reason of surviving the decedent."

The value of a survivorship annuity included in the decedent's gross estate will basically depend on when the decedent retired,[7] whether or not the pension plan is "qualified" under §401a, and whether the annuity is to be paid in periodic installments or in a lump sum.[8] The following summarizes a rather complex set of rules:

1. With regard to *any* annuity whose payments began *after July 17, 1984,* or for which prior to that date the decedent had not made an irrevocable election to designate the beneficiaries, the *entire value* of the annuity will be includable in the gross estate. It will not matter how the survivor elected to receive payment, in a lump-sum or in installments.

2. With regard to certain annuities whose payments began *before July 18, 1984,* and for which prior to that date the decedent had made an irrevocable election designating the beneficiaries, up to $100,000 of the combined value of certain survivorship annuities will be excluded from the gross estate. Annuities qualifying for this exclusion include the following:

    a. Tax-sheltered annuities.

    b. Individual retirement arrangements.

    c. A portion of the value of the periodic payments under pension plans that have been "qualified" under §401. The

---

[7]In community property states, if the non-participant spouse predeceases the participant spouse, his or her community interest in the annuity will be includable in the gross estate.

[8]§401 is quite long and complex, detailing the requirements necessary for plan qualification. The major tax advantages of qualified plans are that employer contributions are tax deductible to the employer but are not reportable as taxable income to the employee. Non-qualified plans do not enjoy these advantages.

amount qualifying the exclusion is that portion attributable to the employer's contributions.

d. A lump-sum payment to a surviving beneficiary if that beneficiary elects to forgo "5-year averaging."[9]

EXAMPLE 2039–1 Decedent died in 1986, three months after retiring from work. At death, decedent was receiving annuities from the former employer's qualified retirement plan, a tax-sheltered annuity, and an individual retirement account, all of which began paying amounts after retirement. The value of the gross estate will include the entire value of all three annuities.[10]

EXAMPLE 2039–2 During his employment, Stan contributed $25,000 to his qualified pension plan, and his employer contributed $75,000. The plan provides that Stan will receive a joint and survivor annuity upon retirement. Twenty years after his retirement in 1965, Stan died and the value of his spouse's survivorship annuity was $300,000. Since Stan's pension payments began prior to July 18, 1984, his gross estate will include $200,000. The amount excluded is lesser of $100,000 or the value of the portion of the annuity attributable to the employer's contributions. That value is: $75,000/($25,000 + $75,000) × $300,000, or $225,000. Thus the amount excluded is $100,000.

§2040: Joint interests. Includability of joint interests in the gross estate of a deceased joint owner depends on whether or not a surviving spouse is the sole co-owner and, if not, whether or not the surviving co-owners can prove contribution.

In general, for decedents dying after 1981, the gross estate will include the *entire* value of property held jointly with others, subject to two very important exceptions. First, if the only surviving joint owner is the decedent's spouse, the property is called a "qualified

---

[9]See §402a. Five-year averaging is a method of reducing the beneficiary's tax burden by enabling the lump sum to be taxed at favorable tax rates in the year of receipt.

[10]TRA 86 imposes an additional 15 percent estate tax on an individual's "excess retirement accumulation," which is the excess of the value of the decedent's interests in qualified plans and IRAs over the present value of an annuity of ordinarily $150,000 payable for the decedent's life expectancy. The excess accumulation can not be reduced by the marital deduction, and the tax can not be offset by the unified credit. Since this accumulation is also subject to income tax (as "income in respect of a decedent") and to the regular estate tax, it is possible that total taxation on this amount could exceed 100 percent!

joint interest," and exactly *one half* of the total value will *always* be included, *regardless* of that spouse's original contribution and regardless whether or not that contribution can be proven. Contribution by the surviving spouse can be as little as 0 percent or as high as 100 percent; but regardless of the amount contributed, exactly one half will be included.

Second, if the jointly owned property is held by the decedent and at least one person who is *not* the decedent's surviving spouse (even if the surviving spouse happens to be another cotenant), the decedent's gross estate will include the entire value of the property, reduced by an amount attributable to that portion of the consideration in money or money's worth which can clearly be shown to have been furnished by the survivors. This is called the "consideration furnished test." It sounds complex, but in most cases its application is rather simple, as shown below:

EXAMPLE 2040–1 At his death, Joel owned a house in joint tenancy with his surviving wife, who is believed to have originally acquired the house with her separate property. Joel's gross estate will include one half of the value of the house. It is a qualified joint interest. The result does not depend on who in fact originally acquired it or in what manner it was acquired. Hence, the result will be the same if the house was purchased with Joel's property, or with co-owned property.

EXAMPLE 2040–2 At her death Jeannette owned a farm worth $100,000 in joint tenancy with her surviving brother Tom. The farm was originally acquired for $50,000 by both, with Jeannette paying $10,000 and Tom paying $40,000. If Tom's contribution cannot be proved, the entire $100,000 will be included in Jeannette's gross estate. If contribution can be proved, under the consideration-furnished test the estate will include only one fifth the farm's value, or $20,000. The percentage excluded would equal: $40,000 ÷ ($10,000 + $40,000), or 80 percent of $100,000, which equals $80,000.

EXAMPLE 2040–3 At her death, Dottie owned $90,000 in common stock in joint tenancy with her husband and her son. The survivors know that Dottie actually contributed only $10,000 to the original $50,000 purchase price, (and the two of them paid $20,000 each) but they are not sure they can prove it. If they can't, Dottie's gross estate will include the full $90,000. If they can, her gross estate will include only her proportional share, or $18,000, which is $90,000 reduced by (($20,000 + $20,000)/$50,000) times $90,000. This is not a qualified joint interest, because at least one non-spouse was also a cotenant.

For purposes of §2040, joint interests encompass only joint tenancies and tenancies by the entirety. In contrast, includability in the gross estate of the two other major forms of co-ownership, tenancies in common and community property, is determined by reference to §2033, discussed earlier.

§2041: Powers of appointment.   As we saw in Chapter 2, a power of appointment is a power to name someone to receive a beneficial interest in property. The grantor of the power is called the "donor." The person receiving the power is called the "holder" or "donee." The parties whom the holder may appoint are called the "permissible appointees." The parties whom the holder actually appoints are called the "appointees."

For federal estate tax purposes, a power of appointment is either a general power or it is not a general power. A *general* power of appointment is a power to designate beneficial enjoyment to a class of people including any one of the following: the holder, the holder's estate, the holder's creditors, or the creditors of the holder's estate. A *nongeneral* power of appointment, often called a "special" or "limited" power of appointment, is a power to designate beneficial enjoyment to a class of people, none of whom consist of any one of those four named above.

Subject to three major exceptions, a decedent's gross estate will include the value of any property subject to a *general* power of appointment held by the decedent-holder at death.[11]

Under the first exception, if the decedent's right to exercise a general power is limited by an *ascertainable standard,* that is, limited for reasons of health, education, support or maintenance, it will not constitute a general power. Second, if the decedent's right to exercise the power depends on the *approval* of the creator of the power or of an adverse party, it will not constitute a general power. According to the Code, an adverse party "is a person having a substantial interest in the property, subject to the power, which is adverse to exercise of the power in favor of the decedent."

Third, if the decedent's right to exercise the power is limited annually to no more than the greater of *$5,000 or 5 percent of the property* in question, it will not constitute a general power. This is

---

[11]Notice that each exception has the effect of substantially restricting the scope of the appointment power.

the so-called "5 and 5 power" and is frequently used in estate planning to carve out an exception for otherwise includable property.

EXAMPLE 2041–1 Decedent died possessing the right to invade the corpus of a trust for the *benefit of herself*. The right is a general power, and the value of the corpus is includable in her gross estate, even though she had not exercised the power at her death. Technically, the power *lapsed* at her death. A general power that lapses at death is included in the decedent-holder's gross estate.

EXAMPLE 2041–2 Facts similar to Example 2041–1, except that the right to invade was on behalf of *anyone except* herself, her creditors, her estate, or the creditors of her estate. This is not a general power, and thus the property subject to the power is not includable under §2041.

EXAMPLE 2041–3 During her lifetime, decedent had been an income beneficiary under a trust, which provides that upon decedent's death, corpus was to be distributed to decedent's son. Decedent could invade corpus on her own behalf only with approval of her son. Her son is an *adverse party;* hence her right to invade is not treated as a general power of appointment.

EXAMPLE 2041–4 During his lifetime, decedent had been an income beneficiary under a trust, which provides that he could invade corpus on his behalf only for reasons of his "health, education, support, or maintenance." Limited by an *ascertainable standard,* this right to invade is not a general power, even if decedent was trustee and had violated his duties by invading for no valid reason.

EXAMPLE 2041–5 Same facts as Example 2041–4, except decedent could invade corpus for reasons of his "health, education, support, maintenance, *or happiness.*" The power is not considered limited by an ascertainable standard, and therefore the invasion right constitutes a general power of appointment.

Why should a general power of appointment over property subject the property to inclusion in the holder's gross estate? Because the rights underlying a general power are considered to be tantamount to ownership of that property. If a person has the right to appoint property to either herself, her creditors, her estate, or the creditors of her estate, she is considered the equivalent of an owner of that property, even though she has died not having exercised that right.

§2042: Insurance on decedent's life. The value of the decedent's gross estate will include the face value of a life insurance policy on the decedent's life under *either* of two circumstances: first, if the policy proceeds were receivable by the decedent's executor, or second, if the decedent, at his or her death, possessed "incidents of ownership" in the policy.

Receivable by the executor. Ordinarily, life insurance proceeds will be receivable by the decedent's executor if (*a*) the decedent-insured names his or her estate to be the primary beneficiary, (*b*) if the decedent-insured names his or her estate to be contingent beneficiary and at the insured's death the primary beneficiary has predeceased the decedent, or (*c*) if at the insured's death no named beneficiaries are living and the proceeds are payable to the estate by default, if the decedent was the policy owner.

Decedent possesses incidents of ownership. Commonly, ownership of a policy gives the owner numerous rights, including the right to assign and to terminate the policy, the right to receive dividends, and the right to change beneficiaries. Possession by the decedent of *any* of the rights to the economic benefits of the policy will subject the proceeds to inclusion in the gross estate.

Payment of part or all of the policy premiums is not, however, an incident of ownership. Nonetheless, if the decedent has incidents of ownership, source of premiums can indicate a shared ownership with another person, which could reduce the amount includable in the gross estate to the amount of the decedent's share. For example, a policy purchased by the decedent but paid for entirely with community property would subject only one half of the proceeds to inclusion in the decedent's gross estate. Example 2042–1, below, illustrates this point.

It is important to distinguish between policies on the decedent's life and policies on the lives of others. §2042 embraces only policies on the decedent's life. If the decedent died owning a policy on someone else's life, the terminal value, if any, of that policy (which was still in force just after the decedent's death) would be included in the decedent's gross estate under §2033, beneficial interests in property owned at death.[12] One way to distinguish these two code sections is to ask whether the insurance company is paying the proceeds as a result of the decedent's death, or whether the policy

---

[12]The true taxable value of a policy in force is called its "interpolated terminal reserve," which is usually nearly equal to its cash surrender value. For simplicity, we shall call it the policy's "terminal value."

has not yet "ballooned" into something worth such a large amount, because at the time of the decedent's death the insured is still alive. If the proceeds are payable because the decedent has died, the decedent is the insured, and the relevant code section to check is §2042.[13] Otherwise, look only to §2033 for possible inclusion of the policy's terminal value.

> EXAMPLE 2042–1 At the moment of his death, decedent *owned* a $100,000 life insurance policy *on his own life*. Under §2042 (incidents of ownership), $100,000 will be includable in his gross estate. However, if all premiums had been paid for with community property, only $50,000 would be includable.

> EXAMPLE 2042–2 Decedent died owning a $60,000 life insurance policy *on the life of her mother,* who is still alive. The policy is still in force and had a terminal value of $14,000 at decedent's death. The proceeds will not be includable in decedent's gross estate under §2042 because the insurance is not on decedent's life. However, the gross estate will include the $14,000 terminal value under §2033, assuming that the policy is separate property. If it is entirely community property, the gross estate will include $7,000.

So far, we have studied Code sections 2033, 2034, 2039, 2040, 2041, and 2042, all of which cover interests owned by the decedent at death and includable in the gross estate. The next section examines a second group of Code sections that are similar to those above in that they make certain interests includable in the gross estate. However, they are different from the sections above because they cover only *strings attached* transfers made by the decedent during lifetime.

Transfers with Retained Interest or Control

A second general type of property interest includable in the gross estate is one that the decedent transferred before death but, in the process, retained the right to control or enjoy it. Such strings-attached transfers are treated by the Code as if the decedent never made the original transfer and, instead, continued to own the property until death. These transfers are the subject of §2036, Transfers

---

[13]Or §2035, as you'll learn in a few pages.

with Retained Life Estate; §2037, Transfers Taking Effect at Death; and §2038, Revocable Transfers.

These three "string" sections have several things in common: First, to fall under these provisions, the transfer must have been made by the *decedent* and must have been made gratuitously, that is, "for less than full and adequate consideration in money or money's worth." Second, if property is includable in the gross estate under §2036, §2037, or §2038, its includable value will be the value as of the *date of death* (or alternate valuation date) rather than the value as of the date of transfer. Third, the amount includable will be only that portion of the transferred property over which the decedent retained control. For example, if the retained control was only over one third of the property, then only one third of its value will be includable in the gross estate. Fourth, transfers with retained controls usually, but not always, arise in the context of a transfer into trust. Fifth, §2036, §2037, and §2038 often overlap. Not infrequently, a single transfer will be includable in the decedent's gross estate under more than one of these sections. If more than one section applies and different amounts are includable under each, the actual amount includable is the one of greatest value.

An examination of each section covering transfers with retained interests and control follows.

§2036: Transfers with retained life estate. A transfer with retained life estate arises when a decedent has made a transfer, by trust or otherwise, for less than full and adequate consideration, under which he or she has both (*a*) retained one or more specified *controls* over assets *and* (*b*) has retained this control for a certain *period of time*.[14] Each aspect will be examined in some detail below.

Retained controls. Essentially, for §2036 to apply, the decedent-transferor must have retained either (1) the possession or enjoyment of, or the right to *income* from, the property transferred

---

[14]In addition, the Revenue Act of 1987 added a subsection to §2036 to discourage so-called valuation freezes. New §2036(c) requires inclusion in the decedent's gross estate of the value of property under which the decedent transferred (within the setting of an "enterprise") a disproportionately large share of the appreciation potential and retained a disproportionately large share of the income or other rights. For a further discussion, see Chapter 9 and Appendix 16A.

or (2) the right, either alone or in conjunction with any person, to *designate* who will enjoy or possess the property or its income.[15]

Period of retention. In addition to the above retained control, §2036 requires that the decedent-transferor have retained that control for any one of three periods: (1) for life, (2) for any period that does not in fact end before the decedent's death, or (3) for any period not ascertainable without reference to the decedent's death.

In the following §2036 examples, assume that decedent D, before death, made a transfer for less than full consideration.

> EXAMPLE 2036–1 D says, "Son, here's title to my vacation home. It's yours now, but I will need to use it occasionally." The date-of-death value of the home will be includable in D's gross estate because D retained the *right to enjoy it,* presumably for life.

> EXAMPLE 2036–2 D transfers property into a *trust,* with income to D for D's life and with remainder to C. The property's value at date of death will be includable in D's gross estate for the same reason as in Example 2036–1; D retained the right to enjoy it, for life.

> EXAMPLE 2036–3 D transfers property into a *trust,* with income to D for 20 years, then remainder to C. D lives 10 years. The property's value will be includable, partly because the *period of retention* did not in fact end before D's death. D would have had to live more than 20 years to avoid inclusion.

> EXAMPLE 2036–4 D transfers property into a trust, with income to D for up to one month before D's death, then remainder to C. This is includable, partly because the retained period is *not ascertainable without reference* to D's death.

> EXAMPLE 2036–5 D transfers property into a trust, with income (for the life of D) to S or C as D chooses, then remainder to C. This is includable, partly because D retained the *right to designate,* presumably for life, who will enjoy the property.

> EXAMPLE 2036–6 Same facts as Example 2036–5, except that the choice between S or C is made by D and Z together. The property's value is includable, partly because D has the right to designate the recipient "alone or *in conjunction with* any other person."

---

[15]Includes the right to vote shares of stock in a corporation over which decedent, alone or with anyone else, has at least 20 percent of the voting power (§2036b).

EXAMPLE 2036–7 Facts similar to any one of the above examples, except that the transfer was of community property. Only one half of the value of the property (D's interst) will be includable.

EXAMPLE 2036–8 D transfers property into a trust, with one quarter of the income to D, the other three quarters to C; then, upon D's death, remainder to C. Only one quarter of the property's entire value will be includable, since D retained an interest over only that portion.

In the following example, let's alter a basic assumption:

EXAMPLE 2036–9 E transfers property into a trust, with income to then living D for life, remainder to C. The value of the property is not includable in D's gross estate under §2036 because D was not the transferor.

The *reciprocal trusts doctrine,* illustrated in the next example, was established by the courts to apply §2036 to situations which in form avoid the literal terms of that section but which in substance do not. In essence, the transferor has made a transfer of property, and at about the same moment has received the right to enjoyment of other property arising from a separate but related transaction.[16]

EXAMPLE 2036–10 Husband transfers $100,000 in property into trust H, with income payable to his wife for her life and remainder to their children. At about the same time, wife transfers $100,000 into trust W, with income payable to her husband for his life and remainder to their children. Under §2036, the corpus of trust H will be includable in husband's gross estate, and the corpus of trust W will be included in wife's gross estate. The trusts leave the spouses in essentially the same economic position that they would have been had they created trusts naming themselves life beneficiaries.

§2037: Transfers taking effect at death.[17] A "transfer taking effect at death" will arise when (1) possession or enjoyment of the

---

[16]The reciprocal trusts doctrine has been applied to gifts, too. Suppose Mr. Garbanzo gives $10,000 to his son and $10,000 to Mrs. Ceci's daughter, and at the same time Mrs. Ceci gives $10,000 to her daughter and $10,000 to Mr. Garbanzo's son. The IRS will treat the cross-family transfers as "mirror images," as if they were made to each donor's own child instead. Thus, each parent will be treated as having made a $20,000 gross gift to their own child. (T.A.M. 8717003.)

[17]This section can be skipped without significant comprehension loss. §2037 is of much more narrow application than §2036 or §2038, and arises much less frequently in planning an estate.

property through ownership can be obtained only by surviving the decedent and (2) the decedent, at the time of the transfer, retained a reversionary interest which, at the decedent's death, exceeded 5 percent of the value of the property. Such reversionary interest is defined as the possibility that the property may return to the decedent or may be subject to a power of disposition by him.

EXAMPLE 2037–1 D transfers property into trust, with income to S for D's life, reversion to D if he survives S, otherwise remainder to C. Assume that D dies, predeceasing S, and that on the date of D's death the value of the trust property was $1 million. Assume further that, using actuarial tables, at D's death there was a 12 percent chance that D would survive S. The value of D's gross estate will include $120,000 (or .12 times $1 million), the value of the reversionary interest, despite the fact that the property can no longer revert to D. Possession and enjoyment through ownership could only be obtained by surviving D, and the value of D's reversionary interest at death was greater than 5 percent of the value of the property.

In the preceding example, D had a 12 percent chance of surviving S at D's death. The reader might find this strange, since D *in fact* did predecease S. However, this calculation must be made without regard to that fact. Thus, the calculation ordinarily assumes that at the moment before D's death, D was in normal health.

§2038: Revocable transfers.   A revocable transfer will be made if a decedent-transferor retained, at death, the power to alter, amend, revoke, or terminate the right to enjoy the property transferred.

EXAMPLE 2038–1 D transfers property into a *revocable living trust,* retaining the power to revoke or amend the trust at any time. D's gross estate will include the value of this property under §2038.

EXAMPLE 2038–2 D transfers property into a trust, with income to S or C, as D chooses. The trust property will be includable in D's gross estate because D retained the power to "alter" the right to enjoy the property.[18]

EXAMPLE 2038–3 D transfers five bonds to C under the state's *Uniform Gift to Minors Act* and appoints herself custodian. If D dies before C reaches majority, the value of the bonds will be includable

---

[18]§2036 would also fit here. Can you see why?

in D's gross estate because, under the Uniform Act, D had the power to terminate the agreement until C reaches majority.

EXAMPLE 2038–4 D transfers cash to the local savings and loan association for an account for C, naming herself as trustee of the account. In the states recognizing it, this is a *Totten trust* arrangement and is includable in D's gross estate under §2038, because D had the right to withdraw it or change the beneficiary at any time.

Application of §2036, 2037 and 2038 to certain gifts. All three "strings attached" sections apply to annual exclusion gifts. An *annual exclusion gift* is a gift of property worth no more than the annual gift tax exclusion. Such gifts will produce very different estate tax results, depending upon whether or not the gift is completed. As we have seen, a *completed* annual exclusion gift is not a taxable gift, so it is not subject to gift taxation. And it is not subject to estate taxation as an adjusted taxable gift. On the other hand, an *incomplete* annual exclusion "gift" is treated, for estate tax purposes, as if it had never been made, and is fully includable in the gross estate at its date of death value.

EXAMPLE A D makes §2036, 2037, and 2038 transfers of real property, each worth $2,000 at date of transfer and $50,000 at date of death. The gross estate will include $150,000. Annual exclusion transfers are not exempt from the *strings attached* provisions.

EXAMPLE B Same facts as example A, above, except that the three transfers were completed gifts. Nothing attributable to the gifts will be includable in the gross estate.

Sections 2036, 2037, and 2038 all involve transfers where the decedent retains some interest in the property. The next section will examine other items includable in the gross estate, including transfers in which no interest whatsoever is retained.

Certain Transfers within Three Years of Death

A third general type of property interest includable in the gross estate arises when the decedent made a completed transfer (i.e., no strings attached), but the transfer occurred within three years of death. Not all transfers within three years of death, however, are so includable. In fact, most are not. §2035 embraces only two types of transfer situations. First, gratuitous transfers of property interests, which, had the interest been retained, would have been includable in the decedent's gross estate under sections 2036, 2037, 2038, or 2042, are includable in the gross estate under §2035. Second, §2035 includes in the gross estate the gift tax paid for any gift made within three years of death. The following material on the "three-year bringback" rule is subdivided into these two parts: relinquishment of certain interests, and gift tax in gross estate.

Relinquishment of certain interests. A decedent's gross estate includes the value of property under which a transfer had been made within three years of death and which would have been includable in the decedent's gross estate under Sections 2036, 2037, 2038, or 2042, had the transfer not been made.

> EXAMPLE 2035–1 D transfers property into trust, with income to S or C for S's life, as D chooses, then remainder to B. If D died possessing this discretionary right to "sprinkle" the trust income, the value of the trust property would be includable in D's gross estate, as we have seen, under both §2036 and §2038. However, if D later irrevocably gave away (relinquished) this right before death, neither §2036 nor §2038 would apply and the property would not be includable, unless D died within three years of relinquishment. If so, the property would be includable under §2035.

> EXAMPLE 2035–2 Within three years of death, D assigned his ownership interest in a *life insurance* policy on his life. At D's death, the value of the proceeds would be includable in his gross estate because (*a*) the transfer occurred within three years of death, and (*b*) the proceeds would have been includable in D's gross estate under §2042 had the assignment not been made.[19]

Most common transfers will not be subject to §2035. For example, *a completed gift* of anything except a life insurance policy made by the decedent within three years of death will never[20] fall within §2035. Had the gift not been made, the property, if still owned by the decedent at death, would only be included in the gross estate under §2033, not one of those sections specified in

---

[19]The IRS takes the position that §2035 will apply even if the decedent-insured never owned the policy, if he or she nonetheless either paid the premiums directly or provided the funds with which to pay the premiums. The IRS is backed by the courts, which treat the decedent as having made a "beamed transfer," that is, as having personally purchased the policy and then made the transfer.

[20]But, as we'll see next, any *gift tax* paid on such a gift will be subject to §2035.

§2035. Thus, except in the case of life insurance, most common gifts, even those made within three years of death, are *not* included in the gross estate.

Just because a lifetime gift is not includable in the gross estate doesn't mean, however, that it won't be includable in the estate tax base. The reader should recall from Chapter 5 that the taxable portion of any post-1976 gift is includable in "adjusted taxable gifts," under §2001. Nevertheless, the distinction between inclusion in the gross estate versus inclusion in adjusted taxable gifts can be quite important for valuation reasons, since all items in the gross estate are included at date-of-death value,[21] while adjusted taxable gifts are included at date-of-gift value.

> EXAMPLE 2035–3 Continuing Example 2035–2, assume that at the time of the transfer the policy's terminal value was $8,000 and its face value was $200,000. If D were to die more than three years after the transfer, the gross estate would be unaffected, and adjusted taxable gifts would include the amount $8,000 less the value of the annual exclusion applicable in the year of the gift. On the other hand, if D were to die within three years of the transfer, the gross estate would include the $200,000 face value, and adjusted taxable gifts would be unaffected.

Gift tax in gross estate: "Grossing up."   §2035 subjects one other important item to inclusion in the gross estate: gift taxes paid on any gifts made within three years of death.

> EXAMPLE 2035–4 The year is 1993, and X and Y, widowers each owning $10 million in property, are planning their estates. They wish to maximize the amount which will pass to their children. X does no planning. If X dies in 1993 owning the entire $10 million, X's net estate tax is $4,583,000, and thus X's children receive $5,417,000. By contrast, Y gives his child $5 million in property shortly before death, paying a gift tax of $2,078,000. Assuming that Y dies within the year owning $2,922,000 ($10 million reduced by the gift and the gift tax paid) and also assuming (incorrectly for the moment) that the gift tax paid is *not* included in the gross estate, Y's tax base will be $7,912,000 (property owned at death plus adjusted taxable gifts), and Y's net estate tax will be $1,461,000. Therefore Y's children will receive at Y's death an additional $1,461,000, which is the difference between the amount of property owned at death ($2,922,000) and the net estate

---

[21]Or alternate valuation date.

tax ($1,461,000). In total, Y's children will have received $6,461,000, which is greater than X's son's net deathtime gift of $5,417,000. The difference, $1,044,000 is explained partly by the $10,000 gift exclusion but mostly by the exclusion from the gross estate of the gift tax paid.

In order to make the point, Example 2035–4 intentionally makes an incorrect assumption: that the gift tax paid is not includable in the donor's gross estate. In 1976, Congress, with the passage of the Tax Reform Act, revised §2035 to include in the gross estate any gift tax paid on gifts made within three years of death. This revision will alter the results in the preceding example.

EXAMPLE 2035–5 Correcting the mistake in Example 2035–4, inclusion of the gift tax in Y's gross estate will give Y's estate a tax base of $9,990,000 and a net tax of $2.5 million. Thus, Y's children will receive a total of $5,422,000 ($10 million minus $2,078,000 minus $2.5 million), which exceeds the total $5,417,000 received by X's children by only $5,000, the amount of the tax advantage of the $10,000 annual exclusion.

The doctrine that requires inclusion in the gross estate of gift taxes paid on lifetime gifts is called *grossing up,* and it prevents wealth used to pay gift taxes from escaping estate taxation. Current law, as we have said, however, requires grossing up only for taxes on gifts made within three years of death. Thus, gift taxes paid on gifts made more than three years before death still escape transfer taxation.

EXAMPLE 2035–6 Continuing the two preceding examples, had Y died at least three years after making the gift, there would be no grossing up, and the tax advantage shown in Example 2035–4 would apply.[22]

Part-Sale, Part-Gift Transfers

Many clients believe that no part of a transfer will be considered a gift if some amount of consideration is received in exchange. They think that a small receipt from the donee will entirely exclude the transfer from gift taxation. As we have learned in Chapter 2, the

---

[22]The tax-saving effect of not having to gross up is also illustrated in Example 9–16 in Chapter 9.

amount of a gift is measured by the difference between the respective values of the consideration exchanged. But when the property is the subject of a §2035, §2038, or §2041 transfer, the consequence of subtracting only the date-of-gift value of the consideration received can be far more disturbing, because of the use of the date-of-death value of the property transferred. Rather unfairly, §2043 provides that the amount of any property included in the gross estate under §2035 through 2038 (and 2041) will be the date-of-death value of the property, reduced only by a "consideration offset," that is, the original value of the consideration received.

> EXAMPLE 2043–1 Continuing Example 2036–1, shown earlier, had D "sold" the vacation home for $1,000, the gross estate would include the date-of-death value of the home, less $1,000, the amount of the consideration received.

> EXAMPLE 2043–2 Continuing Example 2035–3, shown earlier, had D "sold" the policy for $1, the gross estate would include $199,999, the face value of $200,000 less $1, the amount of consideration received.

Most bargain sale-type completed gifts will not be subject to §2043, since they are not usually includable in the gross estate under Sections 2035 through 2038 or 2041. However, they will be includable in the estate tax base at their adjusted taxable gift value, which equals the gross (date of) gift value, less deductions, the annual exclusion, and the value of any consideration received.

> EXAMPLE 2001–1 In 1984, Jessie "sold" her son Charles a parcel of land worth $18,000 for $200. Jessie has made a taxable gift of $7,800, an amount that will be added to Jessie's adjusted taxable gifts when she dies, even though the land may have appreciated since then.

TWO: ESTATE TAX DEDUCTIONS

Estate tax deductions include funeral expenses, expenses in administering the estate, claims against the estate, debts of the decedent, certain taxes, losses incurred during estate administration, charitable bequests, and the marital deduction. In this section we

will examine in detail only the last item, the marital deduction.[23]
The others will be explored somewhat in the context of deduction
planning in Part 3 of the text.

§2056: The Marital Deduction

The gross estate may be reduced by the value of an interest in property that passes from the decedent to the surviving spouse. Thus,
essentially all property properly passing to the surviving spouse
can potentially avoid estate taxation.[24] Subject to several exceptions, a property transfer to a spouse will qualify for the unlimited
marital deduction if it meets the following three requirements:
First, the property must be *includable* in the decedent's gross estate. Second, the property must actually *pass* to the surviving
spouse. For example, if a decedent leaves in her will a $1 million
cash bequest to her husband, but specifies in the will that any federal estate tax will be paid out of this bequest, the amount deductible under the marital deduction will equal the $1 million reduced
by the net tax payable.[25] Third, the interest passing to the surviving
spouse cannot be a *terminable interest*. A terminable interest, defined in §2056, is an interest "which will terminate or fail . . . on
the lapse of time, on the occurrence of an event or contingency, or
on the failure of an event or contingency to occur." The terminable

---

[23]The Tax Reform Act of 1986 allows a new deduction in computing a decedent's taxable estate for an amount equal to 50 percent of the proceeds from the
sale of a decedent's employer's securities to an employee stock ownership plan
(ESOP). The Revenue Act of 1987 restricts application to nonpublicly traded
stock, and further limits the maximum reduction in estate taxes to $750,000. The
purpose of the deduction is to encourage the growth of such retirement plans.

[24]The estate tax marital deduction was first enacted in 1948 to equalize tax
treatment for common law and community property states. Its amount was limited
to one half of the adjusted gross estate. TRA 76 changed this limit to the greater
of $250,000 or one half of the adjusted gross estate, subject to further adjustments
for any gift tax marital deduction taken and for property held as community property. The *adjusted gross estate* was defined essentially as the decedent's separate
property, reduced by certain expenses.

[25]Note the interrelated computations required here: In order to calculate the
amount of the marital deduction, one needs to know the amount of the net tax.
However, in order to calculate the net tax, the amount of the marital deduction
must be calculated. A solution is determinable, but it may require an iterative
sequence of calculations.

interest rule was created to more ensure that spousal property will be subject to estate taxation in at least one of the two spouse's estates. Without it, property could qualify for the marital deduction in the estate of the first spouse and not even show up in the gross estate of the surviving spouse. The next two examples should help clarify the terminable interest rule.

> EXAMPLE 2056–1 In his will, decedent transfers property into a trust, with income to his wife for her life, then remainder to his child. The value of the life interest to the wife will not qualify for the marital deduction because his wife's interest will "terminate . . . on the occurrence of an event or contingency." Her interest will terminate at her death. In general, a life estate interest passing to a surviving spouse does not qualify for the marital deduction.

One exception to the above rule arises when no other person will possess or enjoy any part of the property after the termination of the interest passing to the surviving spouse.

> EXAMPLE 2056–2 At her death, decedent was receiving an annuity that is payable until her husband's subsequent death. If the value of the survivor's annuity is includable in decedent's gross estate under Code §2039, a marital deduction would be allowed because no other person will enjoy the interest at the husband's death.

There are three other important exceptions to the terminable interest rule. First, the rule will not be violated if the decedent-testator conditions a spousal bequest upon surviving up to *six months* after the decedent's death. Thus, the survival clause introduced in the wills in Chapter 3 create terminable interests that still qualify for the marital deduction. Second, a transfer in which the surviving spouse receives a life estate in all of the income, payable at least annually, plus a *general power of appointment,* exercisable during life or by will, does not violate the terminable interest rule.[26] Finally, if the decedent's executor elects to treat certain property as "qualified terminable interest property," or "QTIP," it will qualify for the marital deduction, despite the fact that the surviving spouse may have no power at all to dispose of the property. A further discussion of the estate planning use of these exceptions

---

[26]This arrangement is used in what is called a *power of appointment trust,* an example of one type of marital trust explained in Chapter 12.

will be postponed until Chapter 12, which explores marital deduction and bypass planning.

THREE: ESTATE TAX CREDITS

There are five basic estate tax credits: the unified credit, the credit for state death taxes, the credit for gift tax, the credit for tax on prior transfers, and the credit for foreign death taxes. Since the unified credit has been explained in the preceding chapter, the following material discusses only the four others.

Credit for State Death Taxes

§2011 allows a credit for *state* inheritance or estate taxes actually paid, up to a maximum credit calculated from Table 6 of Appendix A. Procedurally, the actual tax that has been paid is compared with the maximum table credit, and the lesser of the two values is selected. Use of the table requires calculation of the "adjusted taxable estate," which is defined as the taxable estate reduced by $60,000.

> EXAMPLE 2011–1 Assume D died in 1989, having a gross estate of $755,000 and total deductions amounting to $46,000. Also assume that the estate paid a state death tax of $15,000. The federal credit for state death tax is limited to $15,000, which is the lesser of $15,000 or the table amount, calculated to be $18,432. To arrive at this, we obtain the adjusted taxable estate, which equals $649,000 (i.e., $755,000 less $46,000 less $60,000), upon which the rates are calculated. $18,432 equals the sum of $18,000 plus 4.8 percent of $9,000 (i.e., $649,000 less $640,000). Therefore, the lesser amount is $15,000, which is the proper federal credit for state death taxes.

In the above example, the state could have imposed a death tax of $18,432, or $3,432 more, at no extra cost to the estate. This is shown in the next example.

> EXAMPLE 2011–2 Assuming no credits except the unified credit and the credit for state death taxes, the total federal and state death taxes in Example 2011–1 are $40,330. (Tax base: $709,000; tentative tax: $233,130; total credits: $207,800, which is $192,800 plus $15,000; FET: $25,330.) Total state and federal death taxes of $40,330 represent the sum of $15,000 plus $25,330. Alternatively, had the state imposed a tax of $18,432, total state and federal death taxes would still

equal $40,330. (Proof: Tentative tax: $233,130 less unified credit of $192,800 less state death tax credit of $18,432 leaves an FET of $21,898. State tax was $18,432 and total taxes are therefore still $40,330.)

Essentially, any state can impose a death tax as high as the federal "taxable maximum" credit at no extra cost to the estate, since up to that point a higher federal credit will offset, dollar for dollar, a higher state tax. We can conclude from this that to maximize their own fiscal self-interest, the states ought to ensure that each estate pay a state death tax in an amount that is at least equal to the maximum federal credit. As a matter of fact, all states do this, and practitioners call this provision a "pickup," "soakup" or "sponge" tax.[27]

Credit for Gift Tax

The credit for gift tax, line 15 on the federal estate tax return, technically includes only gift taxes paid on pre-1977 gifts which are required to be included in the decedent's gross estate. The reader might be wondering what pre-1977 gifts could possibly show up in the gross estate. Ordinarily, pre-1977 gifts will not in any way affect the estate tax return of post-1981 decedents, since §2035 includes in the gross estate only certain transfers made within three years of death, and §2001 includes in "adjusted taxable gifts" only post-1976 taxable gifts. However, a pre-1977 gift can wind up in the gross estate under §2036, §2037, §2038, or §2035 if the donor-decedent had made a pre-1977 transfer with a retained interest or retained control, or relinquished such an interest within three years of death.

> EXAMPLE 2012–1 In 1962, decedent gave $1 million in common stock to his nephew, subject to only one condition: For as long as decedent lived he could decide whether the dividend income periodically received should be paid to his nephew or his daughter. In the

---

[27]In those one half of the states imposing only a pickup tax, no state death tax will be owed by estates that owe no FET. Among the states that have their own death tax rates, several impose rates high enough to result in a state tax on larger estates that is *higher* than the maximum federal credit. Nonetheless, the estate is still permitted to report only the maximum federally table-determined amount on Form 706. The upshot will be a state tax partially unprotected by the credit.

same year, decedent paid a gift tax of $35,118. If decedent dies in 1990, the gross estate will include the 1990 value of the stock, under §2036. Further, a $235,118 credit for gift tax paid will be allowed in the return.[28]

The purpose of the credit for gift tax is to prevent the imposition of double transfer taxation to the same person on the same property, the first time in the year of the gift and the second time at death.

Credit for Tax on Prior Transfers

A credit is allowed for certain federal estate taxes previously paid on property inherited by a decedent.

EXAMPLE 2013–1 Harold died in 1984, and his entire net estate passed to his mother, Gladys. A federal estate tax was paid on the estate. Gladys died in 1987. Gladys's estate will be allowed a credit for a portion of the federal estate tax paid at Harold's death.

The purpose of the credit for tax on prior transfers is to prevent multiple federal taxation of property that passes by death to successive estates within a brief period. Calculation of the credit is complex; only the two major steps will be summarized:

Step 1: Calculate the amount of the maximum credit before the percentage limitation (Step 2), by determining the *lesser* of (*a*) the amount of the federal estate tax attributable to the transferred property in the transferor's (e.g., Harold's) estate or (*b*) the amount of the federal estate tax attributable to the transferred property in the decedent's (Gladys's) estate.

Step 2: Multiply the amount obtained in Step 1 by the following percentage limitation, which depends upon how long the decedent-transferee survived the deceased transferor:

---

[28]In addition to items such as the one in this example, the federal estate tax base will, of course, include post-1976 taxable gifts. To prevent double taxation, a reduction in the tentative tax for gift taxes paid on these gifts is also allowed. Although the return does not call this reduction a "credit," and includes it on line 7, it has the effect of reducing the tentative tax to an amount called the "gross estate tax," and for our purposes it is the equivalent to a credit. Hence, practically speaking, *any* gift tax paid on *any* gift that is included in the estate tax base will be allowed as a credit or the equivalent of a credit. Either way, it will be subtracted from the tentative tax.

Decedent Survived by	Percent Allowed
0 to 2 years	100%
Over 2 to 4 years	80
Over 4 to 6 years	60
Over 6 to 8 years	40
Over 8 to 10 years	20
Over 10 years	0

Thus, if the decedent-transferee survives the deceased transferor by more than 10 years, no credit for previously taxed transfers is allowed.

Credit for Foreign Death Taxes

A credit is allowed for the foreign death taxes (of many, but not all nations) paid on property that is (*a*) includable in the U.S. gross estate and (*b*) situated in that foreign country.

This chapter has examined the principal items found on the estate tax return, including components of the gross estate, FET deductions, and FET credits. The next chapter examines the components of the gift tax return, and introduces the federal generation-skipping transfer tax.

RECOMMENDED READING

ABRAMS, HOWARD E. "A Reevaluation of the Terminable Interest Rule." *Tax Law Review* 39 (1983), pp. 1–29.

ASHBY, ROBERT S. "Successful Handling of Retirement Benefits: An Estate Planning Overview." *Trusts & Estates,* July 1984, pp. 13–19.

BITTKER, BORIS I. "Transfers Subject to Retained Right to Receive the Income or Designate the Income Beneficiary." *Rutgers Law Review* 34 (1982), pp. 668–99.

BLAKE, JOHN F. "'Control' and the Estate Tax Implications of Retained Voting Rights under Section 2036(b)." *Estate Planning,* January, 1988, pp. 22–26.

CAIRNS, J. DONALD, and STEPHEN W. JONES. "Appraisals, Audits, and Appeals—The Practical Side of Tax Practice." *Probate Notes* 12 (1987), pp. 210–43.

COOPER, GEORGE. "A Voluntary Tax? New Perspectives on Sophisticated Estate Tax Avoidance." *Columbia Law Review* 77 (March 1977), pp. 161–247.

CURZAN, ROBERT L. "Federal Gift and Estate Tax Aspects of Marital Dissolutions." *Gonzaga Law Review* 16 (1981), pp. 923–45.

Estate and Gift Tax Reporter. Chicago: Commerce Clearing House.

Federal Tax Estate and Gift Taxes. Englewood Cliffs, N.J.: Prentice-Hall.

HELLE, STEVEN. "The Impact of Estate Taxes on Independent Daily Newspapers: An Illinois Case Study." *DePaul Law Review* 33 (1984), pp. 323–55.

KINSKERN, DOUGLAS. "When Will Transferees and Executors Be Personally Liable For Estate and Gift Taxes?" *Estate Planning,* March 1987, pp. 106–11.

KISLING, STEPHEN C. "The Life Estate and the Availability of the Section 2013 Credit." *Taxes—The Tax Magazine,* February 1982, pp. 146–53.

LOWE, HENRY T. "Transfer Taxes on Survivor Annuity Benefits." *Missouri Law Review* 50 (1985), pp. 737–58.

MOORE, CHARLES K., JR., and JAMES W. CHILDS. "Econometric Model Useful in Calculating State Death Tax Effect on Marital Deduction." *Journal of Taxation,* October 1985, pp. 252–53.

MOORE, MALCOLM A. "Recognition and Uses of Federal Estate Tax Credits in Estate Planning and Administration." *University of Miami 21st Annual Estate Planning Institute,* 1987.

NEWMAN, JOEL S. "Incompetency and Federal Wealth Transfer Taxation." *Tax Law Journal* 2, no. 1 (1984), pp. 77–87.

NEWMAN, STEPHEN M. "Recent Changes Make It Easier to Keep Nonqualified Plan Benefits Out Of Estate." *Taxation For Accountants,* April 1986, pp. 234–39.

NEWTON, WILLIAM M. III. "Estate, Gift, and Generation-Skipping Transfer Tax Treaties." *Southwestern Law Journal* 37 (1983), pp. 563–99.

OLIVER, HARRY G. "Estate and Gift Tax Planning for Nonresidents." *International Tax Journal* 12:4 (Fall 1986), pp. 299–317.

PENNFIELD, EDWARD B., and CHARLES J. SEIDLER, JR. "Adverse Estate Consequences of Ownership of Reversionary Interests Can Be Avoided." *Estate Planning,* May 1983, pp. 144–47.

REDD, CHARLES A. "When and How to Take Maximum Advantage of the Credit for Tax on Prior Transfers." *Estate Planning,* May 1985, pp. 162–67.

RUANE, THOMAS P. "Federal Estate and Gift Tax Changes under the Economic Recovery Tax Act: An Ideological Retreat." *Loyola Law Review* 28 (1982), pp. 13–33.

STEPHENS, RICHARD B., GUY B. MAXFIELD, and STEPHEN A. LIND. *Federal Estate and Gift Taxation.* 4th ed. Boston: Warren, Gorham & Lamont, 1978.

SURREY, STANLEY S., WILLIAM C. WARREN, PAUL R. McDANIEL, and HARRY L. GUTMAN. *Federal Wealth Transfer Taxation.* 2nd ed. New York: Foundation Press, 1982.

QUESTIONS AND PROBLEMS

1. Explain in general the meaning of the gross estate.

2. (*a*) Identify several "not so obvious" examples of property interests falling and not falling under §2033. (*b*) What common tax principal applies to all of them?

3. (*a*) What is a dower interest? (*b*) How is it taxed?

4. During his lifetime, decedent contributed $30,000 to his pension plan, and his employer contributed $70,000. He retired in 1986. At his death, his wife is entitled to receive a survivor's pension of $1,800 per month for life. The present actuarial value of the pension at decedent's death is $122,000. How much is includable in decedent's gross estate if the pension is (*a*) "nonqualified"; (*b*) "qualified"? (Hint: There is a simple answer to both parts.)

5. Decedent D owned a building worth $200,000 at D's death in joint tenancy with the alternative persons named below. In each case, the surviving cotenant(s) paid two thirds of the purchase price, and D paid one third. Calculate the amounts includable in D's gross estate if the surviving cotenant(s) are:
a. D's spouse, and contribution can be proved.
b. D's spouse, and contribution cannot be proved.
c. D's spouse and D's son, and contribution cannot be proved.
d. D's spouse and D's son, and contribution can be proved.
e. D's son, and contribution cannot be proved.
f. D's son, and contribution can be proved.

6. Can you think of any estate planning reason for creating a power of appointment?

7. (*a*) State the general principles of transfer taxation of powers of appointment. (*b*) What are the three exceptions?

8. At the moment of D's death, an insurance policy having a $150,000 face value and a $70,000 terminal value was in force. In each case in the table below, determine the amount includable in D's gross estate and fill in the reason and the controlling code section. (Note: Uncle and wife are D's surviving uncle and wife. Community property states:

Assume property held as tenancy in common (TIC) is, instead, community property. SP is separate property, that is, property held by someone as an individual.).

	Insured	Owner Named on Policy	Beneficiary	Premiums Paid with	Included in Gross Estate?	Reason
a.	D	D	D's estate	D's SP		
b.	D	D	D's estate	D's and wife's TIC		
c.	D	D	Wife	D and wife's TIC		
d.	D	Wife	D's estate	D's SP		
e.	D	Wife	Wife	D's SP		
f.	Uncle	D	Uncle	D's SP		
g.	Uncle	D	Uncle	D and wife's TIC		
h.	Uncle	Wife	Wife	D and wife's TIC		
i.	Uncle	Uncle	D's estate	Uncle's property		
j.	Uncle	Uncle	Uncle	Uncle		

9. What do Sections 2033, 2034, 2039, 2040, 2041, and 2042 all have in common?

10. What do Sections 2036, 2037, and 2038 have in common?

11. Under §2036 what, technically, is included in the notion "strings attached"?

12. Give three common examples of transfers includable in the gross estate under §2038.

13. Explain the impact of §2035.

14. Redo part e of Question 8 assuming that the policy was purchased two years ago by decedent and given to wife. Assume, alternatively, that the purchase was from (*a*) decedent's property and (*b*) an equal amount of both spouse's property.

15. How would your answers to Question 14 change, if at all, if, alternatively:
    a. the policy was acquired two years ago by wife, but the source of the first year's premiums was the decedent's funds. Why? (Hint: refer to a Chapter 6 footnote).
    b. the policy was acquired four years ago by wife with funds provided by the decedent. Why?

16. Two years before his death, decedent directed the trustee of his revocable living trust to give his daughter a block of

common stock, then worth $10,000. At his death, the stock was worth $100,000. Assuming no other lifetime gifts, will there be any estate tax consequences? (Hint: Consider §2035).

17. (*a*) Terrill owns an estate of $6 million. This year, he gives $3 million to his daughter. Assuming for simplicity no other lifetime gifts, no annual exclusion or deductions, a flat transfer tax rate of 50 percent, a unified credit of $200,000, and no asset appreciation, calculate Terrill's combined transfer taxes if (1) he lives four years; (2) he dies in two years; (*b*) Is grossing up an advantage or a disadvantage?

18. D died in 1985. While alive, he made one outright gift of cash. In each assumed set of facts, indicate how much, if any, would be added to D's (1) gross estate and (2) adjusted taxable gifts.

   a. Gift of any size made in 1976.
   b. Gift of $2,500 made in 1977.
   c. Gift of $2,500 made in 1981.
   d. Gift of $3,500 made in 1983.
   e. Gift of $12,000 made in 1977 (gift tax paid was $300).
   f. Gift of $12,000 made in 1983 (gift tax paid was $300).

19. How would your answer to Parts *c* and *d* in the problem above change if the gift property was a life insurance policy (face value = $100,000) on the decedent's life?

20. In 1973, Mom "sold" $100,000 worth of IBM stock to her son Jim for $10,000, under the condition that if she ever needed it (e.g., for health) she could have it back. (*a*) If Mom dies in 1990 when the stock is worth $420,000, how much, if anything, is includable in her gross estate? (*b*) Would your answer change if in 1989 Mom gave up all right to impose the condition stated above?

21. Frank died with a gross estate of $800,000. During administration, the following checks were written: Partial distribution to Frank's son: $100,000; executor's commission: $16,500; attorney's fee: $20,000; funeral expenses: $4,200; accountant's fee: $4,600. Further, Frank owed $62,000 at his death. During administration a $6,000 auto was stolen and insurance paid $4,100. Frank's will left $8,000 to char-

ity, $200,000 to his wife, and the rest to his mother. He had made no lifetime gifts. Calculate Frank's taxable estate. (Answer: $482,800.)

22. At death, Steve was a man of great wealth. He owned a $2 million hotel in joint tenancy with his wife, Mary. He was also the grantor of a revocable trust (T1), with the principal ($750,000) payable to Mary at his death, if Mary survived him by at least six months. Steven owned a $3 million life insurance policy (L1) on his life, payable to Mary. Mary owned a $1.2 million life insurance policy (L2) on Steve's life (purchased eight years ago), payable to her. A second trust (T2) gave Steve a general power of appointment over $900,000, and in his will Steve appointed Mary. Into a third, :"bypass" trust (T3), Steve left $600,000 at death, with income to Mary for her life, remainder to their son. Mary had a general power of appointment over the trust corpus, limited by the ascertainable standard of health and maintenance. Mary validly disclaimed the remainder of Steve's estate, which amounted to $6 million. Calculate Steve's (a) total gross estate and (b) marital deduction. Be sure to determine whether each transfer either meets the requirements for the marital deduction and/or falls within an exception. (Answer: (a) $12.25 million; (b) $5.65 million.)

23. (a) Calculate the decedent's maximum federal credit for state death taxes under the following conditions:

	Taxable Estate	Total State Death Taxes	Table Credit	Maximum
1.	$ 100,000	$ 1,000		
2.	1,100,000	20,000		
3.	1,100,000	40,000		

(b) If the decedent resided in a state such as Florida, which imposes only a pickup tax, for each part of the preceding table, how much will be the amount of this state tax?

24. (a) What is the purpose of the credit for tax on prior transfers? (b) Why does its amount depend on how recently the transfer occurred?

7

The Federal Gift Tax: The Federal Generation-Skipping Transfer Tax

Chapter 5 introduced the gift tax by outlining how it is calculated and how it is unified with the estate tax. This chapter will examine more qualitative factors, such as the requirements for a valid gift, types of taxable gifts, how gifts qualify for the annual exclusion, and how certain transfers are taxed. The chapter will also introduce the Generation-Skipping Transfer Tax. While reading the chapter, the reader is urged to review both the overview of the gift tax in Table 5–1 and the copy of Form 709, United States Gift Tax Return, which is included in Appendix 5B.

THE FEDERAL GIFT TAX

Requirements for a Valid Gift

A gift may be defined as a completed transfer of an interest in property by an individual for less than full and adequate consideration. To be valid under local law, a gift must ordinarily meet several requirements.[1] First, the donor must be capable of transferring

---

[1]The relationship between federal tax law and local law in regard to the requirements for a valid gift may be stated as follows: Federal law outlines the kinds of transfers constituting *taxable* gifts, while local law dictates whether there has in

property. Second, the donee must be capable of receiving and possessing the property. Third, there must be delivery to, and some form of acceptance by, the donee or the donee's agent.[2] Fourth, under local law, a valid gift ordinarily requires donative intent on the part of the donor. Federal tax regulations, however, explicitly state that donative intent is not required for a transfer to be subject to gift tax.[3] Aspects of federal law which determine the kinds of transfers constituting valid taxable gifts are discussed next.

Types of Taxable Gifts

Under federal law, a gift is taxable whether it is direct or indirect, or whether the property transferred is real or personal, or whether it is tangible or intangible. However, federal gift tax law only applies to property situated within the United States.

The value of the gift for tax purposes is its fair market value at the date of the gift. Any consideration received in exchange is subtracted in determining the gross value of the gift.

> EXAMPLE 2512–1 If Mom "sells" to a son a $10,000 automobile for $1, Mom has made a gross gift in the amount of $9,999.

To be recognized, consideration received in exchange must be measurable in money or money's worth. If it is not reducible to money or money's worth, it will be disregarded.

> EXAMPLE 2512–2 In Example 2512–1, consideration received by Mom is still only $1, even though son gave her incredible amounts of love and affection before and after the gift.

Practically speaking, any transaction made for less than full and adequate consideration between *related parties* is frequently

---

fact been a gift, regardless of taxation. For example, federal law specifically states that an exercise of a general power of appointment constitutes a taxable gift, while state law determines such issues as what action on the part of a holder of a general power constitutes an exercise of that power.

[2]An example of an agent would be an escrow agent who is holding the property on behalf of the donee.

[3]But the existence of donative intent would be strong evidence that a gift had actually been made.

treated with suspicion by the Internal Revenue Service, which will often contend that the transaction is a gift. On the other hand, a transfer made in the ordinary course of business between unrelated parties is usually presumed not to be a gift.

> EXAMPLE 2512–3 Herb, owner of a retail drugstore, sells his aging delivery pickup truck to Karl, a stranger, who read about the truck in the classified section of the newspaper. Karl paid Herb $4,200 and promptly took out a similar ad and sold the truck three days later for $6,700. Herb will probably be considered to have made a bad bargain, but not a gift, because the truck was sold at arm's length "in the ordinary course of business."

> EXAMPLE 2512–4 Same facts as Example 2512–3, except that Herb sold the car for $4,200 to his son Jerry, who shortly thereafter advertised and sold it for $6,700. Herb may have great difficulty establishing to the satisfaction of the IRS that the deal was at arm's length, inasmuch as it was transacted between relatives and not in the ordinary course of business. Herb could possibly succeed if he could establish, among other things, his ignorance of prevailing market conditions.

Deductible Gifts

Four types of gifts are fully deductible, resulting in no tax on the transfer. First, gifts to qualified charities are fully deductible. Second, under the unlimited marital deduction, gifts to a spouse are fully deductible, provided that they are not terminable interests.[4] Third and fourth, any qualified transfer to an educational institution for tuition and any transfer to a provider of medical care on behalf of an individual are fully deductible, provided that the transfers are made directly to these parties, and not the individuals themselves.

---

[4]The gift tax marital deduction was first enacted in 1948, allowing a deduction for up to 50 percent of the value of noncommunity property gifts made to a spouse. TRA 76 changed this limit to 100 percent of the first $100,000, no deduction for the next $100,000, and 50 percent for all amounts exceeding $200,000. The present unlimited gift tax marital deduction became effective in 1982. For an analysis of terminable interests, see the discussion on the estate tax marital deduction in Chapter 6, and the material on the marital trust in Chapter 12.

The Gift Tax Annual Exclusion

The first $10,000 of the total annual value of gifts of a *present* interest to each donee is excluded from the donor's taxable gifts. Present interests are distinguished from future interests, which have been earlier defined as interests whose possession or enjoyment is delayed.

EXAMPLE 2503–1 This year, Mom gave Daughter a corporate bond valued at $24,300. Even though Daughter may not collect the par value until maturity, and even though the periodic interest income is payable in the future, the gift is of a present interest and qualifies for the annual exclusion. Daughter has a present right to enjoy the bond, for example, by selling it. Assuming that Mom, a widow, made no other gifts to Daughter during the year, the taxable value of the gift is $14,300.

EXAMPLE 2503–2 Changing the facts of Example 2503–1, if Mom executed an enforceable contract for a small amount of consideration to deliver the bonds to Daughter in one year, the gift, which is taxable this year, is of a future interest and will not qualify for the annual exclusion. The value of the gift is the present fair market value of the contract, which could be determined by calculating the present discounted value of the bond's forecasted worth one year from now.

Most problems regarding future interest gifts arise in the context of trusts.

EXAMPLE 2503–3 T creates an irrevocable living trust, funding it with dividend-paying common stock worth $8,000. Under the terms of the trust, the trustee is required to accumulate all income for 10 years. Additionally, no principal may be distributed during that time. At the expiration of 10 years, the trust terminates and all principal and accumulated income is payable to B, or if B is dead, to B's estate. Assuming B is currently an adult, T has made a gift of a future interest of $8,000, for which no annual exclusion will be available. Beneficiary B's possession and enjoyment is delayed.

EXAMPLE 2503–4 Altering the facts a bit in Example 2503–3, assume that instead of accumulating the income, the trustee is required to pay all income to A, an adult, at least annually. The result is that a portion of the value of the stock will represent a gift of a present interest and will qualify for the annual exclusion. Upon creation of the trust, two interests arose: a *present interest in the income* for 10 years, and a remainder interest. Using the appropriate table (found in IRS Regulations 25.2512-5) showing the present value of an income interest for a period certain, the value of the interest equals 61.4457 percent of the value of the stock.[5] The product of this amount and $8,000, or $4,916, represents a gift of a present interest. Hence, the total taxable gift equals $3,084, since this represents the value of the future (remainder) interest which does not qualify for the annual exclusion.

The next example illustrates an exception for gifts of future interests on behalf of minors.

EXAMPLE 2503–5 F transfers property into an irrevocable trust with the trustee permitted to expend principal and income for the benefit of her minor son. When son reaches age 21, the trust terminates and all principal and accumulated income will be distributed to him. Under the exception of §2503c, the entire value of the property qualifies for the annual exclusion.

This example represents situations in which grantors choose to accumulate income rather than put it into the hands of minor children. §2503c allows this accumulation without denial of the annual exclusion. In the absence of §2503c, grantors might be encouraged to make outright gifts to minors, a practice that many argue would run contrary to public policy. A further discussion of gifting to minors will be found in Chapter 13. To qualify for §2503c, the provisions of the transfer must specify that (1) the income and principal may be spent for the benefit of the minor before age 21 and (2) any amount not so spent will either pass to the minor when he or she reaches age 21 or, if the minor dies before that age, the amount will be payable to the minor's estate.

Gift Splitting

Gift splitting is conceptually similar to federal spousal income splitting on a joint income tax return. For example, if husband earns $48,000 taxable *income,* and wife earns $2,000, higher income taxes would be paid if each spouse filed a separate return than if both filed a joint return, reporting the single amount $50,000. In effect, a joint return will result in a tax calculated by applying the rate schedule to one half, or $25,000, and multiplying the tax by two. Total income taxes are lower for several reasons, including

---

[5]The values found in Table 10 of Appendix A are similar in amount.

the fact that progressively higher marginal rates may be avoided and, that more importantly, wife might not otherwise be able to enjoy the full benefits of the standard deduction and the personal exemption.[6]

Under federal gift tax law, spouses may also split a *gift*. Thus, a gift by one spouse of his or her individually owned property may, with the consent of the other spouse, be treated as if it were made one half by each spouse.

> EXAMPLE 2513–1 Wife wishes to give $18,000 of her own cash assets to a nephew. Assuming no other gifts and no gift splitting, wife's taxable gift, after the annual exclusion, will be $8,000. Alternatively, wife can *split* this gift with husband, so that each spouse will be considered to have made a gross gift of $9,000. After each donor's annual exclusion, there will be no taxable gift for either spouse. However, a gift tax return must still be filed, and consent of the other spouse is required.

Completing the analogy with income splitting, gift splitting can lower gift taxes because it can permit the deduction of two annual exclusions, rather than one.

Powers of Appointment

Gift taxation of powers of appointment substantially parallels estate tax treatment. Hence, only general powers that are exercised or released, by the holder are taxable.[7] Further, a power won't be treated as a general power if (*a*) it was subject to an ascertainable standard or (*b*) it was exercisable only in conjunction with (1) the creator of the power or (2) an adverse party. Finally, similar to federal estate tax law, §2514 states that the lapse of a power will be considered a release only to the extent that it exceeds the greater of $5,000 or 5 percent of the property.

> EXAMPLE 2514–1 Dad transfers property into trust, with income to Mom for her life, then remainder to anyone Mom chooses during her lifetime or in her will. Although Dad, as donor, created a general power of appointment for Mom, the holder, he did not make a §2514 gift because he did not exercise, release, or let lapse a power he had

---

[6]These terms are explained in Chapter 8.

[7]Recall that a general power is a power by the holder to appoint either oneself, one's creditors, one's estate, or the creditors of one's estate.

originally possessed.[8] Only the holder of a power can exercise, release, or let a power lapse.

EXAMPLE 2514–2 Continuing Example 2514–1, if Mom, during her lifetime, appointed the remainder interest of the trust to anyone, she will have made a taxable gift; that is, she will have exercised a general power.[9]

EXAMPLE 2514–3 Barbara transfers $100,000 in property into an irrevocable trust for the benefit of her daughter, Sara, who is 18 years old. All income is to be accumulated until Sara reaches age 25, except that each year Sara has a noncumulative right to demand the greater of $10,000 or 5 percent of the corpus. At age 25, Sara is entitled to receive all accumulated income and will start to receive all income earned each succceding year for her life. Then, remainder to Sara's daughter, Jane. For every year that Sara fails to exercise her power, that year's power is considered to have lapsed, and Sara will be held to have made a gift (to Jane) of the excess of the amount exercisable over the statutory maximum. In the first year, the amount of the gift is $5,000.

Life Insurance

A taxable gift of life insurance can arise either prior to or at the death of the decedent. First, during the life of the decedent-owner, an *assignment* of ownership rights in a policy may constitute a taxable gift of the value of these rights. Ordinarily, a donor will assign all rights to a policy, and their total value is considered to be the policy's terminal value. However, in contrast to the assignment of ownership interests, the simple naming of a beneficiary by the owner does not constitute a taxable gift since no valuable property rights have been transferred; the beneficiary has a "mere expectancy," contingent upon the owner's not changing the beneficiary designation. The creation of such a contingent future interest does not constitute a taxable gift.

Second, a taxable gift of life insurance can arise at an insured's death. This will occur when the insured, owner, and beneficiary are all different parties.

---

[8]However, Dad may have made a gift (completed transfer for less than full consideration). An example would be if his transfer was into an irrevocable trust.

[9]And when Mom dies, her gross estate will include the date-of-death value of the property, under Sections 2041(a)(2) and 2036(a)(1).

EXAMPLE L–1 Wife purchases with separate property a $100,000 life insurance policy on husband's life, naming son beneficiary. Upon husband's death, wife will be held to have made a $100,000 gift to son.

EXAMPLE L–2 Changing the facts a bit in the preceding example, assume that husband purchased and owned the policy until his death, paying the premiums entirely with jointly owned funds or with community property. At husband's death, wife will be held to have made a $50,000 gift to son, reflecting her one-half interest in the proceeds.[10] Under typical state law, wife can legally require that half of the proceeds be payable to her.

We will see in Chapter 15 that estate planners typically avoid this tax trap by selecting the same person to be owner and beneficiary on a life insurance policy held on the life of another.

Gifts of Property in Joint Ownership

Ordinarily, gifts are made when a fee simple owner of property transfers his or her entire interest to the donee. Sometimes, however, a donor transfers only a fraction of the total interest owned. For example, a donor can transfer his or her property into joint ownership with another person.

The actual moment that a transfer into joint ownership will be deemed to have legally occurred will depend on the nature of the property. In general, ownership and possession of most types of property are usually considered transferred when documents are executed, evidencing a transfer of title. Thus, acquisition of a joint interest by the donee usually arises when the donor simultaneously acquires the asset and names the donee co-owner, or when the donor adds the donee's name as a co-owner of property already owned by the donor. Either way, a gift will usually occur at that time, and the value of the gift will be the net value of the property interest transferred at the time of the gift.

EXAMPLE JT–1 Uncle Charlie buys an automobile for $20,000 cash, *taking title* in joint tenancy with his nephew Brad. Charlie has made a gift of $10,000 to Brad in the year of purchase.

---

[10]The other $50,000 will be includable in husband's gross estate under §2042. Can you see why?

EXAMPLE JT–2 Changing the facts a bit in Example JT–1, assume that Charlie bought the car five years ago for $28,000, taking title as an individual. This year, when the car is worth $20,000, Charlie instructs the motor vehicle bureau to *change the title* to read: "Charlie Jones and Brad Smith, as joint tenants." At that moment, Charlie has made a gift to Brad of $10,000.

EXAMPLE JT–3 This year, Dad purchased a duplex building for $120,000, taking title in joint tenancy with his five adult sons. This year, Dad has made a gift of $20,000 to each son.

There are two principal exceptions to the rule that the inclusion of others as cotenants for less than full consideration results in an immediate gift. First, in the case of *joint bank accounts,* in most states a gift arises upon withdrawal of the funds by the donee, not upon creation of the donee's interest.[11] Second, for jointly held U.S. *government savings bonds,* a gift arises when the bonds are redeemed.

EXAMPLE JT–4 On June 1, last year, Mom deposited $20,000 in a savings account held jointly with Son, who withdrew $6,800 on February 1, this year. In most states, Mom will be considered to have made a gift to Son of $6,800 on February 1, this year.

Disclaimers

Suppose, for some reason, that the donee does not want to accept a gift that has been tendered by a donor. Inasmuch as the unified transfer tax system will include in the donee's tax base any gift property received by the donee and later transferred to another during lifetime or at death, a donee might wish to refuse the gift to minimize his or her own future transfer taxes. Section 2518 allows the donee, in some situations, to "disclaim" a gift. In effect, a valid disclaimer treats the gift as never having been made, and in the case of a deathtime transfer, treats the disclaimant as having predeceased the decedent-donor.

In order to properly disclaim, the following requirements must be met: (1) the disclaimer must be "an irrevocable and unqualified

---

[11]The statutes of a few states, such as New York, however, presume that a gift into a savings account arises at time of deposit, thereby giving rise to immediate federal gift taxation.

refusal . . . to accept" the interest; (2) the refusal must be in writing, (3) the refusal must be received within nine months after the later of (*a*) the date on which the transfer creating the interest was made or (*b*) the day on which the person disclaiming reaches age 21; (4) the intended donee cannot have accepted any interest in the benefits; and (5) as a result of the refusal, the interest will pass, without the disclaiming person's direction, to someone else.

> EXAMPLE 2518–1 Dad gives Son his vacation bungalow, completing the necessary transfer of title. After spending a weekend there, Son retransfers title to Dad, refusing the gift. Dad resumes vacationing there. Son's act is not a valid disclaimer because he *had already accepted* the interest and its benefits. Therefore, two successive completed gifts were actually made, first by Dad and then by Son.

> EXAMPLE 2518–2 Mom died, disposing by will all of her property to Dad. Within nine months of Mom's death, Dad, before receiving any interest or benefit in the property, presented a written refusal of the gift to the executor of Mom's estate. Dad has made a valid disclaimer, and he will not be considered to have ever owned that portion of the property, which will pass by intestate succession to the children.

Chapters 12 and 18 will demonstrate several ways that disclaimers can be used to save estate taxes. Example 2518–2 illustrates one of them, as Dad's disclaimer will reduce the size of his taxable estate at his death.

THE FEDERAL GENERATION-SKIPPING TRANSFER TAX

One fundamental policy objective of federal wealth transfer taxation is to tax all individual wealth in excess of a certain amount each time it passes to the next generation. Can the unified estate and gift tax laws completely achieve that goal? They can not. It is true that they can ensure that property is subject to tax once when it is transferred. But since they both fail to distinguish between transfers made to the next generation and transfers made to more distant generations, they can not possibly meet that goal.

> EXAMPLE 7–1 Grandpa died last year leaving most of his large estate to his *granddaughter*. An estate tax will be imposed on this amount now, but not at the death of any of his children.

Only a tax that explicitly addresses the generational relationship between transferor and transferee can consistently tax wealth as it passes to succeeding generations. The generation-skipping transfer tax is designed to meet that objective.

The first generation-skipping transfer tax was enacted in 1976. Although planners found it quite complicated, they quickly learned that the tax was easy to circumvent.[12] As a result, in 1986, Congress acknowledged its error by repealing it retroactively, and at the same time, enacting the new, more comprehensive law described below.

Nature of the Generation-Skipping Transfer Tax

The current federal Generation Skipping Transfer Tax (GSTT), effective September 1985, imposes a tax on those three types of generation-skipping transfers that would otherwise escape both the estate tax and the gift tax. The GSTT is reported on Form 706 (for gifts) and Form 709 (for transfers at death), which are shown in Appendices 5B and 5C. These transfers are called direct skips, taxable terminations, and taxable distributions. Under each, a transfer or its equivalent is made to or for the benefit of a *skip person;* that is, a beneficiary who is at least two generations younger than the transferor.[13] Contrasting the three: While a taxable termination and a taxable distribution always involve a trust, a direct skip may involve a trust, but it usually will not.

Direct skip.   A direct skip is a transfer to a skip person that is subject to the gift tax or the estate tax. The GSTT is imposed at the time of the direct skip.

> EXAMPLE 7–2 In his will, T, who recently died, left $60,000 cash each to a grandnephew and a granddaughter. Both transfers are direct skips, subject to immediate GSTT taxation.

It should be clear from the definition that direct skips can be simultaneously subject to both estate or gift taxation *and* to the

---

[12]There is widespread speculation among planners that no one ever filed a return under the old Generation-Skipping Transfer Tax.

[13]A "skip person" can also be a *trust,* if all interests in the trust are held by skip persons, or if there is no person holding an interest in the trust and at no time after the transfer may a trust distribution be made to a nonskip person.

GSTT. In effect, a double tax will result, under the rationale that the property (*a*) immediately passes to an individual who is at least two generations younger than the transferor, and (*b*) would not otherwise be taxed to the generation that was skipped.[14]

The *transferor* (or the transferor's estate) is liable for the GSTT on direct skips.

Taxable termination. The Code's definition of a taxable termination is complex.[15] Paraphrasing at the risk of some slight inaccuracy: A taxable termination is a termination of a nonskip person's interest in income or principal of a *trust* with the result that skip persons become the only remaining trust beneficiaries. The GSTT is imposed at the time of the taxable termination.[16]

> EXAMPLE 7–3 T places property in trust, with income to T's daughter D for life, then remainder to T's grandchildren, per stirpes. A taxable termination will occur at *D's* death, because at that time, T's grandchildren, who are all skip persons, become the only remaining trust beneficiaries.

The *trustee* is liable for the GSTT on taxable terminations.

Taxable distribution. A taxable distribution is any distribution of property out of a *trust* to a skip person (other than a taxable termination or a direct skip). The GSTT is imposed at the time of the distribution.

---

[14]Observe that in the context of direct skips, since the current GSTT makes no distinction between a transfer across two generations and one across more than two, it can not fully implement the policy objective stated at the beginning of this section.

[15]Under §2612(a), a taxable termination is "the termination (by death, lapse of time, release of power, or otherwise) of an interest of property held in a trust unless (*a*) immediately after such termination, a nonskip person has an interest in such property, or (*b*) at no time after such termination may a distribution (including distributions on termination) be made from such trust to a skip person."

[16]Unlike a taxable distribution and a taxable termination, a direct skip is taxed on a "tax exclusive" basis. That is, the amount of the tax is excluded from the taxable amount. Mathematically, the tax can be calculated from the following formula: Tax = [(amount of taxable termination) × (tax rate)]/(1 + tax rate). Thus, at a tax rate of 55 percent, the tax on a one dollar taxable termination is about 35 cents, calculated as follows: [($1) × (.55)]/(1 + .55) = $.35. The upshot is a lower, 35 percent rate, derived theoretically in the same manner that the rate is calculated when "grossing up" the FET can be avoided.

EXAMPLE 7–4 H, trustee of a trust established by T, is holder of a power of appointment in which GD, T's granddaughter, is a permissible appointee. This year, H distributed $19,000 to GD. This is a taxable distribution.

The *transferee* is liable for the GSTT on taxable distributions.

GSTT rates. All transfers subject to the GSTT are taxed at the highest marginal unified transfer tax in existence that year. Thus, all taxable generation-skipping transfers will be subject to a 55 percent rate through 1992, and a 50 percent rate thereafter.[17]

Exceptions to GSTT Taxation

The impact of the GSTT is considerably softened by four exceptions: the GSTT annual exclusion; the predeceased parent direct skip rule; the $2 million exemption for direct skips prior to 1990; and the $1 million lifetime exemption for all skips.

GSTT annual exclusion. Similar to the gift tax, a $10,000 annual exclusion per donor per donee is available under the GSTT for *lifetime* generation-skipping transfers. A spouse can consent to *splitting* gifts of up to $20,000 made by the other spouse.

EXAMPLE 7–5 In 1987, Grandpa plans to give granddaughter $10,000 each year for the rest of his life. These generation-skipping transfers will be entirely excluded from computation of the GSTT.

Predeceased parent direct skip rule. Ordinarily, a grandparent and a grandchild are considered two generations apart, and a transfer from the former to the latter will trigger the GSTT. However, if a *parent* predeceases both of them, for purposes of direct skips, the grandparent and the grandchild are treated as if they are only one generation apart.[18]

EXAMPLE 7–6 Sonny lost his dad in an auto accident last year. This year, Sonny's *grandmother* died, and left him the bulk of her sizable

---

[17]See Table 4 in Appendix A at the end of the text.

[18]The Code definitions of parent and grandchild are generous. For the rule to apply, the *parent* of the transferee must be a lineal descendant of either the transferor or the transferor's spouse. And the *grandchild* must be a grandchild of the transferor, the transferor's spouse, or the transferor's former spouse.

estate. The property will be subject to the estate tax but not to the GSTT.

EXAMPLE 7–7 Same facts as Example 7–6 above, except that the decedent-transferor was Sonny's *grandaunt*. At her death, the property will be subject to both the estate tax and the GSTT.

$2 million exemption for direct skips prior to 1990. The first $2 million in *direct skips* by a transferor *to each grandchild* is exempt from the GSTT. And with spousal consent, up to $4 million transferred by one spouse may be "split" by the spouses. This exemption expires at the end of 1989.

EXAMPLE 7–8 Fickett and his wife Audrey, aging owners of a $40 million winery, have six grandchildren. In 1988, the Ficketts make gifts in trust of $4 million in stock in the corporation to each grandchild. The gifts will be subject to gift tax, but not to the GSTT.

$1 million lifetime exemption for all skips. For each individual donor, the first $1 million in direct or indirect lifetime skips to all skip persons combined is exempt from the GSTT. Again, with spousal consent, up to $2 million transferred by one spouse may be split by the spouses.

EXAMPLE 7–9 In each of the years 1986, 1987, and 1988, Beulah, a widow, makes lifetime gifts of $600,000 in property into a trust for her grandniece. In 1986, Beulah allocates $590,000 in transfers to her lifetime GSTT exemption, paying no GSTT. In 1987, Beulah allocates an additional $410,000 to her lifetime exemption, thus leaving $180,000 subject to the GSTT. At this point, she has fully allocated her $1 million exemption. Consequently, in 1988, Beulah can only shelter $10,000 of her last gift, with the result that $590,000 will be subject to the GSTT.

EXAMPLE 7–10 Assume the facts in Example 7–9, and that the trust corpus appreciates to $2 million at Beulah's death in 1992. No additional GSTT will be due. The value of the property is determined at the time the tax is imposed.

This chapter has focused on certain qualitative aspects of the federal gift tax and the Generation-Skipping Transfer Tax. The next chapter will present an overview of the federal income tax.

RECOMMENDED READING

(ANONYMOUS.) "Additional Thoughts on the Impact of the New Generation-Skipping Tax Provision." *Estate Planning,* July 1987, pp. 234–6. Commentary on Mulligan/Boulton articles.

GANS, MITCHELL M. "Gift Tax: Valuation Difficulties and Gift Completion." *The Notre Dame Law Review* 58 (February 1983), pp. 493–536.

HALBACH, EDWARD C. JR. "Generation-Skipping: Planning Opportunities and Drafting Problems." University of Miami 22nd Estate Planning Institute, 1988.

HELLIGE, JAMES R., and WILLIAM C. WEINSHEIMER. "A New Set of Complexities." *Trusts & Estates,* March 1987, pp. 8–26, and April 1987, pp. 10–26. Two-part article on the new GSTT.

KALIK, MILDRED, and PAM H. SCHNEIDER. "The New Generation-Skipping Transfer Tax." *Estate Planning 1987,* California Continuing Education of the Bar.

KATZENSTEIN, ANDREW M. "The New Generation-Skipping Tax: A Road Map." *Taxes,* April 1987, pp. 259–66.

MCCAFFREY, CARLYN S., and MILDRED KALIK. "Using Valuation Clauses to Avoid Gift Taxes." *Trusts & Estates,* October 1986, pp. 47–58.

MULLIGAN, MICHAEL D., and SCOT W. BOULTON. "New Generation-Skipping Tax: Higher Rates, Broadened Scope." *Estate Planning,* January 1987.

———. "Planning Opportunities that Take Advantage of the New Generation-Skipping Transfer Tax." *Estate Planning,* March 1987, pp. 66–71.

ROSENBERG, STANLEY. "Expensive Transfers." (Discusses the new GSTT.) *Financial Planning,* October 1987, pp. 224–29.

SHERMAN, JEFFREY G. "'Tis a Gift to Be Simple: The Need for a New Definition of 'Future Interest' for Gift Tax Purposes." *Cincinnati Law Review* 55, no. 3, pp. 585—675. (Describes how the terms *present interest* and *future interest* have inconsistently evolved through the years, and proposes new definitions.)

SIMINERIO, ANDREW C. "With Strings Attached: Federal Income Tax Consequences to Donors of Conditional Gifts." *Duquesne Law Review* 20 (1982), pp. 463–83.

QUESTIONS AND PROBLEMS

1. List the customary local law requirements for a valid gift.

2. Addie sells her empty lot, appraised at $22,000, to a stranger for $19,500. Is there a gift? Why or why not?

3. Would your answer to Question 2 change if the donee was, in fact, Addie's son? One of her employees?

4. Wayne and his wife Sharon own a parcel of land worth $20,000 as equal tenants in common. This year they give the land to their daughter Christina.
   a. Can this gift be split?
   b. If it could, would it help?

5. Assume that you are the holder of a general power of appointment. What action on your part, if any, might minimize total unified transfer taxes?

6. In 1985, Frank purchased a $280,000-face-value life insurance policy on his own life. A year later he assigned (gave) the policy to his son, when it had a terminal value of $110,000. Four months later, Frank died. Frank's wife had always been beneficiary. Explain all gift and estate tax consequences. (Hint: there are at least three).

7. A client asks you to explain when the acquisition by gift of joint-tenancy property is taxed.

8. Karen and Sal buy 100 shares of ABC Corp. stock for $21,000, writing a check on their joint (or community) checking account and taking title in joint tenancy. Has a gift occurred? Why or why not?

9. Give an example of a way in which a qualified disclaimer can be a valuable estate planning tool.

10. (a) If Jones gives Smith 200 shares of a nondividend-paying stock, is this a gift of a present or a future interest? Why? (b) Why might it matter?

11. Today Lois transfers $10,000 to an irrevocable trust that is required to distribute all income to her son, age 55, for his life. Then, remainder outright to his issue. Calculate the amount of Lois' taxable gift.

12. Explain the public policy reason for the exception under §2503c.

13. (*a*) Explain two reasons why gift splitting can be a valuable estate planning tool. (*b*) Would a "flat rate" gift tax (i.e., the same tax rate regardless of transfer size) eliminate its attractiveness?

14. In 1986, Joe gives $1 million cash to his daughter Mary, who gives it to her son Sal, who gives it to his sister Sue. (*a*) How many taxable gifts have been made? (*b*) Can §2518 help? (*c*) How about §2013?

15. Congratulations! You have just won the $40 million state lottery, entitling you to $2 million cash a year for the next 20 years. You wish to share your winnings equally with your spouse and your 28-year-old daughter.
   a. Are there any tax consequences?
   b. Could there have been any way to avoid them?

16. Five years ago, Francisco and Dagny executed a "joint and mutual will," which is a single will, revocable only by mutual consent. Essentially, it provided that the first to die leaves his or her property to the survivor, who then leaves everything to their children at his or her death. Francisco died today. Can you think of any immediate tax consequences to Dagny?

17. (*a*) Describe the GSTT. (*b*) What are its exceptions?

18. Grandpa Gus, a widower, wishes to leave a substantial amount of his $5 million estate to his two grandchildren. Determine the amount subject to the GSTT, if any, and the date that the tax will be incurred, for the following alternative dispositions.
   a. Outright gift this year of $1 million to each grandchild.
   b. Outright gift in 1990 of $1 million to each grandchild.
   c. Transfer now of $1 million into each of two revocable trusts, with income to Gus for his life, then income to Gus' daughter for her life (expected to be 10 years after Gus' death), then principal outright to the grandchildren. After Gus' death, daughter will have a general power of appointment over the trust property, subject

to an ascertainable standard. Assume that at daughter's death, the aggregate trust assets have doubled in value to $4 million.

d. Same as part *c,* above, except that outright distribution to the grandchildren may be delayed after daughter's death, since distribution will not be made until the youngest grandchild reaches age 30.

8

Introduction to the Federal Income Tax

In contrast to the federal estate tax, which is basically a tax on property owned at one moment of time, the federal income tax is a tax on income earned during a period of time, specifically one year. The income tax was first introduced during the Civil War and was repealed in 1871. It was reenacted in 1913, with the adoption of the 16th Amendment to the Constitution.

Today's income tax laws distinguish four different taxpaying entities: individuals, estates, trusts, and corporations. This chapter will examine principles of taxation of each, with the greatest emphasis on the taxation of individuals.

INCOME TAXATION OF INDIVIDUALS

The general scheme for the federal income taxation of individuals is presented in Table 8–1. Summarizing the table, gross income deductions are subtracted from gross income to arrive at adjusted gross income. Then the standard deduction (or total itemized deductions) and personal exemptions are subtracted, leaving taxable income. The tax is then calculated, from which credits are subtracted to arrive at the net tax.

Let's now examine each item in some detail. While reading this section, you are urged to refer to the copy of Form 1040, U.S. Individual Income Tax Return, included in Appendix 8A.

TABLE 8–1   Federal Income Taxation of Individuals (Form 1040)

Gross Income		$xxx,xxx
Less: Deductions from gross income		xx,xxx
Equals: Adjusted gross income		xxx,xxx
Less: Standard deduction or total itemized deductions	$xx,xxx	
Personal exemptions	x,xxx	xx,xxx
Leaves: Taxable income		xxx,xxx
Calculate the tax		xx,xxx
Less: Credits		x,xxx
Leaves: Net tax		xx,xxx

Gross Income

Code §61 reads, "Except as otherwise provided . . . gross income means all income from whatever source derived." Thus, an item of income will be includable as gross income unless it is expressly excluded by another section of the Code. The most common types of income *included* in gross income are compensation for services rendered (wages, salaries, commissions, etc.), business income, gains from dealings in property, interest, rent, dividends, alimony, annuities, and insurance and pension income. Examples of items *excluded* from gross income are lump-sum life insurance death proceeds, income from investments that represent a return of invested principal, gifts, devises, bequests, and interest on most state and local government obligations.

Deductions from Gross Income

The first group of deductions, called deductions from gross income (or deductions for adjusted gross income), includes trade or business expenses, certain nonreimbursed employee expenses (travel, etc.), losses from the sale of property, alimony payments, and certain retirement contributions.[1] These deductions, subtracted before arriving at adjusted gross income (AGI), may be taken whether or not the taxpayer chooses to "itemize" other deductions.

---

[1]A second group of deductions, called "itemized deductions," will be covered next.

Standard Deduction or Total Itemized Deductions

Since 1987, as a result of the Tax Reform Act of 1986 (TRA 86) individuals have been allowed a choice of deducting from adjusted gross income a fixed lump sum, called the *standard deduction,* or the actual sum of personal itemized deductions.[2] Of course, taxpayers will want to deduct the larger amount.

Standard deduction. The amount of the standard deduction is $2,540 in 1987 and $3,000 in 1988 for single taxpayers and $3,760 in 1987 and $5,000 in 1988 for married individuals filing jointly.

An additional standard deduction is allowed starting in 1987 for taxpayers who are at least 65 years old, or are blind. They are also permitted an additional $600 if married, or $750 if single.

For tax years beginning 1989, standard deduction amounts will be indexed (increased) for inflation, as measured by the consumer price index.

Itemized deductions. Itemized deductions are subdivided into two types. The first type, called *nonmiscellaneous itemized deductions,* include certain personal expenses, such as certain interest on residential loans, taxes, gambling and unreimbursed casualty losses, charitable contributions, and medical expenses. The second group, called *miscellaneous itemized deductions,* include fees paid for tax return preparation, tax planning, investment planning, and certain employee expenses not deductible from gross income, such as job-hunting expenses, union dues, expenses for a home office, and transportation expenses. Miscellaneous itemized deductions are allowed only to the extent that they collectively exceed 2 percent of adjusted gross income.[3]

---

[2]A similar choice was allowed in years prior to 1987, but the standard deduction was built right into the tax table and was called the "zero bracket amount."

[3]Interest expenses may or may not be deductible, depending upon the use of the loan. Interest expense incurred in connection with a trade or business is generally deductible. Interest in connection with investment or the production of income is generally deductible to the extent of net investment income. Interest in the amount of debt secured by the taxpayer's principal residence or second residence (called "qualified residence interest") is deductible up to the amount of the taxpayer's basis plus the cost of any improvements. Interest in connection with "passive" activities may be used only to offset passive income. All other interest is considered "personal interest," the deductibility of which is phased out by 1991. The details are quite complex.

From the above we can see that deductions from gross income are always usable, while itemized deductions are sometimes wasted: The first dollar of deductions from gross income will reduce taxable income, while only those itemized deductions in excess of the standard deduction will further reduce taxable income. Therefore, individuals with modest amounts of total itemized deductions (e.g., less than $5,000 for a married couple filing jointly in 1988) will find that these deductions are entirely wasted, and tax planning would suggest that taxpayers incur such outlays only for nontax reasons.

Personal Exemptions

The following additional amounts are deductible on behalf of the taxpayer, the spouse, and each dependent, as personal exemptions, in calculating taxable income:

Year	Personal Exemption
1987	$1,900
1988	1,950
1989	2,000

Beginning in 1990, the personal exemption will be indexed for inflation.

Starting in 1988, the tax benefit of the personal exemption will be phased out for individuals with larger amounts of taxable income. The phaseout procedure is illustrated in Example 8–3, a bit later.

Persons claimed as dependents on another individual's tax return will not be allowed a personal exemption. And the amount of their standard deduction is further limited to the greater of $500 or the amount of their earned income. Thus, to be able to take a larger standard deduction, dependents must receive earned income. Examples of *earned income* are wages, salaries, tips, and self-employment income. Examples of *unearned income* are interest, dividends, rent, royalties, and capital gains.

Taxable Income

The amount left after subtracting total exemptions is called taxable income.[4] A tax is then calculated, using the proper tax table.

Individual income tax rates are shown in Tables 1 and 2 of Appendix A at the end of the text. Table 1 depicts rates for married couples filing joint returns; Table 2 shows rates for single individuals with no dependents.[5] The trend in rates over time reflects the two-pronged rate revolution of TRA 86. First, TRA 86 "compressed" the number of rate brackets from 15 in 1986 to 5 in 1987 and finally to 2 beginning in 1988. Second, TRA 86 lowered most rates appreciably. From the tables we can see that the maximum unadjusted rate dropped from 50 percent in 1986 to 38.5 percent in 1987, and finally to 33 percent, beginning in 1988.[6]

The reader will note that for the tax year 1988, the maximum marginal tax rate of 33 percent applies to the *next to highest* taxable income bracket rather than the highest. Congress chose to place a 5 percent rate surcharge on a specified amount of joint income in excess of $71,900 to accomplish two tax policy objectives. First, the surtax is intended to eliminate the tax benefit of the 15 percent rate bracket. Second, the surtax is designed to phase out the tax

---

[4]Certain higher-income taxpayers may be subject to an additional tax, called the "alternative minimum tax" (AMT), which has a flat 21 percent rate. In essence, the taxpayer will apply this rate to the excess of "alternative minimum taxable income" over $30,000 ($40,000 for married individuals filing jointly) to arrive at the tentative AMT. The excess, if any, of tentative AMT over the taxpayer's regular tax is the net AMT due. Alternative minimum taxable income is defined as regular taxable income, *plus or minus* "adjustments" (such as excess accelerated depreciation, passive activity losses [both added] and certain itemized deductions [subtracted], *plus* certain "preference items" (such as certain incentive stock option income, tax-exempt interest on newly issued private activity bonds, and untaxed appreciation on charitable contributions of appreciated property). The Congressional purpose of the AMT is to ensure that high income taxpayers who normally pay no tax due to tax preferences will pay at least some federal income tax.

[5]Other rate tables not included in the appendix are for an unmarried head of household, and a married individual filing separately.

[6]As we'll see later, an exception to the rate cuts is the maximum effective tax rate on long-term capital gains, which increased under TRA86 from 20 to 28 percent (a 40 percent jump).

benefit of any personal exemptions taken. Each will be covered briefly.[7]

1. 5 percent surtax to eliminate the 15 percent rate. Beginning in 1988, higher-income taxpayers will pay an additional 5 percent tax on all taxable income exceeding a given amount up to a stated limit. For single taxpayers, this surtax is imposed on taxable income between $43,150 and $89,560. For married couples filing joint returns, it is imposed on taxable income between $71,900 and $149,250.

> EXAMPLE 8–1 The Perkos file a 1988 joint income tax return on taxable income of $80,000. Without the surcharge, their total tax would be $18,532.50, which is the sum of $4,462.50 (= $29,750 × .15) and $14,070 (= ($80,000 − 29,750) × .28). The average tax rate on this tax is 23.17 percent (= $18,532.50/$80,000). A 5 percent surcharge on taxable income in excess of $71,900 will increase the Perkos' tax bill by $405 (= ($80,000 − $71,900) × .05). Thus, their total tax will be $18,937.50, for an average tax rate of 23.67 percent. At the Perkos taxable income level, the surtax did raise their average tax rate a bit, but not to the point at which all income would be taxed at 28 percent.

> EXAMPLE 8–2 The Greers file a 1988 joint income tax return on taxable income of $149,250. Without the surcharge, their total tax would be $37,922.50, which is the sum of $4,462.50 (= $29,750 × .15) *and* $33,460 (= ($149,250 − $29,750) × .28). The average tax rate on this tax is 25.41 percent (= $37,922.50/$149,250). A 5 percent surcharge on taxable income between $71,900 and $149,250 will increase the Greer's tax bill by $3,867.50 (= ($149,250 − $71,900) × .05). Thus, their total tax will be $41,790, for an average tax rate of exactly 28.00 percent.

Example 8–2 should make clear why the surtax to eliminate the 15 percent rate need not be imposed on any joint income in excess of $149,250; at that point the total tax is sufficient to reflect a 28 percent rate on all income. However, the rate table in Appendix A shows a 33 percent rate applied to taxable income in excess of $149,250. This excess is needed to accomplish the second policy objective, described next.

---

[7]The two surtax explanations covered next may be skipped without significant comprehension loss.

2. Phaseout of personal exemptions. Beginning in 1988, the tax benefit of any personal exemptions taken will be gradually phased out for taxpayers having taxable income in excess of the stated limits mentioned above, which are $149,250 of joint return income and $89,560 of single return income. Based on an additional surtax of 5 percent, each $1,950 exemption taken in 1988 ($2,000 in 1989) is totally phased out when the amount $10,920 ($11,200 in 1989) is subjected to the surtax.[8] Thus, a married couple with four exemptions and taxable income of at least $192,930 will find that $43,680 (= 4 × $10,920) will be taxed at 33 percent (= 28 percent + 5 percent). The upshot is an *average* tax rate of exactly 28 percent for joint income of at least $192,930.

> EXAMPLE 8–3 The Brunos, a married couple filing jointly with four personal exemptions, have taxable income of $200,000 in 1988. Their tax is $58,184, which can be calculated in three different ways. First, it is the sum of $4,462.50 (= $29,750 × .15) *and* $11,802 (= $71,900 − $29,750) × .28) *and* $39,939 (= ($192,930 − $71,900) × .33) *and* $1,979.60 (= ($200,000 − $192,930) × .28). Second, it is the sum of $56,204.40 *and* $1,979.60 (= ($200,000 − $192,930) × .28). Third, since their taxable income exceeds $192,930, it should be exactly 28 percent of their taxable income, calculated without subtracting any personal exemptions. (Proof: $58,184 = (.28) [($200,000 + (4 × $1,950)]))

Since the amount of taxable income over which the personal exemption phaseout is applied will depend on the number of exemptions taken, Table 1 in Appendix A shows alternative rates and brackets assuming three different total exemptions taken.

Importance of the marginal rate in planning. From the foregoing, we can observe that the 33 percent marginal tax rate applies over a broad range of base taxable income, and probably represents the actual marginal rate for well over one half of the total estate planning clients. As the next example demonstrates, marginal income tax rates are an important analytical tool in estate planning, especially when examining the impact of incremental income changes on the overall plan.

---

[8]Mathematically, the tax benefit of each personal exemption ($546 = .28 × $1,950) is just equal to the surtax imposed ($546 = .05 × $10,920).

EXAMPLE 8–4 Knudsen expects to earn $120,000 in taxable income next year. His 15-year-old daughter Cheryl will have only a very modest amount of taxable income. Ignoring deductions, Knudsen will save $180 for every $1,000 in taxable income that he can "shift" from his tax return (at 33 percent) to Cheryl's (at 15 percent). For every $1,000 shifted, Knudsen's income tax will fall by $330 (= $1,000 × .33), while Cheryl's income tax will only rise by $150 (= $1,000 × .15).

Chapters 9 and 13 will discuss income shifting in greater detail. For the present it should suffice to understand two basic income shifting principles. First, individuals cannot shift earned income. Second, unearned income can only be shifted by making a complete transfer of the *property* that generates the income, not just by transferring the income itself.

Credits

Credits are subtracted from the calculated tax, resulting in a "total tax," which is the net tax liability. Allowable credits include the child and dependent care credit, and the residential energy credit. There are several others.

At this point it would be useful to compare the tax rates for the income tax with those for unified transfer taxes. If we look at the 1989 income tax rates for married individuals with two dependents filing a joint return, we see that the marginal rates effectively start at 15 percent, rise to 33 percent at $71,900 taxable income, and then drop and level off at 28 percent at $194,050. In contrast, the effective marginal unified transfer tax rate remains at zero percent, due to the exemption equivalent, until the tax base exceeds $600,000 (after 1986) at which point the rate rises from 37 percent to 55 percent (after 1987) for amounts in excess of $3 million. Perhaps the single most outstanding difference is the amount excluded from the tax, $5,000 versus $600,000. This point is important in estate planning because certain expenses associated with death, such as final medical expenses, are deductible either on the estate's estate tax return or on the decedent's income tax return, and a major consideration, of course, will be the alternative tax savings generated by the deduction, an amount that depends on the marginal tax rates for each tax entity. For a further discussion, see Chapter 18.

Form 1040 Summary: An Example

EXAMPLE 8–5 Let's calculate the net income tax liability for Rob and Paula Farrell, who file a joint return for 1989. Income: Rob's salary is $68,000; Paula's salary, $36,000; cash dividends, $4,200; interest received, $3,800; deductions from gross income, $1,000. Itemizable deductions: "qualified residential interest," $8,000; property tax on residence, $5,000; charitable contributions, $2,000; job hunting expenses, $3,000. Assume four personal exemptions but no credits.

Gross income		$112,000.00
Less: Deductions from gross income		1,000.00
Equals adjusted gross income		$111,000.00
Less itemized deductions:		
Qualified residential interest	$8,000.00	
Property tax	5,000.00	
Charitable contributions	2,000.00	15,000.00
Leaves taxable income		96,000.00
Tax (= $16,264.50 + (.33) ($96,000 − $71,900)		$24,217.50
Less credits		—0—
Net income tax		$24,217.50

The Kiddie Tax

Beginning in 1987, all unearned income of children under age 14 in excess of $1,000 is taxed at the parent's marginal rate.[9] The source of the child's unearned income is immaterial; excess unearned income is taxed at the parent's rate even though they were not the original source of the property producing that income.

EXAMPLE 8–F Dale and Josette's joint taxable income in 1988 is $60,000, putting them in the 28 percent marginal rate bracket. Their 12-year-old daughter Lara has $2,100 in unearned income, including $1,300 in dividends from stock received as a gift from Dale's parents, and $800 in interest from a bank savings account, the deposits of which originated from earned income (compensation) to Lara when

---

[9]In 1988, the first $500 is sheltered by the standard deduction (the maximum standard deduction allowable on unearned income is $500 for persons claimed as dependents on another tax return), and the next $500 is ordinarily be taxed at the child's base rate of 15 percent. Both amounts will be indexed for inflation after 1988.

she was a newspaper delivery girl. The amount $1,100, which is the excess of $2,100 over $1,000, will be taxed at 28 percent.

This tax has come to be called the "kiddie tax," and has the effect of moving the federal government a step closer toward taxing the family as a single economic unit.[10] And it restricts income shifting, as we will see in Chapter 9.

Sale or Exchange of Property

In the preceding discussion of gross income, the reader may have noticed that one type of gross income listed appears to be quite different from the others. The item "gains from dealings in property" has many unique features and must be examined in greater detail.

Gain and loss.   Gain and loss realized from the sale of property are both calculated by subtracting an asset's "adjusted basis" from the "amount realized."

EXAMPLE 1001–1 The realized gain on sale of 100 shares of common stock having an adjusted basis of $13,000 and sold for $16,000 net of selling commissions equals $3,000. Had the stock been sold for $11,000, a loss in the amount of $2,000 would be realized.

Amount realized is defined as the fair market value of all money or property received.

EXAMPLE 1001–2 In Example 1001–1, the $16,000 and $11,000 sales proceeds could have been in the form of cash or in kind. Alternatively, the buyer could have canceled an existing debt owed by the seller. Hence, if the buyer actually paid $6,000 in cash and assigned to the seller title to his $8,000 automobile and also tore up a $2,000 IOU held on the buyer-debtor, the total amount realized would still have been $16,000.

Adjusted basis is defined in the Code somewhat tritely, but accurately, as the "basis" that is "adjusted." The initial basis for an asset that is purchased is usually its cost. On the other hand, the initial basis for assets acquired by gift and inheritance have different rules, which will be examined shortly. Adjustments to basis

---

[10]Perhaps the tax should really be called the "Mommy and Daddy tax" to more accurately indicate whose tax rates are, in fact, being used.

include items that reduce basis, such as allowance for depreciation, depletion, and obsolescence. Adjustments that increase basis include capital expenditures for improvement.

> EXAMPLE 1001–3 In Example 1001–1, the adjusted basis of $13,000 was probably simply the original purchase price of the stock. However, had the asset been a machine used in the taxpayer's business, adjusted basis would likely reflect its current book (depreciated) value, including all capital improvements made subsequent to its acquisition. Hence, the $13,000 adjusted basis could, for example, be the net result of a $27,000 original purchase price, less $17,000 in accumulated depreciation, plus $3,000 in capital improvements.[11]

In many cases, no significant adjustments to basis will have been made, so that gain or loss will simply equal the amount realized less the initial unadjusted basis.

Holding period.   A gain or a loss can be either short term or long term, depending on the length of the holding period (that is, how long the asset was held by the seller, and perhaps by prior owners, too). For assets acquired before June 23, 1984, or after December 31, 1987, a gain or loss is *short term* if the holding period is not more than one year; it is *long term* if the property is held more than one year. For assets acquired on or between those two dates, the holding period for long-term treatment is more than six months.[12]

Realized versus recognized gains and losses.   A gain or loss is *realized* when the basic transaction, typically a sale, has occurred. On the other hand, a gain or loss is *recognized* when the taxpayer reports the gain or loss on a tax return. Recognition will commonly occur either because tax law requires recognition in that year or because the taxpayer elects an option to report it that year. Common examples of gains or losses that may be recognized in tax years *after* the year of realization include installment sales (§453),

---

[11]Recapture of depreciation, which arises when a depreciable business asset is sold for greater than its adjusted basis, is beyond the scope of this text.

[12]By repealing the 60 percent deduction for long-term capital gains, TRA 86 has made the short-term versus long-term distinction far less significant. As we shall see a little later in the chapter, short-term and long-term capital gains will always be taxed similarly. In drafting TRA 86, Congress chose not to eliminate the distinction from numerous sections in the code partly to allow for future legislation which might resurrect it.

tax-deferred exchanges of like kind property (§1031), rollover of gain on sale of a principal residence (§1034), involuntary conversion (§1033, e.g., destruction of a house by fire with insurance proceeds used to purchase a replacement home), and certain capital transactions between a corporation and its shareholders.

Sale of property acquired by gift.   As described above, the basis for property acquired by purchase is its cost, which is adjusted by such items as depreciation and capital improvements, if any. In this section we will cover the somewhat more complex rule for determining the basis of property that has been acquired by gift, rather than by purchase. The next section will examine the rule for the basis of property acquired by transfer at death.

A simple rule applies for gift property whose date of gift value is greater than the donor's basis: The donee's basis will equal the amount of the donor's adjusted basis at the date of the gift. This is called the donee's *carryover basis*.

> EXAMPLE 1015–1 Ten years ago, donor purchased common stock for $10,000. Two years ago, donor gave donee the stock when it was worth $11,500. This year, donee sold the stock for $14,500. Since date-of-gift value was greater than donor's basis, donee has realized a gain of $4,500, the difference between the amount realized and donee's basis, which is donor's original basis.

> EXAMPLE 1015–2 Same facts as Example 1015–1, except that donee sold the stock for $7,000. Since date-of-gift value is still greater than donor's basis, donee's basis is still $10,000, the donor's old basis. Therefore, donee has realized a loss of $3,000, the difference between the amount realized and donee's basis.

However, if a donee sells gift property which had a date-of-gift value that is less than the donor's basis, for purposes of calculating a *loss* only, donee's basis will be date-of-gift value. For purposes of calculating a gain, though, the simple rule still applies; donee's basis will be the donor's basis at the date of the gift.

> EXAMPLE 1015–3 Donor acquired property several years ago for $6,000. Last year, when it was worth $4,200, donor gave it to donee, who this year sold it for $3,600. Since date-of-gift value is less than donor's old basis, donee's basis for loss is $4,200, and hence donee has realized a loss of $600.

TABLE 8–2 Summary of Examples 1015–1 to 1015–5

Example	Donor's Old Basis	Date of Gift Value	Amount Realized	Basis for Gain	Basis for Loss	Taxable Gain	Deductible Loss
1	$10,000	$11,500	$14,500	$10,000	$10,000	$4,500	—
2	10,000	11,500	7,000	10,000	10,000	—	($3,000)
3	6,000	4,200	3,600	6,000	4,200	—	(600)
4	6,000	4,200	7,100	6,000	4,200	1,100	—
5	2,000	1,450	1,800	2,000	1,450	—	—

In effect, a donee is not permitted to recognize the portion of the loss resulting from the decline in value while the donor held the property.

EXAMPLE 1015–4 Same facts as Example 1015–3, except that donee sold the property for $7,100. Although date-of-gift value is less than donor's basis, donee's basis for gain is $6,000, which is the donor's basis. Hence donee has realized a gain of $1,100.

Occasionally gift property having a date-of-gift value that is less than the donor's basis will be sold for an amount that is less than the donor's basis but more than date-of-gift value. In such case, the donee will realize neither gain nor loss.

EXAMPLE 1015–5 Several years ago, donor acquired an asset for $2,000 and later gave it to donee when it was worth $1,450. If donee sells the asset for $1,800, no gain or loss will be realized. There is no gain because the amount realized is less than donor's basis for gain, which is donor's old basis. There is no loss because the amount realized is greater than donee's basis for loss, which is the date-of-gift value.

Summarizing, with regard to sale of property acquired by gift, basis for calculating a potential gain is donor's old basis, while basis for calculating a potential loss is the lesser of (a) donor's old basis or (b) date-of-gift value. For comparison purposes, Table 8–2 summarizes the results of the above five examples.

Several additional points should be made with regard to the sale of gift property. First, in determining whether the donee's gain or loss is short term or long term, the length of the donor's holding period is added or "tacked on" to the length of the donee's holding period. Second, if the donor paid a gift tax on the gift, part or all of that tax is added to the donor's adjusted basis at the date of the gift.[13] Now let's incorporate these principles into a summary-type problem.

EXAMPLE 1015–6 In 1985, donor paid $22,000 for a personal computer for use in her business. After spending $1,000 in capital improvements and after depreciating it by $9,000, donor gave it to donee. It was then worth $21,300. Donor paid no gift tax. Fourteen months after acquiring the gift, donee sold it for $12,400. Donee has realized a $1,600 long-term capital loss. Since the amount realized ($12,400) is less than donor's basis ($22,000 − $9,000 + $1,000 = $14,000), a gain is not possible. Donee's basis for loss equals $14,000, the lesser of $21,300 or $14,000. A loss is realized since the amount realized is less than donee's basis. The $1,600 loss is long term because donee's holding period is the length of time the computer was held by both the donee and the donor, a period exceeding one year.

Sale of property acquired by death. When a person sells property that was acquired by death (i.e., bequest, devise, or inheritance), the simple rule for determining basis is that the seller's basis for both gain and loss is the value of the property at the date of the donor's death.[14]

EXAMPLE 1014–1 Frank recently sold a parcel of land for $12,000. The land had been purchased by Frank's dad for $500 in 1930 and passed to Frank by inheritance when Dad died in 1981. At Dad's death, the parcel was worth $11,300. Frank has realized a gain of $700, the difference between the amount realized and value at date of death.

----

[13]The amount added is that portion attributable to the appreciation while in donor's hands, if the gift was made after 1976; otherwise, the full gift tax is added. But in no case can the new basis exceed the fair market value of the gift at the date of the gift.

[14]If the alternate valuation date (discussed in Chapter 18) is elected on the federal estate tax return, then the seller's basis is the value of the property at that date, rather than at date of death. In general, evidence of a step-up in basis is essentially derived from the asset values as stated on the Form 706.

In the trade, a change in the basis of property acquired by death is called a "step-up" or "step-down" in the basis, as the case may be. To simplify expression when making general statements, we will refer to a change in either direction as a *step-up* basis.

If, at death, the decedent was sharing ownership in property, usually only the decedent's share will be stepped-up. The factor that determines whether any *surviving* co-owner can also enjoy a step-up in basis for his or her share depends on the legal form of co-ownership. In general, no surviving co-owner's share will enjoy a step-up in basis unless the asset is owned as community property.

> EXAMPLE 1014–2 At Ricky's death, he and his wife Victoria owned common stock as *joint tenants*. The stock was originally acquired by them for $16,000. When Ricky died, the stock was worth $22,000, and Victoria acquired Ricky's interest by right of survivorship. Four months later, she sold the stock for $29,000. Victoria will realize a gain of $10,000. Victoria's basis is $19,000, the sum of $8,000 (her interest, which is half of the original basis) plus $11,000 (Ricky's one-half interest passing to Victoria at death, stepped-up to one half the date-of-death value).

> EXAMPLE 1014–3 Facts similar to Example 1014–2, except that the stock was owned by Ricky and Victoria as *equal tenants in common*, and at his death, Ricky bequeathed the stock to Victoria. Victoria's gain is still $10,000, calculated in the same manner as Example 1014–2.

Consider the result for *unequal tenancies in common,* illustrated next.

> EXAMPLE 1014–4 In Example 1014–3, had Ricky originally paid $12,000 and Victoria paid $4,000 for the stock, Victoria's gain would be $8,500. Her basis would be $20,500, the sum of $4,000 (her interest, i.e., her purchase price) and $16,500 (Ricky's share of the property stepped-up to date-of-death value, which is $22,000 times the quotient of $12,000 divided by $16,000).

Now consider the different outcome for *community property.*

> EXAMPLE 1014–5 Facts similar to Example 1014–2, except that the stock was owned by Ricky and Victoria as *community property,* rather than in joint tenancy, with Ricky's interest passing to Victoria at his death. Victoria will realize a gain of $7,000. Victoria's basis is

$22,000, since the basis of both halves of community property will be stepped-up to the value at the date of a spouse's death.[15]

Thus, community property states have a decided advantage over common law states with regard to basis adjustments at death, and estate planners often recommend that clients residing in community property states hold growth property in community form, if possible.[16]

The *holding period* for property acquired from a decedent will be considered to have been long term, no matter how long the decedent and the devisee have held it. Thus, a decedent could have purchased the asset shortly before death and the devisee could have sold it shortly after death, and any gain or loss will still be long term.

Character of the gain—capital versus ordinary gains and losses. In general, for tax purposes, property falls into *three* classifications: capital assets, depreciable and real property used in a trade or business, and all other assets. Thus, the Code defines capital assets as all types of property except items such as (*a*) depreciable and real property used in a trade or business, (*b*) inventory, (*c*) copyrights, and (*d*) accounts receivables. Taxation of each of the three classifications will be examined briefly in reverse order in the discussion that follows.

First, gains from the sale of noncapital asset items *b, c,* and *d* are taxed at ordinary rates; that is, the entire gain is included in gross income. Losses from the sale of these items are subtracted from gross income.

Second, taxation of gains from the sale of noncapital asset item *a,* depreciable and real property used in a trade or business, depends on the holding period. For property held not more than one year (or six months, depending on the acquisition date), taxation is similar to that for other noncapital assets. For property held more than one year (six months for certain property), taxation is

---

[15]The IRS takes the position that states recognizing the concept "community property with right of survivorship" (e.g., Nevada and Wisconsin) will not have the advantage of a double step-up in basis.

[16]On the other hand, if a step-down in basis is anticipated, those estate planners will advise clients to convert community property to some other form of ownership to avoid a double step-down.

similar to taxation of long-term capital gains.[17] Principles of taxation of losses from the sale of depreciable business property is similar to the taxation of short-term capital losses, except for the absence of the $3,000 limitation, to be described shortly.

Third, taxation of capital assets depends on the holding period. Assuming that a taxpayer incurs only one capital transaction during the year, the following summarizes the tax consequences:

1. A *short-term gain* is added to gross income and is therefore taxed at ordinary rates.
2. A *long-term gain* is also added to gross income but in no event will be taxed at greater than 28 percent.
3. Both a *short-term loss* and a *long-term loss* can be deducted against gross income up to a maximum of $3,000 per year, with the excess "carried over" to future years.

Taxation of capital gains and losses for a taxpayer involved in more than one transaction in a given year can be complex. An oversimplified summary follows: First, short-term gains are netted against short-term losses, resulting in either a net short-term gain (NSG) or a net short-term loss (NSL). Similarly, the "longs" are netted, resulting in a net long-term gain (NLG) or a net long-term loss (NLL). The two resulting net amounts are then compared, with the following possible consequences:

1. Net long-term gain and net short-term loss:
    a. If NLG exceeds NSL, then the excess is includable in gross income but in no event will be taxed at greater than 28 percent.
    b. If NSL exceeds NSG, then the excess up to a maximum of $3,000 is deductible against current gross income; the rest is carried over.
2. Net long-term loss and net short-term gain:
    a. If NLL exceeds NLG, then up to $3,000 of the excess is used to reduce income; the rest is carried over.
    b. If NSG exceeds NLL, then that excess is included in gross income.
3. Net long-term gain and net short-term gain:
    a. NLG is treated like a long-term gain from a single transaction.

---

[17]Subject, however, to depreciation recapture.

b. NSG is treated like a short-term gain from a single transaction.
4. Net short-term loss and net long-term loss:
   a. NSL is treated like short-term loss from a single transaction.
   b. NLL is treated like a long-term loss from a single transaction.

We turn next to the second and third types of taxable entities discussed in this chapter: estates and trusts.

FEDERAL INCOME TAXATION OF ESTATES AND TRUSTS

Estates of decedents and certain trusts are independent legal and tax entities. Generally speaking, taxable income for these entities is computed in very much the same manner as for an individual. However, income received by an estate or trust may be currently distributed to its beneficiaries, and to avoid imposing double taxation the Internal Revenue Code often treats an estate or trust as a nontaxable *conduit* which merely passes income on from the source of the income to the beneficiaries. The conduit concept, as well as other unique aspects of trusts and estates, gives rise to a few tax principles that are somewhat different from those for the taxation of individuals, and we must examine them briefly. Fiduciaries for estates and all non-grantor trusts report their income on Form 1041, which is reproduced in Appendix 8B.

A simplified outline of the income taxation of estates and trusts is shown in Table 8–3. The general tax computation is quite similar to that for individuals. Essentially, deductions are subtracted from gross income to arrive at taxable income, on which a tax is calculated. Credits are then subtracted to arrive at the net tax.

Two major differences from the taxation of individuals are apparent from the table. First, only one group of deductions, not two, is subtracted. Second, the *distribution deduction* is unique to Form 1041. The distribution deduction implements the conduit principle. It is equal to the lesser of the amount distributed to beneficiaries or the amount of "distributable net income" (described later). Generally speaking, the larger the distribution of income to the beneficiaries, the larger will be this deduction. Correspondingly, the smaller will be the estate or trust tax, and the larger will be the amount the beneficiaries must include in their own tax returns.

TABLE 8–3 Federal Income Taxation of Estates and Trusts (Form 1041)

Gross income		$xx,xxx
Less: Deductions, including:		
Charitable deduction	$xxx	
Administration fees	x,xxx	
Distribution deduction	x,xxx	
Personal exemption	xxx	x,xxx
Equals: Taxable income		xx,xxx
Calculate the tax		xx,xxx
Less: Credits		xxx
Leaves: Net tax		$xx,xxx

Thus, from a tax point of view, the distribution deduction conduits distributed income from the estate or trust, which is not taxed on this income, to the beneficiaries, who are.

Estates

During the administration of the probate estate of a decedent, several income tax returns will probably need to be filed on behalf of the decedent. First, the *decedent's final income tax return* (Form 1040) is filed, covering the period of the decedent's last calendar year of life, from January 1 to date of death. Or, a joint return may be filed with the surviving spouse for the entire year. Second, the first *estate income tax return* (Form 1041) will be filed, covering the part of the year of death from one day after date of death until December 31.[18] Third, *estate income tax returns* (Form 1041) are filed for each succeeding year that the estate is in existence, with the last return covering the period January 1 to date of final distribution of the estate assets.[19] The material following will not cover the decedent's final income tax return; its tax rules are essentially

---

[18]This assumes a calendar tax year (January 1–December 31). Estates are permitted to choose a *fiscal* tax year (i.e., a year ending on the last day of some month other than December). Planning opportunities derived from the choice of tax year are discussed in Chapter 18.

[19]Again, assuming a calendar tax year.

ilar to those covered in detail for individuals. The remainder of this section will focus on income taxation of trusts, including grantor trusts, simple and complex trusts, and income taxation of the decedent's estate. Since decedents' estates are taxed in a manner similar to complex trusts, they will be described in that subsection.

Trusts

For any given tax year, a trust will fall under one of the following three categories: *grantor trust, simple trust,* or *complex trust.* Each will be described briefly.

Grantor trust. A grantor trust is a living trust in which the trustor, also called the grantor, has *retained sufficient interest* in the trust to make the income received by the trust taxable *to the grantor,* not to the trust or its beneficiaries. The income is includable in the grantor's Form 1040 for that year; hence, from an income tax point of view, the trust is treated as if it does not exist. In fact, a separate Form 1041 trust tax return is often not required to be filed.[20] Grantor trusts are therefore not income tax planning devices, and, in fact, in drafting trusts, the estate planning attorney often carefully attempts to avoid grantor trust status.

Grantor trust rules. Generally speaking, the most common categories of interests retained by the grantor (any one of which will subject all income from the property to be taxed to the grantor) are: reversionary interests, the power to control beneficial enjoyment, certain administrative powers, the power to revoke, and the right to trust income. Since the grantor trust rules will become important later when we study trust planning, we must examine each in some detail. Sections 671–678 included in Appendix B at the end of the text, cover these rules.

First, if the grantor of a trust created after March 1, 1986, retains a *revisionary interest* in the trust income or principal that, at the trust's inception exceeds 5 percent of the value of the property, it is a grantor trust.[21] An exception to the revisionary interest rule

---

[20]Regulations require filing of an *information return* by a trust whose trustee is someone other than the grantor. Of course, no tax would be payable.

[21]Prior to TRA 86, a grantor could retain a revisionary interest without risking grantor trust status provided that interest did not take effect until more than 10 years after the date of transfer of the property into the trust. Up to then, planners

is that a trust is not a grantor trust if a reversion can occur upon the death before reaching age 21 of an income beneficiary who is a lineal descendant of the grantor and who holds all present interests in any portion of the trust.

Second, a trust will be a grantor trust if the grantor retains the *power to control beneficial enjoyment* of corpus or income during the first 10 years. Code §674, which covers this rule, has many exceptions. The major exceptions include: (*a*) situations where the grantor can only distribute corpus under a power limited by a "reasonably definite standard" (similar to the "ascertainable standard" under §2041, Powers of Appointment); (*b*) situations where the power may be exercised only after the first 10 years; and (*c*) situations where an independent, nonrelated trustee is used.

Third, a trust will be a grantor trust if the grantor retains certain *administrative powers,* including the power to deal with the trust property for less than full consideration, the power to borrow from it without adequate interest or security, the failure to repay a trust loan before the beginning of the taxable year, and certain voting powers over stock held in the trust corpus.

Fourth, a trust will be a grantor trust if the grantor retains the *power to revoke* the trust within the first 10 years.

Fifth, a trust will be a grantor trust if, for the first 10 years, income from the trust is payable (or accumulated) for the *benefit of the grantor* or the grantor's spouse or if income may be used to pay premiums on a life insurance policy on the life of either the grantor or the grantor's spouse.

Finally, a trust will be a grantor trust if income is actually used to support someone the grantor is *legally obligated to support,* such as purchasing food for a grantor's minor child.

The following examples demonstrate several important grantor trust rules.

EXAMPLE 676–1 Grantor creates a *revocable living trust* which is primarily designed to avoid probate and reduce estate taxes upon death of the surviving spouse. The trust is not an income tax saving device during the grantor's lifetime because the income will be taxed to the grantor, who possesses the right to revoke the trust at any time.

---

widely advocated the use of the short-term or "Clifford" trust as an income-shifting device. TRA 86 killed it. For greater detail, see Example 676–2, and Appendix 14A.

EXAMPLE 676–2 Grantor creates a *short-term trust,* also called a Clifford trust, which is irrevocable for 10 years, with income payable to grantor's mother for the shorter of her life or 10 years, and then reversion to grantor. Created after March 1, 1986, this trust violates the grantor trust rules. The value of grantor's reversion exceeds 5 percent of the value of the trust property. Hence, the income will be taxable to the grantor.

EXAMPLE 677–1 Grantor establishes an irrevocable trust for her 16-year-old son, and the trust is required to use the income to purchase, among other things, clothing for the son. This trust violates the grantor trust rules because the income is required to be used to meet the grantor's *obligation of support.* The income is treated as for the benefit of the grantor, and thus will be taxable to the grantor.

EXAMPLE 677–2 If the son in Example 677–1, had been 18 years old, the grantor trust rules would probably not be violated because parents usually are not legally obligated to support adult children.

Simple trust.   A second category of trusts is the simple trust. For a given taxable year, a simple trust is a trust that is not a grantor trust and is required by its terms to distribute all of its fiduciary accounting income to the trust beneficiaries.[22] *Fiduciary accounting income* (FAI) includes most sources of federal gross income, including cash dividends, interest, and rent (reduced by certain expenses). In contrast, FAI does not include stock dividends, and capital gains, which are considered gains from the sale of corpus. The last two items are examples of income subject to taxation which are included in federal gross income, but which are called *principal,* not FAI. The distinction between FAI and principal derives from state law. Most states have adopted the Revised Uniform Principal and Income Act, which details these differences.

At the risk of overgeneralizing, the amount of FAI is equal to a trust's *distributable net income* (DNI), a tax concept which acts as the measuring rod for estate and trust income taxation.[23] The simple trust best demonstrates the conduit aspect of DNI for estates and trusts: In general, an estate or trust will not be taxed on

---

[22]There is a second requirement for a simple trust: It must have no provisions for charitable contributions.

[23]In this text we'll assume that FAI and DNI are equal. One factor making them somewhat unequal on a tax return is the incurring of expenses in generating tax-exempt income.

DNI received by the trust and paid out (distributed) to beneficiaries in the same taxable year.[24] Although such income is typically included in the trust's gross income, the trust will receive a deduction for that amount, since it is distributed to the beneficiaries. The deduction is called the *distribution deduction,* and it is calculated by finding the lesser of DNI or the amount actually distributed. Thus, in the case of a simple trust, the distribution deduction is equal to its DNI since its DNI equals the amount of income actually distributed. Consequently, a simple trust's only taxable income will be that portion of gross income attributable to principal, or corpus. One example of income taxed to a simple trust is, as we have stated, capital gains.

Continuing the application of the conduit effect, the recipient-beneficiaries of a simple (or complex) trust are required to include in their individual income tax returns their proportional share of the income that was deducted by the trust. Hence, double taxation is prevented because the simple trust acts as an untaxed *conduit* of fiduciary accounting income between the source of the income and the beneficiaries.

Simple trusts are allowed a $300 personal exemption.

EXAMPLE 643–1 The terms of a trust require that all fiduciary accounting income be distributed currently to its sole beneficiary. In the current year, the trust receives $6,000 in dividends, $4,000 in rent, and realizes a $9,000 short-term capital gain and a $1,000 short-term capital loss on the sale of stock. Assuming no deductions except the distribution deduction and the personal exemption, the trust's taxable income is $7,700, calculated as follows:

Trust gross income		$18,000
Less: Distribution deduction (DNI)	$10,000	
Less: Exemption	300	10,300
Leaves: Taxable income		$ 7,700

Notice that the trust is taxed only on the net capital gain, reduced by the amount of the exemption. The beneficiary will include in his or her gross income the amount $10,000, equal to the distribution deduction, which again is the lesser of DNI or the amount actually distributed. In this example these last two amounts are equal.

---

[24]Or within 65 days after the close of the taxable year.

Complex trust or estate. The third type of trust, called the complex trust, is defined as a nongrantor trust which, in a given year, either (*a*) accumulates some FAI (i.e., does not pay out all FAI, which it has received, to the beneficiaries) or (*b*) distributes principal. Essentially, the complex trust will, as in the case of a simple trust, receive a distribution deduction for the amount of its DNI that is actually paid (from income or principal) to the beneficiaries, who will then include that same amount, pro rata, in gross income on their individual tax returns. But unlike the simple trust, the complex trust will be taxed on any undistributed DNI. Finally, like the simple trust, it will be taxed on any amounts included in gross income originating from principal transactions, such as capital gains. With minor exceptions, *estates* are taxed similarly to complex trusts.

Applying the above rules for complex trusts, let's examine the tax effects when an estate or trust accumulates FAI and, alternatively, distributes principal.

An estate or trust that *accumulates income* or, in more exact terms, distributes *less* than its DNI in a given year will receive a distribution deduction equal only to the amount of the distribution and will therefore have to report the amount accumulated as taxable income. The beneficiaries will still report as taxable income only the amount received, which in the aggregate is equal to the amount deducted by the trust. Therefore, a full conduit in the amount paid to the beneficiaries still results, as in the case of a simple trust. The amount conduited however, is less than the amount for a simple trust with the same FAI. This is illustrated in Examples 661–1 and 661–2, below.

Alternatively, an estate or trust that distributes in a given year *more* than its DNI will be allowed a deduction only equal to the full amount of the DNI, which as we have said, essentially equals only the total of its FAI. Therefore, taxable income for such an estate or trust will include only items of gross income that do not constitute FAI (e.g., capital gains). The beneficiaries will be required to include in gross income only their pro rata share of the DNI; all amounts received in excess of DNI constitute a nontaxable receipt of capital (principal). On the other hand, income from principal transactions (e.g., capital gains) is taxable to the estate or trust, whether or not distributed. Again, a full conduit results, in the amount of FAI actually distributed. See Example 661–3, below.

A given trust can be a simple trust in some years and a complex trust in others. For example, a trust's terms could provide that all income shall be accumulated until the sole beneficiary reaches age 21, at which time all income will thereafter be required to be paid to her annually. The trust will be a complex trust during the first period and a simple trust during the second.

A $300 personal exemption is allowed for a trust that is required to distribute all of its income currently, while a $100 exemption is allowed for all other trusts. Estates, on the other hand, receive a $600 exemption.

EXAMPLE 661–1 During the second year of its three-year existence, the *estate* of decedent X earned $52,000 in dividends, $18,000 in interest, and $21,000 in short-term capital gains. During the year, the personal representative distributed $6,000 to the sole beneficiary. Thus, the estate's FAI and DNI equal $70,000. Assuming no deductions except the distribution deduction and the personal exemption, the estate's taxable income is $84,400, calculated as follows:

Estate gross income		$91,000
Less: Distribution deduction	$6,000	
Less: Personal exemption	600	6,600
Leaves: Taxable income		$84,400

The distribution deduction of $6,000 equals the lesser of DNI ($70,000) or the amount actually distributed ($6,000). The beneficiary will include that amount in her gross income.

EXAMPLE 661–2 Facts similar to Example 661–1, except that the entity is a *trust,* not an estate, which permits the trustee to accumulate fiduciary accounting income. All calculations will be the same except, since a complex trust is entitled to personal exemption of only $100, trust taxable income will be $84,900, or $500 greater than that for the estate.

EXAMPLE 661–3 Facts similar to Example 661–1, except the personal representative distributes $115,000 to the beneficiary. The estate's taxable income is $20,400, calculated as follows:

Estate gross income		$91,000
Less: Distribution deduction	$70,000	
Less: Personal deduction	600	70,600
Leaves: Taxable income		$20,400

The beneficiary will include in her gross income the amount $70,000; this is equal to the amount of the estate's distribution deduction, which again equals the lesser of DNI ($70,000) or the amount actually distributed ($115,000). Inasmuch as she received a total of $115,000, the amount $45,000 represents a nontaxable distribution of principal.[25] The net effect is that the estate pays the tax on the capital gain and the beneficiary pays the tax on the fiduciary accounting income.

A certain type of tax planning is eliminated by tax provisions embodied in the so-called *throwback rules*. Suppose a trustee had discretion to distribute or accumulate income, and she chose to accumulate some income in year one when the beneficiary had a high personal marginal income tax rate, and to distribute more than one year of income in year two when the beneficiary had a lower tax rate.[26] If allowed, tax savings could result because each year trustees could direct income to that taxpaying entity having a lower marginal tax rate. The throwback rules thwart this opportunity by requiring excess distributions to a beneficiary to be taxed to the beneficiary as if they had been received in the years in which the trust actually *received* and accumulated them. The throwback rules do not apply, however, to estates or to any accumulations during which a beneficiary was under the age of 21.

Estate and trust taxes are based on a common tax rate schedule, one different from that for individuals. A copy of the schedule is included in Table 3 of Appendix A at the end of the text.

The fiduciary income tax material introduced in the preceding discussion presents a simple overview of a complex subject. As with all tax issues, detailed client questions should be referred to a competent accountant or tax attorney.

THE CORPORATE INCOME TAX

Table 8–4 shows the basic scheme of corporate income taxation.

Corporate income tax rates differ from those for individuals or estates and trusts. The rates for tax years beginning after June 30, 1987, are 15 percent on the first $50,000 of taxable income, 25 per-

---

[25]Or a distribution of previously taxed accumulated income which might now be subject to the throwback rules (described next).

[26]However, the "compression" of tax rates by TRA86 reduces the likelihood of any significant tax saving.

TABLE 8–4 Federal Corporate Income Tax (Form 1120)

Gross income		$xxx,xxx
Less: Deductions	$xx,xxx	
Losses	x,xxx	xx,xxx
Equals taxable income		xxx,xxx
Calculate total tax		xx,xxx
Less: Credits		x,xxx
Leaves: Net tax		xx,xxx

cent on the next $25,000, 34 percent on the next $25,000, 39 percent on the next $235,000, and 34 percent on all taxable income in excess of $335,000.

> EXAMPLE 11–1 If a corporation has a taxable income of $400,000 in 1989, its income tax liability before credits will be $136,000, computed as follows:

15% of first $50,000	$ 7,500
25% of next $25,000	6,250
34% of next $25,000	8,500
39% of next $235,000	91,650
34% of last $65,000	22,100
Total tax liability	$136,000

The higher tax rate of 39 percent, which reflects a surcharge of 5 percent, has the effect of phasing out the tax benefit of the lower tax rates, in a manner similar to that effect on individual tax rates. Thus, the tax of $136,000 is exactly 34 percent of the $400,000 taxable income.

Many deductions and credits for corporations are similar to those for individuals. For deductions, similarities include trade or business expenses, interest, taxes, losses, bad debts, depreciation, charitable contributions, net operating losses, and research expenditures. Differences between individuals and corporations include the dividends-received deduction (explained below), the unavailability of the personal exemption and the nonexistence of the concepts adjusted gross income and itemized deductions.

Regarding capital gains, corporations have a choice as to how to have them taxed. The entire gain may be taxed at 34 percent, or it may be added to all other corporate income and taxed at the ordinary rate. Capital losses may be used to offset capital gains, similar to procedure individuals use, to arrive at a possible net capital loss. However, net corporate capital losses may not be deducted against ordinary income; they may only be carried back, then forward, to offset other years' capital gains.

Finally, corporations are permitted a deduction equal to 80 percent of the amount of dividends received from another corporation. This deduction is 100 percent if the dividend received from a corporation that is a member of a "controlled group" along with the deducting corporation.

This is the last chapter in Part 2 of the text, which has dealt with the *constraints* in estate planning. The next chapter introduces Part 3, the *techniques* of estate planning, by surveying the client goals underlying those techniques.

RECOMMENDED READING

ASCHER, MARK L. "When to Ignore Grantor Trusts: Precedents, a Proposal, and a Prediction." *Tax Law Review* 41 (1986), pp. 253–307.

BAETZ, W. TIMOTHY. "The Indefensible Kiddie Tax." *Trusts & Estates,* April 1987, pp. 27–31, 60.

BARNETT, BERNARD. "The Taxation and Timing of Trusts and Estate Distributions." *The Tax Adviser,* January 1984, pp. 8–24.

HARRIS, PHILIP E. "Allocating Basis for Jointly Owned Property Still Presents Unresolved Questions." *The Journal of Taxation,* April 1983, pp. 234–37.

RANDALL, GARY C. "Basis Considerations in Estate Planning: An Increasingly Important Approach." *Taxes—The Tax Magazine,* July 1983, pp. 459–67.

RHINE, DAVID S. "Planning Tips to Lessen the Adverse Impact of the Throwback Rules on Accumulation Trusts." *Estate Planning,* March 1981, pp. 88–90.

SCHNEE, EDWARD J. "Recent Decisions Restrict the Planning Opportunities of Grantor Trusts." *Taxes,* June 1986, pp. 394–7.

THOMPSON, MARK S., and JEB BROOKS. "The Step-Up Basis: Its Benefits for Estates." *Trusts & Estates,* September 1983, pp. 16–17.

WENIG, MARY M. "Estate Planning: The Name of the Game Is—Basis?" *The Review of Taxation of Individuals,* 1986, pp. 203–27.

West Federal Taxation: Corporations, Partnerships, Estates and Trusts. St. Paul, Minn.: West Publishing, current year.

West Federal Taxation: Individuals. St. Paul, Minn.: West Publishing, current year.

WESTFALL, DAVID. "Grantors, Trusts, and Beneficiaries under the Income Tax Provisions of the Internal Revenue Code of 1986." *Tax Lawyer* 40, no. 3 (1987), pp. 713–32.

QUESTIONS AND PROBLEMS

1. Outline the general scheme for the income taxation of individuals.

2. Contrast the two types of deductions for individuals.

3. Forty years ago, Curtis, now 82 years old, bought 10 acres of raw land for $10,000. Last year, when the land was worth $400,000, Curtis gave it to his son, Wright, who sold it three months later for $450,000.

   a. Assuming no gift tax, calculate any gains or losses from these transfers. Are they short term or long term? Explain.

   b. How would your answer to part *a* be different if instead of giving the land to Wright last year, Curtis died at that time and devised it to Wright? Explain.

   c. How would your answer to part *a* be different if instead of giving the land to Wright last year, Curtis sold it at that time to a stranger and gave (or devised) the cash proceeds to Wright, who in turn immediately repurchased the land and then sold it for $450,000? Explain.

   d. Based on your answers to *a, b,* and *c,* what would you recommend that elderly clients in Curtis' position consider doing?

4. Rework all of Question 3, assuming instead that Curtis originally purchased the land for $500,000.

5. Terry and Chris owned nonbusiness property as joint tenants. They purchased the property for $10,000, and at Chris's death it was worth $18,000. If Terry later sells it for $24,000, calculate the taxable gain.

6. Would your result in Question 5 differ if the property was held as a tenancy in common? As community property?

7. (*a*) Can a person die owning or having an interest in a large amount of property but not leaving an estate subject to income taxation as an independent entity? Why or why not? (*b*) If your answer to part *a* is "yes," how would you define an estate for income tax purposes?

8. Explain the conduit principle as applied to the taxation of estates and trusts.

9. Contrast a simple trust with a complex trust.

10. An *estate* earned $80,000 in dividends, $6,000 in short-term capital gains, and $14,000 in interest during the second of its four-year existence. Assuming no deductions except the distribution deduction and the personal exemption, calculate the estate's taxable income and the beneficiary's gross income related to the estate activity if the beneficiary received a distribution of

    a. $90,000.
    b. $96,000.
    c. $110,000.
    d. Would your answer to parts *b* and *c* change if the facts stated that the actual property distributed in excess of FAI came from corpus or, alternatively, accumulated income?

11. (*a*) How would your answers to Questions 8–10 change if the entity was a *trust* rather than an estate? (*b*) Would it matter how old the beneficiary is?

12. Is a grantor trust an estate planning device?

13. Outline the basic scheme of the corporate income tax.

14. (Note: This is a comprehensive problem requiring an understanding of all of the chapters covered so far.)

    The year is 1988. Brett and Robin are a happily married couple in their late 60s who have two children, Neil, aged 36; and Connie, aged 34. Brett retired last year. Presently, Brett and Robin have the following property interests. In community property states, assume that all tenancies in common (TIC) held by the spouses are actually held as community property.

$210,000	Home: Joint tenancy; cost, $50,000
$500,000	Money market fund: spousal TIC
$21,000	Autos: Brett's property
$160,000	Face value life insurance policy (L1) on Brett's life: cash value $31,000. Robin is owner and beneficiary. Premiums are paid with her separate property.
$90,000	Face value life insurance policy (L2) on Robin's life: cash value $17,000. Brett is owner and beneficiary. Premiums are paid with spousal TIC property.

$130,000 (Replacement value) qualified pension, with income payable to Brett for his life, then to Robin for her life. Brett's contributions (his property) totaled 30 percent of the total contributions made. The employer contributed the rest.

$490,000 Revocable trust (Trust A) was set up in 1982, funded with land, owned by Brett, then worth $180,000. Presently it is worth $490,000. On Brett's death, the trust terminates and all property passes to Connie.

$960,000 Apartment house: Brett's property.

Brett and Robin are planning to have their first wills drafted next month. The wills will basically say "All to surviving spouse."

In 1986, Brett made the following additional gifts: (1) $26,000 cash outright to Neil; (2) $14,500 cash outright to Connie; (3) $700,000 in stock into an irrevocable trust (Trust B) with all income accumulated until Neil reaches age 41. At that time, the trust terminates, and all income and principal will be paid to Neil and Connie equally. Brett has never made any other gifts.

a. Calculate Brett's total taxable gifts for the gift year, assuming gift splitting. This will be a single amount.

b. Calculate Brett's total gift tax liability for 1986. Assume no prior gifts.

c. Assuming that Brett died today, calculate the amount of Brett's probate estate.

d. Assuming that Bred died today, calculate the amount of Brett's gross estate. If applicable, be sure to gross up.

e. Assuming that Brett died today, calculate the amount, if any, of Brett's net estate tax. Assume no debts or expenses. Be sure to consider the marital deduction. Assume intestacy in a UPC state.

f. Assuming that Brett died today, could any of Brett's assets be administered under your state's "summary" probate proceedings? (If unavailable, assume that you are in a UPC state.) Why or why not? Be sure to consider each type.

g. In the fact description, two trusts are mentioned. In the gift year, *each* trust earned $1,000 in fiduciary accounting income and $2,000 in capital gains.

(1) For each trust, who will be taxed on the fiduciary accounting income?

(2) For each trust, who will be taxed on any gain?

h. If Brett died today, calculate the gain or loss if the home is later sold by Robin for:

(1) $400,000.

(2) $40,000.

(Numerical Answers: (*a*) $703,000; (*b*) $75,110; (*c*) $1,239,500; (*d*) $2,039,610; (*e*) $222, 470; (*h*1) $270,000 long-term gain; (*h*2) $90,000 long-term loss.)

APPENDIX 8A

Form **1040**	Department of the Treasury—Internal Revenue Service **1987** (O)		
	U.S. Individual Income Tax Return		

For the year Jan.–Dec. 31, 1987, or other tax year beginning , 1987, ending , 19 . | OMB No. 1545-0074

Label

Use IRS label. Otherwise, please print or type.

Your first name and initial (if joint return, also give spouse's name and initial) | Last name | Your social security number

Present home address (number and street or rural route). (If you have a P.O. Box, see page 6 of Instructions.) | Spouse's social security number

City, town or post office, state, and ZIP code | For Privacy Act and Paperwork Reduction Act Notice, see Instructions.

Presidential Election Campaign

▶ Do you want $1 to go to this fund? . . . . | Yes | No
If joint return, does your spouse want $1 to go to this fund?. . . | Yes | No

Note: Checking "Yes" will not change your tax or reduce your refund.

Filing Status

Check only one box.

1 Single
2 Married filing joint return (even if only one had income)
3 Married filing separate return. Enter spouse's social security no. above and full name here. _____
4 Head of household (with qualifying person). (See page 7 of Instructions.) If the qualifying person is your child but not your dependent, enter child's name here. _____
5 Qualifying widow(er) with dependent child (year spouse died ▶ 19). (See page 7 of Instructions.)

Exemptions

(See Instructions on page 7.)

Caution: If you can be claimed as a dependent on another person's tax return (such as your parents' return), do not check box 6a. But be sure to check the box on line 32b on page 2.

6a ☐ Yourself   6b ☐ Spouse

No. of boxes checked on 6a and 6b ▶ ☐

c Dependents
(1) Name (first, initial, and last name) | (2) Check if under age 5 | (3) If age 5 or over, dependent's social security number | (4) Relationship | (5) No. of months lived in your home in 1987

No. of children on 6c who lived with you ▶ ☐

No. of children on 6c who didn't live with you due to divorce or separation ▶ ☐

If more than 7 dependents, see Instructions on page 7.

No. of parents listed on 6c ▶ ☐

No. of other dependents listed on 6c ▶ ☐

d If your child didn't live with you but is claimed as your dependent under a pre-1985 agreement, check here . ▶ ☐
e Total number of exemptions claimed (also complete line 35) . . . .

Add numbers entered in boxes above ▶ ☐

Income

Please attach Copy B of your Forms W-2, W-2G, and W-2P here.

If you do not have a W-2, see page 6 of Instructions.

7 Wages, salaries, tips, etc. (attach Form(s) W-2) . . . . | 7 |
8 **Taxable** interest income (also attach Schedule B if over $400) . . . | 8 |
9 **Tax-exempt** interest income (see page 10). DON'T include on line 8 | 9 |
10 Dividend income (also attach Schedule B if over $400) . . . . . | 10 |
11 Taxable refunds of state and local income taxes, if any, from worksheet on page 11 of Instructions . | 11 |
12 Alimony received . . . . | 12 |
13 Business income or (loss) (attach Schedule C). . . . . | 13 |
14 Capital gain or (loss) (attach Schedule D) . . . . | 14 |
15 Other gains or (losses) (attach Form 4797) . . . . | 15 |
16a Pensions, IRA distributions, annuities, and rollovers. Total received | 16a |
  b Taxable amount (see page 11) . . . . | 16b |
17 Rents, royalties, partnerships, estates, trusts, etc. (attach Schedule E) | 17 |
18 Farm income or (loss) (attach Schedule F) . . . . | 18 |
19 Unemployment compensation (insurance) (see page 11) . . . . . | 19 |

Please attach check or money order here.

20a Social security benefits (see page 12) . . . . . | 20a |
  b Taxable amount, if any, from the worksheet on page 12 . . . . . | 20b |
21 Other income (list type and amount—see page 12) _____ | 21 |
22 Add the amounts shown in the far right column for lines 7, 8, and 10–21. This is your **total income** ▶ | 22 |

Adjustments to Income

(See Instructions on page 12.)

23 Reimbursed employee business expenses from Form 2106 . . | 23 |
24a Your IRA deduction, from applicable worksheet on page 13 or 14 | 24a |
  b Spouse's IRA deduction, from applicable worksheet on page 13 or 14 | 24b |
25 Self-employed health insurance deduction, from worksheet on page 14 . | 25 |
26 Keogh retirement plan and self-employed SEP deduction . . . | 26 |
27 Penalty on early withdrawal of savings . . . . | 27 |
28 Alimony paid (recipient's last name _____ and social security no. _____) . | 28 |
29 Add lines 23 through 28. These are your **total adjustments** . . . . ▶ | 29 |

Adjusted Gross Income

30 Subtract line 29 from line 22. This is your **adjusted gross income.** If this line is less than $15,432 and a child lived with you, see "Earned Income Credit" (line 56) on page 18 of the Instructions. If you want IRS to figure your tax, see page 15 of the Instructions . . . ▶ | 30 |

APPENDIX 8A *(concluded)*

Form 1040 (1987)   Page **2**

Tax Compu-tation	31	Amount from line 30 (adjusted gross income)	**31**
	32a	Check if: ☐ **You** were 65 or over ☐ Blind; ☐ **Spouse** was 65 or over ☐ Blind.	
		Add the number of boxes checked and enter the total here . . . . . . ▶ ⌐**32a**⌐	
	b	If you can be claimed as a dependent on another person's return, check here . . ▶ **32b** ☐	
	c	If you are married filing a separate return and your spouse itemizes deductions, or you are a dual-status alien, see page 15 and check here . . . . ▶ **32c** ☐	
	33a	**Itemized deductions.** See page 15 to see if you should itemize. If you don't itemize, enter zero. If you do itemize, attach Schedule A, enter the amount from Schedule A, line 26, **AND** skip line 33b . .	**33a**
Caution: ◀—	b	**Standard deduction.** Read **Caution** to left. If it applies, see page 16 for the amount to enter.	
If you checked any box on line 32a, b, or c **and** you don't itemize, see page 16 for the amount to enter on line 33b.		If **Caution** doesn't apply and your filing status from page 1 is: { Single or Head of household, enter $2,540 Married filing jointly or Qualifying widow(er), enter $3,760 Married filing separately, enter $1,880 }	**33b**
	34	Subtract line 33a **or** 33b, whichever applies, from line 31. Enter the result here	**34**
	35	Multiply $1,900 by the total number of exemptions claimed on line 6e or see chart on page 16 . .	**35**
	36	**Taxable income.** Subtract line 35 from line 34. Enter the result (but not less than zero) . . .	**36**
		Caution: If under age 14 and you have more than $1,000 of investment income, check here ▶☐ and see page 16 to see if you have to use Form 8615 to figure your tax.	
	37	Enter tax. Check if from ☐ Tax Table, ☐ Tax Rate Schedules, ☐ Schedule D, or ☐ Form 8615	**37**
	38	Additional taxes (see page 16). Check if from ☐ Form 4970 or ☐ Form 4972	**38**
	39	Add lines 37 and 38. Enter the total . . . . ▶	**39**
Credits (See Instructions on page 17.)	40	Credit for child and dependent care expenses *(attach Form 2441)*	**40**	
	41	Credit for the elderly or for the permanently and totally disabled *(attach Schedule R)*	**41**	
	42	Add lines 40 and 41. Enter the total	**42**
	43	Subtract line 42 from line 39. Enter the result (but not less than zero)	**43**
	44	Foreign tax credit *(attach Form 1116)*	**44**	
	45	General business credit. Check if from ☐ Form 3800, ☐ Form 3468, ☐ Form 5884, ☐ Form 6478, ☐ Form 6765, or ☐ Form 8586 . .	**45**	
	46	Add lines 44 and 45. Enter the total	**46**
	47	Subtract line 46 from line 43. Enter the result (but not less than zero) . . . . . ▶	**47**
Other Taxes (Including Advance EIC Payments)	48	Self-employment tax *(attach Schedule SE)*	**48**
	49	Alternative minimum tax *(attach Form 6251)*	**49**
	50	Tax from recapture of investment credit *(attach Form 4255)*	**50**
	51	Social security tax on tip income not reported to employer *(attach Form 4137)* . . .	**51**
	52	Tax on an IRA or a qualified retirement plan *(attach Form 5329)*	**52**
	53	Add lines 47 through 52. This is your **total tax** . . . . ▶	**53**
Payments Attach Forms W-2, W-2G, and W-2P to front.	54	Federal income tax withheld (including tax shown on Form(s) 1099)	**54**	
	55	1987 estimated tax payments and amount applied from 1986 return	**55**	
	56	Earned income credit (see page 18)	**56**	
	57	Amount paid with Form 4868 (extension request)	**57**	
	58	Excess social security tax and RRTA tax withheld (see page 19)	**58**	
	59	Credit for Federal tax on gasoline and special fuels *(attach Form 4136)*	**59**	
	60	Regulated investment company credit *(attach Form 2439)* . .	**60**	
	61	Add lines 54 through 60. These are your **total payments** . . . . . . ▶	**61**
Refund or Amount You Owe	62	If line 61 is larger than line 53, enter amount **OVERPAID** . . . . ▶	**62**
	63	Amount of line 62 to be **REFUNDED TO YOU** . . . . ▶	**63**
	64	Amount of line 62 to be applied to your 1988 estimated tax . . . ▶ ⌐**64**⌐	
	65	If line 53 is larger than line 61, enter **AMOUNT YOU OWE.** Attach check or money order for full amount payable to "Internal Revenue Service." Write your social security number, daytime phone number, and "1987 Form 1040" on it	**65**
		Check ▶ ☐ if Form 2210 (2210F) is attached. See page 20. **Penalty: $**	

Please Sign Here
Under penalties of perjury, I declare that I have examined this return and accompanying schedules and statements, and to the best of my knowledge and belief, they are true, correct, and complete. Declaration of preparer (other than taxpayer) is based on all information of which preparer has any knowledge.

Your signature ▶		Date	Your occupation
Spouse's signature (if joint return, BOTH must sign) ▶		Date	Spouse's occupation

Paid Preparer's Use Only

Preparer's signature ▶		Date	Check if self-employed ☐	Preparer's social security no.
Firm's name (or yours if self-employed) and address ▶			E.I. No.	
			ZIP code	

U.S. GOVERNMENT PRINTING OFFICE: 1987-0-183-081 E.I. NO. 94-2249262

APPENDIX 8B

Form **1041** Department of the Treasury Internal Revenue Service	**U.S. Fiduciary Income Tax Return** For the calendar year 1987 or fiscal year beginning _____, 1987, and ending _____, 19 ___	OMB No. 1545-0092 **1987**

Check applicable boxes:
- ☐ Decedent's estate
- ☐ Simple trust
- ☐ Complex trust
- ☐ Grantor type trust
- ☐ Bankruptcy estate
- ☐ Family estate trust
- ☐ Pooled income fund
- ☐ Initial return
- ☐ Amended return
- ☐ Final return

Name of estate or trust (grantor type trust, see instructions)

Name and title of fiduciary

Address of fiduciary (number and street)

City, state, and ZIP code

Check if this is for a short taxable year under section 645 ▶ ☐

Employer identification number

Date entity created

Nonexempt charitable and split-interest trusts, check applicable boxes (see instructions):
- ☐ Described in section 4947(a)(1)
- ☐ Not a private foundation
- ☐ Described in section 4947(a)(2)

Income

1	Dividends	1	
2	Interest income	2	
3	Income (or losses) from partnerships, other estates or other trusts (see instructions)	3	
4	Net rent and royalty income (or loss) (attach Schedule E (Form 1040))	4	
5	Net business and farm income (or loss) (attach Schedules C and F (Form 1040))	5	
6	Capital gain (or loss) (attach Schedule D (Form 1041))	6	
7	Ordinary gain (or loss) (attach Form 4797)	7	
8	Other income (state nature of income) _____	8	
9	**Total** income (add lines 1 through 8) ▶	9	

Deductions

10	Interest	10	
11	Fiduciary fees	11	
12	Charitable deduction (from Schedule A, line 6)	12	
13	Attorney, accountant, and return preparer fees	13	
14	Other deductions (including taxes) (attach schedule)	14	
15	**Total** (add lines 10 through 14) ▶	15	
16	Adjusted total income (or loss) (subtract line 15 from line 9)	16	
17	Income distribution deduction (from Schedule B, line 17) (see instructions) (attach Schedule K-1 (Form 1041))	17	
18	Estate tax deduction (including generation-skipping transfer taxes) (attach computation)	18	
19	Exemption	19	
20	**Total** (add lines 17 through 19) ▶	20	
21	Taxable income of fiduciary (subtract line 20 from line 16)	21	

Computation of tax (Please attach check or money order here)

22	**Tax:** ☐ **a** Tax rate schedule or ☐ Schedule D _____; **b** Other tax _____; Total ▶	22c	
23	**Credits:** **a** Foreign tax _____; **b** Nonconventional fuel _____; Total ▶	23c	
24	**Credits:** ☐ Form 3800 ☐ Form 3468 ☐ Form 5884 ☐ Form 6478 ☐ Form 6765 ☐ Form 8586	24	
25	**Total** (add lines 23c and 24) ▶	25	
26	**Balance** (subtract line 25 from line 22c)	26	
27	Recapture of investment credit (attach Form 4255)	27	
28	Alternative minimum tax (attach Form 8656)	28	
29	**Total** (add lines 26 through 28) ▶	29	
30	**Credits: a** Form 2439 _____; **b** Form 4136 _____; **c** Form 6249 _____; Total ▶	30d	
31	**Payments: a** 1987 estimated tax payments ▶ _____		
	b Paid with extension of time to file (attach Form 2758) ▶ _____; **c** Withheld ▶ _____; Total ▶	31d	
32	**Total** (add lines 30d and 31d) ▶	32	
33	**Balance** of tax due (subtract line 32 from line 29) (see instructions)	33	
34	**Overpayment** (subtract line 29 from line 32)	34	
35	Amount of line 34 to be: **a** Credited to your 1988 estimated tax ▶ _____		
	b Treated as paid by trust beneficiaries (Attach Form 1041-T) ▶ _____ Refunded ▶	35c	
	Check ▶ ☐ if Form 2210 (2210F) is attached (see instructions) Penalty: $ _____		

Please Sign Here

Under penalties of perjury, I declare that I have examined this return, including accompanying schedules and statements, and to the best of my knowledge and belief, it is true, correct, and complete. Declaration of preparer (other than fiduciary) is based on all information of which preparer has any knowledge

▶ _____
Signature of fiduciary or officer representing fiduciary

▶ _____
Date

Paid Preparer's Use Only	Preparer's signature ▶	Date	Check if self-employed ▶ ☐	Preparer's social security no.
	Firm's name (or yours if self-employed) and address ▶		E.I. No ▶ ZIP code ▶	

For Paperwork Reduction Act Notice, see page 1 of the instructions.

Form **1041** (1987)

APPENDIX 8B *(concluded)*

Form 1041 (1987)   Page **2**

SCHEDULE A.—Charitable Deduction—*Do not complete for a simple trust or a pooled income fund.*
            (Write the name and address of each charitable organization to whom your contributions total $3,000 or more on an attached sheet.)

1 Amounts paid or permanently set aside for charitable purposes from current year's gross income	**1**
2 Tax-exempt interest allocable to charitable distribution (see instructions)	**2**
3 Balance (subtract line 2 from line 1)	**3**
4 Enter the net short-term capital gain and the net long-term capital gain of the current tax year allocable to corpus paid or permanently set aside for charitable purposes	**4**
5 Amounts paid or permanently set aside for charitable purposes from gross income of a prior year (see instructions)	**5**
6 Total (add lines 3, 4, and 5). Enter here and on page 1, line 12	**6**

SCHEDULE B.—Income Distribution Deduction

1 Adjusted total income (Enter amount from page 1, line 16.) (If net loss, enter zero.)	**1**
2 Adjusted tax-exempt interest (see instructions)	**2**
3 Net gain shown on Schedule D (Form 1041), line 17, column (a) (If net loss, enter zero.)	**3**
4 Enter amount from Schedule A, line 4	**4**
5 Long-term capital gain included on Schedule A, line 1	**5**
6 Short-term capital gain included on Schedule A, line 1	**6**
7 If the amount on page 1, line 6, is a capital loss, enter here as a positive figure	**7**
8 If the amount on page 1, line 6, is a capital gain, enter here as a negative figure	**8**
9 Distributable net income (combine lines 1 through 8)	**9**
10 If a complex trust, amount of income for the tax year determined under the governing instrument (accounting income) **10**	
11 Amount of income required to be distributed currently (see instructions)	**11**
12 Other amounts paid, credited, or otherwise required to be distributed (see instructions)	**12**
13 Total distributions (add lines 11 and 12). (If greater than line 10, see instructions.)	**13**
14 Enter the total amount of tax-exempt income included on line 13	**14**
15 Tentative income distribution deduction (subtract line 14 from line 13)	**15**
16 Tentative income distribution deduction (subtract line 2 from line 9)	**16**
17 Income distribution deduction (Enter the smaller of line 15 or line 16 here and on page 1, line 17.)	**17**

Other Information

	Yes	No
1 If the fiduciary's name or address has changed, enter the old information ▶		
2 Did the estate or trust receive tax-exempt income? (If "Yes," attach a computation of the allocation of expenses.) Enter the amount of tax-exempt interest income ▶		
3 Did the estate or trust have any passive activity loss(es)? (If "Yes," enter the amount of any such loss(es) on **Form 8582**, Passive Activity Loss Limitations, to figure the allowable loss.)		
4 Did the estate or trust receive all or any part of the earnings (salary, wages, and other compensation) of any individual by reason of a contract assignment or similar arrangement?		
5 At any time during the tax year, did the estate or trust have an interest in or a signature or other authority over a financial account in a foreign country (such as a bank account, securities account, or other financial account)? (See the Instructions for exceptions and filing requirements for Form TD F 90-22.1 If "Yes," enter the name of the foreign country ▶		
6 Was the estate or trust the grantor of, or transferor to, a foreign trust which existed during the current tax year, whether or not the estate or trust has any beneficial interest in it? (If "Yes," you may have to file Form 3520, 3520-A, or 926.)		
7 Check this box if this entity has filed or is required to file **Form 8264**, Application for Registration of a Tax Shelter. ▶ ☐		
8 Check this box if this entity is a complex trust making the section 663(b) election ▶ ☐		
9 Check this box if a section 643(e)(3) election is made (attach Schedule D (Form 1041)) ▶ ☐		
10 Check this box if the decedent's estate has been open for more than 2 years (see instructions) ▶ ☐		

☆ U.S. GPO: 1987-183-156

PART 3

The Techniques of Planning

9

Introduction to Part 3:
The Goals of Estate Planning

OVERVIEW AND CAUTION

This chapter is an introduction to the many specific estate planning techniques to be covered in the remainder of the text. It will isolate the general goals that these techniques have in common. The goals can be categorized into two broad groups, non-financial and financial. Within the financial group, they can be further subdivided into tax and nontax goals.

In reading this chapter, it would be well to keep in mind that the client has one very fundamental goal, one far more general than saving taxes or attaining any other specific goal described in this chapter. The client's primary goal is happiness and peace of mind, and specific estate planning strategies may conflict with it. For example, gift giving reduces client wealth and may jeopardize happiness by imperiling financial security and comfort. The planner should be especially attuned to the client's emotional and psychological preferences and should be sure not to persist in recommending techniques that appear to be inconsistent with them. Planning strategies are not ends in themselves; they are means to an end: happiness.

NONFINANCIAL GOALS

Some specific objectives in estate planning are not strictly financial in nature; they can't be measured in dollars and cents. These nonfinancial goals will be examined first. They include care of future dependents, privacy and speed in the property transfer process, and maintaining control over assets.

Care of Future Dependents

One of the client's objectives should be to provide care for family members affected by the client's disability or death. For example, *disability* of the client may trigger the need to select others to care for the client and the client's property. In addition, *death* of a client who was the single parent of a minor child will require court selection of one or more persons to care for that child. In either case, prior planning can permit the evetual selection process to reflect the current wishes of the client, the individual who is currently in the best position to arrange for future care. Methods of planning for care at death and disability are examined in Chapter 17, covering miscellaneous lifetime planning.

Privacy in the Property Transfer Process

Other things equal, clients would prefer that their wealth be transferred as privately as possible. They realize that their intended beneficiaries will experience less stress by avoiding public scrutiny. We have seen in Chapter 4 that the methods of property transfer are characterized by different degrees of privacy, with the probate process considerably more public than the process of transferring property by trust. Of course, if privacy were the only criterion, no one would consciously prefer the probate alternative. Probate does, however, offer unique advantages, and the client should weigh them against its disadvantages. The decision whether or not to avoid probate is the main focus of Chapter 10.

Speed in the Property Transfer Process

Similar to privacy, speed in property transfer is desired by most clients and is often less attainable with the probate alternative. The decision to avoid probate requires a weighing of the benefits against the drawbacks, as outlined in Chapter 10.

Maintaining Control over Assets

As we shall see in later chapters, many lifetime estate planning strategies require that the client relinquish beneficial interests in property by making actual transfers. Few clients relish this; other things the same, they would rather keep their property. They usually seek to protect their economic interests, and wish to prevent their children from gaining unrestricted control over their wealth. But other goals may change their mind. Their desire to accomplish other estate planning goals can motivate them to make lifetime transfers.

Further, different lifetime transfer strategies require different degrees of transfer. Usually, the more complete the transfer, the more likely other goals can be accomplished. As you cover the remainder of the text, you should contemplate the degree of transfer involved in the various strategies covered, and ask what kind of clients would be most willing to undertake them.

FINANCIAL GOALS

Financial goals include nontax and tax considerations and will be covered in that order.

Nontax Financial Goals

Financial goals that are not tax-related include minimizing nontax estate transfer costs, maintaining a satisfactory standard of living, ensuring proper disposition by careful drafting, preserving business value, and attaining pre- and postmortem flexibility.

Minimizing nontax estate transfer costs. Nontax estate transfer costs include attorney and trustee fees, executor commissions, court costs, and several other probate fees, such as the bond premium. Chapter 10 will examine these costs while exploring the decision to avoid probate.

Maintaining a satisfactory standard of living. We shall see that many tax objectives can be achieved with lifetime transfers. The planner should ensure, however, that clients will retain sufficient assets and income to maintain a satisfactory standard of living. This may require forgoing certain tax-saving transfers, such as outright gifts, in favor of retaining property. Or it may call for making other transfers, such as an installment sale, which, in return, can generate valuable consideration. These alternatives will be explored in detail in Chapters 13 and 14, covering lifetime transfers.

Ensuring proper disposition by careful drafting. In the planning process, clients normally assume that no matter what happens, their intended beneficiaries will in fact receive their accumulated wealth. Clients trust the attorney to draft transfer documents properly. However, attorney drafting skill varies greatly, and poor drafting can frustrate a client's dispositive preferences in many ways. The examples below are merely illustrative.

EXAMPLE 9–1 A simple will fails to include a brief survival period, creating the risk that a client's property will be inherited by her *in-laws*, rather than by her parents.

EXAMPLE 9–2 To minimize estate taxes, Francis leaves all of his property outright to his second wife, running the risk that she may neglect to adequately provide for her *stepchildren* (Francis' children of the former marriage), who are living with Francis' first wife.

EXAMPLE 9–3 A trust-will is drafted for a client, in which estate property will be held in trust until the youngest of the client's grandchildren reaches age 25. The disposition may be ruled invalid for violating the *rule against perpetuities*.

EXAMPLE 9–4 Donald's attorney drafts a tax-saving testamentary trust into which nearly all of Donald's estate is intended to pass. However, because much of Donald's property is still held in *joint tenancy* with his wife, that property will not pass to the trust at his death but will go outright to his wife by automatic right of survivorship. At that point, the only way for her to move the property into the trust will be by making a taxable gift.

In each of these situations, more careful planning and drafting could have eliminated the risk of unintended disposition without significantly altering the client's objectives. Careful planning and drafting is an essential prerequisite to the achievement of dispositive goals. The client should be assisted in locating an attorney experienced in drafting estate planning documents.

Preserving business value. Death of an active closely held business-owning client can precipitate a serious decline in the amount of wealth receivable by the client's survivors. In Chapter 16, we shall see that *prearrangements* can minimize this decline and increase the survivors' likelihood of receiving the material fruits of the client's productive career.

Attaining pre- and postmortem flexibility. Flexibility in estate planning means that as circumstances change, arrangements can be intelligently altered to continue to accomplish desired goals. While the client is still alive and mentally competent, flexibility can easily be maintained by periodically reviewing the estate plan and revising it when necessary. After the client either loses mental capacity or dies, flexibility, although not entirely impossible, is more difficult to sustain. Yet, as we shall see next, considerable flexibility can be maintained if the client anticipates the problem by providing in advance for *surrogate decision makers.*

The need for flexibility emerges often in the context of providing for young adult children in the event that the parents die prematurely. For example, without planning, the parent's property is usually required by law to be held by a legal guardian, and transferred outright to the children when they reach legal adulthood, typically at age 18. Most parents would prefer to delay distribution until the children are older and more mature. We shall see that they can accomplish this by designating responsible parties, such as trustees, to act on their behalf, parties who can make such an important decision after the parents are gone. Other examples of providing for extended flexibility through the use of surrogate decision

---

[1]And, a §2036 problem can arise if the gift is made into a trust *for her benefit.* An example is the bypass trust, to be introduced in Chapter 11.

makers include the power of appointment (Chapters 11 and 12), the durable power of attorney (Chapter 17), and the disclaimer (Chapter 18).

Maximizing benefits for the surviving spouse. Tax factors may impel a client to arrange future transfers to minimize the transfer tax bite to the surviving spouse. Different transfer devices accomplish this goal with different degrees of success. As the next example demonstrates, poor planning can result in an inefficient transfer, one that risks forgoing other benefits which could otherwise be enjoyed by the surviving spouse.

> EXAMPLE 9–5 Realizing that any property owned by Mom at her later death will be subject to transfer taxation, Dad *writes his own will,* one that will transfer a substantial amount of property outright to their middle-aged children in the event that he dies before Mom. Dad has succeeded in arranging for some property to bypass Mom's taxable estate, but in so doing, he has foolishly denied to her all legal rights to the property.

> EXAMPLE 9–6 Continuing Example 9–5, an estate planner might instead recommend that Dad leave the property in *trust* for the benefit of Mom and the children. The trust would give Mom the following rights, without precipitating any greater transfer tax: (1) right to income from the property for her life; (2) right to invade the trust corpus for reasons of health, education, or support; and (3) right to determine how much of the property to distribute outright to the children at her death.

As we'll see in Chapters 11 and 12, careful planning for the spouse's welfare can often maximize tax saving without sacrificing other important objectives.

Tax-Saving Goals

Income taxes and transfer taxes represent the largest cause of estate shrinkage to medium- and large-sized estates. Most of the specific planning strategies covered in this text will seek to reduce these taxes. Next, let's isolate the general tax goals they share in common.

Income tax saving goals.   The goals of those planning strategies designed to save income taxes include obtaining a stepped-up basis, shifting income to a lower bracket taxpayer, and deferring recognition of income.

Obtaining a stepped-up basis.   Achieving a step-up in income tax basis on transferred property can be especially important to a transferee who wishes to sell a rapidly appreciating asset. As we have seen in Chapter 8, a step-up is the normal tax consequence when a transferee makes an ordinary purchase for full consideration. However, much of estate planning favors lifetime gifts, that is, lifetime transfers for less than full consideration, and the basis rule for them is different: The transferee receives not a step-up, but a carryover basis. On the other hand, a step-up is normally available for gifts received at death. Thus, other things the same, planners are sometimes inclined to recommend deferring the transfer of an appreciating asset until death. This is just one of many basis considerations involved in making lifetime transfers, a subject that will be more thoroughly explored in Chapters 13 and 14.

Shifting income to a lower-bracket taxpayer.   Estate planning clients are often in the highest income tax bracket, while other family members, such as parents and children, are in lower brackets. As we have seen, under our progressive income tax rate structure, marginal and average rates of tax increase with increasing taxable income.

TRA 86 directed a three-pronged attack on the popular methods of shifting of income to a lower-bracket family member. First, it adopted the *kiddie tax,* described in Chapter 8. The kiddie tax virtually eliminates any successful shifting of income to children who haven't reached age 14 by the end of the calendar year. Second, by lowering the maximum marginal income tax *rate* to 33 percent, TRA 86 made income shifting relatively less attractive. And third, as will be described in Appendix 14A, two major lifetime *incomplete* transfer devices, the short-term trust and the spousal remainder trust, have been all but destroyed by two brief but sweeping revisions to the *grantor trust rules*. However, *completed* transfers (gifts) can still shift some income effectively, subject to the first two factors mentioned above.

What *transferors* are currently most suited to making income shifting transfers? Of course, taxpayers in the highest tax bracket.

Based on Table 1 of Appendix A at the end of the text, a married couple with joint taxable income between $71,900 and $192,930 (assumes four personal exemptions) are taxed at the top (33 percent) marginal rate.

Which *transferees* will be most able to benefit taxwise from income shifting? Those whose unearned income will be taxed at the zero or 15 percent marginal tax bracket. They include minor children over age 13, young adults in college, and, perhaps, the client's parents.

How much income can be shifted to another *person* and still be taxed at the 15 percent marginal rate? Up to $17,850 per year, assuming that the donee has no other taxable income. On the other hand, any taxable income earned by a *trust* in excess of $5,000 will be subject to the higher 28 percent rate.

EXAMPLE 9–7 Dad, a surgeon, projects before-tax earnings from two sources next year: $120,000 from his surgical practice, and $64,000 from dividends on common stock. He wishes to use some of this income to help support a daughter in college. Assuming that Dad will have a marginal income tax rate of 33 percent, and that daughter's rate is 15 percent, each dollar of Dad's income up to $17,850 that can instead be taxed to daughter will save 18 cents in tax.

Can all income potentially receivable by one person be taxed to another? The answer is no, because tax law distinguishes two types of income: personal service income and other income. Under the *assignment of income doctrine,* earnings from services performed will always be taxable to the person performing those services. However, income from nonservices, such as property, can be taxed to another if the underlying property is satisfactorily transferred for their benefit before the income is realized.

EXAMPLE 9–8 Continuing Example 9–7, Dad will not be able to tax shift his surgical services income to anyone. However, by properly transferring beneficial interest in some of the common stock to daughter, the stock's dividend income can be shifted to her, making it taxable at her lower rate.

Can a client gain by shifting income to a *spouse?* Not ordinarily, because most spouses file a joint income tax return, which subjects both of their income to taxation at the same marginal rate.[2] Thus, spousal income shifting will not usually save income taxes.

Must a transfer of property be complete and outright, such as by gift or sale, to effect a valid tax shift? Not necessarily. Examples of incomplete or nonoutright transfer devices covered in later chapters which can successfully shift income include the custodial gift and the irrevocable trust.

We shall also see in Chapter 18 that income shifting can be arranged between nonindividuals. Transfers can be made in connection with estates and trusts to save income taxes.

Occasionally, multiple taxpaying entities can be created to spread income around, thereby possibly subjecting each entity to lower marginal rates.

> EXAMPLE 9–9 Andy's will creates three trusts, one for each of his three children, transferring a total amount of property worth $450,000 and generating approximately $30,000 in taxable income a year. Assuming that each trust is taxed as a separate entity and that all of the first year's income is accumulated, each trust will pay an income tax of approximately $2,150, for a combined total tax of $6,450. If, instead, only one trust had been created, and if that trust was taxed as a single taxpaying entity, its income tax would total $8,400, which is $1,950 higher than the tax on the three trusts.

Estate planners call this three "trips up the rate ladder."

> EXAMPLE 9–10 Continuing the three-trust situation in Example 9–9, instead of accumulating all income, let's consider two alternatives. First, assume instead that each trust distributes all income to the children, who are also in relatively low brackets. Rates and income will still be split among the children, with similar tax savings.
>
> As a second alternative to complete accumulation, assume that each trust accumulates one half of the income and distributes the other half to the children. Rate splitting will be further enhanced, since the income will be divided among six rather than three taxpayers. However, because of the throwback rule, discussed briefly in Chapter 8, this bonus will work only in special circumstances, such as when the income is being accumulated for beneficiaries under age 21, or when the distributing entity is an estate. However, multiple taxpaying estates for one decedent are not possible.

---

[2]Filing separately will usually result in a higher combined income tax.

Deferring recognition of income. When a property transaction results in the realization of a gain, that gain will usually be subject to immediate recognition, that is, included in that year's gross income. However, careful planning can defer the gain to later years. By exploiting the time value of money, deferral of the tax enables the taxpayer to temporarily earn greater income. Examples of transfer that defer taxable gain are the installment sale and the private annuity, covered in Chapter 14. And in Chapter 18 we will see that an estate can defer income by carefully choosing its fiscal year end.

Transfer tax saving goals and planning. As with income tax saving techniques, devices designed to reduce transfer taxes all seek to accomplish just a few general goals. They include reducing and freezing the estate tax value and delaying the payment of the transfer tax. This section will first briefly describe those goals, each with a specific example. Then it will explore, with an ongoing example, the aspects of transfer tax theory underlying transfer tax saving goals by examining the meaning of transfer tax unification and how current imperfections in our unified transfer tax system give rise to tax planning.

Reducing the estate tax value. Certain planning arrangements can actually reduce an estate's tax value. Estate reduction subjects less of the client's wealth to transfer taxation.

> EXAMPLE 9–11 Sharon, a widow, gave her son James $10,000 cash last year. Due to the annual exclusion, the gift was not taxable and no gift tax was owed. Sharon's gross estate is now $1 million rather than $1,010,000, which means that if she were to die today, her FET will be lower by $4,100, which is the product of 41 percent, her marginal FET rate, times the value of the gift.

Other techniques of estate reduction to be examined in later chapters include gifts into trust (Chapter 13), use of the unlimited marital deduction (Chapters 11 and 12), bypass planning (Chapters 11 and 12), election of the alternate valuation date (Chapters 15 and 18), and special-use valuation of farm or closely held business property (Chapter 15).

Freezing the estate tax value. Certain property arrangements have the effect of freezing the future taxable value of a portion of the client's wealth at its *current value*. Thus, all future appreciation is excluded from transfer taxation.

TABLE 9–1 Illustration of FET Savings from Estate Freeze on One Half of Total of Four Hypothetical Estates

Assuming No Estate Freeze

Assumed Present Estate Size	Inheritable Estate in 10 Years, 8 Percent Growth per Year on Entire Present Estate (= Estate Tax Base)	FET in 10 Years	FET As Percent of Inheritable Estate in 10 Years
$ 1,000,000	$ 2,158,925	$ 665,873	30.8%
2,500,000	5,397,312	2,281,656	42.3
5,000,000	10,974,625	4,980,312	45.4
10,000,000	21,589,250	10,377,625	48.1

Assuming Estate Freeze of One Half of Present Estate

Assumed Present Estate Size	Inheritable Estate in 10 Years, 8 Percent Growth per Year on Only One Half of Present Estate	FET in 10 Years	FET as Percent of Inheritable Estate	FET Saved Due to Freeze
$ 1,000,000	$ 1,579,460	$ 398,758	18.5%	$ 267,115
2,500,000	3,948,650	1,557,328	28.9	724,328
5,000,000	7,897,300	3,531,656	32.2	1,448,656
10,000,000	15,794,600	7,480,312	34.6	2,897,313

EXAMPLE 9–12 Dwaine, a single parent, makes a *gift* of one of his vacation homes, worth $128,000, to his son Manu. Assuming Dwaine has made no other taxable gifts this year, he will file a gift tax return and report a taxable gift of $118,000. Assuming no prior taxable gifts, no gift tax will be due because of the shelter of the unified credit. If Dwaine dies 20 years later when the value of the vacation home is $500,000 (or, for that matter, any amount over $118,000), Dwaine's estate tax base will include the home at its taxable gift value, $118,000. With regard to that particular asset, Dwaine's tax base has been frozen at its taxable date-of-gift value.

The FET benefit of freezing is further illustrated in Table 9–1. It calculates the effect of an estate freeze of one half of each of four hypothetical estate sizes, assuming an annual growth rate in all estate assets of 8 percent over a period of 10 years. For example, at

8 percent, a present estate of $1 million will grow to about $2.16 million in 10 years. Assuming no estate freezing technique is used, the FET on 2.16 million will be $665,873, or 30.8 percent of the total inheritable estate. Instead, assuming a present estate freeze on $500,000. Although the total inheritable estate in 10 years will still be $2.16 million, the estate tax base will be only $1.579 million, or the sum of $500,000, the frozen half, plus $1,079,460, the appreciated date-of-death value of the other unfrozen half. Thus, FET will be only $398,758, which is only 18.5 percent of the total inheritable estate. Estate freezing saved over $267,000. As Table 9–1 indicates, larger estate sizes will save correspondingly larger amounts of FET.

Other transfer devices covered in later chapters that can freeze taxable estate values include the private annuity (Chapter 14), the installment sale (Chapter 14), the joint purchase of a life estate and a remainder interest (Chapter 14), and the business buyout agreement (Chapter 16).

The passage of *Section 2036(c)* in the *Revenue Act of 1987* has made it more difficult to successfully effect a freeze by means of certain transfers, including the sale of a remainder interest, and two devices discussed in Appendix 16A: the corporate recapitalization and the partnership capital freeze. Summarizing this complex provision, a decedent's gross estate will include the date-of-death value of property if he (or any member of his family) held a substantial interest in an enterprise connected with that property, and he (or his spouse) made a transfer after December 17, 1987, (even for full and adequate consideration), where (1) the property interest transferred had a disproportionately large share of the *potential appreciation* in his interest in the enterprise, and (2) the property interest retained had a disproportionately large share in the *income or other rights* in that enterprise.

This provision is quite far-reaching for at least two reasons. First, the term *enterprise* is interpreted broadly to include any business or other property that can produce income or gain. Thus, it can extend to nonbusiness types of property transfers, such as the sale of a remainder interest to a family member. Second, the term *transfer* is meant to include any passing or conferrence on another, regardless of the means or device employed in its accomplishment. Thus, it includes transfers that are not complete for gift tax purposes.

EXAMPLE 9–13 During her lifetime, decedent *gave* her son outright IBM stock worth $100,000. At her death, the stock was worth $1,000,000. Despite the fact that the portion of her transferred estate attributable to the stock was frozen at the adjusted taxable gift value of $90,000, this transfer is not subject to §2036(c) because the decedent did not retain any income or rights in the stock.

EXAMPLE 9–14 Facts similar to the above example, except that the arrangement had the decedent *sell the remainder interest* to her son for its fair market value and retain the right to the stock's dividend income for life. At her death, the $1,000,000 will be includible in her gross estate under §2036(c). Decedent made a transfer of property under an arrangement that would be considered an enterprise, retaining a disproportionately large share of the income while transferring a disproportionately large share of the appreciation. The fact that consideration was paid is immaterial.

In many cases, the statute can be avoided with careful planning, as we'll see in later chapters.

Delaying payment of the transfer tax. In certain situations, transfer taxes can be deferred, even though a completed taxable transfer has taken place.

EXAMPLE 9–15 Danny is contemplating several transfers of property from his large estate. His wife, Barbara, has an equally large estate and can live very comfortably off her own wealth. If Danny gives his wealth to Barbara at his death, there will be no immediate FET on that property, since the transfer will be totally sheltered by the unlimited estate tax marital deduction. But the FET will only be deferred, not eliminated, since the property will probably be taxed at Barbara's later death. In fact, the gift to her will probably increase the overall FET on that property (compared to the amount of tax that Danny's estate would pay if he left the property outright or in trust to the children) since the gift (a) foregos the use of the unified credit at Danny's death; and (b) will increase the size of Barbara's gross estate, possibly subjecting it to a higher tax rate. Thus, Danny faces the alternative of either deferring a potentially larger tax or, more immediately, incurring a smaller estate tax on his wealth.

Factors to consider in answering the question of whether or not to defer the FET by means of the unlimited marital deduction are examined in Chapters 11 and 12. Those chapters also discuss the interrelationship of the marital deduction and the unified credit.

Other transfer tax deferral devices covered in later chapters include the application of §6166, dealing with the payment of the FET in future installments for a decedent-owner of a closely held business (Chapter 16), and the simple practice of delaying property transfers (Chapter 13).

Now, let's examine in some detail the theory underlying these basic transfer tax saving goals.

The meaning of unification. Many transfer tax saving techniques take advantage of the fact that our unified transfer tax system is imperfect, that is, not completely unified. To appreciate fully how these strategies work, the reader must clearly understand both how a system of perfect unification would function and how the planner can exploit the imperfections inherent in our unified system. The following material will first portray what a tax world of perfect unification would be like, and then describe our present, imperfectly unified system. An ongoing example will illustrate the major points.

Perfect unification. Perfect unification of gift and estate taxes would mean that an individual would be *indifferent,* from a total transfer tax planning point of view, between making lifetime and deathtime gifts. Under perfect unification, total transfer taxes would be the same whether an individual owned property at death or whether that person gifted the property away during lifetime. Perfect unification would require all of the following conditions:

1. A uniform system of *deductions and credits* for all transfers. Otherwise, individuals would prefer to make that transfer which enjoyed the shelter of higher deductions or credits.

2. A *tax on all completed transfers,* whether made during lifetime or at death, no matter the size of the gift and no matter how long ago the transfer was made. Otherwise, individuals would seek to make that transfer which would be tax-free. This would require complete imposition of the *cumulative gift doctrine,* described in Chapter 5, and would entail the following specific procedures:

   a. *All prior gifts* made by the transferor would be added to the transferor's current transfer tax base. No gifts would be excluded, including gifts of very small value and gifts made many years ago.

b. All prior gifts would be included in the estate tax base at their *current market value,* not date-of-gift value.

c. All *gift taxes* paid would be grossed up; that is, added to the estate tax base.

Failure to completely accumulate prior transfers and taxes in each of these ways would enable an individual to save taxes by timing transfers to make them subject to less transfer taxation.

3. A world in which the *time value of money* is negligible. Otherwise, individuals would prefer to pay the same (or even greater) transfer tax later rather than sooner.

4. Finally, only *one tax rate schedule* applicable to all transfers. Otherwise, individuals would seek to make transfers that would be subject to the lower tax rates.

To see the operation of perfect unification, consider the following numeric example, which reflects all of the above assumptions. While reading it, please keep in mind that the present tax system does not include all of these assumptions; these calculations are made for illustration purposes only. All transfers will be assumed to be made after 1987.

EXAMPLE 9–16 Howard, a widower, died owning $2 million in property, consisting of $1 million in land and $1 million in cash. Ignoring all deductions and credits except the unified credit, Howard's FET is $588,000, calculated as follows:

Gross estate	$2,000,000
Less: Deductions	—0—
Taxable estate	2,000,000
Tentative tax	780,800
Less: Unified credit	192,800
Net estate tax	$ 588,000

Continuing the example, assume that instead of dying owning all of his wealth, Howard gave the land to his son four years before his death. At that time the land was worth $800,000. Under perfect unification, Howard's total combined transfer taxes would still be

$588,000. First, Howard would have paid a gift tax of $75,000, calculated as follows:

Current gross gift	$800,000
Less: Exclusions and deductions	—0—
Taxable gift	800,000
Tentative tax	267,800
Less: Unified credit	192,800
Net gift tax	$ 75,000

Howard's subsequent death would have resulted in a net estate tax of $513,000 calculated as follows:

Gross estate (date-of-death value of property plus gift tax paid)*	$1,000,000
Less: Deductions	—0—
Taxable estate	1,000,000
Plus: Prior gifts (date-of-death value)	1,000,000
Estate tax base	2,000,000
Tentative estate tax	780,800
Less: Gift tax paid	75,000
Less: Unified credit	192,800
Net estate tax	$ 513,000
Total transfer taxes	$ 588,000

*The gross estate of $1 million is the sum of property owned at death plus the gift tax paid. At death, Howard owned $925,000 in cash, which is the difference between the $1 million cash initially owned and the $75,000 gift tax paid. Grossing up then increases the gross estate back to $1 million.

Summarizing, under perfect unification, total transfer taxes would be the same whether an individual retained all property until death or whether he or she had made lifetime gifts. In Example 9–16, the gift tax plus the estate tax in the case of a lifetime gift equals $588,000, which is the estate tax in the case of no lifetime gift.

Our present imperfectly unified system. Comparing our present transfer tax world with the list of conditions required for perfect unification, we see one similarity and several differences. The real world and the perfect system are similar with regard to item 4 (the existence of one transfer tax rate schedule applied to both lifetime and deathtime transfers). However, the two "worlds" are different with regard to all other conditions; our present transfer tax scheme does not fully reflect any of them. The dissimilarities are described in the following outline which, for ease of comparison, is numerically structured to parallel the previous list.

1. Some *deductions and credits* are not uniformly applied to all transfers. For example, as we have seen, the estate tax credit for tax on prior deathtime transfers is not allowable for prior lifetime transfers.

2. The *cumulative gift doctrine* has not been completely incorporated into our transfer tax system. Major omissions include the following:

   a. *Not all prior gifts* made by the transferor are added to the transferor's current transfer tax base. In fact, some gifts are not included at all.

      (1) Except in unusual situations, only *post-1976* gifts are added to the estate tax base.[3] Pre-1977 gifts are usually totally excluded from the estate tax base. The major exception applies to pre-1977 transfers subject to retained interests and control under Code Sections 2036, 2037, and 2038.

      (2) Ordinarily, only the taxable gift value is added to the gift tax base or estate tax base, not the value of the entire gift. Taxable gift value is the net gift value after subtraction of deductions and exclusions, including the $10,000 annual exclusion. Hence, the estate tax base will be lower by the amount of the annual exclusions taken, creating an advantage to making lifetime transfers.

   b. Prior gifts that are included in the current tax base reflect the *value of the transfer at the date of the gift*, not the current value. In many, perhaps most, circumstances, date-of-gift value will be lower than current value, thereby enabling individuals, as shown in Example 9–12 to make gifts of appreciating assets—to freeze the taxable value by eliminating estate taxation on their subsequent appreciation.

   c. Not all *prior gift taxes* paid are grossed up, that is, added to the estate tax base. Only gift taxes paid on gifts made within three years of death are so included. We have seen in Chap-

---

[3]Internal Revenue Code §2001 defines *adjusted taxable gifts* as the total of all *post-1976* taxable gifts.

ter 6 examples illustrating the tax advantage created by non-inclusion of gift taxes in the gross estate.[4]

3. Finally, our transfer tax structure can not ever be perfectly unified because we live in a world having a significant *time value of money*. Thus, other things the same, individuals will prefer to delay the payment of transfer taxes.

To see how real-world imperfections 2a(2), 2b, and 2c affect the unified transfer tax, let's rework the numbers in Example 9–16. First, assuming no lifetime gifts, Howard's net estate tax will still be $588,000, calculated in exactly the same manner as shown in the original example. However, the lifetime gift alternative under today's imperfect unification has markedly different results. Howard's gift tax, at the time of the gift, will be $71,100, calculated as follows:

Current gross gift	$800,000
Less: Exclusions and deductions	10,000
Taxable gift	790,000
Tentative tax	263,900
Less: Unified credit	192,800
Net gift tax	$ 71,100

Assuming simply that Howard dies owning $928,900 cash ($1 million less gift tax paid of $71,100), Howard's net estate tax will be $390,405, calculated as follows:

Gross estate (date-of-death value of cash property owned at death—excludes the gift tax paid)	$928,900
Less: Deductions	—0—
Taxable estate	928,900
Plus: Adjusted taxable gifts (from gift tax return)	790,000
Estate tax base	1,718,900
Tentative estate tax	654,305
Less: Gift tax paid	71,100
Less: Unified credit	192,800
Net estate tax	$ 390,405

---

[4] Examples 2035–4 and 2035–6.

Howard's total transfer tax will be $461,505, the sum of $71,100 (gift tax) and $390,405 (estate tax). Hence the use of the lifetime gift has saved $126,495 in transfer taxes. Imperfect unification has enabled Howard to *freeze* the tax value of the land at its taxable gift value and to *reduce* his taxable estate by the amount of the annual exclusion and the gift tax paid. Thus, a total of $281,100 escaped transfer taxation. This represents the sum of three amounts: the $10,000 annual exclusion, the $71,100 gift tax paid, and $200,000 in postgift appreciation in the land. We can check our result, since the total tax saved will be the product of 0.45, the marginal estate tax rate, and $281,100. That product does in fact equal the tax saving of $126,495.

Thus, careful exploitation of the present system's failure to completely unify estate and gift taxes can yield substantial tax savings for clients with medium to larger amounts of wealth. Further discussion of these issues will be deferred to the chapters on planning for lifetime transfers.[5]

This chapter has introduced the specific techniques of estate planning by presenting the main goals underlying them. The next chapter begins our detailed study of the techniques with an examination of the decision to avoid probate.

RECOMMENDED READING

EUBANK, J. THOMAS. "Gifts and Other Bread and Butter Freezes." *Real Property, Probate and Trust Journal*, 1983, pp. 566–95.

FRAZER, DAVID R. "Five Myths of Estate Planning." *Trusts & Estates*, December 1985, pp. 16–18.

RHINE, DAVID S. "Personal Financial Planning: A Map to the Minefield." *Trusts & Estates*, December 1985, pp. 20–22.

STUKENBERG, M. W., and D. L. GIBLEN. "Techniques for Obtaining the Tax Benefits of More than One Trust for the Same Beneficiary." *Taxation for Lawyers*, November–December 1983, pp. 162–65.

---

[5]Chapters 13 and 14.

QUESTIONS AND PROBLEMS

1. (*a*) What is the client's principal goal in estate planning? (*b*) Give your own example of how a more specific goal described in this chapter can conflict with it.

2. List and briefly describe a client's nonfinancial estate planning goals.

3. List and briefly describe a client's nontax financial estate planning goals.

4. Describe the advantage of selecting a surrogate decision maker in the estate planning process.

5. List and briefly describe a client's income tax saving goals.

6. Mom and Dad are in the 33 percent marginal income tax bracket. Based on actual tax rates, how much income tax can the family save each year if they can shift $20,000 in taxable income to the following alternate taxpayers which, we will assume, have no current taxable income? Also, for each taxpayer, state the maximum total income taxable at that taxpayer's lowest rate bracket.
   a. Shift to their 12-year-old daughter.
   b. Shift to their 18-year-old son.
   c. Shift to an irrevocable trust that distributes all the income annually to their 12-year-old daughter.
   d. Shift to an irrevocable trust that accumulates all income annually for the benefit of their 18-year-old son.
   e. Shift to an irrevocable trust that accumulates $5,100 and distributes the balance annually to their 18-year-old son.
   f. Shift to a new corporation owned by their 18-year-old son. No dividend is paid.

7. List and briefly describe a client's transfer tax saving goals.

8. (*a*) What is the meaning of perfect unification? (*b*) Why is our present unified transfer tax system imperfect?

9. Compare the *gift* tax calculations for Howard in Example 9–16 in the text, contrasting perfect unification with the present tax system.
   a. On a piece of paper, list the major numerical gift tax calculations, in side-by-side columns.
   b. Which lines are different in amount? Why?

10. Now compare the *estate* tax calculations for Howard's estate in Example 9–16 of the text, contrasting perfect unification with the present tax system, under both the no-gift and the gift alternatives.

    a. On a piece of paper, list the major numerical calculations, in side-by-side columns.

    b. Which lines are different in amount? Why?

11. Revise the numerical answers in Example 5–7 in the text of Chapter 5 to include the influence of the $10,000 annual gift tax exclusion. In addition, calculate the net tax on a single gift of $500,000. What conclusions can be drawn? (Answer: Total gift taxes for both gifts combined = $149,000; tax for the single gift = $152,400.)

12. Without doing any further calculations, explain what effect you think the following alternative *additional* gifts would have on your calculation of total taxes in Problem 11 at the end of Chapter 5:

    a. $10,000 to a different person in 1982.

    b. Instead, 48 equal lifetime gift amounts of $9,810.83, totaling $470,920. Assume that these gifts were made to eight children and grandchildren over a six-year period beginning in 1982. (Why the amount $470,920? To help answer this, refer to the amounts in your answer to Problem 11 in Chapter 5 for the gross estate and adjusted taxable gifts.)

    c. Instead, $470,920 all to one son in one year.

    What planning conclusions can be drawn?

10

The Decision to Avoid Probate

OVERVIEW

As we have seen, probate is a legal court process by which the state supervises the orderly distribution of a decedent's probate property. Since probate has significant drawbacks, some clients may prefer to avoid it by planning the disposition of property with one of its two major alternatives, joint tenancy and the living trust. This chapter can help make this decision; it surveys the advantages and disadvantages of all three vehicles. We shall see that to a great degree the choice of the best method is subjective, depending on the client's personal assessment of the pros and cons. The choice also depends in part on the client's personal circumstances. Although generalization is difficult, we will conclude the chapter with a summary of several client circumstances which are apt to favor a particular alternative.

Several other limited alternatives to probate will not be discussed. Contracts such as life insurance and retirement plans can avoid probate but have limited general application for two reasons. First, the decision whether or not to utilize these contracts is usually independent of the decision whether or not to avoid probate. For example, life insurance is purchased for reasons other than avoiding probate—such as the need for cash at someone's death; acquiring it is not influenced by the method chosen to transfer property. In contrast, probate and the living trust each are means of transferring virtually any asset owned by the client. Second, these limited alternatives to probate are "asset specific"; that is, they cannot be used to help other client assets avoid probate. For example, a Totten trust only avoids probate for that particular bank account. On the other hand, while joint tenancy also applies to specific assets, many more types of property qualify.

We begin by examining the pros and cons of probate.

THE BENEFITS AND DRAWBACKS OF PROBATE

The probate alternative for property transfer is very controversial, especially among lawyers. Below, we describe its major benefits and drawbacks. For a more thorough understanding of the probate process, the reader is urged to first review the material in Chapter 4.

The Benefits of Probate

The major benefits of probate include fairness promoted by court supervision, orderly administration of assets, greater protection from creditors, and income tax savings.

Court supervision promotes fairness.   Formal probate requires substantial court supervision, a process which, at its best, promotes fairness. Through the use of petitions, accountings, hearings, and court orders, probate seeks to ensure that asset distribution is fair. No other estate transfer procedure is so controlled by public authorities.

The public-forum nature of probate encourages evaluation by numerous observers. Judges and official clerks are called on to approve major estate activities. In addition, other interested persons have an opportunity to object to perceived inequities in estate administration. For example, they can object to many activities, including admission of a certain will to probate, appointment of a certain personal representative, payment of a certain creditor, and distribution of estate assets to a certain individual. They can raise these objections in the probate court itself; the parties need not seek a remedy elsewhere and they can often do it without hiring a lawyer. In contrast, objections to disposition by joint tenancy and by the living trust require a different, procedurally more complicated legal action.

Critics of probate contend that the additional degree of equity fostered by probate administration is, at best, minimal. They argue that judges and other public officials too often give only superficial rubber-stamp approval of estate activities and even occasionally dispense with certain onerous procedural requirements of their state's probate code. Supporters of probate respond to this criticism saying that judges implicitly rely on the interested parties, who are formally notified of the proceedings, to speak up in court if they feel they are being treated unfairly. Critics contend, however, that the average person may not be aware of certain inequities.

The claim that probate encourages fairness is also subject to challenge because of the recent trend in the direction of reduced supervision. In Chapter 4, we learned that many states permit "informal" or "summary" probate procedures that can greatly reduce court surveillance. Also, we saw that UPC states permit the estate's interested parties to select the degree of supervision they desire. If they choose "informal probate," the estate will receive no direct supervision by the court. In UPC states, the risk of misadministration in probate is therefore greater because of the opportunity to avoid the public forum. Of course, the ability to request greater formal supervision later in probate reduces the risk of any noticeable mismanagement.

In conclusion, through supervision, probate promotes fairness. However, the strength of this generalization has been weakened by the degree to which the courts only superficially oversee administrative activities and the recent movement of the states to reduce the degree of mandatory court supervision.

Orderly administration of assets.   Probate offers an orderly administration of estate assets. Supervision by the court and by other public officials ensures further that property transfers and title clearance will be done correctly. Once again, however, this advantage is less pronounced to the extent that court approval is given only perfunctorily.

Greater protection from creditors.   As we saw in Chapter 4, probate procedures typically require creditors to formally file their claims against probate assets within a certain period of time, such as four months from date of issuance of Letters Testamentary. Failure to timely file a creditor's claim can forever bar collection from those assets. Nonprobate assets, on the other hand, are protected only by the state's general limitations period, which can be several years. Thus, asset disposition by probate can offer distributees nearly complete protection from creditors much sooner, at least by the time of distribution.

Clients who anticipate more claims after their death may find the shorter limitations period a great advantage. For example, professionals such as lawyers and accountants are potentially vulnerable to malpractice claims which, if instituted after their death, stand a greater chance of succeeding, partly because the defense's best witness, the client, is not available to testify. The shorter creditors' period can minimize this undesired outcome.[1] Most other clients, however, will find the benefit of the shorter creditors' period to be of little value. And, in view of the fact that probate publicly exposes a pot of assets for creditors to reach, some clients may prefer more private and more decentralized methods of asset distribution.[2]

In UPC states, clients' estates can have the same claims protection without supervised probate. For example, informal UPC probate offers the four-month creditors' period, because its provisions allow for the filing of a legal notice to creditors.[3] Certain other forms of summary probate in non–UPC states do not offer this protection.[4]

Income tax savings. The probate estate is considered a separate tax entity during its existence, taxable at its own rates. Hence, income shifting with an additional taxpaying entity is possible. For example, during estate administration, undistributed income earned on estate property will be taxed to the estate rather than to the beneficiaries. This can reduce total income taxes if the estate is in a lower tax bracket than its beneficiaries. However, as mentioned in Chapter 9, the advantage has been severely undercut by

---

[1] However, the limitations period on medical malpractice claims often starts when the negligence was or could have been discovered. Thus, the shorter creditors' period may be unavailable for physicians.

[2] For a discussion of the protection from creditors of a deceased cotenant's property under joint tenancy agreements, see below in the section "advantages of joint tenancy"—"reduced creditor's claims".

[3] As mentioned in Chapter 4, if the notice is not issued, the UPC imposes a three-year creditors' limitations period, starting at date of death.

[4] For example, in California, the creditors' period is not available under summary distribution to the surviving spouse, described in Appendix 4A.

TRA 86, which lowered and compressed the income tax rate brackets. Income tax planning for estates is described in Chapter 18.

The Drawbacks of Probate

Probate has several distinct disadvantages, including complexity, cost, lack of privacy, delay, and danger of unintended disposition.

Complexity. As we saw in Chapter 4, probate can be a complex process, requiring petitions, accountings, hearings, and other complicated legal procedures. Most laypersons understand neither their purpose nor their operation and are forced to hire specialists to meet their requirements. Critics argue that supervised probate is usually an unnecessary, clumsy process offering considerable makework for the legal profession. Others respond that the movement by many states toward less formal probate procedures has made probate no more complex than administration for a decedent whose assets had been placed in a living trust.

Cost.[5] The cost of legal supervision under probate can be high. Studies have found that total probate administration expenses range between about 2 and 10 percent of estate assets, with larger estates subject to informal UPC administration experiencing the lowest rates.

The personal representative's commission usually constitutes the largest probate expense. Of course, a surviving beneficiary who acts as personal representative may wish to waive the commission.[6] The statutes of most states either provide for "reasonable" compensation of the personal representative or make no provision at all. A few states have enacted statutory commissions, based on a percentage of estate assets, such as the one included in Table 4–1. In general, personal representatives' commissions for formal probate range between 3 and 5 percent.

The next largest probate administration expense is usually the attorney's fee. Most states' statutes do not set attorneys' fees;

---

[5]Contrary to popular belief, probate does *not* increase a decedent's estate's FET. Nor does avoiding probate necessarily reduce FET. The probate estate and the gross estate are independent (but not mutually exclusive) concepts.

[6]For a discussion of the tax factors in deciding whether or not to waive the personal representative's commission, see Chapter 18.

their probate courts approve what they consider a "reasonable" fee. In general, attorneys' fees range between 2 and 4 percent of estate assets.

Other probate administration expenses include bond fees, accountants' and appraisers' fees, and court costs, including filing fees. In a later section we will present a method for comparing the total costs of formal probate and the living trust.

Probate administration fees will be higher for estates containing real property located in other states. Under what is called *ancillary administration,* that property must ordinarily be probated in the state in which it is located. This will usually require hiring an attorney who practices in that state to handle the probate.

Lack of privacy. Probate is a public process; all probate proceedings are subject to public scrutiny. For example, any citizen willing to take a trip to the county offices can inspect a decedent's probate file, which will eventually include such personal documents as the will, the inventory and appraisement, and the order for final distribution. Those particularly interested in inspecting include survivors who are fighting and members of the press seeking a story about a newsworthy resident.[7]

How much publicity can a typical client reasonably expect? The probate files for most decedents are probably not examined by anyone other than the executor, certain county officials, and one or two of the decedent's relatives. Keep in mind, however, that clients receiving estate planning advice are typically the wealthier, more prominent citizens, who are likely to arouse greater than average curiosity. And even in cases where invasion of privacy is not expected, it is always possible. Because probate is by nature a public process, privacy cannot be assured.[8]

---

[7]Commonly cited examples of celebrities receiving embarrassing publicity which arguably could have been avoided include the estates of Natalie Wood and John Wayne and the controversy surrounding the conservatorship for Groucho Marx.

[8]In some situations, a client may actually prefer the lack of privacy inherent in probate. For example, the public aspects of probate might discourage or uncover fraudulent dealings undertaken by unscrupulous survivors. See the earlier discussion of fairness.

Delay. Even for smaller estates, probate administration takes considerable time, ranging from nine months to several years before final distribution is made.[9] And in any particular case, the delay can be quite unpredictable. Delay can be especially hard on grieving survivors, partly because it can increase tension and conflicts among them. As a specific example of delay in probate, payment of proceeds of life insurance on the decedent's life to the decedent's testamentary trust will be delayed until the trust takes effect, which usually can be no sooner than the expiration of the creditor's period, or several months after date of death. Thus, immediate liquidity cannot be provided to survivors.

Danger of unintended disposition. The nature of probate may in some cases increase the risk of an undesired will contest, one which may be settled with a distribution of assets in a manner that conflicts with testator intent. For example, a person named only in a prior will might contest the decedent's last will on a technicality. The person might, for example, claim that the decedent failed, at the time of execution, to verbally request that the witnesses sign the will. In contrast with probate, other nonprobate documents of transfer can be much more difficult to contest, partly because execution requirements are less stringent; thus a mistake in an execution formality is far less likely to void the transfer.

With a better understanding of the pros and cons of probate, let us now consider the two principal alternatives to probate. We first turn to the simpler alternative, disposition by joint tenancy.

ONE ALTERNATIVE TO PROBATE: JOINT TENANCY

Disposition by automatic survivorship under title held in joint tenancy is one major alternative to probate.[10] It, too, has several advantages and disadvantages, which we consider next.

---

[9] However, preliminary distributions of significant amounts can usually be made earlier. Often, probate attorneys will delay closing an estate for income tax reasons. See Chapter 18.

[10] We should mention in passing the "pay on death" bank account, which is an account payable to one or more persons during their lifetime (usually the depositor's), and payable on their death to one or more other persons (the survivors). Pay-on-death accounts also avoid probate.

Advantages of Joint Tenancy

Joint tenancy has a number of distinct advantages, including low administrative cost; convenience, speed and privacy; clear, undisputed disposition; the ability to reduce creditor's claims; and income shifting.

Low administrative cost.   Joint tenancy is inexpensive, both to create and to terminate. Both actions typically involve simply adding or deleting names on a legal certificate of ownership. Financial institutions and others holding record of title will usually do this, eliminating the need for an attorney. Later removal of a deceased cotenant's name from title to property often simply requires the presentation of a death certificate and perhaps the completion of a short, preprinted form signed by the surviving cotenants.

Convenience, speed, and privacy.   The simplicity inherent in creating and terminating joint tenancies makes them a convenient, easily understood, and speedy dispositive device. And since joint tenancy combines a method of disposition at death with a method of holding title, the property owner will not need to execute a relatively complex document, such as a will or a trust, to dispose of property held jointly.[11] In fact, at time of disposition, any existing will or trust will be disregarded as irrelevant to the automatic survivorship inherent in joint tenancy. Finally, unlike probate property, which is a matter of public record, joint tenancy property will pass to the surviving cotenants in relative privacy. Joint tenancy documents are not made public.

Clear, undisputed disposition.   Ordinarily, surviving joint tenants need not worry about not succeeding to ownership of the deceased cotenant's interest. Suits contesting joint tenancies are rare, partly because the legal formality requirements for taking title in joint tenancy are clear and minimal. There is little to challenge. In addition, the method of holding title in joint tenancy is usually clearly indicated. For example, some states require the words, "joint tenancy with right of survivorship and not as tenants in common," a description that further minimizes confusion. In contrast, interested parties are more able to challenge the validity of a will, in part because its execution requirements are far more complex.

---

[11] This characteristic of joint tenancy explains why some call it "the poor man's will."

A few joint tenancies, however, have been successfully challenged. In some cases, courts have held that the decedent created a joint tenancy "for convenience only," and did not intend to leave his or her interest to the surviving cotenants. For example, elderly people may create a joint tenancy solely to seek assistance in property management. Another person may be included as a cotenant simply to help write checks on the elder's bank funds. As another example, consider the facts of an actual court case, in which a husband took title to his own stock in joint tenancy with his wife, in order to avoid probate. At their later divorce, the wife was required to release her interest in the stock. The court reasoned that the husband had not created the joint tenancy with donative intent. To safeguard against any controversy over unintended gifts in these types of situations, the client might wish to write a letter clearly indicating actual intent.

Reduced creditors' claims. Property held in joint tenancy is not subject to the claims of a deceased cotenant's unsecured creditors, because death results in an instantaneous and automatic transfer of ownership to the surviving cotenants.[12] Thus, joint tenancy can be one method of insulating property from some creditors.

> EXAMPLE 10–1 Three years ago, Starfield financed the purchase of a car, which was used as collateral against the loan. Starfield died this year owning, among other things, the car (a probate asset), and some securities held in joint tenancy with his sister. If the bank loan goes into default, the bank will be able to recover the car. If proceeds from the sale of the car are not sufficient to pay off the loan, the bank may be able to reach other assets in Starfield's probate estate, but it probably will not be able to seize the securities, which now belong to the sister.

Income shifting. By placing property in joint tenancy with other family members, the client is able to shift income to lower-bracket taxpayers. Ownership interest is immediately transferred to them, and, consequently, income generated by the transferred

---

[12]However, a creditor may be able to recover under the theory that the deceased cotenant made a transfer considered to be "fraudulent" as to creditors. In addition, the property will be subject to claims resulting from debts incurred by the surviving cotenants, whether or not incurred jointly with the decedent.

property belongs to them, too. If the cotenant is in a lower tax bracket than the creator, the combined tax on generated income may be reduced. However, we shall see shortly that the relinquishment of so much control can be a serious drawback to joint tenancy.

Disadvantages of Joint Tenancy

The disadvantages of joint tenancy as a dispositive device include nontax factors such as inflexible disposition and loss of ownership and control, as well as tax disadvantages, including the basis problem and the risk of higher transfer taxes. After studying them, the reader will probably conclude that joint tenancy is not usually suitable for wealthier clients.

Inflexible disposition. Joint tenancy is an inflexible dispositive device. Disposition is clear but rigid: The surviving cotenants take outright the deceased cotenant's interest. Thus, joint ownership prevents the client from making other, less direct types of transfers at death, such as giving an interest to a nonowner or splitting the interest by giving an income interest to one person and a remainder interest to another. And the property passing to the surviving cotenant will not be subject to those protective provisions often included in wills and trusts regarding responsible asset management. As a consequence, by selecting joint tenancy, clients often risk asset depletion by inexperienced cotenants having complete discretion over care and management of the property. Most of the planning arrangements to be discussed in the remaining chapters of this book require types of transfers not possible with joint tenancy.

As just one example of the many distribution problems that can arise, consider joint tenancy between a childless couple. If both were to die in fairly rapid succession, such as in a common accident, all of the property could wind up in the hands of the *surviving cotenant's* heirs or beneficiaries. As illustrated in Chapter 3, this unlimited disposition can be avoided with a will or a trust, documents that can explicitly provide for the contingency with a survival clause.[13] By taking title in joint tenancy, spouses empower the survivor to totally disregard the other's dispositive wishes.

---

[13]But only if the assets disposed of in these documents are not held in joint tenancy!

Surrender of ownership and control. Creating an interest in joint tenancy will usually constitute an immediate, completed gift to any cotenant who has not contributed an equal share of the consideration. Thus, each donee-cotenant will become the legal owner of an equal portion of the property. By receiving a (vested) present interest, each has the right to convert his or her share of the property into a tenancy-in-common interest, capable of being sold or devised to noncotenants. This is not usually a problem for joint tenancies between happily married spouses or between people who contribute equal shares of property. Between others, however, the probate avoidance of joint tenancy may not be worth the client's immediate surrender of significant property interests.

In contrast with joint tenancy, other documents of transfer such as the will and the trust can delay the making of an outright gift at least until death. Instead of creating present interests, they provide for future interests, ones that are contingent upon future events, such as the client's not revoking those interests in the future. Most clients do not wish to make outright gifts at the time they are planning to avoid probate.

The basis problem. As we have seen in Chapter 8, the rule for basis adjustment for joint tenancy property at the death of one cotenant is clear and unalterable: Only the deceased cotenant's share of the property will receive a step-up in basis to date-of-death value. The surviving cotenant's basis will remain unchanged.

Avoiding joint tenancy may open up opportunities to achieve a step-up in basis for the entire value of the property. For example, the property could be *given to a donee* who is expected to die before the donor. At the donee's death, the entire property, which is then devised back to the donor, will receive a full step-up in basis. This strategy will work satisfactorily only in situations where the donee can be trusted to actually devise the property to the donor, such as where the parties are happily married. It will also succeed only if the donee's death occurs at least one year after the initial gift. Under Internal Revenue Code §1014(e), failure of the donee to survive by at least a year will cause the gift to be treated, for purpose of basis adjustment, as if the original transfer never occurred. A further discussion of this strategy will be found in Chapter 13.

The second way in which avoiding joint tenancy can open up an opportunity for a step-up in basis for the entire value of property involves the ownership of *community property* between spouses. As we saw in Chapter 8, unlike joint tenancy property, both halves of community property receive a step-up in basis at the death of the first spouse. Thus, married clients in community property states (even those of modest wealth) may be especially interested in avoiding joint tenancy arrangements, choosing instead to dispose of community property by will or trust.

Possible higher estate tax. Joint tenancies can increase FET for two reasons: because of the somewhat harsh provisions of §2040 and because of their effect on the size of the surviving spouse's gross estate.

In Chapter 6 we learned that under §2040, the *entire value* of property held in joint tenancy by a decedent is includable in the decedent's gross estate, except in two situations. First, if the joint tenancy was held solely with the surviving spouse, exactly one half will always be included. Second, if the joint tenancy was held by the decedent and at least one person who is not the decedent's spouse, the decedent's gross estate will include the entire value of the property, reduced only by an amount attributable to that portion of the consideration which can be shown to have been furnished by the survivors. Thus, a higher than necessary FET can result if a joint tenancy has a nonspouse cotenant and if the surviving cotenants are unable to prove contribution.

Joint tenancies between spouses can also result in a higher than necessary FET for the estates of *surviving spouses* because their gross estates will be quite large, having been loaded up with the other spouse's property passing to them by automatic right of survivorship. We shall see in Chapter 11 that in some cases, total spousal FET can be reduced by rejecting such a "one hundred percent marital deduction" plan, and instead passing less property outright to the surviving spouse. Such a "bypass" can only be arranged satisfactorily with a will or a trust. And as we have learned, neither document can dispose of property held in joint tenancy.

Gift taxation. Creation of joint tenancies between nonspouses can result in a taxable gift if an unequal material contribution is made and if the value of the gift exceeds the annual exclusion. In contrast, disposition by will or by the typical living trust produces no immediate gift during the client's lifetime because, as we have said, the documents only create contingent interests.

In view of the many significant drawbacks to joint tenancy, especially for clients with medium to large estates, planners almost universally prefer to recommend the other alternative to probate, the living trust, which is discussed next.[14]

THE OTHER ALTERNATIVE TO PROBATE: THE LIVING TRUST

The more popular alternative to probate for many estate planning clients is the living trust. As mentioned in Chapter 3, it is a trust created during the trustor's lifetime and funded with some or all of the family wealth. While the trustor is alive, the living trust is usually revocable,[15] which means that its terms are amendable and, if desired, its assets can be retransferred to the trustor's name.[16] At the trustor's death, the revocable trust becomes irrevocable and either terminates with the corpus distributed to the remaindermen, or remains in existence until a later date. In the case of a typical revocable living trust created by a husband and wife, all assets are placed in one trust, which is revocable by either of them during their lifetimes. At the first spouse's death, different things can happen, depending on the plan. If the spouses want a distribution pattern similar to that found in the living trust in Exhibit 3-2, then the decedent's share of the trust property is left in trust to the spouse, so that the trust becomes one large pot belonging entirely to the surviving spouse. Then, at his or her later death, the trust, which has avoided two probates, is either terminated or continued for the benefit of the children. Other distribution arrangements, particularly those designed to reduce FET at the surviving spouse's death, will be discussed in Chapter 11.

Taxation of a living trust depends on whether or not it is revocable. A revocable living trust has no tax consequences during the trustor's lifetime. A transfer to it does not constitute a taxable gift

---

[14]The client may not be able to avoid joint tenancy with regard to certain property. For example, some bank lenders may require that title to a borrower's home be held in joint tenancy with the spouse for certain reasons, including the need to have both spouses responsible for the debt.

[15]Irrevocable living trusts also avoid probate. Not as commonly used as the revocable living trust, they will be discussed at length in Chapters 13 and 15, in the context of gift giving and life insurance.

[16]Most trustors name themselves trustee of their living trust during their lifetime. However, under a doctrine called *merger,* a few states do not recognize trusts that name the same person to be trustor, trustee, and beneficiary.

since the transfer is not complete. And under the grantor trust rules, all income earned by a revocable trust is taxable to the grantor, that is, the trustor. In contrast, an irrevocable living trust is usually a separate income-taxpaying entity; all transfers into it usually constitute completed gifts, and, except when either the grantor trust rules or the kiddie tax apply, all distributed FAI income is usually taxed to the beneficiaries.

Advantages of the Living Trust

The living trust has several distinct advantages over other transfer devices. They include lower total costs, greater privacy and speed, the opportunity to test the future, the ability to use the trust as an alternative to a conservatorship, and reduced litigation.

Lower total cost than probate. Compared to will preparation and probate, the overall cost of preparation and administration of the living trust is usually significantly less. The following material discusses preparation costs and total cost.

Oddly, the *cost of preparing* the living trust may be a bit higher than the cost of preparing a will for at least two reasons. First, the trust is usually a more complicated document. Its provisions must arrange for the immediate receipt of property, for management of that property, and for the proper distribution of the property and its income for a period that might span several generations of beneficiaries.[17]

The cost of preparing the living trust is also higher than for planning for probate with a will because in addition to drafting a trust, the attorney must *also* draft a type of will. Unfortunately, the establishment of the living trust does not totally eliminate the need for a will. Because clients often fail to take the additional step necessary to fund the trust in a manner to be explained shortly, most clients will die owning some property in their own name, rather than in the name of the trustee. Planners provide for disposition of this property with what is called a *pour-over will*, specifying that any of the testator's assets not in the trust shall be distributed or "poured over" into the trust at the client's death. The

---

[17]However, if the probate alternative to a living trust embodies a *trust will*, the difference in drafting costs may not be as large.

pour-over will is usually a brief, simple document, adding little to the preparation cost of avoiding probate with the living trust.

While the specific cost of preparing the living trust may be higher, the *total cost* of the living trust alternative is usually lower, due to the relatively high cost of *formal* probate administration at death. In contrast with formal probate, administration of a living trust at the client's death involves minimal or no legal work in court. However, some other postmortem legal duties that are required under the probate alternative may also have to be performed under the trust alternative. They include obtaining appraisals, preparing an informal inventory of assets, filing death tax returns, paying creditors, distributing assets, and obtaining receipts.

But the total cost of probate isn't always greater. The efficiency of *informal* probate administration in UPC states can make probate an attractive alternative to the living trust, measured by the criterion of cost.

As mentioned earlier, a detailed quantitative comparison of the costs of the living trust versus formal probate is presented later in the chapter.

Greater privacy. A trust is usually a very private document, not subject to public inspection. Although property transfers into and out of a living trust may require examination of the trust instrument by financial and other institutions, the document usually need not be made publicly accessible. County recorders may require a filing of the trust in the public records, but usually only brief sections of the document need be submitted. However, some states that impose an inheritance tax on trust property may require the public filing of an inventory, which can reveal the nature and value of the trust's assets and the names of its beneficiaries. In addition, in the litigation process, a determined contestant can gain access to the contents of a living trust through "discovery."

As mentioned earlier, privacy may be especially desired by particularly wealthy or prominent clients. They may wish to avoid any additional publicity and any inspection by disinherited or contentious survivors, who may be seeking the opportunity to initiate a will contest.

Speed. Property can usually be transferred out of a trust rapidly because the transfer process is not ordinarily subject to supervision by the courts. However, in those states where creditors' claims can be made against trust assets, some delay before distribution may be required.

Speed of disposition of real property located in another state can be more rapid if that property is held in a living trust rather than disposed of by will, because ancillary administration can often be avoided. Real property held in a living trust is considered by most states to be intangible personal property, not subject to ancillary administration.[18]

Opportunity to test the future.   By placing assets into a revocable living trust, the client has the opportunity to test the future by making the estate plan largely operational during lifetime. The client can obtain a preview of how the assets will be managed after death and of how the beneficiaries can be expected to react to the receipt of family property. By naming another party trustee, the client can observe firsthand how well the assets are being managed and can make needed adjustments in management provisions before death. In addition, the trustee can be given the opportunity to become familiar with the trust assets during the client's lifetime, thus increasing the likelihood of both more efficient future management and a more smooth transition period after the client's death. Finally, by initiating a predictable pattern of asset distributions to beneficiaries during lifetime, the client can help a family member learn to use assets more maturely. Of course, a program of gifting is possible without a living trust, but having the terms of distribution in writing further ensures a continuous and consistent transfer program. It is these reasons why a few commentators have called the revocable living trust a "living will."[19]

Alternative to conservatorship.   We shall see in Chapter 17 that a client who becomes physically or mentally incapable of managing assets will need someone to provide that management. Just as a guardianship may have to be established to manage a minor's estate, a conservatorship may be necessary to manage the estate of an incapacitated adult. Like probate, guardianships and conservatorships are carefully supervised by the court, which usually re-

---

[18]However, most states impose a death tax on such property, and some states require reporting procedures quite similar to the probate process. Nevertheless, such real property may be able to avoid death tax in the state in which it is located if the property is owned by a corporation rather than directly by the decedent.

[19]This should not be confused with the universally known "living will," which is a document containing directions regarding health care decisions. See Chapter 17.

quires periodic accountings and formal court approval for many acts of asset management.

Used in lieu of a conservatorship, the living trust can thus be seen as a vehicle to avoid probate-type administration before the client's death.[20] The typical living trust begins with the client acting as trustee. Subsequently, a successor trustee takes over when the client relinquishes the role, becomes incapacitated, or dies. Thus, the living trust has an additional application not directly available with a will: It can be easily structured to provide for the client's incapacity.

Minimize litigation. As we have seen, the probate process can offer a relatively convenient opportunity for a dissatisfied survivor to initiate a will contest. On the other hand, the living trust is quite difficult to contest, since it requires a separate legal action in a different court, one often with more onerous legal requirements. In general, trusts are more difficult and more expensive to challenge.

Disadvantages of the Living Trust

The living trust has several disadvantages, including the burden of funding, possibly greater legal uncertainty, and some minor tax factors.[21]

Funding burden. Establishment of a joint tenancy is a one-step process. The very act of creation of the joint interest creates the appropriate title. On the other hand, establishment of the living trust to avoid probate is a two-step process. First, the trust document must be executed, somewhat like that of a will. Second, the trust must be *funded;* that is, legal title to the property intended to avoid probate must be formally transferred from the trustor to the trustee. Some trustor-clients never do it, because they are unaware that the additional step of funding is necessary. Others are aware of it but simply never get around to it. Most find it downright inconvenient, because it requires trips to the bank and to other places where title is officially kept. And clients who actively trade

---

[20]Another less expensive alternative to the conservatorship is the durable power of attorney, also discussed in Chapter 17.

[21]One other disadvantage is that in some states, property held in a living trust may not be secured as collateral against a loan.

their property, such as those involved in frequent real estate deals and securities transactions, may especially dislike the greater complexity inherent in keeping property in trust name.

Failure to fund the trust will cause that property not to be subject to the trust's terms. As a result, at the client's death the property will usually pass through probate, under the will or by intestate succession. Some attorneys carefully avoid this undesired outcome by insisting on funding the living trust themselves, rather than leaving the responsibility to the client. This may increase somewhat the legal cost of setting up the living trust.

Greater legal uncertainty.   Unlike the will, the living trust has not had the benefit of centuries of testing by the courts to resolve the inevitable conflicts that can arise. In the future, we can expect some continuing litigation in the area of the living trust, a prospect that raises uncertainty over the outcome of any unresolved issues.

Tax factors.   There are a number of minor tax disadvantages to the living trust.[22]

> Compared to the $600 available to an estate, a trust, after the grantor's death, has a smaller personal income tax exemption, at either $100 or $300.
>
> After the grantor's death, a trust cannot recognize net capital losses. An estate can.
>
> A trust is subject to the income tax throwback rules, while an estate is not.
>
> For income tax purposes, the trustee of a living trust cannot select the close of the trust's taxable year, while the executor of an estate can. The advantage of selecting a fiscal tax year is illustrated in Chapter 18.
>
> Finally, the IRS has taken the position that property transferred from a revocable trust within three years of the grantor's death will be included in his or her gross estate under §2035. The service argues that the property would have been included un-

---

[22]Not included among these disadvantages of a revocable living trust is the loss of a *basis set-up* at the grantor's death. Property held in a revocable living trust *will* receive a step-up because it is treated, from an income tax point of view, as owned by the grantor.

der §2038 had the transfer not been made.[23] To overcome this consequence, commentators recommend a two-step transfer: first the grantor should withdraw the amounts from the trust; second, he or she should directly make the gift.

A QUANTITATIVE COMPARISON OF THE COSTS OF PROBATE VERSUS THE LIVING TRUST

This section applies the principles of finance to develop a method of comparing the costs of probate with the costs of the living trust. The technique used will incorporate the "time value of money" concept known as present value.

> EXAMPLE 10–2 Patty is evaluating the decision whether to avoid probate of her assets, worth $1 million, by setting up a revocable living trust. With regard to costs, she has made the following estimates:
>
> Under the probate alternative: drafting her will, $600; probate administration, $25,000; other costs at death, including accountant's fees, $1,000.
>
> Under the trust alternative: drafting the trust and the pour-over will, $1,600; annual record-keeping until death, $300 per year; non-probate administration cost at death, $9,000; costs in higher income taxes due to inability to use a probate estate as a separate taxpayer, $1,100; other costs at death, including accountant's fees, $1,000.
>
> Her life expectancy is 10 years.

In calculating the total cost for each alternative, Patty could simply add up the expenses. That would result in a forecasted total cost under the probate alternative of $26,000, and a forecasted total cost under the trust of $17,600. Simple summation, however, does not take into account the time value of money. To correctly compare amounts incurred at different points in time, we must make adjustments to reflect the fact that money not payable today can be invested profitably until the time that it is payable. We can do this by calculating the sum of the *present values of the costs for each alternative*. The present value of a cost is the amount that would have to be invested today to accumulate the actual amount of that cost payable in the future.

To better understand the present value concept, consider an intuitively simple illustration. At an assumed annual rate of invest-

---

[23]I.R 8609005.

ment of 10 percent, one would need to invest $100 today to accumulate the amount $110 payable in one year. In other words, at 10 percent, the present value of $110 payable in one year is $100. Present values of any amount can be derived from present value tables such as Tables 11 and 12 of Appendix A at the end of the text. Table 11 depicts the present values of a single $1 amount to be paid in the future, assuming certain investment rates. Thus, the present value of $1 in one year at 10 percent is $0.909, or a bit less than 91 cents. Since we have been calculating the present value of the amount $110, not $1, our answer must be the product of $110 and 0.909, or $100. With regard to Patty's actual figures, at 10 percent, the present value of $1 to be paid in 10 years is $0.386. We will use this lump-sum discount factor in the calculations that follow.

How can we calculate the present value of the amount $300 payable each year for the next 10 years, with the first payment due in one year? Described in other words, we must calculate the total amount to be invested today which will enable us to fund this annuity, that is, to fund this entire progression of equal payments. To do this, we calculate the present value of the annuity. Table 12 in book Appendix A shows the present values of a $1 annuity for specified periods, assuming certain investment rates. The "annuity factor," as it is called, corresponding to 10 years and 10 percent, can be seen to 6.145. Since we wish to determine the present value of an annuity of $300, not $1, the answer must be the product of $300 and 6.145, or $1,844.

We are now ready to calculate Patty's total costs for the two alternatives in a manner which adjusts for the time value of money. The figures are included in Table 10–1 and Table 10–2.

Thus the sum of the present values of the costs are $10,636 for probate and $8,461 for the trust.[24] These represent the total amounts that Patty would have to invest today, at 10 percent, to properly accumulate and pay all of the individual forecasted costs when they are due.[25]

---

[24]The analysis could be refined slightly to include the tax deductibility of these expenses. For example, as we shall see in Chapter 18, administration costs may be deducted on the estate tax return. Thus, if T represents the marginal estate tax rate, the after-tax cost of an FET deductible expense is the product of that expense times the expression one minus T.

[25]The estimates in Example 10–2 have been made for illustration purposes only and should not be used as a general indicator of costs. Actual costs will vary

TABLE 10–1 Present Value of Costs of Probate

Item	Year	Amount	Discount Factor	Present Value
Drafting	Now	$ 600	1.0000	$ 600
Administration	10	25,000	.386	9,650
Other costs	10	1,000	.386	386
Total present value of probate costs				$10,636

TABLE 10–2 Present Value of Costs of Living Trust

Item	Year	Amount	Discount Factor	Present Value
Drafting	Now	$1,600	1.0000	$1,600
Record-keeping	1–10	300	6.145	1,844
Administration	10	9,000	0.386	3,474
Higher tax	10	1,100	0.386	425
Other costs	10	1,000	0.386	385
Total present value of living trust costs				$7,728

WHICH ALTERNATIVE IS BEST?

From the material covered so far, the reader can gather that the decision whether or not to avoid probate is not always a simple one. It requires that the client examine and subjectively weigh the advantages and disadvantages of each. It should be clear that there is no absolutely correct answer for all situations. Perhaps we can conclude with a description of a few of the circumstances in which clients are likely to favor a particular alternative.

considerably, depending on specific factors, such as the laws of the decedent's particular residence state and the cost of professional services in the decedent's locale. However, at the risk of overgeneralizing, in this author's experience, the present-value cost of formal probate is typically higher than the present-value cost of the living trust by at least 20 percent.

Probate

Clients who will be inclined to lean toward the probate alternative include:

1. Professionals, such as self-employed lawyers, engineers, and accountants, who stand to gain considerable security from the short creditors' limitations period.
2. Those who have large, complicated estates or who expect family disharmony after their death may benefit from the extra protection potentially available through greater court supervision.
3. Wealthier residents of UPC states where the cost advantage to avoiding probate is minimal.

Joint Tenancy

Since joint tenancy has some very significant disadvantages, clients are inclined to prefer it only if one, or perhaps all, of the following circumstances apply:

1. The client wants the property to pass outright to the surviving joint tenants. This implies that there is no need for tax-saving trusts after death.
2. A complete step-up in income tax basis at the client's death is not needed. This may include situations where property has not appreciated substantially, or where the survivors do not plan to sell the property, or where they expect any gain from sale of the property to be sheltered by provisions of the Internal Revenue Code.[26]
3. The creation of the joint tenancy interest does not result in an immediate gift.

These circumstances usually apply only to smaller estates.

---

[26]Common methods of sheltering an otherwise taxable gain include the IRC §1034 rollover of gain on sale of principal residence and the §121 one-time exclusion of $125,000 of a gain from sale of the principal residence by an individual who has attained age 55.

Living Trust

Clients who will tend to prefer the living trust typically include those who want to avoid probate but do not like joint tenancy because of its significant disadvantages. For example:

1. Those with larger estates who wish to avoid the FET consequences of joint tenancy.
2. Those who want privacy and speed in the property transfer process.
3. Clients for whom the total cost of the living trust is expected to be considerably lower than the cost of probate; reasons include the following:
   a. Probate administration expenses are expected to be high, perhaps because an independent executor must be named.
   b As trustee, the client will not need to pay for record-keeping.
   c. Nonprobate administration fees are low, perhaps because a private individual can be named trustee.

The next chapter will explore marital deduction and bypass planning, two major methods of reducing the FET.

RECOMMENDED READING

BOSTICK, CHARLES D. "The Revocable Trust: A Means of Avoiding Probate in the Small Estate?" *University of Florida Law Review* 21 (1968), pp. 44–58.

BRINK, RHONDA H. "Planning Perspectives for Creditor-Conscious Clients." University of Miami Estate Planning Institute, 1988.

DALY, JOHN K. "How Fiduciary Fees Are Determined." *Trusts & Estates*, May 1977, pp. 348–49.

DOUSSARD, JOSEPH E. "The Effect of the Uniform Probate Code on Estate Administration and Tax Planning." *Estate Planning*, May 1981, pp. 142–44.

ELLWANGER, THOMAS J. "ERTA Gives New Impetus to the Use of Joint Tenancy in Planning for Gifts and Estates." *Estate Planning*, March 1982, pp. 84–89.

ELZER, ROBERT W. "Using a Revocable Trust to Minimize Probate Proceedings or Avoid Them Entirely." *Estate Planning*, September 1987, pp. 286–94.

FETTERS, SAMUEL M. "An Invitation to Commit Fraud: Secret Destruction of Joint Tenant Survivorship Rights." *Fordham Law Review*, 1986, pp. 173–202.

GIBBER, ALLAN J. "Effective Use of Probate Procedure Can Ease Administration, Saving Costs and Time." *Estate Planning*, July 1984, pp. 230–34.

JOHNSON, MICHAEL L. "Survivorship Interests with Persons Other than a Spouse: The Costs of Probate Avoidance." *Real Property, Probate And Trust Journal,*

20 (1985), pp. 985–1007. (Discusses problems with joint and survivorship bank accounts.)

KEIDEL, FREDERICK R. "The Revocable Trust Revisited." Fifth Annual Southern California Tax and Estate Planning Forum, 1985.

KESSLER, RICHARD P., and ZOE M. HICKS. "Protecting a Professional Client's Assets from the Potential Claims of Creditors." *Estate Planning,* November 1986, pp. 340–44.

LANGBEIN, JOHN H. "The Nonprobate Revolution and the Future of the Law of Succession." *Harvard Law Review* 97 (1984), pp. 1108–41.

LYNN, ROBERT J. "Problems with Pour-Over Wills." *Ohio State Law Journal* 47, pp. 47–64.

MENNELL, ROBERT L. "Community Property with Right of Survivorship." *San Diego Law Review* 20 (1983), pp. 779–800.

MOORE, MALCOLM A. "The Will Regenerate: From Whipping Boy to Workhorse." *The Probate Lawyer* 7 (Summer 1981), pp. 5–48.

RUEBEL, RICHARD J. "Planning for the Impact of Creditor's Claims against a Client's Nonprobate Property." *Estate Planning,* January 1988, pp. 38–42.

TERRAZZANO, JEANN R. "Joint Tenancy Is Simple Way of Holding Property but May Not Produce the Best Tax Results." *Taxation for Accountants,* June 1983, pp. 348–51.

THORNE, JACK F. "Form of Joint Ownership Controls Results for Estate and Gift Tax and Income Tax Planning." *Taxation for Lawyers,* March–April 1985, pp. 308–13.

TOPOLNICKI, DENISE M. "Which Assets Should Be in Whose Name?" *Money,* September 1984, pp. 105–10.

WELLMAN, RICHARD V. "The Uniform Probate Code: A Possible Answer to Probate Avoidance." *Indiana Law Journal* 44 (1969), pp. 189–205.

WINN, EDWARD B. "The Estate Lawyer: Relic of the Past or Firm Fixture of the Future?" *Probate Lawyer* 9 (Summer 1983), pp. 1–84.

WOODRUM, V. L. "A Planner's Guide to Probate." *Financial Planning,* February 1985, pp. 203–7.

YU, DIANE C. "Revocable Trusts as an Alternative to Conservatorships." *California Lawyer,* September 1983, pp. 23–26.

QUESTIONS AND PROBLEMS

1. Discuss the validity of the claim that probate promotes fairness.

2. (*a*) Why isn't probate private? (*b*) Is the living trust always private?

3. (*a*) Who might wish to contest an invalidly executed will? (*b*) Why might it be easier to do than to challenge a living trust?

4. You wish to advise client Brush about the income tax advantage to probate. Assuming that all of Brush's survivors will be in the 28 percent marginal rate bracket, a) how much income in the future Brush estate could be subject to a lower rate? b) what is the maximum amount of tax that could be saved by using the Brush estate as a separate tax entity? c) reanswer parts a and b assuming a 33 percent marginal rate for all survivors.

5. One of your clients asks you to summarize the advantages and disadvantages of using joint tenancies to avoid probate.

6. (*a*) Why should the living trust cost less than the formal probate alternative? (*b*) Are all cost components lower?

7. Curley has just received his lawyer's bill for developing a plan that avoids probate with a living trust. Included is a charge for drafting a will. Did the lawyer make a billing mistake?

8. Today Dennis executed a living trust, with his sister as the only remainder beneficiary. Upon driving home from the lawyer's office, Dennis is killed in an auto accident. All of his property is still held in joint tenancy with his brother, Elmer. Is there a problem? Why or why not?

9. Evaluate the cost factor in the decision whether or not to avoid formal probate with a living trust, under the following assumed set of facts.

    For the probate alternative: drafting the will, $1,300; formal probate administration, $60,000; other costs at death, including accountants' fees, $2,300.

For the trust alternative: drafting costs, $2,200; record-keeping until death, $500 per year; nonprobate administration costs at death, $3,100; costs in higher income taxes due to the inability to use a probate estate as a separate taxpayer, $1,000; other costs at death, including accountants' fees, $3,600.

Assume an investment rate of return of 10 percent, and that the client will live 12 years. (Answers: Present value of total costs: probate, $21,174; trust, $8,063.)

10. Now evaluate the cost of *informal* probate versus the living trust. Assume all facts given in problem 9, above, except that informal probate administration will cost $25,000.

11. (*a*) What types of clients are most likely to prefer probate? (*b*) To avoid probate with joint tenancies? (*c*) To avoid probate with the living trust?

11

Marital Deduction and Bypass Planning: I

<hr>

OVERVIEW

As we have seen, estate planning embraces numerous goals. For medium size or larger estates, one of the most important goals is to minimize the impact of the federal estate tax. Several techniques seek to accomplish FET minimization, including planning with the marital deduction, bypass planning, using lifetime transfers, and freezing the estate. This chapter and Chapter 12 will focus on the first two, use of the marital deduction and bypass planning to defer or completely eliminate the federal estate tax.[1]

Beginning in 1987, any decedent's estate will be able to transfer as much as $600,000, tax free. Thus, in the family plan that incorporates a simple will, a husband and wife with a total estate as high as $600,000 will be able to transfer their entire estate outright to their survivors, free of federal tax.

EXAMPLE 11–1 Husband (H) owns $600,000 in property and wife (W) owns nothing. Each has a simple will. If their order of death is first H, then W, H will be able to leave his entire estate outright to W, estate tax free. Upon her later death, she can pass the entire

<hr>

[1]Lifetime transfers are the subject of Chapters 13 and 14. Freezing the taxable estate as a technique was described in Chapter 9.

amount to her children, tax free. In fact, the children will be able to receive the full $600,000 free of tax, no matter how ownership of the property is divided among the spouses and no matter which spouse dies first. No federal estate tax will be owed at either death because neither spouse will have died owning greater than the amount of the exemption equivalent of the unified credit.

Thus, planning to minimize the federal estate tax will be a concern only for families whose total estates are expected to exceed $600,000.[2]

> EXAMPLE 11–2 Increasing the asset size in example 11–1 a bit, assume H and W own a family estate of $800,000. Under a simple will arrangement, although the marital deduction will entirely shelter the estate of the first spouse to die from FET, the estate of the second spouse to die will have a gross estate of $800,000 and thus will pay an FET of $75,000, under simple assumptions.

This chapter will focus on planning for these wealthier individuals.

In the following material, we will often refer to the "first spouse to die," and "second spouse to die."[3] To relieve the tedium of excessive wording, let's call these individuals S1 and S2, respectively. Further, we will continue to use FET as a shorthand for federal estate tax.

Planning to minimize the FET through the use of the marital deduction and the bypass arrangement traditionally involves applying at least one of four different planning options, to be described in considerable detail next. They are called the *100 percent marital deduction,* the *credit shelter bypass,* the *bypass with estate equalization,* and the *100 percent marital deduction with disclaimer into bypass.*

---

[2]Because of the possibility of lifetime taxable gifts and the likelihood of certain FET deductions, especially administration expenses and debts, estates somewhat larger than $600,000 can be transferred at death, completely tax free. Thus, more accurately, we will be focusing on those estates having a tax base exceeding the exemption equivalent.

[3]In most of the discussion that follows, we won't make assumptions about whether the husband or wife dies first. From a tax point of view, the crucial factor is not the sex of the decedent, but wealth of the decedent. However, order of death has, of course, very significant nontax implications. Statistics indicate that there is a 75 percent probability that the wife will outlive the husband an average of 10 years.

PLANNING OPTION 1: 100 PERCENT MARITAL DEDUCTION

One way to eliminate entirely the FET on all property owned by S1 at death is to leave all of it to S2. It will be sheltered by the unlimited marital deduction. Types of transfers by an S1 to an S2 that will qualify for the marital deduction include all outright transfers and, as we shall see, many types of transfers in trust for the benefit of S2.

Advantages of the 100 percent Marital Deduction

The 100 percent marital deduction is attractive to many clients who do not wish to burden an S2 with paying any avoidable taxes at the first death. And it can be a simple plan, easy to understand and inexpensive to establish. For example, the preparation of a simple will ordinarily will meet the objective of a zero FET for S1. In fact, even joint tenancy ownership of property solely between husband and wife will produce a full marital deduction for S1's share.

Finally, the 100 percent marital deduction can give S2 *total dispositive control* over all of the family property.[4] For example, the outright receipt of a *fee simple interest* will enable S2 to do anything with the property, including totally possess it, consume it, gift it, and exercise any other rights permitted such an owner.

Disadvantages of the 100 percent Marital Deduction

The 100 percent unlimited marital deduction has several significant drawbacks. First, and perhaps most important is a *higher total FET.* Since the entire estate will be sheltered by the marital deduction and will ordinarily pass outright to S2, it will all be subject to inclusion in S2's gross estate, barring remarriage or a program of gifting or consumption.[5]

---

[4]Not all 100 percent marital deduction plans need to, however. We will see shortly that certain nonoutright transfers for the benefit of S2 can restrict his or her control over the property and still qualify for the marital deduction. One commonly used technique is the transfer of qualified terminable interest property (a QTIP transfer).

[5]Under federal transfer tax law, even a *nonoutright transfer* by S1 that qualifies for the marital deduction will be included in the S2 gross estate. The universal

EXAMPLE 11–3 H and W own a family estate of $2 million, with each owning one half. Assuming simple wills, upon S1's death there will be no FET, inasmuch as the entire $1 million passing to S2 will be sheltered by the marital deduction. However, assuming that S2 doesn't remarry and neither transfers nor consumes the property prior to death, S2's $2 million taxable estate will be subject to an FET of $588,000.

In effect, complete use of the unlimited marital deduction will only *defer* the FET, not eliminate it. And because it fails to take advantage of the unified credit in the estate of S1, 100 percent marital deduction planning can have the effect of "overqualifying" or overusing the marital deduction, resulting in "loading up" of the taxable estate of S2, and later subjecting a greater amount to tax at the second death. And due to its progressive rate structure, an even greater FET will result by subjecting the entire property to taxation at S2's death.

Another disadvantage of the 100 percent marital deduction planning option is the possibility that more family assets will be *subject to probate,* and therefore to creditor's claims, while they reside in S2's probate estate. However, this will happen only if S2 disposes of the property by will rather than by a will substitute.

Three Impracticable Alternatives to a Bypass

For many wealthier individuals, the major deterrent to using the 100 percent marital deduction is the FET cost at S2's death. The second option, discussed shortly, called the credit shelter bypass, is the most common method used to reduce this cost. Before examining it, let's first touch on three simpler, though not usually practical, alternatives to a bypass that could work with the 100 percent marital deduction option to defer or reduce the FET for S2.

Remarriage. First, S2, having received all of S1's property outright, could anticipate remarrying and leaving the entire estate to the new spouse, S3, enabling the family to again secure the shelter of the marital deduction.

---

rule in this area is that, barring remarriage, gifting, or consumption, any property qualifying for the S1 marital deduction will inexorably be included in the S2 gross estate.

There are several problems with the anticipation of remarriage as a planning device. First, there is no assurance that it will occur. Demographically, the odds are against it. Second, an outright transfer from S2 to S3 may not be desirable, especially if the marriage occurred recently, because our former S2 would often have less than complete assurance that S3 would leave the property to survivors who are acceptable to S2, usually the children of the S1–S2 marriage. To solve this disposition problem, our S2 could create a more complex 100 percent marital deduction plan that would leave the estate in a QTIP trust (described in greater detail later in the chapter), with income payable to the new spouse for life and the remainder to S2's chosen survivors. The property would become "qualified terminable interest property" (QTIP), resulting in a marital deduction for S2's estate. However, the tax laws covering qualified terminable interest property require that it must be taxed as if it were includable in the surviving spouse's (here, S3's) gross estate.

This last point brings up the third drawback to remarriage as a planning solution. Whether S2 leaves the property outright to S3 or in a QTIP trust, the property will eventually be taxed once before it is received by the younger-generation beneficiaries.

In conclusion, planning to take advantage of a possible remarriage may delay the FET until the new surviving spouse dies, but it will not reduce or eliminate it. And, of course, there is no assurance that a remarriage will occur. Finally, the assumption of remarriage creates a potential, though surmountable, problem of an undesirable disposition.

Consumption. A second simple yet often improbable method of deferring or reducing the S2 FET in the context of a 100 percent marital deduction is for S2 to plan to consume the property. Substantial consumption will in fact reduce the tax because it effectively depletes the estate. But expecting S2 to carry this out is usually unrealistic because old habits die hard. People grow accustomed to a standard of living and usually feel uncomfortable spending a great deal more. Also, clients usually want to pass on all or most of their wealth to their survivors, not deplete it. Moreover, they may need the extra feeling of security that accompanies the act of continued ownership of the bulk of their wealth until death. Finally, an older client might find it downright impossible to consume the estate in such a short period of time. For all of these reasons, substantial consumption is not usually a realistic expectation.

Lifetime gifts. As an alternative to consumption or remarriage, S2 could make lifetime gifts of the property, reducing the estate tax base to less than $600,000. For some clients, this is an ideal solution. Yet many clients will be reluctant, for the same reasons, to make the sizable lifetime transfers needed to substantially reduce a future FET. Lifetime gifting is the subject of Chapter 13 and will not be discussed further here. In this and the next chapter, we will assume that S2 will not make significant lifetime gifts.

We turn now to the most preferred method of reducing the S2 FET.

PLANNING OPTION 2: THE CREDIT SHELTER BYPASS

The credit shelter bypass is usually a more desirable method of reducing the FET for S2 than is a 100 percent marital deduction for S1, combined with S2 remarriage, consumption, or lifetime gifting. Unlike remarriage, it can truly reduce the FET, not just defer it. And unlike consumption and lifetime gifting, it does not require a significant disposition of the family estate before the death of S2.

The customary version of the credit shelter bypass originates with a deathtime transfer by S1, under which S2 is left an amount equal to S1's entire estate, reduced by $600,000, the amount of the exemption equivalent of the federal unified credit.[6] Since the $600,000 is not received by S2, it will not become part of S2's gross estate at death. That amount is said to *bypass* the S2 estate. This plan will reduce or, possibly, eliminate the S2 FET, without subjecting the S1 estate to any tax. S1's estate will incur no FET because the portion of S1's estate passing to S2 will be sheltered by the marital deduction, and the portion not passing to S2 will be sheltered by the unified credit.

---

[6]Actually, the disposing document usually provides that the bypass amount be determined by a complex verbal *formula* designed to take account of the influence of other factors besides the unified credit, such as the deduction for debts and administration expenses. In this text, we will ignore this complication.

EXAMPLE 11–4 As in Example 11–3, H and W own a family estate of $2 million, with each owning one half. However, instead of a simple will in which S1 would have left all property to S2, assume that S1's will leaves only $400,000 (S1's estate reduced by $600,000) to the spouse. S1's estate will still incur no FET, since $400,000 will be sheltered by the marital deduction, and the other $600,000 will be sheltered by the unified credit. Yet the expected FET for S2's taxable estate (of $1.4 million) will be reduced from $588,000 to $320,000, a saving of $268,000.

Thus, under the credit shelter bypass option, S2's estate will be loaded up less than it would have been if the 100 percent marital deduction option had been chosen. This option enables the estate of *each spouse* to take advantage of the unified credit, rather than denying it to the S1 taxable estate. In the language of the trade, this option will "zero out" or "reduce to zero" the S1 FET, and there will be "two trips up the rate ladder," rather than one.

In Example 11–4, S2 received $600,000 less of S1's estate. The reader may ask at this point, is it really worth saving $268,000 in FET if the transfer requires that S2 lose the right to receive $600,000, especially in view of the fact that the tax saving will not occur until both spouses have passed away? Surprisingly, the answer is often yes, for reasons developed next.

The Bypass Trust

The bypass plan often works because the disposition to someone other than S2 can be arranged to conform to S2's overall objectives. The bypass property could be transferred to those individuals who are sometimes described as "the natural objects of (S2's) bounty." Usually, these individuals are the children of the S1–S2 marriage. As a potential S2, neither spouse will usually object to naming his or her children to be the bypass recipients since in all likelihood, they would have been chosen to ultimately receive the entire family estate under a simple will plan.

S1 and S2 might, however, have some reservations about the bypass plan if, at S1's death, it gave rise to an immediate, outright transfer to the children. They may feel that the survivors may be too young to receive that amount of property. Or S2 may need either the income from the property, or the property itself, for support. Or S2 might prefer to retain control over the management of those assets ultimately intended for the children. These are common objections to the use of an immediate, outright transfer to the children to effect a bypass. Happily, the bypass can be salvaged and these objections can be overcome by means of a transfer into *trust*.

Used in the context of bypass planning, a trust can take on at least two somewhat different names. In general, when incorporated in a plan to bypass S2's gross estate, it is called a *bypass trust*.[7] More specifically, when the amount included in the bypass trust is set equal or nearly equal to the amount of the exemption equivalent of the unified credit, it is called a *credit shelter bypass trust*.[8]

Used in lieu of an outright transfer of the bypass share to the children, however, the trust does not save one additional cent of FET. The same saving could be achieved by an outright transfer of property to them. Instead, the bypass trust vehicle is employed to overcome some major nontax problems inherent in outright transfers to children, some of which were mentioned in the above discussion. The trust solves those problems in a number of ways, some of which are described next.

Immaturity.   First, if at S1's death the children are too young to properly handle an outright transfer, the trustee can be directed to manage the property until they are considered sufficiently mature.

Income and principle for S2.   Second, if S2 needs funding from the trust for support, the trust could be made to last at least until S2's death, for example, during which time S2 could enjoy a life estate in part or all of the *income* earned by the trust. Further, S2 could be granted a power to invade the *principal* of the trust for certain needs. Recall from Chapter 6 that a power to invade for the benefit of the holder, which is limited by an "ascertainable stan-

---

[7]A bypass trust is also known as a *nonmarital trust* to relate it to and distinguish it from the marital trust, described in Chapter 12.

[8]In planning for division of the estate into the bypass and the marital share, attorneys will usually choose one of two types, called the pecuniary and the fractional share distributions. Under a *pecuniary distribution,* complete interests in specific assets will pass to one or the other share. Under a *fractional share distribution,* both bypass and marital shares will receive a fractional interest in each and every asset in the estate. Factors in deciding which type of provision to use include expected estate and income taxes. The rules are complicated. For a detailed treatise, see the Covey book cited at the end of Chapter 12.

dard," will not be taxed as a general power of appointment. Hence, S2 could have the right to invade for her benefit for reasons of his or her "health, education, support, or maintenance," without subjecting the property to inclusion in S2's gross estate.[9]

S2 as trustee. Third, the trust will often be preferable to an outright transfer if S2 wishes to *manage* the property during his or her lifetime. S2 could be named trustee of the bypass trust, without adverse FET consequences.[10]

S2 as surrogate decision maker. Besides having a limited power to invade and the power to act as trustee, S2 could also be given certain other powers over the bypass trust. S2 could be given a nongeneral power of appointment to dispose of the assets to certain *third parties* during lifetime or at death. Thus, S2 may be given the power to appoint anyone except S2, S2's estate, S2's creditors, or the creditors of S2's estate. For example, S2 could be granted the power to determine the amount of property each child should receive, and when each should receive it, perhaps long after S1's death. In this way, S1 would be giving S2, as surrogate decision maker, the opportunity to respond, perhaps long after S1's death, to changed circumstances.

"Five and five" power for S2. Another power that S2 could be granted over the bypass trust is the right for any reason to withdraw the greater of $5,000 or 5 percent of the corpus each year. This "five and five" power adds some flexibility to bypass planning, without subjecting the value of the corpus to inclusion in S2's gross estate as property subject to a general power of appointment.

---

[9]The words "health," "education," "support," and "maintenance" are carefully chosen from the IRS Regulations under §2041. Draftsmen purposely avoid including other terms, such as "any other special need," "comfort," "welfare," "emergency," and "happiness." Unfortunately, resignation by S2 as trustee of a *tainted* trust will not solve the problem. S2 will be considered to have made a gift by releasing a general power of appointment over the property, and as a trust income beneficiary, S2, at death, will be considered to have made a §2036 transfer with a retained life estate. For a discussion of some other perils in using the word "emergency," see the Schlenger article cited at the end of Chapter 12.

[10]However, naming an independent party, such as a bank, to be trustee can enhance flexibility by giving the trustee greater freedom to distribute trust principal and income without adverse income, gift, and estate tax consequences. For example, an "independent" trustee could distribute corpus to S2 for his or her "happiness" without risking inclusion of the trust corpus in S2's gross estate.

However, S2's gross estate will include the value of the unexercised right in the year of death.

S2 discretion over income distribution. Finally, in circumstances where S2 does not need the income from the bypass trust, S2 could also be given the power of discretion over distribution of the trust income. Called a *discretionary bypass trust,* it offers greater flexibility and can save income taxes if, for example, the children are in a lower tax bracket than S2. However, the discretionary trust has some significant tax traps and must be planned carefully.

For these and other nontax reasons, planners usually implement bypass planning with a trust.

PLANNING OPTION 3: BYPASS WITH ESTATE EQUALIZATION

Although the credit shelter bypass can totally eliminate the S1 FET, and can reduce the S2 FET, it may not succeed in minimizing the combined FET for both deaths. To illustrate, consider the effect of reducing the marital deduction in Example 11–4 by $1. Notice that S1's estate has a marginal tax rate of 37 percent (taxable estate of $600,000) and S2 has a marginal tax rate of 43 percent (taxable estate of $1.4 million). Accordingly, reducing the S1 marital deduction to $399,999 should, other things the same, increase the S1 FET by 37 cents and reduce the S2 FET by 43 cents, resulting in a net savings of 6 cents, or 6 percent of the reduction. Similarly, reducing the S1 marital deduction by a greater amount should continue to yield a net saving until the point is reached where the marginal tax rates are equal. At that point, the combined FET for both S1 and S2 will be lowest.

> EXAMPLE 11–5 As in Examples 11–3 and 11–4, H and W own a family estate of $2 million, with each owning one half. Instead of leaving all or some property to the spouse, as in the examples above, let's assume that S1 plans to leave nothing to S2. Instead, S1 bequeaths his or her entire $1 million estate, outright or in trust, to the children, via bypass. S1's FET will be $153,000, the net tax on a $1 million taxable estate subject to no marital deduction. S2's FET will also be $153,000, because it too will have a taxable estate of $1 million. S1 and S2's combined FET will be $306,000, which is $14,000 less than the amount resulting from the credit shelter bypass option.

In the above example, reducing the S1 marital deduction to zero had the effect of *equalizing the taxable estates* of S1 and S2, consequently equalizing the marginal tax rates and thereby minimizing the combined tax for both spouses.[11] This third option, bypass with estate equalization, seeks to minimize total FET by means of a bypass which attempts to equalize both spouse's total taxable estates and marginal tax rates.

To summarize options 1, 2, and 3, consider the illustrations in Figure 11–1. For each option, circles represent property held in an estate. For example, in option 2, which illustrates the facts described in Example 11–4, S1 dies owning $1 million in property. S1's estate will incur no FET, and thus $400,000 will pass to S2 and $600,000 will pass to the bypass share. S2 will then die owning an estate of $1.4 million, which will incur an FET of $320,000. The children will receive $1,680,000, representing $1,080,000 from S2 and $600,000 from the bypass share.

The last two options described above, credit shelter bypass and bypass with estate equalization, demonstrate the trade-off the planner and client must face. The former seeks to *defer* the FET as much as possible, at the possible cost of a greater total tax, while the latter, by equalizing the taxable estates, seeks to *equalize* the two tax rates and thereby minimize the total tax at the cost of a greater S1 tax. Some commentators call this the trade-off between estate tax deferral and estate tax equalization.

---

[11]Making several simplifying assumptions, the determination of the amount of the marital deduction needed to equalize the taxable estates for S1 and S2 can be arrived at with the following formula:

$$\text{S1 taxable estate} = \text{S2 taxable estate}$$
$$\text{S1 gross estate} - \text{S1 marital deduction} = \text{Property presently owned by S2} + \text{S1 marital deduction}$$

Solving, in our example,

$$\$1 \text{ million} - \text{marital deduction} = \$1 \text{ million} + \text{marital deduction}$$
$$2 \times \text{Marital deduction} = 0$$
$$\text{Marital deduction} = 0$$

This formula is crude, however, and does not take into account many specific factors, such as the presence of other estate tax deductions and certain credits. Its value is mostly pedagogical.

FIGURE 11-1 Illustration of Planning Options 1, 2, and 3 (no asset appreciation)

OPTION 1	OPTION 2	OPTION 3
100% marital deduction	Credit shelter bypass	Bypass with estate equalization
(Example 11-3)	(Example 11-4)	(Example 11-5)

OPTION 1

S_1 $1,000,000

Less $0 FET

Leaves $1,000,000 (= M.D.)

S_2 $2,000,000

Less $588,000 FET

Leaves $1,412,000

Children $1,412,000

OPTION 2

S_1 $1,000,000

Less $0 FET

Leaves $1,000,000

$600,000 → Bypass share $600,000 → $600,000

$400,000 (= M.D.) → S_2 $1,400,000 → Less $320,000 FET → Leaves $1,080,000

Children $1,680,000

OPTION 3

S_1 $1,000,000

Less $153,000 FET

Leaves $847,000

$847,000 → Bypass share $847,000 → $847,000

(zero M.D.) → S_2 $1,000,000 → Less $153,000 FET → Leaves $847,000

Children $1,694,000

Factors Influencing Deferral versus Equalization

In deciding between deferral and equalization, we must keep in mind the client's goals. If a major goal is simply to save as much S2 FET as possible while not incurring a single penny of S1 FET, then equalization is not possible and the plan must usually seek full deferral by means of the credit shelter bypass. On the other hand, if a primary goal is to minimize the combined effect of both estate taxes, then attempts at equalization may be practicable. Finally, if a major goal is to maximize the amount passing to the next generation, equalization may be inefficient due to the effect of the time value of money, discussed further below. Thus, the choice of a bypass planning strategy will depend partly on the client's specific FET reduction goal. Some of the factors that will influence these goals are explored next.

Avoidance of tax while spouses are alive. A factor that often motivates spouses to choose the goal of minimizing S2's FET subject to the requirement of a zero S1 FET is a strong opposition to incurring any avoidable taxes during their lifetimes. Other reasons include the hope that the FET is repealed or reduced, and the anticipation that S2, during lifetime, may consume or gift the estate assets. These factors favor deferral but do not rule out a bypass of the credit shelter amount.

Time value of money. Clients may be willing to incur an S1 FET, provided that significant offsetting benefits will result. Example 11–5 demonstrated how equalization can lower the combined S1–S2 FET. However, that arrangement may be financially inefficient, due to the effect of the time value of money. In that example, we saw that equalization by means of reducing S1's marital deduction to zero resulted in a total tax saving of $14,000. However, the cost of this result was to tax S1's estate by $153,000 more than the amount taxed to S1 by deferral. At a 10 percent rate of return, assuming that S2 survived S1 by 10 years, this represents a before-tax *opportunity income loss* in 10 years of over $36,000. Proper planning must therefore consider the effect of the time value of money, since a substantial opportunity income loss from the early payment of the transfer tax may favor deferral.

Another aspect of the time value of money concerns the effect of *asset appreciation* on the S2 FET. It is reasonable to assume that family assets will grow in value after the death of S1 due to the combined influence of inflation and real capital appreciation. This growth will generate a larger S2 taxable estate, and greater deferral will make it even larger. Alternatively, increased equalization will result in a greater bypass and thereby reduce the S2 buildup. Hence, the expectation of greater asset appreciation justifies greater equalization by means of a larger bypass.

FIGURE 11–2 Illustration of Planning Options 1, 2, and 3 (5 percent asset appreciation)

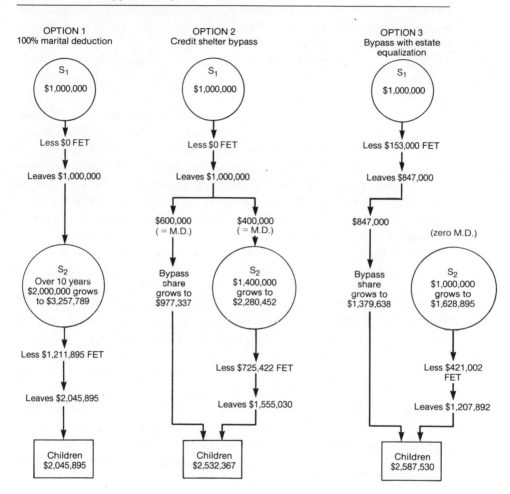

Numerical illustration of effect of asset appreciation. To adequately reflect the influence of opportunity income loss and asset
appreciation on the estate plan, clients must adopt the goal of maximizing the amount *passing to the next generation,* rather than
minimizing the combined estate taxes. To see the effects of the
time value of money on the amount that can pass to the next generation, refer to the illustrations in **Figure 11–2**, which assume that

the family estate assets will appreciate an average of 5 percent a year during the assumed 10-year span between S1's and S2's death. Otherwise, the illustrations use the same initial estate sizes and plans incorporated in Examples 11–3, 11–4, and 11–5, and shown in Figure 11–1.

Several conclusions can be drawn. First, appreciation will increase substantially the net amount passing to the children for all three plans. Second, compared to Option 1, Option 2, the credit shelter bypass, still results in a large FET saving for S2 and thus generates a much larger net transfer to the children. Third, Option 3, bypass with reduced marital deduction, still beats Option 2 in terms of the total amount passing to the children. Appreciation apparently increases Option 3's relative advantage from $14,000 to $55,163. In summary, the opportunity income loss on the S1 FET of $153,000 is more than offset by the gain from the S2 FET saving resulting from a complete bypass.

Other factors.   At least two factors influence the choice of deferring or equalizing, in light of the client's goals. First, *liquidity* can be a concern. The choice of greater deferral reduces the liquidity problem at S1's death. In the extreme case, complete elimination of S1's FET will eliminate what constitutes the typical medium- and larger-size estate's greatest cash need. Other methods of meeting liquidity needs will be discussed in Chapter 15.

Second, in considering whether to defer or to equalize, we should consider the benefits of the *step-up in basis* received by all property included in the S2 estate. Complete use of the marital deduction under planning Option 1 will maximize the property subject to this adjustment. Deferral by means of the use of the credit shelter bypass will result in a step-up, at S2's death, of less property (all of S2's assets owned at death, which include all but $600,000 of S1's assets). Equalization through the use of a substantially reduced marital deduction will further reduce the amount subject to an S2 step-up. Since bypass property will not be stepped-up at S2's death, income tax basis rules favor deferral rather than equalization through bypass.

In conclusion, when deciding whether to defer or to equalize, although generalization is difficult, practitioners have developed a rough rule of thumb essentially based on the considerations discussed above: Equalization should be seriously considered if either the assumed surviving spouse is not expected to live very long or if the estates contain relatively large amounts of highly appreciating property. Otherwise, deferral will probably be more desirable.

In our discussions of bypass planning so far, we have examined the various factors that influence the choice to defer with the marital deduction or to equalize with the bypass. At this point, the reader might wonder what plans clients are actually using. Experience indicates that most clients do not wish to equalize, if the result will be the incurrence of an S1 FET. Further, most clients are willing to plan for a bypass, by means of a trust, but again only as long as the plan generates no S1 FET. The upshot is that most clients use planning Option 2, credit shelter bypass. In addition to the other two options, a few clients are selecting a fourth option, which is described at the beginning of Chapter 12.

RECOMMENDED READING

(Please refer to the end of Chapter 12 for Recommended Readings.)

QUESTIONS AND PROBLEMS

1. What is the largest estate size that an individual can transfer, FET free, with a simple will to a (*a*) spouse; (*b*) nonspouse? Explain, and state any assumptions made.

2. (*a*) Under simple assumptions, what is the largest family estate size that a husband and wife can transfer, FET free, with simple wills to their children? (*b*) Does it make any difference how much is owned by each spouse? Explain.

3. (*a*) Under simple assumptions, what is the largest family estate size that a husband and wife can transfer, FET free, with a credit shelter bypass plan to their children? (*b*) Does it make any difference how much is owned by each spouse? Explain.

4. In this question, assume that H owns $1 million in property and W owns nothing to speak of, and at the moment we are planning for the possibility that H will survive W.
   a. Why won't the credit shelter bypass arrangement work?
   b. What is the minimum amount of property that either spouse as S1 must own to take full advantage of that bypass?
   c. Can you think of any device that will make the bypass work in this situation? Perhaps one with an income tax advantage, as well?
   d. Regarding the device in part *c*, how much should be involved?

5. A client asks you to describe the advantages of the 100 percent marital deduction.

6. How can each of the following defer or reduce the FET for S2: (*a*) remarriage; (*b*) consumption. Explain the drawbacks to each as an estate planning device.

7. How does the credit shelter bypass plan help overcome the limitations of the two devices mentioned in Question 6?

8. (*a*) In selecting the amount of property to place into the bypass share, what factors should be considered? (*b*) Must this amount be precisely specified prior to S1's death?

9. H and W have come to you to help them do some FET planning. They own a family estate of $3 million, with H

owning two thirds. Presently they have simple wills. Calculate the amount which, under simple assumptions, will pass to their children under the following plans: (*a*) the present arrangement; (*b*) a 100 percent marital deduction; (*c*) a credit shelter bypass; (*d*) bypass with estate equalization. Be sure to do your calculations twice, reflecting a reversal in the order of deaths. Assume that the first death will occur in 1990 and the second death ten years later. (One answer: Under equalization, if H dies first: children will receive $2,274,000.) What conclusions can be drawn?

10. Regarding Question 9, could H and W wind up having very different plans? Why or why not?

11. (*a*) Rework parts *a, b* and *c* of Question 9, assuming that between the first and second deaths all property doubles in value. (*b*) What conclusions can be drawn?

12. (*a*) What factors help determine whether a bypass should entail an outright transfer or a transfer into trust? (*b*) Is FET savings a factor? Why or why not?

Marital Deduction and
Bypass Planning: II

OVERVIEW

This chapter continues our discussion of marital deduction and by-pass planning. We begin with a fourth popular planning option, one using a disclaimer. Next, we'll focus on the marital trust, and then we'll cover a brief case study in marital deduction and bypass planning. The chapter concludes with an examination of bypass plans involving nonimmediate family members, with emphasis on the impact of the generation-skipping transfer tax on marital deduction and bypass planning.

PLANNING OPTION 4: 100 PERCENT MARITAL DEDUCTION WITH DISCLAIMER INTO BYPASS

Clients often fail to properly revise wills and other planning documents when necessary. Too often, facts and circumstances change substantially between the date those documents are drafted and the date of the client's death. Yet the decedent's immediate, predeath *verbal* desires or apparent wishes must be legally disregarded. The law requires that the terms of the documents themselves, however dated, be strictly observed to control asset transfer. For example, if Congress substantially reduced FET rates just after a potential S1 developed a plan that incorporated a credit shelter bypass, the bypass might become less desirable. Under the changed circumstances, the clients might prefer to transfer, at death, more property outright to S2 rather than to the bypass share. Yet unless the documents were revised prior to S1's death, this modification would not be possible. However, the provision for a disclaimer makes a constructive revision after death entirely possible.

Anticipating a disclaimer, instead of providing for a reduced marital deduction, the document could specify that all property shall pass to the surviving spouse, except that amount which S2 validly disclaims, which will pass to the bypass share. This would permit S2, just after S1's death, to decide how much equalization to arrange. The disclaimer would thus offer the estate plan an additional degree of flexibility, giving S2, just after S1's death, a second look at the entire family and legal situation.[1]

Disadvantages

The use of Option 4, 100 percent marital deduction with disclaimer into bypass, has some drawbacks.

Emotional burden. First, the 100 percent marital deduction with disclaimer into bypass is a complex plan with which unsophisticated, grieving survivors may not be capable of dealing. During this difficult time, they might choose to do nothing. Or they might act imprudently. The wishes of an S1 who felt strongly about the benefits of the bypass could be completely frustrated by an S2 who elected to do nothing. S2 might be unable to understand the meaning of a bypass or, in a period of insecurity, might feel emotionally unwilling to "jeopardize my financial security." By default, failure to disclaim would result in a 100 percent marital deduction, which, as we have learned, invariably results in a larger S2 FET. Imposing on a grieving S2 this additional burden of having to decide whether or not to disclaim within nine months of the death of his/her spouse can also result in a hasty decision, additional pressure on S2, and conflicts between S2 and other survivors.

---

[1]For an alternative means of selecting the degree of equalization, see Note 4 describing the QTIP election.

Loss of dispositive control by S1. Another drawback to Option 4 is that S1 must relinquish some or all ability to influence the manner of disposition of his or her property after the death of S2. For example, if S1 had created a bypass arrangement without a disclaimer provision, S1 would have had complete control over the ultimate disposition of the property channeled to the bypass. S1 could feel certain that the property would pass to chosen named survivors, such as S1's children, at a future date. However, use of the disclaimer enables S1's spouse to direct more property to him or herself outright, thereby enabling the spouse, as S2, to later transfer it to anyone S2 chooses.[2] Of course, in practice, S1's and S2's distribution interests are usually similar, but they could be different, as is so often the case when there has been marital strife, when S1 has children of a former marriage, or when S1 anticipates the possibility that S2 could be "persuaded" after S1's death to make alternate dispositions.

Reduced S2 control. Another drawback to use of the 100 percent marital deduction with disclaimer is that tax law will not allow S2 to retain the right to direct beneficial enjoyment of the disclaimed bypass property. For example, if the clients create a plan to permit S2 to disclaim property into a bypass trust, S2 cannot be given a special power of appointment over the trust corpus. However, the power to invade principal under an ascertainable standard is permitted, and the spouse can be trustee of the trust. Thus, while the disclaimer adds some flexibility in the area of *FET saving,* it also removes some flexibility to the plan in the area of subsequent *S2 control.*

PLANNING SOFTWARE

From the preceding discussion of the four planning options and the choice between FET deferral and FET equalization, it should be clear that selection of the proper estate plan will depend on many factors, both quantitative and qualitative. Recently, elaborate com-

---

[2]As an alternative, S1 could have incorporated a credit shelter bypass plan which gave S2 the right to disclaim additional property into the bypass share. This would ensure a minimum FET saving via bypass, enable S1 to retain dispositive control over that amount, yet still offer some flexibility to S2. This fifth option, *credit shelter bypass with disclaimer,* is becoming increasingly popular.

puter programs have been developed which attempt to take account of the quantitative factors. Developed primarily by independent software publishers, insurance companies, certified public accounting firms, and securities houses, the programs analyze the client's personal and financial position and, after making certain assumptions, suggest an optimal plan that usually incorporates a bypass. While a great many planners, especially attorneys, are reluctant to overwhelm their clients with complex computer printouts which often only confuse them all the more, others use these plans extensively, especially with knowledgeable clients.

THE MARITAL TRUST

So far we have assumed that all property that we wish to qualify for the marital deduction will pass outright to the surviving spouse. However, that property could still qualify for the marital deduction if, instead of being transferred outright, it was transferred into a *marital trust,* which is simply defined as a trust structured to qualify for the marital deduction. Several different types of marital trusts are commonly used, with the most popular being the power of appointment trust and the QTIP trust (both will be described shortly). They differ in at least one important manner: how they qualify for one of the statutory exceptions to the *terminable interest rule*.

In Chapter 6, you learned that, in general, transfers to a surviving spouse of property that is subject to a terminable interest will not be treated as property "passing" to that surviving spouse and therefore will not qualify for the marital deduction. A common example is the transfer, at death, of a life estate. A deathtime transfer of property by S1 into a trust giving S2 only a life estate in the property's income would not qualify the property for the marital deduction in S1's estate, because a life estate is a terminable interest.

You should now be able to see more clearly the rationale for the terminable interest rule. In creating the marital deduction, Congress intended that if the deduction was taken in a donor-spouse's estate, then the property qualifying for the deduction must stand a good chance of eventually being included in the recipient spouse's estate. The intent was to tax property owned by the spouses at one of the two deaths. Therefore, if an S1 leaves to S2 property that is subject to a terminable interest, an S1 marital deduction will be disallowed. Without the rule, property could be both deducted from S1's gross estate and excluded from S2's gross estate if S2's interest in it was set to terminate before S2's death. Thus, the property transferred would escape taxation at both spouse's deaths.

Without any exceptions, however, the terminable interest rule would be too sweeping and could deny the marital deduction for property that would in fact be destined for inclusion in the gross estate of the surviving spouse.

> EXAMPLE 12–1 S1's will provides for a transfer of property into a trust, with all income to S2 for life, then remainder to whomever S2 appoints. In the absence of the exceptions to the terminable interest rule, the property might not qualify for the marital deduction in S1's estate because S2 has been left property subject to a terminable interest. Nonetheless, the property would be included in S2's gross estate because S2 possessed, at death, a general power of appointment over the property. Hence, without any exceptions to the terminable interest rule, the property would probably be included in both S1's *and* S2's gross estate.

> EXAMPLE 12–2 S1's will provides for a transfer of property into trust, but only if S2 survives S1 by at least six months. If S2 does not live that long, then the property immediately passes outright to X. Without an exception to the terminable interest rule, the property would be subject to tax in both estates for reasons mentioned in the previous example.

To prevent these undesired results, Congress created several exceptions to the terminable interest rule, thereby saving the marital deduction for S1 in certain situations. These exceptions, introduced in Chapter 6, enable planners to use the marital trust with life income to S2 as an alternative to an outright transfer to the surviving spouse.

As mentioned earlier, today planners commonly use two different types of marital trusts.[3] The *power of appointment trust,* is one type. As in the facts in Example 12–1 it grants S2 the right to re-

---

[3]A third type of marital trust called the *estate trust* is occasionally used. Under its terms the trust corpus is made payable to S2's estate. Its unique feature is that during S2's lifetime, some or all of the income may be payable to someone other than S2. The estate trust may be particularly useful when S1 wishes to provide temporary support to someone other than S2.

ceive all income from the property for life, payable at least annually. It also gives S2 a general power of appointment over the
principal, exercisable alone and in all events, at death or during
life.[4]

The second and more frequently used marital trust is called the
QTIP trust, a trust funded with qualified terminable interest property.[5] To qualify for the marital deduction, a QTIP trust must provide that the surviving spouse is entitled to all of the income from
the trust property, payable at least annually. In addition, the trust
cannot give anyone a power to appoint any of the property to anyone other than the surviving spouse. In other words, only S2 can
be a permissible appointee.[6] The executor of S1's estate is given
the right to make what is called the *QTIP election.* If the executor
so elects, the QTIP property will be part of the S1 marital deduction and will automatically be included in the gross estate of S2. If
the executor does not so elect, the property will not qualify for the
marital deduction in S1's estate, but will likely avoid inclusion in
the S2 gross estate. Thus, as with a disclaimer, the QTIP election
offers flexibility by enabling someone, at S1's death, to decide
whether to defer or to equalize.[5]

Both trusts enable the property to qualify for the marital deduction at S1's death, but do not entail an outright transfer to the
surviving spouse. They are employed to give S1 some post-death
control over the disposition of the property, at least until the death
of S2. The power of appointment trust can prevent S2 from hastily
disposing of the property during life, because it can provide that
the power may be exercisable only at S2's death.[7] The QTIP trust
enables S1 to designate who will receive the property upon S2's
death[8]; it is most useful if S1 wishes to be absolutely certain that

---

[4]The exception to the terminable interest rule allowing for a power of appointment marital trust is found in §2056(b)(5). For additional discussion, see Chapter
18.

[5]For additional discussion, see Chapter 18.

[6]§2056(b)(7).

[7]The power of appointment trust is sometimes preferred because the death tax
of some states exclude property from taxation in the estate of the holder of the
power.

[8]The reader should keep in mind that the bypass trust, like the QTIP trust, will
permit S1 to control disposition of certain (bypass) property at S2's death.

S1's intended beneficiaries will actually receive the property.[9] The QTIP trust is commonly used in situations where there has been a remarriage, where the spouses are experiencing marital difficulties, where the client wishes to protect the estate from possible consequences of S2's immaturity or senility, or where the client strongly wishes to ultimately dispose of property to charity.

The marital trust (also called the "A" trust) and the bypass trust (also called the "B" trust) are the products of essentially different planning motives, and are legally two different trusts. Often, both trusts are incorporated into one estate plan, and the combination is commonly called the "A-B" trust plan.[10]

A CASE STUDY IN MARITAL DEDUCTION AND BYPASS PLANNING

Let's now apply the principles of this chapter to a hypothetical fact situation.

Jim and Mary Clark are both age 49 and have been happily married for 23 years. They have a son Joe, age 20, a junior at the local university, and a daughter, Donna, age 16. Jim is financial vice president of a Fortune 500 corporation and is currently earning an annual salary of $168,000. Mary, a research chemist for a fertilizer company, earns an annual salary of $32,000. From sizable inheritances and successful investing, the Clarks own a fair amount of property, with Jim's interests having a total fair market value of $1,660,000 and Mary's interests worth $980,000. Joe handles the management of all of the family estate assets. Most of the investment property is real estate, but some is common stock and other securities. The balance consists of the home, personal effects, and cash. The Clarks had a simple will prepared about 10 years ago, and now they would like to inquire about the possibility of reducing transfer taxes at the

---

[9]In common law states, the QTIP trust may be viewed as potentially unfair, if it results in totally depriving the non-acquiring spouse from dispositive control over the family wealth. After all, assert some commentators, the accumulation of wealth is usually the product of both spouses, not just the one who legally earned it.

[10]In fact, more and more plans are incorporating three trusts, the bypass trust and the two major types of marital trusts. One marital trust disposes of property over which the surviving spouse is given the power to control disposition (e.g., power of appointment trust), and the other trust disposes of QTIP property over which the surviving spouse has no dispositive control (QTIP trust). This arrangement is sometimes called the "A-B-C" or "A-B-Q" trust plan.

FIGURE 12–1 Case Study: Effect of Planning Options 1, 2, and 3

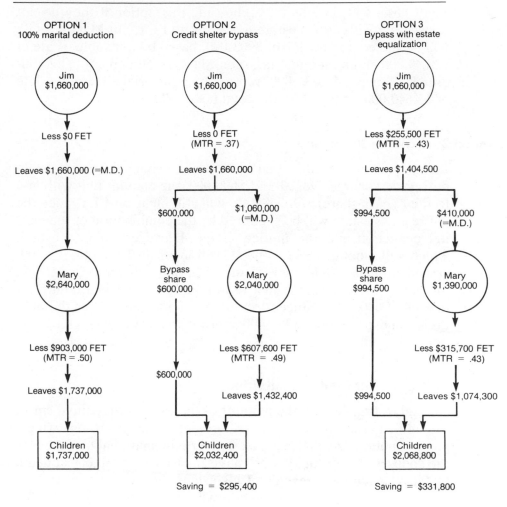

second death. Mary knows little about investing and would have difficulty managing the family estate by herself. The Clarks are not presently interested in initiating a lifetime program of gifting to their children.

Applying each of the four planning options introduced earlier to the Clarks' situation produces substantially different results, which are described next. The first three are illustrated in Figure 12–1. For each alternative, we shall assume that Jim will be the S1, dying this year, and Mary will live a normal life expectancy.

Option 1: 100 Percent Marital Deduction

The Clarks will, in effect, be choosing this option if they do not revise their wills. Jim's estate will incur no FET, but Mary's estate will be subject to an FET of $903,000, based on a taxable estate of $2,640,000 and a marginal tax rate (MTR) of 50 percent. The children will receive $1,737,000, representing the original family estate of $2,640,000, reduced by the total tax of $903,000.

Option 2: Credit Shelter Bypass

If Jim's will is revised so that instead of receiving his entire estate outright, Mary receives all but $600,000 (the amount that will pass to the bypass share), Jim's estate will still incur no FET since the entire gross estate will be sheltered by the combination of the marital deduction and the unified credit. However, Mary's estate, which will amount to $2,040,000, will incur an FET of $607,600, considerably less than the FET under Option 1. Joe and Donna will ultimately receive $2,032,400, representing the original family estate of $2,640,000, reduced by the tax of $607,600. Thus the children stand to receive $295,400 more if the credit shelter bypass option is implemented.

Option 3: Bypass with Estate Equalization

Instead of transferring the amount of the exemption equivalent of the unified credit to the bypass share, let's consider transferring a larger amount, one that will just equalize the marginal tax rates for the spouses. Accordingly, we'll have Jim transfer $410,000 at death to Mary, leaving the residue of his estate after payment of the tax to the bypass share.[11] Jim's estate will incur an FET of $255,500, and Mary's estate, which will amount to $1,390,000, will pay an FET of $315,700, so that the children will later receive $2,068,000,

---

[11] The amount of the marital deduction necessary to equalize the S1 and S2 taxable estates calculated by the formula in Note 9 in Chapter 11 would be different from $410,000:

$$\$1,660,000 - \text{Marital deduction} = \$980,000 + \text{Marital deduction}$$
$$2 \times \text{Marital deduction} = \$680,000$$
$$\text{Marital deduction} = \$340,000$$

an amount that exceeds Option 1 by $331,800 and Option 2 by $36,400.

Option 4: 100 Percent Marital Deduction with Disclaimer into Bypass

Option 4, 100 percent marital deduction with disclaimer into by-pass, is not shown in Figure 12–1 because it represents numerically a choice of one of many options, including the three outlined ear-lier. For example, if Mary elected to make no disclaimer, the num-bers would be identical to Option 1. If Mary chose to disclaim the amount of the exemption equivalent, then the figures in Option 2 would apply. Instead, if Mary disclaimed all but $600,000, then Op-tion 3 would apply. Of course, Mary could be permitted to disclaim other amounts.

Mary and Jim should be better able to weigh their choices after being presented with these figures. Of course, the order of deaths might be the reverse, so it is important to perform the same type of calculations assuming that Mary died first. This would probably also lead to a revision in Mary's will.

This amount is not as desirable as a $410,000 marital deduction, because the formula fails to take account of both the impact of the time value of money and the fact that the same marginal tax rate will apply over a range of taxable estates. Consider first the time value of money. In contrast with a marital deduction of $410,000, a marital deduction of $340,000 will generate a higher S1 FET (of $285,600 versus $255,500) and a lower S2 FET (of $285,600 versus $315,700), al-though it will still produce the same total combined S1–S2 FET of $571,200 and the same total amount received by the children ($2,068,800). The time value of money would suggest the larger S1 marital deduction in order to defer payment of the tax. To determine how much larger, we must examine the second issue, the influence of the tax rate brackets. The $410,000 marital deduction represents the greatest marital deduction possible which can still maintain equal spousal mar-ginal tax rates. Examining Table 4 of Appendix A, the FET marginal tax rates for the $340,000 marital deduction alternative would be 43 percent for both spousal estates since the taxable estates would be the same ($1,320,000). Increasing the marital deduction by $1 will reduce S1's taxable estate by $1 and will increase S2's taxable estate by the same amount. In fact, since the marginal tax rate of 43 percent would apply to all taxable estates between $1.25 million and $1.5 million, S1's taxable estate could be reduced to $1.25 million (by a marital deduction of $410,000) before the marginal tax rate dropped. S2's taxable estate could be raised to $1.5 million (by a marital deduction of $520,000) before the S2 marginal tax rate rose. Thus, the maximum marital deduction that could be taken before either mar-ginal tax rate changed is $410,000.

The analysis above suggests some possible recommendations for the Clarks. Based on the numbers, there is good reason for Jim to revise his current will. A bypass of at least $600,000 would save nearly $300,000 in federal estate taxes, which amounts to over 11 percent of the family estate.

But there are some *drawbacks* to this plan. The spouses will not live to enjoy this tax saving; it will be of benefit only to the children. Further, Mary and Jim must be willing to relinquish some control over the assets in the bypass. If Jim made an outright transfer to the children, they would, of course, become fee simple owners of the property and, in the extreme, could refuse to assist Mary in the event she became needy. If, instead, Jim made the transfer into trust, Mary could still have invasion rights over the corpus, but those rights would have to be limited to the standards of "health, education, support, or maintenance," factors Mary might consider too restrictive. Usually, though, spouses do not have difficulty living with these terms. However, since we have assumed that Mary is not an effective asset manager, even if Mary did object, Jim might prefer to have some of his assets protected from the potential peril of her mismanagement. Option 3, bypass with estate equalization, may be attractive to Jim because it would place less property outright into Mary's hands and save a larger FET. Finally, Option 4, the spousal disclaimer, is not likely to work very well in this situation, in view of Mary's limited financial management skills. Jim might well prefer to avoid the discretion inherent in a disclaimer to ensure that FET at S2's death will, in fact, be saved and that the children will be assured of receiving some portion of the family wealth. Summing up, Jim will probably wish to choose Option 2 or 3, alternatives involving a substantial bypass.

Regarding the marital deduction share, Jim might choose to direct that that property be placed in a *marital trust* in view of Mary's apparent lack of desire or inability to handle the management responsibilities. And assuming that Jim is confident that, at her death, Mary would leave the family property to the children, a power of appointment trust would probably be preferable to a QTIP trust because of its greater flexibility: at her death, Mary could act as *surrogate decision maker* for Jim, properly disposing of his property perhaps decades after he dies.

The facts in the case assumed no appreciation in asset values. If they were projected to increase between the deaths of the two spouses, the benefits of a bypass arrangement over the simple will would mount. Further, the benefits of the bypass with reduced marital deduction over the credit shelter bypass option would also be expected to increase. The Clarks would have even more reason to implement a bypass estate plan.

Other Factors

The Clarks' fact pattern oversimplifies reality in other ways besides assuming no property appreciation. The material below examines several other factors that, by altering the numerical results, can complicate bypass and marital deduction planning.[12]

State death tax. In this chapter we have ignored the influence of state death taxes. Typically, their effect will be relatively small, in view of the impact of the federal credit for the state death tax. Since they represent another tax resulting from the death of a property owner, however, planners will have reason to avoid them, and in many states a bypass device will succeed in this goal. The numbers will change but will usually show a greater saving if a bypass is utilized.[13]

Revocable living trust. To avoid probate, the spouses may wish to establish a revocable living trust, which can be coordinated with bypass planning, or even planning with a 100 percent marital deduction plan. At S1's death, the trust can be directed to transfer its contents into three new trusts, which we can call X, Y, and Z. Property belonging to S1 which is intended to qualify for the marital deduction will pass to trust X, the marital trust. Property belonging to S1 which is intended to bypass S2's estate will pass to trust Y, the bypass trust. And finally, property belonging to S2 will pass to trust Z, which can continue to be revocable until S2's death. All trust property will thus avoid probate at both S1's and S2's deaths and will also accomplish all of the FET savings described in this chapter.[14]

---

[12]For a technical discussion of the planning trade-off between the S1 marital deduction and a possible S2 credit for tax on prior transfers, see the Malcolm Moore article cited at the end of Chapter 6.

[13]An example of the influence of state death taxes can be found in note 5.

[14]A poorly drafted spousal *joint grantor trust* can give rise to estate and gift tax consequences for wealthier clients, particularly when the spouses fund the trust with different amounts of individually owned property. For example, the spouse contributing the greater amount may be deemed to have made a gift of a termin-

The evolution of a typical client-decedent's revocable trust estate plan is illustrated in Figure 12–2. At death, the decedent's probate property interests pass to the estate, while the decedent's nonprobate property interests flow into the revocable trust, which then terminates. This trust property is then apportioned between the nonmarital (bypass) and marital trusts, based on principles covered in this chapter. At the surviving spouse's death, all trust property then passes outright to the children if they have reached the specified age, commonly 25, 30, or 35. On the other hand, if the children are younger, then the two trusts terminate and the property is merged into a single "pot" trust and then subdivided into equal shares, or into one trust for each child when the children reach their early 20s (here, age 23). Pot trusts are further discussed in Chapter 17.

Debts and expenses. Of course, any estate will have deductible debts and expenses, which will alter the calculations. As we have seen in Chapter 10, expenses in administering a decedent's estate typically range between 5 and 10 percent of the total estate. Ordinarily, estate planners handle debts and expenses in the following manner: Regarding *debts,* in performing the calculations, planners use net worth as the value of the estate property; regarding *expenses,* planners either estimate the expenses or simply ignore them. Often, planners want to keep the calculations simple to avoid confusing the client. The net effect of the existence of debts will be to increase the size of the gross family estate that can pass FET free. The net effect of expenses will be to reduce the amount passing to survivors and to increase the desirability of the revocable living trust as a probate avoidance device.

BYPASS PLANS INVOLVING NONIMMEDIATE FAMILY MEMBERS

Up to now, we have been focusing our discussion of FET saving on the family unit, including S1, S2, and the children. The same type of planning will often work as well with nonimmediate family members, too. For example, a childless S1 and S2 may develop a

---

able life interest in a portion of the trust to the other spouse, one not qualifing for the marital deduction. These and other problems are avoidable with careful drafting, as explained by Flanagan in his article cited at the end of the chapter.

FIGURE 12–2   A Typical Revocable Trust Estate Plan*

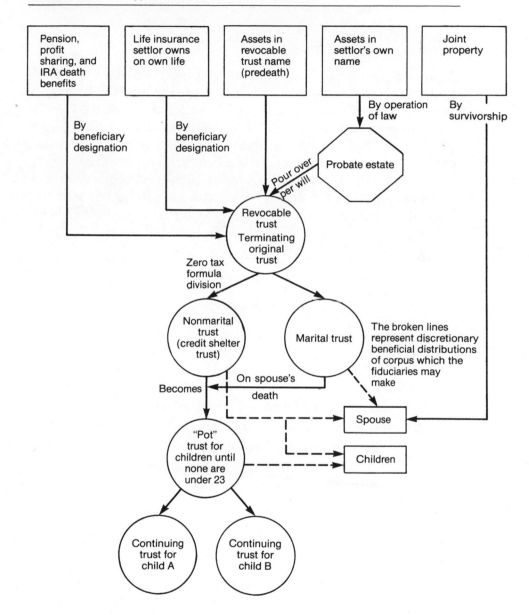

*Reprinted, with permission, from the Keidel article cited at the end of Chapter 10.

bypass plan for their nephews and nieces. In fact, such a plan will work as well for any survivors who belong to the next generation.

Generation-Skipping Bypass Planning

A problem can arise, however, when the purpose of a bypass is to skip not only the estate of a spouse but also the estate of a younger-generation beneficiary. In Chapter 7, we learned that the Generation-Skipping Transfer Tax (GSTT) will be imposed on direct skips, taxable terminations, and taxable distributions to or for the benefit of a skip person. A skip person is a beneficiary who is at least two generations younger than the transferor. Thus, in the usual bypass situation, the GSTT will not be a factor; it will be imposed only when the remainder beneficiaries are skip persons, not the client's children.

> EXAMPLE 12–3 A client creates a bypass trust to take effect upon his death and directs that all income will be payable to his wife for her life, then remainder to his living children. If a child survives, the GSTT would not apply because the child is not a skip person. However, if no children survive, or if the disposition were also to the issue of deceased children, then the GSTT may apply.

Exceptions to GSTT taxation. We also learned of four exceptions to the GSTT that considerably soften its impact:

1. $10,000 annual exclusion for lifetime gifts to a skip person.
2. Predeceased parent direct skip rule.
3. $2 million exemption for direct skips to a grandchild until 1990.
4. $1 million lifetime exemption per donor for all skips.

> EXAMPLE 12–4 The GSTT transfers in Example 12–3 will not result in a GSTT to the extent that they can be sheltered, for example, by allocating all or a portion to the decedent's $1 million lifetime exemption.

Thus, we can see that there are several methods of at least partially circumventing the GSTT, particularly through lifetime transfers and the GSTT lifetime exclusion.[15] The upshot is that only larger

---

[15]For a detailed discussion of planning for the GSTT, see the Kalik-Schneider article cited at the end of the chapter.

estates will be prevented from making generation-skipping transfers GSTT free. For a discussion of planning for *lifetime* generation-skipping gifts, see Chapter 13.

RECOMMENDED READING

(Anonymous) "Surviving the Surviving Spouse: Accommodating the Wives' Concerns." *Trusts & Estates,* April 1986, pp. 29–30.

ARNOLD, RICHARD S., and PETER S. CREMER. "The Unlimited Marital Deduction: Some Community Property/Common Law Disparities Still Remain." *Community Property Journal* 12 (Spring 1985), pp. 129–40.

BLATTMACHER, JONATHAN C., and IRA H. LUSTGARTEN. "Alexander v. Commissioner: The Ultimate Marital Deduction Freeze May Be Here." *Trusts and Estates,* March 1984, pp. 51–55.

COVEY, RICHARD B. "Marital Deduction and Credit Shelter Dispositions and The Use of Formula Provisions," 1985, U.S. Trust Co.

DOBRIS, JOEL C. "Marital Deduction Estate Planning: Variations on a Classic Theme." *San Diego Law Review* 20 (1983), pp. 801–35.

ECK, E. EDWIN. "Drafting Considerations in Appointing the Surviving Spouse as Trustee of the Nonmarital Trust." *Montana Law Review* 45 (1984), pp. 215–44.

EVANS, DANIEL B. "Administrative Powers and the Marital Deduction." *Real Property, Probate, and Trust Journal* 20 (1985), pp. 1161–87.

FLANAGAN, TIMOTHY L. "Designing Trusts for Couples Owning a Substantial Amount of Jointly Held Assets." *Estate Planning,* March 1988, pp. 84–89.

FRUEHWALD, KRISTIN G. "Credit Shelter Trusts Should Not Be Limited to Just the Unified Credit." *Estate Planning,* July 1983, pp. 200–205.

GENEVA, LOUIS B. "Simplifying Qualified Terminable Interest Property Use Planning Considerations." *Review of Taxation of Individuals* 8 (1984), pp. 3–22.

GUTIERREZ, MAX JR. "Marital Deduction: An Update." (Covering the impact of the final disclaimer regulations on the marital deduction.) *University of Miami's 21st Annual Estate Planning Institute,* 1987.

HALBACH, JR., EDWARD C. "Generation Skipping: Planning Opportunities and Drafting Problems." University of Miami 22nd Estate Planning Institute, 1988.

————. "Tax-Sensitive Trusteeships." *Oregon Law Review* 63 (1984), pp. 381–429.

JONES, JOHN T. "Marital Deduction Planning with QTIP after the 1984 Tax Reform Act: The Flexibility, and Some Problems, Continue." *Boston University Journal of Tax Law* 4 (1986), pp. 139–56.

KALIK, MILDRED, and SCHNEIDER, PAM H. "The New Generation-Skipping Transfer Tax." *Estate Planning 1987,* California Continuing Education of the Bar.

KETCHUM, ROBERT S., and KAY I. JOHNSON. "Traditional Simultaneous Death

Planning Must Be Reviewed in Light of ERTA, Social Changes." *Estate Planning,* March 1983, pp. 90–94.

KURTZ, SHELDON F. "Marital Deduction Estate Planning Under the Economic Recovery Tax Act of 1981: Opportunities Exist, but Watch the Pitfalls." *Rutgers Law Review* 34, no. 4 (Summer 1982), pp. 591–667.

LANDROCHE, MARIE. "The Qualified Terminable Interest Rule: An Overview." *University of Florida Law Review* 34 (1982), pp. 737–63.

LANGSTRAAT, CRAIG J. "Considerations in Valuation of Marital Deduction Assets." *Trust & Estates,* February 1986, pp. 18–19.

LEIMBERG, STEPHAN R. "Choosing Estate Planning Software for your Practice: Eight Programs Compared." *Estate Planning,* November 1987, pp. 322–31.

MARTIN, MARY JILL LOCKWOOD. "Multiple Options Provide Great Flexibility in Choosing the Proper Marital Deduction Form." *Taxation for Lawyers,* July–August 1984, pp. 30–36.

MILLER, RALPH G. "Using Computers to Present Estate Plans." *Trusts & Estates,* April 1986, pp. 50–56.

MOORE, MALCOLM A. "The New Marital Deduction Qualified Terminable Interest Trust: Planning and Drafting Considerations." *Probate Notes* 8 (1982), pp. 56–60.

MULLIGAN, MICHAEL D. "Spouse's Use of Disclaimer on Outright Bequest Maximizes Credit and Adds Flexibility." *Estate Planning,* November 1984, pp. 328–34.

MULLIGAN, MICHAEL D., and SCOT W. BOULTON. "New Generation-Skipping Tax: Higher Rates, Broadened Scope." *Estate Planning,* January 1987.

————. "Planned Opportunities that Take Advantage of the New Generation-Skipping Transfer Tax." *Estate Planning,* March 1987, pp. 66–71.

SCHLENGER, JACQUES T; ROBERT E. MADDEN; and WILLIAM G. MURRAY. "Power to Invade a Trust Corpus for Emergency Purposes Is Not Limited by an Ascertainable Standard under Sections 2036 and 2038. Letter Ruling 8606002." *Estate Planning,* September 1986, pp. 300–04.

SCHNEE, EDWARD J., and PAULA WIEHRS. "Using the Marital Deduction: A Simulation." *Tax Adviser,* February 1984, pp. 76–84.

WESTFALL, DAVID. "Lapsed Powers of Withdrawal and the Income Tax." *Tax Law Review* 39 (1983), pp. 63–76.

WRIGHT, EARL L., and MARILYN K. RENNINGER. "Bringing Automation into the Estate Planning Process." *Trusts & Estates,* January 1986, pp. 26–29.

ZABEL, WILLIAM D., and KIM E. BAPTISTE. "Marital Dissolution and the Lifetime QTIP Trust." *Trusts & Estates,* April 1984, pp. 19–22.

QUESTIONS AND PROBLEMS

1. Describe the advantages and disadvantages of Option 4, 100 percent marital deduction with disclaimer into bypass.

2. (*a*) What factors help determine whether marital deduction property should pass outright or in trust? (*b*) Is FET savings a factor? Why or why not?

3. (*a*) Explain the Congressional purpose of the terminable interest rule. (*b*) Describe the common marital trust plans used to take advantage of the exceptions to this rule.

4. True or false: A bypass trust and a marital trust cannot coexist in the same state plan. Explain.

5. A bypass trust provides for income to the trustor's wife for her life, then remainder outright to his daughter, if she survives her mother; otherwise, to the daughter's *issue*.
   a. Could there be a potential GSTT problem?
   b. Is the size of the trust a factor?

13

Lifetime Transfers I: Overview and Survey of Gift Planning

OVERVIEW

This chapter will introduce the study of planning for lifetime transfers of property and will examine the techniques utilized in *gifting*, the most popular type of intrafamily lifetime transfer. The techniques of planning for other lifetime transfers, including incomplete transfers, completed transfers for consideration, and charitable transfers, will be described in Chapter 14.

Lifetime transfers take many forms and are undertaken for many reasons. For example, they can be made to individuals or to charity. They can be made outright or to a fiduciary such as a trustee or custodian. They can take the form of a completed transfer, like a sale or a gift, or they can remain incomplete, as in the case of a transfer with a retained interest or control. They can be a transfer of a total interest in property or of just a partial interest. And they can be made for many different motives, most of which have already been outlined in Chapter 9.

While you read this and Chapter 14, you will want to keep in mind two important principles. First, different types of transfers will accomplish different types of goals. And second, the less complete the transfer, the less likely the transfer will achieve desired *tax* goals. This latter point cannot be overemphasized because clients tend to prefer to make incomplete transfers in order to retain some control over the transferred property. By definition, however, every lifetime transfer requires the relinquishment of some control; the client must part with some interest in property for some period of time. Gifts mean loss of access, control and flexibility, and clients who are especially reluctant to make them take a greater tax risk and are more likely to feel uncomfortable with their estate plan, no matter what the magnitude of the financial rewards. Planners must be particularly sensitive to this issue.

We begin our discussion of lifetime transfers with an examination of completed lifetime gifts, hereafter called *gifts*. For present purposes, we shall define a gift as any transfer that gives rise to potential gift taxation. As explained in Chapter 7, a gift is *complete* for tax purposes when there is surrender of dominion and control and delivery by a donor capable of transferring property to an accepting donee capable of receiving and possessing property.

Essentially, a gift may be made outright, or it may be made to another party, usually a fiduciary, for the benefit of the donee. An *outright* gift results ordinarily in the receipt by the donee of a fee simple interest in the gift property, yielding to the donee all of the rights which accompany that type of interest. Thus, an outright gift extends to the donee the greatest flexibility of ownership and control. However, the donor may not wish to bestow that degree of flexibility. For example, a donor, mainly for tax reasons, may presently wish to make a sizable gift to help a preteenaged son finance future college expenses. An outright gift to such a young person would ordinarily be out of the question.

The customary alternative to an outright gift is the transfer to a *fiduciary,* who would be responsible for managing the property and distributing its income and principal in accordance with the legal conditions either contained in the underlying document or established by local law. Gifts to adult donees are usually outright but are sometimes made in trust. Gifts for a minor are usually to a fiduciary, such as a custodian, a trustee, or occasionally to a guardian.

The next section will describe, with illustrations, the major tax considerations in making gifts. For the most part, the discussion will assume that an outright gift is being made. Some unique aspects of nonoutright gifts to children will be examined in greater detail at the end of the chapter.

TAX CONSIDERATIONS IN MAKING GIFTS

Let's now examine the death tax and income tax advantages and disadvantages of making gifts.

Tax Advantages of Gifting

Gifts are commonly made to save death taxes and income taxes. In the examples that follow, look for two common tax threads. First, many gifts can be made at no gift-tax cost. Second, even if a gift tax is incurred, gifts may still be desirable because they often have the potential of reducing death and income taxes.

Death tax advantages. Death tax advantages include the ability to reduce or freeze the taxable estate in three ways: using the shelter of the annual exclusion, avoiding grossing up, and excluding postgift appreciation.

Shelter of annual exclusion. Most clients about to embark upon a program of gifting will be able to transfer a significant portion of their estate, gift tax and death tax free. The gift tax and GSTT annual exclusions, of course, enables a donor to gift, free of tax, $10,000 per donee per year. And spousal gift splitting doubles this amount to $20,000.

> EXAMPLE 13–1 Mom and Dad wish to gift maximum equal amounts to their three children and three grandchildren. Each of the six donees can receive $20,000 each year, tax free, adding up to a current aggregate annual tax-free gift total of $120,000.

In the above example, because total gross gifts to any one donee during a given calendar year will amount to no more than the annual exclusion, the donors need not even file a gift tax return.

Actually, donors can gift a much larger amount, gift tax free, but only at the expense of "using up" their unified credits.

> EXAMPLE 13–2 In Example 13-1, if Mom and Dad instead gave $50,000 to each person, they will have made six taxable gifts of $30,000, or total taxable gifts for the year of $180,000. Assuming that the donors had made no prior taxable gifts, the tentative tax on their joint gift-tax return will be $48,400. Although the application of the unified credit would result in a zero current net tax, the amount of the spousal combined unused unified credit would be reduced by $48,400, from $385,600 (two times $192,800) to $337,200, which could be applied to amounts of tentative taxes in later years. Each would be able to gift an additional $510,000 in excess of all annual exclusions, with-

out incurring a gift tax outlay, since each has used up only $90,000 of the $600,000 exemption equivalent of each of their unified credits.

The upshot of these examples is that jointly a husband and wife can gift, tax free, a sizable portion of their family estate, amounting to $1.2 million during their lifetimes, plus $20,000 times the number of suitable beneficiaries, per year. Thus, spouses with five suitable donees can give away, tax free, a total of $2.2 million over the span of 10 years. Of course, the spouses would thereby totally use up their unified credits, making the transfer of the next dollar in excess of the annual exclusion after this period subject to tax at a minimum marginal rate of 37 percent.

EXAMPLE 13–3 Corey, a bachelor, has already made total lifetime taxable gifts of $600,000. This year, he makes a single gift of $20,000. His gift tax will be $3,700, determined as follows:

Gross gift	$ 20,000
Less: Annual exclusion	10,000
Equals: Current taxable gift	10,000
Plus: Prior taxable gifts	600,000
Equals: Total taxable gifts	610,000
Tentative tax on total gift	196,500
Less: Tentative tax on prior gifts	192,800
Equals: Tentative tax on current gifts	3,700
Less: Unused unified credit	-0-
Equals: Net gift tax payable	$ 3,700

A somewhat different result would occur if the most recent transfer was made at death.

EXAMPLE 13–4 Assume the same basic facts as in Example 13-3, except that Corey dies owning $20,000 and therefore transfers that amount at death. The FET due will be $7,400, calculated as follows:

Gross estate	$ 20,000
Plus: Adjusted taxable gifts	600,000
Equals: Taxable estate	620,000
Tentative tax	200,200
Less: Unified credit	192,800
Equals: Net FET	$ 7,400

The difference in the net tax between the two examples, $3,700, is due to the absence in estate tax law of a gift tax-like annual exclusion for property transferred at death. Otherwise, the outcome is similar; each additional dollar is taxed at 37 percent, the marginal unified transfer tax rate.

Summarizing, the making of annual exclusion gifts is a simple estate planning device which can enable many clients to substantially reduce their gross estate, by the time of their death, at no gift tax cost.

No grossing up. Another estate tax advantage of gifting derives from the ability to exclude from the gross estate, at death, the amount of any gift tax paid on gifts made longer than three years before death. At this point, please take a few minutes to review Examples 2035-4 through 2035-6 in Chapter 6, which illustrate the estate tax advantage to paying a gift tax.

Postgift appreciation. A third tax advantage of gifting is the ability to exclude postgift appreciation of the gifted property from the donor's gross estate at death. Its unique tax-saving effect was shown in Example 9-12, which the reader is also urged to review at this point.

By way of a complete review of these three major tax advantages of making lifetime gifts, consider the following comprehensive example. Assume that all transfers occur after 1987.

> EXAMPLE 13–5 Burt, a widower, owns $3 million in property. His estate planner predicts that the property will double in value to $6 million in 10 years, the length of Burt's expected life span. The adviser recommends a plan of periodic gifting. Let's assume, however, for simplicity, that Burt is advised to make only one gift before he dies: one half of his entire estate to his only child, this year. Burt's total transfer taxes will be $1,469,300 if the gift is made, rather than the $2,583,000 that will be due if the gift is not made.

Burt makes the gift. If Burt makes the gift, and assuming that he has made no prior taxable gifts, Burt will pay a gift tax of $358,700, calculated as follows:

Gross gift	$1,500,000
Less: Annual exclusion	10,000
Taxable gift	1,490,000
Tentative tax	551,500
Less: Unified credit	192,800
Net gift tax	$ 358,700

In 10 years, when Burt is assumed to die, he will own property worth $2,282,600, calculated in the following manner. First, at the time of the gift, Burt's estate is reduced by $1,500,000, the value of the gift, and by $358,700, the amount of the gift tax paid. The remainder $1,141,300, while in his hands, will double over the decade to $2,282,600. Burt's FET will be $1,110,600, calculated as follows:

Gross estate	$2,282,600
Plus: Adjusted taxable gifts	1,490,000
Equals: Estate tax base	3,772,600
Tentative tax	1,662,100
Less: Gift tax payable	358,700
Less: Unified credit	192,800
Net FET	$1,110,600

Burt's donee and beneficiaries will wind up receiving and owning a total of $4,172,000, which is the sum of $1,172,000, the value of his net estate after subtracting the FET, plus $3 million, the current value of the gift property.

Burt does not make the gift. Alternatively, if Burt does not make the gift, his beneficiaries will wind up with only $3,417,000, which is the $6 million assumed value of the property owned at death, reduced by the FET of $2,583,000, calculated as follows:

Gross estate	$6,000,000
Plus: Adjusted taxable gifts	-0-
Equals: Estate tax base	$6,000,000
Tentative tax	2,775,800
Less: Unified credit	192,800
Net FET	$2,583,000

Let's analyze the tax savings from this gift plan. As a result of Burt's gift, his donee and beneficiaries will receive $755,000 more in combined lifetime and deathtime gifts. This amount represents the mathematical difference between $1,113,700, the saving in total transfer taxes, and $358,700, the forgone appreciation in the property that will be used to pay the gift tax. The saving in transfer taxes can be explained as follows: The FET tax base in the no-gift alternative exceeds the FET tax base under the gift scenario by $2,227,400. At a marginal tax rate of 50 percent, this means an FET reduction of $1,113,700.

Why will the gift alternative shelter $2,227,400 from transfer taxes? The answer has four components. First, $10,000 is sheltered by the gift tax *annual exclusion*. Second, $1.5 million will escape taxation because it represents the amount of the untaxed *appreciation* of the gift property after Burt makes the gift. Third, since Burt is not expected to die within three years of the date of the gift, there will be *no grossing up*. Thus, $358,700, the amount of the gift tax paid, is not added to Burt's gross estate at death. Finally, since a gift tax will actually be paid, Burt's gross estate will not include the $358,700 appreciation in the property used to pay the gift tax, an amount that would be includable if no gift is made. The sum of these four components equals $2,227,400, the amount of the total reduction in the tax base generated from Burt's $1.5 million gift.

This example assumed that Burt will make only one lifetime gift to only one person, thereby reaping the benefit of only one annual exclusion. Substantially more transfer tax will be saved if Burt can make smaller gifts to several persons *each year* until his death, utilizing the ongoing shelter of multiple annual exclusions.

In conclusion, a program of gifting can result in substantial transfer tax savings and, commonly, the ultimate transfer of a larger amount of wealth, tax free, to succeeding generations. The gifts can be tax sheltered by the annual exclusion as well as by the excludability of both the gift tax and postgift appreciation from the donor's taxable estate.

Income tax advantages.   The making of gifts also offers some income tax advantages. As we saw in Chapter 9, gifts can result in some income shifting. In general, since the donee becomes the owner of gifted property, any income earned on that property will be taxed to the donee, who is usually subject to a lower marginal income tax rate.[1] Further, the reduced taxable income to the donor might put her or him in a lower tax bracket.

As explained in Chapter 8 and 10, outright gifts to children under age 14 will not shift much taxable income, due to the *kiddie tax*.

EXAMPLE 13–6 The Gerards are in the 33 percent marginal income tax bracket, and wish to shift taxable income to their 13-year-old son, Wayne, who is in the 15 percent bracket. They transfer $10,000 in 10 percent coupon bonds to Wayne, who will be taxed on the $1,000

---

[1]Due to the kiddie tax, this is not true for donees under age 14. See below.

interest received each year.[2] After subtracting $500, the maximum standard deduction amount allowable against unearned income of a dependant, Wayne's income tax for the first year on the remaining $500 would be $75, which is $255 less than the $330 tax that would have been owed by the Gerards. The Gerards realize that it would not make any income tax sense at this time to shift additional income to Wayne by transferring a greater amount of securities since the additional income would be all taxed at their rate, not Wayne's.

Beginning in the taxable year that a child reaches age 14, the kiddie tax will not apply and all unearned income of the child's will be taxable to the child.

EXAMPLE 13–7 Continuing Example 13-6 above, in the following year Wayne turns 14, and the Gerards transfer an additional $45,000 in 10 percent coupon bonds for Wayne's benefit. Wayne's income tax on the taxable $5,000 will be $750, which is $1,065 less than the tax of $1,815 otherwise payable by the Gerards (i.e., .33 × $5,500 = $1,815).[3]

Tax Disadvantages of Gifting

There are several tax dangers and disadvantages of making lifetime gifts, including prepaying the transfer tax, adverse §2035 consequences, the danger that the gift is later ruled incomplete, and loss of step-up in basis.

Prepaying the transfer tax.   The making of a large gift can result in an immediate gift tax liability, thereby preventing the client-donor from investing the funds that have been used to pay the tax.[4] However, as we have seen, prepayment of the transfer tax will

---

[2]The securities would typically be transferred to a fiduciary, such as a custodian or a trustee, on behalf of the child. See the discussion on techniques for transferring property to minor children later in this chapter.

[3]Actually, as much as $18,350 in income could be shifted to a 15 percent tax bracket *person* reporting no other income, assuming a standard deduction of $500. On the other hand, a *trust's* 15 percent bracket ends at $5,000, reflecting Congress's strong interest in discouraging the use of trusts to shift income.

[4]Even if the gift is small enough to be totally or partially sheltered by the unified credit, it will have the effect of reducing the amount that can be transferred at death, free of tax, since it will be included in the estate tax base as an "adjusted taxable gift."

often be tax-justifiable if it has the effect of substantially reducing the client's FET. This will happen if the gift property appreciates greatly before the client's death or if it appreciates modestly and the client can avoid grossing up under §2035 by surviving at least three years after making the gift. On the other hand, gifting property and prepaying the transfer tax may turn out to have been a costly mistake, particularly in situations where the property fails to appreciate or actually declines in value and the client dies within three years of making the gift. Then little or no transfer taxes will have been saved, and the client will have forfeited the ability to use both the prepaid tax money and the gift property that was transferred. Thus, to assess the likelihood of financial success resulting from a sizable gift, the planner must consider factors such as life expectancy of the client-donor, expected appreciation potential, as well as future transfer tax rates.

An additional adverse Section 2035 consequence: Unsheltering postgift appreciation. We have already mentioned in the preceding discussion that if a gift is made within three years of death, the amount of any gift tax paid will be included in the donor's gross estate under the grossing-up rule. In addition to this adverse consequence, the entire *date-of-death value* of the gift property will be included in the donor's gross estate, under Section 2035, if the property or interest transferred would have subjected the property to be included in the gross estate under Sections 2036, 2037, 2038, and 2042 had the transfer not been made. This consequence is illustrated in Examples 2035-1 through 2035-3 in Chapter 6, covering the federal estate tax.

In summary, §2035 can have the effect of denying two of the three major advantages of gifting. It can require grossing up of gift taxes, and, in the case of life insurance and transfers in which retained controls were recently relinquished, it can include all postgift appreciation in the taxable estate.[5]

---

[5]As mentioned in Chapter 10, a potentially common pitfall under §2035 can arise when a trustee of a revocable living trust makes a gift within three years of the trustor's death. The IRS takes the position that the gift constitutes a relinquishment of revocability which under the combined influence of Sections 2035 and 2038 will subject the date-of-death value of the gift to inclusion in the trustor's gross estate (LR 8609005). To avoid this result, the gift should be made directly by the trustor, after withdrawal from the trust.

Gift later ruled incomplete. If it is later ruled that a gift transaction was not really complete, the date-of-death value of the property will be includable in the donor's gross estate in spite of the fact that the donor, in all good faith, paid a gift tax at the time of the gift. The estate will receive the equivalent of a credit for the gift tax paid, but from every other tax perspective the gift will be considered as not having been made, thereby completely frustrating the donor's intentions. One example of an incomplete gift is a §2036 transfer with retained interest or control, described in Chapter 6. Another is illustrated in the following example:

> EXAMPLE 13–8 On her deathbed, decedent made a gift by writing a check on her bank account. She died before the check was cashed. In her state, because she had the power to revoke by stopping payment, the gift was not complete, and therefore includable in her gross estate under §2038.

Loss of step-up in basis. A fourth tax disadvantage of making lifetime gifts is the loss in the step-up in income tax basis that would have been received on property owned by the decedent at death. This can be a major drawback for a donee who wishes to sell appreciated gift property. On the other hand, if the donee has no plans to sell the property during his or her lifetime, the problem disappears since there will likely be a new step-up in basis before it is sold, at the donee's death.

> EXAMPLE 13–9 Granny has always wanted to do something nice for her loving, adult grandson, and today she gives him some real property that she and her deceased husband acquired in the 1920s. When Granny dies, the gift property will not receive a step-up in basis, and grandson will own an asset with a sizable unrealized gain to be recognized if he sells it prior to his death. However, this potential taxable gain will vanish if grandson dies owning the property.

Another major consideration in gifting is the selection of the best gift assets, described next.

TYPES OF ASSETS TO GIVE

In gifting, the client is often able to select among a number of assets to give. With careful selection, a more efficient estate plan can result since, from tax and other perspectives, some assets make better gifts than others. The following constitutes a basic set of guidelines for selecting gift property.

Basis Considerations

Other things the same, high-basis assets make better gifts than do low-basis assets, if the donee is likely to sell the asset before death. As we have seen, the basis of property received by gift, in the hands of the donee, will retain the donor's old basis. Later sale by the donee at a price above this basis will result in a taxable gain. Thus, the higher the donor's original basis in the gift property, the lower the taxable gain.

> EXAMPLE 13–10 Donor wishes to give donee $100,000 in marketable securities and conveniently happens to own two different blocks of common stock with which to do this. Both are worth $100,000. Stock A was purchased two years ago for $95,000, while stock B was acquired 15 years ago for $20,000. Assuming that each stock's present basis in donor's hands is its cost, and that donee plans to sell the stock in about two years when each is expected to appreciate to $110,000, donee will realize a gain of $15,000 on the sale of stock A and a gain of $90,000 on the sale of stock B.

On the other hand, gifting low-basis assets makes more sense in some circumstances. For example, if for liquidity or other reasons a donor *plans to sell* a retained asset at the time of gifting another asset, he or she should consider gifting a lower-basis asset and retaining and selling the higher-basis asset in order to personally incur a lower tax outlay. This strategy will be especially productive if the donee either is in a lower tax bracket or has no immediate plans to sell the gift asset. Any gain realized upon later sale by the donee will at least be deferred, and may be totally eliminated, if the donee dies before the asset is sold, due to the step-up-at-death principle. Further, if the donee is *quite old,* and if there is every likelihood that the donee will die owning the gift property, there is additional incentive to give the low-basis property since it can be expected to receive a full step-up soon. The scope of this planning opportunity has recently been narrowed by Congress a bit, however, as the next example illustrates.

> EXAMPLE 13–11 Husband gives his terminally ill wife his interest in raw land, purchased many years ago for $400, and currently worth $10,000. Wife, who dies two months later, devises the land back to husband, who then sells it for $10,500. Husband's realized gain is $10,000 not $500. Code Section 1014(e) provides that when a person inherits property which he or she had gifted to a decedent within one year of decedent's death, for purposes of sale, the adjusted basis of

the property to the donor will be decedent's adjusted basis immediately before the donee's date of death. Thus, wife's adjusted basis just before death is $400, which is also donor's old basis. In this set of facts donor winds up receiving his old basis back.

Hence, the advantage of gifting low-basis property works, in the case of a donor-heir, only if the donee-decedent lives *at least one year* after the date of gift.[6] This strategy will work even if the original donor is not the spouse of the decedent.

If the donor has no choice other than gifting low-basis assets, he or she can take steps to maximize the likelihood that the donee *will not sell* the gift property before death by selecting assets that the donee is more likely to retain. Assets having sentimental or utilitarian value may more likely ensure a step-up in basis in the future. A gift of such an asset may make basis considerations largely unnecessary.

Although high-basis assets usually make good gifts from an income tax point of view, they make unattractive gifts if their basis is higher than their date-of-gift value. Property in which the owner has an *unrealized loss* is not a good asset to give because the donee, upon selling it, will not be able to recognize that loss. Examples 1015-3 and 1015-5 in Chapter 8 demonstrate this effect, which prevents the donee from recognizing that portion of the loss resulting from the decline in value while the donor held the property. A better strategy would be to retain assets having an unrealized loss, or to sell them first to realize the loss and then gift the cash proceeds.

Postgift Appreciation

If FET reduction is a major goal, the generous client should consider gifting *growth assets,* that is, assets expected to appreciate substantially, rather than assets whose value will remain stable or fall. As we have seen, a gift of an appreciating asset will cause future appreciation to inure to the donee and will avoid inclusion in the donor's gross estate. Some assets have greater inherent ap-

---

[6]But Section 1014e does not apply if the original donor (or the donor's spouse) is not the person who later acquires the property from the decedent-donee. Thus, A can gift an appreciated asset to D, the decedent, who can then transfer it, at death, to B, and obtain the step-up free of the one-year restriction.

preciation potential than others, although in most cases this determination represents pure speculation. However, assets such as life insurance, or equity interests in either a closely held business or real estate may be likely prospects, while assets such as patent rights, whose value usually declines over time, would not make good gift assets in this context. Cash and cash equivalents are also less than highly desirable, because their value cannot be expected to rise. In general, from a transfer-tax point of view, assets having a combined low gift tax value and high estate tax value make the best gifts.

An excellent example of a type of gift of highly appreciating assets is called *opportunity shifting*. It involves the transfer of a wealth- or an income-producing opportunity before it is objectively ascertainable. For example, business clients may be able to recognize the prospect of a profitable commercial enterprise before it blossoms sufficiently into a verifiably valuable opportunity. By transferring ownership during its early stages, a value shift can occur without transfer-tax cost and before the income the venture generates is considered attributable to the client.

> EXAMPLE 13–12 Dad, owner of a successful computer component firm, has just established a new corporation to pursue the viability of a recently developed engineering idea. The new firm is capitalized at $50,000, and Dad gives an adult daughter 20 percent of the stock and places another 20 percent in an irrevocable trust for the benefit of his minor son.

This example demonstrates the creation of *additional taxpaying entities,* the new corporation and the trust, as well as the *splitting up of anticipated income* and wealth among more family members. Similar techniques can be arranged for any assets that are expected to appreciate in value or generate significantly higher income, but for which these expectations have not yet become objectively verifiable. Good hunches by savvy clients are the major sources of intrafamily opportunity shifting.

Administration Problems

Assets that are likely to create problems in estate administration can make good gift assets. For example, oil paintings, especially those currently worth somewhat less than the annual gift tax exclusion, may not need to be valued if transferred by lifetime gift, but could create valuation disputes, a potentially higher FET, and additional costs of valuation if transferred at death. Further, illiquid assets such as real estate may need to be sold to pay death taxes, if transferred at death. Alternatively, a lifetime gift of these assets may avoid a later problem.

Other Asset Choice Considerations

Where *income shifting* is an estate planning goal, high income-earning assets make better gifts. As we have seen, income tax law in general requires an actual transfer of the "tree" (asset) in order to effect a transfer of the "fruit" (income) from that tree.

The well-heeled donor should ordinarily consider gifting assets that do not have *built-in tax benefits* such as income exclusions, deductions, or credits which would be of less value to a lower-bracket donee. The client should consider retaining assets such as tax shelters, municipal bonds, and income-producing real property in his or her own portfolio.[7]

Gifting of *nonbusiness* holdings offer certain death and income tax advantages by virtue of reducing the decedent's taxable estate so that certain very specific provisions of the Internal Revenue Code can apply. These provisions allow the following tax saving opportunities: (*a*) reduced income tax when a business interest is redeemed. Income proceeds from the redemption of the decedent's closely held business stock used to pay death taxes can be taxed as a capital gain rather than as a dividend, enabling the estate to deduct basis from the proceeds (§303); (*b*) special reduced valuation of the decedent's closely held business, in FET calculations (§2032A); and (*c*) deferral of paying the FET attributable to the value of the decedent's closely held business (§6166). In each case, the Code requires that the value of the decedent's business must be at least a certain percentage of the total estate, commonly 35 percent. One way of increasing the likelihood of meeting this percentage requirement is to reduce the estate size by gifts of nonbusiness assets. For greater detail on the business liquidity boosting techniques available under the Code, see Chapter 15.

---

[7]However, when a tax-shelter property reaches the "crossover point" and begins to throw off "phantom income" to the investor, it may be a good time to gift the property, to shift the income to a lower bracket.

There are other assets which, if transferred, could result in *adverse tax consequences* and therefore would not make good gift assets. For example, consider an asset for which the donor has taken the investment tax credit.[8] If the donor gifts the asset before the end of its useful life, he or she will be required to "recapture" part of the credit, that is, repay part of the taxes saved from the credit.

In at least one situation, gifts to children can generate a tax benefit otherwise unavailable to the parents.

> EXAMPLE 13–13 Because of the size of their income, the Hornes are not qualified to contribute before-tax dollars to an *Individual Retirement Account* (IRA). And while their young adult son, Jason, is qualified, he can't afford to. Jason enters in an agreement with his parents, who will give him $1,950 a year, to help contribute $2,000 to his own IRA. This annual arrangement is to continue indefinitely, so long as Jason does not make a single premature withdrawal. The Hornes have both deferred and reduced their son's income tax, and have some reassurance that in a small way they will have increased the comfort of his later years.

As a result of the kiddie tax, generous parents may wish to transfer to their children property that *does not generate taxable income,* at least until they reach age 14. Possible assets include U.S. government EE bonds; municipal bonds, interests in land, and growth stocks. In many situations, the parent can then determine the timing of the tax "hit" by choosing which year to liquidate the assets and, consequently, which year to realize the likely gain.

While the material up to now has centered on a discussion of the tax and nontax aspects of gifting to individuals in general, the next section discusses the making of gifts to two specific classes of donees, the spouse and the minor children. We choose to focus on them because several tax and nontax implications of gifts to them are unique and require further explanation. Gifts to spouses are different in part because of the additional tax saving available through the use of the federal gift tax marital deduction. Gifts to minors are unique in part because of the techniques by which the transfer is often arranged, usually with the assistance of a fiduciary.

---

[8]The investment tax credit was repealed by TRA 86.

GIFTS TO THE SPOUSE: TECHNIQUES AND CONSIDERATIONS

This section will explore the tax characteristics of lifetime gifts between spouses. We shall see that the gift tax marital deduction offers unique planning opportunities to reduce taxes, in some cases by an even greater amount than for gifts to a nonspouse. The following material discusses interspousal gift considerations involved in saving death taxes and income taxes.[9]

Interspousal Gifts to Save Death Taxes

In the last two chapters, we examined in some detail several death-time marital deduction techniques designed to minimize the FET for a family estate. We saw that four planning options are commonly used: the 100 percent marital deduction, the credit shelter bypass, the bypass with estate equalization, and the 100 percent marital deduction with disclaimer into bypass. We will now see that when one spouse is substantially wealthier than the other and there is a significant chance that the less wealthy spouse will die first, even more death taxes can be saved by means of a deathtime bypass plan which is coupled with a program of interspousal gifting. However, this strategy will not work if the basic testamentary scheme involves a nonbypass, 100 percent marital deduction, as the following example shows.

> EXAMPLE 13–14 Husband and wife have a $2 million estate, all owned by husband. If the spouses prefer an estate plan with a *100 percent estate tax marital deduction* (simple will, etc.), then a restructuring of the distribution of wealth between them by means of completed gifts will result in no additional FET saving. The first spouse to die, whether husband or wife, will leave an estate subject to no FET, either because there is no gross estate (no gifts, wife dies first) or because the entire gross estate is sheltered by the 100 percent marital deduction (all other situations). Thus, either spouse, as S2, will wind up owning the entire $2 million at death no matter how much each spouse owned prior to their deaths, and a lifetime interspousal gift will not change the total projected FET.

---

[9]For a description of the use of interspousal gifts designed to qualify a spouse under long-term medical care for medicaid benefits, see the Gilfix article cited at the end of the chapter, and the Schlesinger article cited in Chapter 17.

However, if the spouses instead elected a bypass type of plan, FET may be saved by means of lifetime interspousal gifts, as the following examples demonstrate. First we'll see the effect if no gift is made, and then we'll calculate the FET saving from an interspousal gift.

> EXAMPLE 13–15 Let's assume that our couple in Example 13-14 wishes to create a *credit shelter bypass*. If *no lifetime gifts are made,* the family wealth will devolve in the following manner. S1 will incur no FET no matter which spouse dies first, either because that spouse owns no property or because of the combined shelter of the marital deduction and the unified credit. If husband dies first, wife will receive $1.4 million and $600,000 will pass to the bypass share. Upon wife's later death, her estate will incur an FET of $320,000, leaving a net combined amount to the children of $1,680,000, which is the sum of $1,080,000 from her, plus 600,000 from the bypass share. Alternatively, if wife dies first, husband's $2 million estate at his later death will incur an FET of $588,000, leaving a total of only $1,412,000 to pass to the children. No bypass could be created if wife died first since wife had no assets to put into a bypass.

Now consider the effect of an interspousal gift upon this credit shelter bypass plan.

> EXAMPLE 13–16 Assume that husband in Example 13-15 presently *gives* wife one half of his wealth. The effects on FET under a credit shelter bypass plan are as follows. Since the gift was made between the spouses, no gift tax will be due, as the unlimited gift tax marital deduction will reduce the amount of the taxable gift to zero. The gift will not even be listed on husband's estate tax return as an "adjusted taxable gift" because the gift tax scheme subtracts the marital deduction amount in arriving at this concept.
>
> If husband dies first, the results will be the same as in the no-gifts Example 13-15: there will be no FET upon husband's death, and an FET of $320,000 upon wife's later death. However, if wife dies first, a markedly different result will occur. Wife's estate will still incur no FET, but on husband's later death there will be an FET of $320,000, an amount that is $268,000 less than the Example 13-15 result in which no gift had been made. Thus, the children will be able to receive a total of $1,680,000, rather than $1,412,000. Husband's gift of one half of his wealth to wife will, if wife predeceases husband, generate a transfer tax saving of $268,000.

The interspousal gift described in the example above saved FET because it enabled the less wealthy S1 to devise property into the bypass, thereby reducing S2's gross estate and FET. Similarly, other interspousal gifts can also generate large tax savings for other types of bypass arrangements, but will not be detailed here.

Drawbacks.   In spite of the large potential FET saving, the wealthier spouse may have some reservations about making a sizable spousal gift.

Relinquishment of control.   First, for the transfer to be complete, the donor spouse must be willing to surrender complete dominion and control to his or her spouse. In this age of high rates of marital dissolution, planners should be mindful of the possibility of future marital strife and its effect on the overall plan: It could generate a bitter regret by the donor that the gift was ever made. Further, even if the spouses are happily married, the wealthier spouse may still be reluctant to relinquish control over so much wealth.[10]

FET saving unlikely.   Second, demographic statistics indicate two salient facts: Many more wives survive their husbands than vice versa. And husbands in most noncommunity property states are generally wealthier than their wives. Thus, in the likely situation where the wealthier spouse (husband) dies first, a gift to the less affluent spouse (wife) will have saved no FET, as Example 13-16 demonstrated. Apparently, interspousal gifts designed to maximize FET saving through bypass plans will work in only a minority of family situations.

In conclusion, completed interspousal gifts, when added to a testamentary bypass plan, can occasionally result in an even larger FET saving. The strategy will work best in situations where the less wealthy spouse is expected to die first and where the spouses are happily married, elderly, and reasonably confident in each other's ability to handle such an undertaking.

Interspousal Gifts to Save Income Taxes

Ordinarily, there is no lifetime income tax advantage to interspousal gifts. As we have seen, the joint income tax return, filed by the overwhelming majority of spouses, has the effect of combining spousal income and produces one tax, no matter which

---

[10]As a possible solution, the donor spouse could instead transfer the property into a living QTIP trust, which could effectively prevent the donee spouse from exercising dispositive control over the corpus. However, if the donee spouse does

spouse earned the income. However, a completed gift from one spouse to the other can often save income taxes after the donee's earlier death, if the gift property is later sold at a gain. The tax-saving results from the opportunity to experience a step-up in basis before sale and was illustrated earlier in this chapter.

> EXAMPLE 13–17 In Example 13-11 husband was unable to obtain a step-up basis upon the death of his wife on property he had given her two months before her death, due to the restriction in Code Section 1014(e). However, had wife *lived longer than one year,* husband's taxable gain upon later sale will be $500 rather than $10,100, because of the resulting step-up in basis.[11]

Next, we turn to considerations in making gifts to minor children.

GIFTS TO MINOR CHILDREN: TECHNIQUES AND CONSIDERATIONS

Gifts to minor children are somewhat unique, not in their tax-saving potential so much as in the techniques by which their transfer is usually arranged. As mentioned earlier in this chapter, gifts to minors are usually not made outright but are made instead through a fiduciary in the form of a guardianship, a custodianship, or a trust.

Outright gifts transfer the greatest amount of control to the donee, invite the least amount of potential challenge from the Internal Revenue Service regarding the completeness of the transaction, and are the least complicated to make. But an outright gift to a person, whether a minor or an adult, will only work satisfactorily when the donee has sufficient maturity to rationally possess, conserve, and enjoy the gift property. In other circumstances, the transfer should be made to a fiduciary.[12] It should be arranged to

---

in fact die first, Section 2036 may require later inclusion of the corpus in the donor's (S2's) gross estate to the extent that the latter retained any benefits or controls (such as a life estate in the income).

[11]In community property states, of course, since the surviving spouse receives a step-up in basis for all community property owned, this gifting strategy need only be considered for the client's separate property.

[12]In fact, many states have statutes requiring outright gifts made to a minor in excess of a certain value to be held for the minor by a fiduciary.

achieve the same tax advantages available with an outright gift, to protect the donee from the risks of his or her own immaturity, and, in the case of minors, also to confirm to any restrictions state law may place on the ownership and use of property by minors.

Before examining types of fiduciary gifts that can meet these objectives, it might be helpful to review a tax issue that will influence the *use* of property given on behalf of minors. If income from a gift is used to discharge the *obligation of support* of the donor-parent to the donee-minor, that income will be taxable to the parent. For example, if Dad gives 14-year-old Junior $500 so that Junior can purchase lunch during his freshman year in high school, and Junior deposits the money in his own savings account, subsequently withdrawing interest as well as principal to buy the lunches, the interest income will be taxable to Dad as income used in discharge of a support obligation.[13] Thus, in order to enjoy the full tax advantages of a completed gift to a minor, income from the gift must not be used in this manner. Ordinarily, parents are not obligated to support their adult children, so the issue does not usually apply to adult donees.[14]

Gifts under Guardianship

Individuals may make completed gifts to themselves or others as guardians for the benefit of minor children. Gifts under guardianships have some *drawbacks*. First, to be legally valid, the transfer must be made with local (probate) court supervision, which usually involves the expense of time and money in securing court approval, a bond, an annual accounting, and other legal burdens. State laws vary on specific requirements. Further, property held in a guardianship is difficult to manage efficiently because many actions, including the purchase and sale of property, often require

---

[13]The rule subjecting income used for the support of a minor child to taxation of the parent even applies where the source of the income is not the parents (for example, income from a trust).

[14]There has been a recent trend in the case law, however, to impose on parents the duty of support of *higher education* for an adult child. So far, most of the decisions have been in the divorce, rather than the tax, arena. Nonetheless, caution should be exercised in advising clients, and local law should be checked. For more information, see the Blase article in this chapter's Recommended Reading section, and the Kline article at the end of Appendix 14A.

court approval. Court-supervision does afford the ward greater potential protection from misuse of the property by the adult fiduciary, but protection is rarely a major consideration. Finally, another disadvantage of guardianships is that the guardian must turn over the property outright to the ward at majority, an age donors usually consider too immature to receive a fee simple interest in gift property.

Custodial Gifts

The Uniform Gifts to Minors Act (UGMA), adopted in one form or other in all states, allows a relatively simple method of making fiduciary gifts of certain property. The gift property is transferred in the name of someone, acting "as custodian for (minor's name) under the (state name) Uniform Gift to Minors Act." Commonly, permissible property includes securities, cash, life insurance, and annuities, but there is legislative movement by several states to greatly expand this list.[15] The custodian acts, in effect, like a trustee; but title to the property rests in the minor. State law specifies when the property must be turned over to the donee, usually at age 21.[16] No court supervision is required.

In 1983 the National Conference on Uniform Laws adopted the Uniform Transfers to Minors Act (UTMA) which revised and expanded UGMA. Major changes include the following: (1) allows any property interests to be transferred, including real estate, partnership interests, patents, royalty interests, and intellectual property; (2) allows a fiduciary (executor or trustee) to establish a custodianship if authorized in a governing will or trust; (3) authorizes transfers to a custodian from persons other than the transferor who are obligated to the minor (examples include a personal injury recovery and a joint bank account of which the minor is a surviving cotenant); (4) allows a transferor to revocably nominate a custo-

---

[15]The major type of property that cannot be gifted under UGMA in most states is real estate.

[16]Upon receiving the property outright in fee simple, the donee may (or may not) be able to be successfully persuaded to immediately transfer the assets into an irrevocable trust for his or her future benefit.

dian to receive property in the future. At least 16 states have adopted UTMA without significant alterations.[17]

Custodial gifts achieve essentially all of the tax advantages of completed outright transfers, except that the custodial property will be included in the donor's gross estate if the donor both acts as custodian and predeceases the minor. In that case, the donor will be deemed to have made a §2036 transfer with retained control over the property.

Gifts to an Irrevocable Trust

Although both gifts under guardianships and custodial gifts are usually an improvement over larger outright gifts to minors, they have some serious drawbacks. They usually terminate at or shortly after the donee's age of majority, at which time the donee enjoys fee simple ownership of the property. And they are restrictive, either in the red tape involved to create and continue them (gifts under guardianships) or in the type of property that usually may be given (custodial gifts) under the laws of many states. They are also inflexible in that the controlling state law usually is not or cannot be modified by private document. Thus, the donor under a guardianship arrangement usually cannot provide, by private document, that court supervision will not be required. The presence of these and other drawbacks leads many donors to consider making sizable gifts to minors using the irrevocable trust.[18]

In structuring gifts in trust for the benefit of minors, planners seek to obtain all of the tax benefits available to other outright gifts. The four major tax objectives are: (1) taking the annual gift tax exclusion; (2) excluding the nontaxable value of the gift from the donor's gross estate at death; (3) excluding postgift appreciation in the value of the gift property from the donor's estate tax

---

[17]Including Arkansas, California, Colorado, Florida, Idaho, Illinois, Montana, Missouri, Nevada, New Hampshire, North Dakota, Oregon, and Rhode Island. For further details, see the Ledwith-Robinson article cited at the end of the chapter.

[18]The trust may also have the advantage of more successfully insulating the gift property from the parents' creditors.

base; and (4) shifting the taxable income earned on the gift property to the donee.

Drafting an irrevocable trust takes great care because the non-outright nature of transfers into it makes it vulnerable to challenge by the Internal Revenue Service. For example, the donor will often wish to act as trustee of the trust. Also, the donor will usually want to restrict the minor child's enjoyment of the trust principal and income for some period of time. These requirements reflect the donor's desire to retain a greater degree of control over the gift property. The problem is that often only a very fine line exists between Code-acceptable and Code-unacceptable controls by the donor. Earlier in this chapter we saw some situations in which the transferor was penalized by income and estate tax provisions for retaining too much control. To this list we must add certain ill-designed transfers into a trust for the benefit of minors. The following discusses particular tax hurdles facing the planners of an irrevocable trust and several methods for dealing with them, including qualifying for the annual exclusion, an estate tax caution, and an income tax concern.

Qualifying for the annual exclusion.   As we have mentioned, to qualify for the gift tax annual exclusion, a gift must be one of a "present interest," that is, an unrestricted right to the immediate use, possession, or enjoyment of property or the income from property. The reader might ask how a gift into trust for the benefit of a minor can qualify for the annual exclusion when, after all, the minor is not typically given the unrestricted right to the immediate use of either the principal *or* the income. After all, most or all of the property is usually withheld from the child for some period of time. The answer lies in three exceptions carved out by the Internal Revenue Code and the courts that form the basis for an added clause in the trust document. The three alternatives are called the 2503(c) provision, the Crummey provision, and the 2503(b) provision.

2503(c) provision: Under Section 2503(c), a gift in trust is not a gift of a future interest if three conditions are met. First, the property and income may be expended by or for the benefit of the donee before the donee attains age 21. Second, any portion of the property not so expended will pass to the donee at age 21. Third, the property is made payable to the donee's estate (or as the donee may appoint under a general power of appointment) if the donee dies before age 21.[19] As mentioned in Chapter 7, the 2503(c) exception was created to discourage the adoption of trusts which pay out income to presumably immature minors immediately upon the trustee's receipt, for the sole purpose of taking advantage of the annual exclusion. Thus, "2503(c) trusts," as they are called, are normally expected to terminate when the child reaches age 21.[20]

The Crummey provision: Crummey is the name of a taxpayer who succeeded in federal court in getting an annual exclusion for each year's transfer into a trust for the benefit of the minor children. The typical Crummey trust clause provides that the child has the right to withdraw, for a brief period each year, the lesser of the amount of the annual exclusion or the value of the gift property transferred into the trust. Thus, since the child has the right to withdraw that amount, it is considered a gift of a present interest, and the donor will receive an annual exclusion for gifts of property into the trust.[21]

2503(b) provision: A trust that requires mandatory distribution of income annually to the beneficiary as the way of entitling the donor to the annual exclusion is called a 2503(b) trust or a "minor's income trust."[22] The gift is considered as comprising two parts, the

---

[19]In many states, a minor may not legally execute a will. Thus, in the event of the death of the minor, the property would likely revert, by intestacy, to the grantor-parent, thereby defeating the estate-reducing objective in making the gift. The Crummey provision, discussed next, does not have this drawback.

[20]The §2503(c) trust need not terminate at age 21 as long as the beneficiary can request a complete distribution at age 21 (LR 8507017).

[21]Use of a Crummey power can result in undesired gift tax and income tax consequences. For example, a beneficiary's failure to exercise a Crummey power in a given year may mean that the beneficiary has made a *taxable gift* by permitting a general power of appointment to lapse. The gift tax value would be the amount that the value permitted to lapse exceeded the greater of $5,000 or 5 percent of the aggregate value of the assets subject to the power. For example, if $120,000 was contributed as an initial gift in trust, with a $20,000 demand right, $14,000 would be considered a taxable gift (the amount that $20,000 exceeds the greater of $5,000 or 5 percent of $120,000). The gift will not qualify for the annual exclusion. Commentators think that most planners ignore this tax consequence. For a detailed discussion, see the Tarlow-Vacca article, as well as several others cited at the end of the chapter.

[22]However, the mandatory distribution of income from a §2503(b) trust may be deposited in a custodial account for the benefit of a minor and left to accumulate until majority.

income portion and the gift portion. Tax law considers the income portion of the gift to be a present interest qualifying for the annual exclusion. The alternative fractions making up the gift are derived from tables found in the Internal Revenue Service regulations (25.2512-5), similar to Table 8 in Appendix A. For example, .098066, or 98.066 percent of a gift into trust for the benefit of a 14-year-old having solely a life estate in the trust income represents the present interest income portion. Thus, $1 - 0.98066$, or 0.01934 (1.934 percent) represents the remainder portion which does not qualify for the annual exclusion.

The 2503(b) and 2503(c) trusts have become less attractive since the Crummey decision. Prior to Crummey, planners had to choose between an arrangement requiring annual distribution of all trust income to the minor and one effectively requiring distribution of the entire trust corpus at age 21. Although many planners favored 2503(b) for larger trusts, the choice was usually not enthusiastically made. Happily, the Crummey provision solved this dilemma by enabling the donor to give the child the *right to demand* a modest amount from the trust annually, without handing a lot of income or principal over to the child, even after age 21. Usually the child is made to realize that there is much to lose by exercising the demand right. For example, the child might lose a greater inheritance in the future, or the parent might simply refuse to make further transfers into the trust.[23]

Estate tax caution.   In designing the irrevocable trust, the estate planner must be mindful of the dangers of letting the donor retain prohibited controls that would subject the date-of-death value of the gift property to be included in the donor's gross estate. For example, naming the grantor to be trustee of a §2503(b) or (c) trust will cause estate tax inclusion of the trust assets at the grantor's death. The underlying Code provisions have been covered in Chapter 6 and include §2036, transfers with retained life estate; §2037, transfers taking effect at death; and §2038, revocable transfers. The reader is urged to review them at this point.

---

[23]Of course, parents sometimes will approve of withdrawals, such as when the money will be used for college expenses.

Income tax concern. The donor of a gift in trust for a minor child usually wishes to avoid being taxed on the income received by the trust, preferring instead to let the trust be taxed to the extent the income is accumulated, or to let the child be taxed to the extent that the income is paid to the child. However, the trust must be designed so as not to conflict with the grantor trust rules, described in Chapter 8. For example, reservation by the donor of the unlimited right to make withdrawals from the trust will cause the income to be taxed to the donor.[24]

This chapter has introduced the planning for lifetime transfers, devoting considerable detail to gifts. Chapter 14 will explore another group of lifetime transfers: ones different from gifts in that they are either incomplete or are completed transfers to charity.

RECOMMENDED READING

ADAMS, RAY M., and SCOTT BIEBER. "Making '5 and 5' Equal 20: Crummey Powers after ERTA." *Trusts & Estates,* September 1983, pp. 22–25.

BLAKE, JOHN FREEMAN, and LYNN K. PEARLE. "New Decision Expands Scope of Support a Parent May Be Required to Furnish." *Estate Planning,* November 1984, pp. 322–26.

BLASE, JAMES G. "College Education and the Duty to Support." *Trusts & Estates,* March 1984, pp. 45–48.

BLATTMACHR, JONATHAN, G. "Child's Income May Be Taxed at Parent's Tax Rate," *Journal of Taxation,* January 1987, pp. 48–52.

BUTTITA, JOHN J. "Another Look at Income Shifting: The Qualified Subchapter S Trust," *Chicago Bar Record* 66 (January 1985), pp. 194–202.

DANIEL, R. MICHAEL, and WILLIAM R. NEE. "Pre-death Planning Techniques for Clients without a Surviving Spouse." *Estate Planning,* May 1985, pp. 168–71.

DELORIO, MAJ. DOMINIK J. "Uniform Gifts to Minors Act." *Military Law Review* 112 (1986), pp. 159–73.

DEVINE, JAMES D. "How Trusts for Minors Can Be Structured to Meet Grantors' Tax and Nontax Objectives." *Taxation for Accountants,* March 1984, pp. 140–46.

---

[24]However, as a result of TRA 86, the grantor trust rules will not apply if the grantor retains a reversion that can only occur on the death of a beneficiary (before age 21) who is a lineal descendant of the grantor and holds all present interests in any portion of the trust.

DYE, DOUGLAS G. "Several Routes Exist to Avoid IRS' Income Tax Roadblock to Use of Crummey Trust Provisions." *Estate Planning,* July 1983, pp. 220–24.

GILFIX, MICHAEL "Medicaid and Estate Planning: Asset Preservation and Long-Term Care." *Estate Planning for the Aging or Incapacitated Client 1986,* Practicing Law Institute.

GOGGANS, TRAVIS P., and CANDACE J. GARCIA. "Family Gifts of Real Estate: Avoiding Inclusion under Sec. 2036." *Tax Adviser,* July 1984, pp. 394–402.

LEDWITH, JAMES R., and MARY ANN ROBINSON. "Expanded Opportunities Available under Uniform Transfers to Minors Act." *Estate Planning,* September 1986, pp. 258–62.

LOBENHOFER, LOUIS F. "Who Do You Trust?—Planning Opportunities for Parents Making Gifts to Their Children with Themselves as Trustees." *Ohio Northern University Law Review 9,* no. 2 (1982), pp. 171–203.

McCUE, HOWARD M. III, and DANIEL W. LUTHER. "New Rules Create New Problems." (Income and Value Shifting after TRA 86) *Trusts & Estates,* October 1987, pp. 10–18.

MEADE, JANET A. "Section 1014(e) and the Lock-In Problem: Basis Considerations in Transfers of Appreciated Property." *Taxes—The Tax Magazine* 64 (September 1986), pp. 588–94.

METZ, LEROY, and WESLEY YANG. "Goal Tending Called on Net Gifts." *Taxes—The Tax Magazine,* January 1983, pp. 13–19.

MEZZULLO, LOUIS A. "New Regulations Make It Difficult, but Not Impossible, to Shift Income to Minors." *Estate Planning,* January 1988, pp. 2–5.

MOORE, MALCOLM A. "Tax Consequences and Uses of "Crummey" Withdrawal Powers: An Update," University of Miami 22nd Annual Estate Planning Institute, 1988.

MORRIS, MALCOLM L. "The Tax Posture of Gifts in Estate Planning: Dinosaur of Dynasty?" *Nebraska Law Review* 64 (1985), pp. 25–82.

NECHIN, HERBERT B. "Gifts of Real Estate to Minors Can Shift Income While Satisfying Clients' Other Needs." *Taxation for Lawyers,* March–April 1985, pp. 302–6.

OFFICER, DENNIS T., and WARREN E. BANKS. "Estates vs. Gifts in a Period of Inflation." *Taxes—The Tax Magazine,* January 1980, pp. 68–72.

SPENCER, PATTI S. "Advantages Remain to Making Gifts in Trust to Minors that Qualify for Annual Exclusion." *Estate Planning,* September 1987, pp. 264–68. (Covers the 2503(c) trust.)

TARLOW, EDWARD D., and CATHERINE M. VACCA. "Recent Developments Clarify Tax Effects of Lapse of Crummey Powers, but Problems Remain." *Estate Planning,* September 1986, pp. 272–75.

VORSATZ, MARK L. "Trust with Beneficiary's Power of Withdrawal Adaptable for Use in Many Family Situations." *Taxation for Accountants,* February 1986, pp. 98–103.

"What to Give Away." *Real Property, Probate and Trust Journal* 18 (1983), pp. 678–707. (Report of the Committee on Estate Planning and Drafting: Inter Vivos Transfers and Property Ownership.)

WICKER, WILLIAM H. "Spendthrift Trusts Are an Excellent Way to Leave Money to Someone Who Can't Handle It." *Estate Planning*, Summer 1975, pp. 202–5.

WINTRISS, LYNN. "Gift-Splitting Can Increase Tax Effectiveness of Gift Program that Is Part of an Estate Plan." *Estate Planning*, November 1982, pp. 340–45.

QUESTIONS AND PROBLEMS

1. Good planning requires that the client feel comfortable with a proposed lifetime transfer. How can lifetime transfers be a source of discomfort?

2. One of your clients explains to you that she'd like to make a lifetime transfer to her child, perhaps in the form of a gift. But she is not clear on how gifts differ from other lifetime transfers. Inform her.

3. Now that your client is aware of the unique nature of a gift, explain to her the difference between an outright and a non-outright gift.

4. Carrie, a rich elderly widow, expects to live 10 years. She would like to begin a program of lifetime gifting to her four children.
   a. What equal amount can Carrie give to each child, per year, without paying any gift tax, while fully using up her unified credit? Assume no prior taxable gifts.
   b. Why might Carrie be willing to use up her unified credit?

5. Why is the ability to avoid grossing up a tax advantage to gifting?

6. Two years ago, Zack gave his daughter Luna a one-acre plot of desert land in Nevada, then worth $9,000. Subsequently, oil was found, making the plot worth $900,000.
   a. How much attributable to this land will be included in Zack's estate tax base if he dies today? Explain.
   b. If he died four years ago? Explain.
   c. How much would be included if, instead, Zack made the gift in 1981 and dies today? Explain.
      Assume no prior gifts.

7. How would your answers to Question 6 change, if at all, if at the time of the transfer Zack reserved the right to camp out on the land whenever he liked? (Assume further that Zack just died of a heart attack after discovering that shortly after receiving the land, Luna quickly sold it to a third party for $10,000.)

8. Describe the attributes of those clients who would be most willing to make sizable gifts.

9. Summarize the major tax disadvantages to gifting.

10. "Higher basis assets make better gifts." True, false, or uncertain?

11. Discuss any significant reasons why each of the following assets have particularly attractive or unattractive gift potential.
    a. Stock: donor's basis, $60,000; fair market value, $20,000.
    b. Stock: donor's basis, $20,000; fair market value, $800,000. Does age of the donee matter at all?
    c. Life insurance on the donor's life.
    d. Rights to a patent.
    e. Raw land.
    f. A bond having a coupon rate of 18 percent.
    g. Clipped bond coupons.

12. Under what circumstances can an interspousal gift save FET? (b)Under what circumstances can an interspousal gift save income tax?

13. Contrast the advantages and disadvantages of the alternative methods of making gifts to minors.

14. Paradiso, a client, asks you to review the recommendation of one of your competitors. That planner proposed transferring $10,000 per year for life into an irrevocable trust, whose terms provide that all income will be accumulated until Paradiso's son Max (age 4) reaches age 35. At that time all accumulated income will be distributed to Max, who will thereafter receive all income currently until Paradiso's death, at which time the trust will terminate and all principal will be distributed outright to Max.
    a. Will this arrangement reduce Paradiso's future FET or freeze any part of his estate? Why or why not?
    b. Will the periodic transfers be free of gift tax? Why or why not?
    c. If the answer to b is no, suggest three alternative provisions in the trust that will change the result.

    d. Which of the three provisions in part *c* reduces the maximum life of the trust?

    e. Which of the three provisions in part *c* will probably be most appealing to Paradiso, who is quite reluctant to allow distribution of income or principal until Max reaches age 35?

    f. How much income shifting, if any, will your answer in part *e* accomplish?

15. A client of yours needs some planning advice. She wants to start a college fund for her 8-year-old daughter. Her goal is to accumulate approximately $50,000 in 10 years, at which time equal monthly payments will be made to daughter over a period of the following 4 years.

    a. if neither income shifting nor estate reduction are important, is a program of gifting necessary? Why or why not?

    b. if your client wishes to shift income to daughter (who for simplicity, we'll assume, has no taxable income of her own), recommended strategies for each of the following alternative sets of assumptions:

      (1) Client wishes to accumulate a fund that can revert to her if her daughter later decides not to attend college.

      (2) Client would like an arrangement under which she can continue funding after her daughter's graduation.

    c. In part *b* above, recommend suitable investments to purchase.

14

Lifetime Transfers II: Other Intrafamily Transfers; Charitable Transfers

OVERVIEW

Gift planning, the subject of the last chapter, is often rejected by clients for two reasons. First, by their very nature, gifts entail a lack of consideration received in exchange. Gifting reduces wealth which, in turn, reduces the client's income-earning capacity, a situation many clients are unwilling to experience. Second, gifting requires complete relinquishment of dominion and control over the gift property, a difficult thing for just about any donor to do.

Happily, the reluctant but interested client can select from other, less painful alternatives to the outright gift. In this second of two chapters on lifetime transfers, we'll explore two other types of attractive intrafamily arrangements. The first type involves the client's receiving consideration, as in the installment sale and the private annuity. The second type, such as the grantor retained income trust, are incomplete transfers which permit the client to retain some degree of control over the transferred property. The chapter will also cover the popular types of lifetime charitable transfers, including outright charitable transfers and charitable transfers in trust, such as the annuity trust, the unitrust, and the pooled income fund.

COMPLETED INTRAFAMILY TRANSFERS FOR CONSIDERATION

In this section, we'll study lifetime transfers that are unique in two ways. First, they differ from gifts because they generate consideration to the transferor. Second, they differ from the second type of lifetime intrafamily transfer to be covered in this chapter in that they are complete, that is, they entail *total* transfer of all interests in the asset.

Ordinary Sale

The client can simply sell property for cash to a family member at a fair market price. Under certain circumstances, an ordinary sale can be especially beneficial to both family members. The client may truly wish to sell at a fair price but would prefer to keep the asset in the family. And the related buyer will be spared the effort and expense of looking for a similar, relatively unique asset. As a true sale, of course, there will probably be income tax consequences to the seller. Careful records should be kept, since intrafamily sales are often subject to greater IRS review, especially if the transaction is sizable. The buyer, of course, has the burden of acquiring the cash or other acceptable property needed for the purchase. And the seller is not allowed to deduct any loss incurred in the sale, due to the Code's prohibition against loss recognition on sales between related parties.[1]

Bargain Sale

If the client has mixed transfer motives, on the one hand wishing to gift a particular asset to a family member, and on the other hand not willing to completely forgo the receipt of all consideration in return, a bargain sale may be appropriate. As described in Chapter 2, under a bargain sale the client sells the asset for an amount less than what would be regarded full and adequate consideration. The difference between the consideration received by the client-donor and the value of the asset transferred is a gift, for tax purposes. Regarding income tax, the client would recognize a gain in proportion to the consideration received if the asset's value exceeded its

---

[1]Section 267.

adjusted basis. The buyer-donee's basis in the asset would be the price paid.

> EXAMPLE 14–1 Mom owns property with a basis of $90,000 and a current value of $240,000, which she sells to her son for $80,000. The transaction is ⅓ sale and ⅔ gift. Mom's taxable gain is $50,000, the difference between $80,000 and $30,000, with the latter figure being one third of her total basis. Son's new basis is $140,00, which is $80,000, the purchase price, plus $60,000, the carry-over basis on the gifted two thirds portion (i.e., ⅔ of $90,000).

As a compromise between a gift and a sale, the bargain sale can be arranged to closely reflect the degree of generosity that the client feels.

Installment Sale

Instead of selling the asset to a family member for cash or other tangible property, the client could sell it in exchange for an installment note, in which the buyer agrees to make periodic payments of principal and interest, based on a fair market rate of interest. Under income tax law, the seller may spread recognition of the gain over the collection period. The gain would be recognized in proportion to the amount of each payment. Losses do not qualify for installment reporting.

> EXAMPLE 14–2 Mom, a widow, sells her rental house to her daughter for $80,000, payable with a down payment of $10,000. Interest is payable monthly, with five equal annual $14,000 payments on principal. Mom's current adjusted basis in the house is $20,000. Her gross profit is $60,000, and each year she will recognize a capital gain of $60,000/$80,000, or 75 percent of the amount received.[2] Thus, in the year of sale, she'll receive the $10,000 and her reportable gain will be $7,500. In each of the succeeding five years she can expect to report a gain of $10,500.

---

[2]Any interest received on the balance due will also be taxable income. But under TRA 86, subject to phase-in by 1991, interest paid will be fully deductible by the buyer only if it is considered either business interest or investment interest which is offset by investment income, interest on a debt secured by a primary or secondary residence, or some other type of qualified interest. In addition, TRA 86 places restrictions on deferral of gain on an installment sale of certain trade or business property. Section 453(C)(e)(1)(A)(i)(III).

At least two different events will trigger an *immediate recognition* of the entire remaining gain. If the seller sells or "otherwise disposes" of the installment note, or if the seller cancels the note, then he or she will have to report currently the remaining gain from the original transaction.

The buyer, as in any valid sale, will enjoy a step-up in basis in the property to the amount of the purchase price. However, with regard to the seller's note, transfer of the note at the death of the seller *will not generate a step-up basis* in the note. The legatee-heir will continue to report installment gain in the same manner as the seller.

If the installment transaction is a bona fide sale for full and adequate consideration, there will be *no gift tax* consequences to the lender.[3] However, we already know that family transactions are often scrutinized more carefully by the IRS, and the client is well advised to determine the value of the asset by qualified appraisal and to use a market rate of interest.

A generous seller may wish to *forgive* one or more of the purchaser's future payments. In the usual case, only the amount forgiven constitutes a taxable gift in the year forgiven. The gift will qualify for the annual exclusion.

> EXAMPLE 14–3 Continuing Example 14-2, if daughter fails to make the third annual payment of $14,000 because she uses the money instead to make a down payment on a home, and Mom sanctions the omission, Mom has made a gift of that amount. Ordinarily, after the annual exclusion, her taxable gift will be $4,000. If Mom had been married and she and her husband elected to split the gift, the taxable gift would have been zero.

A more serious tax problem can arise, however, when the seller is considerably more generous. The IRS maintains that if the seller, at the time of the sale, *intended not to enforce* the note, the entire value of the property would then be taxable as a gift. However the IRS has rarely prevailed, especially when the note has been drafted carefully to be legally valid and enforceable.

---

[3]On the other hand, if the lender is deemed to have made a gift, §2036 may subject the entire date-of-death value of the property sold to later inclusion in the lender's gross estate.

Ordinarily, when the seller in an installment sale dies, only the current value of the installment note is included in his or her *gross estate*.

> EXAMPLE 14–4 Continuing Example 14-3, if Mom dies just before the fourth payment is due, her gross estate will include the discounted value of the note. If the current discount rate is 12 percent, then the note's value would equal $23,661, the present value of the right to receive $14,000 a year for two years, discounted at 12 percent. Of course, Mom's gross estate will also include any proceeds from receipt of earlier payments from daughter, to the extent retained by Mom, or any assets she purchased with those proceeds. However, her gross estate will not include the value of the installment asset sold.

Self-canceling provision. The client may seek to avoid inclusion of the value of the note in his or her gross estate by incorporating a self-canceling provision, specifying that no further payments will be made after his or her death. Since the initial value of a *self-canceling installment note* (SCIN) is less than one whose payments can not be prematurely canceled, the payor will have to give additional alternative consideration, usually in the form of a higher principal amount or a higher interest rate. And, of course, the older the client, the greater the additional consideration. Otherwise, the IRS could assert the existence of a gift element in the transaction, creating the risk of §2036 application. The SCIN represents aggressive planning and should be used only when the client is willing to be subject to potentially greater tax exposure.

Tax deferral through installment sales have recently become more attractive for two reasons.[4] First, TRA 86's elimination of the preferential rate on capital gains has made tax rates for property transactions in current years higher. Second, rates on *ordinary in-*

---

[4]On the other hand, TRA 86 placed restrictions on installment reporting of certain sales. Sales of publicly traded property (e.g., stocks and bonds) will no longer qualify. In addition, a portion of the following sales may not qualify (under the so-called "proportional disallowance rule") if the sales price exceeds $150,000: sales of property held primarily for sale to customers in the ordinary course of business, sales of real property used in a business, and any sales of real rental property. In general, sales of other personal-use property will still qualify for installment reporting.

come are expected to be raised in future years, while capital gains rates are expected to be lowered.

Thus, the client has a number of ways to arrange the intrafamily sale of a high appreciating asset. The sale can help to freeze the client's estate, since postsale appreciation will inure not to the client but to the new owner, whose gross estate is probably far smaller than the client's and who will probably live considerably longer. Intrafamily sales, whether of the ordinary, bargain, or installment variety, can be significant value-shifting devices.[5]

Private Annuity

Much like an installment sale, a private annuity usually involves the sale of an asset by the client in exchange for the unsecured promise of a life annuity by another family member. It is distinguished from a commercial annuity, which is purchased from an insurance company or other financial institution.

> EXAMPLE 14–5 Schwab, age 65 and in poor health, agrees to transfer a $100,000 asset to his son, under a private annuity arrangement. Based on valuation tables essentially similar to those shown in Table 9 of Appendix A, Schwab will receive $14,712.37 a year for life ($14,712.37 = $100,000/6.7970).

Tax aspects of the private annuity are as follows. If the transaction is designed properly, there will be *no taxable gift* as long as the value of the property transferred equals the discounted present value of the annuity promised. With regard to income taxation, *no gain* is immediately recognizable because the amount realized (i.e., the value of the unsecured promise to pay an annuity for someone's life) is not considered immediately ascertainable. Thus, as with the installment sale, gain is reported as the annuity payments are *received*.

Regarding death taxation, upon death of the client-annuitant, *nothing* connected with the transaction should be included in the estate tax base, inasmuch as he or she no longer has an interest in the property transferred. As with any life estate on the life of its owner, the life annuity terminates, becoming valueless at the death

---

[5]One exception is the bargain sale in connection with a transfer subject to §2043, which embraces all transfers covered by Sections 2035–38 and 2041. See Chapter 6.

of its owner.[6] However, if the original transfer were to be ruled a *gift* because the value of the annuity promised the client is less than the value of the property transferred, the client's gross estate will include the *entire* date-of-death value of that property as a Section 2036 transfer with a retained life estate. Such effect would wipe away the major tax justification for the transaction, a danger that can be minimized by securing a qualified professional appraisal.

> EXAMPLE 14–6 In Example 14-5, above, if Schwab lives for two years, his son will have paid less than $30,000 for an asset worth $100,000. In connection with this transaction, Schwab's estate tax base will include nothing more than the amount of the two cash payments that Schwab retained at death.

While the private annuity has many of the characteristics of the installment sale, and although it may have the relative advantage of complete excludability from the annuitant's estate tax base, it has several *disadvantages*. First, while the seller in an installment sale can require security, the annuitant under a private annuity will lose the advantage of deferrability of the gain if any *collateral* is involved. Thus, private annuity arrangements are always unsecured, a distinct disadvantage to the annuitant-client. Lack of security will increase the risk of not being repaid, a result that could be unsettling, especially to an annuitant who was more or less depending on the payments for support.[7] Second, interest paid by the purchaser under an installment sale may be tax deductible, while *no part* of the annuity payment under a private annuity is deductible. Third, if the annuitant lives a very long life, the payor will have made a *bad bargain*.

----

[6]The private annuity can work very well for nonterminal clients having shorter than average life expectancies. For example, one person arranged a private annuity prior to open-heart surgery, which was successful. He died 17 months later. In court the IRS lost its argument that the value of the property transferred exceeded the present value of the annuity payments, which had been determined using IRS tables. Ordinarily, only in cases where death is "imminent" will actual life expectancies be required (Estate of Fabric 83TC932). For a discussion of when the tables will and will not be used, see the Blattmachr-Cavalieri article cited at the end of the chapter.

[7]For a discussion of placing the transferred property in a trust managed by a trustee until the property is made available to the ultimate beneficiaries, see the Loftis article cited at the end of the chapter.

EXAMPLE 14–7 Continuing Example 14-6, above, if Schwab regains his health and lives 20 years, his son will have paid more than $294,000 for the $100,000 asset. Schwab's gross estate will include this amount (which is nearly three times the value of the asset transferred) if he doesn't consume or gift it during his lifetime.

Finally, since the private annuity is a complicated tax-sheltering family transaction subject to the risk of the application of Section 2036, it must be carefully structured to pass careful IRS scrutiny, a factor that increases the tax danger of a foul-up. However, because it can accomplish significant estate freezing without gift tax consequences, the private annuity can be a very attractive transaction if the parties are willing to assume the inherent risks.

Sale of a Remainder Interest and Joint Purchase

The ordinary sale, bargain sale, installment sale, and private annuity may all be unacceptable to some clients, who, during their lifetimes, do not want to surrender the present enjoyment of property. All of these sales techniques involve the immediate transfer of the right to possession and enjoyment. Another type of sale, however, the sale of a remainder interest, does not have this drawback and may be an attractive alternative. Like the other sales devices, it can be expected to freeze estate tax values, generate cash inflow, and assist a family member. But unlike the others, it will permit the client to retain the right to possession and enjoyment of the property "sold," at least for life.

EXAMPLE 14–8 A 62-year-old parent has some valuable jewelry and has a physician-son who agrees to purchase the remainder interest in the gems. Based on Table A in Treasury Regulation 25.2512-5(e) (similar to the value in Table 9 of Appendix A), the son will now pay 27.998 percent of the current value of the jewelry for the right to receive it outright at the client's death. The client will be able to own and enjoy the jewelry for life. And the FET value of the asset should still be effectively frozen, since the client's gross estate ought to include only the amount of the sale proceeds that has been retained at death. Of course, the son will not receive possession of the jewelry until the client's death, but he probably would have received it no sooner anyway.

If the purchaser is unwilling to pay cash for the asset, an installment sale could be arranged, and the client even occasionally forgive a payment, an action which would constitute a taxable gift, but one that would probably qualify for the annual exclusion, so long as the acts of forgiveness are not frequent and are not planned at the time of the sale. Use of the installment sale will also postpone recognition of the client's gain, if any, in the same manner as described earlier. In determining gain or loss, the client's tax basis is apportioned between the remainder interest and the retained life estate. Thus, in our example, the client's tax basis will become 27.998 percent of the former basis.

Exclusion of the remainder interest from the seller's gross estate is not guaranteed, however, as the IRS may contend that the only way to escape the trap of §2036 is for the purchaser to pay the full value of the property, not just the value of the remainder interest. Of course, this would make the transaction even less attractive to the buyer than an ordinary sale. And the passage of §2036(c) in the Revenue Act of 1987 has increased the likelihood of inclusion, due to the emphasis of that section on estate freezing transfers.[8] But the risk of §2036 can be greatly minimized if, instead of making a transfer of property, the client and the family member join in purchasing property from a *third party,* with the client purchasing a life interest and the family member acquiring the remainder interest.[9] This "joint purchase" or "split purchase" agreement is rapidly replacing the sale of a remainder interest as the preferred transfer.

Thus, the sale of a remainder interest in property or joint purchase for family members can be an attractive tool for a client who seeks an estate freeze, does not with to part with property until

---

[8]S2036(c) uses the word "enterprise," but commentators believe that the subsection will apply to many nonbusiness agreements, including the type discussed here. In addition, the "full and adequate consideration" exception in the S2036(a)(1) does not apply to S2036(c) transfers to family members. (S2036(c) (2)). For a further discussion of §2036(c) in connection with the estate freezing recapitalization, see Appendix 16A.

[9]Another attractive application of the joint purchase involves the purchase of the life estate by the trustee of the marital deduction trust and purchase of the remainder interest in the residence by the trustee of the bypass trust.

death, and has a younger-generation family member with the desire and the wherewithal to acquire it.

INCOMPLETE INTRAFAMILY TRANSFERS

This section briefly covers two currently used incomplete intrafamily transfers, the gift-leaseback and the grantor income trust. Several other incomplete transfers, including the interest-free loan, the short-term trust, and the spousal remainder trust, were popular income-shifting devices until tax reform activity of the mid-1980s destroyed their usefulness. Appendix 14A examines these defective incomplete transfers in some detail, and the student is urged to read it, partly to gain a historical perspective, partly because some clients will still be involved in prior-consummated transfers of this kind, and partly to be aware of formerly popular devices about which clients will be curious for some time to come.

Gift-Leaseback

When a business-owning parent wishes to establish a program of gifting but is held back for lack of available assets, he or she might find the answer in a gift-leaseback arrangement. As its name suggests, the parent gives a business asset outright or in trust to a lower-bracket family member and leases the asset back for use in the business. The parent is able to continue using the asset, can take a deduction for the lease payment, and can still enjoy all the other advantages inherent in gifting.

The ability to *deduct* the lease payments under a gift-leaseback will depend in part on the client's residence state, and in part on how carefully the arrangement is structured. Federal appellate courts in certain areas of the country have disallowed the deduction, while others have allowed it as a legitimate business expense. Even there, however, the deduction could be denied if the transaction is structured poorly. Some requirements for success include having a legitimate business purpose, charging a reasonable lease payment, having a written and enforceable lease, and making sure that the trustee, if any, is independent, not subservient to the donor.

Grantor Retained Income Trust

Under the grantor retained income trust (GRIT), also called the grantor lead trust, the client transfers property into an irrevocable trust, retaining the right to income for a period of years. Distribution of corpus at the client's death depends upon whether or not the client survived this period. If not, the corpus reverts to the client-grantor's estate. If the client did survive the period, the corpus passes to a younger-generation beneficiary.

The GRIT has the following tax consequences. At creation of the GRIT, the present actuarial value of the remainder interest will constitute a *taxable gift,* one that will not qualify for the annual exclusion.[10] If the client dies before the expiration of the income period, §2036 will subject the date-of-death value of the corpus to *inclusion* in the client's gross estate. If the client dies after the end of the stated period, the corpus will not be included in the gross estate.[11] However, any taxable gift value will be included in the estate tax base. Regarding income tax, since the trust is initially a grantor trust, all income will be taxed to the client until the end of the stated period.

> EXAMPLE 14–9 Haney, who is 58 years old, just created a GRIT, funding it with $50,000 in the common stock of his closely held business. The trust terms provide that all income will be payable at least annually to Haney for the lessor of 12 years or Haney's life. If Haney dies before the end of the 12-year period, the trust will terminate and the corpus will revert to his estate. If Haney survives the period, the trust will terminate at the end of 12 years and the corpus will then be distributed outright to Haney's son. As a result of this plan, Haney has made a *taxable gift* of the remainder interest in the stock, which is valued at $11,589 (= $50,000 times .23178. See Table 9 of Appendix

---

[10]Some commentators argue that there is no clear statutory basis for valuing the gift at less than the full current market value. This would reduce its attractiveness in transfer tax reduction. However, if the partial valuation is permitted, FET reduction is substantial in view of the use of 10 percent present value tables to generate an artificially low remainder interest value.

[11]One commentator has suggested, however, that to be totally protected from the impact of §2036(c), the grantor will need to survive at least three years after the end of the period.

A). He will owe no gift tax, however, because of the availability of a sufficient amount of unused unified credit.

EXAMPLE 14–10 Continuing the above example, if Haney *dies four years later,* the date of death value of the corpus will be included in Haney's gross estate, and the trust will have served no useful function. In fact, Haney's estate tax base will be higher than if the GRIT had not been established, because of the addition of $11,589 in adjusted taxable gifts.

EXAMPLE 14–11 Examining the consequences of the alternative outcome in the above example, if Haney instead *dies thirteen years later* when the stock is worth $350,000, his gross estate will include nothing in connection with this stock (although adjusted taxable gifts will include the amount $11,589). Haney has succeeded in freezing the transfer tax value of this stock at the original gift tax value of the remainder interest.

The GRIT can be an attractive incomplete transfer to reduce FET. It can accomplish an estate tax freeze at no more than a relatively modest, although earlier, gift tax cost.

PLANNING FOR CHARITABLE TRANSFERS

We now shift gears and examine transfers designed primarily to assist charitable institutions.

Introduction

Transfers to charity, whether lifetime or testamentary, are supported by several provisions of the Internal Revenue Code, which normally allows generous deductions on a contributor's income tax, gift tax, and estate tax returns. While charitable transfers can be made during lifetime or at death, lifetime transfers will be the primary focus of this section, partly for consistency with the chapter theme, partly because lifetime charitable transfers often are more complex and need greater elaboration, and partly because they have a significant tax advantage over deathtime charitable transfers, as we shall see. Lifetime gifts to charity are of essentially two types, the outright gift and the split-interest gift, offering to clients considerable flexibility in the amount and type of interest in a given piece of property that can be donated.

Income tax consequences. The Code contains rather complex *limitations* on the amount of charitable contributions deductible from income by individuals in any given tax year. As shown next, there are limitations on both the total amount deductible and on the specific amount deductible for any particular gift.

Limitations on total amount deductible. In general, total deductible charitable contributions may not exceed 50 percent of a taxpayer's "contribution base," the name for an amount that is approximately equal to adjusted gross income. However, there are some major exceptions with regard to this 50 percent limitation. Taxpayers are limited to 30 percent of adjusted gross income for donations to public charities of "capital gain property" (20 percent to private foundations), and to 20 percent for contributions of cash to private foundations. Contributions in excess of these limits may be carried over, to be deducted during the next five years. This summary of the annual limitations has been merely a capsule overview; individuals wishing to make contributions of this relative size should consult with a competent tax adviser.

Amount deductible for a particular gift. The amount deductible from adjusted gross income for any particular charitable gift is usually its *fair market value,*[12] subject to the total annual limitation outlined above. However, there are several *exceptions for noncash gifts.* First, if sale of the property would have resulted in ordinary income or in short-term capital gain, then the individual is limited to deducting the *adjusted basis* of the property.[13] Second, if sale of any property except publicly traded stock would have resulted in a long-term capital gain, then one of two alternative tax consequences will occur.[14] If the property is given to a public charity which can *properly use it* in its activities, then the entire *fair market value* is deductible. If, on the other hand, the charity is a private foundation, or if it is a public charity which *cannot* properly use the donated property in its activities, then the amount deductible is limited to the donor's *basis.*

---

[12]Presently, a charitable donor of property exceeding $5,000 in value is required to obtain a "qualified appraisal" and supply additional information detailing the transaction.

[13]Called "ordinary income property."

[14]Called "capital gain property."

EXAMPLE 14–12 Charles, a real estate developer earning $400,000 in adjusted gross income this year, has four assets (each currently worth $100,000), one of which he is considering donating to a public charity. Besides *cash*, Charles has a parcel of *real estate* which his business purchased three years ago and which currently has an adjusted basis of $20,000. Charles also has two blocks of *common stock*, each of which cost $20,000. Stock A was purchased three years ago, and Stock B was acquired last month. The following describes the amount deductible if Charles contributes, alternatively, each asset to the charity which, for the moment we shall assume, can properly use any of the assets in its activities.

1. Cash: $100,000 deduction.
2. Business real estate: $20,000 deduction.[15]
3. Stock A: $100,000 deduction.[16]
4. Stock B: $20,000 deduction.

In many cases, contributing *capital gain property* to a public charity is more advantageous than contributing cash.

EXAMPLE 14–13 Edna, who is in the 33 percent income tax bracket, wishes to contribute $5,000 to her favorite public charity. Edna could give an original oil painting, acquired for $1,000 and now worth $5,000, or she could sell the painting and donate the cash proceeds. If Edna contributes the painting, her after-tax cost will be $3,350 which is the $5,000 value of the painting, less the $1,650 tax savings from the deduction. Alternatively, if Edna sells the painting, her after-tax cost will be $4,470, which is the $5,000 amount of the donated cash, plus the $1,120 tax on the gain, minus the $1,650 tax saving from the deduction.[17]

Gift tax consequences. Similar to the unlimited marital deduction there is an unlimited gift tax deduction for the present value of gifts to qualifying charities. However, unlike the marital deduction, the rules covering the charitable deduction require that a gift tax return must be filed if total gifts, including those to charity, exceed the amount of the annual exclusion.

---

[15]The charitable deduction is limited to the developer's basis because the property represents his business inventory.

[16]Stock A could have been the stock of Charles' real estate development corporation. The charity could be given the right to redeem the stock for cash.

[17]TRA 86 made the appreciation portion of the charitable deduction ($4,000 in this example) a tax preference item, subject to the *alternative minimum tax*. In

Estate tax consequences.   Similar to lifetime interspousal gifts, lifetime gifts to charity are not included in the donor's estate tax base. They are not includable in the gross estate because they are not owned by the decedent at death. And they are not an adjusted taxable gift because they were deducted in arriving at that amount.

Deathtime gifts to charity are totally deductible from the gross estate. Thus, a multimillionaire could give all (or all but $600,000) of his or her entire estate to charity and ensure total avoidance of the FET. Of course, he or she could also accomplish this goal by making a series of lifetime charitable transfers. In fact, lifetime charitable transfers are preferable to donations at death, as the next example illustrates.

> EXAMPLE 14–14 Sampson wishes to make a gift of $100,000 to his church which has been a source of continuous spiritual support to Sampson and his family for many years. Sampson's estate planner recommends a lifetime transfer, reasoning as follows. If Sampson donates the property at his death, his gross estate will be reduced by the amount of the gift, but he will enjoy no income tax shelter. Alternatively, if Sampson makes the gift during his lifetime (perhaps a death-bed gift), not only will his gross estate and estate tax base be lower by the date-of-death value of the gift property he no longer owned, but Sampson will also be able to deduct some or all of the value of the gift against his income.

Gifts of Split Interests

Despite the added income tax advantage of lifetime charitable gifts, clients with strong charitable motives are often reluctant to make outright gifts to charity because they are not willing to *relinquish total control* of an asset. For example, they may be relying on an asset as a source of income, or they may have been planning to pass the asset on to the children. Reluctant clients may be more willing, however, to make what could be called a compromise charitable gift; that is, a split-interest gift in which only part of an interest in property is given to charity. The client will often be able to accomplish *three objectives:* retain a much-desired portion of the interest, transfer the less-needed part, and still enjoy substantial income tax and death tax savings.

the example we'll avoid the result by assuming that Edna's total alternative minimum taxable income is less than the exempt amount.

A split interest arrangement divides the asset into two separate property interests, the income interest and the remainder interest. The client has the ability either to retain the right to the income from the asset, and presently gift the remainder interest to charity, or to gift the income interest to charity and designate a private party to take the remainder. Each type is described below.

Arrangements for donating remainder interests to charity. Three devices recognized by tax law are commonly used by clients to retain an income interest in an asset and to gift the remainder interest to charity.[19] Two of them, broadly called *charitable remainder trusts,* are the annuity trust and the unitrust. The third is called the *pooled income fund.* For each, the charity presently receives an irrevocable (vested) remainder interest in the asset.

Charitable remainder annuity trust. Under the charitable remainder annuity trust (CRAT), the client receives a fixed annuity income of at least 5 percent of the *original value* of the assets transferred into trust, payable at least annually, usually for life. The value of the deductible interest is calculated from tax tables essentially similar to Table 9 and 10 in Appendix A.

> EXAMPLE 14–15 Carrie, age 74, creates a CRAT, funding the trust with $100,000 cash. The trust provides for a 5 percent annual payment to Carrie for her life. The value of Carrie's retained income interest, derived from Table 9 of Appendix A, is $26,931, the product of the table value (5.3862) and $5,000, the annual trust income. Therefore, Carrie's deductible remainder interest is $73,069, the difference between the total value of the property and the value of the retained income interest.

Charitable remainder unitrust. The charitable remainder unitrust (CRUT) is much like the CRAT, above, except that the annual income depends on a fixed percentage of the current *fair market value* of the assets in the trust, determined annually. Thus, the amount of the annual income paid to the client will vary (hopefully upward) from year to year.[20] Calculation of the amount of the deductible remainder interest is complex and will not be shown here.

---

[18]This area of tax law is extremely complicated and mistakes in drafting can result in total denial of the deduction. For a discussion of methods of salvaging the deduction by reforming defective documents, see the Baltz article cited at the end of the chapter.

[19]The CRUT can provide for the income to be the lesser of the unitrust amount or the amount actually earned on the trust property, with any deficiencies payable

Pooled income fund. Instead of a separate trust created by the client, a pooled income fund is an investment fund created and maintained by the *target charity,* which "pools" property from many similar contributors. This arrangement ordinarily provides that the charity will pay to the grantor an income for life and, if desired, for the life of the grantor's spouse, based on the rate of return actually earned by the fund as a whole. At their death, the property passes to the charity. Valuation of the charitable deduction is calculated using Treasury tables available from the IRS.

Comparison of the three techniques. The CRAT may appeal to clients who desire the certainty of a fixed income, while the CRUT may be preferred by those willing to risk fluctuating income for the opportunity to realize higher income payments. However, assets in a CRUT require an annual valuation, a possible extra trust cost. The pooled income fund may be preferred by those who would like to avoid having to establish and maintain a trust. Pooled income funds, however, are not permitted to invest in tax-exempt securities. Not all qualifying charities have created pooled income funds. Most educational institutions, however, use them to encourage charitable contributions by well-heeled alumni.

Arrangement for donating income interests to charity: The charitable lead trust. Instead of contributing a remainder interest, the client can donate an asset's income interest to charity, with the remainder interest passing to a private party after a specified length of time. The estate or its beneficiaries will receive an income tax deduction for the value of the income interest, based on Treasury valuation tables. However, the trust must be set up as a grantor trust, making the income taxable to grantor, the estate or its beneficiaries. Thus, the charitable lead trust is usually designed to take effect after the client's death.

Charitable lead trusts have become less attractive tax shelters since the revision of the Treasury valuation tables which, based on a higher discount rate, now contain less attractive valuation percentages.

This chapter has focused on viable nongift lifetime intrafamily transfers and on charitable gifts. Appendix 14A examines defective

---

in later years when earnings are higher. Thus, the owner of a rapidly appreciating, low-dividend-paying corporation can contribute stock to a CRUT and enjoy a large stream of income years later, after retirement, when the stock starts paying dividends.

incomplete transfers. The next chapter will survey the principles of liquidity planning.

RECOMMENDED READING

AUSTER, ROLF. "Estate Planning Strategies after 1986." *Taxes—the Tax Magazine,* February 1987, pp. 116–23.

BAETZ, TIMOTHY W. "Making Something Out of Nothing or How to Achieve Charitable Deduction by Repairing Defective Split Interest Trusts." *University of Miami 21st Annual Estate Planning Institute, 1987.*

BAILEY, LESTER D. "Tax Results of Many Transfers of Property Will Change When Made between Husband and Wife." *Taxation for Accountants,* July 1984, pp. 38–40.

BANOFF, SHELDON I., and MICHAEL O. HARTZ. "It's No Sin to SCIN! A Reply to Professor Blum on Self-Cancelling Installment Notes." *Taxes—The Tax Magazine,* March 1982, pp. 187–96.

————"Self-Cancelling Installment Notes: New IRS Rulings Expand Opportunities." *Journal of Taxation,* September 1986, pp. 146–54.

BILANSKY, LAWRENCE J. "Making the Most of Private Annuity Arrangements to Transfer Property and Reduce Estate Tax." *Estate Planning,* March 1981, pp. 102–7.

BLATTMACHR, DOUGLAS J., and JONATHAN G. BLATTMACHR. "Estate Planning for Individuals with Short Life Expectancies." *Trusts & Estates,* August 1985, pp. 22–28.

BLATTMACHR, JONATHAN G. and VIVIAN L. CAVALIERI. "To Apply or Not to Apply the Treasury Department Valuation Tables—That Is the Question." *New York University 45th Annual Institute on Federal Taxation, 1986.*

BLUM, WALTER J. "Self-Cancelling Installment Notes—The New SCIN Game." *Taxes—The Tax Magazine,* March 1982, pp. 183–96.

CAMPISI, DOMINIC J. "Estate of Buck: Frustration of a Charitable Purpose." *Trusts & Estates,* January 1985, pp. 70–76.

COMSTOCK, PAUL L. "Planned Giving Issues and Techniques under Tax Reform." CLU Journal, January 1988, pp. 60–65.

CORNFELD, DAVE L. "The Latest in Capital Freezes: Installment Sales, Private Annuities,and Transfers Involving Life Estates and Remainders." *Probate Notes* 9 (1983), pp. 20–47.

GELBER, LAWRENCE R. "Annuities: An Overview for the Estate Planner." *New York Law School Law Review* 26 (1981), pp. 1059–87.

GLEITMAN, STEVEN L. "Using Insurance Trusts to Increase Unified Credit, Avoid Kiddie Tax, and Fund Education." *Taxation for Accountants,* July 1987, pp. 37–7.

GOGGANS, TRAVIS P., and JOHN TENBRUNSEL. "Trustee Independence in Trust-Leaseback Arrangements." *Trust & Estates,* December 1984, pp. 29–32.

HARRISON, MELINDA J., and EDWARD D. TARLOW. "How to Use Trusts and Estates to Maximize Deductions for Charitable Contributions." *Estate Planning*, March 1986, pp. 66–73.

HARTZ, MICHAEL O., and SHELDON I. BANOFF. "Planning Opportunities Available Using a Private Annuity for a Term of Years." *Journal of Taxation*, November 1986, pp. 302–12.

HASS, FREDERICK W., and JOSEPH C. SKALCKI. "The Charitable Lead Trust: New Appeal as an Executive Perk." *Trusts & Estates*, September 1986, pp. 44–45.

HERBERT, MARCEL G., and MARY SUE GATELY. "Gift-Leaseback Still Effective Income and Estate Tax Saver Despite IRS Opposition." *Taxation for Accountants*, April 1985, pp. 240–44.

JOHANSON, STANLEY M. "'Now You See It, Now You Don't'—Intra-Family Transfers, Sales of Remainder Interests, Split-Interest Purchases, Grantor Trusts, and Other Value-Shifting Arrangements." *Fifth Annual Southern California Tax and Estate Planning Forum*, 1985.

LEIMBERG, STEPHEN R., and JEFF A. SCHNEPPER. "SPLIT Interest Purchase of Property." *CLU Journal*, November 1987, pp. 44–55.

LERNER, RALPH E. "How to Coordinate Income and Estate Tax Savings of Donating a Collection to Charity." *Estate Planning*, May 1984, pp. 144–48.

LICHTER, JONATHAN M. "The Effects of the Proposed Regulations on Charitable Remainder Trusts." *Trusts & Estates*, June 1984, pp. 41–50.

LOFTIS, ROBERT O., JR. "When Can a Trust Be Used to Fund a Private Annuity without Creating a Retained Interest?" *Estate Planning*, July 1987, pp. 218–27.

McCOY, JERRY J. "Private Foundations and Related Entities in the Post Tax Reform Era." *University of Miami 21st Annual Estate Planning Institute*, 1987.

MELFE, THOMAS A. "When to Make Outright Gifts of Partial, Undivided Interests in Property." *Estate Planning*, July 1986, pp. 330–33.

MONZO, ANTHONY P., and ROBERT N. POLANS. "Interest-Free Loans and Other Planning Tools Can Still be Used to Shift Income." *Taxation for Accountants*, August 1987, pp. 82–8.

"More on Intra-Family Sales of Remainder Interests to Freeze Asset Values." *Estate Planning*, May 1981, pp. 164–67.

MOSES, JAMES O. "Intra-Family Sales of Remainder Interests Can Freeze Asset Values and Reduce Estate Taxes." *Estate Planning*, January 1981, pp.22–28.

OSHINS, RICHARD A. "GRITS and Splits: Turning The Tables in the IRS and Insuring the Victory." *CLU Journal*, November 1987, pp. 84–93.

————. "Grits, Splits and Tidbits." *Trusts & Estates*, March 1987, pp.28–51.

PORCANO, THOMAS M. "Private Annuities and Estate Planning." *The Tax Adviser*, February 1983, pp. 72–82.

ROLFE, ROBERT J. "Trust-Annuity Plans Can Offer Substantial Income and Estate Tax Savings." *Taxes—The Tax Magazine*, July 1984, pp. 482–88.

SCHLESINGER, MICHAEL, and R. ARNOLD HANDLER. "Recent Developments May

Expand the Use of Private Annuities, but Problems Still Exist." *Estate Planning,* March 1986, pp. 106–10.

SCHNEE, EDWARD J. "Partial Gifts to Charity: Estates Claim Larger Deductions." *Taxes—The Tax Magazine,* March 1983, pp. 219–24.

SHUBERT, ROY A., and LINDA J. REPH. "How to Reduce the Tax Cost When an Individual Wants to Benefit Charity. *Taxation For Accountants,* September 1986, pp. 150–53.

STRIZEVER, WILLIAM J. "Self-Cancelling Notes Increase Planning and.Risks of a Sale over Private Annuities." *Taxation for Accountants,* January 1984, pp. 20–25.

TIDD, JONATHAN G. "Using a Charitable Income Trust Provides More Flexibility than Lead Annuity or Unitrusts." *Estate Planning,* July 1986, pp. 214–18.

TREBBY, JAMES P. "Current Approaches to Shifting Value through Sales and Purchases of Remainder Interests." *Estate Planning,* November 1986, pp. 362–5.

VERES, JOSEPH A. "Using Pooled Income Funds to Pass ITC and Depreciation through to Life-Income Donors." *Journal of Taxation,* July 1984, pp. 28–33.

WEINBAUM, PETER M. "Are Sales of Remainder Interests Still Available in Light of a New Decision?" *Estate Planning,* September 1987, pp. 258–63.

WEINSTOCK, HAROLD. "Beyond Freezes—Planning to Reduce the Taxable Estate." *1982 Institute on Estate Planning,* Chap. 5, pp. 1–29.

QUESTIONS AND PROBLEMS

1. Why are many planning-minded clients disinclined to make gifts?

2. How can a bargain sale add flexibility to gift planning?

3. (*a*) Describe the installment sale. (*b*) What tax advantage does it have over the ordinary sale?

4. Summarize the major advantages and disadvantages of the private annuity.

5. Crucible, a wealthy 60-year-old, asks you for advice on lifetime transfers. His daughter is interested in acquiring his antique car, which is worth $40,000 and has a basis of $10,000. In each of the following alternatives, calculate Crucible's taxable gain for each future year.
   a. Ordinary sale.
   b. Installment sale, over 10 years (no down payment), with equal annual payments on principal, plus interest at a rate of 10 percent on the outstanding balance.
   c. Private annuity. Additional information: 7.6953 percent of the payment is excluded from Crucible's taxable income for life (return on principal invested, based on annuity table in Treasury regulations 1.72-9). During the first 24 years, 4.1322 percent of the gross profit will be taxed as capital gain (thereafter, it is taxed as ordinary income). The balance of the annuity will be taxable as ordinary income.

6. The Platos are a husband and wife in their 70s, with an adult daughter age 45. They wish to make a lifetime transfer of a considerable amount of wealth to her, and you recommend five alternatives for consideration:
   Large outright gift.
   Installment sale.
   Private annuity.
   Sale of a remainder interest.
   Joint purchase of a life estate/remainder interest.
   a. Which transfer probably would involve the greatest present value of total costs to daughter? Why?
   b. Which one will probably save the most FET? Why?

     c. Which is probably the safest, in terms of IRS challenge? Why?

     d. In which have the Platos retained the greatest interest? Why?

     e. Name several other factors that will influence which transfer, if any, the Platos will ultimately select.

7. Why is the sale of a remainder interest or joint purchase agreement often considered an attractive alternative to the ordinary sale, bargain sale, installment sale, and private annuity?

8. Chico Butte is 60 years old, and wishes to sell the remainder interest in his house. This house is currently appraised at $100,000. Discuss all transfer tax consequences if Butte sells this interest for

     a. $10,000.

     b. $25,000.

     c. $26,000.

9. Under what circumstances will a gift-leaseback work well?

10. Discuss the income-shifting and FET-reducing ability of the grantor retained income trust.

11. In this question, you will compare the advantages of the lifetime transfers you have studied in the last two chapters. In each box on the next page, place the code number which you think describes how well that transfer accomplishes that goal. Code: 3 = excellent; 2 = good; 1 = fair; 0 = poor. (See Table 14–1.)

12. Explain the reason for the advantage of each of the following *charitable* transfers.

     a. Gift of appreciated property rather than cash derived from sale of the property.

     b. Lifetime gift rather than gift at death.

     c. Gift of a split interest rather than a whole interest.

13. Stover is 70 years old and is currently in the 28 percent marginal income tax bracket. He wishes to gift to charity his block of ABC Corp. stock, currently worth $20,000. His adjusted basis in the stock is $2,000.

     a. Calculate Stover's "after (income) tax cost" if he be-

TABLE 14–1 Comparative Advantages of Lifetime Transfers

Types of Transfers	Goals									
	Ability to Retain:		Ability to Avoid Taxation:				Taxable Estate:			Absence of IRS Scrutiny and Tax Risk
	Control	Income	Income Tax	Gift Tax	Step-Up in Basis	Shift Income	Reduce	Freeze	Avoid Probate	
Annual exclusion gift										
Large outright gift										
Ordinary sale										
Bargain sale										
Installment sale										
Private annuity										
Joint purchase										
Grantor retained income trust										
Gift-leaseback										

queaths the stock to the charity and dies shortly thereafter.

b. Perform the same calculation as in part *a*, above, assuming that Stover sells the stock and gives the cash to charity during his lifetime.

c. Calculate Stover's after-tax cost, assuming instead that Stover makes a lifetime gift of the stock to charity.

d. Would it matter at all in *a, b,* or *c,* above if Stover is president and controlling owner of ABC? Why or why not?

14. Compare the advantages of the CRAT, the CRUT, and the pooled income fund.

Defective Incomplete Transfers

OVERVIEW

This appendix will describe four defective transfer devices that, for one of two reasons, are presently not recommended by planners. The first three were virtually legislated out of existence by Congress in the mid-1980s. And the fourth has always been riddled with tax defects, making it inherently defective.

The evolution of income tax law in the last few years has resulted in depriving taxpayers of the major tax benefits earlier available through the use of the *interest-free loan,* the *short-term trust,* and the *spousal remainder trust.* The interest-free loan was first to go with the passage of TRA 84. The other two were killed by TRA 86. They were all vulnerable to attack because, unlike the transfers covered in Chapter 13 and 14, they shifted income and yet still enabled the transferor to retain substantial interest or control over the transferred assets. The *family estate trust* has never worked, since its operation clearly violates major holdings of case law and provisions of the Internal Revenue Code.

This appendix has been written for three reasons. First, it will give the reader a better historical perspective on lifetime transfers. Second, these strategies may have been employed by some clients in the past, and may still be in use. The reader should be aware of their operation since questions will be raised about their efficacy. Finally, the planner can expect even uninvolved clients to be curious about these formerly popular devices, for years to come.

INTEREST-FREE LOAN

Until 1984, the interest-free loan was considered to be an attractive, although somewhat tax-risky, device to shift income to a lower-tax-bracket family member. However, the Tax Reform Act of 1984 all but destroyed its appeal. The following material presents and overview of the major tax and nontax considerations in making IFLs and describes the few areas in which IFLs still might be put to use.

An arm's-length loan, in which the lender charges a fair market rate of interest, does not achieve many estate planning objectives. It does not shift income significantly, although it may provide for the borrower an otherwise unavailable loan opportunity. An interest-free loan (IFL) of cash, on the other hand, may be able to shift taxable income from the lender to the borrower. Since the borrower is free to use the loaned property to generate income without incurring a financing charge, the loan may put the borrower in a higher standard of living. Further, the income generated may be taxed at a significantly lower rate. Unfortunately, other tax consequences often render IFLs largely unattractive.[1] As the following material suggests, tax controversy has highlighted their brief history.

Gift Tax Consequences

In 1984, the U.S. Supreme Court settled a longstanding conflict between taxpayers and the IRS by ruling that an IFL constitutes a taxable gift of the reasonable value of the use of the money loaned.[2] In calculating the taxable gift value, the taxpayer is required to use a federal rate of interest, which is published and revised semiannually by the IRS and set approximately equal to the rate that had been paid by the U.S. Treasury on securities of similar maturity several months earlier.

---

[1] Actually, any loan made at a rate of interest below an acceptable market rate will be subject to taxation. However, we will continue to use the term *IFL* to refer to all below-market loans.

[2] *Dickman v. Commissioner,* 104 S. ct. 1086.

IFLs can be made for a fixed term, or they can have a demand provision. If the loan is made for a *fixed term,* the gift is considered as having been made as of the loan inception, with the gift amount equal to the difference between the amount loaned and the discounted present value of the note.

> EXAMPLE 14A–1 Dad and Mom lend $100,000 cash, interest-free, to Mary who has just graduated dental school and wishes to start a practice. Mary signs a 10-year note, with no principal payable until maturity. Assuming that the current federal long-term rate is 10 percent, the present discounted value of the note is approximately $38,500, and Mom and Dad are deemed to have made a gift of approximately $61,500, the difference between the amount transferred and the value received.

If, on the other hand, an interest-free loan incorporates a nonmaturing *demand loan,* with the loan callable by the lender at any time, then at the end of each year the lender will have made a gift of one year's imputed interest.

> EXAMPLE 14A–2 Assume the facts in Example 14A-1, except that the note is a demand loan, having no maturity. If the loan is still outstanding at the end of their first taxable year, Mom and Dad will have made a gift of one year's interest, imputed to be $10,000, calculated on the basis of the assumed 10 percent short-term federal rate. For every year that the loan remains outstanding, a similar gift computation will have to be made.

Thus, in order to minimize the gift tax, an IFL must have no maturity. And, to prevent the entire transfer from being treated as an outright gift, the nonmaturing loan must have a demand provision.

If an interest-free demand loan becomes unenforceable, a more significant taxable event will have occurred.

> EXAMPLE 14A–3 Assume the facts in Example 14A-2. Four years go by, and the state's statute of limitations on collection on the original note expires. In that year, a taxable gift of the entire loan principal is triggered.

Thus, IFLs must be redrafted periodically to prevent this unfortunate tax consequence.

Despite the court decision subjecting interest-free loans to gift taxation, many client-lenders will not owe any gift tax because of the combined shelter of the annual exclusion and the unified credit. Thus, the parents in the above examples will incur no gift tax liability.[3] In general, the gift tax issue should not discourage many from the use of interest-free loans as a method of shifting income to a lower tax bracket. However, the income tax issues, discussed next, usually will.

Income Tax Consequences

The IRS has argued, in a business context, that the interest forgone by a corporate lender constitutes taxable income to an employee-executive borrower. To date, the IRS has had little success in the courts,and unless it can influence Congress to act, imputed interest income on an interest-free loan will not likely be taxed to the *borrower.*

In 1984, Congress did act, however, to tax to the *lender* the amount of the interest forgone under an IFL.[4] This forgone interest is treated as if it had been received by the lender and paid by the borrower. Thus, the lender is deemed to have received taxable interest, which is includable in gross income. Similarly, the borrower is deemed to have paid interest, which, under TRA 86, ordinarily would not be tax deductible, unless it is considered business interest, investment interest which is offset by investment income, or interest on a debt secured by a primary or secondary residence. The upshot will usually be greater taxable income without the corresponding deduction. And the compression of tax rates under TRA 86 further reduced the income shifting attractiveness of the IFL.

> EXAMPLE 7872–1 Dad, in the 33 percent income tax bracket, makes a $20,000 interest-free demand loan to his son, who is in the 15 percent bracket and is able to invest the proceeds in a bank time deposit yielding an annual return of 8 percent. Assuming a federal rate

---

[3]Unless they have already made taxable gifts large enough to have fully used up their unified credits.

[4]Code Section 7872.

of 10 percent, the tax consequences in the first full year are as follows:

Gift tax treatment: At the end of each year, Dad will be deemed to have made a gross gift of $2,000, the amount of the calculated forgone interest. Because of the annual exclusion, there will be no taxable gift.

Income tax treatment in the absence of the 1984 Act: Each year, son would earn $1,600 taxable income on the deposit, paying a tax of $240. Instead, had Dad invested the loan money, he would have paid a tax of $528. Thus, in the absence of the 1984 act, under TRA 86 tax rates the family would have saved $288 in income tax.

Income tax treatment under the 1984 Act: Son will still pay a tax of $240. In addition, Dad will pay a tax of $660 on the $2,000 of imputed interest. The total tax paid by both will be $900, which is $272 *more* than Dad's tax on the bank income had the IFL not been made.

The 1984 Act incorporated four exceptions, which may provide the basis for a very modest degree of income shifting. First, where the proceeds of an IFL between individuals are invested by the borrower to yield less than $1,000 income in any given year, forgone interest will not be imputed. Thus, at an assumed 8 percent investment return, the client could lend $12,500 interest free, without being subject to income taxation.

The second exception to the 1984 Act applies to a loan balance of $10,000 or less to any individual, which is not subject to imputed interest unless it is used to purchase income-producing assets.

Third, the amount of the imputed interest is limited to the borrower's net investment income for the year in cases where the aggregate amount of outstanding loans between two individuals does not exceed $100,000, provided that one of the principal purposes of the loan is not federal tax avoidance.

The fourth exception to the 1984 Act applies to loans to employees and to corporate shareholders, who are permitted to owe up to $10,000 without imputing forgone interest, provided that one of the principal purposes of the loan is not federal tax avoidance.

Interest-free demand loans should be made in the form of cash, rather than other property. A transfer of noncash in exchange for a note might be treated as a taxable *sale* to the extent of the consideration received.

Estate Tax Consequences

At the lender's death, the gross estate will include the current value of the note. The market value of a *demand note* will equal the face amount of the note, since the decedent, just prior to death, could have demanded full repayment.[5] On the other hand, the market value of a *term note* will usually be different from the face amount and is calculated, as in Example 14A-1, by using a market rate of interest to discount the value of the future payments. In executing either kind of note, the lender has not really been able to reduce his or her gross estate significantly. The interest-free loan was never designed to reduce death taxes.

In conclusion, because of its serious tax consequences and the compression of income tax rates, the IFL will no longer be used much.

SHORT-TERM TRUST

Prior to March 2, 1986, the short-term trust was a very popular device to shift income to a lower-bracket taxpayer. Also called the Clifford trust, after the taxpayer whose court case originally set the standards for satisfactory construction, it is arranged in the following manner.[6] The transferor creates and funds a living trust, irrevocable for at least 10 years, for the benefit of a lower-bracket beneficiary, who will receive all of the income earned on the trust property during that time.[7] At the end of 10 years, the principal reverts to the transferor and the trust terminates.

---

[5] If the executor is not a family member, he or she (or it, in the case of a bank) may choose to call the note due and payable after the death of the lender in order to properly manage the estate. Borrowers should be made aware of this possibility.

[6] Clifford lost the case, however. Subsequent to the Clifford decision, Congress added the 10-year requirement to the Code, under Section 673, et. seq.

[7] In this discussion, we'll assume 10 years.

Gift Tax Consequences

The transferor in a short-term trust is irrevocably parting with a 10-year income interest in the property, and the actuarial value of this income interest is taxable as a gift. Its calculation is derived by multiplying the total value of the property by a fraction representing the proportion of the total value of the property constituting that income interest. The fraction is obtained from U.S. Treasury Gift Tax Table B, found in Treasury Regulations 25.2512-5, which is similar to Table 10 of Appendix A. For a 10-year income interest, the fraction equals 0.614457. Thus, approximately 62 percent of the transfer represents the income interest, and about 38 percent represents the remainder interest. Since the remainder portion will revert to the trustor, it does not constitute a gift, for tax purposes.

> EXAMPLE 14A–4 Dr. Jones and his wife set up a short-term trust for the benefit of their daughter, who is 11 years old, to defray her future college expenses. They fund the trust with high-income stock, worth $32,000. The trust provides that all income will be accumulated until daughter reaches her 18th birthday. Then daughter will receive approximately equal amounts each year for the next four years, with all remaining accumulated income payable to her on her 21st birthday. At that time all principal will revert to the parents. Upon creation of the trust, the Joneses have made a gift of an income interest worth $19,662.62, which is $32,000, the total value of the stock, multiplied by 0.614457. However, no gift tax is owed, due to the annual exclusion of $20,000 available to spouses making a split gift.

The annual exclusion is available to the parents, above, despite the fact that technically the gift of the income to be accumulated is a future interest, because the short-term trust is structured to meet an exception under Section 2503(b) or 2503(c), mentioned in the discussion of trusts for minors in Chapter 13.

Income Tax Consequences

Grandfathered trusts. Income earned on the property placed in a 10-year short-term trust on or before March 1, 1986, will not be taxable to the transferor-grantor, except when the kiddie tax applies. Instead, the income will be taxed to the trust or to the beneficiary, depending on whether it is accumulated or distributed. And the accumulated income later distributed to the beneficiary could be subject to some additional tax, under the throwback rules, unless the beneficiary is under age 21.

The reader will recall from Chapter 8 that failure to avoid the grantor trust provisions of the Internal Revenue Code will cause income received by the trust to be taxable to the grantor. Thus, the short-term trust had to be carefully drafted to avoid running afoul of the grantor trust rules. For example, the trust had to be irrevocable for at least 10 years from the date the trust was *funded* with the property, not from the date the document was executed. For the other major grantor trust rules, refer to Chapter 8.

Non-grandfathered trusts.   TRA 86 destroyed the income tax benefit of the short-term trust by deleting the 10-year exception under Internal Revenue Code (IRC) Section 673. Thus, for any transfers into trust after March 1, 1986, the grantor will be treated as the owner of any portion of a trust in which the grantor has any *reversionary interest which exceeds 5 percent* of the value of such portion. Based on the present values in Table 10 of Appendix A, the grantor of a 10-year short-term trust has a reversionary interest that is about 38.55 percent of the value of the trust. Thus, the typical new short-term trust will be treated as a grantor trust. Nonetheless, the new kiddie tax will apply even to these grandfathered trusts, subjecting most or all trust income for the benefit of a child under age 14 to taxation at the parent's marginal rate.

How long must a short-term trust created after March 1, 1986, last so that the present value of the remainder interest does not exceed 5 percent of the corpus? Table 10 indicates that the reversion can't occur for at least 32 years! Although several commentators are suggesting that there may be situations where this period is acceptable, in most cases, grantors will not wish to make an irrevocable transfer of property for such a long time. Most clients will no longer wish to shift income with the short-term trust. Thus, the short-term trust is no longer able to save significant income tax by shifting income.

Estate Tax Consequences to the Grantor

Several estate tax consequences may occur when the grantor dies. First, if creation of the trust resulted in a "taxable gift," that is, the transfer of an amount in excess of the annual exclusion and other deductions, then that taxable value will be added to the estate tax base, as an "adjusted taxable gift." Of course, a credit will be applied for any gift tax paid, but the taxation of adjusted taxable gifts along with the rest of a decedent's estate may subject the gift to a higher marginal rate of taxation than that incurred when the gift tax was calculated.

A second estate tax consequence at the grantor's death will be the addition to the gross estate of the actuarial value of the decedent-grantor's interest in the trust property. Determination of that amount will depend on when the decedent dies, as explained next.

If the grantor of a short-term trust dies *before the trust reverts,* the value of the gross estate will include the value of the grantor's reversionary interest at death. Derived from the U.S. Treasury estate tax valuation table found in Treasury Regulations 20.2031-7, included in Table 10 of Appendix A, the value depends on the assumed rate of interest and the number of years remaining to reversion. For example, assuming a 10 percent discount rate, if a grantor dies exactly four years prior to reversion, the gross estate will include 68.3013 percent of the decedent's share of the trust property.

If the grantor of a short-term dies *at or after reversion,* the value of the gross estate will include the deathtime market value of the property that had reverted, if still owned, or the value of any other assets acquired with the property.

From the above we can see that the value of the grantor's taxable estate may exceed the value of the trust principal, a decided estate tax disadvantage to the short-term trust. This will always happen when the grantor outlives the trust and the funding of the trust has created a taxable gift. It should be clear now why, the short-term trust was never designed to reduce death taxes.

As an income tax planning device, the short-term trust was often used for two common types of beneficiaries: children and elderly parents. Both are individuals whom many clients wish to assist, and who are often in a lower income tax bracket. Unfortunately, due to tax reform, the short-term trust will hardly ever be used in the future.

SPOUSAL REMAINDER TRUST

A popular income-shifting device prior to TRA 86 was the spousal remainder trust (SRT). As in the case of the short-term trust, the grantor, typically a high-income-tax-bracket parent, transferred income-earning property to an irrevocable trust, which for a specified period paid all income to a low-income-tax-bracket family member, typically a young adult child, and remainder to the grantor's spouse. Properly arranged, the value of the income interest, which is valued in a manner similar to the short-term trust, would qualify for the annual gift tax exclusion. However, unlike the short-term trust, whose property reverted to the grantor, the SRT corpus then passed to the grantor's spouse. Although the value of the remainder interest will not qualify for the annual exclusion, it will not be subject to gift tax, due to the unlimited gift tax marital deduction.

> EXAMPLE 14A–6 In 1985 Dad created an SRT, funding it with $30,000 in bonds. Income is required to be paid semiannually to daughter, a college freshman, for the next four years. At the end of the fourth year, the corpus will pass outright to Mom. Based on the valuation tables, the value of a gift of an income interest for a four-year term certain represents 31.6987 percent of the total value of the property transferred. Thus, Dad has made a gross gift to daughter of $9,510. There will be no taxable gift, since the gift of the income interest is sheltered entirely by the annual exclusion, and the gift of the remainder interest is sheltered entirely by the marital deduction.

Prior to TRA 86, the SRT had several advantages over the short-term trust. First, because the corpus does not revert to the grantor, the trust was not required, under the grantor trust rules, to remain in existence for at least 10 years. Thus, the trust could terminate at any time, and if it terminated sooner than 10 years, the relative value of the transferred income interest would be less than that for the short-term trust. This meant that a greater amount of property could be transferred to the SRT free of gift tax. Further, earlier termination might have encouraged grantors to make successive annual gift tax-free transfers into the trust, unimpeded by the requirement of waiting 10 years after date of the most recent transfer to terminate the trust.

The SRT often facilitated the client's estate tax planning objectives.It helped to equalize the spouses' estates in order to minimize the combined estate tax, and remainder interests were transferred to the less wealthy spouse by means of the SRT.

Compared with the short-term trust, the SRT had one potentially major disadvantage: At the termination of the trust, the property passes to the grantor's spouse, rather than the grantor. Thus, the SRT worked best in a harmonious family setting. And any SRT having an agreement in which the remainderman spouse agreed to immediately retransfer the remainder interest to the grantor was attacked by the IRS, which claimed that the grantor in fact retained a reversion, thereby destroying all income and transfer-tax benefits.

TRA 86 destroyed the usefulness of the spousal remainder trust by amending Section 672 to treat any power or interest held by a spouse (who lives with the grantor) as if that interest were held by the grantor. Thus, the traditional spousal remainder trust funded after March 1, 1986, will be treated as if it will revert to the grantor, making it a *grantor trust,* and thereby preventing the shifting of income to the lower-bracket-income beneficiary. Few clients will now choose this once appealing transfer strategy.

THE FAMILY ESTATE TRUST: A TRAP FOR THE UNWARY

The reader should be cautioned against recommending one so-called estate planning device, the family estate trust. Also called a constitutional trust, an equity trust, and an ABC trust, the family estate trust is an arrangement fraught with tax danger. Many variations have been created, but they all have the following characteristics:

1. The same person acts in four different capacities: grantor, trustee, trust employee, and beneficiary.
2. The grantor transfers assets into the trust in exchange for "certificate units." The trustee leases the employees' services to others (typically including the individual's current employer), who pay a salary directly to the trustee.
3. The certificate units entitle the grantor to share in the income "earned" by the trust.
4. Upon the grantor's death, the trust assets pass to others, not to the grantor's estate.

The family estate trust has been touted as a great tax saver. It is said to be able to reduce income tax by shifting income to a lower bracket (the trust and other family members), and to reduce the client's death taxes by shifting assets before death to other beneficiaries. In fact, just the opposite is true. The IRS has been aggressively and successfully challenging family estate trusts in the courts, which have regularly upheld the following tax consequences:

1. Under the *assignment-of-income doctrine,* explained in Chapter 9, wages assigned to the trust are still taxable to the client-wage earner, not to the trust.
2. Personal living expenses are not deductible.
3. Fees to set up the trust are not deductible.
4. The deathtime value of the property owned by the trust is subject to inclusion in the *gross estate* of the client-trustor as an incomplete transfer.
5. At least two tax *penalties* will be imposed. First, if negligence is proven against the taxpayer, a negligence penalty of 5 percent of the additional tax due will be assessed. Second, tax preparers will be charged penalties of hundreds of dollars for each return found to exhibit negligent or willful attempts to understate the tax liability.

In view of the tax exposure, clients would do well to steer clear of the family estate trust.

APPENDIX 14A   RECOMMENDED READING

ADAMS, ROY M. "Estate Planner's Guide to the Time Value of Money: Neither Borrower nor Lender Be." *Trusts & Estates,* June 1986, pp. 46–59.

BALK, MARK D. "Interest-Free No Longer." *Trusts & Estates,* September 1984, pp. 39–42.

KLINE, TERRANCE A. "Clifford Trusts and the Parental Duty to Provide a College Education: *Braun* v. *Commissioner.*" *University of Pittsburgh Law Review* 46 (1985), pp. 537–54.

McCUE, HOWARD M. and PATRICIA BROSTERHOUS. "Interest-Free and Below-Market Loans after Dickman and the Tax Reform Act of 1984." *Taxes—The Tax Magazine,* December 1984, pp. 1010-21.

ORBACH, KENNETH N.; FIREMAN, HARVEY B.; and HOWARD A. LEVINSON. "Planning for Tax Advantages under Proposed Below-Market Loan Regs." *Journal of Taxation,* March 1986, pp. 144–50.

PLUTCHOCK, JONATHAN. "Long Live Clifford!" *Financial Planning,* September 1987, pp. 130–34.

WEINDRUCH, LINDA, and KIM SMITH. "Interest-Free Loans after the Deficit Reduction Act of 1984." *The Tax Adviser,* November 1984, pp. 642–52.

15

Liquidity Planning

OVERVIEW

This chapter will explore the role of liquidity in estate planning. It will summarize the liquidity needs at death, examine the sources of liquidity available to the estate before and after death, and describe the planning techniques commonly undertaken with these sources. Planning devices covered include sale of assets during lifetime, life insurance, flower bonds, and several strategies unique to business owners, including sale of the business and three techniques arising from specific provisions of the Internal Revenue Code.

SUMMARY OF CASH NEEDS

Death will usually trigger the need for liquidity. Cash may be needed to pay a variety of obligations. There may be *taxes,* including federal and state income and transfer taxes. There may be expenses of administration, payable to lawyers, executors, accountants, appraisers, and trustees. There may be *debts and claims* against the decedent, including last illness and funeral expenses. There may be immediate cash *needs* for the maintenance and welfare of the *surviving family.* There may be the need for funds to continue *running the family business.* And finally, there may be *cash bequests* and other transfers to the decedent's heirs and beneficiaries.

Cash needs can be influenced by estate size and family situation. In general, cash needs rise with increasing estate size. For larger family estates, the FET usually constitutes the greatest cash need at the death of the surviving spouse. Most wealthier clients will probably choose an estate plan incorporating either a 100 percent marital deduction or a credit shelter bypass, both of which will result in a zero FET for S1. This delay in cash needs can influence the choice of the liquidity source, as we shall see.

In contrast to clients with larger estates, young families with smaller estates will often have *relatively* large cash needs at the death of *either* spouse. (For a discussion of the cash needs of the two career family with minor children, see the Kinskern article cited at the end of the chapter.) Although transfer taxes may not be due, there will be the need to replace the economic value of the income or services that had been provided by the deceased spouse in the role of parent or breadwinner. As the children get older, the total amount of this cash need will decline.

Next, we turn our attention to the sources of estate liquidity.

SALE OF ASSETS DURING LIFETIME

We will begin our discussion of the sources of estate liquidity with one of the simplest liquidity-generating devices. During lifetime, the client might be able to sell particularly illiquid assets. High-basis assets are preferable, because they result in little or no taxable gain. In fact, assets that have a built-in loss make the best assets for sale, because the client can use the loss before death to offset other gains or to reduce taxable income. Death eliminates this potential tax benefit by *stepping down* the basis to date-of-death value.

Low-basis assets, on the other hand, do not make the most desirable assets for sale because of the tax on the gain (a prospect which can be largely eliminated if the client dies owning the assets). However, the client might be able to offset the gain with losses, whether incurred during the present taxable year or carried over from previous years. Or the sale may be practical in situations where other factors justify paying a tax whose maximum marginal rate on long-term capital gains is 28 percent. For example, an interest in a closely held business will often command a substantially higher price if it is sold prior to the owner's death.

Thus, sale of assets during the client's lifetime can provide liquidity by converting an illiquid asset into cash in anticipation of the cash need.

LIFE INSURANCE

Next, we turn our attention to perhaps the most commonly used estate liquidity source, life insurance.

Introduction

Let's review the basic terminology. In its simplest form, a life insurance policy is a contract owned by the person called the *owner,* which pays an amount called the *face value* to the person called the *beneficiary,* upon the death of the person called the *insured.* Life insurance has several uses, but in estate planning its major purpose is to provide funds to cover cash needs arising at the client's death.

We'll cover three major topics in this section. First, we'll survey the various types of insurance policies commonly used.[1] Next, we'll review the major concepts in the income, gift, and estate taxation of insurance. Finally, we'll examine the insurance planning techniques frequently used to provide needed liquidity.

Types of Insurance

Hundreds of different insurance policies are sold in the United States today. However, most are simply minor variations of each other, and the number of really different types, for our purposes, are two. They are term insurance and cash value insurance. Each is briefly described next.

Term insurance. The simplest form of insurance is a one-year policy whose premium is based on the likelihood of death in that year. If the insured dies, the beneficiary is paid the face value. If the insured does not die, the company owes nothing and the contract terminates. This is the essence of term insurance; whether or

---

[1] In this chapter, the word *insurance* will be used as shorthand to mean life insurance.

not the company is financially obligated to pay depends solely on whether or not the insured dies during the contract period.

Most term insurance is *renewable;* that is, the company is obligated to sell another year's insurance at a previously agreed-upon price, at the option of the policy owner.[2] Another physical exam cannot be required. The premium, or cost, of *annually renewable* term insurance policies rises annually with increasing age, reflecting the continuing increase in the likelihood of death. Other term insurance policies have premiums that remain constant for 5, 10, or 20 years, and then rise to a new plateau for another similar period, etc., until termination date. Regardless of how often the premium rises, all term insurance is characterized by rising premiums and by the uncertainty as to whether the company will ever be financially obligated to pay the face value.

Cash value insurance.   In contrast with term insurance, cash value insurance is characterized by a constant (level) premium. It is also characterized by certainty: When a cash value insurance contract ends, either because the insured dies or because the policy owner no longer wants coverage, the company will ordinarily be obligated to pay a significant amount of money. If the insured *dies*, the company will pay the face value, of course, as it does on its term insurance policies. If, on the other hand, the owner *surrenders* the policy before the insured's death, the company will be obligated to pay an amount called the *cash surrender value,* described later. Actuarially, insurers can afford to do this because they charge a much higher initial premium for cash value insurance.

Cash value insurance originated as a solution to a problem of early lapsation perceived to be inherent in term insurance. Many years ago, when term insurance was just about the only policy sold, agents found that policy owners frequently terminated their insurance as it got more and more expensive with increasing age. To retain clients, companies started offering cash value insurance, charging a constant premium over time. Evidence has since shown

---

[2]Most policies are renewable to age 65 or 100 if they are term policies, and to age 95 or 100 if they are cash value policies. Regarding premiums, most *illustrated* term insurance premiums are guaranteed for one, three, five, or ten years. Thereafter, premiums can be raised up to a guaranteed maximum.

that such policies are not as frequently surrendered by policyholders, despite advancing age. Essentially, the earlier year's premiums are more than the company actuarially needs to fund death and other claims, and the later years' premiums are less than the company needs. The overcharge in early years enables the company to accumulate a type of actuarial reserve, some of which is made contractually available as a cash value to the policyholder, either to borrow, to pledge, or in the event of surrender prior to the insured's death, to receive outright.

Today's cash value policy premiums typically range between three and five times the initial premium charged for annually renewable term insurance for a given policyholder. This is a substantial difference, and today all states have what are called *nonforfeiture laws,* which specify how to calculate the minimum cash surrender value that the company must legally make available to the policy owner at the end of each policy year. Competition usually compels carriers to offer more than the minimum statutory requirement. Cash surrender values are listed, year by year, in the policy itself.

> EXAMPLE 15–1 Audrey, an insurance salesperson, offers Gerard, aged 45, a choice of two policies, each having a face value of $100,000. First, she describes a cash value *whole life* policy, sold by the ABC Co., which has a level annual premium of $2,700. Its cash surrender value at the end of the fifth policy year will be $7,500. At the end of the 20th policy year, the cash value will be $43,500. Audrey then describes an annually renewable to age 100 term policy that is sold by the XYZ Co. The policy's first five years of premiums will be $500, $550, $610, $680, and $750. The premiums, which will be listed in the policy, rise annually until age 100. For example, Gerard's annual premiums will rise to $1,735, $4,620, $13,100, and $31,400 at ages 60, 70, 80, and 90, respectively.

Whole life policy.   All cash value policies have a maturity date, that is, a date at which, if the insured reaches it alive, the face value will be paid. A whole life cash value policy, as its name implies, has a maturity date that extends beyond the "whole life" of most insureds, typically the insured's 95th or 100th birthday. Thus, in Example 15-1, if Gerard purchases the whole life policy and keeps it in force, under simple assumptions ABC will send him a check for $100,000 if he reaches age 100 alive.

Endowment policy. In contrast to a whole life cash value policy, an endowment cash value policy has a much earlier maturity date, usually the insured's 65th birthday, a date designed to be coincident with retirement. Since the typical surviving insured will be paid the face value at a much earlier age, the insurer must charge a substantially higher premium for endowment insurance than for whole life insurance. Per dollar of insurance protection, endowment insurance is one of the most expensive policies sold.

Universal life policy. During periods of high inflation, traditional cash value policies such as whole life and endowment are not as attractive because their contractually guaranteed cash values are typically designed to appreciate at a relatively modest rate of growth in comparison with returns available on other short-term interest-sensitive, investments. Naturally, applicants are more attracted to other products, including term insurance, where the cash saved from the significantly lower initial premiums can be personally invested with other financial institutions to earn higher yields.

In response, the insurance industry developed a product called universal life insurance, which is essentially a third type of cash value insurance that offers the policyholder greater flexibility and, often, greater investment yield. It offers greater flexibility because the policyholder is permitted to vary the amount of the face value and the premium payments from time to time to meet changing financial conditions. It can offer greater investment yield because the insurer invests premium dollars in a portfolio of securities having a shorter average maturity. Thus, during periods of greater inflation, the insurer can often earn greater income, which it can pass on to the policyholder in the form of higher cash values. The typical universal life policy offers a guaranteed rate of appreciation of some low amount, commonly 4 percent, with the provision that a higher rate will be earned if the investments are more profitable. Universal life insurance is an attractive product, and it has the potential to become even more popular than the conventional guaranteed cash value whole life policy.[3]

---

[3]Some commentators dislike variable life insurance because its complexity and flexibility makes it virtually impossible to evaluate numerically and undertake cost comparisons with term policies and traditional cash value policies.

Taxation of Life Insurance

This section will survey the major concepts in the income, gift, and estate taxation of insurance. Many of these topics were covered in greater detail in Part 2 of the text, and the reader is referred there for elaboration and clarification.

Income taxation. Two major income tax aspects of life insurance are the taxation of the cash value accumulation and the taxation of the policy proceeds.[4]

Income taxation of cash value accumulation. Increases in cash value buildup will not ordinarily be subject to income taxation while the policy is in force, primarily because the taxpayer-policyholder cannot effectively receive these amounts outright without borrowing them or surrendering the policy.

When a cash value policy is surrendered, any excess of the cash surrender value (amount realized) over the total premiums paid (adjusted basis) will be includable in the owner's gross income. Usually this difference, if positive, will be quite small and will not be a significant tax burden.

Income taxation of policy proceeds. The Code[5] generally excludes from gross income all proceeds received from a life insurance policy paid by reason of the insured's death.

The Code has carved out an exception to the proceeds exclusion rule for policies that have been transferred for valuable consideration. The amount includable in the transferee-owner's gross income in the year of the transfer will equal the policy proceeds, reduced by the amount of consideration paid and the total premiums paid by the new owner. This *transfer for value rule,* as it is called, does not apply to policy transfers to the following parties:

- The insured.
- A partner of the insured.

---

[4]To qualify for the two favored tax treatments described next, an insurance policy must meet the requirements under recently enacted code Section 7702, which was enacted to discourage the popularity of certain universal life-type policies containing an unusually large investment element relative to the size of the death protection component.

[5]Section 101.

- A partnership in which the insured is a partner.
- A corporation in which the insured is a shareholder or officer.
- A transferee whose basis will be determined by reference to the transferor's basis.

> EXAMPLE 101–1 For over 15 years, Terry had been owner of a $10,000 face value insurance policy on his life. Last year, he gave the policy to his beneficiary-son Ralph, who began to pay the premiums. Terry died last month. No portion of the proceeds will be includable in Ralph's gross income because Ralph did not give valuable consideration for the policy.

> EXAMPLE 101–2 If, in Example 101-1, we assume instead that Terry sold the policy to Ralph for $100, and that the premiums paid by Ralph totaled $400, Ralph's gross income will include $9,500.

> EXAMPLE 101–3 Ulysses and Xeno are business partners. For years, each had owned an insurance policy on his own life. Now, their attorney is drafting a buy-sell contract, and the partners have agreed to exchange policies, with some cash also included as part of the transaction. Thus, Ulysses will become owner and beneficiary of the policy on the life of Xeno, and Xeno will become owner and beneficiary of the policy on the life of Ulysses. Upon the death of either partner, no part of the proceeds will be includable in the other's gross income.

The last example illustrates the use of existing insurance policies to fund a business "buyout" agreement, which is discussed further in the next chapter.

Gift taxation. As illustrated in Chapter 7, there are two common situations where insurance can be the subject of gift taxation. First, a taxable gift of the policy's replacement value will arise prior to the death of the decedent-owner when an assignment of ownership rights to a policy is made. Ordinarily, the gift of an insurance policy will qualify for the annual exclusion, unless the donee is an irrevocable trust.

Second, a taxable gift of the policy proceeds will arise at the death of a decedent-insured if the insured, owner, and beneficiary are all different parties. The effect of this rule is to compel planners to recommend that the same noninsured party be both owner and beneficiary.

Estate taxation. Life insurance is most commonly included in a decedent's federal estate tax base under Code Sections 2033, 2042, 2001, and 2035. Since this material was covered and illustrated in Chapter 6, each section will be reviewed only briefly here.

Under §2033 (property owned at death), the terminal value of a life insurance policy on the *life of someone other than the decedent* will be included in the decedent's gross estate to the extent of the decedent's ownership interest in the policy.

Under §2042, proceeds on the *life of the insured* will be includable in the decedent's gross estate if, at the insured's death, either the proceeds were receivable by the decedent's executor or the decedent possessed incidents of ownership in the policy.

Under §2001, the decedent's *adjustable taxable gifts* will include the date-of-gift taxable terminal value of any life insurance policy for which the decedent made a completed transfer more than three years before death.

Finally, under §2035, the proceeds of a life insurance policy on the life of the decedent will be included in the decedent's gross estate if, within three years of death, the decedent made a completed transfer of incidents of ownership in the policy.

With these tax rules in mind, let us turn to the techniques of insurance planning.

Life Insurance Planning

The fundamental goal in using life insurance in liquidity planning is to provide for cash needs while minimizing income, gift, and estate taxation, as well as other costs. This multifaceted criterion will be employed next to help determine who should be chosen to be the insured, the owner, and the beneficiary of a proposed life insurance policy. Throughout this section we will assume an estate's need for cash will be met with insurance, rather than some other source of liquidity.

Selecting the insured. Proper family planning would provide for insurance on the life of that spouse whose death is expected to create a cash need. For smaller estates, this could occur at the death of either or both spouses, depending on certain factors, such as the size of their economic contribution to the family.

For larger estates, as mentioned earlier, use of the marital deduction and the credit shelter bypass will usually minimize cash needs at the death of the first spouse, but will create a relatively large need at the surviving spouse's death. Thus, ordinarily, little or no insurance will be required on S1's life.[6] However, since most clients do not know for certain whether the husband or the wife will be the surviving spouse, both may need to be insured. Several commonly used purchase arrangements are discussed next.

One simple but costly plan would be to insure *both* spouses for the *full amount* of protection needed at the surviving spouse's death.

An alternative method of insuring the spouses is to purchase immediately a *small amount* of insurance on *both* spouses which, upon either's first death, can be used to purchase a fully paid larger policy on the life of the survivor. This can eliminate the cash flow drain on the surviving spouse's assets that would otherwise be used to pay the premium.

A third and theoretically attractive method of insuring both spouses for cash needs at the survivor's death is to purchase a joint life policy of *second death insurance,* which pays the proceeds only upon the death of the second spouse. This alternative should save premium dollars in two ways: First, only one policy need be purchased. Second, the contingency insured against is more remote in time than that insured against under a single-death policy; the policy proceeds are not payable until both of the insureds have died, not just the one. Unfortunately, many second-death policies cost nearly as much as a single-life policy, so careful cost comparison is necessary.

A final alternative is to insure only the *wife,* usually the probable survivor, for the required liquidity. If she survives her husband, the contract becomes, de facto, a second-death policy. If she predeceases him, the proceeds can be invested and then made available to pay the FET at his later death.

Let's shift gears now to examine the very different factors involved in selecting the best policy owner and beneficiary.

---

[6]However, some insurance may be needed to meet nontax needs, such as to replace the breadwinner's income. This will be particularly important for clients supporting younger children with a large amount of earned income.

Selecting the owner and beneficiary. Selecting the owner and beneficiary of insurance on the lives of the spouses of a *smaller estate* is rather simple, since death taxation will not usually be a significant issue. The client and the client's spouse will be able to own policies on their own lives, making the proceeds payable to either of them without generating an FET. However, it would be advisable not to make the proceeds payable to the decedent-insured's estate, so as not to needlessly subject those proceeds to *probate* administration. Instead, the noninsured spouse could be named the primary beneficiary. The contingent beneficiary could be the client's children, if sufficiently mature, or it could be a trust, perhaps the same trust provided for in an uncomplicated trust-will, similar to the one illustrated in Chapter 3.

Selection of owner and beneficiary of insurance on the spouses of a *larger estate* requires greater care in order to minimize the effects of transfer costs. We consider next the effect of naming various parties as owner and beneficiary of policies on the lives of the spouses.

Spouse as owner and beneficiary. Naming one or the other spouse as owner or beneficiary will not minimize transfer costs. It will usually subject the proceeds either to a transfer tax or to probate administration or to both, depending on which spouse dies first. To see why, consider the tax consequences for each of the possible outcomes.

First, if the *insured spouse dies first and is either owner or beneficiary,* the proceeds will be includable in his or her gross estate under §2042. If the proceeds qualify for the marital deduction, thereby avoiding S1 taxation, they will inexorably be included in S2's gross estate, barring consumption, gifting, or remarriage. If the proceeds do not qualify for the marital deduction, then the only way they will escape taxation is by disposition of the proceeds to a credit shelter bypass. If the amount passing to the bypass without insurance already exceeds the amount of the exemption equivalent, then the insurance proceeds cannot be sheltered. If they can be sheltered because the estate size is less than the exemption equivalent, then the insured spouse can be named beneficiary without subjecting the proceeds to spousal estate taxation. However, the proceeds will be subject to probate administration. One way to avoid probate is to name as beneficiary the trustee of the bypass trust. This designation may be challenged, however, in a few states that do not authorize it by statute. Local law must be checked. Summarizing, if the insured spouse is owner or beneficiary and dies first, the insurance proceeds will be subject to estate taxation and possibly to probate administration, except in a few situations where the proceeds can be sheltered by a bypass trust whose trustee is named beneficiary of the policy. Thus, in the usual larger family estate, the insured spouse should not be named either owner or beneficiary.

Second, if the *insured spouse dies first and the noninsured spouse is beneficiary,* then the proceeds will likely be included in that S2's estate.[7] Or if the noninsured spouse is named *owner* and someone other than a spouse is named beneficiary, then that spouse will be deemed to have made a taxable gift to the beneficiary of the proceeds upon the death of the insured spouse. Thus, in the usual larger family estate, even the noninsured spouse should not be named either owner or beneficiary.

Finally, if the *decedent-insured spouse dies second and is either owner or beneficiary,* then the proceeds will be includable in his or her gross estate, again under §2042.

Several conclusions can be drawn from the above. First, subject to one minor exception, the naming of either spouse as owner or beneficiary of a policy on the life of a spouse will subject the proceeds to transfer taxation and, perhaps, probate administration. Further, probate costs may be greater. Thus, to minimize spousal transfer costs, neither spouse of a larger estate should usually be designated as either owner or beneficiary of an insurance policy on the life of a spouse. And second, a taxable gift will occur whenever a noninsured owner is not the beneficiary. Thus, whoever is selected should be named both owner and beneficiary to avoid gift consequences. Designation of other parties, including a child and two types of trusts, is evaluated next.

---

[7]The proceeds may escape estate taxation entirely, however, if the spouses die simultaneously. Under a provision of the Uniform Simultaneous Death Act, the owner-beneficiary will be deemed to have predeceased the insured. Thus, only the policy's terminal value, if any, would be includable, and the proceeds would pass to the contingent beneficiaries (usually to the children or in trust for them), estate tax free.

Child as owner and beneficiary. Instead of a spouse, one of the client's children could be named owner and beneficiary. The child could be *requested* to use the proceeds to provide liquidity to the estate upon the death of the insured. This alternative will work best when the child is sufficiently mature to handle such a responsibility. Nonetheless, there will always be a risk that the child may permit the policy to lapse. Or the child, having received the policy proceeds upon the death of the insured parent, may be unwilling to provide the funding needed by the estate. And since the child will become the legal owner of the proceeds, any gratuitous transfer of the funds to the estate or to the surviving spouse will likely be treated as a taxable gift.[8] Additionally, the proceeds may inevitably wind up in the child's own gross estate.

Revocable trust as owner and beneficiary. To eliminate any doubts over whether a named beneficiary will cooperate to make the proceeds available to the estate and to remove the chance that the insurance proceeds will be subject to probate in a spouse's estate, the client could name a revocable trust to be the owner and beneficiary. However, the power to revoke in the hands of the client or the client's spouse will cause the proceeds to be includable in the insured's *gross estate*. Thus, although avoiding probate of the proceeds, the revocable insurance trust offers no transfer tax advantage over the owner-beneficiary arrangements considered so far.

Irrevocable trust as owner and beneficiary. The irrevocable trust offers what many commentators consider to be the ultimate solution. With regard to a spouse owning an estate whose value exceeds the exemption equivalent of the unified credit, only the designation of an irrevocable trust as owner and beneficiary can achieve all of the following goals:[9]

- Exclude the insurance proceeds from income taxation and from the taxable estates of both spouses.
- Exclude the insurance proceeds from the probate estates of both spouses.

---

[8]However, the child could purchase estate assets, or lend the money to the estate.

[9]The irrevocable life insurance trust can also be effectively used by a single person to achieve similar tax and nontax goals.

- Enjoy the shelter of the gift tax annual exclusion for transfers to the trust of both the policy and the funds needed to pay policy premiums.
- Ensure that a responsible party will in fact provide the needed post-death liquidity.
- Make the proceeds available to the surviving spouse for health or certain other reasons.

The irrevocable trust is usually structured in the following manner. Created by the insured, the trustee is named the owner and beneficiary of the policy.[10] Upon the death of the insured, the trustee is authorized to lend the proceeds to the insured's estate or to purchase assets from the estate.[11] If the insured is S1, then the trust corpus usually continues to provide benefits to S2 in the form of a bypass trust, similar to the one introduced in Chapter 11. At the death of S2, the trust is again authorized to lend cash to the S2 estate or to purchase estate assets. Then the trust is either terminated, with corpus payable to the children, or it is continued, distributing income to the children until they reach a specified age or, in the case of a generation-skipping trust qualifying for the $1 million lifetime exemption, until the grandchildren reach a specified age.[12]

Ownership of insurance by an irrevocable trust requires that the clients be willing to surrender all future interest in the policy owned by the trust.[13] As mentioned in the chapter on gifting, clients

---

[10]The grantor should not be named a trust beneficiary, because of possible §2036 problems. And since the noninsured spouse is usually one of the beneficiaries of an irrevocable life insurance trust, he or she should not be a grantor. This will require greater care in preparation in community property states.

[11]An insured spouse who is also grantor should not be named trustee, since this would constitute an incident of ownership in the policy. The noninsured spouse could be named trustee without this adverse result.

[12]For a discussion of the "private marital deduction annuity," see the Guiterréz article cited at the end of Chapter 12. At S1's death, the trustee of the QTIP trust is directed to purchase an annuity for the life of S2 from the life insurance trust. Its advantages include an S1 marital deduction, S2 estate reduction, and the use of the life insurance trust as a generation-skipping trust that is not subject to the generation-skipping transfer tax.

[13]The gift of a policy to an irrevocable trust will not ordinarily qualify for the annual exclusion because it is not considered a gift of a present interest. However,

may have reservations about gifting any assets. However, insurance having little or no cash value is usually one of the least distasteful assets to gift, for several reasons. First, the gift tax value is minimal.[14] A policy can have little or no cash value either because it is a term policy or because it is a cash value policy that has been recently purchased or has a sizable outstanding loan.[15] Second, in contrast with its gift tax value, its estate tax value will be very large, making it a desirable asset to exclude from the estate. And third, because it is merely a document, clients will not experience much loss in the pleasure of ownership commonly felt when they gift tangible or other intangible property.

Whether an existing policy is transferred to the trust, or whether a new policy is created when the trust is established, the client-trustor-insured must live *three years* thereafter to ensure the avoidance of inclusion of the proceeds in the gross estate under §2035.[16] If the client transfers an existing policy, the annual exclusion will not be available unless the beneficiaries have a Crummey-type power to invade.

Who should pay the premiums on the trust-owned policy? One alternative is to fund the trust with sufficient income-earning assets

---

both that transfer and the payments into a trust to fund the insurance premiums can be made to qualify with the use of a Crummey-type provision.

[14]The gross gift tax value of a newly issued policy is simply the first year's premium.

[15]The best type of insurance with which to fund the irrevocable life insurance trust is a term policy. Not only will there be no initial gift tax consequences, but the trust will have greater flexibility. If circumstances were to later change, making the need for life insurance unnecessary, a term policy could be permitted to lapse simply by making the trust unable to pay the premiums. Thus, the trust would be terminated. On the other hand, failure to pay the premiums of a cash value policy might not result in lapsation, or even if it did the trust would likely be left holding a valuable asset that was inaccessible to the grantor.

[16]The trust can include a *contingent marital deduction clause,* so that if the three-year rule caused the proceeds to be included in the insured's gross estate, then the proceeds would be paid outright to the spouse (or to a marital trust). This would save the marital deduction. On the other hand, if the insured lived longer than three years, causing the three-year rule not to apply, then the proceeds would be used to fund the bypass share. This would exclude the proceeds from the estates of both spouses, one of the main goals of the irrevocable life insurance trust. For a further discussion, see the Brand–LaPiana article cited at the end of the chapter.

to enable the trust to pay them. Unfortunately, the grantor trust rules will make that income taxable to the client-grantor rather than to the trust.[17] A preferred alternative has the client making annual gifts to the trust in amounts sufficient to pay the premiums.[18] By including a Crummey provision, these gifts can qualify for the annual exclusion.[19]

If the trust is *required* to use insurance proceeds to pay the decedent's estate debts, including taxes, the proceeds will be includable in the decedent's gross estate, under §2042. Thus, as we have said, the trustee should instead be simply advised that it may lend the proceeds to the estate or purchase estate assets to achieve funding.

Life insurance can be a potential liquidity source because it rather efficiently supplies cash exactly when it is needed: at death of the client. Planned carefully, it can also be structured to avoid spousal transfer costs.

Next we examine a long-used source of liquidity, but one that is steadily declining in importance.

FLOWER BONDS

Flower bonds are certain issues of long-term U.S. Treasury bonds which, if owned by the decedent at death, can be used at par value to pay the FET.[20] Their appeal lies in the fact that they can be purchased at discount, thus effectively reducing the FET owed. The par value of those flower bonds actually used to pay the FET are included in the decedent-owner's gross estate.

Table 15-1 lists the Treasury issues which are flower bonds. As the table indicates, flower bonds have not been issued since 1963, which means that the length of time to the most distant maturity

---

[17]Section 677(a)(3).

[18]Insured-clients in community property states should make the periodic gifts from his or her separate property to keep the proceeds out of the estate of the noninsured spouse, who is beneficiary of the trust.

[19]If each spouse is an insured, then two trusts will have to be established, with each owning one policy. These trusts must be drafted especially carefully to avoid §2036 problems and the reciprocal trust doctrine, as illustrated in Example 2036-10 in Chapter 6.

[20]Actually, redemption is made at par plus accrued interest.

TABLE 15–1 U.S. Treasury Flower Bonds

Series	Year Issued	Maturity Date
3½% 1990	1958	February 15, 1990
4½% 1987–92	1962	August 15, 1992
4% 1988–93	1963	February 15, 1993
4⅛% 1989–94	1963	May 15, 1994
3% 1995	1955	February 15, 1995
3½% 1998	1960	November 15, 1998

---

date is falling with every passing day, causing market prices to more or less gravitate toward the bond's par value. Thus, flower bonds have become less and less attractive and will continue to decline in appeal in the future, except during periods when market interest rates are high. Several years ago it was possible to buy some issues at less than 70 percent of par value, which meant that the estate would enjoy more than a 30 percent FET saving. More recently however, discounts have dropped to less than 7 percent below face value, often making the tax-saving value of flower bonds marginal.

To work, flower bonds must be owned by the decedent prior to death. However, they may be purchased very shortly before death by someone else, on the decedent's behalf. In fact the use of flower bonds has been upheld even when purchased by a comatose or incompetent person's agent, trustee, or attorney-in-fact under a durable power of attorney, acting with proper prior written authorization.[21] Delaying their purchase as long as possible makes sense, as the following example suggests, since flower bonds are such low-yielding investments.

> EXAMPLE 6312–1 One day before her death, decedent's attorney-in-fact purchased flower bonds under authority of a durable power of attorney. Decedent was a widow, owning a taxable estate of $1 million. In anticipation of an FET of $153,000, bonds totaling $150,000 in face value were purchased. The bonds were bought at about 93 percent of par, costing $139,500 including commissions. One day before the due date of the tax, which is nine months after date of death, decedent's executor mailed the bonds to the Treasury, in partial pay-

---

[21]The durable power of attorney is discussed in Chapter 17.

ment of the FET. Decedent's taxable estate is $1,010,500 (the sum of $1 million originally owned, less the $139,500 cash spent on the bonds, plus $150,000, the par value of the bonds). Thus, the FET paid was actually $157,328 (which is $153,000, the FET on $1 million, plus $4,328, the addition tax on the $10,500, which is subject to a marginal tax rate of 41 percent).

Decedent's net benefit from the use of the bonds can be calculated as follows. The net FET saved from the bonds is $6,172, which is the amount $10,500, (the FET saved by using bonds costing $139,500 to pay $150,000 in tax), reduced by $4,328 (the additional tax on the increment in the taxable estate resulting from inclusion of the bonds on the gross estate at face value). Further, during the nine-month period when the bonds were held, the estate experienced an opportunity income loss since it could have been earning a considerably higher return on other investments. If the flower bonds were purchased to yield 2 percent on an after-income tax basis, and if other Treasury bonds yielding 5 percent after tax had been available, then the estate has lost the opportunity to earn $3,139. This amount is the product of $139,500 times 0.03 times three-fourths, representing the loss of three quarters of a year of the interest differential on the amount of the money invested. In conclusion, the estate's net benefit from the purchase of the flower bonds is $3,033, the difference between the FET saved, $6,172, and the after-tax opportunity income loss, $3,139. The use of flower bonds increased the estate's cash flow by $3,033.

Flower bonds are a source of liquidity to the estate because they reduce the effective FET owed. They will continue to be used only as long as their market price is sufficiently below par so that the net FET saved more than offsets the opportunity income loss.

LIQUIDITY PLANNING DEVICES UNIQUE TO BUSINESS OWNERS

Many owners of closely held businesses can anticipate a potentially severe liquidity problem. Not infrequently, their principal estate consists of the interest in the business, which is usually quite illiquid. The need to pay the FET in cash within nine months after date of death acts as a cloud that could force the survivors to sell the business at distress prices, probably to outside parties. And failure to make a timely payment of the tax will result in penalties and can give the IRS the power to seize estate assets and sell them at public auction. In view of these factors, the business owner should plan in advance to minimize future liquidity problems. The following presents several devices that uniquely apply to the business-owning client.

Sale of the Business

First, consideration should be given to the predeath sale of the business or to a merger with a publicly held firm, as a means of converting a relatively illiquid asset into a liquid one. A predeath sale has a tax drawback, which was covered earlier in the chapter, and a client who chooses not to sell or merge should consider executing a funded buyout agreement with the other owners. The buyout contract, discussed in some detail in the next chapter, will obligate the other owners to pay the client's estate a cash amount in exchange for the client's interest in the firm.

Three other liquidity-generating devices explicitly created by the Internal Revenue Code for the business-owning client are discussed next.

§6166: FET in Installments

To help reduce the risk of an immediate liquidity crisis at the business owner's death, Congress enacted Code Section 6166, which permits the estate of a decedent-owner of a closely held business to defer payment[22] of the FET for four years, with interest owing at only 4 percent per year.[23] The estate then can pay that FET in 10 installments starting in the fifth year.[24]

---

[22]The IRS also has discretion under Code Section 6161 to grant an extension of up to 10 years to pay the FET upon a showing of "reasonable cause." Examples of situations satisfying this requirement include: (a) the estate has liquid assets but they are located in other states, not immediately available to the executor, (b) a large part of the estate is in the form of assets which consist of rights to receive payments in the future (royalties, accounts receivables, etc.), and (c) the estate includes a claim to substantial assets which cannot be collected without litigation. Reasonable cause will not be found merely because common assets must be sold at distress prices.

[23]Only the FET attributable to the first $1 million of taxable estate value in the interest in the business is subject to the 4 percent rate. The excess is subject to the current "federal rate," which is approximately equal to the long-term rate at which the U.S. Treasury recently borrowed. (§6601(j)).

[24]All interest on §6166 debt is still entirely deductible from income, and not subject to the "personal interest" limitations under TRA 86. (§163(h)(2)(e)).

There are several important requirements and conditions for qualification under §6166. First, the value of the decedent's interest in the business must be at least 35 percent of the value of the adjusted gross estate, which is the gross estate reduced by debts, expenses, taxes, and losses. Second, the decedent's interest must have been in a *closely held business*, which is defined as

1. Sole proprietorship; or
2. A partnership:
    a. In which at least 20 percent of the capital interest is included in the decedent's gross estate, or
    b. Which has 15 or fewer partners; or
3. A corporation:
    a. In which at least 20 percent of the voting stock is included in the decedent's gross estate, or
    b. Which has 15 or fewer shareholders.

Third, to qualify, the sole proprietorship, partnership, or corporation must have been actually engaged in carrying on a trade or business at the time of the decedent's death. Finally, the sale, redemption, or other disposition of all or a portion of the business, or the failure to make timely interest or principal payments, will result in immediate acceleration of the deferred payments.

> EXAMPLE 6166–1 Decedent died owning 40 percent of the stock in a corporation, with the decedent's interest worth $600,000. Decedent had a gross estate of $1 million and an adjusted gross estate of $900,000. Assume that the FET is $120,000. Under the above rules, the estate will qualify under §6166, since the business qualifies as a closely held business, and decedent's interest is at least 35 percent of the adjusted gross estate. The amount of the tax that may be deferred is calculated to be $80,000, which is the amount of the FET ($120,000) times the ratio of the value of the business interest ($600,000) divided by the adjusted gross estate ($900,000).

Estate tax deferral under §6166 can be a source of estate liquidity by reducing the amount of the immediate cash needs of the decedent's estate. It is particularly attractive to the client who anticipates the risk of a forced sale of the business at his or her death.

Section 303 Redemption

The Internal Revenue Code provides for another method to lessen the impact of taxes on the estates of business-owning decedents. Section 303 permits the estate of a decedent-shareholder of a corporation to redeem the decedent's shares with favorable *income tax* treatment. Specifically, the transaction will be treated as a disposition of a capital asset rather than the receipt of a dividend.

> EXAMPLE 303–1 Decedent's estate redeemed decedent's 1,000 shares of stock in a closely held corporation. Immediately before death, each share had an adjusted basis of $100. The date-of-death value of each share was $150. Upon redemption, the estate received $158,000 cash. If the redemption does not qualify for capital gains treatment, the estate may be deemed to have received a dividend of as much as $158,000, treated as ordinary income.[25] Alternatively, if the redemption qualifies under §303, the estate will have a taxable long-term gain of $8,000, reflecting the step-up in basis at date of death.[26]

There are two major requirements to qualify under §303. First, as with the §6166 deferral, the value of the decedent's interest in the stock must be at least 35 percent of his or her adjusted gross estate. Second, the amount paid by the corporation in redemption of the shares may not exceed the sum of federal and state death taxes and funeral and administration expenses.

A §303 redemption can provide liquidity to the estate by encouraging a postdeath cash-generating transaction which would otherwise produce very undesirable income tax consequences.

By means of lifetime planning, Sections 6166 and 303 may be made available to a client who had anticipated not qualifying because he or she did not expect the estate to meet the 35 percent test. The client can be urged to acquire additional interest in the firm or to reduce the size of the nonbusiness estate by gifting in

---

[25] If the distribution exceeds the amount of the corporation's earnings and profits, the excess is considered a nontaxable return of capital.

[26] TRA 86, by taxing most capital gains at ordinary income rates, reduced somewhat the tax advantage of the Section 303 redemption. But the ability to exclude the amount of the adjusted basis for taxation, as illustrated in this example, continues to make the strategy often quite attractive, especially when a step-up in basis is still available.

order to increase the proportion of the estate represented by the business.

§2032A: Special Use Valuation

One other liquidity source explicitly provided by the Code is available to the business owner's estate. Its purpose might be best explained with a hypothetical fact situation.

Suppose a client has owned a farm for many years, one that had originally been well outside of the city limits. But with the progress of urban growth, the farm is presently in the heart of one of the high-rent districts. Although the general value of the land is considerably greater than the specific value of the farm as a business, the client has no interest in selling; she and her survivors are determined to remain working the farm in the indefinite future.

The reader might be wondering which value will be included in the client-owner's gross estate at her death. Will it be the value of the farm in its *present use* or the value of the property in its *highest and best use,* available, for example, for construction of a high-rise building? Valuation at its highest and best use might force the survivors to sell the land to pay the large FET. On the other hand, valuation at its present use might enable the survivors to carry on the business.

Section 2032A permits qualifying estates to value property in such situations at its present, *qualified-use value,* as a farm or other trade or business.

The major requirements and conditions under §2032A include the following. First, the property must have been held for qualified use and actively managed by the decedent or the decedent's family for five out of the eight years prior to the decedent's death.[27] Second, at least 50 percent of the value of the gross estate must consist of real or personal property devoted to the qualifying use. Third, the value of the real property portion must constitute at least 25 percent of the adjusted gross estate. Fourth, the qualifying property must pass to a qualifying heir and must continue to be used for a qualified use for at least 10 years after the decedent's death.

---

[27]For example, *passive leasing* by the decedent of the property for farming by others will later disqualify the estate from §2032A.

Fifth, the maximum amount by which the gross estate can be reduced by this election is $750,000.

The §2032A election can reduce the need for liquidity by reducing the size of the gross estate and, therefore, the amount of the FET cash requirement. It is being used frequently.

OTHER LIQUIDITY SOURCES

Two other sources of liquidity to the estate deserve brief mention.

Employee Benefits

As an employee, the client may have accumulated substantial retirement benefits on the job. If some of these benefits are payable after the client's death, the estate or the employee's spouse could be m de beneficiary to provide a degree of needed liquidity.

Postmortem Liquidity Planning Techniques

There are a host of techniques that can be undertaken after death over which the client has little or no control during lifetime. Postmortem devices, such as disclaimers and the alternate valuation date, will be examined in Chapter 18, which surveys postmortem tax planning.

This chapter has examined the planning for liquidity. Chapter 16 will present the principles of planning for the closely held business.

RECOMMENDED READING

BLAKE, JOHN F. "Current Approaches to Avoiding Estate Tax Where Insured Dies within Three Years." *Estate Planning,* November 1986, pp. 346–48.

BLASE, JAMES. "Structuring Insurance Trusts to Avoid Estate Inclusion under Section 2035." *Journal of Taxation,* March 1985, pp. 154–59.

————. "Maximizing the Advantages of Life Insurance as a Funding Device and as an Investment." *Estate Planning,* January 1986, pp. 2–7.

BLATTMACHR, JONATHAN G., and DOUGLAS J. BLATTMACHR. "Determining If Flower Bonds Are Warranted for a Client's Estate, and How Much to Buy." *Estate Planning,* September 1986, pp. 264–68.

BRAND, RONALD A., and WILLIAM P. LAPIANA. "Using Disclaimers Add More

Flexibility to Escape Clauses for Taxable Insurance." *Estate Planning*, September 1986, pp. 278–81.

CHANDLER, DARLENE K. "The Irrevocable Life Insurance Trust and Section 2035: New Guideposts to Effective Planning." *C.L.U. Journal*, July 1987, pp. 52–55.

CHANDY, P. R., and SHARON GARRISON. "Planning for Death with Flowers." *Journal of The Institute of Certified Financial Planners*, Fall 1986, pp. 187–91.

CHASMAN, HERBERT. "Life Insurance As an Estate and Financial Planning Tool." University of Miami 22nd Annual Estate Planning Institute, 1988. An excellent summary of the characteristics of universal life, variable life, single premium life, and other insurance products.

CHRISTENSEN, BURKE A. "The Unfunded, Irrevocable Life Insurance Trust." *Trust & Estates*, March 1984, pp. 72–73.

DAVIS, HERBERT J., and DONALD R. DANN. "Life Insurance in the '80s." *Trust & Estates*, July 1984, 23–28.

GORFINKLE, ROBERT A. "Many Choices Available to Owner Wishing to Transfer Business to Younger Family Members." *Estate Planning*, March 1986, pp. 98–103.

GRUDZINSKI, CHESTER W., and STEVEN E. EISENBERG. "Coordinating 303's Redemption Benefits with the Estate Tax Deferral Rules of 6166." *Taxation for Accountants*, July 1984, pp. 32–36.

HOLDMANN, LEE F. "Income and Estate Planning Advantages of Life Insurance Enhanced by TRA 86 Changes." *Estate Planning*, May 1987, pp. 130–36.

HORN, JEROLD I. "Proper Form of Life Insurance Gift Can Improve Tax Savings Significantly." *Estate Planning*, September 1981, pp. 258–66.

JENSEN, DAVID E., and ROBERT O. SMITH. "How to Determine Whether Proposed Life Insurance Makes Economic and Tax Sense for a Client." *Taxation for Accountants*, December 1985, pp. 350–56.

KINSKERN, DOUGLAS. "Two Career Families Causing Significant Changes in Estate Planning for Younger Couples." *Estate Planning*, March 1988, pp. 92–98.

LEVAN, GERALD. "Passing the Family Business to the Next Generation—Resolving Family Conflicts." University of Miami 22nd Annual Estate Planning Institute, 1988.

LEW, HARRY J. "Buyer's Market" Financial Planning, May 1988, pp. 79–83. (Describes the evolution of term life insurance products since the early 1970s.)

"Life Insurance—How to Protect Your Family." *Consumer Reports*, June, July, and August 1986 issues. Three-part series.

LOWE, HENRY T. "Combining Life Insurance Proceeds with Other Estate Assets" *Missouri Law Review* 47 (1982), pp. 661–92.

MELTZER, ALAN L. "Implications of Survivorship Whole Life in Estate Planning." *Trust and Estates*, August 1984, pp. 48–50.

MILLAR, SANFORD I. "Life Insurance for the Closely Held Business." In *The*

Closely Held Business: Financial Planning for the Owners, 1986, Practising Law Institute, pp. 139–226.

OLINEY, DAN. "Flower Bonds: Are the Flowers Wilting?" *Estate Planning & Probate News,* Winter 1985, p. 9.

PAIK, SOO BONG. "Estate Tax Deferral: An Assessment." *UCLA Law Review* 29 (1982), pp. 642–60.

PAOLA, SUZANNE. "New Policies: Many Insurance Agencies Are Favorably Poised to Begin Offering Planning Services, but the Transition to This More Service-Oriented Outlook May Drastically Change the Way They Look and Feel." *Financial Planning,* February 1985, pp. 110–14.

PETRIE, LINDA C. "Increasing the Liquidity of an Estate Involves Combination of Pre- and Post-Death Planning." *Estate Planning,* March 1984, pp. 98–103.

PRICE, JOHN R. "Life Insurance: New Products—Old Problems." *1986 Southern California Tax and Estate Planning Forum.*

RESNICK, JOEL. "Application of Incidents of Ownership Test to Life Insurance Trusts." *Wayne Law Review* 27 (Spring 1981), pp. 1151–99.

SAWYER, W. WHITNEY. "Irrevocable Life Insurance Trust Offers Tax Savings, Liquidity at Small Cost to Flexibility." *Estate Planning,* March 1981, pp. 72–81.

SCHECHTMAN, RICHARD G. "New Concepts in Life Insurance Planning: Universal Life." *Cumberland Law Review* 13 (1982), pp. 219–37.

SCHLESINGER, SANFORD J. "How to Get the Maximum Benefit Out of Life Insurance." *The Practical Accountant,* October 1986, pp. 97–104.

SHAW, RANDALL L. "Universal Life Insurance—How it Works." *American Bar Association Journal* 71 (February 1985), pp. 68–70.

SPEWAK, STEVEN B., and BENNETT S. KELLER. "Deferral Can Still Be Combined with Corporate Redemptions to Provide Liquidity, Tax Benefits." *Estate Planning,* September 1987, pp. 296–301.

QUESTIONS AND PROBLEMS

1. How will the following factors influence liquidity needs at death?

   a. Size of the family estate.

   b. Whether the decedent is S1 or S2.

   c. Age of the family members.

2. "High-basis assets make desirable assets for a predeath sale designed to generate liquidity." True, false, or uncertain? Explain.

3. (*a*) What traits distinguish cash value insurance from term insurance? (*b*) Universal life insurance from other types of cash value insurance?

4. Is life insurance ever subject to income taxation? Explain.

5. Explain the two primary ways in which life insurance can be subject to gift taxation.

6. Life insurance can be subject to estate taxation under Sections 2001, 2033, 2042, and 2035. Briefly explain the application of each.

7. Who, if anyone, should be the insured of a policy designed to provide liquidity to a family estate of $250,000, assuming the following alternative facts?

   a. Spouses in their 30s; husband working; wife at home with two young children.

   b. Spouses in their 30s; both working; no children.

   c. Spouses in their 50s; both working; children are adults living elsewhere.

   d. Single adult; no children.

   e. Single parent of one six-year-old child.

   f. Retired couple; adult children living elsewhere.

8. Reanswer parts *a, d,* and *f* of Question 7, assuming instead a $2 million family estate owned by spouses who wish to set up a credit shelter bypass plan. In each case, would it matter how liquid the family wealth was?

9. What factors influence the selection of the owner and primary and contingent beneficiaries of an insurance policy on the life of a spouse in a small family estate situation?

10. (*a*) Describe the characteristics of the irrevocable life insurance trust. (*b*) What are its advantages?

11. A well-heeled client of yours is about to acquire life insurance on his life and is thinking of naming his wife owner and beneficiary. They each own $1 million. Advise him.

12. Would any of your answers to Question 11 change if the family estate was $800,000? Why or why not?

13. Five years ago, Mary assigned ownership of an insurance policy on the life of her husband, Bud, to Bud's living trust, which provided that at Bud's death Mary was entitled to a life estate in the trust income. If Mary survives Bud, could there be an estate tax problem? (Hint: the answer is in a chapter footnote.)

14. April, age 40, is a recently divorced single mother of two young children. She is not on friendly terms with her ex-husband who, in her opinion, is a "selfish spendthrift." April owns few assets, and asks your estate planning advice to help achieve her goal of financial security for her children.

15. Great-Aunt Rachel is dying. She has a taxable estate of $2 million. Using the salient facts found in Example 6312-1 in the chapter, calculate the net benefit or cost to the estate of purchasing $100,000 in flower bonds. (Answer: Net benefit = $1,478.)

16. As an alternative method of solving the problem posed in Question 15 above, assume instead that the attorney-in-fact purchases 3½ percent Treasury bonds maturing on November 15, 1998, for the price listed in *The Wall Street Journal* (see the index on the first page under "Treasury issues") on the most recent Wednesday prior to the date this assignment is due.

17. How are the arrangements based on Sections 6166, 303, and 2032A designed to provide estate liquidity?

—16——————————————————

Planning for Closely Held
Business Interests

———————————————————————————————

OVERVIEW

A closely held business is a firm privately owned by one or a few individuals who actively participate in its management. Unique estate planning problems can arise for owners of a closely held business. Typically, the firm generates the major source of its owners' income and represents the single largest part of their family wealth. Too often, however, the firm can sustain that level of income and value only if the owners continue to be actively involved in its management.[1] Thus, this income and value can be jeopardized by two events, each of which is certain to occur. First, each owner's involvement with the firm is destined to end, and the enterprise will lose his or her economic contribution. Second, the ownership interest in the business must eventually be transferred, subjecting it to possible transfer taxation. Estate planning seeks to minimize the adverse impact of these significant events by attempting to achieve four basic objectives:

1. To generate sufficient *income* for the owner and the owner's family after the owner's active involvement in the business terminates.

———————

[1]For example, a nondividend-paying closely held corporation is rarely in a position to start paying a dividend after the client-owner dies.

2. To transfer to the owner's chosen beneficiaries the maximum *value* attributable to that business.

3. To minimize the *costs* of making this transfer.

4. To provide sufficient *liquidity* to pay the transfer costs.

These objectives are more easily accomplished for owners of *publicly* held corporations, for two reasons. First, withdrawal of any one owner will usually have a far less depressing effect on business value and income. Publicly traded firms usually employ far more personnel, making business success much less dependent on the efforts of any one individual. Second, the goal of liquidity is easier to achieve for owners of publicly held firms because the client's survivors will receive liquid securities, readily tradable in the securities markets.

Thus, owners of closely held businesses have unique problems, and this chapter will survey the major principles and techniques of estate planning devoted to assisting them.[2] The chapter will first present an overview of general planning in this area, and then examine in greater detail the business buyout agreement. Appendix 16A will examine two business estate freezing techniques, the corporate recapitalization and the partnership capital freeze, and the repressive impact on their use of recent tax legislation.

PLANNING IN GENERAL FOR CLOSELY HELD BUSINESS INTERESTS

All estate planning for closely held business interests is premised on the fact that the client-owner cannot carry on forever. As mentioned earlier, we are certain of the occurrence of two future events: that the client's active *involvement* in the management of the firm will terminate, and that the client's *ownership* interest will have to be transferred. Since these events have major economic implications for the four objectives mentioned earlier, we shall begin with a further discussion of them.

---

[2]For example, statistics indicate that only 35 percent of successful family businesses survive in the second generation, and only 20 percent in the third generation. In many cases, this is due primarily to unresolved family conflict. For an excellent overview of the unique sociological aspects of families in business, see the LeVan article cited at the end of Chapter 15.

Minimizing Decline in Value Resulting from Withdrawal from the Firm

Client-owners have the ability to choose when to terminate their active management of the firm. Some elect to remain active until disability or death. The rest withdraw sooner, for any number of reasons, including the desire to adopt a new lifestyle, to consume more of the wealth that time and hard work have created, and to step aside to provide a business opportunity for a son or daughter. No matter when the client plans to withdraw, if the departure is expected to reduce the value and income derived from the business, the client can take several steps to minimize the decline.

First, the owner can plan early to *delegate* greater and greater responsibility to those who may one day be able to replace his or her contribution. To provide an *incentive* to assume this responsibility, the business can contribute to certain tax-favored fringe benefit plans, including medical expense contracts, group term life insurance, and retirement plans. In general, contributions to these plans are income tax deductible by the firm and are either tax free or tax deferred to the employee.

Second, the owner can use current business value to raise his or her own future *income* by executing certain *contracts,* such as a deferred compensation plan,[3] disability income insurance, and a retirement plan.

Third, the firm may be able to undertake a corporate recapitalization or create a partnership capital freeze. These are intricate transfer devices which, in addition to sustaining value and income, can *reduce transfer taxes*. Each can offer additional employment incentives to family members, and each may be able to freeze the value of the clients' interest in the business, and still continue to provide him or her with rights to substantial income and voting power in the business affairs. However, as Appendix 16A describes, recent tax legislation has severely restricted their potential value, and the client should be advised to seek expert tax counsel when exploring these techniques.

---

[3]Deferred compensation is an agreement under which the employer agrees to pay the employee in the future for services rendered presently. Tax law permits the income tax to be similarly deferred. The professional athlete, a person with a brief but often lucrative career, is a frequent party to the deferred compensation contract.

Finally, if no amount of planning can be expected to prevent substantial post-withdrawal depreciation in the value and income derived from the business, the client might consider, while still active, selling or negotiating a contract for future sale of the business prior to the onset of that depreciation. The selling alternative will be explored in some detail shortly.

In summary, by planning early, the client can usually take one or more significant steps to forestall a large decline in the future income from, and the value of, interests that will pass to his or her chosen beneficiaries.

Transferring the Business Interest

As well as minimizing the decline in business value resulting from withdrawal from the firm, the client will want to choose when and to whom to transfer the business interest. Planning for the transfer will depend in large part on whether the client wishes to transfer the equity interest itself to a family member or whether the client intends to sell it to a nonrelated party and later transfer the sale proceeds to the chosen beneficiaries. The next two sections will probe these alternatives.

Transfer of an equity interest to a family member. Some clients will want to make a lifetime or deathtime transfer of some or all of the business interest itself to a particular family member who is willing and potentially able to take over its management. Many lifetime and deathtime transfer devices are available, and the most common ones are discussed next.

Lifetime transfer strategies. As mentioned earlier, to encourage the family member to adopt a long-term commitment and to prevent deterioration in business value and income, the client should consider starting early to develop a program to prepare the family member for eventual ownership and control. In addition to delegating increasing amounts of responsibility, the owner can offer incentives, such as the *lifetime gift* of an ownership interest in the business, possibly in the form of stock or stock options. The transfer can be outright, or it can be in trust, with the client and family member acting as cotrustees. A transfer into trust can promote a more orderly transition by enabling the client to monitor and develop the family member's interest, abilities, and commitment.

Instead of a completed gift, the client may wish to arrange a gift-leaseback, an installment sale,[4] a sale-leaseback, or a private annuity. In general, most aspects of gifts and other transfers of business interests can be analyzed in a manner similar to lifetime transfers of business interests that are not closely held. The reader is referred to Chapters 13 and 14 for greater detail.

Transfer devices at death. Instead of making a lifetime gift of the business interest to a family member, the client, to retain complete control, may prefer to delay and pass it on at death.[5] However, there are several drawbacks to making deathtime transfers of closely held business interests. First, estate *liquidity problems* may arise if a nonspouse survivor winds up owning a relatively illiquid asset having a substantial taxable value. For a discussion of several methods of handling liquidity problems, review the material on liquidity planning in Chapter 15.

Second, transfers at death of closely held business interests to *nonactive beneficiaries* who do not intend to sell out are often ill-advised if the beneficiaries have no desire to manage the firm in the future. By its nature, the closely held business requires active cooperation among its owners, cooperation which usually necessitates constant interaction. Unaware of the firm's precise manner of operation, uninvolved owners can often generate *uncertainty and friction* among the manager-owners and other employees, especially if they offer opinions as to how the business should be run.

---

[4]In fact, an installment sale can be a simple, inexpensive, and relatively tax-safe estate freezing alternative to the corporate recapitalization or the partnership capital freeze. The latter two are discussed in Appendix 16A.

[5]We might mention in passing that if a client's interest in "S corporation" stock is to be distributed at death to a trust, such as a bypass or a marital trust, that trust must be designed to qualify as a "Qualified Subchapter S Trust" in order not to jeopardize the corporation's Subchapter S status. Under §1361(d)(3), requirements include the naming of only one income beneficiary. Essentially, an S corporation is a corporation that is treated by federal income tax law as if it does not exist; income is conduited and taxed to the individual shareholders, rather than the corporation. Clients may be particularly interested in S corporation status as a result of TRA 86, which has resulted in a lower maximum marginal tax rate for individuals (33 percent) than for so-called C corporations (34 percent). For a discussion of planning with the S Corporation, see the Lang article cited at the end of the chapter.

Third, transferring business interests at death can create sizable *problems for surviving transferees* who do wish to sell out. In structuring the terms of the sale, survivors will not be able to take advantage of the client's knowledge and experience. The business may no longer be as productive, a fact that could substantially lower the bid price. The surviving owners may not be willing to pay the surviving beneficiaries a fair value for the client's interest, particularly if it is a minority interest. The survivors will have little bargaining power, in view of both their apparent need for cash and the illiquidity of the interest they hold. Additional problems may include finding a buyer and deciding on a reasonable asking price.

Finally, *disputes with the IRS* over the FET valuation of a closely held business are common and often result in litigation or settlement at higher than expected values.[6] A predeath sale avoids this prospect.

For these and many other practical reasons, the client would normally be well-advised not to delay gifting a business interest to a family member until after death.

Sale to a nonrelated party. Instead of transferring an ownership interest to the surviving beneficiaries, the client could arrange the sale of the business interest to a nonrelated party. Potential buyers include the client's key employees, and other firms, including competitors. In addition to eliminating potential friction, this alternative can result in the beneficiaries receiving other far more liquid assets that require less effort to generate income. The following material explores several aspects of the sale option, including timing and tax effects.

Timing. The business could be sold before or after the client withdraws from active management. *While the client is still active,* the entire firm could be sold outright, or some of its assets could be sold and then leased back to the firm. Or *prearrangements* could be made to sell the firm when the client withdraws at retirement, disability, or death. Actual timing of the sale will often depend largely on the personal, noneconomic preferences of the client. The material below discusses the economic and tax factors influencing that decision.

---

[6]And IRC §6660 imposes an FET penalty ranging from 10 to 30 percent of the underpayment for valuation understatements exceeding 50 percent.

In general, the greater the expected decline in the value of the firm resulting from the client's withdrawal, the greater the economic motive to sell it while it is still being actively run by the client. Value will fall most for single-owners, especially those offering professional services, such as physicians, accountants, and attorneys. Other closely held businesses, such as product-oriented firms and service firms with more than one owner, may be more able to retain their value after departure of the owner-client. Sale of the business interest prior to the owner's withdrawal will often bring a higher price since potential buyers can observe that the business is operating successfully under the direction of an active owner-client. Further, the client's firsthand appreciation of the firm's identity and its earnings potential will provide additional bargaining power during the negotiations. And if the sale is completed while the client is alive, the agreement may include an obligation of the new owner to retain the client as an "adviser" or "consultant," as a way of increasing the client's future income. Finally, sale of a closely held business prior to the client's death can avoid unsettling disputes with the IRS over the firm's actual FET fair market value.

In the alternative, the business interest could be sold at or *after the client's withdrawal* from the firm. If the sale is structured in advance to take effect at the client's disability or death, it is called a *business buyout agreement,* an arrangement to be discussed shortly.

Taxable gain. Selling the business for cash prior to the owner's death will give rise to the immediate recognition of a taxable gain, unless the transaction is an installment sale or other tax-deferred exchange. On the other hand, transferring the interest at death can eliminate most or all of the taxable gain because of the step-up basis that the interest will receive at death. However, at a maximum tax rate of 33 percent, the tax impact of a predeath sale for cash may turn out to be a reasonable price to pay to achieve substantial estate liquidity, in view of the high costs of alternate liquidity sources, such as insurance on the life of an elderly client.[7]

---

[7]Regarding tax rates, a substantial portion of the business gain should be *capital gain,* subject to a maximum 28 percent rate. In addition, most commentators expect the ordinary income-capital gain distinction to be resurrected by Congress,

Form of the transaction.   Sale of the business can take one of several forms. It can be for *present cash,* either to one or a few individuals, or to many individuals, as in a public offering. It can be in the form of an installment sale for *future cash,* with the client's taxable gain spread over the collection period. Or the sale can be for *stock,* in a tax-deferred exchange with a publicly held firm.[8]

A common planning device employed to sell a closely held business to one or a few individuals is the *business buyout,* or buy-sell agreement, in which the firm, one or more other owners, employees, or other parties contract in writing with the client in advance to purchase the client's interest in the business, usually at the client's death or disability. The buyout agreement offers many advantages, including future liquidity, a guaranteed market, and greater certainty over the selling price. Often, the purchase is funded with life and disability insurance. The business buyout is covered in the next major section.

If an unincorporated client insists on retaining the business for an indefinite period, consideration should be given to *incorporating.*[9] Incorporating will generate divisible shares of ownership which may be easier to transfer or liquidate when the need arises. Incorporating will also enhance continuity, since a corporation has an indefinite existence, one that might be more able to survive the client's departure. One disadvantage of incorporating is that almost any distribution of corporate property to the shareholders will be taxable as a dividend and thus subject to double taxation.[10]

---

which should enact an even lower maximum rate on capital gains, similar to the 20 percent maximum rate in effect prior to TRA 86.

[8]Of course, the tax on the deferred gain may be eliminated entirely by a step-up in basis if the new stock is transferred at death.

[9]For a discussion of whether or not to elect "S Corporation" status, see the article by Russell cited at the end of the chapter.

[10]Two exceptions are the §303 redemption to pay death taxes, covered in Chapter 15, and a complete redemption of the deceased shareholder's stock.

The Need for Early Planning

When should planning for closely held business interests begin? Planning should begin early, when the client is still active and in good health, for many reasons. First, the client can more clearly express specific estate planning *objectives* at this point, and the client's knowledge and expertise can provide professional planners with greater help in reaching these objectives. Second, the client will be able to take advantage of planning concepts that are available only to *healthy* clients, including relatively inexpensive life and disability insurance. Third, as implied earlier, if the business will eventually have to be sold, *careful planning* can eliminate the need for a sudden forced sale at a time when the business, having lost the client's services, is clearly less valuable.

With these general principles in mind, let's examine several of the specific legal arrangements to which we have been referring.

BUSINESS BUYOUT AGREEMENT

Earlier we learned that placing upon one's survivors the burden of selling the business after the client's death can create sizable problems. These problems can be either totally eliminated or at least greatly minimized with the client's careful preparation of a business buyout agreement. Executed by the client and one or more prospective purchasers, the buyout agreement obligates the other parties to purchase[11] the interest of the client upon the occurrence of specific future events, such as the client's death and, often, the onset of his or her permanent disability.[12]

---

[11] One type of contract, the cross-purchase plan, to be discussed soon, usually also obligates the client to purchase the interest of each of any other contracting owners at the latter's death or disability.

[12] In an attempt to accommodate buyout agreements, more and more insurance companies are offering disability policies promising to pay a *lump sum* at the onset of disability, rather than the usual income stream. Other, usually uninsurable events triggering the buyout could be retirement, divorce, insolvency of an owner, criminal activity, and loss of a professional license. However, without adequate funding, buyouts under such circumstances may be financially difficult to honor.

Determining the Selling Price

The buyout contract will provide for an objective method of determining the selling price, one usually defined in terms of a specific dollar amount or one determined either by an appraisal or by a formula.

If a *specific dollar amount* is stated, provision is normally made for periodic review so the owners can agree to revise the amount as conditions change. Without provision for a review, if, for example, the value of the business subsequently increased, the purchasing owners would receive a windfall at the expense of the selling owner.

If the purchase price is determined by *appraisal,* the terms usually specify that a qualified appraiser will determine the value of the business shortly before the sale date. The appraisal method has the advantage of ensuring that a current value will be used. However, since the value will not be known in advance, owners could have difficulty planning their estates. For example, their planners may be unable to predict the amount of their gross estate as accurately, making bypass and other tax planning less precise.

If the *formula* method of valuing the business interest is used, the terms ordinarily call for valuation to be a specified percentage of book value or a multiple of current earnings. A formula is more flexible than a specific amount since the derived selling price can vary with economic conditions. However, because a formula is less flexible than an appraisal, it may later turn out not to be reflective of current economic conditions. And again, planning will be more difficult with a formula, because the price is not fixed.[13]

However determined, a reasonable contract price provided in a properly drafted buyout contract will set the value of the business for estate tax purposes, if the following U.S. Treasury regulation requirements are met.[14]

---

[13]The discussion above applies more to buyout agreements between *nonfamily members,* where approximate fair market value may be an important goal. Family members executing a buyout contract, in an attempt to minimize the FET, may not mind setting a fixed price which may turn out to be significantly less than fair market value, provided that price sets the value for FET purposes, as described next.

[14]Some commentators seriously doubt that the appraisal method can ever be considered "reasonable."

1. The agreement must provide for a specifically determinable *price,* either in amount or by formula, which need not necessarily be fair market value.[15]
2. The surviving parties must be given at least the *option to buy* the deceased owner's interest.
3. The client is *not free to dispose of* the interest during lifetime at a price other than the one provided in the agreement.[16]
4. The agreement is a *bona fide business arrangement* and not a device to pass the client's shares "to the natural objects of his bounty" for less than full and adequate consideration.[17]

An agreement under which the surviving owner, a son, is obligated to purchase the client's $1 million business interest for $1,000 will not meet requirement Number 4. On the other hand, prices set between nonrelated owners are not usually subject to intense scrutiny if the transaction otherwise appears to be made at arm's length.

The two most common types of buyout agreements are distinguished by the identity of the contracting parties. The first type, called the *cross-purchase* agreement, provides that the owners, usually all of them, purchase the interest of a particular owner. The second, type, called the *entity* or *redemption* agreement, has the business itself purchase the interest of one or more owners.

Funding

How can a buyout agreement be funded? How can the owners ensure that when the triggering event of death or disability occurs, the surviving owners will possess sufficient funds to complete the purchase? To eliminate any uncertainty, most clients use *insur-*

---

[15]The advantage of avoiding valuation disputes with the IRS can be significant. Subsequent litigation over business value can be very expensive and unpredictable.

[16]Of all the terms and conditions of the buyout agreement, this one may be the most difficult for the client to swallow. It prevents him or her from selling out at a higher price during lifetime.

[17]A buyout agreement executed between family members will be very closely examined by the IRS. However, many below-market valuations have passed IRS scrutiny.

ance. The following material discusses insurance arrangements that fund a buyout.

The principles of the acquisition of insurance to fund a business buyout agreement will be influenced by the type of buyout chosen. Under an entity agreement, the firm purchases and acts as beneficiary of a policy on the life of each owner, each policy in the amount of money that that owner can expect to pay.[18] In a cross-purchase agreement, each contracting party purchases and acts as beneficiary of a policy on the life of each of the other contracting owners.

> EXAMPLE 16–1 Sol and Harry are equal shareholders of a corporation that has a net worth of $300,000. The men have executed an *entity* buyout arrangement. The corporation will own and be the beneficiary of two $150,000 face value policies, one on Sol's life and one on Harry's life. The men plan to review and update this amount periodically, as the value of the business changes.

> EXAMPLE 16–2 Facts essentially similar to those in Example 16-1, except that a *cross-purchase* plan is adopted. Sol will own and be beneficiary of a $150,000 policy on Harry's life, and Harry will own and be beneficiary of a $150,000 policy on Sol's life.

A cross-purchase arrangement funded with life insurance becomes unwieldy when the agreement includes numerous owners, because each contracting party will have to purchase a policy on the life of each contracting owner. For example, although only 2 policies would have to be purchased for a firm with two contracting owners, 6 policies would have to be purchased for three owners, and 12 policies for four owners. In general, the number of policies purchased under a cross-purchase plan would be $n(n-1)$, where n equals the number of contracting owners.[19] Under an entity plan, the business itself would simply purchase one policy on the life of

---

[18]The proceeds of corporate-owned life insurance on the life of a shareholder, although not includable in corporate gross income, will be subject to the TRA 86 corporate alternative minimum tax.

[19]Besides the problem of purchasing numerous policies, an income tax problem can arise under the *transfer for value rule*, if on the death of one corporate owner the surviving owners purchase the remaining decedent-owned policies. Tobisman, in an article cited at the end of the chapter, suggests a solution to both problems: the creation of a trust to acquire only one policy on each owner's life. However, there may be a §2042 risk.

each contracting owner. Thus, only *n* policies would have to be purchased.

There are several other methods of funding a buyout agreement. The parties can agree to an *installment sale* of the business interest. The installment sale can make the purchase of life insurance unnecessary and can be a source of periodic income to the client and the client's family. However, installment payments carry the risk that the purchasers will be unable to make the payments, a situation that can lead to disaster if the family again winds up owning a business that is now failing. Further, a decedent owner's family may dislike receiving deferred payments if the estate has the need for immediate liquidity to pay a large FET or other outlay incurred at death. Finally, an installment note fails to completely avoid a potentially stressful creditor–debtor relationship between the decedent's surviving family and the surviving business owners.

A third method of funding an entity arrangement is with the firm's own *cash or noncash assets*. This can also make life insurance unnecessary, but too often the business will not own sufficient distributable assets, particularly the amount of cash that may be needed to pay estate debts.

Income Tax Effects

One significant advantage to a corporate cross-purchase plan for a corporation is that the surviving purchasers will receive a step-up in the basis of the interest purchased. No corresponding step-up will ordinarily result from a purchase pursuant to an entity arrangement.

> EXAMPLE 16–3 Stan and Oliver, equal owners of a corporation, are trying to decide whether to arrange a cross-purchase or an entity-buyout plan. The adjusted basis of each of their stock in the business is $20,000. They project that the business will be worth $200,000 when the first owner dies. Thus, under either arrangement, the purchase price, which will be determined by appraisal, is expected to be $100,000, and the total value of the surviving owner's stock will equal $200,000, the total value of the business. However, the survivor's basis will be different, depending on which arrangement is selected. If a *cross-purchase* plan is chosen, the surviving shareholder's basis in his stock will increase to $120,000, which is $20,000, the basis of the preowned stock, plus $100,000, the purchase price of the decedent's stock. Alternatively, if an entity arrangement is chosen, the basis of

the surviving shareholder's stock will still be $20,000, because he will not have actually purchased any more shares.

In conclusion, the advantages of the business buyout agreement include liquidity, a guaranteed market, and greater certainty over the selling price. The preceding overview material merely highlights the general principles of a complex subject. A business buyout agreement should not be executed without the help of expert legal advice.

This chapter has focused on estate planning for owners of closely held business interests, featuring the business buyout agreement. For a discussion of two estate freezing business techniques, see Appendix 16A.

RECOMMENDED READING

ABBIN, BYRLE M. "Mitigating the Chernobyl Syndrome of Asset Value Freeze Meltdown." *University of Miami 21st Annual Estate Planning Institute,* 1987.

ADAMS, ROY M.; ALLAN J. SWEET; and SCOTT BIEBER. "Recapitalizations Revisited." *Trust & Estates,* August 1984, pp. 21–25.

AKRE, STEVEN H. "Buy-Sell Agreement Can Meet the Conflicting Needs of Parties When a Shareholder Departs." *Taxation for Accountants,* November 1985, pp. 308–15.

BLACKBURN, JOSEPH, and R. THOMAS BLACKBURN. "Estate Planning with Recapitalizations: Realistic Expectations." *Cumberland Law Review* 12 (1981), pp. 1–26.

BUCHANAN, JEFFREY D. and MALCOLM A. MOORE. "Valuation Readjustment Clauses: What's Possible?" *New York University 45th Annual Institute on Federal Taxation,* 1986.

CEZER, FREDERICK. "Planning for Retirement, Disability or Death of the Owner of a Small Business Interest." *Estate Planning,* January 1984, pp. 32–37.

CHECKOWAY, ALLAN B. "Insuring the Disability Hazard in the Small Closely Held Corporation." *Journal of American Society of CLU,* January 1985, pp. 44–51.

CHRISTENSEN, BURKE A. "Funding a Buy-Sell Agreement." *Trusts & Estates,* July 1984, pp. 57–59.

DRANEAS, JOHN H. "S Corp. or Partnership: Which Meet Clients' Business and Estate Planning Objectives?" *Estate Planning,* January–February 1986, pp. 30–36.

EASTLAND, S. STACY. "Use of Partnerships As an Alternative to Trusts in Estate

Planning." *Ninth Annual UCLA/CEB Estate Planning Institute, 1987*, California Continuing Education of the Bar.

FOWLER, ANNA C. "Planning for Recapitalizations in Light of Recent Administrative and Legislative Developments." *Taxes—The Tax Magazine*, March 1985, pp. 202–9.

GERSON, DAVID. "How Family Partnerships Can Be Used to Shift Income and Capital Appreciation." *Estate Planning*, March 1983, pp. 86–9.

GOLDSTEIN, ARNOLD S. *Business Transfers—An Accountant's and Attorney's Guide.* New York: John Wiley and Sons, 1986.

GORFINKLE, ROBERT A. "Many Choices Available to Owner Wishing to Transfer Business to Younger Family Members." *Estate Planning*, March 1986, pp. 98–103.

HARL, NEIL E. Handling Risk and Debt Resolution in Farm Estates in an Era of Declining Asset Values." *20th Annual University of Miami Estate Planning Institute*, 1986.

HARMON, MICHAEL R. "Should Partnership Interests Gifted in a Multi-Level Freeze Be Included in the Donor's Gross Estate under Section 2036?" *Taxes—The Tax Magazine*, November 1986, pp. 741–45.

HIGGINS, DAVID M. "Installment Sales, Private Annuities, Recapitalizations, and Charitable Lead Trusts." In *The Closely Held Business: Financial Planning for the Owners*, Practicing Law Institute, 1986, pp. 507–643.

KLINGER, LESLIE S. "Compensation Planning Techniques in Estate Planning for Owners of Closely Held Businesses." In *The Closely Held Business: Financial Planning for the Owners*, Practicing Law Institute, 1986, pp. 227–440.

KOWALSKI, LAWRENCE W., and BRENT B. NICHOLSON. "Buy-Sell Agreements Can Avoid Disputes As to the Value of a Minority Interest." *Taxation for Lawyers*, July–August 1984, pp. 56–60.

LANDSMAN, STEPHEN A. "Divorce Planning in the Closely Held Business Context." *Trust & Estates*, May 1984, pp. 41–6.

LANG, DUDLEY M., "Subchapter S in Estate Planning," presented at the 10th Annual UCLA/CEB Estate Planning Institute. Article published in *Estate Planning, 1988*, California Continuing Education of the Bar.

LEVUN, CHARLES R. "Partnerships—The Preferred Form of Doing Business after the Tax Reform Act of 1986." *Taxes—The Tax Magazine*, September 1987, pp. 600–03.

MATHIAS, BRUCE R. "How Buy-Sell Agreements Can Produce The Best Tax Results for Both the Partners and Partnership." *Taxation for Accountants*, October 1986, pp. 246–52.

MELGREN, ERIC. "No Mere Yeoman: Incorporating the Family Farm—Considerations and Consequences." (Pre-TRA 86 discussion.) *Washburn Law Journal* 24 (1985), pp. 546–73.

PETRIE, LINDA C. "Partnership Freezes: Determining When and How This Estate Planning Technique Should Be Used." *Taxation for Accountants*, April 1985, pp. 226–31.

PUDLIN, DAVID. "Maximizing the Income Shifting and Estate Planning Potentials of Family Partnerships." *Taxation for Accountants,* November 1985, pp. 286–91.

RUSSELL, WALTER J. "The New Impetus to Elect S Status Requires Prompt Review of Shareholder's Planning." *Estate Planning,* March 1987, pp. 98–102.

SAPER, MICHAEL S. "Strategies for Managing a Closely Held Business during the Period of Administration." *Estate Planning,* September 1985, pp.266–73.

SCHLENGER, JACQUES T.; STEPHEN L. OWEN; and JOHN B. WATKINS V. "Freezing the Value of Closely Held Business Interests." *Taxes—The Tax Magazine,* November 1983, pp. 719–42.

SCHMIDT, L. WILLIAM. "How to Plan a Recapitalization that Will Meet a Client's Needs and Withstand IRS Scrutiny." *Estate Planning,* September 1982, pp. 274–79.

TARLOW, EDWARD D., and ANDREW M. CURTIS. "How to Overcome Complications of Ownership Attribution for Closely Held Corporations." *Estate Planning,* September 1987, pp. 270–78.

THATER, WILLIAM, C. "Buy-Sell Agreements: A New Funding Vehicle," *CLU Journal,* September 1986, pp. 82–4. Discusses life insurance product whose face value can vary as much as 25 percent per year.

TOBISMAN, STEWART P. "Corporate Buy-Sell Agreements." In *The Closely Held Business: Financial Planning for the Owners,* Practicing Law Institute, 1986, pp. 7–137.

WOOD, HARLESTON R. "Estate Planning for the Professional Corporation Shareholder." *Journal of Taxation,* October 1987, pp. 222–26.

ZANKEL, JEFFREY A. "Choosing the best Method of Handling the Partnership of a Deceased Partner." *Estate Planning,* July 1986, pp. 198–202.

ZATT, MARK E. "Structuring Shareholder Buyout Agreements to Meet Business, Tax and Estate Planning Goals," *Taxation for Accountants,* September 1985, pp. 170–74.

QUESTIONS AND PROBLEMS

1. What could you say to client owning a closely held business who respects your advice but seems to be stubbornly refusing even to consider estate planning?

2. What unique estate planning problems are common to owners of closely held businesses?

3. Identify the objectives of estate planning for owners of closely held business interests.

4. One of your clients is worried about the possible future decline in the value of his firm upon his departure. Recommend ideas that can help minimize that decline.

5. (*a*) Describe the inter vivos methods of transferring business interests to a family member. (*b*) Under what conditions will such transfers be ill-advised?

6. (*a*) You are trying to encourage one of your clients to consider selling her business to a third party while she is still alive. Describe the benefits of this strategy. (*b*) Is planning for a sale after death always unwise? Why or why not?

7. Horne, a closely held business-owning client, requests your advice. He has a simple will, but has done no other planning. Neither his wife nor his children have any interest in continuing the business after his death. Horne does not wish to retire. Recommend alternative solutions for his consideration.

8. Describe the alternative methods for payment that can be arranged when a business is sold.

9. When should planning for closely held business interests begin? Why?

10. (*a*) Describe the essential characteristics of the typical business buyout agreement. (*b*) What are its advantages?

11. What is the tax advantage of including a method for determining the selling price in a properly drafted business buyout agreement?

12. (*a*) Describe the three methods by which a business buyout agreement can be funded. (*b*) Why might types of funding influence the choice of whether a cross-purchase or an entity plan is adopted?

13. Why might income taxation influence the choice of whether a cross-purchase or an entity plan is adopted?

14. McQueen is the surviving shareholder of the M-C Corporation. Forty years ago, he and Cross acquired the business, and just prior to Cross's death two years ago each had a $46,000 basis in their stock. McQueen purchased Cross's shares from the Cross estate for $180,000, pursuant to a buyout agreement. Presently, McQueen is thinking of selling the firm. Analyze the overall economic desirability of each of the following alternatives. Be sure to consider all of the objectives of planning for closely held business interests, including income taxation. Assume a rate of 33 percent for income tax and 50 percent for FET.

    a. McQueen presently sells his shares for $600,000 cash.

    b. McQueen presently exchanges his shares for 6,000 shares of the publicly traded XYZ Corporation, which is currently trading at $100 per share.

    c. McQueen continues to own the shares until death, which is actuarially expected to occur in five years. The shares, worth $600,000 at death, will be bequeathed to his wife, who we believe may be able to sell them for $400,000 cash.

    d. McQueen continues to own the shares until death (date of death value is still $600,000), at which time the KR Corporation, a competitor of M-C, purchases the shares from McQueen's estate for $700,000 cash, pursuant to a buyout agreement, executed presently.

    e. Can you recommend any alternative methods of disposition? (Hint: the M-C Corporation currently has an ESOP.)

Freezing Business Wealth with the Corporate Recapitalization and the Partnership Capital Freeze: An Uncertain Future

OVERVIEW

The world contains more than just a few outstandingly successful owners of closely held corporations. Some have amassed a degree of wealth that they themselves consider to be more than adequate to provide for their income and capital needs for the rest of their lives. To them, the prospect of acquiring more property may be relatively unimportant. Few of them, however, look forward to relinquishing control of their business interests. They may be having too much fun, or they may have been unable as yet to sufficiently groom a younger-generation family member.

Prior to the Revenue Act of 1987, highly successful entrepreneurs had several relatively safe, although complicated methods of effecting a transfer of most or all of their business interest to a younger generation without much transfer tax. The most common methods are called the corporate recapitalization and the partnership capital freeze. Through a reorganization of the firm's capital accounts, these techniques enabled the owner to retain complete voting control of the firm and continue to receive the same amount of income from the firm, yet freeze future transfer taxes by arranging for other family members to benefit from a large part of the future appreciation of the business.

By enacting Section 2036(c), in the Revenue Act of 1987, the federal government severely restricted the use of these and other estate freezing devices. This brief appendix will summarize how these techniques were usually structured, how they had succeeded in freezing business wealth, and how §2036(c) is currently influencing planning in this area.

The Corporate Recapitalization

Recapitalizations prior to §2036(c). Prior to the new act, corporate recapitalizations (recaps) were structured in varying manners. A commonly used variation has the following characteristics: Prior to the recap, the client possessed controlling interest in the firm through the ownership of the voting common stock. After the recap, the client will usually own a combination of some voting shares, usually common, and nonvoting preferred shares, which are entitled to a substantial dividend. The younger-generation family members to whom the client wishes to transfer future wealth are issued nonvoting common shares and, if the client wishes, some voting shares. In the following three examples, assume the date to be prior to December 18, 1987.

EXAMPLE 16A–1 Alfred is sole owner of a highly successful computer software corporation, owning all 1,000 shares of common stock, valued at $2,000 per share. Presently, this is the only class of stock. This year, the company will earn a net income of $260,000. Within the next six months, the company expects to be releasing a revolutionary new software package, one that can triple the company's sales and net worth. Alfred is divorced and has two children, Kyle and Maude. Kyle, age 32, has worked for the firm for 10 years and shows great promise to take over when Alfred departs. Maude, age 31, is a tenured biology professor and has never been interested in working for the company. At his death, Alfred wishes to leave his entire estate to the children in approximately equal shares.

A recapitalization of the firm is undertaken. In exchange for Alfred's 1,000 shares of common stock, the corporation issues three classes of new stock:

1. 20,000 shares of nonvoting, 13 percent *preferred stock,* all to Alfred. The stock is noncumulative and has a par value of $100 per share.

2. 480 shares of nonvoting common stock, one half to Kyle and one half to Maude.

3. 20 shares of voting common stock, all to Alfred.

Both types of common stock will share, pro rata, in any income available after payment of the preferred dividend.

> EXAMPLE 16A–2 Continuing the facts in Example 16A–1, assume that Alfred will die in 10 years when the business is worth $6 million. The value of Alfred's business interest included in his gross estate is expected to be $2,160,000. This is the sum of $2 million (the value of the preferred stock) plus $160,000 (the value of the 20 shares of voting common), derived in the following manner: Of the $6 million market-value capitalization, since the preferred stock is still expected to be worth $2 million at Alfred's death, the total value of the common shares will be worth $4 million, or $8,000 per share. Thus, nearly all of Alfred's interest in the firm will be frozen at its value as of the date of recapitalization, and nearly the entire postrecapitalization appreciation will inure to Kyle and Maude free of transfer tax.

> EXAMPLE 16A–3 In Example 16A–2 instead of passing the voting common shares at his death, Alfred could make periodic lifetime gifts of them to Kyle in amounts not exceeding the annual gift tax exclusion. In this way, Alfred would have both given additional incentive to Kyle to remain with the firm and, at the same time, reduced even further the value of the business interest taxable in his estate at his death.

The ideal recap was intended to have the following tax-related benefits:

1. No taxation to the corporation arising from the recap.
2. No taxable income to the client upon receipt of the new shares.
3. No taxable gift by the client at the time of the recap.
4. At death, the amount included in the client's estate tax base attributable to the firm will approximately equal the value of the client's interest in the business at the date of the recap.

Under item 3, a taxable gift can arise either because the younger-generation transferees are deemed to have initially received stock valued at an amount greater than the amount of the annual exclusion, or because the client is deemed to be making an annual gift to them of some portion of the annual appreciation in the common stock.

Even prior to the passage of §2036(c), one or more of these benefits could have been lost with an improperly structured recap. In fact, even a state-of-the-art recap may not have been able to achieve all of them in view of the zeal with which the IRS had been attacking them, especially with regard to the taxable gift issues to be discussed next.[1]

The IRS takes the position that the value of the shares transferred to the former nonowners cannot possibly equal zero because the value of the preferred shares cannot be made to equil the total value of the firm. Consequently, some positive value will remain in the common stock, value which is therefore transferred as a taxable gift to the other family members. Referring to Example 16A–2, if the preferred stock is actually determined to be worth $1.6 million, rather than $2 million, the 500 shares of common stock will have a total fair market value of $400,000. Thus, if each share is worth $8000, Alfred will be deemed to have made a gift of $384,000.

The tragedy of this determination is that the entire fair market value of the firm at Alfred's death may be included in his gross estate, because he may be deemed to have made a §2036(a) transfer; that is, a transfer for less than full and adequate consideration in which he had retained either a voting-control interest or a dividend income interest for life. Thus, the gift consequence is one that planners take careful precautions to avoid, especially by securing an accurate appraisal of the value of the preferred shares so as to be sure that their value is made equal or nearly equal to the total value of the firm.[2]

---

[1]Another drawback to the recap is that a *decline* in business value can result in an *inflated,* rather than a frozen, client gross estate. See the Harl article cited at the end of Chapter 16.

[2]As we have seen, the §2036 risk also endangers the private annuity and the sale of a remainder interest (and certain installment sales). For some protection, several commentators have suggested incorporating as a provision in the transaction a "valuation readjustment" or "savings"-type clause. One such clause would require the purchaser to pay additional consideration if the IRS determines that a gift had been made. The IRS has attacked these clauses, arguing that (1), as completed gifts, the transactions can't be altered, and (2) they are contrary to

Impact of Section 2036(c). New section 2036(c) of the Internal Revenue Code will strongly discourage the use of recaps.[3] Ones of the type illustrated in the examples above that have been created after December 17, 1987, will clearly subject the value of the stock transferred to inclusion in the transferor's gross estate at death, for the following reasons. Prior to the transfer, the client owned a "substantial" interest in the "enterprise." The client transferred "property having a disproportionately large share of the potential appreciation," since the future appreciation in the value of the corporation will be attributed to the transferred stock. Finally, the client retained "a disproportionately large share in the income of, or rights in, the enterprise" by receiving voting preferred shares out of the transaction.

It is in this setting that planners must decide whether to totally refrain from establishing recaps or to recommend to clients recaps that are modified to conform to the new law. The following describes the possible solutions being offered by some planners.

Some planners take a very pessimistic view of the impact of §2036(c), believing that it will be applied to all recaps (and to sales of remainder interests, private annuities and installment sales as well!). Others have more hope for saving the recap. The following briefly describes the possible solutions being offered by some planners.

Some commentators are suggesting a recap using two classes of common stock but *no preferred*. They reason that §2036(c) should not apply, since a "disproportionately large share of the potential appreciation" is not transferred; the share of the potential appreciation inherent in both the transferred and the retained interests is the same, because both the client and his other children will own essentially the same type of asset, each of which bear a porportionate share of the total appreciation.

The above "common on common" type of recap will not be able to immediately freeze as much of the business value as the old

---

public policy. The case law is scant, but there is reason to believe that in some situations, the IRS would lose. For a discussion, see the Buchanan–Moore paper cited at the end of Chapter 16.

[3]At this point, the reader is strongly urged to review the brief description of §2036(c) in Chapter 9.

preferred stock recap. Thus, some planners recommend a program of lifetime annual exclusion *gifts* of the stock to further help, for the reasons mentioned in Chapter 13. In addition, the client can undertake an immediate *installment sale* of some of the stock to freeze more of the value.

A technique being recommended to salvage a tainted preferred stock recap is to have the client *dispose* of the retained interest prior to death, as a way of avoiding the impact of §2036(c). However, retained interests must be disposed of sooner than three years before death, under §2036(c)(4). Further, disposition by transferring the interest to the client's spouse will not likely avoid §2036, because under §2036(c)(3)(C), an individual and the spouse will be treated as one person.

Quite similar to disposition, some planners are recommending a preferred stock recap under which the preferred is retained by the client only for a *fixed period,* such as ten years. The transfer tax effects are quite similar to the grantor retained income trust, discussed in Chapter 14. If the client dies before the end of the period, §2036(c) will apply. On the other hand, if the client survives the period, the section will not apply because at death the client had not retained any benefits from or rights to the stock.

From the above, we can see that the recap is an endangered species, one that will be undertaken only for the most aggressive tax avoiding clients. At this point the future application of §2036(c) is quite uncertain; only time will tell how pervasive its impact will be.

The Partnership Capital Freeze

Prior to the passage of §2036(c), it was possible to reorganize an unincorporated firm to achieve the same results as the estate-freezing recap. Conceptually similar to the recap, under the partnership capital freeze two classes of partnership interests were created, one for the client and one for the younger family members. The client's interest could similarly be frozen at its present value, with future appreciation in the business accruing to the other share. As with the recap, the partnership capital freeze dealt in a complex, rapidly changing area of tax law, subject to frequent IRS attack. Experts believe that §2036(c) has all but totally destroyed its estate-freezing effectiveness.

RECOMMENDED READING

BETTIGOLE, BRUCE J. "Use of Estate Freeze Severely Restricted by Revenue Act of 1987," *Journal of Taxation,* March 1988, pp. 132–34.

KINYON, RICHARD S. "Provisions in the Revenue Act of 1987 Affecting Estate Planning and Administration," *Estate Planning & California Probate Reporter,* California Continuing Education of the Bar, February 1988, pp. 81–85.

PLUTCHOK, Y. JONATHAN "Recaptured Recaps," *Financial Planning,* April 1988, pp. 101–3.

—17——

Miscellaneous Lifetime Planning

OVERVIEW

In the past seven chapters, we have covered five major lifetime planning topics: avoiding probate, marital deduction and bypass planning, lifetime transfers, liquidity planning and planning for closely held business interests. This chapter will explore a number of more narrow topics, many of which are interrelated only because they influence the preparation of a client's will or trust. Examples include those provisions that provide for the care of minor children, select the executor and trustee, and deal with survival clauses and the allocation of death taxes. A final section will cover planning for the client's own incapacity, and includes a discussion of the durable power of attorney.

WILL AND TRUST PLANNING

By now the reader should agree that the will and the trust are the major documents used in estate planning. Both have been referred to in every chapter so far, especially those in Part 3 outlining the techniques of planning. The material below describes several other types of planning frequently undertaken in drafting the will and the trust. In reading this material, the reader is urged to refer back to the documents illustrated in Exhibits 3-1, 3-2 and 3-3, which detail their construction.

Planning for the Care of Family Members: An Introduction

The occurrence of both disability and death of the client can require the making of important decisions as to how to care for affected family members who are unable to care for themselves. Disability of the client may necessitate the selection of others to care for the client and the client's property, and death of the surviving client-parent of a minor child will require selection of one or more persons to care for that orphaned child. In either case, prior planning can enable the selection process to reflect the wishes of the client, whose direct input can better ensure that the proper care will be provided. Planning for care of minor orphaned children will be discussed in the next section. Planning for the disabled client's care will be surveyed at the end of the chapter. We begin, however, with a discussion of factors common to both.

Planning for the care of both the incapacitated client and the orphaned child have three factors in common. First, by not making prearrangements, clients force their local court to assume greater responsibility in arranging for this care. Without help from the client, the court, in its attempt to act in the dependent's best interest, must rely on secondhand information obtained from other family members and from friends. To best ensure that the court's decisions reflect his or her wishes, the client should plan to express those wishes in writing, before it is too late.

Second, for both minors and incapacitated adults, the law distinguishes two types of care: care of the person and care of the property. An individual legally responsible for care of the *person* is charged with providing everyday physical and psychological needs. An individual legally responsible for care of the *property* of a minor or incapacitated person is charged with safeguarding, investing, and expending that person's wealth.

Third, because care of the person and care of the property entail such dissimilar responsibilities, different parties will often be nominated and appointed to perform each, as we shall see.

Planning for the Care of the Client's Minor Children

As we have said, planning for the client's incapacity will be discussed later in the chapter. The material below explores the prearrangements that can be undertaken to provide care for the client's minor children in the event that both parents die prematurely.

Planning for the minor's personal care: The parental guardian. In the typical household, the married parents of a child are the *natural* and *legal guardians* of their children. Thus, upon the death of one parent, the other parent will routinely carry on as sole guardian. Only in the most unusual situations will the courts act to deny this right. On the other hand, when a minor child survives the death of *both* parents, the state must select a successor parental guardian. The selection process typically culminates in an order by a judge of the probate or similar court after a noticed hearing. The court will usually appoint the person nominated in the parent's will, unless the nominee is unwilling or unable to perform. If the will contains no nomination, the court must examine the family situation more carefully, relying on other information, including a list of willing friends and relatives, as well as the expressed preferences of any older, more mature minor. Since the court's main criterion is the best interests of the child, it seeks to appoint that person who is best capable of providing the minor with such basics as food, clothing, shelter, medical care, and schooling, as well as providing psychological well-being, love, and attention.

Since the court's selection of a guardian may not reflect the parent's unexpressed wishes, the client-parent should clearly assert that preference by nominating a person guardian in the will. Considering the stakes, it can be the most important estate planning action made by young parents.

Whom should the client nominate? An ideal parental guardian will possess the following qualities:

1. The *integrity, maturity, physical stamina,* and *experience* needed to be a permanent parent.
2. A strong *concern* for the minor's welfare.
3. The ability to provide a *stable personal environment* conducive to raising a child in a manner consistent with the client's particular moral, religious, social, and financial situation.

Of course, these attributes are ideals; the usual client will have difficulty identifying more than one or two capable and willing nominees, neither of whom will probably be ideal. But however imperfect, the nomination greatly reduces the risk of an undesired appointment. And nominating more than one parental guardian will allow for an alternate/successor guardian who will serve in the event that the preferred person named is unwilling or unable to serve or continue to serve.

Once the choice is made, the client should be encouraged to periodically review the nomination in light of both the minor's changing needs and the nominee's changing personal and financial situation.

Planning for the minor's financial care. Anticipating the possibility that their spouse will not survive them, clients will usually want to provide for adequate financial care for their orphaned minor children. They will ordinarily want to transfer all or most of their probate and nonprobate property for the benefit of the children. Common nonprobate sources of property for the children include life insurance proceeds, survivorship under joint tenancy arrangements, trust property, and gifts from others.

While most states allow a minor to receive outright a modest amount of property, larger amounts will be required to be turned over to a fiduciary who is legally responsible for their care and custody. What legally acceptable fiduciary arrangements are available? While the law recognizes parental guardianships as the only legal arrangement for the minor's *personal* care, it recognizes several arrangements for the minor's *financial* care. The client may choose a financial guardianship, a trust, or a custodianship under the Uniform Gift to Minors Act. Each is surveyed briefly.

Financial guardianship. A financial guardian, also called an estate guardian, is typically appointed by the court in a manner similar to the procedures used for appointment of a parental guardian. Usually required to file a formal accounting with the court every one or two years, the financial guardian must obtain written permission from the court to undertake nonroutine transactions, such as the sale of real property.[1]

In general, the *criteria* for selecting a financial guardian are radically different from those used in selecting a parental guardian. As we have mentioned, while the primary consideration in selecting the parental guardian is parental ability, the primary focus in selecting the estate guardian is skill in financial management. Since skill in financial management is also the primary criterion used to

---

[1]Reflecting the general trend in probate reform, some states have enacted streamlined guardianship proceedings to minimize court involvement.

select a trustee, we shall defer further discussion of its attributes to the section on selecting the trustee.

Trust for the minor. Instead of a financial guardian, a trustee can be chosen to manage the client's property left for the benefit of a minor child. The trust can be created and funded during the client's life. Or it can be created by the client's will and funded with probate and nonprobate property.

The trust has several advantages over the financial guardianship. First, it is a *private* arrangement, not usually subject to court supervision and control.[2] Second, the trust offers great *flexibility*; the client can tailor it to his or her personal wishes. For example, while guardianship property usually must be surrendered outright to the minor upon reaching the age of majority, trust property can easily be retained in trust until any date after that age, one specified by the client. Further, while a separate guardianship must usually be established for each minor, a single trust can have multiple beneficiaries, as in the case of the family pot trust, described later in the chapter. Also, the trust is more flexible because it can include such things as a spendthrift provision, a protective clause to be further described later. Financial guardianships are not usually established with such a refinement.

A third advantage of the trust over the financial guardianship rests on the fact that the statutory and case law of trusts is much more well defined. Thus, a trustee will often feel less uncertain than a guardian about the potential adverse consequences of a particular fiduciary act or decision.

Financial guardianships usually arise by default when the client dies having done no planning. Because of its drawbacks, the financial guardianship is rarely preferred over a trust.

Custodianship under the Uniform Gifts to Minors Act. Finally, the client may wish to leave property to a custodian for the benefit of a minor child under the Uniform Gifts to Minors Act in the manner described in Chapter 13. Like trusts, custodianships offer far greater privacy than financial guardianships, since they are not subject to court supervision. However, like guardianships, custodianships are quite inflexible because they are usually controlled

---

[2]However some states require ongoing probate court supervision of testamentary trusts after the trustor's death. But the trend has been to eliminate this requirement.

by statute. For example, in most states property held by the custodian must be turned over to the minor upon reaching age 21. Also, most states limit the kinds of property that can be transferred under the Uniform Act.

Executor

As we have said, the executor is responsible for representing and managing a decedent's probate estate. Below, we examine factors influencing both the selection of an executor and the choice of the executor's powers.

Selection. Whom should the client consider in selecting an executor? An ideal executor will possess the following qualities:

1. *Longevity,* that is, the likelihood of being able to serve after the death of the client, perhaps many years hence.
2. *Skill in managing* legal and financial affairs.
3. *Familiarity* with the testator's estate and the testator's wishes.
4. Strong *integrity,* coupled with *loyalty* to the testator and the testator's family.

Let us use these criteria to evaluate the types of potential candidates who are normally available to serve.

Nominating a *family member* or *friend* to be executor can often reduce administration costs paid to nonbeneficiaries. And family members and friends usually possess a strong degree of familiarity and loyalty. However, they often have only modest legal and financial skills. And while they can normally delegate most of their work to the estate attorney, they cannot delegate their legal responsibility, since the executor cannot normally avoid personal liability for many types of mistakes made in administration. Nonetheless, in smaller estates most mistakes are not very costly, and, in general, nominating as executor the spouse, an adult child, or a good friend makes the best sense.

The testator may prefer to select a *corporate executor* such as a bank trust department. Reasons include inability to find and select a responsible family member or friend, conflict among family members, or a complex estate. Banks usually do a technically satisfactory job in managing estate assets. However, because they are usually unfamiliar with the decedent's family, they cannot offer much of a personal touch in the administration process. For example, they may have difficulty deciding whom should be given minor personal effects of which the decedent made no specific mention.

Should an *attorney,* such as the testator's attorney, be considered for nomination as executor? Probate attorneys will usually do a satisfactory job in managing assets during the probate period, because they commonly possess a substantial degree of expertise acquired over the years by doing the work delegated by their executor-clients. Nomination of the testator's attorney, however, may increase the risk of a will contest. Dissatisfied with the will provisions, an aspiring beneficiary might allege that the nomination is further evidence that the testator was subject to "undue influence" by overpersuasion and intimidation, and might petition that the will not be admitted to probate.[3] In addition, nominating an attorney will not usually reduce administration costs, since most attorney-executors will hire other attorneys to represent the estate. In general, caution should be exercised when considering the nomination of an attorney.

Finally, acting as an executor can create potential conflicts of interest for the attorney in the areas of drafting, confidentiality, and the duty to deal impartially with beneficiaries. For example, an attorney who anticipates becoming a fiduciary may be tempted to insert in the client's document an unconventional, self-serving exculpation (hold harmless) clause for all simple negligence acts.[4]

Where possible, the testator should also nominate an *alternate* or "backstop" executor to serve in case the primary nominee is unwilling or unable to serve. Many clients nominate a bank as the alternate because they are confident that a corporate executor will always be available to serve.

Regardless of the choice of executor, the testator should always consult with the nominees to get their consent and should periodically review the choice in light of changing circumstances.

---

[3]But it would be well to keep in mind that successful will contests are rare.

[4]For an example of a hold harmless clause in a trust exculpating the attorney-trustee for acts or omissions other than intentional breaches of trust, gross negligence, bad faith, or reckless indifference, etc., see the Alvarez article cited at the end of the chapter.

Executor's powers. What powers should be explicitly granted to an executor? Most simple wills either do not delineate the powers of the executor, or they list just a few powers. The will in Exhibit 3-1 explicitly grants to the executor the powers to distribute principal and income; to sell, lease, mortgage, pledge, assign, invest, and reinvest estate property; and to operate a business.

When a will is silent regarding a specific proposed action of the executor, we look for authority first to the provisions of the state's probate code, which usually delineates many executor's powers. If nothing relevant is found in the probate code, the executor may feel obliged to request permission from the probate court. For example, in the absence of explicit permission in the will, executors in many states must seek formal written permission to be able to sell real property. Thus, specifying powers explicitly in the will can offer the executor greater *flexibility* by minimizing unnecessary delays in probate. And enumerating powers in the will can reveal more to the survivors about the testator's *wishes,* especially with regard to the degree of court supervision originally envisioned by the testator.

Allocation of Death Taxes

Which beneficiaries should bear the burden of death taxes? All of them, or only some? If only some, which ones? If all, should the taxes be shared equally or proportionately? A number of important considerations in determining the allocation of death taxes are examined next.

In the absence of a provision in the will, both federal and state law determine which beneficiaries will share the cost of death taxes. Federal law controls the burden on a few types of assets. The Internal Revenue Code provides that the FET on life insurance, QTIP property and property subject to a general power of appointment is payable out of those assets. Under state law, with regard to other assets owned by the decedent, an old common law rule provides that death taxes are paid from the residuary probate estate. However, most states have changed this rule by enacting a type of *equitable apportionment statute,* which spreads the tax burden more or less proportionately among *all* of the beneficiaries receiving the taxed assets. Thus, even recipients of nonprobate assets, such as property held by the decedent in joint ownership, would owe a portion of the tax.

The client can override federal and state law by expressly including a *tax clause* in the will. Most attorneys routinely draft wills containing a tax clause that directs all taxes to be paid out of the residuary estate. The trust-will in Exhibit 3–3 contains such a provision. Payment of taxes from the residue can speed up the probate process by making it unnecessary to obtain reimbursement from nonresiduary and nonprobate beneficiaries. In addition, recipients of specific bequests of illiquid assets won't be forced to search for the required cash. And paying the taxes out of the residue may be especially helpful if the will specifically bequeathes certain assets over which the testator does not wish the tax burden to fall. For example, if the testator leaves only one relatively illiquid asset, such as a piano, to a particular beneficiary, should that person have to pay any transfer taxes attributable to it? Most clients would probably say no, unless the beneficiary is known to have considerable wealth or at least access to a reasonable amount of discretionary liquid assets.

Yet there are numerous situations where a residuary-type tax clause will conflict with the testator's wishes. For example, the testator may specifically bequeath an asset such as a closely held business that comprises a very large portion of the entire estate. If the tax clause allocates the entire tax burden to the residue, the effect may be to radically reduce the total of net after-tax residuary gifts.

> EXAMPLE 17–1 Livingston's estate consists of a closely held business currently worth $800,000 and other assets worth $200,000. The will bequeaths the business to Livingston's son and the residue to a brother. If the will provides that the tax is to be paid from the residue, the brother's after-tax bequest will be reduced to less than $50,000. And if the value of the business increased by about 10 percent before death, the brother's after-tax bequest could be reduced to zero. On the other hand, if the tax clause apportioned the death tax, the value of the brother's after-tax bequest will be substantially larger.

Further, many clients view their residuary legatees as the primary "objects of their bounty"; such clients often want them to receive as much wealth as possible. An apportionment-type tax clause would more closely meet this objective.[5]

---

[5]Another consideration is the effect of the tax allocation upon a bypass plan that provides for determination of the amount of the marital deduction by formula.

Whatever the provisions of state law, the client would be well-advised to consider including a desired tax clause in the will for greater certainty. Determining the best tax clause can be a difficult job, particularly when there are several beneficiaries. An undesired provision can mean unnecessary delay or a pattern of property distribution radically different from that envisioned by the testator. Yet rarely will the courts override the provisions of a will or the applicable statute to prevent an undesired result. Consequently, the client should consider the alternatives carefully.

Survival Clauses

The phrase "If A survives me by X days, I give her . . ." is a survival clause and is commonly included in wills, partly to avoid the consequences of lapsation and difficulties encountered when the intended beneficiary survives the decedent by only a short period.

Lapsation occurs when a beneficiary named in a will fails to survive the testator. Each state's probate code contains sections which determine, in the absence of a provision in the will, to whom a lapsed testamentary bequest will pass. A very common type of "antilapse statute," as they are called, provides that bequests to one of the testator's predeceased blood relatives will instead pass to that relative's surviving issue.

> EXAMPLE 17–2 Rudolph died recently, and his will simply left his car to his predeceased brother, Randall, and the residue of his estate to his friend James. The bequest will lapse. Due to the state's particular antilapse statute, the lapsed bequest will pass to Randall's only son, Jeremy.

If the state has *no antilapse statute,* or if the particular statute does not apply, perhaps because the lapsed bequest was to a nonrelated beneficiary, then a lapsed nonresiduary bequest will ordinarily pass to the residuary beneficiary.

> EXAMPLE 17–3 In Example 17-2, if the car was left to Rudolph's predeceased *friend* Josef instead of Randall, because that particular state's antilapse statute applies only to relatives, the car will pass to James, the residuary beneficiary.

To minimize FET, such plans invariably incorporate an allocation clause placing the burden of the tax on the property that is not subject to the estate tax.

This result is unfortunate if the testator actually wished to leave the property to the beneficiary's survivors, an example of which might be a son- or daughter-in-law, such as the dearly loved ex-spouse of the testator's child who is raising the testator's grandchild.

If a *residuary gift lapses* in the absence of a specific antilapse statute provision, the property will pass by intestate succession.

> EXAMPLE 17–4 In Example 17-3, if James had also predeceased Rudolph, the residuary bequest will lapse, and the car, as well as the rest of the estate, will pass in accordance with that state's intestacy laws.

Lapsation can usually be avoided with a *survival clause* designating an alternate taker.

> EXAMPLE 17–5 Continuing the series of examples above, if Rudolph's will alternatively left the car to Isaac "in the event that Randall fails to survive me," and Isaac survives Rudolph, then Isaac, the alternate taker, will receive the car.

A survival clause may require survival for some period beyond the testator's death. An example would be the phrase, "if she survives me by 30 days."[6] Extending the survivorship requirement reduces the likelihood that bequeathed property will be subject to two successive probates in situations when the beneficiary dies shortly after the decedent.

> EXAMPLE 17–6 In Example 17-2, if Randall survived Rudolph by only one month, the car will still pass to Randall and also be subject to administration in his estate. If, instead, Rudolph's will bequeathed the car to Randall "if he survives me by six months, otherwise to Isaac," then Isaac will receive the car, which will be subject to administration only in Rudolph's estate.

---

[6]However, there may be an estate tax reason for providing that in a common accident the *beneficiary* will be presumed to have survived the testator. For example, to achieve *estate equalization* (see Chapter 11) in a common accident situation, the wealthier spouse (W) can be specified to have predeceased the less wealthy spouse (L). In that event, W's estate will receive a marital deduction, reducing the taxable estate, while L's gross estate will increase by the amount of the bequest. And to prevent property from passing to L's named beneficiaries, W's bequest can be structured to qualify as a QTIP transfer. For greater detail, see the Clary–Anderson article cited at the end of the chapter.

How long should the survival period be? Making it at least several months in duration will provide for the event which, relatively speaking, probably occurs most frequently: death of the decedent and the intended beneficiary in a common accident. However, specifying too long a survival period can delay distribution of estate assets since the executor will be required to wait that long to determine whether or not the named beneficiary in fact survived that period. Further, a marital bequest will not qualify for the marital deduction if it is contingent on the spouse's surviving the decedent by greater than six months.[7]

Many planners use a survival period of about one month for tangible personal property and between four and six months for other property. The shorter period for tangible personal property reflects the usual testator's desire to permit the surviving beneficiary to be able to use such property almost immediately, if even for only a short while, to avoid storage and other additional costs.

Selection of the Trustee

Earlier we saw that a good executor is characterized by longevity, skill in managing, familiarity, integrity, and loyalty. In general, these traits also apply to selecting a trustee, except that greater weight is accorded to skill in financial management. Since the trustee's job can turn out to be a long-term responsibility, the trustee's ability to manage and invest property over a long period becomes a major criterion.[8] As in the case of the executor, potential nominees include family members, friends, the family attorney, and a corporate fiduciary.

Selecting a *family member* or *friend* to be trustee can minimize costs, maximize administrative speed, and may ensure a personal

---

[7]Bypass planning also influences the decision whether or not to include a survival clause. One rule of thumb used is to insert a survival requirement in the wills or trusts of both spouses unless their estates are substantially unequal in amount. In that case use it only in the document of the less wealthy spouse. The basic rationale is twofold: first, to take advantage of both unified credits, where practical; second, to avoid unnecessarily loading up a wealthier S2's gross estate.

[8]For a brief examination of the history of the "prudent person rule" and its inconsistency with current trustee investment management practices in the face of inflation and modern portfolio theory, see the Cheris article cited at the end of the chapter.

relationship with the survivors. But it can also result in mismanagement, since few family members have much experience in investing, accounting for, and maintaining an investment portfolio, all critical responsibilities of the trustee. In addition, family conflicts can arise. For example, nominating the client's children of a former marriage to be trustees of a QTIP trust can create a difficult situation for S2, the client's second and surviving spouse.

Selecting an *attorney* to be trustee can create the same minor risk of a will contest as in nominating an attorney to be executor. In addition, since management of the trust may become a long-term assignment, the client should determine whether the attorney has the time and expertise required to perform effectively. By training and experience, most attorneys are not investment managers.

Selecting a *corporate trustee,* such as a bank, will increase the likelihood that an impartial, technically satisfactory job will be performed. The corporate trustee, however, is often relatively expensive, excessively conservative in asset management, and unable to establish a personal relationship with the beneficiaries.

As in nominating an executor, the client should always nominate an alternate-successor trustee and should always consult with the intended trustee to ensure that the job would be accepted. Many bank trust departments set minimum asset amounts below which they will not accept, which creates the possibility that they may refuse to manage small trusts.[9]

Determining the Age of Outright Distribution from a Trust

All commonly used trusts specify a time when the corpus will be distributed outright to the beneficiaries. Determining in advance the best time can be difficult for a client with minor children, because the client cannot accurately predict their rates of future maturation.[10] The trust-will found in Exhibit 3–3 uses age 21 as the basic reference for distribution. Thus, if the client dies leaving orphan minor children, the property will remain in trust. Then, when

---

[9]Minimum amounts can range between $50,000 and $350,000, depending upon the bank.

[10]For an interesting discussion of alternative distribution strategies for presently immature children, see the Gallo article cited at the end of the chapter.

the youngest of the client's children reaches age 21, the assets will be divided into equal shares, with one share being distributed outright, at that time, to each child.[11]

A client may prefer to delay distribution of corpus to a later age. Others prefer staggered ages. For example, the client may choose age 30, or may select multiple ages, such as one third distributed at age 21, one third at age 25, and one third at age 30. Other clients may prefer to delay distribution to beneficiaries until age 50 or so, by which time they will have fully established their own lives. Finally, a few clients may prefer to leave the bulk of their wealth to charity.

For clients with more than one child, a separate trust can be established for each child, or a single trust can include all children. Creating a separate trust for each child adds flexibility but increases administration costs. In addition, separate trusts may be considered unfair to the younger children for the following reason. If the client lives, expenses in raising all children will ordinarily come from family property in general, not just from one "share" reserved for each child. Thus, expenses to raise even the youngest child will come from what could be called the family "pot" of wealth. On the other hand, if the client dies leaving orphan minor children, and if a separate trust is immediately created for each child, the pot will likely be split before all expenses in raising the children have been made. Thus, each child's expenses will be financed out of his or her own predetermined share, rather than from the pot. Consequently, the younger children will receive a relatively smaller final distribution upon reaching adulthood because living expenses over a longer period of time will have been charged only to their shares.

The name given by some attorneys to a type of single trust created for more than one child, one that retains the "pot" characteristic, is the *pot trust* or family pot trust. Under its usual terms, the trust remains undivided until the youngest child reaches age 21, the age at which parental obligations are commonly perceived to terminate. At that time, the assets are divided into equal separate shares, one for each child.[12] The assets are distributed out-

---

[11]Under that trust-will, not all trust property will be distributed at this time if there are surviving minor issue of the client's deceased children.

[12]Some attorneys recommend dividing the corpus into separate shares when the oldest child reaches age 18, reasoning that each child should bear subsequent

right, or they are held for distribution at some older age. Thus, the trust-will in Exhibit 3-3 provides for a pot trust.

The choice of the age at which the assets are divided into separate shares involves a *trade-off* between inequality and delay. The younger that age, the more *unequal* will be the amounts distributed to the children, but the *sooner* will the older children receive their outright distributions. Conversely, the older the age at which the assets are divided into separate shares, the less the inequality, but the later the distributions will be made.

> EXAMPLE 17–7 Mrs. Hunsaker, who is a widow, and her attorney are pondering the type of distribution clause to be included in her trust-will, which is similar in many ways to that found in Exhibit 3-3. She has two children, Colleen, aged 20, and Nancy, aged 15. Colleen is a senior in college and is engaged to be married, and Nancy is a sophomore in high school. Nancy wishes to attend college. Mrs. Hunsaker is considering two different distribution plans for the girls, her only beneficiaries. The first alternative would split the trust into two equal shares for the girls immediately upon her death, with outright distribution when each reaches age 21. The second alternative would delay dividing the assets into equal shares until Nancy reaches age 21, at which time both children would receive the property outright. Assume that Mrs. Hunsaker dies just after the will is executed. If the first alternative is chosen, Colleen will receive her distribution in less than one year, at age 21. None of the distribution will have been used to finance Nancy's living expenses. If the second alternative is selected, assuming that Nancy does not die, Colleen will have to wait until age 26 to receive her distribution. This distribution will be smaller, since one half of her sister's living expenses will have been charged to it. Nancy's distribution, at age 21, will be correspondingly larger.

Restrictions against Assignment

As mentioned in Chapter 3, the client may wish to include a *spendthrift clause,* insulating the trust from the claims of the beneficiaries creditors and restricting beneficiaries from transferring their interests in trust income or principal prior to their receipt.[13]

(perhaps very unequal) costs (e.g., college, graduate school) only out of his or her own share.

[13]For an interesting application of the spendthrift clause, see the Ross article

Spendthrift clauses are legally recognized in the majority of American jurisdictions, even if the beneficiary is not a "spendthrift." However, such clauses are not foolproof. Although they often can deny a creditor of the beneficiary the right to demand that the trustee directly hand a distribution over to it, they do not prevent the creditor from exercising the usual legal remedies (i.e., action in court) against a beneficiary *after* the beneficiary receives a distribution.[14] In addition, all states will enforce a promise made by the beneficiary prior to a distribution that the beneficiary will hand it over to a creditor once it is received. Thus, while a spendthrift clause can discourage excessive spending, it cannot completely prevent the beneficiary from "spending" trust property prior to receiving it, as long as there are potential creditors around who are willing to risk having to seek payment from the spender.

Perpetuities Savings Clause

Appendix 3A discusses the *rule against perpetuities,* which is a common law principle invalidating a dispositive clause if a contingent interest transferred may vest in the transferee too long after the client's death. The reader is referred to that section for a discussion of ways in which the rule can be violated, as well as a description of savings clauses that can be used in wills and trusts to prevent the operation of the rule.

Powers of the Trustee

The client has at least three commonly used options in deciding what trustee powers to confer in a trust document. First, the client can specify *no powers,* relying entirely on that state's statutory and case-law framework, which explicitly confers some powers to

---

cited at the end of the chapter. Ross describes a *discretionary spendthrift trust* used for the benefit of a developmentally disabled child after the parents' death, and designed to avoid rendering the child ineligible for public benefits, including Supplemental Security Income (SSI), Medicaid, and Social Security Disability Insurance (SSDI). This trust may not work in some states.

[14]Several states, including California, have recently enacted exceptions to the general rule that spendthrift trust assets are not subject to the claims of beneficiaries. Common exceptions apply to the following situations: revocable trusts, if

trustees.[15] This approach is often used for clients having relatively small estates and no assets requiring difficult administration, such as a closely held business.

The second approach is to rely on the state's laws in general but also *explicitly grant* some other desirable powers not found in the statute, ones that may facilitate asset administration. This is the approach used in Exhibit 3-3, the trust-will.

A third approach is to not rely at all on state law and instead draft a document that *exhaustively includes* all powers that the trustee should be permitted to have. The resulting independent tailor-made document eliminates certain risks, such as future legislative and judicial revision of the law, and the uncertain consequence of a change in the client's residence state. On the negative side, a custom-drafted form will be a more complex document, more difficult to read and perhaps more prone to internal inconsistency.

We turn next to the second major topic of the chapter: principles of planning for the client's own incapacity.

PLANNING FOR THE CLIENT'S INCAPACITY

Disability often precedes death. When the client's death is not sudden, his or her disability can create the need for care by another party. Since the client will usually have specific preferences regarding care, planning for incapacity while the client is physically and mentally fit can increase the likelihood of more happy final years.

As in the case of minors, the law commonly distinguishes two types of persons who care for incapacitated adults: those who care for the client's property and those who care for the client.

---

the trustor is beneficiary; in cases involving spousal and child support judgments; and for creditors that are government agencies. In addition, California has established a procedure similar to wage garnishment for judgment creditors of up to 25 percent of amounts distributable in excess of support needs.

[15]Many states have adopted the Uniform Trustees Powers Act, which codifies many trustee powers.

Planning for the Care of the Incapacitated Client's Property

As in the case of caring for the minor's property, several devices are available to care for the property of an incapacitated client. These include the guardianship or conservatorship, the trust, and the durable power of attorney.

Guardianship or conservatorship of the client's property. Similar to the guardianship of the estate of a minor, all states recognize a formal, court-supervised arrangement to manage the property of an incapacitated client. Called a guardianship or a conservatorship, appointment of either normally requires a court hearing, and the appointee is ordinarily subject to continuing court supervision. The guardian or conservator is required to give periodic accountings to the court, and is typically required to obtain court permission before engaging in most property transactions. Most guardians and conservators have little or no discretionary authority.[16]

For reasons similar to those for avoiding probate, many clients will plan to avoid the necessity of having a property guardian or conservator. A few clients, however, may prefer the protection offered from their closer court supervision. Clients owning larger estates, or those who cannot recommend a friend or relative to manage property, might prefer a court-administered alternative. In most cases, though, clients will prefer one of the two alternatives described next.

Trust. In planning for incapacity, the client could create a revocable living trust, with the client-trustee funding it with family assets. The trust could provide for a successor trustee when the client became unable to manage the trust's financial affairs.[17] The

---

[16]However, some states are reducing court involvement in guardianships and conservatorships in the same way they are for probate proceedings. For example, see California Probate Code §2590-95.

[17]For a discussion of the use of "discretionary support trusts" and other transfer devices designed to provide benefits for an elderly disabled person and still qualify that person for *state and federal aid,* see the Schlesinger paper cited at the end of the chapter. In view of the government's maximum-assets test required to qualify, the primary objective is to eliminate all nonexempt assets from the impaired client's estate by spending, gifting, and converting them into exempt assets, such as a car, a home, and improvements to the home. One commentator

successor trustee could be the spouse, an adult child, another relative, a trusted friend, or a corporate trustee.[18]

In comparison with a guardianship or conservatorship, a living trust offers the advantages of privacy, flexibility, and freedom from court appearances and accountings. On the other hand, since the trust is a private, noncourt-supervised arrangement, there exists a greater potential for undiscovered fraud and mismanagement by the trustee and the beneficiaries. It should be clear to the reader that this choice will depend on many of the same factors used in deciding whether or not to avoid probate, the main subject in Chapter 10.

One additional disadvantage of the trust arrangement to handle incapacity is the possible requirement of a formal legal determination of the trustee-client's incapacity before a successor trustee can be named. Embarrassing litigation can develop between the client and a family member who is attempting to publicly establish that the client is incompetent. However, this conflict can also arise if a guardianship or conservatorship is being established. To minimize the problem, the trust can contain a clause providing for a private determination of incapacity, in the same manner provided by the springing durable power of attorney, discussed next.[19]

Durable power of attorney for property. Creation and administration of a trust can be relatively expensive. Clients owning smaller estates may prefer to execute a simpler document, known as a durable power of attorney for property. Popularized by the Uniform Probate Code, the durable power of attorney for property

---

has suggested the following planning scenario: H, who is expected to have to go to a nursing home, gives all of his assets to W. After waiting the required period to qualify for Medicaid, H enters the home. Then W and her children make a joint purchase of a portfolio of securities with a substantial part of the family wealth. At her death, W leaves little or no assets against which Medicaid can file a claim. And since she did not "transfer" any assets to the children, no claim can be made against them.

[18]To avoid the risk of the grantor's sudden incapacity triggering a *completed gift*, the grantor or grantor's agent should hold a general power of appointment over the trust assets.

[19]Perhaps the only sure way to avoid the potential for conflict is for the client, *while still competent*, to place his or her property in the hands of a respected

has been recognized by the statutes of every state except the District of Columbia.[20]

First, let's generalize. The durable power of attorney for property (DPOA) is one type of a legal relationship called more simply a power of attorney. A power of attorney can be defined as a document executed by one person, called the *principal,* authorizing another person, called the *attorney-in-fact,* to perform designated acts on behalf of the principal.

Nondurable powers of attorney are not practicable alternatives for caring for the property of elderly clients because they become legally invalid just when they are needed most: at the onset of the client's incapacity.[21] The durable type was developed to overcome this deficiency. Thus, a DPOA is durable because it survives the client's incapacity. Exhibit 17-1 illustrates the common provisions of a DPOA. The underlined sentence makes it "durable."

EXHIBIT 17–1 Durable Power of Attorney (for property)

TO WHOM IT MAY CONCERN:

I, John Jones, a resident of Anytown, Anystate, in the county of Anycounty, do hereby constitute and appoint Aaron Agent, a resident of Anytown, Anystate, to be my attorney-in-fact, with full power to name and stead and on my behalf and with full power to

---

trustee or an attorney-in-fact. The client may be unwilling, however, to relinquish control that soon.

[20]The durable power of attorney for property is different from the durable power of attorney for health care, described in the next section. And for each, state laws vary somewhat; the reader is strongly urged to examine the law of his or her particular state. For a description of some peculiarities in state law, see the Brown article cited at the end of the chapter.

[21]In one situation, an attorney-in-fact under a *nondurable* power of attorney gifted property after the principal became mentally incompetent. The IRS ruled that the gift was potentially voidable under local law (by a court-appointed guardian), and therefore was later includable in the principal's gross estate under §2038 (LR 8623004).

EXHIBIT 17–1 *(continued)*

---

substitute at any time or times for the purposes described below one
or more attorneys and to revoke the appointment of my attorney so
substituted and to do the following:

1. To manage my affairs; handle my investments; arrange for the
   investment, reinvestment, and disposition of funds; exercise all
   rights with respect to my investments; accept remittances of income and disburse the same, including authority to open bank
   accounts in my name and to endorse checks for deposit therein
   or in any bank where I may at any time have money on deposit
   and sign checks covering withdrawals therefrom.
2. To endorse and deliver certificates for transfer of bonds or other
   securities to be sold for my account and receive the proceeds
   from such sale.
3. To sign, execute, acknowledge, and deliver on my behalf any
   deed of transfer or conveyance covering personal property or
   real estate wherever situated (including transfers or convey-
   ances to any trust established by me), any discharge or release
   of mortgage held by me on real estate or any other instrument
   in writing.
4. To negotiate and execute leases of any property, real or personal, which I may own, for terms that may extend beyond the
   duration of this power and to provide for the proper care and
   maintenance of such property and pay expenses incurred in
   connection therewith.
5. To subdivide, partition, improve, alter, repair, adjust boundaries
   of, manage, maintain, and otherwise deal with any real estate
   held as trust property, including power to demolish any building
   in whole or in part and to erect buildings.
6. To enter into a lease or arrangement for exploration and removal
   of minerals or other natural resources or to enter into a pooling
   or unitization agreement.
7. To hold securities in bearer form or in the name of a nominee or
   nominees and to hold real estate in the name of a nominee or
   nominees.
8. To continue or participate in the operation of any business or
   other enterprise.
9. To borrow money from time to time in my name and to give
   notes or other obligations therefore, and to deposit as collateral,
   pledge as security for the payment thereof, or mortgage any or
   all my securities or other property of whatever nature.

EXHIBIT 17–1 *(continued)*

10. To have access to any and all safe deposit boxes of which I am now or may become possessed, and to remove therefrom any securities, papers, or other articles.
11. To make all tax returns and pay all taxes required by law, including federal and state returns, and to file all claims for abatement, refund, or other papers relating thereto.
12. To demand, collect, sue for, receive, and receipt for any money, debts, or property of any kind, now or hereafter payable, due or deliverable to me; to pay or contest claims against me; to settle claims by compromise, arbitration, or otherwise; and to release claims.
13. To employ as investment counsel, custodians, brokers, accountants, appraisers, attorneys-at-law, or other agents such persons, firms, or organizations, including my said attorney and any firm of which my said attorney may be a member or employee, as deemed necessary or desirable, and to pay such persons, firms, or organizations such compensation as is deemed reasonable and to determine whether or not to act upon the advice of any such agent without liability for acting or failing to act thereon.
14. To expend and distribute income or principal of my estate for the support, education, care, or benefit of me and my dependents.
15. To make gifts to any one or more of my spouse and my descendants (if any) of whatever degree (including my said attorney who is a spouse or descendant of mine) in amounts not exceeding $10,000 annually with respect to any one of them and gifts to charity in amounts not exceeding 20 percent of my federal adjusted gross income in any one year.
16. To renounce and disclaim any interest otherwise passing to me by testate or intestate succession or by inter vivos transfer.
17. To exercise my rights to elect options and change beneficiaries under insurance and annuity policies and to surrender the policies for their cash value.

In general I give to my said attorney full power to act in the management and disposition of all my estate, affairs and property or every kind and wherever situate in such manner and with such authority as I myself might exercise if personally present.

This power of attorney shall be binding on me and my heirs, executors, and administrators and shall remain in force up to the time of the receipt of my attorney of a written revocation signed by me.

EXHIBIT 17–1 *(concluded)*

This power of attorney shall not be affected by my subsequent disability or incapacity.

IN WITNESS THEREOF, I have hereunto set my hand and seal on this day of March 19, 1999.

_____ (Signature) _____

Executed in counterparts

STATE OF ANYSTATE

County of Anycounty

_____, 19_____

Then personally appeared the above-named _____ and acknowledged the foregoing instrument to be his free act and deed,

Before me,

_____

Notary Public

My commission ex-pires:

_____

This is a slightly modified version of the sample form contained in Charles M. Hamann, "Durable Powers of Attorney," *Trusts and Estates*, February 1983, pp. 30–31. Reprinted with permission.

There are two common types of DPOAs. The first type becomes effective as soon as it is executed. The second type, called a "springing" DPOA, becomes effective *at* the principal's incapacity.[22] It will contain the following clause, in addition to those found in Exhibit 17-1:

> This power of attorney shall become effective upon my disability or my incapacity. I shall be deemed disabled or incapacitated upon the election of my said attorney to accept the certificate of a physician (who, in his opinion, is qualified) which states that such physician has examined me and that I am incapacitated mentally or physically and am therefore incapable of attending to my business affairs.[23]

To be valid, any DPOA must be executed prior to the principal's incapacity. To ensure competent execution, many advisers recommend the preparation of a DPOA for an older client at the time the will is being prepared.

The DPOA has several advantages over the other devices designed to manage an incapacitated client's property. Compared to a guardianship or conservatorship, the DPOA is less expensive to create and to administer. And the nonspringing type can avoid the necessity of a court-held incompetency proceeding, an event that can be painful and embarrassing to all parties, especially the client. Compared with the trust, the DPOA is also less expensive to create and administer. And some clients who flatly refuse to set up a trust will not mind executing a DPOA, because of its relative simplicity. However, the trust and the DPOA need not be considered alternatives; greater flexibility may result if a DPOA authorizes the attorney-in-fact to fund an existing unfunded revocable living trust

---

[22]Springing powers are authorized by most, but not all, states. Clients in states not authorizing springing powers, such as in New York, have no choice but to execute a nonspringing DPOA while they are competent and then hope that their attorney-in-fact does not improperly act on their behalf prior to their incapacity. Delaying delivery of the document may help.

[23]Reprinted with permission from Charles M. Hamann, "Durable Powers of Attorney," *Trusts & Estates*, February 1983, pp. 30–31. Some attorneys recommend that, instead of a physician, a "trusted committee" of three of the client's trusted friends and relatives determine when the power of attorney becomes effective.

(called a "standby trust") with the client's assets at the onset of incapacity. Upon funding, the assets could be managed by a skilled trustee. Thereafter, the attorney-in-fact may be permitted to perform other duties that were not given to the trustee, including funding other trusts, purchasing flower bonds, making gifts and disclaimers, and appearing at tax audits.

The DPOA has at least two potential estate tax drawbacks, either of which might subject the principal's property to inclusion in the attorney-in-fact's gross estate in the event the attorney-in-fact dies first.[24] First, the attorney-in-fact may be deemed to have a general power of appointment over the principal's property. Eliminating this danger may require either prohibiting entirely the ability of the attorney-in-fact to make gifts to him or herself, or limiting such gifts to an ascertainable standard, or to the greater of $5,000 or 5 percent of the value of the property.

A second estate tax problem concerns insurance on the life of the attorney-in-fact, who may be deemed to have acquired from the principal taxable incidents of ownership, thereby subjecting the proceeds to inclusion in the attorney-in-fact's gross estate at death, under IRC §2042. At present the tax rules are in dispute, and until the courts resolve the issue in the taxpayer's favor, it might be best to explicitly deny the attorney's power of control over such policies.

One nontax drawback to the DPOA concerns its acceptance. Certain financial institutions may be unwilling to recognize a legally valid DPOA, especially if it is more than six months to a year old. Increasing use of the DPOA should substantially minimize that result.[25]

A second, nontax drawback of the DPOA is that it can be misused. Lawyers will attest to numerous situations where attorneys-in-fact, particularly the children of clients, have used the property

---

[24]For a discussion of a potential §2036 problem involving spousal "cross powers," see the Brown article cited at the end of the chapter.

[25]The attorney can minimize acceptance problems with careful and specific custom-drafting of enumerated powers, and by having the client periodically reexecute the DPOA to prevent it from appearing outdated. Nevertheless, some institutions won't accept a DPOA, and some banks and the IRS will, but require the use of their own forms. New York has recently adopted a statute making it unlawful to refuse to recognize the New York statutory form DPOA.

in a manner clearly contrary to the client's best interests. Although such behavior is actionable, it is rarely challenged. Because the DPOA delegates very fundamental property rights, the client should think long and hard about the possible consequences.

Planning for the Care of the Incapacitated Client

Similar to the procedure for selecting the guardian of a minor child, the procedure for selecting the person who will care for an incapacitated adult is usually undertaken in the county probate court after a noticed hearing. Some states call this fiduciary a *guardian* or *committee,* while others use the name *conservator.*[26] In either case, the court chooses the party only after careful, formal consideration.

Whom should the client recommend to provide personal care in the event of his or her incapacity? Ordinarily, the client has few choices. The spouse, if able, usually makes the best first choice. Next come other family members, especially adult children. However, the children often lead busy lives and are often neither capable nor willing to do all the work required. This is especially true for a client in an advanced stage of incapacity, such as at the onset of incontinence.

Older clients would be well-advised to visit nursing homes and other institutions for care of the elderly in their area. Some organizations will even sell to the client the right to occupy, for life, an apartment in a large residential health-care facility, which also provides on the premises all meals and round-the-clock nursing, medical, and hospital services.

Delegation of health care decisions. For many years, clients have been able to execute documents such as wills and trusts, empowering surrogate decision makers to make personal *wealth* decisions when they no longer could. Until recently however, clients did not have the same ability to delegate the power to make *medi-*

---

[26]States define guardian, conservator, and committee differently. In some states, such as California, a conservator deals with either or both the person and the property of someone unable to either provide for personal needs or manage financial resources. In other states, such as New York, a conservator concerns itself primarily with an "impaired" person's property, while a committee cares for both the person and the property of an "incompetent" person. The UPC parallels

cal decisions. Today, almost all states recognize an individual's ability to delegate to some degree important medical decisions, or at least to state in writing what those decisions should be. The two most commonly used documents are called the durable power of attorney for health care and the living will.

Durable power of attorney for health care. Like the durable power of attorney for property (DPOA), the durable power of attorney for health care (DPOAHC) appoints a person as attorney-in-fact to make decisions on behalf of the principal. However, the documents are different in several important respects. First, of course, the DPOAHC concerns *medical,* not property decisions. Examples include placement in or removal from a medical facility, withholding of future medical treatment, use or nonuse of medication, performance or nonperformance of surgery, and use or nonuse of artificial life-sustaining methods, such as respiration, nourishment, and hydration.[27] Second, the DPOAHC ordinarily creates only a *springing* power, one that becomes effective upon the principal's incapacity, that is, his or her inability to make a particular health care decision.[28] Third, while it is theoretically possible to include the legal content of a DPOAHC within a DPOA document, attorneys choose instead to draft them separately. Appendix 17A shows an example of a DPOAHC. The DPOAHC is statutorily recognized in only four states: California, Illinois, Nevada, and Rhode Island.[29]

---

the New York terminology and, in addition, permits a guardian to be appointed to oversee the person and the property of an "incapacitated" person.

[27]Reflecting an increasingly popular dissatisfaction with the zealous use of artificial life-sustaining methods, Dubler, in the article cited at the end of the chapter, emphatically states that rapid advances in medical technology combined with the implicit premise of medicine to "do everything" for the patient, has led some to conclude that "doing everything" might violate rather than support the rights of the patient, and "could condemn a body to endless non-sapient, non-relational existence in a dehumanizing antiseptic setting," one actually not preferable to death.

[28]Thus, the DPOAHC does not apply only to situations when the principal is terminally ill. It usually applies to all situations where the principal is unable to give "informed consent" with respect to a particular medical decision.

[29]However, several other states seem to recognize such a power to one degree or another. For a complete list, see the Collin article cited at the end of the chapter. California's statutory scheme is particularly flexible in terms of both the scope of the authority of the attorney in fact to act on behalf of the client and the pro-

Living will. In contrast with the as yet limited acceptance of the DPOAHC, about three quarters of the states explicitly recognize some variation of the living will, which essentially deals with only one of the two features of the DPOAHC: it details those health care interventions that the person does or does not wish to be subjected to in situations when he or she is no longer capable of making those decisions.[30] Appendix 17B illustrates one example of a living will. The reader will notice that this particular one, reflecting the modern trend, enables the signer to name another person, called a "proxy," to act on his or her behalf to make certain medical decisions. Many attorneys in states where living wills aren't yet statutorily recognized urge their clients to execute them, under the expectation that the courts would approve them if and when tested.

When compared to the DPOAHC, living wills have several disadvantages. First, many living wills do not appoint a surrogate decision maker, which restricts its flexibility considerably. Second, living wills are typically very brief, covering only a few possible outcomes, mostly in the area of life-sustaining treatment. Third, most living will statutes apply only to terminal patients. Finally, the language of living wills are usually quite vague, failing to carefully define important terms, leaving the physician and the family to disagree over proper care.

This chapter has described miscellaneous lifetime estate planning techniques not covered earlier. Chapter 18 will examine tax planning techniques which can be employed on behalf of the client after the client's death.

---

tection afforded to all health-care providers who act on those decisions. For a discussion of post-drafting experience with the DPOAHC in California, see the West paper, cited at the end of the chapter. The American Medical Association has recently backed this trend in ruling that it is appropriate for doctors to withdraw life-supporting, artificial feeding systems from hopelessly comatose patients.

[30]Several states, including Virginia, recognize a variation on the living will, called the "directive to physicians" giving instructions with regard to the use of life-sustaining treatment. A copy of one such document is in Appendix 17C. At least one state, however, severely limits its application by requiring that the patient, before signing the form (*a*) be diagnosed as terminally ill, (*b*) wait an additional 14 days, and (*c*) then have the capacity to execute the document.

RECOMMENDED READING

ANONYMOUS. "Who Can Afford a Nursing Home?" *Consumer Reports*, May 1988, pp. 300–309 (includes ratings of nursing home insurance policies).

ADAMS, FRANK T. "Estate Planning for the Elderly." *Trusts & Estates*, February 1986, pp. 37–40.

ADAMS, ROY M., and CARTER, HOWARD. "Coping with a New Threat." (Increasing liability exposure to professional fiduciaries.) *Trusts & Estates*, October 1987, pp. 25–36.

ALVAREZ, EDNA R. "The Attorney as Fiduciary: Problems When You Say 'Yes.'" *Estate Planning, 1988*, California Continuing Education of the Bar. Also, paper presented at the 10th annual UCLA/CEB Estate Planning Institute, May 1988.

BAER, SUSAN T. "Avoiding Estate Depletion in the Face of Catastrophic Illness." *Pace Law Review* 47 (1984), pp. 783–826.

BECKMAN, GAIL MCKNIGHT. "Changes Highlight Need for Making Special Provisions for Adopted or Illegitimate Children." *Estate Planning*, November 1985, pp. 352–55.

BERTEAU, JOHN T. "Steps to Avoid Beneficiary Conflicts over Bequests of Tangible Personal Property." *Estate Planning*, November 1985, pp. 356–61.

BLAKE, JOHN F. "Drafting a QTIP Trust Where Extended Medical Care for the Surviving Spouse Is Foreseeable." *Estate Planning*, July 1987, pp. 200–05.

BLATTMACHR, DOUGLAS J., and JONATHAN G. BLATTMACHR. "Estate Planning for Individuals with Short Life Expectancies." *Trusts & Estates*, August 1985, pp. 22–28.

BROWN, KENNETH R. "Options Available to the Estate Planner in Anticipating a Client's Disability," *Estate Planning*, September 1986, pp. 282–87.

CHERIS, SAMUEL D. "Making Responsible Investment Decisions in Light of the Evolving Prudent Person Rule." *Estate Planning*, November 1987, pp. 338–42.

CLARY, DUANE A., and KEVIN R. ANDERSON. "Anticipating the Possibility of Simultaneous Deaths in Light of Uniform Act's Presumptions." *Estate Planning*, September 1987, pp. 280–84.

COLLIN, FRANCIS F. "Planning and Drafting Durable Powers of Attorney for Health Care." University of Miami 22nd Annual Estate Planning Institute, 1988.

COLLIN, FRANCIS J.; JOHN J. LOMBARD; ALBERT L. MOSES.; and HARLEY J. SPILTER. *Drafting the Durable Power of Attorney: A Systems Approach." Colorado Springs:* Shepard's/McGraw-Hill, 1987.

DAVIS, A. KIMBROUGH. "Proper Planning Can Reduce Estate Taxes in the Event of the Simultaneous Death of Spouses." *Taxation for Lawyers*, July–August 1984, pp. 10–13.

DUBLER, NANCY N. "Health Care Decisions: Enforcing Autonomy and Delegating Authority." *Estate Planning for the Aging or Incapacitated Client 1986.* Practicing Law Institute.

EDWARDS, MARK B. "Long-Term Care for the Elderly: A Primer for the Estate Planner." University of Miami 22nd Estate Planning Institute, 1988.

FRENCH, SUSAN F. "Antilapse Statutes Are Blunt Instruments: A Blueprint For Reform," *Hastings Law Journal* 37, November, 1985, pp. 335–75.

FROLIK, LAWRENCE A. "Discretionary Trusts for a Disabled Beneficiary: A Solution or A Trap for the Unwary?" *University of Pittsburg Law Review* 46, no. 335 (1985), pp. 335–71.

GALLO, JOHN J., and EILEEN F. GALLO. "Incentive Estate Planning For the Postponed Child." *Estate Planning 1987,* California Continuing Education of the Bar.

GAMBLE, RICHARD H. "Estate Planning For the Unmarried Person. *Trusts & Estates,* April 1986, pp. 25–28.

GENTLE III, EDGAR C. "Lawyers as Executors and Trustees: Snakes and Ladders." *The Alabama Lawyer,* March 1987, pp. 94–5.

GILMAN, SHELDON. "Trustee Selection: Corporate vs. Individual." *Trusts & Estates,* June 1984, pp. 29–36.

GRANELLI, L. F., JANET WRIGHT; and JOHN SCHOOLING. "Treating Children Equally (An Estate Planning Challenge)." *Estate Planning, Trust & Probate News* (State Bar of California publication) 6 (Winter 1985), p. 1.

HADDLETON, RUSSELL E. "How to Provide for the Surviving Spouse and Children during Administration of an Estate." *Estate Planning,* January 1988, pp. 14–18.

HALBACH, EDWARD C., JR. "Issues About Issue: Some Recurrent Class Gift Problems," *Missouri Law Review* 48 (1983), pp. 333–70.

HAMANN, CHARLES M. "Durable Powers of Attorney." *Trusts & Estates,* February 1983, pp. 28–32.

————. "More Durable Powers of Attorney." *Trusts and Estates,* August 1983, pp. 30–32.

"Isn't it Time You Wrote a Will? Seven Out of Ten Americans Don't Have Wills. They Should." *Consumer Reports,* February 1985, pp. 103–8.

KIRKLAND, RICHARD I., JR. "Should You Leave It All to the Children?" *Fortune,* September 29, 1986, pp. 18–26.

LEIMBERG, STEPHAN R., and CHARLES K. PLOTNICK. "What a Probate Attorney Must Know about the Psychological Aspects of Death and Dying." *The Practical Lawyer,* October 1986, pp. 38–46.

LEVIN, JOEL A. "Sufficient Administrative Authority May Require Special Provisions beyond State Fiduciary Powers." *Estate Planning,* November 1984, pp. 336–41.

LOMBARD, JOHN J. "Asset Management under a Durable Power of Attorney—The Ideal Solution to Guardianships or Conservatorships." *Probate Notes* 9 (1983), pp. 189–212.

————. "Planning for Disability: Durable Powers, Standby Trusts and Preserving Eligibility for Governmental Benefits." *1986 University of Miami Institute on Estate Planning,* chap. 16.

LUNDERGAN, BARBARA. "Elderly Clients Require Special Lifetime Planning." *Trusts & Estates,* February 1986, pp. 33–35.

MILANI, KEN, and CLAUDE D. RENSHAW. "Tax Strategies Especially Designed for Disabled or Handicapped Individuals." *Taxation for Accountants,* October 1987, pp. 256–66.

MOSES, A. L., and ADELE J. POPE. "Estate Planning, Disability, and the Durable Power of Attorney." *South Carolina Law Review* 30 (1979), pp. 511–55.

NADLMAN, JAY. "Spendthrift Trusts: Enforceability of Agreements to Pay Over on Receipt" *UMKC Law Review* 52, no. 1 (1983), pp. 115–27.

NEUWIRTH, GLORIA S. "Steps a Client Can Take to Plan for Future Medical Treatment Decisions." *Estate Planning,* January 1985, pp. 14–20.

NORDSTRON, KENNETH V. "Estate Planning for Unmarried Individuals," *CLU Journal,* September 1987, pp. 38–46.

OLSEN, RORY R., and DAVID C. SHARMAN. "Practical and Tax Considerations in Deciding Who Should Be a Trustee." *Estate Planning,* July 1981, pp. 214–20.

OWENS, RODNEY J., and RAYMOND C. JORDAN. "Estate Planning for Parents of Mentally Disabled Children." *Trusts & Estates,* September 1987, pp. 41–8.

PENNELL, JEFFREY N. "Avoiding Tax Problems for Settlors and Trustees When an Individual Trustee Is Chosen." *Estate Planning,* September 1982, pp. 264–72.

————. "Tax Payment Provisions And Equitable Apportionment: Drafting to Span Legal Voids." University of Miami 22nd annual Estate Planning Institute, 1988. A complex, exhaustive analysis of state laws, and document planning.

PIERSON, DONALD R. II. "Steps a Practitioner Can Take to Facilitate the Planning and Probate of a Client's Estate." *Estate Planning,* March 1987, pp. 88–95.

ROSS, STERLING L. "The Special-Needs Trust and Its Use in Estate Planning for Families with Disabled Children." *Estate Planning for the Aged or Incapacitated Client 1986,* Practising Law Institute.

SCHLESINGER, SANFORD J. "Estate Planning for Elderly or Disabled Clients after the Tax Reform Act (Internal Revenue Code of 1986)." *New York University Institute on Federal Taxation, 1986.*

SELIGMANN, WILLIAM A. "Distributions to Children in the Sprinkling Trust." *Trusts & Estates,* February 1975, pp. 78–80.

SIMPSON, SAMUEL S. "Living Wills: A Matter of Life and Death." *Trusts & Estates,* April 1986, pp.10–20.

Solomon, Lewis D. "Planning Estates for the Forgotten Middle Class." *1982 University of Miami Institute on Estate Planning,* chap. 13, pp. 1–41.

Suter, Philip H. "Techniques to Apportion Estate Taxes Will Have to Be Reviewed to the New Tax Law." *Estate Planning,* March 1982, 96–100.

Van Houten, Margaret D. "Divorce Negotiations Carry Substantial Estate Planning Implications." *Estate Planning,* November 1987, pp. 344–49.

West, Suzanne F. "Practical Experience with Durable Powers of Attorney for Health Care." *Estate Planning 1986,* California Continuing Education of the Bar.

Wicker, William H. "Spendthrift Trusts Are an Excellent Way to Leave Money to Someone Who Can't Handle It." *Estate Planning,* Summer 1975, pp. 202–5.

Williams, John C. ". . . but Some Are More Equal than Others: Factors to Consider in Creating Trusts for Groups of Children or Grandchildren." *Trusts & Estates,* March 1975, pp. 140–44.

QUESTIONS AND PROBLEMS

1. (*a*) Describe the attributes of a good parental guardian, executor, and trustee. (*b*) Why are they different?

2. One of your clients asks you to describe the legal alternatives available to provide for her young son's financial care. Be sure to mention the advantages and disadvantages of each.

3. What factors will influence which beneficiaries a testator should choose to bear the burden of death taxes?

4. (*a*) What is a survival clause? (*b*) How does it overcome the consequences of lapsation?

5. Cassie's will simply says, "I leave all my securities to John, and everything else to Mary." If John predeceases Cassie, analyze the possible recipients of the securities, using the alternative assumptions made in the text about the contents of the will and the influence of state law.

6. Describe the family pot trust and the trade-off involved in determining the age of distribution to young adult beneficiaries.

7. Why isn't a spendthrift clause foolproof?

8. What legal alternatives does a client have in property planning for his or her own incapacity? Describe the advantages and disadvantages of each.

9. Your 86-year-old mentally competent client wishes to plan for her incapacity but refuses to immediately transfer her assets to anyone. Is planning impossible, or does this refusal merely create a particular problem?

10. An attorney jokingly tells a client: "Today you'll be signing two documents, one for wealth and one for health. One gives someone the power to steal from you, while the other gives someone the power to kill you." (*a*) What two documents is she talking about? (*b*) Is there any truth to her cynicism?

Durable Power of Attorney for Health Care*

---

*Reproduced with permission of the California Medical Association.

APPENDIX 17A

DURABLE POWER OF ATTORNEY
FOR HEALTH CARE©
(California Civil Code Sections 2410-2443)

This is a Durable Power of Attorney for Health Care form. By filling in this form, you can select someone to make health care decisions for you if for some reason you become unable to make those decisions for yourself. A properly completed form provides the best legal protection available to help ensure that your wishes will be respected.

READ THIS FORM CAREFULLY BEFORE FILLING IT OUT. EACH PARAGRAPH IN THE FORM CONTAINS INSTRUCTIONS. IT IS IMPORTANT THAT YOU FOLLOW THESE INSTRUCTIONS SO THAT YOUR WISHES MAY BE CARRIED OUT.

The following checklist is provided to help you fill out this form correctly. You may use this checklist to double check sections you may be unsure of as you fill in the form. You may also use this checklist to help make sure you have completed the form properly. If you have properly completed this form, you should be able to answer **yes** to each question in the checklist.

_____ 1. I am a California resident who is at least 18 years old, of sound mind and acting of my own free will.

_____ 2. The individuals I have selected as my agent and alternate agents to make health care decisions for me are at least 18 years old and are **not:**

  my **treating** health care provider.

  an employee of my **treating** health care provider, unless the employee is related to me by blood, marriage or adoption.

  · an operator of a community care facility (Community care facilities are sometimes called board and care homes. If you are unsure whether a person you are thinking of selecting operates a community care facility, you should ask that person.)

  · an employee of a community care facility, unless the employee is related to me by blood, marriage or adoption.

_____ 3. I have talked with the individuals I have selected as my agent and alternate agents and these individuals have agreed to participate. (You may select someone who is not a California resident to act as your agent or alternate agent, but you should consider whether someone who lives far away will be available to make decisions for you if and when that may become necessary.)

_____ 4. I have read the instructions and completed paragraphs 4, 5, 6, 7, 8, and 9 to reflect my desires.

_____ 5. I have **signed** and **dated** the form.

_____ 6. I have either _____ had the form notarized; **or** _____ had the form properly witnessed:

  _____ 1. I have obtained the signatures of two adult witnesses who personally know me.

  _____ 2. Neither witness is:

    · my agent or alternate agent designated in this form.

    · a health care provider, or the employee of a health care provider.

    · a person who operates or is employed by a community care facility.

  _____ 3. At least one witness is not related to me by blood, marriage, or adoption, and is not named in my will or so far as I know entitled to any part of my estate when I die.

_____ 7. I HAVE GIVEN A COPY OF THE COMPLETED FORM TO THOSE PEOPLE INCLUDING MY AGENT, ALTERNATE AGENTS, FAMILY MEMBERS AND DOCTOR, WHO MAY NEED THIS FORM IN CASE AN EMERGENCY REQUIRES A DECISION CONCERNING MY HEALTH CARE.

SPECIAL REQUIREMENTS

_____ 8. **Patients in Skilled Nursing Facilities.**
If I am a patient in a skilled nursing facility, I have obtained the signature of a patient advocate or ombudsman. (If you are not sure whether you are in a skilled nursing facility, you should ask the people taking care of you.)

_____ 9. **Conservatees under the Lanterman-Petris-Short Act.**
If I am a conservatee under the Lanterman-Petris-Short Act and want to select my conservator as my agent or alternate agent to make health care decisions, I have obtained a lawyer's certification. (If you are not sure whether the person you wish to select as your agent is your conservator under the Lanterman-Petris-Short Act, you should ask that person.)

If you change your mind about who you would like to make health care decisions for you, or about any of the other statements you have made in this form, you should take all of the following steps: 1. Complete a new form with the changes you desire; 2. Tell everyone who got a copy of the old form that it is no longer valid and ask that copies of the old form be returned to you so you may destroy them; 3. Give copies of the new form to the people who may need the form to carry out your wishes as described above in number 7. If after reading this material you still have unanswered questions, you should talk to your doctor or a lawyer.

1   ©California Medical Association 1986 (revised)

APPENDIX 17A *(continued)*

DURABLE POWER OF ATTORNEY
FOR HEALTH CARE DECISIONS
(California Civil Code Sections 2410-2443)

WARNING TO PERSON EXECUTING THIS DOCUMENT

This is an important legal document. Before executing this document, you should know these important facts:

This document gives the person you designate as your agent (the attorney-in-fact) the power to make health care decisions for you. Your agent must act consistently with your desires as stated in this document or otherwise made known.

Except as you otherwise specify in this document, this document gives your agent the power to consent to your doctor not giving treatment or stopping treatment necessary to keep you alive.

Notwithstanding this document, you have the right to make medical and other health care decisions for yourself so long as you can give informed consent with respect to the particular decision. In addition, no treatment may be given to you over your objection, and health care necessary to keep you alive may not be stopped or withheld if you object at the time.

This document gives your agent authority to consent, to refuse to consent, or to withdraw consent to any care, treatment, service, or procedure to maintain diagnose, or treat a physical or mental condition. This power is subject to any statement of your desires and any limitations that you include in this document. You may state in this document any types of treatment that you do not desire. In addition, a court can take away the power of your agent to make health care decisions for you if your agent (1) authorizes anything that is illegal, (2) acts contrary to your known desires or (3) where your desires are not known, does anything that is clearly contrary to your best interests.

Unless you specify a shorter period in this document, this power will exist for seven years from the date you execute this document and, if you are unable to make health care decisions for yourself at the time when this seven-year period ends, this power will continue to exist until the time when you become able to make health care decisions for yourself.

You have the right to revoke the authority of your agent by notifying your agent or your treating doctor, hospital, or other health care provider orally or in writing of the revocation.

Your agent has the right to examine your medical records and to consent to their disclosure unless you limit this right in this document.

Unless you otherwise specify in this document, this document gives your agent the power after you die to (1) authorize an autopsy, (2) donate your body or parts thereof for transplant or therapeutic or educational or scientific purposes, and (3) direct the disposition of your remains.

If there is anything in this document that you do not understand, you should ask a lawyer to explain it to you.

1. CREATION OF DURABLE POWER OF ATTORNEY FOR HEALTH CARE

By this document I intend to create a durable power of attorney by appointing the person designated above to make health care decisions for me as allowed by Sections 2410 to 2443, inclusive, of the California Civil Code. This power of attorney shall not be affected by my subsequent incapacity.

2

APPENDIX 17A *(continued)*

2. DESIGNATION OF HEALTH CARE AGENT

(Insert the name and address of the person you wish to designate as your agent to make health care decisions for you. None of the following may be designated as your agent: (1) your treating health care provider, (2) a nonrelative employee of your treating health care provider, (3) an operator of a community care facility, or (4) a nonrelative employee of an operator of a community care facility.)

I, _____
(insert your name)

do hereby designate and appoint: Name: _____

Address: _____

Telephone Number: _____ as my attorney-in-fact (agent)
to make health care decisions for me as authorized in this document.

3. GENERAL STATEMENT OF AUTHORITY GRANTED

If I become incapable of giving informed consent to health care decisions, I hereby grant to my agent full power and authority to make health care decisions for me including the right to consent, refuse consent, or withdraw consent to any care, treatment, service, or procedure to maintain, diagnose or treat a physical or mental condition, and to receive and to consent to the release of medical information, subject to the statement of desires, special provisions and limitations set out in paragraph 4.

4. STATEMENT OF DESIRES, SPECIAL PROVISIONS, AND LIMITATIONS

(Your agent must make health care decisions that are consistent with your known desires. You can, but are not required to, state your desires in the space provided below. You should consider whether you want to include a statement of your desires concerning decisions to withhold or remove life-sustaining treatment. For your convenience, some general statements concerning the withholding and removal of life-sustaining treatment are set out below. If you agree with one of these statements, you may INITIAL that statement. READ ALL OF THESE STATEMENTS CAREFULLY BEFORE YOU SELECT ONE TO INITIAL. You can also write your own statement concerning life-sustaining treatment and/or other matters relating to your health care. BY LAW, YOUR AGENT IS NOT PERMITTED TO CONSENT ON YOUR BEHALF TO ANY OF THE FOLLOWING: COMMITMENT TO OR PLACEMENT IN A MENTAL HEALTH TREATMENT FACILITY, CONVULSIVE TREATMENT, PSYCHOSURGERY, STERILIZATION OR ABORTION. In every other respect, your agent may make health care decisions for you to the same extent you could make them for yourself if you were capable of doing so. If you want to limit in any other way the authority given your agent by this document, you should state the limits in the space below. If you do not initial one of the printed statements or write your own statement, your agent will have the broad powers to make health care decisions on your behalf which are set forth in Paragraph 3, except to the extent that there are limits provided by law.)

I do **not** want my life to be prolonged and I do **not** want life-sustaining treatment to be provided or continued if the burdens of the treatment outweigh the expected benefits. I want my agent to consider the relief of suffering and the quality as well as the extent of the possible extension of my life in making decisions concerning life-sustaining treatment.	I want my life to be prolonged and I want life-sustaining treatment to be provided **unless I am in a coma** which my doctors reasonably believe to be irreversible. Once my doctors have reasonably concluded I am in an irreversible coma, I do **not** want life-sustaining treatment to be provided or continued.	I want my life to be prolonged to the greatest extent possible without regard to my condition, the chances I have for recovery or the cost of the procedures.
If this statement reflects your desires, initial here _____.	*If this statement reflects your desires, initial here _____.*	*If this statement reflects your desires, initial here _____.*

Other or additional statements or desires, special provisions, or limitations.

_____

_____

_____

(You may attach additional pages if you need more space to complete your statement. If you attach additional pages, you must DATE and SIGN EACH PAGE.)

3

APPENDIX 17A (continued)

5. CONTRIBUTION OF ANATOMICAL GIFT

(You may choose to make a gift of all or part of your body to a hospital, physician, or medical school for scientific, educational, therapeutic or transplant purposes. Such a gift is allowed by California's Uniform Anatomical Gift Act. If you do not make such a gift, you may authorize your agent to do so, or a member of your family may make a gift unless you give them notice that you do not want a gift made. In the space below you may make a gift yourself or state that you do not want to make a gift. If you do not complete this section, your agent will have the authority to make a gift of all or a part of your body under the Uniform Anatomical Gift Act.)

If either statement reflects your desires, sign on the line next to the statement. **You do not have to sign either statement.** If you do not sign either statement, your agent and your family will have the authority to make a gift of all or part of your body under the Uniform Anatomical Gift Act.

(_____)
(signature)

Pursuant to the Uniform Anatomical Gift Act, I hereby give, effective upon my death:

☐ Any needed organ or parts; or

☐ The parts or organs listed:

_____

_____

_____

(_____)
(signature)

I do not want to make a gift under the Uniform Anatomical Gift Act, nor do I want my agent or family to do so.

6. AUTOPSY AND DISPOSITION OF MY REMAINS

I understand that my agent will be able to authorize an autopsy (an examination of my body after my death to determine the cause of my death) and to direct the disposition of my remains unless I limit that authority in this document. I also understand that my agent or any other person who directs the disposition of my remains must follow any instructions I have given in a written contract for funeral services, my will or by some other method.

(OPTIONAL: If you do not want your agent to be involved in these matters, you should state your desires concerning an autopsy and the person you would like to direct the disposition of your remains. If any of the statements below reflect your desires, sign next to that statement. If none of these statements reflect your desires and you want to limit the authority of your agent to consent to an autopsy and/or to dispose of your remains, you should write your own statement in paragraph 4, above.)

Autopsy

(_____)
(signature)

I hereby consent to an examination of my body after my death to determine the cause of my death.

(_____)
(signature)

My agent may not authorize an autopsy.

Disposition of Remains

(_____)
(signature)

My agent may not direct the disposition of my remains and I would prefer that _____
(name and address)

direct the disposition of my remains.

(_____)
(signature)

I have described the way I want my remains disposed of in (circle one):

1. A written contract for funeral services with _____

(name of mortuary cemetery)

2. My will

3. Other: _____

4

APPENDIX 17A *(continued)*

7. DESIGNATION OF ALTERNATE AGENTS

(You are not required to designate any alternate agents but you may do so. Any alternative agent you designate will be able to make the same health care decisions as the agent designated in Paragraph 2, above, in the event that agent is unable or unwilling to act as your agent. Also, if the agent designated in Paragraph 2 is your spouse, his or her designation as your agent is automatically revoked by law if your marriage is dissolved.)

If the person designated in Paragraph 2 as my agent is not available and willing to make a health care decision for me, then I designate the following persons to serve as my agent to make health care decisions for me as authorized in this document, such persons to serve in the order listed below:

A. First Alternative Agent

Name: _____

Address: _____

Telephone Number: _____

B. Second Alternative Agent

Name: _____

Address: _____

Telephone Number: _____

8. DURATION

I understand that this power of attorney will exist for seven years from the date I execute this document unless I establish a shorter time. If I am unable to make health care decisions for myself when this power of attorney expires, the authority I have granted my agent will continue to exist until the time when I become able to make health care decisions for myself.

(Optional) I wish to have this power of attorney end before seven years on the following date: _____ . (Fill in this space ONLY if you want the authority of your agent to end EARLIER than the seven-year period described above.)

9. NOMINATION OF CONSERVATOR OF MY PERSON

(A conservator of the person may be appointed for you if a court decides that you are unable properly to provide for your personal needs for physical health, food, clothing or shelter. The appointment of a conservator may affect, or transfer to the conservator your right to control your physical care, including under some circumstances your right to make health care decisions. You are not required to nominate a conservator but you may do so. The court will appoint the person you nominate unless that would be contrary to your best interests. You may, but are not required to, nominate as your conservator the same person you named in paragraph 2 as your health care agent. You can nominate an individual as your conservator by completing the space below.)

If a conservator of the person is to be appointed for me, I nominate the following individual to serve as conservator of the person:

Name: _____

Address: _____

Telephone Number: _____

10. PRIOR DESIGNATIONS REVOKED

I revoke any prior durable power of attorney for health care.

APPENDIX 17A *(continued)*

Date and Signature of Principal

(YOU MUST DATE AND SIGN THIS POWER OF ATTORNEY)

I sign my name to this Durable Power of Attorney for Health Care on _____ at

(Date)

_____, _____

(City)   *(State)*

_____

(Signature of Principal)

(THIS POWER OF ATTORNEY WILL NOT BE VALID FOR MAKING HEALTH CARE DECISIONS UNLESS IT IS EITHER: (1) SIGNED BY TWO QUALIFIED ADULT WITNESSES WHO ARE PERSONALLY KNOWN TO YOU AND WHO ARE PRESENT WHEN YOU SIGN OR ACKNOWLEDGE YOUR SIGNATURE OR (2) ACKNOWLEDGED BEFORE A NOTARY PUBLIC IN CALIFORNIA.)

CERTIFICATE OF ACKNOWLEDGEMENT OF NOTARY PUBLIC

(You may use acknowledgment before a notary public instead of the statement of witnesses which appears on the following page.)

State of California   )

) ss.

County of _____)

     On this _____ day of _____, in the year _____,

before me, _____

(here insert name of notary public)

         personally appeared _____,

(here insert name of principal)

personally known to me (or proved to me on the basis of satisfactory evidence) to be the person whose name is subscribed to this instrument, and acknowledged that he or she executed it. I declare under penalty of perjury that the person whose name is subscribed to this instrument appears to be of sound mind and under no duress, fraud, or undue influence.

NOTARY SEAL

_____

(Signature of Notary Public)

6

APPENDIX 17A *(continued)*

STATEMENT OF WITNESSES

(If you elect to use witnesses instead of having this document notarized, you must use two qualified adult witnesses. None of the following may be used as a witness: (1) a person you designate as your agent or alternate agent, (2) a health care provider, (3) an employee of a health care provider, (4) the operator of a community care facility, (5) an employee of an operator of a community care facility. At least one of the witnesses must make the additional declaration set out following the place where the witnesses sign.)

I declare under penalty of perjury under the laws of California that the person who signed or acknowledged this document is personally known to me to be the principal, that the principal signed or acknowledged this durable power of attorney in my presence, that the principal appears to be of sound mind and under no duress, fraud, or undue influence, that I am not the person appointed as attorney-in-fact by this document, and that I am not a health care provider, an employee of a health care provider, the operator of a community care facility, nor an employee of an operator of a community care facility.

Signature: _____ Residence Address: _____

Print Name: _____ _____

Date: _____ _____

Signature: _____ Residence Address: _____

Print Name: _____ _____

Date: _____ _____

(AT LEAST ONE OF THE ABOVE WITNESSES MUST ALSO SIGN THE FOLLOWING DECLARATION.)

I further declare under penalty of perjury under the laws of California that I am not related to the principal by blood, marriage, or adoption, and, to the best of my knowledge I am not entitled to any part of the estate of the principal upon the death of the principal under a will now existing or by operation of law.

Signature: _____

(Optional Second Signature): _____

COPIES

YOUR AGENT MAY NEED THIS DOCUMENT IMMEDIATELY IN CASE OF AN EMERGENCY THAT REQUIRES A DECISION CONCERNING YOUR HEALTH CARE. YOU SHOULD KEEP THE EXECUTED ORIGINAL DOCUMENT AND GIVE A COPY OF THE EXECUTED ORIGINAL TO YOUR AGENT AND ANY ALTERNATE AGENTS. YOU SHOULD ALSO GIVE A COPY TO YOUR DOCTOR, MEMBERS OF YOUR FAMILY, AND ANY OTHER PEOPLE WHO WOULD BE LIKELY TO NEED A COPY OF THIS FORM TO CARRY OUT YOUR WISHES. PHOTOCOPIES OF THIS DOCUMENT CAN BE RELIED UPON AS THOUGH THEY WERE ORIGINALS.

7

APPENDIX 17A *(concluded)*

SPECIAL REQUIREMENTS

(Special additional requirements must be satisfied for this document to be valid if (1) you are a patient in a skilled nursing facility or (2) you are a conservatee under the Lanterman-Petris-Short Act and you are appointing the conservator as your agent to make health care decisions for you. If you are not sure whether you are in a skilled nursing facility, which is a special type of nursing home, ask the facility staff. If you are not sure whether the person you want to choose as your health care agent is your conservator under the Lanterman-Petris-Short Act, ask that person.)

1. If you are a patient in a skilled nursing facility (as defined in Health and Safety Code Section 1250(c)) at least one of the witnesses must be a patient advocate or ombudsman. The patient advocate or ombudsman must sign the witness statement **and** must also sign the following declaration:

I further declare under penalty of perjury under the laws of California that I am a patient advocate or ombudsman as designated by the State Department of Aging and am serving as a witness as required by subdivision (f) of Civil Code 2432.

Signature: _____   Address: _____

Print Name: _____   _____

Date: _____   _____

2. If you are a conservatee under the Lanterman-Petris-Short Act (of Division 5 of the Welfare and Institutions Code) and you wish to designate your conservator as your agent to make health care decisions, you must be represented by legal counsel. Your lawyer must also sign the following statement:

I am a lawyer authorized to practice law in the state where this power of attorney was executed, and the principal was my client at the time this power of attorney was executed. I have advised my client concerning his or her rights in connection with this power of attorney and the applicable law and the consequences of signing or not signing this power of attorney, and my client, after being so advised, has executed this power of attorney.

Signature: _____   Address: _____

Print Name: _____   _____

Date: _____   _____

California Medical Association
P.O. Box 7690, San Francisco 94103-7690

8

Living Will Declaration*

---

*Reproduced with permission of the Society for the Right to Die.

APPENDIX 17B

Society for the Right to Die

250 West 57th Street/New York, NY 10107

Living Will Declaration

To My Family, Doctors, and All Those Concerned with My Care

INSTRUCTIONS
Consult this column for help and guidance.

I, _____, being of sound mind, make this statement as a directive to be followed if I become unable to participate in decisions regarding my medical care.

This declaration sets forth your directions regarding medical treatment.

If I should be in an incurable or irreversible mental or physical condition with no reasonable expectation of recovery, I direct my attending physician to withhold or withdraw treatment that merely prolongs my dying. I further direct that treatment be limited to measures to keep me comfortable and to relieve pain.

You have the right to refuse treatment you do not want, and you may request the care you do want.

These directions express my legal right to refuse treatment. Therefore I expect my family, doctors, and everyone concerned with my care to regard themselves as legally and morally bound to act in accord with my wishes, and in so doing to be free of any legal liability for having followed my directions.

You may list specific treatment you do not want. For example:

Cardiac resuscitation
Mechanical respiration
Artificial feeding/fluids by tubes

Otherwise, your general statement, top right, will stand for your wishes.

I especially do not want: _____
_____
_____
_____
_____
_____

You may want to add instructions for care you do want—for example, pain medication; or that you prefer to die at home if possible.

Other instructions/comments: _____
_____
_____
_____

Proxy Designation Clause: Should I become unable to communicate my instructions as stated above, I designate the following person to act in my behalf:

If you want, you can name someone to see that your wishes are carried out, but you do not have to do this.

Name_____
Address_____

If the person I have named above is unable to act in my behalf, I authorize the following person to do so:

Name_____
Address_____

Sign and date here in the presence of two adult witnesses, who should also sign.

Signed:_____Date:_____
Witness:_____Witness:_____

Keep the signed original with your personal papers at home.
Give signed copies to your doctors, family, and to your proxy.

Directive to Physicians*

---

*Reproduced with permission of the Society for the Right to Die.

APPENDIX 17C

=== **CALIFORNIA** ===

DIRECTIVE TO PHYSICIANS

Directive made this _____ day of _____ (month, year).

I, _____ , being of sound mind, willfully and voluntarily make known my desire that my life shall not be artificially prolonged under the circumstances set forth below, and do hereby declare:

1. If at any time I should have an incurable injury, disease, or illness certified to be a terminal condition by two physicians, and where the application of life-sustaining procedures would serve only to artificially prolong the moment of my death and where my physician determines that my death is imminent whether or not life-sustaining procedures are utilized, I direct that such procedures be withheld or withdrawn, and that I be permitted to die naturally.

2. In the absence of my ability to give directions regarding the use of such life-sustaining procedures, it is my intention that this directive shall be honored by my family and physician(s) as the final expression of my legal right to refuse medical or surgical treatment and accept the consequences from such refusal.

3. If I have been diagnosed as pregnant and that diagnosis is known to my physician, this directive shall have no force or effect during the course of my pregnancy.

4. I have been diagnosed at least 14 days ago as having a terminal condition by

   _____ , M.D., whose address is

   _____ , and whose

   telephone number is _____ . I understand that if I have not filled in the physician's name and address, it shall be presumed that I did not have a terminal condition when I made out this directive.

5. This directive shall have no force or effect five years from the date filled in above.

6. I understand the full import of this directive and I am emotionally and mentally competent to make this directive.

Signed _____

City, County and State of Residence _____

The declarant has been personally known to me and I believe him or her to be of sound mind.

Witness _____ Witness _____

This Directive complies in form with the 'Natural Death Act' California Health and Safety Code, Section 7188.

— 18 ——————————————————————

Postmortem Tax Planning

———————————————————————————————————

OVERVIEW

The estate planning process does not end at the client's death. Assets must still be marshalled, preserved, and distributed by the decedent's representatives, a group that includes executors, trustees, accountants, attorneys, and survivors. In the transmission process, tax law often enables these aides to recommend and make choices. This chapter focuses on the tax elections available to them as parties dealing in the decedent's property. It will begin with an overview of the principles of postmortem tax compliance. Next, it will survey those planning devices primarily designed to reduce income taxes, including estate expense elections, choice of tax year, and distribution-planning strategies. Finally, the chapter will present those planning devices primarily designed to save death taxes, including the alternate valuation date, the use of disclaimers, and the application of the QTIP election.

TAX RETURNS AFTER DEATH

We already know that death of an individual may trigger estate and inheritance taxes. Transfer of a decedent's property is often not a transfer tax-free procedure. But can the work be done free of income tax? Will the death of an income-earning individual terminate the obligation to pay taxes on all income received thereafter? Of course, the answer to both questions is no, because income subject to taxation will be received by survivors, estates, and trusts. If income subject to taxation is being received, you can be sure that the Internal Revenue Code imposes a tax on that income to one or another recipient in the year received.

Since death can create or continue the obligation to pay transfer and income taxes, we must first study the nature of these tax obligations and their effects on the survivors. This section will introduce principles of postmortem federal tax compliance, that is, the completion of federal tax returns and the payment of federal taxes on income and on property in connection with the death of a decedent.

Several transfer tax and income tax returns will usually be filed after the client's death. With regard to *transfer taxes,* the decedent's representatives may be required to file a state estate or inheritance tax return, and a Form 706, federal estate tax return, which is due within nine months after date of death.[1]

With regard to *income taxes,* the representatives may be required to file state returns and the following two types of federal returns. First, the decedent's final income tax return will be reported on Form 1040, covering all income for the last tax year up to date of death. Second, if the decedent leaves a probate estate, one estate fiduciary income tax return, Form 1041, will be filed for each tax year of the estate's existence. The fiduciary return for the first year will report all income from the decedent's date of death to the end of the first tax year. When the estate is terminated, usually by final distribution, the last estate income tax return will be

---

[1]As mentioned in Chapter 6, a federal estate tax return must be filed for decedents dying with a total gross estate plus adjusted taxable gifts equaling or exceeding the amount of the exemption equivalent of the unified credit for the year of death. For example, the estate of a decedent who died in 1985 having a gross estate of $355,000 and adjusted taxable gifts of $100,000 must file a return because their sum exceeds $400,000. Unfortunately, filing is required even though no FET will be due, as in the case where the entire estate is left to a surviving spouse.

One further point regarding the estate tax return: Since evidence of a step-up in basis is essentially derived from the information on Form 706, many tax practitioners will recommend filing this return for smaller estates in order to ensure that the death value of appreciated property will be recognized as its new basis. However, the IRS is not bound by such FET values in an income tax dispute.

filed for a "short" year, from the beginning of the tax year to date of distribution. After estate termination, the beneficiaries will report income from distributed estate property on their own tax returns.

The following example summarizes these federal income tax rules and assumes that all taxpayers report taxes on a *calendar year* basis; that is, their tax year begins January 1 and ends December 31.[2]

> EXAMPLE 18–1 Farley, a widower, died on May 12, 1986. In his will, Farley left 100 shares of Xerox stock to his son Jordan and the residue of his estate in trust for the benefit of his granddaughter Sheila. The date of final estate distribution was February 25, 1988. The following postdeath tax returns were filed. All income earned by the decedent from January 1 through May 12, 1986, was reported by the executor on the decedent's final income tax return, Form 1040. All income earned by the estate between May 13 and December 31, 1986, was reported by the executor on the first estate income tax return, Form 1041. The executor also filed a Form 1041 return for all estate income for the entire year 1987 and a third for income earned during the period from January 1 to February 25, 1988. Jordan reported on his Form 1040 all income received after February 25, 1988. Trust property income, or DNI, earned after that date will be reported by the trust, on Form 1041, and by Sheila on her Form 1040, if the income is distributed to her.[3]

A *joint return* may be filed for a decedent and the surviving spouse for the year of death, covering income of the decedent to date of death and income of the spouse for the entire year. In the alternative, returns may be filed for each spouse separately. In most situations, filing jointly will save total taxes in the same way it does when both spouses are alive. The greater the difference between the two spousal incomes, the greater the tax usually saved by filing jointly.[4]

Next, we turn to postmortem income tax planning ideas.

---

[2]Actually, an estate needn't use a calendar year. Planning with the use of a fiscal rather than calendar year will be discussed later in the chapter.

[3]All trusts must use a calendar tax year.

[4]The surviving spouse will also be permitted to enjoy the lower rates applicable to joint returns for two years after the decedent's death, provided that he or she

PLANNING DEVICES PRIMARILY DESIGNED TO SAVE INCOME TAXES

Some postmortem planning strategies are primarily undertaken to reduce the income tax bite. They include various expense elections, selection of probate estate tax year, and distribution planning. Before examining these techniques, let us survey three tax principles on which most of them will be based.

First, greater income tax can be saved when taxable income can be spread among more taxpaying entities. This idea was first mentioned and developed in Chapter 9. Proper premortem planning can result in the creation of *additional taxpaying entities* after the client's death. These tax entities can include the estate, several trusts (with at least one trust for each beneficiary), and the beneficiaries themselves. After death, proper timing of distributions among these entities can often save significant tax dollars, as we shall see.

A second tax principle on which postmortem income tax planning is based is the notion of the *conduit*, introduced in Chapter 8. The conduit principle prevents double taxation of estate or trust income. It is derived from the concept of distributable net income, or DNI, which is roughly equal to the estate or trust's fiduciary accounting income, and which constitutes the maximum amount of income taxable to the beneficiaries, as well as the maximum amount deductible by the estate or trust. The amount taxable to an estate or trust roughly equals its total income, including capital gains and losses, reduced by the distribution deduction, which roughly equals the lesser of the amount distributed or its DNI. Thus, a trust or estate that distributes all of its income will be taxed only on its capital gains. Consequently, under the conduit principle, DNI earned by an estate or trust which is distributed to the beneficiaries in the year earned will be taxed to the beneficiaries and not to the estate or trust, which simply acts as a conduit for delivering income from the source to the beneficiaries. Conversely, any DNI retained by the estate or trust will not be offset by a distribution deduction, which will make that DNI taxable to it rather

---

(*a*) has not remarried and (*b*) maintains a home for one or more dependent children.

than to the beneficiaries. Further, all capital gains are taxed to the estate or trust, except in the last taxable year.

A third tax principle on which postmortem income tax planning is based is that in the year in which an estate or trust makes its final distribution, all income, including capital gains, will be *carried out* to and taxable to the beneficiaries. Thus in its *termination year,* a trust or estate will have no taxable income.

These tax principles represent only the briefest summary of the principles of income taxation of estates and trusts detailed in Chapter 8. The reader is strongly urged to review that more comprehensive section before continuing.

Expense Elections Available to the Executor

During administration, the executor is able to make several informal elections with regard to estate expenses.[5] These include the medical expense election, the administration expense and losses election, and the election to waive the executor's commission. They are covered next.

Medical expense election.   Any of the decedent's unreimbursed medical expenses which are unpaid at death may be deducted either on the decedent's final income tax return or on the federal estate tax return, but not on both.

The choice of where to deduct unpaid medical expenses will depend on which alternative will yield the greater tax saving. The size of the tax saving will be a function of the marginal tax rate which, in turn, will be influenced by the size of the estate tax base. However, smaller estates may be unable to benefit from a deduction on either return. On the *income tax return,* only the excess of the medical expense amount over 7.5 percent of adjusted gross income is deductible, and any remaining undeductible amount may not be deducted on the FET return. With regard to the *estate tax return,* no estate tax may be due for smaller estates, even without the deduction, either because no estate tax return need be filed or

---

[5]We will refer to the executor's ability to make elections because the executor is the person having that legal authority. Of course, most executors rely on their attorney or accountant to apprise them of the tax alternatives.

because other deductions, including the marital deduction, may independently reduce the taxable estate to zero.

Administration expense and losses election.   Expenses in administering the decedent's estate, including executor's commission,[6] attorney's fees, and casualty losses, are deductible either on the federal estate tax return or on the estate income tax return, or partly on each. However, double deductions are not allowed.

Again, the choice of where to deduct these items will usually turn on which return will produce the greater tax saving. And again, smaller estates may be unable to enjoy a deduction on either return. Casualty losses are deductible against income only to the extent that they exceed 10 percent of adjusted gross income. And there may be no FET to save in the case of a small estate, or any size estate for that matter, which will essentially pass to the surviving spouse. Larger estates often will be able to choose because they can save taxes on either return, but there may be situations, as in the next example, when the deduction should be divided between the two returns.[7]

> EXAMPLE 18–2 Let's assume that Maggie, owning a gross estate of $5 million, will die in 1990 leaving everything to her husband, Earl. Expenses in administering Maggie's estate are expected to total $700,000. If the estate's marginal income tax rate exceeds the marginal FET rate, greater taxes would be saved by deducting the entire amount on Form 1041. On the other hand, if the marginal FET rate is higher, a greater tax saving would result if only $100,000, not the entire amount, is deducted on Form 706 and the rest is deducted on Form 1041. To see why, consider the effect of the expense outlay on the amount of the maximum marital deduction. Since the actual amount "passing" to Earl will be only $4.3 million, this amount will constitute the maximum allowable marital deduction. If the executor deducts all of the administration expenses on the estate income tax return, the estate will wind up incurring an FET, despite the fact that Maggie left her entire estate to her spouse, since the taxable estate of $700,000 will exceed $600,000, the 1990 exemption equivalent of the unified credit. Alternatively, if the executor deducts at least $100,000

---

[6]We'll see in a moment that the executor may want to waive the commission.

[7]Again, of course, unless there is a 100 percent marital deduction.

of these expenses on the estate tax return, the FET will be zero since the taxable estate will have been reduced to the amount of the exemption equivalent. Since no more than $100,000 is needed to do this, the other $600,000 can be deducted on the income tax return.

Thus, if an amount is deductible on another return, it would be imprudent to deduct it on any FET return that can already shelter all taxable estate property with the unified credit or some other shield.

Election to waive executor's commission. The executor's commission, as a deductible administration expense, will be taxable as income to the executor. However, the executor may elect to waive (i.e., refuse) that commission. Waiver of the commission may be worthwhile if the executor is residuary beneficiary of the estate and if his or her personal marginal income tax rate exceeds the marginal tax rate for both the estate FET and the estate income tax. If the executor is not residuary beneficiary of the estate, a waiver of the commission will mean a complete forfeit of that amount. Thus, the nonresiduary executor will usually prefer to receive the commission, no matter the tax cost.

EXAMPLE 18–3 An estate has been left entirely to the decedent's *daughter,* who is the executor. The executor's commission will be $10,000. The estate's marginal FET rate is 41 percent and its marginal income tax rate is 28 percent. The daughter's marginal income tax rate is 33 percent. *Not waiving* the commission will lower the FET by $4,100 and raise daughter's income tax by $3,300, for a net tax saving of $800.

EXAMPLE 18–4 Facts similar to Example 18-3, except that decedent left his entire estate to his *spouse,* who is executor. Due to the unlimited marital deduction, the effective marginal FET rate is 0 percent. Regarding income tax rates, assuming that spouse's marginal rate is 33 percent, and the estate's marginal rate is 28 percent, *waiving* the commission will raise estate income tax by $2,800 and lower spouse's income tax by $3,300, for a net tax saving of $500.

EXAMPLE 18–5 Facts similar to Example 18-4, except that the entire estate has been left outright *to the decedent's children* of a former marriage. Waiving the executor's commission would mean totally forfeiting the receipt of that amount. As executor, spouse, not wishing to forfeit all cash flow from the estate, elects *not to waive* the commission. Instead of nothing, spouse will receive $6,700, after tax, from the estate.

Selection of Estate Taxable Year

The executor of a probate estate has considerable flexibility in choosing its taxable, or tax, year. Although all income tax years except the first and the last must be 12 months long, the executor can choose the estate's tax year to end on the last day of any month. If it ends on December 31, the estate is said to be on a *calendar year,* with the first tax year running from date of death to December 31. All other tax years will then run from January 1 to December 31, except for the year of final distribution of the estate assets, which will run for a "short year," from January 1 to date of distribution. Alternatively, if the estate's tax year ends on the last day of any month other than December, it is said to be on a *fiscal year.*

Whether an estate is on a calendar year or fiscal year, two basic income tax benefits are available to it. First, it can be made a separate taxpaying entity, capable of *splitting income* with the other tax entities involved in the estate distribution process.[8] Second, further tax saving can be realized in the first and last tax years of an estate's life, since both years are usually shorter than 12 months. The first tax year is shorter because date of death does not usually coincide with the last day of the tax year. The last tax year is shorter than 12 months because date of final distribution doesn't usually coincide with the last day of the tax year. A *short tax year* produces income tax savings because proportionately less income will ordinarily be taxed in those years, at proportionately lower rates.

In contrast to the tax benefits available to all estates, some benefits are available only to estates having a carefully selected fiscal year. In each of the next two examples, assume that the decedent died on March 10, 1987.

---

[8] By lowering tax rates, TRA 86 reduced the tax saving benefit of splitting income.

EXAMPLE 18–6 The estate of a decedent is planning the distribution of income to its beneficiary, the surviving spouse. It elects a fiscal year ending January 31. If the estate distributes income earned on March 15, 1988, to the spouse during the month of January, 1989, the spouse may not have to report the income until April 1990 more than two full years after the income was initially received by the estate. This assumes that no quarterly estimated tax payments will have to be filed by the spouse.

EXAMPLE 18–7 An estate, which has a lower marginal income tax rate than its beneficiaries, expects to receive an income of $30,000 every three months starting in June 1988, until estate termination on November 30, 1990. To spread the income out over as many tax years as possible, the estate elects to have its fiscal year close just before the expected date of final distribution. Thus, it chooses a fiscal year ending September 30. Estate taxable income (DNI) for each year will be the following: first year, $60,000; second year, $120,000; third year up to September 30, 1990, $120,000. Thus, for each of the first three tax years, the estate will be taxed on all of this accumulated income, and DNI carried out to beneficiaries will be zero. In the final year, the beneficiaries will receive the after-tax accumulation, tax free. In contrast, more total tax would be owed if the estate elected a fiscal year that effectively prevented it from being a taxpaying entity in the third year. For example, had the estate elected a fiscal year ending November 30, the pattern of estate taxable income would be as follows: first year, $60,000; second and last estate taxable year ending November 30, 1987, $120,000. DNI to the beneficiaries would be $120,000. The beneficiaries would receive tax free the after-tax accumulation on $180,000 of income, but the last year's $120,000 would constitute taxable DNI to them, not to the estate. In the last taxable year of an estate, DNI is totally carried out to the beneficiaries.

If the executor of an estate expects an unusually large income receipt shortly after the period of administration begins, he or she may wish to elect a year end which would give it a rather short first year, so that other taxable income received later will be taxed during the following year rather than lumped with the large receipt and taxed at a higher rate.

EXAMPLE 18–8 Decedent Malley was an accountant who died on May 19 owning, among other things, account receivables amounting to $50,000. The estate elects a fiscal year ending July 31 to include most of this income in the first tax year, while causing most other income to be taxed in the second and later years.

On the other hand, a relatively long first tax year would be desirable if a large deduction is expected within 6 to 12 months from date of death.

> EXAMPLE 18–9 Combined with a large amount of early income, as in Example 18-8, the estate expects to make a large distribution to the beneficiaries in April of the following year. The estate instead elects a fiscal year closing on April 30, so that the deduction can be used to reduce estate taxable income.

Distribution Planning

Although TRA 86 reduced income tax rates substantially for all tax entities, an estate or trust may be able to save some income tax for its beneficiaries by properly planning the amount and timing of beneficiary distributions. Much of distribution planning hinges on the existence of differentials in marginal tax rates, and thus one of the planner's tasks is to compare the tax rates of the various entities and allocate taxable income to those in lower brackets. In this section, we will consider situations where the beneficiaries are, alternatively, in a higher bracket and in a lower bracket in comparison with the distributing estate or trust. This section will also examine the income tax advantage of prolonging the estate's life.

Estate or trust in lower bracket than beneficiaries. When the estate or trust is in a lower income tax bracket than its beneficiaries, consideration should be given to distribution arrangements that will generate a greater taxable income to itself and a correspondingly lesser taxable income to its beneficiaries.

Accumulation of income. The most common device used accumulates income by reducing and delaying distributions of DNI. In some cases, excess accumulations will be subject to the *throwback rules,* which, as mentioned in Chapter 8, seek to prevent a trustee from delaying a distribution to a beneficiary in years when the beneficiaries' tax rate is high, only to distribute the income in later years when the rate is expected to be lower. The throwback rules require excess distributions to a beneficiary in later years to be taxed to the beneficiary as if they had been received in the years in which the trust actually received and accumulated them. However, the throwback rules do not apply to estates nor to any trust accumulations made for a beneficiary when under the age of 21.

EXAMPLE 667–1 Jonathan died earlier this year, leaving his entire estate to his wife, Kathleen. The estate has earned some income this year but elects *not to distribute* it to Kathleen until next year. This year Kathleen, who has earned considerable income herself, is also recipient of a large lump-sum pension distribution from Jonathan's employer. Therefore, she is in the 33 percent marginal tax bracket. The estate, on the other hand, is subject to a 15 percent marginal tax rate, partly because the executor has elected a fiscal year that will give the estate a very short first taxable year. The accumulated income will be distributed to Kathleen in later years when her tax rate is likely to be lower. The throwback rules will not apply.[9]

Nonapplication of the throwback rules to estates can constitute a reason not to avoid probate. Without probate, there is no taxpaying estate capable of accumulating income in one year and making an accumulation distribution in another. Since the probate-avoiding revocable living trust is usually subject to the throwback rules, it cannot usually exploit this tax strategy. With the lower rates brought about by TRA 86, however, the decision to elect probate cannot rest solely on income tax savings.

Realization of a gain. Another way to benefit from the estate or trust having a lower tax rate than the beneficiaries is through the realization of a gain. If an estate asset has appreciated after death and is expected to be quickly sold upon receipt by the designated beneficiary, the executor of a lower-bracket estate should give consideration to selling the asset prior to distribution so that the estate can recognize the gain. The after-tax proceeds can be distributed to the beneficiary tax free. However, to be taxed to the estate, the sale will have to be made before its last taxable year so that the gain is not automatically carried out to the beneficiary.

Despite having a lower marginal tax rate, the executor of an estate may wish to distribute rather than sell the asset if the beneficiary has a *realized loss* that is presently unusable for lack of any offsetting gains. The beneficiary, who could sell the asset, then would not have to carry over an unused loss to future years.

Estate or trust in higher marginal tax bracket than beneficiaries. In cases where an estate or trust is subject to a higher marginal income tax rate than one or more of its beneficiaries, the executor or trustee may prefer to *distribute income* to them in the year the income is received, so that it is taxed at the beneficiaries' lower

---

[9]However, probate fees might substantially wipe out the tax saving.

rate. In addition, when the estate or trust's tax year overlaps those of the beneficiaries, the executor or trustee can time the distribution so that it is made in one of two years in which the beneficiaries' tax rate is lower.

> EXAMPLE 18–10 It is the month of November, and the beneficiary of an estate just lost his job as a law firm associate and expects to be unemployed for about six months. Instead of distributing $50,000 of income to him in late December, the executor distributes it early next January, during a year in which the beneficiary's taxable income is expected to be substantially lower. The estate has a fiscal year ending February 28, so the choice to distribute in either December or January has no effect on its own taxation; both months are in the same tax year, the year in which the income is received.

Tax planning of distributions from estates and trusts are subject to some other tax constraints, one of which is described next.

Unduly prolonging the estate life. By now, the reader is aware of several potential income tax advantages to having a probate estate. This will encourage some executors to delay closing their estates. Since termination of an estate by final distribution cuts off the tax benefits available to this separate taxpayer, tax planning would suggest undertaking this ploy by delaying the estate's date of final distribution. Unfortunately, the IRS has authority to treat an estate as *terminated* for tax purposes if it concludes that the estate's life had been "unduly" prolonged.

How long can an estate usually be kept open without generating IRS disapproval? Some authorities believe that a reasonable life is about 3 to 4 years for an ordinary estate, and as long as 15 years for an estate which elects to defer payment of taxes under Section 6166.

PLANNING DEVICES PRIMARILY DESIGNED TO SAVE DEATH TAXES

We turn now to an examination of several postmortem tax planning strategies which have their greatest impact on death taxes. They include the alternate valuation date, disclaimers, and the QTIP election.

Alternate Valuation Date

The size of the FET for an estate will, of course, often be a direct function of the value of its assets. An intelligent executor or estate adviser will try to keep valuation as low as possible. Often, conflicts with the IRS arise regarding the correct valuation of particular estate assets and deductions. While such conflicts make the entire subject of estate valuation seem quite subjective, there is one area in this field that offers objective certainty. The Code allows the executor the option to value estate assets and deductions at either one of two different points in time.

Under Section 2032, the value of the assets included in the gross estate (and corresponding liabilities) may be determined as of date of death, or they may be determined as of the alternate valuation date (AVD), which is six months after date of death. This section was enacted after the Great Depression to limit the adverse tax and liquidity effect that radical changes in market values could have on an estate. For example, consider a decedent who died in mid- to late 1929 owning a considerable amount of stock, which had to be included in the gross estate at high, precrash date-of-death values. Such an estate could have wound up owing, nine months after death, an FET that was considerably larger than its total current market value!

Under AVD rules, the executor may not pick and choose which assets to value at which of the two dates. If the election is made, *all* assets must be valued at the AVD. However, any assets sold or distributed after death and before the AVD must be valued as of date of sale.

Disclaimers

We have already studied disclaimers in two earlier chapters. First, in Chapter 7, covering the federal gift tax, we examined the transfer tax aspects of disclaimers, including the requirements for a valid disclaimer. Second, in Chapter 12, surveying marital deduction and bypass planning, we saw how a disclaimer provision could be included in a bypass arrangement to add postmortem flexibility to the client's estate plan. That discussion also mentioned several disadvantages of the use of disclaimers. The purpose of the present discussion is to further describe the marital deduction disclaimer and to give an overview of how disclaimers can be used to correct defective or inefficient dispositive documents.

Disclaimers to reduce the marital deduction. We have seen how a spousal disclaimer of a marital deduction bequest can add postmortem flexibility by enabling the surviving spouse to choose the amount of the marital bequest to disclaim to the bypass share, thereby self-determining the amount of FET to defer to the second death. That section was described as Option 4, "full marital deduction with disclaimer into bypass," in which the surviving spouse was bequeathed the entire amount of the decedent spouse's estate, subject to S2's ability to disclaim all or part of it in the event that a bypass eventually became desirable.

The marital deduction disclaimer can be used for any size estate but probably works best for smaller estates. For example, a plan for an estate that is currently too small to justify the use of a bypass could include a disclaimer provision, available in the event that the estate grew large enough to warrant a bypass distribution.

Factors that may help the surviving spouse decide whether and how much to disclaim include S2's needs and his or her income tax bracket. First, the greater S2's perceived *need* for S1's assets to live comfortably, the less S2 will probably be willing to disclaim. This, in turn, will depend on the size of S2's estate. Of course, by disclaiming, S2 would not ordinarily be relinquishing all interests in the property, since the typical bypass trust provides for some invasion powers and for most or all income to be paid to S2. However, many S2s often feel emotionally that by disclaiming, they are in reality making a complete relinquishment.

Second, S2's willingness to disclaim will also depend on his or her marginal income *tax rate,* since the higher S2's rate, the more desirable will be a disclaimer if it has the effect of redirecting taxable income to other beneficiaries.

For a further discussion of the benefits and drawbacks of providing for a spousal disclaimer into a bypass, see Chapter 12.

Disclaimers to increase the marital deduction. A disclaimer can be used to raise a marital deduction that is subsequently found to be inadequate. For example, a client may have died with an estate plan that neither included a bypass nor took full use of the unlimited marital deduction. This can occur when a person dies intestate or dies owning a considerable amount of property in joint tenancy with someone other than a spouse. The nonspouse beneficiary may be encouraged to disclaim the interest so that it may qualify for the marital deduction by passing to the surviving spouse. However, problems in implementation may arise. First, only a *donee* of property held in joint tenancy may disclaim. Thus, such a disclaimer will work only if the decedent was the original donor of the property. Second, courts may be unwilling to allow the guardian of a minor child to disclaim rights to property, reasoning that full relinquishment of property is not in the child's best interest.[10,]

Disclaimers to correct defective and inefficient dispositive documents. Occasionally, wills and trusts are drafted erroneously. One always hopes that these mistakes will be discovered during the client's lifetime. If not, they can still often be corrected by disclaimer.

> EXAMPLE 2518–1 Kirby, a widower, died earlier this year, leaving all of his $2 million estate in trust, with income payable to his son Klaus for his life, and then remainder to his granddaughter Harriet, who is Klaus's daughter. This is an undesirable *generation-skipping transfer,* because it will subject all but $1 million of the corpus to an immediate generation-skipping tax. To avoid this result, Klaus could disclaim his rights to all of the income except that amount that $1 million in corpus would generate. Whether Klaus would want to disclaim would depend on several factors, including Klaus's age, the amount of his other income in comparison with his needs, and whether Harriet is one of Klaus's intended beneficiaries.

A disclaimer can also be used to overcome an inefficient disposition, thereby increasing the size of a charitable contribution.

> EXAMPLE 2518–2 Sally, a widow, was 90 years old when she died six months ago. She left one surviving relative, her son Abbott, who is aged 73 and in failing health. Sally's will, paraphrased somewhat, reads, "All to Abbott, but if he does not survive me by 30 days, then all to the Girl Scouts of America." Abbott, who should be able to live for 30 days but is not likely to live more than six months, has no issue

---

[10]An additional problem with disclaiming joint tenancy property is that IRS regulations require the disclaimer to be made within nine months of the date the joint tenancy is *created*. (An exception is made for joint bank accounts and savings certificates. T.A.M. 8625001.) One court has recently reached a contrary conclusion, reasoning that joint tenancies are unilaterally revocable during the cotenants' lifetimes, *Kennedy* v. *Commissioner,* 7 cir, (1986) 804 F2d 1332. But another court has ruled otherwise, *McDonald* 89TC26(1987).

and would not mind leaving all of the property inherited from his mother to the Girl Scouts. To avoid taxation of the property in Sally's estate, Abbott could disclaim all interest in Sally's bequest. Consequently, the property would pass to the Girl Scouts without being subject to taxation in Sally's estate.

A disclaimer may also be used to refuse an undesirable bequest of a general power of appointment.

EXAMPLE 2518–3 Barbara died seven months ago leaving a will that provides for a bypass trust for the benefit of her husband, Jake. The will gives Jake the right to invade the trust for reasons of "health or happiness." Since courts have consistently held that the term *happiness* does not constitute an ascertainable standard, Jake will be deemed to be the holder of a general power of appointment over the entire trust corpus, which will be includable in Jake's gross estate at his later death. Jake may be able to prevent this unfortunate result by properly disclaiming his power over the corpus.

These examples are merely illustrative of the many situations where postmortem disclaimers can be used to alter estate dispositions to obtain more desirable results. It should be noted that this is a rapidly changing area of the law, and the client is encouraged to seek competent counsel prior to attempting to make a qualified disclaimer.

QTIP Election

As mentioned in Chapter 6, property normally can qualify for the marital deduction only if it "passes" to the spouse. In other words, the spouse cannot ordinarily receive an interest that might terminate; the interest cannot be terminable. Over the years, however, the Code has carved out several exceptions to this rule. Up to 1982, the most commonly used exception involved giving the spouse a life estate in the income and a general power of appointment over the corpus. Since then, the QTIP election, effective in 1982, has become even more popular. It is found in Code Section 2056(b)(7) and provides that property subject to a terminable interest can qualify for the marital deduction if it meets the following two requirements for "qualified terminable interest property":

1. The surviving spouse must be entitled to receive all income from the property for life, payable at least annually.

2. No person may have the power to appoint the property to anyone other than the surviving spouse.

Why might clients wish to bequeath only a terminable interest to their spouse? Why wouldn't clients always prefer to give property to the spouse outright, or in trust with the spouse receiving a general power of appointment over the property? Why restrict the spouse's ability to control disposition of the property? There are several possible reasons, including the desire to protect the estate from the consequences of S2's immaturity or senility, but perhaps the most common reason is a desire by S1 to absolutely *guarantee the ultimate disposition* to an intended beneficiary. The typical S1 choosing a QTIP arrangement has children of a former marriage and wishes to provide for the surviving spouse's income needs during lifetime, yet still absolutely ensure that his or her own children will eventually receive the property after the surviving spouse's death. Only a QTIP-type arrangement will do all this and still qualify the property for the marital deduction.[11]

In contrast with the decision as to who will ultimately receive the property outright, the final decision whether to elect to include QTIP property in the S1 marital deduction will not be up to the S1-transferor. And in contrast with the spousal disclaimer, that decision will not be up to S2. Instead, *S1's executor* is required to make the choice on the S1 FET return. If the election is made, the property can qualify for the S1 marital deduction, and S1's taxable estate and FET can be reduced. However, at S2's death, the S2 date-of-death value of the qualifying property *must* be taxed as though it were included in S2's gross estate. Thus, in making the election, the S1 executor must choose one of the following consequences: (1) making the election will defer the FET by reducing the S1 taxable estate and increasing the S2 taxable estate, and alternatively (2) not making the election will accelerate the FET by producing a larger S1 taxable estate and a smaller S2 taxable estate. The choice whether or not to make the election essentially boils down to the choice *to defer or to equalize* spousal FET. The reader is directed

---

[11]Some planners recommend the QTIP plan for clients still married to their first spouse to eliminate the risk that their surviving spouse might remarry and leave substantial property to the new spouse rather than the children. Others disagree, pointing out that most widows either do not remarry or act prudently when they remarry.

back to Chapter 12 for an extended discussion of the factors influencing this decision.

> EXAMPLE 2056(b)(7)–1 Kenneth died three months ago. He is survived by his ex-wife, his second wife (S2), and three adult children of the first marriage. There are no children from the second marriage. At death, Kenneth owned $2 million in property. Kenneth's will creates two trusts, trust B and trust A. Trust B is a bypass trust and will receive an amount equal to the exemption equivalent of the unified credit. Trust A will receive the residue of Kenneth's estate. The trustees of both trusts are to pay all income monthly to S2 for her life. At S2's death, the amount of each corpus will pass outright in equal shares to Kenneth's three children. S2 is given a power to invade the corpus of trust B, subject to an ascertainable standard. S2 is given no power over the corpus of trust A. The property in trust A meets the requirements for qualified terminable interest property. As executor of Kenneth's estate, *S2 elects* to include the value of this property in the S1 marital deduction. By so electing, S2 has made it certain that the property will be included in her gross estate at her death. During his lifetime, Kenneth created a plan which ensures that the children of his first marriage will eventually receive all of his property.

> EXAMPLE 2056(b)(7)–2 Modifying the facts in the preceding example a bit, assume that S2, as executor of the S1 estate, *does not elect* to include the trust property in the S1 marital deduction. The property will still pass to the children upon S2's death, but will neither be deducted from S1's gross estate nor be included in S2's gross estate. By not electing, S2 has chosen not to defer the FET. Both trusts, not just the B trust, will bypass S2's estate.

> EXAMPLE 2056(b)(7)–3 Again modifying the facts in Example 2056(b)(7)-1 a bit, assume that S2, as executor of Kenneth's estate, makes a QTIP election as to only one half of the trust A property. Kenneth's marital deduction will then be $700,000.

Tax law permits *partial QTIP elections* with regard to fractional asset shares.[12]

---

[12]Disclaimers and QTIP elections can also frequently be used to remedy the problem illustrated in Example 1–10 in Chapter 1. In essence, they can partially raise the marital deduction for an S1 in spite of the forced application of the pre–1982 marital deduction rules for certain wills and trusts executed before September 12, 1981. For a further discussion, see the Alvarez article cited at the end of the chapter.

Thus, as an alternative to the power of appointment marital trust described in Chapter 12, the QTIP election offers greater flexibility in bypass planning while enabling the client, as a potential S1, to retain total dispositive control over the property.[13]

Other Postmortem Death Tax-Saving Devices

Three other postmortem tax elections often available to the estates of business owners include the §6166 election to pay the FET in installments, the §303 redemption of stock, and the §2032A special use valuation election. These elections were covered in some detail in Chapter 16 and will not be discussed further here.

This chapter has focused on postmortem planning techniques designed to reduce income and death taxes. They have been the subject of this last chapter because they represent, conceptually, the final phase of planning undertaken on behalf of a client.

RECOMMENDED READING

ALVAREZ, EDNA. "Post-Mortem Reconstruction of the Marital Deduction: QTIPs, Disclaimers and Other Tools." *18th Annual Institute on Estate Planning 1987,* Practising Law Institute.

ASCHER, MARK L. "The Fiduciary Duty to Minimize Taxes." *Real Property, Probate & Trust Journal* 20 (1985), pp. 663–717.

BARNETT, BERNARD. "Estate and Trust Distributions in Kind after TRA '84." *Trusts & Estates,* October 1984, pp. 32–38.

---

[13]The astute reader will observe that the disclaimer and the QTIP election are both strategies that can enable a surrogate decision maker to decide on behalf of the client whether or not to defer the FET. One advantage of the QTIP alternative over the disclaimer is the ability to dclay the decision an additional six months. While a disclaimer is made on the federal estate tax return which, when including an automatically granted 6-month extension to file, will be due 15 months after date of death. An advantage of the disclaimer over the QTIP election is that under the QTIP election, the spouse's right to income can not be made contingent upon the election being made (LR861106).

BETTIGOLE, BRUCE J. "Post-Mortem Remedies Can Salvage the Problem of Underfunded and Overfunded Marital Bequests." *Estate Planning,* March 1985, pp. 66–71.

DEVERAUX, JAMES F. "Understanding Grief and the Grieving Process." *Trusts & Estates,* August 1985, pp. 30–32.

DIRKES, GEORGE R. "Post Mortem Tax Planning." *18th Annual Institute on Estate Planning 1987,* Practising Law Institute.

EDWARDS, MARK B., and DAVID L. THOMAS, "Post-Mortem Tax Planning: Income Tax Aspects—The Overlooked Opportunities." *Trusts & Estates,* January 1985, pp. 46–51.

EGGLESTON, JON R. "Post-Mortem Election of Subchapter S Can Benefit Estate with Closely Held Stock." *Estate Planning,* March 1984, pp. 104–7.

EUBANK, J. THOMAS "When the Estate Plan Must Be Made Final: An Overview of Decisions and Techniques Shortly after the Decedent's Death." *1983 Institute on Estate Planning,* Chap. 20, pp. 1–31.

FERGUSON, BARBARA B. "Disclaimers Can Adjust Tax Consequences to Reflect Post-Mortem Changed Circumstances." *Taxation for Accountants,* January 1985, pp. 30–36.

FEVURLEY, KEITH R. "Planning Must Be Revised to Obtain Maximum Benefits of Special-Use Valuation." *Estate Planning,* January 1986, pp. 14–19.

FRIMMER, PAUL N. "Qualified Disclaimers." *Estate Planning, 1987,* California Continuing Education of the Bar.

GEU, THOMAS E. "Post-Mortem Recognition of Informal Family Partnerships." *Nebraska Law Review* 63 (1984), pp. 314–44.

HASTINGS, DAN T. "The Discriminate 'No'." (On the final Section 2518 Disclaimer Regulations), *Trusts & Estates,* October 1986, pp. 39–46.

KASNER, JERRY A. *Post Mortem Tax Planning,* New York: Shephard's/McGraw-Hill, 1982.

KINSKERN, DOUGLAS. "When Will Transferees and Executors Be Personally Liable for Estate and Gift Taxes?" *Estate Planning,* March 1987, pp. 106–11.

MARIANI, MICHAEL M. "Form 1041 vs. Form 706: Where to Deduct Administration Expenses." *Trusts & Estates,* June 1984, pp. 37–40.

MAYS, R. L., JR. "How to Stay Flexible in Estate Tax Decisions." *Trusts & Estates,* December 1985, p. 32.

PENA, EMMA. "Internal Revenue Code Section 2518 Disclaimers and the 1981 Economic Recovery Tax Act: Continued Unequal Treatment of Taxpayers." *Santa Clara Law Review* 22 (1982), pp. 1179–1204.

PETERS, JEFFREY A. "Deferral Strategies Still Exist Despite New Calendar Year and Estimated Tax Requirements." *Estate Planning,* July 1987, pp. 194–99.

RAABE, WILLIAM A. "Sec. 6166: Computing the Estate's Interest Deduction." *The Tax Adviser,* August 1984, pp. 458–65.

RHINE, DAVID S., and JOHN H. LAVELLE. "Post-Mortem Adjustments Affecting

Estate and Beneficiaries are Significant in Planning Wills." *Estate Planning,* July 1984, pp. 210–15.

SALZARULO, W. PETER. "When to Elect to Recognize Gain or Loss on Distributions of Estate or Trust Property." *Estate Planning,* January 1986, pp. 38–44.

SUMERFORD, REES M. "Administration Expenses Offer Opportunities for Planning to Maximize the Available Tax Benefits." *Taxation for Accountants,* July 1984, pp. 26–31.

UCHTMANN, D. L., and P. K. ZIGTERMAN. "Disclaimers of Joint Tenancy Interests Revisited." *Creighton Law Review* 18 (1985), pp. 333–56.

QUESTIONS AND PROBLEMS

1. List the federal tax returns that may have to be filed during a period of administration of a decedent's property.

2. Maxie, a widower, died recently, leaving his $2 million gross estate to his brother Morey. Maxie spent the last six months in a hospital, paying $50,000 of the $80,000 hospital bill before he died. Marginal tax rates for the taxpaying entities are as follows: Maxie's final Form 1040, 33 percent; the Form 1041, 28 percent; the Form 706, 41 percent. How much in tax will Maxie's estate save if the allowable expense is deducted, alternatively, on
   a. The Form 706?
   b. The final Form 1040?
   c. The estate's Form 1041?

   On which return should the deduction be made?

3. Moose died recently, leaving his entire $2 million gross estate to his wife, Trixie, who is named executor. Assume that the only estate expense is the executor's commission of $100,000. Marginal tax rates for the taxpaying entities are: Trixie's Form 1040, 33 percent; the final Form 1040, 15 percent; the Form 1041, 28 percent; the Form 706, 41 percent.
   a. Should Trixie accept or waive the commission? Why?
   b. Where, if at all, should the estate deduct the commission? Why?
   c. Would your answers to parts *a* and *b* change if Moose owned a $200,000 estate, and Trixie's Form 1040 marginal rate was 28 percent?
   d. Would your answers to parts *a* and *b* probably change if Trixie, the executor, was Moose's cousin to whom Moose left nothing by will or otherwise? Assume a $2 million gross estate.

4. Describe the income tax advantages available to all estates and those advantages available only to estates having a carefully chosen fiscal year.

5. How can the executor of an estate or the trustee of a trust reduce income taxes by planning the distributions to bene-

ficiaries if the beneficiaries marginal tax rates are:

a. Higher than that of the estate or trust?

b. Lower than that of the estate or trust?

6. What is the benefit of prolonging an estate's life, and what is the tax consequence if it is "unduly" prolonged?

7. Explain the tax advantage of the alternate valuation date election.

8. Give two specific examples where a disclaimer can reduce the FET.

9. (a) Can "qualified terminable interest property" wind up not being part of the S1 marital deduction? (b) If yes, can the QTIP arrangement be considered a bust?

10. Describe the unique contribution of a QTIP arrangement to estate planning.

11. (a) Can a QTIP arrangement and a disclaimer provision be alternative methods of achieving the same objective? Why or why not? (b) Which will place greater property rights in the hands of S2? Why?

Tax and Valuation Tables

TABLE 1 Federal Individual Income Tax Rates: Married Individuals Filing Joint Returns and Surviving Spouses

Taxable Income		Base Amount	+	Percent	On Excess Over
Over	But Not Over				

1984–1986

Over	But Not Over	Base Amount	Percent	On Excess Over
$ 0	$ 3,400	$ 0	0%	$ 0
3,400	5,500	0	11	3,400
5,500	7,600	231	12	5,500
7,600	11,900	483	14	7,600
11,900	16,000	1,085	16	11,900
16,000	20,200	1,741	18	16,000
20,200	24,600	2,497	22	20,200
24,600	29,900	3,465	25	24,600
29,900	35,200	4,790	28	29,900
35,200	45,800	6,274	33	35,200
45,800	60,000	9,772	38	45,800
60,000	85,600	15,168	42	60,000
85,600	109,400	25,920	45	85,600
109,400	162,400	36,630	49	109,400
162,400	—	62,600	50	162,400

1987

Over	But Not Over	Base Amount	Percent	On Excess Over
$ 0	$ 3,000	$ 0	11%	$ 0
3,000	28,000	330	15	3,000
28,000	45,000	4,080	28	28,000
45,000	90,000	8,840	35	45,000
90,000	—	24,590	38.5	90,000

1988 and later
(2 personal exemptions)

Over	But Not Over	Base Amount	Percent	On Excess Over
$ 0	$ 29,750	$ 0	15%	$ 0
29,750	71,900	4,462.50	28	29,750
71,900	171,090	16,264.50	33	71,900
171,090	—	48,997.20	28	171,090

(3 personal exemptions)

Over	But Not Over	Base Amount	Percent	On Excess Over
$ 0	$ 29,750	$ 0	15%	$ 0
29,750	71,900	4,462.50	28	29,750
71,900	182,010	16,264.50	33	71,900
182,010	—	52,600.80	28	182,010

TABLE 1 (*concluded*)

Taxable Income		Base Amount	+	Percent	On Excess Over
Over	But Not Over				
(4 personal exemptions)					
$ 0	$ 29,750	$ 0		15%	$ 0
29,750	71,900	4,462.50		28	29,750
71,900	192,930*	16,264.50		33	71,900
192,930*	—	56,204.40		28	192,930

*Will be $194,050 in 1989, reflecting additional taxable income needed to phase out the larger personal exemption.

TABLE 2 Federal Individual Income Tax Rates: Single Individuals with No Dependents

Taxable Income		Base Amount	+	Percent	On Excess Over
Over	**But Not Over**				
		1984–1986			
$ 0	$ 2,300	$ 0		0%	$ 0
2,300	3,400	0		11	2,300
3,400	4,400	121		12	3,400
4,400	6,500	241		14	4,400
6,500	8,500	535		15	6,500
8,500	10,800	835		16	8,500
10,800	12,900	1,203		18	10,800
12,900	15,000	1,581		20	12,900
15,000	18,200	2,001		23	15,000
18,200	23,500	2,737		26	18,200
23,500	28,800	4,115		30	23,500
28,800	31,100	5,705		34	28,800
31,100	41,500	7,507		38	31,100
41,500	55,300	10,319		42	41,500
55,300	81,800	16,115		48	55,300
81,800	108,300	28,835		50	81,800
108,300	—	42,085		50	108,300
		1987			
$ 0	$ 1,800	$ 0		11%	$ 0
1,800	16,800	198		15	1,800
16,800	27,000	2,448		28	16,800
27,000	54,000	5,304		35	27,000
54,000	—	14,754		38.5	54,000
		1988 and later			
$ 0	$ 17,850	$ 0		15%	$ 0
17,850	43,150	2,677.50		28	17,850
43,150	100,480	9,761.50		33	43,150
100,480	—	28,680.40		28	100,480

TABLE 3 Federal Income Tax Rates: Estates and Trusts

Taxable Income		Base Amount	+	Percent	On Excess Over
Over	But Not Over				
		1984–1986			
$ 0	$ 1,050	$ 0		11%	$ 0
1,050	2,100	115		12	1,050
2,100	4,250	241		14	2,100
4,250	6,300	542		16	4,250
6,300	8,400	870		18	6,300
8,400	10,600	1,248		22	8,400
10,600	13,250	1,732		25	10,600
13,250	15,900	2,395		28	13,250
15,900	21,200	3,137		33	15,900
21,200	28,300	4,886		38	21,200
28,300	41,100	7,584		42	28,300
41,100	53,000	12,960		45	41,100
53,000	79,500	18,315		49	53,000
79,500	—	31,300		50	79,500
		1987			
$ 0	$ 500	$ 0		11%	$ 0
500	4,700	55		15	500
4,700	7,550	685		28	4,700
7,550	15,150	1,483		35	7,550
15,150	—	4,143		38.5	15,150
		1988 and later			
$ 0	$ 5,000	$ 0		15%	$ 0
5,000	13,000	750		28	5,000
13,000	26,000	2,990		33	13,000
26,000	—	7,280		28	26,000

TABLE 4 Federal Unified Transfer Tax Rates Since 1977

If the Amount Is:		Tentative Tax			
Over	But Not Over	Base Amount	+	Percent	On Excess Over
All years after 1976–taxable amounts up to $2,500,000					
$ 0	$ 10,000	$ 0		18%	$ 0
10,000	20,000	1,800		20	10,000
20,000	40,000	3,800		22	20,000
40,000	60,000	8,200		24	40,000
60,000	80,000	13,000		26	60,000
80,000	100,000	18,200		28	80,000
100,000	150,000	23,800		30	100,000
150,000	250,000	38,800		32	150,000
250,000	500,000	70,800		34	250,000
500,000	750,000	155,800		37	500,000
750,000	1,000,000	248,300		39	750,000
1,000,000	1,250,000	345,800		41	1,000,000
1,250,000	1,500,000	448,300		43	1,250,000
1,500,000	2,000,000	555,800		45	1,500,000
2,000,000	2,500,000	780,800		49	2,000,000
1977–1981					
$2,500,000	$3,000,000	$1,025.800		53%	$2,500,000
3,000,000	3,500,000	1,290,800		57	3,000,000
3,500,000	4,000,000	1,575,800		61	3,500,000
4,000,000	4,500,000	1,880,800		65	4,000,000
4,500,000	5,000,000	2,205,800		69	4,500,000
5,000,000	—	2,550,800		70	5,000,000
1982					
$2,500,000	$3,000,000	$1,025,800		53%	$2,500,000
3,000,000	3,500,000	1,290,800		57	3,000,000
3,500,000	4,000,000	1,575,800		61	3,500,000
4,000,000	—	1,880,800		65	4,000,000
1983					
$2,500,000	$3,000,000	$1,025,800		53%	$2,500,000
3,000,000	3,500,000	1,290,800		57	3,000,000
3,500,000	—	1,575,800		60	3,500,000
1984–1992					
$2,500,000	$3,000,000	$1,025,800		53%	$2,500,000
3,000,000	—	1,290,800		55	3,000,000
1993 and later					
$2,500,000	—	$1,025,800		50%	$2,500,000

TABLE 5 Federal Unified Credit

Year	Amount of Credit	Amount of Exemption Equivalent
1977	$ 30,000	$120,667
1978	34,000	134,000
1979	38,000	147,333
1980	42,500	161,563
1981	47,000	175,625
1982	62,800	225,000
1983	79,300	275,000
1984	96,300	325,000
1985	121,800	400,000
1986	155,800	500,000
1987 and thereafter	192,800	600,000

TABLE 6 Maximum Credit against Federal Estate Tax for State Death Taxes

Adjusted Taxable Estate		Maximum Credit			
At Least	But Not Over	Base Amount	+	Percent	On Excess Over
$ 40,000	$ 90,000	$ 0		.8%	$ 40,000
90,000	140,000	400		1.6	90,000
140,000	240,000	1,200		2.4	140,000
240,000	440,000	3,600		3.2	240,000
440,000	640,000	10,000		4.0	440,000
640,000	840,000	18,000		4.8	640,000
840,000	1,040,000	27,600		5.6	840,000
1,040,000	1,540,000	38,800		6.4	1,040,000
1,540,000	2,040,000	70,800		7.2	1,540,000
2,040,000	2,540,000	106,800		8.0	2,040,000
2,540,000	3,040,000	146,800		8.8	2,540,000
3,040,000	3,540,000	190,800		9.6	3,040,000
3,540,000	4,040,000	238,800		10.4	3,540,000
4,040,000	5,040,000	290,800		11.2	4,040,000
5,040,000	6,040,000	402,800		12.0	5,040,000
6,040,000	7,040,000	522,800		12.8	6,040,000
7,040,000	8,040,000	650,800		13.6	7,040,000
8,040,000	9,040,000	786,800		14.4	8,040,000
9,040,000	10,040,000	930,800		15.2	9,040,000
10,040,000	—	1,082,800		16.0	10,040,000

TABLE 7   Federal Estate Tax Rates for Decedents Dying prior to 1977

Taxable Estate (after exemption)		Estate Tax			
At Least	But Not Over	Base Amount	+	Percent	On Excess Over
$ 0	$ 5,000	$ 0		3%	$ 0
5,000	10,000	150		7	5,000
10,000	20,000	500		11	10,000
20,000	30,000	1,600		14	20,000
30,000	40,000	3,000		18	30,000
40,000	50,000	4,800		22	40,000
50,000	60,000	7,000		25	50,000
60,000	100,000	9,500		28	60,000
100,000	250,000	20,700		30	100,000
250,000	500,000	65,700		32	250,000
500,000	750,000	145,700		35	500,000
750,000	1,000,000	233,200		37	750,000
1,000,000	1,250,000	325,700		39	1,000,000
1,250,000	1,500,000	423,200		42	1,250,000
1,500,000	2,000,000	528,200		45	1,500,000
2,000,000	2,500,000	753,200		49	2,000,000
2,500,000	3,000,000	998,200		53	2,500,000
3,000,000	3,500,000	1,263,200		56	3,000,000
3,500,000	4,000,000	1,543,200		59	3,500,000
4,000,000	5,000,000	1,838,200		63	4,000,000
5,000,000	6,000,000	2,468,200		67	5,000,000
6,000,000	7,000,000	3,138,200		70	6,000,000
7,000,000	8,000,000	3,838,200		73	7,000,000
8,000,000	10,000,000	4,568,200		76	8,000,000
10,000,000	—	6,088,200		77	10,000,000

TABLE 8 Federal Gift Tax Rates for Gifts Made prior to January 1, 1977

Taxable Gifts		Gift Tax		
At Least	But Not Over	Base Amount +	Percent	On Excess Over
$ 0	$ 5,000	$ 0	2¼%	$ 0
5,000	10,000	112.50	5¼	5,000
10,000	20,000	375.00	8¼	10,000
20,000	30,000	1,200.00	10½	20,000
30,000	40,000	2,250.00	13½	30,000
40,000	50,000	3,600.00	16½	40,000
50,000	60,000	5,250.00	18¾	50,000
60,000	100,000	7,125.00	21	60,000
100,000	250,000	15,525.00	22½	100,000
250,000	500,000	49,275.00	24	250,000
500,000	750,000	109,275.00	26¼	500,000
750,000	1,000,000	174,900.00	27¾	750,000
1,000,000	1,250,000	244,275.00	29¼	1,000,000
1,250,000	1,500,000	317,400.00	31½	1,250,000
1,500,000	2,000,000	396,150.00	33¾	1,500,000
2,000,000	2,500,000	564,900.00	36¾	2,000,000
2,500,000	3,000,000	748,650.00	39¾	2,500,000
3,000,000	3,500,000	947,400.00	42	3,000,000
3,500,000	4,000,000	1,157,400.00	44¼	3,500,000
4,000,000	5,000,000	1,378,650.00	47¼	4,000,000
5,000,000	6,000,000	1,851,150.00	50¼	5,000,000
6,000,000	7,000,000	2,353,650.00	52½	6,000,000
7,000,000	8,000,000	2,878,650.00	54¾	7,000,000
8,000,000	10,000,000	3,426,150.00	57	8,000,000
10,000,000	—	4,566,150.00	57¾	10,000,000

TABLE 9 Single Life, Unisex, Present Worth at 10 Percent of an Annuity, a Life Interest, and a Remainder Interest (Table A from Reg. §20.2031-7 and Reg. §25.2512-5(e))

Age	Annuity	Life Estate	Remainder	Age	Annuity	Life Estate	Remainder
0	9.7188	.97188	.02812	55	8.0046	.80046	.19954
1	9.8988	.98988	.01012	56	7.9006	.79006	.20994
2	9.9017	.99017	.00983	57	7.7931	.77931	.22069
3	9.9008	.99008	.00992	58	7.6822	.76822	.23178
4	9.8981	.98981	.01019	59	7.5675	.75675	.24325
5	9.8938	.98938	.01062	60	7.4491	.74491	.25509
6	9.8884	.98884	.01116	61	7.3267	.73267	.26733
7	9.8822	.98822	.01178	62	7.2002	.72002	.27998
8	9.8748	.98748	.01252	63	7.0696	.70696	.29304
9	9.8663	.98663	.01337	64	6.9352	.69352	.30648
10	9.8565	.98565	.01435	65	6.7970	.67970	.32030
11	9.8453	.98453	.01547	66	6.6551	.66551	.33449
12	9.8329	.98329	.01671	67	6.5098	.65098	.34390
13	9.8198	.98198	.01802	68	6.3610	.63610	.36369
14	9.8066	.98066	.01934	69	6.2086	.62086	.37914
15	9.7937	.97937	.02063	70	6.0522	.60522	.39478
16	9.7815	.97815	.02185	71	5.8914	.58914	.41086
17	9.7700	.97700	.02300	72	5.7261	.57261	.42739
18	9.7590	.97590	.02410	73	5.5571	.55571	.44429
19	9.7480	.97480	.02520	74	5.3862	.53862	.46138
20	9.7365	.97365	.02635	75	5.2149	.52149	.47851
21	9.7245	.97245	.02755	76	5.0441	.50441	.49559
22	9.7120	.97120	.02880	77	4.8742	.48742	.51258
23	9.6986	.96986	.03014	78	4.7049	.47049	.52951
24	9.6841	.96841	.03159	79	4.5357	.45357	.54643
25	9.6678	.96678	.03322	80	4.3659	.43659	.56341
26	9.6495	.96495	.03505	81	4.1967	.41967	.58033
27	9.6290	.96290	.03710	82	4.0295	.40295	.59705
28	9.6062	.96062	.03938	83	3.8642	.38642	.61358
29	9.5813	.95813	.04187	84	3.6998	.36998	.63002
30	9.5543	.95543	.04457	85	3.5359	.35359	.64641
31	9.5254	.95254	.04746	86	3.3764	.33764	.66236
32	9.4942	.94942	.05058	87	3.2262	.32262	.67738
33	9.4608	.94608	.05392	88	3.0859	.30859	.69141
34	9.4250	.94250	.05750	89	2.9526	.29526	.70474
35	9.3868	.93868	.06132	90	2.8221	.28221	.71779
36	9.3460	.93460	.06540	91	2.6955	.26955	.73045
37	9.3026	.93026	.06974	92	2.5771	.25771	.74229
38	9.2567	.92567	.07433	93	2.4692	.24692	.75306
39	9.2083	.92083	.07917	94	2.3728	.23728	.76272
40	9.1571	.91571	.08429	95	2.2887	.22887	.77113
41	9.1030	.91030	.08970	96	2.2181	.22181	.77819
42	9.0457	.90457	.09543	97	2.1550	.21550	.78450
43	8.9855	.89855	.10145	98	2.1000	.21000	.79000
44	8.9221	.89221	.10779	99	2.0486	.20486	.79514
45	8.8558	.88558	.11442	100	1.9975	.19975	.80025
46	8.7863	.87863	.12137	101	1.9532	.19532	.80468
47	8.7137	.87137	.12863	102	1.9054	.19054	.80946

TABLE 9 (concluded)

Age	Annuity	Life Estate	Remainder	Age	Annuity	Life Estate	Remainder
48	8.6374	.86374	.13626	103	1.8437	.18437	.81563
49	8.5578	.85578	.14422	104	1.7856	.17856	.82144
50	8.4743	.84743	.15257	105	1.6962	.16962	.83038
51	8.3874	.83874	.16126	106	1.5488	.15488	.84512
52	8.2969	.82969	.17031	107	1.3409	.13409	.86591
53	8.2028	.82028	.17972	108	1.0068	.10068	.89932
54	8.1054	.81054	.18946	109	.4545	.04545	.95455

TABLE 10   Present Worth at 10 Percent of an Annuity for a Term Certain, of a Life Estate for a Term Certain, and of a Remainder Interest Postponed for a Term Credit (Table B from Reg. §20.2031-7 and Reg. §25.2512-5(e))

Years	Annuity	Life Estate	Remainder	Years	Annuity	Life Estate	Remainder
1	.9091	.090909	.909091	31	9.4790	.947901	.052099
2	1.7355	.173554	.826446	32	9.5264	.952638	.047362
3	2.4869	.248685	.751315	33	9.5694	.956943	.043057
4	3.1699	.316987	.683013	34	9.6086	.960857	.039143
5	3.7908	.379079	.620921	35	9.6442	.964416	.035584
6	4.3553	.435526	.564474	36	9.6765	.967651	.032349
7	4.8684	.486842	.513158	37	9.7059	.970592	.029408
8	5.3349	.533493	.466507	38	9.7327	.973265	.026735
9	5.7590	.575902	.424098	39	9.7570	.975696	.024304
10	6.1446	.614457	.385543	40	9.7791	.977905	.022095
11	6.4951	.649506	.350494	41	9.7991	.979914	.020086
12	6.8137	.681369	.318631	42	9.8174	.981740	.018260
13	7.1034	.710336	.289664	43	9.8340	.983400	.016600
14	7.3667	.736669	.263331	44	9.8491	.984909	.015091
15	7.6061	.760608	.239392	45	9.8628	.986281	.013719
16	7.8237	.782371	.217629	46	9.8753	.987528	.012472
17	8.0216	.802155	.197845	47	9.8866	.988662	.011338
18	8.2014	.820141	.179859	48	9.8969	.989693	.010307
19	8.3649	.836492	.163508	49	9.9063	.990630	.009370
20	8.5136	.851356	.148644	50	9.9140	.991481	.008519
21	8.6487	.864869	.135131	51	9.9226	.992256	.007744
22	8.7715	.877154	.122846	52	9.9296	.992960	.007040
23	8.8832	.888322	.111678	53	9.9360	.993600	.006400
24	8.9847	.898474	.101526	54	9.9418	.994182	.005818
25	9.0770	.907704	.092296	55	9.9471	.994711	.005289
26	9.1609	.916095	.083905	56	9.9519	.995191	.004809
27	9.2372	.923722	.076278	57	9.9563	.995629	.004371
28	9.3066	.930657	.069343	58	9.9603	.996026	.003974
29	9.3696	.936961	.063039	59	9.9639	.996387	.003613
30	9.4269	.942691	.057309	60	9.9672	.996716	.003284

TABLE 11 Present Value of $1 Lump Sum

Period	1%	2%	3%	4%	5%	6%	7%	8%	9%	10%	11%	12%
1	0.990	0.980	0.971	0.962	0.952	0.943	0.935	0.926	0.917	0.909	0.901	0.893
2	0.980	0.961	0.943	0.925	0.907	0.890	0.873	0.857	0.842	0.826	0.812	0.797
3	0.971	0.942	0.915	0.889	0.864	0.840	0.816	0.794	0.772	0.751	0.731	0.712
4	0.961	0.924	0.885	0.855	0.823	0.792	0.763	0.735	0.708	0.683	0.659	0.636
5	0.951	0.906	0.863	0.822	0.784	0.747	0.713	0.681	0.650	0.621	0.593	0.567
6	0.942	0.888	0.837	0.790	0.746	0.705	0.666	0.630	0.596	0.564	0.535	0.507
7	0.933	0.871	0.813	0.760	0.711	0.665	0.623	0.583	0.547	0.513	0.482	0.452
8	0.923	0.853	0.789	0.731	0.677	0.627	0.582	0.540	0.502	0.467	0.434	0.404
9	0.914	0.837	0.766	0.703	0.645	0.592	0.544	0.500	0.460	0.424	0.391	0.361
10	0.905	0.820	0.744	0.676	0.614	0.558	0.508	0.463	0.422	0.386	0.352	0.322
11	0.896	0.804	0.722	0.650	0.585	0.527	0.475	0.429	0.388	0.350	0.317	0.287
12	0.887	0.788	0.701	0.625	0.557	0.497	0.444	0.397	0.356	0.319	0.286	0.257
13	0.879	0.773	0.681	0.601	0.530	0.469	0.415	0.368	0.326	0.290	0.258	0.229
14	0.870	0.758	0.661	0.577	0.505	0.442	0.388	0.340	0.299	0.263	0.232	0.205
15	0.861	0.743	0.642	0.555	0.481	0.417	0.362	0.315	0.275	0.239	0.209	0.183
16	0.853	0.728	0.623	0.534	0.458	0.394	0.339	0.292	0.252	0.218	0.188	0.163
17	0.844	0.714	0.605	0.513	0.436	0.371	0.317	0.270	0.231	0.198	0.170	0.146
18	0.836	0.700	0.587	0.494	0.416	0.350	0.296	0.250	0.212	0.180	0.153	0.130
19	0.828	0.686	0.570	0.475	0.396	0.331	0.277	0.232	0.194	0.164	0.138	0.116
20	0.820	0.673	0.554	0.456	0.377	0.312	0.258	0.215	0.178	0.149	0.124	0.104
25	0.780	0.610	0.478	0.375	0.295	0.233	0.184	0.146	0.116	0.092	0.074	0.059
30	0.742	0.552	0.412	0.308	0.231	0.174	0.131	0.099	0.075	0.057	0.044	0.033
40	0.672	0.453	0.307	0.208	0.142	0.097	0.067	0.046	0.032	0.022	0.015	0.011
50	0.608	0.372	0.228	0.141	0.087	0.054	0.034	0.021	0.013	0.009	0.005	0.003

Percent

TABLE 11 *(concluded)*

Percent

Period	13%	14%	15%	16%	17%	18%	19%	20%	25%	30%	35%	40%	50%
1	0.885	0.877	0.870	0.862	0.855	0.847	0.840	0.833	0.800	0.769	0.741	0.714	0.667
2	0.783	0.769	0.756	0.743	0.731	0.718	0.706	0.694	0.640	0.592	0.549	0.510	0.444
3	0.693	0.675	0.658	0.641	0.624	0.609	0.593	0.579	0.512	0.455	0.406	0.364	0.296
4	0.613	0.592	0.572	0.552	0.534	0.515	0.499	0.482	0.410	0.350	0.301	0.260	0.198
5	0.543	0.519	0.497	0.476	0.456	0.437	0.419	0.402	0.320	0.269	0.223	0.186	0.132
6	0.480	0.456	0.432	0.410	0.390	0.370	0.352	0.335	0.262	0.207	0.165	0.133	0.088
7	0.425	0.400	0.376	0.354	0.333	0.314	0.296	0.279	0.210	0.159	0.122	0.095	0.059
8	0.376	0.351	0.327	0.305	0.285	0.266	0.249	0.233	0.168	0.123	0.091	0.068	0.039
9	0.333	0.308	0.284	0.263	0.243	0.225	0.209	0.194	0.134	0.094	0.067	0.048	0.026
10	0.295	0.270	0.247	0.227	0.208	0.191	0.176	0.162	0.107	0.073	0.050	0.035	0.017
11	0.261	0.237	0.215	0.195	0.178	0.162	0.148	0.135	0.086	0.056	0.037	0.025	0.012
12	0.231	0.208	0.187	0.168	0.152	0.137	0.124	0.112	0.069	0.043	0.027	0.018	0.008
13	0.204	0.182	0.163	0.145	0.130	0.116	0.104	0.093	0.055	0.033	0.020	0.013	0.005
14	0.181	0.160	0.141	0.125	0.111	0.099	0.088	0.078	0.044	0.025	0.015	0.009	0.003
15	0.160	0.140	0.123	0.108	0.095	0.084	0.074	0.065	0.035	0.020	0.011	0.006	0.002
16	0.141	0.123	0.107	0.093	0.081	0.071	0.062	0.054	0.028	0.015	0.008	0.005	0.002
17	0.125	0.108	0.093	0.080	0.069	0.060	0.052	0.045	0.023	0.012	0.006	0.003	0.001
18	0.111	0.095	0.081	0.069	0.059	0.051	0.044	0.038	0.018	0.009	0.005	0.002	0.001
19	0.098	0.083	0.070	0.060	0.051	0.043	0.037	0.031	0.014	0.007	0.003	0.002	0
20	0.087	0.073	0.061	0.051	0.043	0.037	0.031	0.026	0.012	0.005	0.002	0.001	0
25	0.047	0.038	0.030	0.024	0.020	0.016	0.013	0.010	0.004	0.001	0.001	0	0
30	0.026	0.020	0.015	0.012	0.009	0.007	0.005	0.004	0.001	0	0	0	0
40	0.008	0.005	0.004	0.003	0.002	0.001	0.001	0.001	0	0	0	0	0
50	0.002	0.001	0.001	0.001	0	0	0	0	0	0	0	0	0

TABLE 12 Present Value of $1 Annuity

Period	1%	2%	3%	4%	5%	6%	7%	8%	9%	10%	11%	12%
1	0.990	0.980	0.971	0.962	0.952	0.943	0.935	0.926	0.917	0.909	0.901	0.893
2	1.970	1.942	1.913	1.886	1.859	1.833	1.808	1.783	1.759	1.736	1.713	1.690
3	2.941	2.884	2.829	2.775	2.723	2.673	2.624	2.577	2.531	2.487	2.444	2.402
4	3.902	3.808	3.717	3.630	3.546	3.465	3.387	3.312	3.240	3.170	3.102	3.037
5	4.853	4.716	4.580	4.452	4.329	4.212	4.100	3.993	3.890	3.791	3.696	3.605
6	5.795	5.601	5.417	5.242	5.076	4.917	4.767	4.623	4.486	4.355	4.231	4.111
7	6.728	6.472	6.230	6.002	5.786	5.582	5.389	5.206	5.033	4.868	4.712	4.564
8	7.652	7.325	7.020	6.733	6.463	6.210	5.971	5.747	5.535	5.335	5.416	4.968
9	8.566	8.162	7.786	7.435	7.108	6.802	6.515	6.247	5.995	5.759	5.537	5.328
10	9.471	8.983	8.530	8.111	7.722	7.360	7.024	6.710	6.418	6.145	5.889	5.650
11	10.368	9.787	9.253	8.760	8.306	7.887	7.499	7.139	6.805	6.495	6.207	5.938
12	11.255	10.575	9.954	9.385	8.863	8.384	7.943	7.536	7.161	6.814	6.492	6.194
13	12.134	11.348	10.635	9.986	9.394	8.853	8.358	7.904	7.487	7.103	6.750	6.424
14	13.004	12.106	11.296	10.563	9.899	9.295	8.745	8.244	7.786	7.367	6.982	6.628
15	13.865	12.849	11.939	11.118	10.380	9.712	9.108	8.559	8.061	7.606	7.191	6.811
16	14.718	13.578	12.561	11.652	10.838	10.106	9.447	8.851	8.313	7.824	7.379	6.974
17	15.562	14.292	13.166	12.166	11.274	10.477	9.763	9.122	8.544	8.022	7.549	7.102
18	16.398	14.992	13.754	12.659	11.690	10.828	10.059	9.372	8.756	8.201	7.702	7.250
19	17.226	15.678	14.324	13.134	12.085	11.158	10.336	9.604	8.950	8.365	7.839	7.366
20	18.046	16.351	14.877	13.590	12.462	11.470	10.594	9.818	9.129	8.514	7.963	7.469
25	22.023	19.523	17.413	15.622	14.094	12.783	11.654	10.675	9.823	9.077	8.422	7.843
30	25.808	22.396	19.600	17.292	15.372	13.765	12.409	11.258	10.274	9.427	8.694	8.055
40	32.835	27.355	23.115	19.793	17.159	15.046	13.332	11.925	10.757	9.779	8.951	8.244
50	39.196	31.424	25.730	21.482	18.256	15.762	13.801	12.233	10.962	9.915	9.042	8.304

Percent

TABLE 12 (concluded)

Percent

Period	13%	14%	15%	16%	17%	18%	19%	20%	25%	30%	35%	40%	50%
1	0.885	0.877	0.870	0.862	0.855	0.847	0.840	0.833	0.800	0.769	0.741	0.714	0.667
2	1.668	1.647	1.626	1.605	1.585	1.566	1.547	1.528	1.440	1.361	1.289	1.224	1.111
3	2.361	2.322	2.283	2.246	2.210	2.174	2.140	2.106	1.952	1.816	1.696	1.589	1.407
4	2.974	2.914	2.855	2.798	2.743	2.690	2.639	2.589	2.362	2.166	1.997	1.849	1.605
5	3.517	3.433	3.352	3.274	3.199	3.127	3.058	2.991	2.689	2.436	2.220	2.035	1.737
6	3.998	3.889	3.784	3.685	3.589	3.498	3.410	3.326	2.951	2.643	2.385	2.168	1.824
7	4.423	4.288	4.160	4.039	3.922	3.812	3.706	3.605	3.161	2.802	2.508	2.263	1.883
8	4.799	4.639	4.487	4.344	4.207	4.078	3.954	3.837	3.329	2.925	2.598	2.331	1.922
9	5.132	4.946	4.772	4.607	4.451	4.303	4.163	4.031	3.463	3.019	2.665	2.379	1.948
10	5.426	5.216	5.019	4.833	4.659	4.494	4.339	4.192	3.571	3.092	2.715	2.414	1.965
11	5.687	5.453	5.234	5.029	4.836	4.656	4.486	4.327	3.656	3.147	2.752	2.438	1.977
12	5.918	5.660	5.421	5.197	4.988	4.793	4.611	4.439	3.725	3.190	2.779	2.456	1.985
13	6.122	5.842	5.583	5.342	5.118	4.910	4.715	4.533	3.780	3.223	2.799	2.469	1.990
14	6.302	6.002	5.724	5.468	5.229	5.008	4.802	4.611	3.824	3.249	2.814	2.478	1.993
15	6.462	6.142	5.847	5.575	5.324	5.092	4.876	4.675	3.859	3.268	2.825	2.484	1.995
16	6.604	6.265	5.954	5.668	5.405	5.162	4.938	4.730	3.887	3.283	2.834	2.489	1.997
17	6.729	6.373	6.047	5.749	5.475	5.222	4.988	4.775	3.910	3.295	2.840	2.492	1.998
18	6.840	6.467	6.128	5.818	5.534	5.273	5.033	4.812	3.928	3.304	2.844	2.494	1.999
19	6.938	6.550	6.198	5.877	5.584	5.316	5.070	4.843	3.942	3.311	2.848	2.496	1.999
20	7.025	6.623	6.259	5.929	5.628	5.353	5.101	4.870	3.954	3.316	2.850	2.497	1.999
25	7.330	6.873	6.464	6.097	5.766	5.467	5.195	4.948	3.985	3.329	2.856	2.499	2.000
30	7.496	7.003	6.566	6.177	5.829	5.517	5.235	4.979	3.995	3.332	2.857	2.500	2.000
40	7.634	7.105	6.642	6.233	5.871	5.548	5.258	4.997	3.999	3.333	2.857	2.500	2.000
50	7.675	7.133	6.661	6.246	5.880	5.554	5.262	4.999	4.000	3.333	2.857	2.500	2.000

Internal Revenue Code of 1986: Selected Edited Sections*

Sections Included

671: Trust Income, Deductions, and Credits Attributable to Grantors and Others As Substantial Owners

672: Definitions and Rules

673: Reversionary Interests

674: Power to Control Beneficial Enjoyment

675: Administrative Powers

676: Power to Revoke

677: Income for Benefit of Grantor

678: Person Other than Grantor Treated As Substantial Owner

2001: Imposition and Rate of Tax

2002: Liability for Payment

2031: Definition of Gross Estate

2032: Alternate Valuation

2033: Property in Which the Decedent Had an Interest

2034: Dower or Curtesy Interests

2035: Adjustments for Gifts Made within 3 Years of Decedent's Death

---

*Note: Omitted passages are marked with five asterisks (*****).

2036: Transfers with Retained Life Estate

2037: Transfers Taking Effect at Death

2038: Revocable Transfers

2039: Annuities

2040: Joint Interests

2041: Powers of Appointment

2042: Proceeds of Life Insurance

2043: Transfers for Insufficient Consideration

2056: Bequests, etc., to Surviving Spouse

2503: Taxable Gifts

CHAPTER 1J; SUBPART D: GRANTOR TRUST RULES

SEC. 671: TRUST INCOME, DEDUCTIONS, AND CREDITS ATTRIBUTABLE TO GRANTORS AND OTHERS AS SUBSTANTIAL OWNERS

Where it is specified in this subpart that the grantor or another person shall be treated as the owner of any portion of a trust, there shall then be included in computing the taxable income and credits of the grantor or the other person those items of income, deductions, and credits against tax of the trust which are attributable to that portion of the trust to the extent that such items would be taken into account under this chapter in computing taxable income or credits against the tax of an individual. Any remaining portion of the trust shall be subject to subparts A through D.

*****

SEC. 672: DEFINITIONS AND RULES

(a) ADVERSE PARTY.—For purposes of this subpart, the term "adverse party" means any person having a substantial beneficial interest in the trust which would be adversely affected by the exercise or nonexercise of the power which he possesses respecting the trust. A person having a general power of appointment over the trust property shall be deemed to have a beneficial interest in the trust.

(b) NONADVERSE PARTY.—For purposes of this subpart, the term "nonadverse party" means any person who is not an adverse party.

(c) RELATED OR SUBORDINATE PARTY.—For purposes of this subpart, the term "related or subordinate party" means any nonadverse party who is—

  (1) the grantor's spouse if living with the grantor;

  (2) any one of the following: The grantor's father, mother, issue, brother or sister, an employee of the grantor, a corporation or any employee of a corporation in which the stock holdings of the grantor and the trust are significant from the viewpoint of voting control; a subordinate employee of a corporation in which the grantor is an executive.

For purposes of sections 674 and 675, a related or subordinate party shall be presumed to be subservient to the grantor in respect of the exercise or nonexercise of the powers conferred on him unless such party is shown not to be subservient by a preponderance of the evidence.

(d) RULE WHERE POWER IS SUBJECT TO CONDITION PRECEDENT.— A person shall be considered to have a power described in this subpart even though the exercise of the power is subject to a precedent giving of notice or takes effect only on the expiration of a certain period after the exercise of the power.

(e) GRANTOR TREATED AS HOLDING ANY POWER OR INTEREST OF GRANTOR'S SPOUSE.—For purposes of this subpart, if a grantor's spouse is living with the grantor at the time of the creation of any power or interest held by such spouse, the grantor shall be treated as holding such power or interest.

SEC. 673: REVERSIONARY INTERESTS

(a) GENERAL RULE.—The grantor shall be treated as the owner of any portion of a trust in which he has a reversionary interest in either the corpus or the income therefrom, if, as of the inception of that portion of the trust, the value of such interest exceeds 5 percent of the value of such portion.

(b) REVERSIONARY INTEREST TAKING EFFECT AT DEATH OF MINOR LINEAL DESCENDANT BENEFICIARY.—In the case of any beneficiary who—

(1) is a lineal descendant of the grantor, and

(2) holds all of the present interests in any portion of a trust, the grantor shall not be treated under subsection (a) as the owner of such portion solely by reason of a reversionary interest in such portion which takes effect upon the death of such beneficiary before such beneficiary attains age 21.

SEC. 674: POWER TO CONTROL BENEFICIAL ENJOYMENT

(a) GENERAL RULE.—The grantor shall be treated as the owner of any portion of a trust in respect of which the beneficial enjoyment of the corpus or the income therefrom is subject to a power of disposition, exercisable by the grantor or a nonadverse party, or both, without the approval or consent of any adverse party.

(b) EXCEPTIONS FOR CERTAIN POWERS.—Subsection (a) shall not apply to the following powers regardless of by whom held:

(1) POWER TO APPLY INCOME TO SUPPORT OF A DEPENDENT.—A power described in section 677(b) to the extent that the grantor would not be subject to tax under that section.

(2) POWER AFFECTING BENEFICIAL ENJOYMENT ONLY AFTER OCCUR-RENCE OF EVENT.—A power, the exercise of which can only affect the beneficial enjoyment of the income for a period commencing after the occurrence of an event such that a grantor would not be treated as the owner under section 673 if the power were a reversionary interest; but the grantor may be treated as the owner after the occurrence of the event unless the power is relinquished.

(3) POWER EXERCISABLE ONLY BY WILL.—A power exercisable only by will, other than a power in the grantor to appoint by will the income of the trust where the income is accumulated for such disposition by the grantor or may be so accumulated in the discretion of the grantor or a nonadverse party, or both, without the approval or consent of any adverse party.

(4) POWER TO ALLOCATE AMONG CHARITABLE BENEFICIARIES.—A power to determine the beneficial enjoyment of the corpus or the income therefrom if the corpus or income is irrevocably payable for a purpose specified in section 170(c) (relating to definition of charitable contributions).

(5) POWER TO DISTRIBUTE CORPUS.—A power to distribute corpus either—

  (A) to or for a beneficiary or beneficiaries or to or for a class of beneficiaries (whether or not income beneficiaries) provided that the power is limited by a reasonably definite standard which is set forth in the trust instrument; or

  (B) to or for any current income beneficiary, provided that the distribution of corpus must be chargeable against the proportionate share of corpus held in trust for the payment of income to the beneficiary as if the corpus constituted a separate trust.

A power does not fall within the powers described in this paragraph if any person has a power to add to the beneficiary or beneficiaries or to a class of beneficiaries designated to receive the income or corpus, except where such action is to provide for after-born or after-adopted children.

(6) POWER TO WITHHOLD INCOME TEMPORARILY.—A power to distribute or apply income to or for any current income beneficiary or to accumulate the income for him, provided that any accumulated income must ultimately be payable—

  (A) to the beneficiary from whom distribution or application is withheld, to his estate, or to his appointees (or persons named as alternate takers in default of appointment) provided that such beneficiary possesses a power of appointment which does not exclude from the class of possible appointees any person other than the beneficiary, his estate, his creditors, or the creditors of his estate, or

  (B) on termination of the trust, or in conjunction with a distribution of corpus which is augmented by such accumulated income, to the current income beneficiaries in shares which have been irrevocably specified in the trust instrument.

Accumulated income shall be considered so payable although it is provided that if any beneficiary does not survive a date of distribution which could reasonably have been expected to occur within the beneficiary's lifetime, the share of the deceased beneficiary is to be paid to his appointees or to one or more designated alternate takers (other than the grantor or the grantor's estate) whose shares have been irrevocably specified. A power does not fall within the powers described in this paragraph if any person has a power to add to the beneficiary or beneficiaries or to a class of beneficiaries designated to receive the income or corpus except where such action is to provide for after-born or after-adopted children.

(7) POWER TO WITHHOLD INCOME DURING DISABILITY OF A BENEFICIARY.—A power exercisable only during—

  (A) the existence of a legal disability of any current income beneficiary, or

  (B) the period during which any income beneficiary shall be under the age of 21 years,

to distribute or apply income to or for such beneficiary or to accumulate and add the income to corpus. A power does not fall within the powers described in this paragraph if any person has a power to add to the beneficiary or beneficiaries or to a class of beneficiaries designated to receive the income or corpus, except where such action is to provide for after-born or after-adopted children.

(8) POWER TO ALLOCATE BETWEEN CORPUS AND INCOME.—A power to allocate receipts and disbursements as between corpus and income, even though expressed in broad language.

(c) EXCEPTION FOR CERTAIN POWERS OF INDEPENDENT TRUST-EES.—Subsection (a) shall not apply to a power solely exercisable (without the approval or consent of any other person) by a trustee or trustees, none of whom is the grantor, and no more than half of whom are related or subordinate parties who are subservient to the wishes of the grantor—

(1) to distribute, apportion, or accumulate income to or for a beneficiary or beneficiaries, or to, for, or within a class of beneficiaries; or

(2) to pay out corpus to or for a beneficiary or beneficiaries or to or for a class of beneficiaries (whether or not income beneficiaries).

A power does not fall within the powers described in this subsection if any person has a power to add to the beneficiary or beneficiaries or to a class of beneficiaries designated to receive the income or corpus, except where such action is to provide for after-born or after-adopted children.

(d) POWER TO ALLOCATE INCOME IF LIMITED BY A STANDARD.—Subsection (a) shall not apply to a power solely exercisable (without the approval or consent of any other person) by a trustee or trustees, none of whom is the grantor or spouse living with the grantor, to distribute, apportion, or accumulate income to or for a beneficiary or beneficiaries, or to, for, or within a class of beneficiaries, whether or not the conditions of paragraph (6) or (7) of subsection (b) are satisfied, if such power is limited by a reasonably definite external standard which is set forth in the trust instrument. A power does not fall within the powers described in this subsection if any person has a power to add to the beneficiary or beneficiaries or to a class of beneficiaries designated to receive the income or corpus except where such action is to provide for after-born or after-adopted children.

SEC. 675: ADMINISTRATIVE POWERS

The grantor shall be treated as the owner of any portion of a trust in respect of which—

(1) POWER TO DEAL FOR LESS THAN ADEQUATE AND FULL CONSID-ERATION.—A power exercisable by the grantor or a nonadverse party, or both, without the approval or consent of any adverse party enables the grantor or any person to purchase, exchange, or otherwise deal with or dispose of the corpus or the income therefrom for less than an adequate consideration in money or money's worth.

(2) POWER TO BORROW WITHOUT ADEQUATE INTEREST OR SECU-RITY.—A power exercisable by the grantor or a nonadverse party, or both, enables the grantor to borrow the corpus or income, directly or indirectly, without adequate interest or without adequate security except where a trustee (other than the grantor) is authorized under a general lending power to make loans to any person without regard to interest or security.

(3) BORROWING OF THE TRUST FUNDS.—The grantor has directly or indirectly borrowed the corpus or income and has not completely repaid the loan, including any interest, before the beginning of the taxable year. The preceding sentence shall not apply to a loan which provides for adequate interest and ad-

equate security, if such loan is made by a trustee other than the grantor and other than a related or subordinate trustee subservient to the grantor.

    (4) GENERAL POWERS OF ADMINISTRATION.—A power of administration is exercisable in a nonfiduciary capacity by any person without the approval or consent of any person in a fiduciary capacity. For purposes of this paragraph, the term "power of administration" means any one or more of the following powers: (A) a power to vote or direct the voting of stock or other securities of a corporation in which the holdings of the grantor and the trust are significant from the viewpoint of voting control; (B) a power to control the investment of the trust funds either by directing investments or reinvestments, or by vetoing proposed investments or reinvestments, to the extent that the trust funds consist of stocks or securities of corporations in which the holdings of the grantor and the trust are significant from the viewpoint of voting control; or (C) a power to reacquire the trust corpus by substituting other property of an equivalent value.

SEC. 676: POWER TO REVOKE

(a) GENERAL RULE.—The grantor shall be treated as the owner of any portion of a trust, whether or not he is treated as such owner under any other provision of this part, where at any time the power to revest in the grantor title to such portion is exercisable by the grantor or a non-adverse party or both.

(b) POWER AFFECTING BENEFICIAL ENJOYMENT ONLY AFTER OC-CURRENCE OF EVENT.—Subsection (a) shall not apply to a power the exercise of which can only affect the beneficial enjoyment of the income for a period commencing after the occurrence of an event such that a grantor would not be treated as the owner under section 673 if the power were a reversionary interest. But the grantor may be treated as the owner after the occurrence of such event unless the power is relinquished.

SEC. 677: INCOME FOR BENEFIT OF GRANTOR

(a) GENERAL RULE.—The grantor shall be treated as the owner of any portion of a trust, whether or not he is treated as such owner under section 674, whose income without the approval or consent of any adverse party is, or, in the discretion of the grantor or a nonadverse party, or both, may be—

    (1) distributed to the grantor or the grantor's spouse;

    (2) held or accumulated for future distribution to the grantor or the grantor's spouse; or

    (3) applied to the payment of premiums on policies of insurance on the life of the grantor or the grantor's spouse (except policies of insurance irrevocably payable for a purpose specified in section 170(c) (relating to definition of charitable contributions)).

This subsection shall not apply to a power the exercise of which can only affect the beneficial enjoyment of the income for a period commencing after *the occurrence of an event* such that the grantor would not be treated as the owner under section 673 if the power were a reversionary interest; but the grantor may be treated as the owner after *the occurrence of the event* unless the power is relinquished.

(b) OBLIGATIONS OF SUPPORT.—Income of a trust shall not be considered taxable to the grantor under subsection (a) or any other provision of this chapter merely because such income in the discretion of another person, the trustee, or the grantor acting as trustee or co-trustee, may be applied or distributed for the support or maintenance of a beneficiary (other than the grantor's spouse) whom the grantor is legally obligated to support or maintain, except to the extent that such income is so applied or distributed. In cases where the amounts so applied or distributed are paid out of corpus or out of other than income for the taxable year, such amounts shall be considered to be an amount paid or credited within the meaning of paragraph (2) of section 661(a) and shall be taxed to the grantor under section 662.

SEC. 678: PERSON OTHER THAN GRANTOR TREATED AS SUBSTANTIAL OWNER

(a) GENERAL RULE.—A person other than the grantor shall be treated as the owner of any portion of a trust with respect to which:

(1) such person has a power exercisable solely by himself to vest the corpus or the income therefrom in himself, or

(2) such person has previously partially released or otherwise modified such a power and after the release or modification retains such control as would, within the principles of sections 671 to 677, inclusive, subject a grantor of a trust to treatment as the owner thereof.

(b) EXCEPTION WHERE GRANTOR IS TAXABLE.—Subsection (a) shall not apply with respect to a power over income, as originally granted or thereafter modified, if the grantor of the trust or a transferor (to whom section 679 applies) is otherwise treated as the owner under the provisions of this subpart other than this section.

(c) OBLIGATIONS OF SUPPORT.—Subsection (a) shall not apply to a power which enables such person, in the capacity of trustee or co-trustee, merely to apply the income of the trust to the support or maintenance of a person whom the holder of the power is obligated to support or maintain except to the extent that such income is so applied. In cases where the amounts so applied or distributed are paid out of corpus or out of other than income of the taxable year, such amounts shall be considered to be an amount paid or credited within the meaning of paragraph (2) of section 661(a) and shall be taxed to the holder of the power under section 662.

(d) EFFECT OF RENUNCIATION OR DISCLAIMER.—Subsection (a) shall not apply with respect to a power which has been renounced or disclaimed within a reasonable time after the holder of the power first became aware of its existence.

*****

CHAPTER 11: ESTATE TAX

SEC. 2001: IMPOSITION AND RATE OF TAX

(a) IMPOSITION.—A tax is hereby imposed on the transfer of the taxable estate of every decedent who is a citizen or resident of the United States.

(b) COMPUTATION OF TAX.—The tax imposed by this section shall be the amount equal to the excess (if any) of—

(1) a tentative tax computed in accordance with the rate schedule set forth in subsection (c) on the sum of—
(A) the amount of the taxable estate, and
(B) the amount of the adjusted taxable gifts, over

(2) the aggregate amount of tax which would have been payable under chapter 12 with respect to gifts made by the decedent after December 31, 1976, if the rate schedule set forth in subsection (c) (as in effect at the decedent's death) had been applicable at the time of such gifts.

For purposes of paragraph (1)(b), the term "adjusted taxable gifts" means the total amount of the taxable gifts (within the meaning of section 2053) made by the decedent after December 31, 1976, other than gifts which are includable in the gross estate of the decedent.

(c) RATE SCHEDULE
(Editor's note: Transfer tax rates will be found in the textbook Appendix A.)

*****

(d) ADJUSTMENT FOR GIFT TAX PAID BY SPOUSE.

*****

(e) COORDINATION OF SECTIONS 2513 AND 2035.

*****

SEC. 2002: LIABILITY FOR PAYMENT

Except as provided in section 2210, the tax imposed by this chapter shall be paid by the executor.

SEC. 2031: DEFINITION OF GROSS ESTATE
(a) GENERAL.—The value of the gross estate of the decedent shall be determined by including to the extent provided for in this part, the value at the time of his death of all property, real or personal, tangible or intangible, wherever situated.

(b) VALUATION OF UNLISTED STOCK AND SECURITIES.

*****

(c) CROSS REFERENCE.

*****

SEC. 2032: ALTERNATE VALUATION
(a) GENERAL.—The value of the gross estate may be determined, if the executor so elects, by valuing all the property included in the gross estate as follows:

(1) In the case of property distributed, sold, exchanged, or otherwise disposed of, within six months after the decedent's death such property shall be valued as of the date of distribution, sale, exchange, or other disposition.

(2) In the case of property not distributed, sold, exchanged, or otherwise disposed of, within six months after the decedent's death such property shall be valued as of the date six months after the decedent's death.

(3)

*****

(b) SPECIAL RULES.

*****

(c) ELECTION MUST DECREASE GROSS ESTATE AND ESTATE TAX.—
No election may be made under this section with respect to an estate unless such election
shall decrease—

(1) the value of the gross estate, and
(2) the amount of the tax imposed by this chapter (reduced by credits allowable
against such tax).

(d) ELECTION

*****

SEC. 2033: PROPERTY IN WHICH THE DECEDENT HAD AN INTEREST

The value of the gross estate shall include the value of all property to the extent of the
interest therein of the decedent at the time of his death.

SEC. 2034: DOWER OR CURTESY INTERESTS

The value of the gross estate shall include the value of all property to the extent of any
interest therein of the surviving spouse, existing at the time of the decedent's death as
dower or curtesy, or by virtue of a statute creating an estate in lieu of dower or curtesy.

SEC. 2035: ADJUSTMENTS FOR GIFTS MADE WITHIN 3 YEARS OF DECEDENT'S DEATH

(a) INCLUSION OF GIFTS MADE BY DECEDENT.—Except as provided for in
subsection (b), the value of the gross estate shall include the value of all property to the
extent of any interest therein of which the decedent has at any time made a transfer, by
trust or otherwise, during the three-year period ending on the date of the decedent's
death.

(b) EXCEPTIONS.—Subsection (a) shall not apply—

(1) to any bona fide sale for an adequate and full consideration in money or money's
worth, and
(2) to any gift to a donee made during a calendar year if the decedent was not required by section 6019 [other than by reason of section 6019(2)] to file any gift
tax return for such year with respect to gifts to such donee. Paragraph (2) shall
not apply to any transfer with respect to a life insurance policy.

(c) INCLUSION OF GIFT TAX ON CERTAIN GIFTS MADE DURING 3
YEARS BEFORE DECEDENT'S DEATH.—The amount of the gross estate (determined without regard to this subsection) shall be increased by the amount of any tax
paid under chapter 12 by the decedent or his estate on any gift made by the decedent or
his spouse made after December 31, 1976, and during the three-year period ending on
the date of the decedent's death.

(d) DECEDENT'S DYING AFTER 1981—

(1) IN GENERAL.—Except as otherwise provided in this subsection (a) shall not
apply to the estate of a decedent dying after December 31, 1981.

(2) EXCEPTIONS FOR CERTAIN TRANSFERS.—Paragraph 1 of this subsection and paragraph (2) of subsection (b) shall not apply to a transfer of an interest in property which is included in the value of the gross estate under section 2036, 2037, 2038, or 2042 or would have been included under any of such sections if such interest had been retained by the decedent.

(3) THREE-YEAR RULE RETAINED FOR CERTAIN PURPOSES.

*****

(4) COORDINATION OF THREE-YEAR RULE WITH SECTION 6166(a)(1).

*****

SEC. 2036: TRANSFERS WITH RETAINED LIFE ESTATE

(a) GENERAL RULE.—The value of the gross estate shall include the value of all property to the extent of any interest therein of which the decedent has at any time made a transfer (except in case of a bona fide sale for an adequate and full consideration in money or money's worth), by trust or otherwise, under which he has retained for his life or for any period not ascertainable without reference to his death or for any period which does not in fact end before his death—

(1) the possession or enjoyment of, or the right to the income from, the property, or

(2) the right, either alone or in conjunction with any person, to designate the persons who shall possess or enjoy the property or the income therefrom.

(b) VOTING RIGHTS

(1) IN GENERAL.—For purposes of subsection (a)(1), the retention of the right to vote (directly or indirectly) shares of stock of a controlled corporation shall be considered to be a retention of the enjoyment of transferred property.

(2) CONTROLLED CORPORATION.

*****

(3) COORDINATION WITH SECTION 2035.

(c) INCLUSION RELATED TO VALUATION FREEZES.—

(1) In General.—For purposes of subsection (a), if—
   (A) any person holds a substantial interest in an enterprise, and
   (B) such person in effect transfers after December 17, 1987, property having a disproportionately large share of the potential appreciation in such person's interest in the enterprise while retaining a disproportionately large share in the income of, or rights in, the enterprise,

then the retention of the retained interest shall be considered to be a retention of the enjoyment of the transferred property.

(2) Special Rule for Sales to Family Members.—The exception contained in subsection (a) for a bona fide sale shall not apply to a transfer described in paragraph (1) if such transfer is to a member of the transferor's family.

(3) Definitions.—For purposes of this subsection—
   (A) Substantial Interest.—A person holds a substantial interest in an enterprise if such person owns (directly or indirectly) 10 percent or more of the voting

power or income stream, or both, in such enterprise. For purposes of the preceding sentence, an individual shall be treated as owning any interest in an enterprise which is owned (directly or indirectly) by any member of such individual's family.

(B) Family.—the term "family" means, with respect to any individual, such individual's spouse, any lineal descendant of such individual or of such individual's spouse, any parent or grandparent of such individual, and any spouse of any of the foregoing. For purposes of the preceding sentence, a relationship by legal adoption shall be treated as a relationship by blood.

(C) Treatment of Spouse.—An individual and such individual's spouse shall be treated as 1 person.

(4) Coordination with Section 2035.—For purposes of applying section 2035, any transfer of the retained interest referred to in paragraph (1) shall be treated as a transfer of an interest in the transferred property referred to in paragraph (1).

(5) Coordination with Section 2043.—In lieu of applying section 2043, appropriate adjustments shall be made for the value of the retained interest.

(d) LIMITATION ON APPLICATION OF GENERAL RULE.

*****

SEC. 2037: TRANSFERS TAKING EFFECT AT DEATH

(a) GENERAL RULE.—The value of the gross estate shall include the value of all property to the extent of any interest therein of which the decedent has at any time after September 7, 1916, made a transfer (except in case of a bona fide sale for an adequate and full consideration in money or money's worth), by trust or otherwise, if—

(1) possession or enjoyment of the property can, through ownership of such interest, be obtained only by surviving the decedent, and

(2) the decedent has retained a reversionary interest in the property (but in the case of a transfer made before October 8, 1949, only if such reversionary interest arose by the express terms of the instrument of transfer), and the value of such reversionary interest immediately before the death of the decedent exceeds 5 percent of the value of such property.

(b) SPECIAL RULES.

*****

SEC. 2038: REVOCABLE TRANSFERS

(a) IN GENERAL.—The value of the gross estate shall include the value of all property—

(1) Transfers after June 22, 1936- To the extent of any interest therein of which the decedent has at any time made a transfer (except in case of a bona fide sale for an adequate and full consideration in money or money's worth), by trust or otherwise, where the enjoyment thereof was subject at the date of his death to any change through the exercise of a power (in whatever capacity exercisable) by the decedent alone or by the decedent in conjunction with any other person (without regard to when or from what source the decedent acquired such power), to alter, amend, revoke, or terminate, or where such power is relinquished during the three-year period ending on the date of the decedent's death.

(2) TRANSFERS ON OR BEFORE JUNE 22, 1936.

*****

(b) DATE OF EXISTENCE OF POWER.

*****

SEC. 2039: ANNUITIES

(a) GENERAL.—The gross estate shall include the value of an annuity or other payment receivable by any beneficiary by reason of surviving the decedent under any form of contract or agreement entered into after March 3, 1931 (other than as insurance under policies on the life of the decedent), if, under such contract or agreement, an annuity or other payment was payable to the decedent, or the decedent possessed the right to receive such annuity or payment, either alone or in conjunction with another for his life or for any period not ascertainable without reference to his death or for any period which does not in fact end before his death.

(b) AMOUNT INCLUDABLE.

*****

(c) EXCEPTION OF CERTAIN ANNUITY INTERESTS CREATED BY COMMUNITY PROPERTY LAWS.

*****

SEC. 2040: JOINT INTERESTS

(a) GENERAL RULE.—The value of the gross estate shall include the value of all property to the extent of the interest therein held as joint tenants with right of survivorship by the decedent and any other person, or as tenants by the entirety by the decedent and spouse, or deposited, with any person carrying on the banking business, in their joint names and payable to either or the survivor, except such part thereof as may be shown to have originally belonged to such other person and never to have been received or acquired by the latter from the decedent for less than an adequate or full consideration in money or money's worth: *Provided,* That where such property or any part thereof, or part of the consideration with which such property was acquired, is shown to have been at any time acquired by such other person from the decedent for less than an adequate and full consideration in money or money's worth, there shall be excepted only such part of the value of such property as is proportionate to the consideration furnished by such other person: *Provided further,* That where any property has been acquired by gift, bequest, devise, or inheritance, as a tenancy by the entirety by the decedent and spouse, then to the extent of one half of the value thereof, or, where so acquired by the decedent and any other person as joint tenants with right of survivorship and their interests are not otherwise specified or fixed by law, then to the extent of the value of a fractional part to be determined by dividing the value of the property by the number of joint tenants with right of survivorship.

(b) CERTAIN JOINT INTERESTS OF HUSBAND AND WIFE.—

    (1) INTERESTS OF SPOUSE EXCLUDED FROM GROSS ESTATE.—Notwithstanding subsection (a), in the case of any qualified joint interest, the value included in the gross estate with respect to such interest by reason of this section is one half of the value of such qualified joint interest.

(2) QUALIFIED JOINT INTEREST DEFINED.—For purposes of paragraph (1), the term "qualified joint interest" means any interest in property held by the decedent and the decedent's spouse as—
(A) tenants by the entirety, or
(B) joint tenants with right of survivorship, but only if the decedent and the spouse of the decedent are the only joint tenants.

SECTION 2041: POWERS OF APPOINTMENT

(a) IN GENERAL.—The value of the gross estate shall include the value of all property.

(1) POWERS OF APPOINTMENT CREATED ON OR BEFORE OCTOBER 21, 1942.

*****

(2) POWERS CREATED AFTER OCTOBER 21, 1942.—To the extent of any property with respect to which the decedent has at the time of his death a general power of appointment created after October 21, 1942, or with respect to which the decedent has at any time exercised or released such a power of appointment by a disposition which is of such a nature that if it were a transfer of property owned by the decedent, such property would be includable in the decedent's gross estate under section 2035 to 2038, inclusive. For purposes of this paragraph (2), the power of appointment shall be considered to exist on the date of the decedent's death even though the exercise of the power is subject to a precedent giving of notice or even though the exercise of the power takes effect only on the expiration of a stated period after its exercise, whether or not on or before the date of the decedent's death notice has been given or the power has been exercised.

(3) CREATION OF ANOTHER POWER IN CERTAIN CASES.

*****

(b) DEFINITIONS.—For purposes of subsection (a)—

(1) GENERAL POWER OF APPOINTMENT—The term "general power of appointment" means a power which is exercisable in favor of the decedent, his estate, his creditors, or the creditors of his estate; except that—
(A) A power to consume, invade, or appropriate property for the benefit of the decedent which is limited to an ascertainable standard relating to the health, education, support, or maintenance of the decedent shall not be deemed a general power of appointment.
(B) A power of appointment created on or before October 21, 1942, which is exercisable by the decedent only in conjuntion with another person shall not be deemed a general power of appointment.
(C) In the case of a power of appointment created after October 21, 1942, which is exercisable by the decedent only in conjunction with another person—
(i) If the power is not exercisable by the decedent except in conjunction with the creator of the power—such power shall not be deemed a general power of appointment.
(ii) If the power is not exercisable by the decedent except in conjunction with a person having a substantial interest in the property, subject to the power, which is adverse to the exercise of the power in favor of the

decedent—such power shall not be deemed a general power of appointment.

*****

(iii)

*****

For purposes of clauses (ii) and (iii), a power shall be deemed to be exercisable in favor of a person if it is exercisable in favor of such a person, his estate, his creditors, or the creditors of his estate.

(2) LAPSE OF POWER—The lapse of a power of appointment created after October 21, 1942, during the life of the individual possessing the power shall be considered a release of such power. The preceding sentence shall apply with respect to the lapse of powers during any calendar year only to the extent that the property, which could have been appointed by exercise of such lapsed powers, exceeded in value, at the time of such lapse, the greater of the following amounts:
 (A) $5,000, or
 (B) 5 percent of the aggregate value, at the time of such lapse, of the assets out of which, or the proceeds of which, the exercise of the lapsed powers could have been satisfied.

(3) DATE OF CREATION OF SUCH POWER

*****

SEC. 2042: PROCEEDS OF LIFE INSURANCE

The value of the gross estate shall include the value of all property—

 (1) RECEIVABLE BY THE EXECUTOR.—To the extent of the amount receivable by the executor as insurance under policies on the life of the decedent.

 (2) RECEIVABLE BY OTHER BENEFICIARIES.—To the extent of the amount receivable by all other beneficiaries as insurance under policies on the life of the decedent with respect to which the decedent possessed at his death any of the incidents of ownership, exercisable either alone or in conjunction with any other person.

*****

SEC. 2043: TRANSFERS FOR INSUFFICIENT CONSIDERATION

(a) IN GENERAL.—If any one of the transfers, trusts, interests, rights, or powers enumerated and described in sections 2035 to 2038, inclusive, and section 2041 is made, created, exercised, or relinquished for a consideration in money or money's worth, but is not a bona fide sale for an adequate and full consideration in money or money's worth, there shall be included in the gross estate only the excess of the fair market value at the time of death of the property otherwise to be included on account of such transaction, over the value of the consideration received therefore by the decedent.

(b) MARITAL RIGHTS NOT TREATED AS CONSIDERATION.

*****

SEC. 2056: BEQUESTS, ETC., TO SURVIVING SPOUSE

(a) ALLOWANCE OF MARITAL DEDUCTION.—For purposes of the tax imposed by section 2001, the value of the taxable estate shall, except as limited by subsection (b), be determined by deducting from the value of the gross estate an amount equal to the value of any interest in property which passes or has passed from the decedent to his surviving spouse, but only to the extent that such interest is included in determining the value of the gross estate.

(b) LIMITATION IN THE CASE OF LIFE ESTATE OR OTHER TERMINABLE INTEREST—

(1) GENERAL RULE.—Where, on the lapse of time, on the occurrence of an event or contingency, or on the failure of an event on contingency to occur, an interest passing to the surviving spouse will terminate or fail, no deduction shall be allowed under this section with respect to such interest—

(A) if an interest in such property passes or has passed (for less than an adequate and full consideration in money or money's worth) from the decedent to any person other than such surviving spouse (or the estate of such spouse); and

(B) if by reason of such passing such person (or his heirs or assigns) may possess or enjoy any part of such property after such termination or failure of the interest so passing to the surviving spouse;

and no deduction shall be allowed with respect to such interest [even if such deduction is not disallowed under subparagraphs (A) and (B)]—

(C) if such interest is to be acquired for the surviving spouse, pursuant to directions of the decedent, by his executor or by the trustee of a trust.

*****

(2) INTEREST IN UNIDENTIFIED ASSETS.

*****

(3) INTEREST OF SPOUSE CONDITIONAL ON SURVIVAL FOR LIMITED PERIOD—For purposes of this subsection, an interest passing to the surviving spouse shall not be considered as an interest which will terminate or fail on the death of such spouse if—

(A) such death will cause a termination or failure of such interest only if it occurs within a period not exceeding six months after the decedent's death, or only if it occurs as a result of a common disaster resulting in the death of the decedent and the surviving spouse, or only if it occurs in the case of either such event; and

(B) such termination or failure does not in fact occur.

(4) VALUATION OF INTEREST PASSING TO SURVIVING SPOUSE.

*****

(5) LIFE ESTATE WITH POWER OF APPOINTMENT IN SURVIVING SPOUSE—In the case of an interest in property passing from the decedent, if his surviving spouse is entitled for life to all the income from the entire interest, or all the income from a specific portion thereof, payable annually or at more frequent intervals, with power in the surviving spouse to appoint the entire interest, or such specific portion (exercisable in favor of such surviving spouse, or of the estate of such surviving spouse, or in favor of either, whether or not in

each case the power is exercisable in favor of others), and with no power in any other person to appoint any part of the interest, or such specific portion, to any person other than the surviving spouse—

(A) the interest or such portion thereof so passing shall, for purposes of subsection (a), be considered as passing to the surviving spouse, and

(B) no part of the interest so passing shall, for purposes of paragraph (1)(A), be considered as passing to any person other than the surviving spouse.

This paragraph shall apply only if such power in the surviving spouse to appoint the entire interest, or such specific portion thereof, whether exercisable by will or during life, is exercisable by such spouse alone and in all events.

(6) LIFE INSURANCE OR ANNUITY PAYMENTS WITH POWER OF APPOINTMENT IN SURVIVING SPOUSE.

*****

(7) ELECTION WITH RESPECT TO LIFE ESTATE FOR SURVIVING SPOUSE—

(A) IN GENERAL.—In the case of qualified terminible interest property—

(i) for purposes of subsection (a), such property shall be treated as passing to the surviving spouse, and

(ii) for purposes of paragraph (1)(A), no part of such property shall be treated as passing to any person other than the surviving spouse.

(B) QUALIFIED TERMINABLE INTEREST PROPERTY DEFINED.—For purposes of this paragraph—

(i) IN GENERAL.—The term "qualified terminable interest property" means property—

(I) which passes from the decedent,

(II) in which the surviving spouse has a qualifying income interest for life, and

(III) to which an election under this paragraph applies.

(ii) Qualifying Income Interest For Life- The surviving spouse has a qualifying income interest for life if—

(I) the surviving spouse is entitled to all the income from the property, payable annually or at more frequent intervals

*****

and

(II) no person has a power to appoint any part of the property to any person other than the surviving spouse.

Subclause (II) shall not apply to a power exercisable only at or after the death of the surviving spouse.

*****

(iii) PROPERTY INCLUDES INTEREST THEREIN.

*****

(iv) SPECIFIC PORTION TREATED AS SEPARATE PROPERTY.

*****

(v) ELECTION.—An election under this paragraph with respect to any property shall be made by the executor on the return of tax imposed by section 2001. Such an election, once made, shall be irrevocable.

(8) SPECIAL RULE FOR CHARITABLE REMAINDER TRUSTS.

*****

(9) DENIAL OF DOUBLE DEDUCTION.

*****

CHAPTER 13: GIFT TAX

SEC. 2503: TAXABLE GIFTS

(a) GENERAL DEFINITION.—The term "taxable gifts" means the total amount of gifts made during the calendar year, less the deductions provided in subchapter C (section 2522 and following).

(b) EXCLUSIONS FROM GIFTS.—In the case of gifts (other than gifts of future interests in property) made to any person by the donor during the calendar year, the first $10,000 of such gifts to such person shall not, for purposes of subsection (a), be included in the total amount of gifts made during such year. Where there has been a transfer to any person of a present interest in property, the possibility that such interest may be diminished by the exercise of a power shall be disregarded in applying this subsection, if no part of such interest will at any time pass to any other person.

(c) TRANSFER FOR THE BENEFIT OF A MINOR.—No part of a gift to an individual who has not attained the age of 21 years on the date of such transfer shall be considered a gift of a future interest in property for purposes of subsection (b) if the property and the income therefrom—

(1) may be expended by, or for the benefit of, the donee before his attaining the age of 21 years, and

(2) will to the extent not so expended—
   (A) pass to the donee on his attaining the age of 21 years, and
   (B) in the event that the donee dies before attaining the age of 21 years, be payable to the estate of the donee or as he may appoint under a general power of appointment as defined in section 2514(c).

(d) Repealed.

(e) EXCLUSION FOR CERTAIN TRANSFERS FOR EDUCATIONAL EXPENSES OR MEDICAL EXPENSES.—

(1) IN GENERAL—Any qualified transfer shall not be treated as a transfer of property by gift for purposes of this chapter.

(2) QUALIFIED TRANSFER.—For purposes of this subsection, the term "qualified transfer" means any amount paid on behalf of an individual—
   (A) as tuition to an educational organization described in section 170(b)(1)(A)(ii) for the education or training of such individual, or
   (B) to any person who provides medical care [as defined in section 213(e)] with respect to such individual as payment for such medical care.

GLOSSARY

Adjusted basis   The amount subtracted from the amount realized to calculate gain or loss on sale or exchange of property.

Adjusted taxable gifts   In federal estate tax (FET), the sum of post-1976 taxable gifts. It is added to the taxable estate on the federal estate tax return to arrive at the estate tax base.

Administrator   A personal representative who was not nominated in the will.

After-born child   A child who was born after the execution of a parent's will.

Alternate valuation date   Under FET law, the date that is six months after date of death. Assets may be valued on this date or on date of death.

Annual exclusion   Under the federal gift tax, a deduction, up to $10,000, from gross gifts for gifts by any donor to each donee in a given year.

Annual exclusion gift   A gift of property worth no more than the annual exclusion.

Antilapse statute   A state statutory provision that specifies, in the absence of a provision in the will, to whom a lapsed testamentary bequest will pass.

Appointee (of a power of appointment)   The party or parties whom the holder of a power of appointment actually appoints.

Apportionment statute   See *Equitable apportionment statute*.

Ascertainable standard   Wording in a will or trust intentionally limiting the freedom of holder of a power of appointment over property. The most common words of limitation are, "health," "education," "support," and "maintenance," derived from Section 2041. Use of the words avoid FET taxation to the holder of the power as a general power of appointment.

Assignment   Any type of passing of property in which the transferor gives up some kind of interest to the transferee. See transfer.

Assignment of income doctrine   Under income tax law, a doctrine holding that earnings from services performed will always be taxable to the person performing those services.

Bargain sale   The sale of an asset for some amount less than what would be regarded full and adequate consideration. The difference between the consideration received by the client-donor and the value of the asset transferred constitutes a gift, for tax purposes.

Beneficial interest   An interest that carries an economic benefit. Examples of beneficial interests in property include the temporary or permanent right to possess, consume, and pledge the property.

Beneficiary   A person who is receiving or will receive a gift of a beneficial interest in property. See *Donee*.

Bequest   A gift, by will, of personal property. Also called a legacy.

Business buyout agreement   An agreement between one or more owners of a closely held business and one or more other persons that obligates one or more of the parties to purchase the interest of one of the others upon the occurrence of specific future events, such as the latter's death and, often, the onset of his or her permanent disability.

Buyout agreement   See *Business buyout agreement*.

Buy-sell agreement   See *Business buyout agreement*.

Bypass   An arrangement under which property owned by a decedent and intended for the lifetime benefit of the surviving spouse does not actually pass to the surviving spouse, thereby avoiding inclusion in the latter's gross estate.

Bypass trust   A trust designed to contain property that bypasses the surviving spouse's estate. See *Bypass*.

Cash value life insurance policy   A policy that accumulates economic value because the insurer charges a constant premium that is considerably higher than mortality costs required during the earlier years. Part of this overpayment accumulates as a cash surrender value which, prior to the death of the insured, can be enjoyed by the owner, basically in one of two ways. First, at any time the owner can surrender the policy and receive this value in cash. Second, the owner can make a policy loan and borrow up to the amount of this value.

Charitable lead trust   A trust under which the client donates an asset's income interest to charity, with the remainder interest passing to a private party after a specified length of time. The estate or its beneficiaries will receive an income tax deduction for the value of the income interest.

Charitable remainder annuity trust (CRAT)   A trust into which the client transfers assets in exchange for a fixed annuity income of at least 5 percent of the original value of the assets transferred into trust, payable at least annually, usually for life. The value of the remainder is deductible on the income tax return.

Charitable remainder unitrust (CRUT)   A trust that is much like the charitable remainder annuity trust, except that the annual income depends on a fixed percentage of the current fair market value of the assets in the trust, determined annually.

Chose in action   A claim or debt recoverable in a lawsuit.

Codicil   A separate written document that amends or revokes a prior will. It is executed if the testator wishes to change or add to the will.

Collateral A relative who shares a common ancestor with a person but who is neither a descendant nor an ascendant of that person. Contrast with *issue*.

Committee See *Guardian*.

Community property In the eight states recognizing it, any property that has been acquired by either of the spouses during their marriage, but not by gift, devise, bequest or inheritance, or, in most of the community property states, by the income therefrom. The eight states are: Arizona, California, Idaho, Louisiana, Nevada, New Mexico, Texas, and Washington. In addition, Wisconsin has recently adopted a form of community property known as "marital partnership property."

Completed gift A gift involving a total transfer of all interests in the asset transferred.

Complex trust A nongrantor trust which, in a given year, either (*a*) accumulates some fiduciary accounting income (FAI) (i.e., does not pay out all FAI, which it has received, to the beneficiaries) or (*b*) distributes principal.

Conduit principle In the income taxation of estates and trusts, the rule that fiduciary accounting income distributed to beneficiaries will be taxed to them, rather than to the estate or trust.

Consanguinity Degrees of blood relationship between a decedent and the decedent's relatives.

Conservator A court-appointed fiduciary responsible for the person or property of an elderly incompetent person, or both.

Consideration furnished test Under the federal estate tax, the proposition that includes in a decedent's gross estate the entire value of property held by the decedent in joint tenancy, reduced only by an amount attributable to that portion of the consideration in money or money's worth which can clearly be shown to have been furnished by the survivors.

Contingent interest A future interest that is not vested; that is, an interest whose possession and enjoyment are dependent on the happening of some future event, other than the passage of time.

Corpus The property in a trust. Also called *principal*.

Creator The person who creates the trust and whose property usually winds up in it. Also called *grantor, settlor,* or *trustor*.

Credit An amount deductible from the tax. See also *Unified credit*.

Credit shelter bypass A bypass of an amount approximately equal to $600,000, the exemption equivalent of the unified credit.

Crummey provision A clause in an irrevocable trust for the benefit of a minor child giving the child the right to withdraw, for a limited period of time each year, the lesser of the amount of the annual exclusion or the value of the gift property transferred into the trust.

Cumulative gift doctrine The requirement that all lifetime gifts be accumulated; that is, that prior taxable gifts be added to current taxable transfers to determine the estate or gift tax base.

Curtesy   A surviving husband's life interest in a portion of the real property owned by his deceased wife.

Custodial gift   A gift to a custodian for the benefit of a child, under the Uniform Gifts to Minors Act or the Uniform Transfers to Minors Act.

Death tax   A tax levied on certain property owned or transferred by the decedent at death. Either an estate tax or an inheritance tax.

Decedent   In estate planning nomenclature, the person who has died.

Deferral   A term used in this text to mean delaying payment of the FET by using the marital deduction.

Devise   A gift, by will, of real property.

Devisee   A beneficiary, under a will, of a devise, i.e., a gift of real property.

Direct skip   Under federal generation-skipping tax law, a transfer to a skip person that is subject to the gift tax or the estate tax.

Disclaimer   An unqualified refusal to accept a gift. In estate planning, a valid disclaimer must meet the requirements of both local law and IRC Section 2518.

Distributable net income (DNI)   An amount more or less equal to fiduciary accounting income (FAI) that acts as the measuring rod for estate and trust income taxation.

Distribution deduction   In the income taxation of estates and trusts, an amount equal to the lesser of distributable net income or the amount actually distributed to beneficiaries.

Distribution planning   Planning the amount and timing of beneficiary distributions from an estate or irrevocable trust, usually with the objective of reducing income tax.

DNI   See *Distributible net income*.

Donee   A person who is receiving or will receive a gift of a beneficial interest in property. See *Beneficiary*.

Donor   A person making a gift.

Dower   A surviving wife's life interest in a portion of the real property owned by her deceased husband.

Durable power of attorney   A power of attorney that does not become legally invalid at the onset of the principal's incapacity.

Durable power of attorney for health care   A durable power of attorney granting to the attorney-in-fact the power to make medical decisions on behalf of the principal. Recognized in only a few states.

Durable power of attorney for property   A durable power of attorney granting to the attorney-in-fact the power to make decisions concerning the property of the principal.

Equalization   A term used in this text to mean a plan of property disposition by the spouses so that the taxable estates (or estate tax base) of the two are more or less equal.

Equitable apportionment statute   A state statute that spreads the death tax burden more or less proportionately among all of the beneficiaries receiving the taxed assets.

Escheat The reversion of an intestate decedent's property to the state, because either the decedent left no next of kin, or all surviving relatives are considered under state law to be too remote for purposes of inheritance.

Estate A quantity of wealth or property. See also *Net estate, Gross estate,* and *Probate estate.*

Estate tax A federal or state tax on the decedent's right to transfer property.

Estate tax base On the estate tax return, the taxable estate plus adjusted taxable gifts. The amount used to calculate the tentative estate tax.

Estate trust One type of *marital trust* under which the corpus is made payable to the estate of the surviving spouse at his or her death. Its unique feature is that during the surviving spouse's lifetime, some or all of the income can be made payable to someone else.

Execute To complete a document (i.e., to do what is necessary to render it valid).

Executor A personal representative who was nominated in the will.

Exercise a power of appointment To invoke the power by appointing a permissible appointee.

FAI See *Fiduciary accounting income.*

FET Federal estate tax.

Family pot trust See *Pot trust.*

Fee simple interest The greatest interest that a person can have over property, corresponding to the layperson's usual notion of full ownership.

Fiduciary A person in a position of trust and confidence. Examples include executor, trustee, attorney-in-fact, and custodian.

Fiduciary accounting income (FAI) In the income taxation of estates and trusts, most sources of federal gross income, including cash dividends, interest, and rent (reduced by certain expenses) but not including stock dividends and capital gains.

Fiscal year An income tax year that ends on the last day of any month except December.

Flower bonds Certain issues of long-term U.S. Treasury bonds which, if owned by the decedent at death, can be used at par value to pay the federal estate tax.

Freezing the tax value estate Using estate planning to effectively ensure that the value of certain property includable in the estate will not be significantly higher than its current value.

Future interest A beneficial interest in property in which the right to possess or enjoy the property is delayed, either by a specific period of time or until the happening of a future event.

General bequest A gift payable out of the general assets of the estate, but not one that specifies one or more particular items.

Generation-skipping transfer tax (GSTT) A federal tax on certain transfers to succeeding generations that would otherwise usually escape both the gift tax and the estate tax.

Gift   A lifetime or deathtime transfer for any amount that is less than full consideration.

Gift tax   A tax on a lifetime transfer of property for less than full consideration.

Grantor   The person who creates the trust and whose property usually ends up in it. Also called *creator, settlor,* or *trustor.*

Grantor retained income trust (GRIT)   A trust under which the client retains the right to income for a period of years. Distribution of corpus at the end of the period depends upon whether or not the client survived this period. If not, the corpus reverts to the client-grantor's estate. If the client did survive the period, the corpus passes to a younger-generation beneficiary.

Grantor trust   A living trust in which the trustor, also called the grantor, has retained sufficient interest in the trust to make the income received by the trust taxable to the grantor, not to the trust or its beneficiaries.

Grantor trust rules   The federal income tax rules concerning grantor trusts. They are located in Internal Revenue Code Sections 671–78.

Gross estate   An FET term indicating property owned by the decedent at death, property transferred by the decedent under which the decedent retained an interest or control, and certain amounts in connection with property transferred within three years of death.

Grossing up   Inclusion in the gross estate of gift taxes paid on any gifts made within three years of death.

GSTT   See *Generation-skipping transfer tax.*

Guardian   A court-appointed fiduciary responsible for the person or property of a minor or, in some cases, an incompetent adult, or both. In some states, a guardian is called a *committee.*

Heir   A beneficiary who will receive property that passes by intestacy.

Holder (of a power of appointment)   The person who has received the power of appointment, i.e., the one who has the right to appoint designated property to a permissible appointee. Also called the donee of the power.

Holding period   In income tax law, the length of time that property is held. It determines whether a gain is short term or long term. The current threshold is one year.

Holographic will   A will, recognized in many states, that is usually required to be written entirely in the hand of the testator. It need not be witnessed.

Incidents of ownership   Powers and interests over an insurance policy on decedent's life that would subject the policy to inclusion in the decedent's gross estate under Section 2042.

Income beneficiary   The beneficiary of a trust who has a life estate or estate for years in the trust income.

Income shifting   See *Shifting income.*

Income tax   A tax levied on income earned by a taxpayer during a given year.

Incomplete gift   A gift that is not complete, i.e., either not involving a total transfer of all interests in the asset transferred, or subject to a contingency.

Inheritance tax   A state tax on the right of a beneficiary to receive property from a decedent.

Installment sale   The sale of an asset in exchange for an installment note, in which the buyer agrees to make periodic payments of principal and interest, based on a fair market rate of interest.

Intangible personal property   Personal property that is not in itself valuable, but derives its value from that which it represents.

Inter vivos transfer   A transfer made while the transferor is alive.

Inter vivos trust   A trust taking effect during the life of the trustor. Also called a *living trust*.

Interest by the entirety   An interest in property similar to a joint interest; however, it can be created only between husband and wife. And unlike joint tenancy, neither spouse may transfer the property without the consent of the other.

Interest for years   An interest in property giving the transferee the right to possess it for a fixed period.

Interest-free loan   A demand loan, having no interest charge, usually to a family member in a lower income tax bracket. TRA 86 virtually destroyed its use.

Interest in common   An interest in property held by two or more persons, each having an equal undivided right to possess property. Unlike a joint interest, however, an interest in common may be owned in unequal percentages, and when one owner dies the remaining owners do not automatically succeed in ownership. Instead, the decedent's interest passes through his or her estate, by will, by some other document, or by the laws of intestate distribution.

Intestate   Having died leaving probate property not disposed of by a valid will.

Instrument   Any legal document.

Inventory and appraisement   A probate document that delineates all probate assets at their fair market value.

Issue   A person's direct descendants, or offspring, including children, grandchildren, great-grandchildren, and the like. Also called *descendants*. Contrast with *Collaterals*.

Itemized deductions   In federal income tax law, deductions from adjusted gross income that are specifically listed, and taken in lieu of the standard deduction.

Joint interest   A form of equal, undivided ownership in property that, upon death of one owner, automatically passes to the surviving owner(s). Also called *joint tenancy*.

Joint tenancy   See *Joint interest*.

Kiddie tax   In federal income tax law, the taxation of the unearned income of a minor child at the parent's marginal income tax rate.

Lapse or Lapsation   The result when a beneficiary named in a will fails to survive the testator. Also, a power of appointment is said to *lapse* if the holder does not exercise it within the permitted period.

Leasehold   An interest in property entitling the lessee to possess and use the property for a specified time, usually in exchange for a fixed series of payments.

Legacy A gift, by will, of personal property. Also called a *bequest*.

Legatee A beneficiary, under a will, of a gift of personal property.

Letters testamentary A document in probate indicating the court's formal authorization of the person named to be personal representative for the estate.

Life estate An interest in property that ceases upon someone's death.

Life insurance policy A contract in which the insurance company agrees to pay a cash lump-sum amount (the face value or policy proceeds) to the person named in the policy to receive it (the beneficiary) upon the death of the subject of the insurance (the insured).

Living trust A trust taking effect during the life of the trustor. Also called an *inter vivos trust*.

Living will A document detailing those health care interventions that a person does or does not want to be subjected to in situations when he or she is no longer capable of making those decisions.

Marital deduction In federal gift and estate taxation, the deduction for certain transfers to a spouse.

Marital trust A trust designed to contain property qualifying for the marital deduction.

Net estate The net worth of a person; i.e., total assets minus total liabilities.

Omitted child See *Omitted heir*.

Omitted heir Any spouse, child, or issue of any deceased child who was not provided for in the decedent's will.

Omitted spouse See *Omitted heir*.

Opportunity shifting The transfer of a rapidly appreciating wealth- or an income-producing opportunity to a family member before it is objectively ascertainable.

Outright transfer A transfer in which the transferee receives both legal interests and all beneficial interests, subject to no restrictions or conditions.

Partnership capital freeze Like a recapitalization, the reorganization of a partnership for the purpose of freezing the FET value of the client's partnership interest. Severely restricted by the Revenue Act of 1987.

Permissible appointee (of a power of appointment) A party whom the holder may appoint by exercising the power of appointment.

Per capita A scheme of distribution from a will or trust requiring that issue of a decedent of all degrees share equally.

Per stirpes A scheme of distribution from a will or trust requiring that certain issue of a decedent, as a group, inherit the share of an estate that their immediate ancestor would have inherited if he or she had been living.

Perpetuities saving clause A clause in a will or trust that prevents interests from being ruled invalid under the rule against perpetuities.

Personal exemption In federal income tax law, amounts deductible on behalf of the taxpayer, the spouse, and each dependent, in calculating taxable income.

Personal property All property except fee simple and life estates in land and its improvements.

Personal representative   The person appointed by the probate court to represent and manage the estate.

Pickup tax   A state death tax set at least equal to the federal credit for state death taxes.

Pooled income fund   An investment fund created and maintained by the target charity, which "pools" property from many similar contributors. This arrangement ordinarily provides that the charity will pay to the grantor an income for life and, if desired, for the life of the grantor's spouse, based on the rate of return actually earned by the fund as a whole. At their death, the property passes to the charity.

Pot trust   A trust established for the benefit of minor children which typically remains undivided until the youngest child reaches age 21. At that time, the assets are divided into equal separate shares, one for each child. The assets are distributed outright, or they are held for distribution at some older age. Also called a *Family pot trust*.

Pour-over will   A will that distributes, at the testator's death, probate assets to a trust that had been created during the testator's lifetime.

Power of appointment   A power to name someone to receive a beneficial interest in property.

Power of appointment trust   A marital trust that gives to the surviving spouse the right to receive all income from the property for life, payable at least annually. It also gives him or her a general power of appointment over the principal, exercisable alone and in all events, at death or during life.

Power of attorney   A document executed by one person, called the principal, authorizing another person, called the attorney-in-fact, to perform designated acts on behalf of the principal.

Present interest   An immediate right to possess or enjoy property.

Principal   The property in a trust. Also called *corpus*.

Private annuity   A transfer of property under which the seller receives an unsecured promise of a life annuity.

Probate   A legal process that focuses on the will and the probate estate, that is, property which will be disposed of by, and only by, either the will or by the state laws of intestate succession. It is the entire process of administration of a decedent's estate.

Probate estate   All of the decedent's property passing to others by means of the probate process. This includes all property owned by the decedent except joint tenancy interests. In addition, the probate estate does not include property transferred by the decedent before death to a trustee, life insurance proceeds on the decedent's life, and the decedent's interest in pension and profit sharing plans.

QTIP election   An election by the executor of the estate of the first spouse to die to treat certain property as QTIP property, thereby qualifying it for the marital deduction.

QTIP trust   A marital trust which provides that the surviving spouse is entitled to all of the income from the trust property, payable at least annually. In addition, the trust cannot give anyone a power to appoint any of the property to anyone other than the surviving spouse.

Real property   Fee simple or life estate interests in land and any improvements.

Recapitalization   A reorganization of a closely held corporation for the purpose of freezing the value of the client's interest in the firm. Severely restricted by enactment of new §2036(c) under the Revenue Act of 1987.

Remainder   A type of future interest held by someone other than the transferor; it will become a present interest when all other interests created at the same time have ended.

Remainderman   The beneficiary of a trust who will receive the remainder at the termination of all other interests.

Residuary bequest   A gift of that part of the testator's estate not otherwise disposed of by the will.

Reversion   A future interest in property that is retained by the transferor; it will become a present interest when all other interests created at the same time have ended.

Rule against perpetuities   A common law principle invalidating a dispositive clause in a will or a trust if the contingent interest transferred may vest in the transferee too long after the client's death.

S1   The author's nomenclature for the first spouse to die.

S2   The author's nomenclature for the second spouse to die.

Sale   A transfer of property under which the transferor receives an amount of consideration that is regarded equivalent to the value of the property transferred.

Self-canceling installment note (SCIN)   An installment note which provides that no further payments will be made after the seller's death.

Self-proved will   A will containing a formal affidavit by witnesses stating that all formalities have been complied with. It eliminates the need for the witnesses to later testify in probate.

Separate property   In community property states, all property that is not community property. That is, all property acquired by a person not during marriage, and all property acquired during a marriage by gift, devise, bequest or inheritance, or, in most community property states, income earned on property so acquired.

Settlor   The person who creates the trust and whose property usually winds up in it. Also called *creator, grantor,* or *trustor.*

Shifting income   In estate planning, saving income tax by enabling income otherwise taxable to the client to be taxable to a family member in a lower tax bracket.

Short-term trust   An irrevocable trust that reverts to the grantor sometime after 10 years. TRA 86, in subjecting this trust to the grantor trust rules, virtually destroyed its further use.

Simple will   A will prepared for a family having a small estate, one for whom death tax planning is not a significant concern.

Skip person   In federal generation-skipping transfer tax law, a beneficiary who is at least two generations younger than the transferor.

Soakup tax   See *Pickup tax.*

Special use valuation   A provision in federal estate tax law (Section 2032A) that permits qualifying estates to value farm or other trade or business property at its present "qualified-use value" rather than at its "highest and best use" value.

Specific bequest   A gift of a particular item of property which is capable of being identified and distinguished from all other property. Contrasted with *general bequest* and *residuary bequest.*

Spendthrift clause   A clause in a trust that restricts the beneficiary from transferring any of his or her future interest in the corpus or income. For example, a typical spendthrift clause would not permit the beneficiary to pledge the interest as collateral against a loan.

Splitting a gift   Treating a gift of the property owned by one spouse, on the federal gift tax return, as if it were made one half by each spouse.

Sponge tax   See *Pickup tax.*

Spousal remainder trust   An irrevocable trust providing for income for a period to a lower-income tax bracket family member, then remainder to the trustor's spouse. Future use of this trust was virtually destroyed by TRA 86, which subjected it to the grantor trust rules.

Springing durable power of attorney   A durable power of attorney that becomes effective at the onset of the principal's incapacity.

Standard deduction   In federal income tax law, a fixed amount that may be deducted from adjusted gross income. It may be used instead of specifically subtracting actual "itemized" deductions.

Statutory will   A will whose format is entirely specified by statute.

Step-up in basis   In income tax law, the upward adjustment in basis resulting from the acquisition of property from a decedent.

Surrogate decision makers   Individuals capable of making decisions regarding a client's property and family at times when the client is unable, either due to incapacity or death. Examples include attorney-in-fact, trustee, and executor.

Survival clause   A disposition provision in a will or trust naming an alternate taker of certain property if the donee fails to survive the donor.

Takers in default   Persons who receive property subject to a power of appointment if the holder permits the power to lapse.

Tangible personal property   Personal property which has value of its own.

Taxable estate   In federal estate tax law, the gross estate reduced by total deductions.

Taxable distribution   In federal generation-skipping transfer tax law, any distribution of property out of a trust to a skip person (other than a taxable termination or a direct skip).

Taxable gift   In federal gift tax law, for a given year, total gross gifts reduced by total deductions and exclusions.

Taxable termination   In federal generation-skipping transfer tax law, a termination of a nonskip person's interest in income or principal of a trust, with the result that skip persons become the only remaining trust beneficiaries.

Tax clause   A provision in a will specifying which property bears the burden of paying taxes.

Terminable interest   An interest which will terminate or fail on the lapse of time, on the occurrence of an event or contingency, or on the failure of an event or contingency to occur. Property otherwise qualifying for the marital deduction will not qualify if the interest passing to the spouse is terminable.

Terminal value   Used in this text to indicate the value of a cash value life insurance policy that is currently in force. Formally called the policy's interpolated terminal reserve value, its amount is nearly equal to its cash surrender value.

Term life insurance   A type of life insurance policy that has no value prior to the death of the insured because the premium charged, which increases over time with increasing risk of death, simply buys pure protection: if the insured dies during the policy term, the company will pay the face value; otherwise, it will pay nothing.

Testamentary capacity   The mental ability required of a testator to validly execute a will.

Testamentary transfer   A transfer at death by will.

Testamentary trust   A trust established by a trust-will into which probate property is transferred at the testator's death.

Testate   Dying with a valid will.

Testator   The person who executes a will.

Throwback rules   In the income taxation of trusts, rules that subject income accumulated by a trust in one year and distributed to a beneficiary in another year to possible additional taxation to that beneficiary.

TRA 86   Tax Reform Act of 1986.

Transfer   Any type of passing of property in which the transferor gives up some kind of interest to the transferee. Also called an *assignment*.

Trust   A legal arrangement that divides legal and beneficial interest in property among two or more people.

Trust beneficiary   A person who is named to enjoy a beneficial interest in the trust.

Trust-will   A will disposing of some or all of the testator's probate property to a trust, the terms of which are described in the document. The trust usually takes effect at the testator's death.

Trustor   The person who creates the trust and whose property usually winds up in it. Also called *Creator, Grantor, Settlor*.

Undue influence   Influence of another which has the effect of impeding the testator's free will. A will can be denied probate if it can be established that the testator, at execution, was subject to undue influence.

Unification of gift and estate taxes   The efforts by Congress to tax lifetime and deathtime transfers equally, so that an individual would be indifferent, from a total transfer tax planning point of view, between making lifetime and deathtime gifts.

Unified credit   Presently $192,800, a reduction in the tentative gift tax and tentative estate tax.

Uniform Gifts to Minors Act Like the Uniform Transfers to Minors Act, a statute in many states permitting custodial gifts for the benefit of a minor.

Uniform Probate Code (UPC) A set of probate laws originally promulgated by legal scholars and practitioners and currently adopted in whole or in part by about two fifths of the states.

Uniform Simultaneous Death Act (USDA) A statute providing that when transfer of title to property depends on the order of deaths, and that when no sufficient evidence exists that two people died other than simultaneously, the property of each is disposed of as if each had survived the other.

Uniform Transfers to Minors Act See *Uniform Gifts to Minors Act.*

Vested interest A nonforfeitable future interest whose possession and enjoyment are delayed only by time and not dependent on the happening of any future event.

Wait-and-see statute A provision in some state statutes that can overcome the effect of the rule against perpetuities by finding an interest void only if its turns out, in fact, not to vest within the required period.

Will A written document disposing of a person's probate property at death.

Witnessed will A written will, recognized in all states, that must be signed by two or more witnesses who acknowledge, among other things, that the testator asked them to witness the will, that they in fact did witness the testator's signing, and that the testator is mentally competent to execute a will (in accordance with state law).

Index

Acquiring client facts and objectives, 5–7
Adjusted basis, calculation, 244–50
Adjusted taxable gifts, 131, 137–38, 186, 203, 289
Administration; *see* Probate
Administrator, defined, 26
Adopted child, 108
Advice of proposed action, 117
Affidavit of right, 127–28
Affinity, degrees of; *see* Consanguinity, degrees of
Afterborn child, 108
Allocation of death taxes, 481–83
Alternate valuation date, 532
Alternatives to probate; *see* Probate
Amount realized, 244
Ancillary administration, 299, 309
Annual exclusion, 134, 220–22, 358–60
generation-skipping transfer tax, 229
gift tax, 134, 220–21
Annually renewable term insurance, 425
Annuities, survivorship, estate taxation, 189–91
Antilapse statute, 483
Appointee of power of appointment, defined, 38
Apportionment statute, 481
Ascertainable standard; *see* Power of appointment
Assignment, defined, 24
Assignment of income doctrine, 280, 421
Attorney-in-fact, 493
Avoiding probate; *see* Probate

Bargain sale, 24, 388–89
Basic concepts, survey of; *see* Estate planning, basic concepts
Basis
property acquired by death, 248–50
property acquired by gift, 248–48
Basis problem of joint tenancy, 304
Beneficial interest, defined, 24, 37
Beneficiary, defined, 25
Bequest, defined, 26
Bond, probate, 114
Business buyout agreement, 457–62

Buyout agreement (business), 457–62
Bypass planning; *see* Marital deduction and bypass planning
Bypass trust, 326–29

Calendar year, 522, 527
California statutory wills, 83–95
Capacity, testamentary, 51–52
Care of client's minor children; *see* Miscellaneous lifetime planning
Case study in marital deduction and bypass planning, 344–50
Cash surrender value, 28, 425
Cash value life insurance, 27, 425–27
Character of gain or loss, income tax, 250
Charitable lead trust, 403–4
Charitable remainder annuity trust, 402
Charitable remainder unitrust, 402
Charitable transfers; *see* Lifetime transfers
Chose in action, defined, 32
Clifford trust, 415–18
Closely held business, general planning for, 449–62
business buyout agreement, 457–62
determining the selling price, 458–59
funding, 459–60
income tax effects, 461–62
corporate recapitalization, 468–72
liquidity planning, 440–44
section 303 redemption, 442–43
section 2032A special use valuation, 443–44
section 6166: FET in installments, 440–41
minimizing decline in value from withdrawal from firm, 451–52
need for early planning, 457
objectives, 449–50
partnership capital freeze, 472
transferring the business interest, 452–56
to family member, 452–54
lifetime strategies, 452–53
transfer devices at death, 453–54
sale to a third party, 454–56
form of the transaction, 456

Closely held business, general planning for, corporate recapitalization, transferring the business interest, sale to a third party—*Cont.*
  taxable gain, 455
  timing, 454–55
Codicil, 56
Collateral, 100
Common law states, 35
Community property, defined, 34
Community property with right of survivorship, 250
Completed intrafamily transfers for consideration, 388–96
Complex trusts and estates, income taxation, 258–60
Concurrent ownership, defined, 32
Conduit, 252, 257, 523
Consanguinity, degrees of, 100–101
Conservatorship, 491
  trust as alternative to, 309–10
Consideration
  completed intrafamily transfers for, 388–96
  defined, 24
Consideration furnished test, 192
Contingent remainder, defined, 40
Contract, property disposal by, 49
Corporate income tax, 260–62
Corporate recapitalization, 468–72
Corpus; *see* Principal
Creator; *see* Trustor
Credit, defined, 133
Credit, tax; *see* Estate tax, federal; Gift tax, federal; *and* Income tax
Creditors
  claim, 116
  period, 116
  probate protection from, 296–97
Credits
  estate tax, 208–11
  income tax, 242–43
Credit shelter bypass plan; *see* Marital deduction and bypass planning
Cross-purchase agreement, 459
Crummey provision, 379
Cumulative gift doctrine, 135, 289
Curtesy interest, 110, 189
Custodial gifts, 376–77, 478–79
Cy pres, 80

Death tax, defined, 28
Decedent, defined, 25
Decision to avoid probate, 294–316, *see also* Probate
Deductible gifts, 219
Deductions
  defined, 153
  estate tax, 205–8
  gift tax, 219
  income tax, 236–38
Deferral, 330
Deferred compensation, 451
Deferring recognition of income, 282
Degrees of consanguinity; *see* Consanguinity, degrees of

Descent and distribution laws, 59
Developing an estate plan, 5–9
  acquiring client facts and objectives, 5
  following up, 8–9
  implementing the plan, 8
  reviewing the facts and preparing the plan, 7–8
Devise, defined, 26
Devisee, defined, 26
Directive to physicians, 501, 519
Direct skip, 227
Disclaimer
  gift tax, 225–26
  planning, 338–40, 532–35
Discretionary bypass trust, 329
Discretionary spendthrift trust, 498–99
Discretionary support trust, 491
Distributable net income, 256
Distribution deduction, 257
Distribution planning, 529–31
Donee, 25
Donor, 25
Dower interest, 110, 189
Durable power of attorney for health care, 500, 508–15
Durable power of attorney for property, 492–99

Employee benefits, as liquidity source, 444
Employee stock ownership plan, 206
Entity agreement, 459
Equalization, 330–33
Escheat, 106
Estate, defined, 23
Estate planning, basic concepts, 23–41
  beneficiaries, 25
  estates, 23–24
  life insurance, 27–28
  property interests, 29–41
    basic interests in property, 29–31
    classification by physical characteristics, 31–32
    concurrent ownership, 32–37
    legal versus beneficial interests, 37–38
    power of appointment, 38
    present versus future and vested versus contingent, 39–41
  taxation, 28–29
  wills, trusts and probate, 25–27
Estate planning, defined, 3
Estate planning team, 9–11
  accountant, 10
  attorney, 9
  financial planner, 11
  life underwriter, 10
  trust officer, 10
Estate tax, federal
  comprehensive outline, 186
  credits, 208–11
    foreign death taxes, 211
    gift taxes, 209–10
    state death taxes, 208–9
    tax on prior transfers, 210–11
  deductions, 205–8
  defined, 28
  Form 706, 149–84

Estate tax, federal—*Cont.*
　gross estate components, 186–205
　interests owned at death, 187–96
　　section 2033: property owned by
　　　decedent, 187–89
　　section 2034: dower and curtesy
　　　interests, 189
　　section 2039: survivorship annuities,
　　　189–91
　　section 2040: joint interests, 191–93
　　section 2041: powers of appointment, 193–
　　　94
　　section 2042: insurance on decedent's life,
　　　194–96
　part-sale, part-gift transfers, 204–5
　transfers with retained interest or control,
　　　196–201
　　section 2036: transfers with retained life
　　　estate, 197–99
　　section 2037: transfers taking effect at
　　　death, 199–200
　　section 2038: revocable transfers, 200–201
　transfers within three years of death (section
　　　2035), 201–4
　　gift tax in gross estate: "grossing up," 203–
　　　4
　relinquishment of certain interests,
Estate trust, 432
Execute, 8, 202–3
Executor
　clause in simple will, 54, 57–58
　clause in trust-will, 69
　defined, 26
　powers of, 55, 59, 72, 481
　selection, 479–81
　waive commission, 526–27
Exemption equivalent of unified credit, 133
Exemptions, personal income tax, 238
Exercise a power of appointment, 38
Expense elections by executor; *see* Postmortem
　　　tax planning

Family estate trust, 420–21
Family pot trust; *see* Pot trust
Federal estate tax; *see* Estate tax, federal
Federal gift tax; *see* Gift tax
Federal unified wealth transfer taxation; *see*
　　　Estate tax, federal; Gift tax,
　　　federal; *and* Transfer taxation
Fee simple, defined, 29
Fiduciary, 26
Fiduciary accounting income, 256
Fiscal year, 522, 528
"5 and 5 power," 194, 328
Flower bonds, 437–39
Following up with an estate plan, 8–9
Formal UPC administration, 121
Format requirements for wills, 52–53
Formula marital deduction clause, 325
Fractional share distribution, 327
Freezing the estate tax value, 282–85
Freezing wealth with corporate recapitalization
　　　and partnership capital freeze,
　　　467–72
Future interest, defined, 39

General bequest, defined, 27
Generation-skipping bypass planning, 352–53
Generation-skipping transfer tax, 226–30
　direct skip, 227–28
　exceptions to GSTT taxation, 229–30
　taxable distribution, 228–29
　taxable termination, 228
Gift, defined, 25
Gifting, 356–83; *see also* Lifetime transfers
Gift-leaseback, 396
Gift splitting, 221–22
Gift tax, federal, 217–26
　annual exclusion, 220–21
　deductible gifts, 219
　defined, 28
　disclaimers, 225–26
　Form 709, 145–48
　gift splitting, 221–22
　jointly held property, 224–25
　life insurance, 223–24
　marital deduction, 134, 219
　powers of appointment, 222–23
　requirements for a valid gift, 217–18
　types of taxable gifts, 218–19
Goals of estate planning, 273–91
　financial goals, 275–91
　　nontax, 275–78
　　　benefits for surviving spouse, 278
　　　business value, 277
　　　nontax estate transfer costs, 276
　　　pre- and postmortem flexibility, 277–78
　　　proper disposition by careful drafting,
　　　　276
　　　satisfactory standard of living, 276
　　tax saving, 278–91
　　　income tax, 279–82
　　　　deferred income recognition, 282
　　　　shifting income to lower-bracket
　　　　　taxpaper, 279–81
　　　　stepped-up basis, 279
　　　transfer tax, 282–91
　　　　delaying payment, 285–86
　　　　freezing the taxable estate, 282–85
　　　　reducing the taxable estate, 282
　nonfinancial goals, 274–75
　　care of future dependents, 274
　　maintaining control over assets, 275
　　privacy, 274
　　speed, 275
Grantor; *see* Trustor
Grantor lead trust; *see* Grantor retained income
　　　trust
Grantor retained income trust, 397–98
Grantor trust, income taxation, 254–56
Gross estate, 186
Grossing up, 204
Guardianship
　clause in simple will, 54, 57
　clause in trust-will, 69
　gifts, 375–76
　planning, 4, 476–77, 499

Hearing, probate, 115
Heir, defined, 26, 100
Highest and best use, 443

Holder of power of appointment, defined, 38
Holding period, 245
Holographic will, 52–53

Implementing an estate plan, 8
Incapacity, client; *see* Miscellaneous lifetime planning
Incidents of ownership, 195
Income, of a trust (FAI), 60–61, 256
Income beneficiary, defined, 41, 61
Income shifting, 302, 369
Income splitting, 368, 527
Income tax
  corporations, 260–62
    tax rates, 261
  defined, 28
  estates and trusts, 252–60
    complex trusts and estates, 258–60
    distributable net income, 256
    distribution deduction, 257
    fiduciary accounting income, 256
    grantor trusts, 254–56
    simple trusts, 256–57
    throwback rules, 260
  individuals, 253–52
    credits, 242
    deductions, 236–38
      deductions from gross income, 236
      itemized deductions, 237
      personal exemptions, 238
      standard deduction, 237
      taxable income, 239
    general scheme, 235–36
    gross income, 236
    kiddie tax, 243–44
    sale or exchange of property, 244–52
      gain and loss, 244–45
        adjusted basis, 245
        amount realized, 244
        character of gain or loss, 250–52
        holding period, 245–46
        property acquired by death, 248–50
        property acquired by gift, 246–48
        realized versus recognized, 245–46
        summary example, 243
        taxable income, 239–42
Independent Administration of Estates Act, 113, 117
Informal U.P.C. administration, 120–21
Inherit, 100
Inheritance tax, defined, 28
Installment sale, 389–92, 461, 472
Instrument, defined, 25
Insured
  defined, 27
  selecting, 430–31
Intangible personal property, defined, 31
Interest by the entirety, defined, 33–4
Interest for years, defined, 29
Interest-free loan, 411–15
Interest in common, defined, 33
Inter vivos, defined, 25, 37, 60
Intestate, defined, 26
Intestate succession, state laws, 100–108
  non–UPC states, 107–8

Intestate succession—*Cont.*
  UPC states, 103–7
Inventory and Appraisement, 116
Irrevocable trust
  gifts into, 377–81
  life insurance trust, 434–37
Issue, defined, 26, 71
Itemized deductions, 237

Jointly-held property, joint interest
  alternative to probate, 300–6, 315
  contrasted with community property, 36–37
  defined, 32
  estate taxation, 191–93
  gift taxation, 224–25
  transfer at death, 48
Joint purchase of a life estate and remainder interest, 395–96
Joint return, 522
Joint tenancy; *see* Jointly-held property

Kiddie tax, 244, 279

Lapsation of a bequest, 483–85
Lapsation of a power of appointment, 38
Large estate, 50
Laughing heirs, 106
Leasehold, 31
Legacy, defined, 26
Legal interest, defined, 24, 37
Legatee, defined, 26
Letters testamentary, 113
Life estate, defined, 30
Life in being, 78
Life insurance
  defined, 27
  estate taxation, 194–96
  gift taxation, 223–24
  planning; *see* Liquidity planning, life insurance
Lifetime exclusion
  generation-skipping transfer tax, 229
  gift tax, 134, 220
Lifetime transfers, 357–81, 387–404
  charitable transfers, 398–404
    gifts of split interests, 401–4
      donating income interests: charitable lead trust, 403–4
      donating remainder interests, 402–3
        charitable remainder annuity trust, 402
        charitable remainder unitrust, 402
        pooled income fund, 403
    tax consequences, 399–401
      estate tax, 401
      gift tax, 400
      income tax, 399–400
        amount deductible for a particular gift, 399–400
        limitations on deductible, 399
  completed intrafamily transfers for consideration, 388–96
    bargain sale, 388–89
    installment sale, 389–92
      self-cancelling provision, 391
    ordinary sale, 388

Lifetime transfers, completed intrafamily
transfers for consideration—*Cont.*
private annuity, 392–94
sale of a remainder interest and joint
purchase, 394–96
defective incomplete transfers, 410–21
family estate trust, 420–21
interest-free loan, 411–15
estate tax consequences, 415
gift tax consequences, 411–13
income tax consequences, 413–14
short-term trust, 415–18
estate tax consequences to grantor, 417–
18
gift tax consequences, 416
income tax consequences, 417–18
spousal remainder trust, 418–20
gifting, 356–83
opportunity shifting, 267
to minor children, 374–81
custodial gifts, 376–77
under guardianship, 375–76
via irrevocable trust, 377–81
annual exclusion, 378–80
Crummey provision, 379
2503b provision, 379–80
estate tax caution, 380
income tax concern, 381
2503c provision, 378–79
to spouse, 371–74
save death taxes, 371–73
control relinquished, 373
FET saving unlikely, 373
save income taxes, 373–74
tax considerations, 358–65
advantages, 358–63
death tax, 358–62
annual exclusion shelter, 358–60
comprehensive example, 360–62
no grossing up, 360
postgift appreciation, 360–62
income tax, 362–63
disadvantages, 363–65
gift later ruled incomplete, 365
loss of step-up in basis, 365
prepaying the transfer tax, 363–64
§2035 consequence, 364
types of assets to give, 365–70
administration problems, 368–69
basis considerations, 366–67
other considerations, 369–70
postgift appreciation, 367–68
incomplete intrafamily transfers, 396–98
gift leaseback, 396
grantor retained income trust, 397–98
Lineal line of descent, 100
Liquidity planning, 422–44
cash needs at death, 422
devices unique to business owners, 439–44
sale of the business, 440
section 303 redemption, 442–43
section 2032A: special use valuation, 443–
44
section 6166: FET in installments, 440–41
flower bonds, 437–39

Liquidity planning—*Cont.*
life insurance, 424–37
planning, 430–37
selecting insured, 430–31
selecting owner and beneficiary, 432–37
child, 434
irrevocable trust, 434–37
revocable trust, 434
spouse, 432–33
taxation, 428–30
estate taxation, 430
gift taxation, 429
income taxation, 428–29
of cash value accumulation, 428
of policy proceeds, 428–29
types of, 424–27
cash value insurance, 425–27
endowment, 427
universal life, 427
whole life, 426
term insurance, 424–25
other liquidity sources, 444
employee benefits, 444
postmortem techniques, 444, 532–38
alternate valuation date, 532
disclaimers, 532–35
QTIP election, 535–38
sale of assets during lifetime, 423–24
summary of cash needs, 422
Living trust, 37, 60–68, 306–16, 349–51, 491–92,
497; *see also* Probate,
alternatives to
Living will, 501, 517

Marital deduction, 134, 206–8
Marital deduction and bypass planning, 320–35,
338–53
bypass with estate equalization, 329–35
factors influencing deferral versus
equalization, 331–35
avoidance of tax while spouse alive, 332
other factors, 334–35
time value of money, 332–33
asset appreciation, 332
opportunity income loss, 332
bypass with nonimmediate family members,
350–53
case study, 344–50
credit shelter bypass, 325–29
bypass trust, 326–29
debts and expenses, 350
discretionary bypass trust, 329
marital trust, 341–44
power of appointment trust, 342
QTIP trust, 343
numerical illustration of asset appreciation,
333–34
100 percent marital deduction, 322–25
advantages, 322
disadvantages, 322–23
three impracticable alternatives, 323–25
consumption, 324–25
lifetime gifts, 325
remarriage, 323–24

Marital deduction and bypass planning—*Cont.*
100 percent marital deduction with disclaimer
into bypass, 338–40
disadvantages, 339–40
revocable trust estate plan (diagram), 351
software, 340–41
Marital trusts, 341–44
estate trust, 342
power of appointment trust, 342
QTIP trust, 343
Measuring life, defined, 30
Medium estate, 50
Minors
trusts, 377–81
Uniform Gift To Minors Act, 376–77
Miscellaneous lifetime planning, 474–501
client incapacity, 490–501
care of incapacitated client, 499–501
durable power of attorney for health
care, 500
living will, 501
care of incapacitated client's property, 491–
99
conservatorship, 491, 499
durable power of attorney for property,
492–99
guardianship, 491
trust, 491–92
will and trust planning, 474–90
allocation of death taxes, 481–83
care of client's minor children, 475–79
financial care, 477–79
custodianship, 478–79
financial guardianship, 477–78
trust for the minor, 478
personal care: the parental guardian,
476–77
care of family members, introduction, 475
determination of age of outright
distribution from trust, 486–88
executor, 479–81
powers of, 481
selection, 479–80
perpetuities savings clause, 489
restrictions against assignment, 488–89
survival clauses, 483–85
trustee powers, 489–90
trustee selection, 485–86

Nonforfeiture laws, 426
Notice of Death and of Petition to Administer
Estate, 114

Obligation of support, 375
Omitted child, 108
Omitted spouse, 109
One hundred percent marital deduction; *see*
Marital deduction and bypass
planning
Opportunity shifting, 368
Order for Probate, 115
Ordinary sale, 388
Organization of the book, 11–13
Outright transfer, defined, 24

Parental guardian, 376–77
Partial intestacy, 109
Partnership capital freeze, 472
Part-sale, part-gift transfers, 204–5
Pay on death bank account, 300
Pecuniary distribution, 327
Per capita, 101–3
Perfect unification, 286
Permissible appointee, defined, 38
Perpetuities savings clause, 65, 68, 71, 78, 80,
489
Personal exemptions, 238
Personal property, defined, 31
Personal representative, 26
Per stirpes, 101–3
Petition for Final Distribution, 118
Petition for Preliminary Distribution, 118
Petition for probate, 113
Pickup tax, 28, 208–9
Pooled income fund, 403
Postmortem tax planning, 520–38
devices to save estate taxes, 531–38
alternate valuation date, 532
disclaimers, 532–35
to correct defective documents, 534–35
to increase marital deduction, 533–34
to reduce marital deduction, 533
QTIP election, 535–38
partial election, 537
devices to save income taxes, 523–31
distribution planning, 529–31
expense elections by executor, 524–27
administration expenses and losses, 525–
26
medical expenses, 524–25
to waive executor's commission, 526–27
selection of estate taxable year, 527–29
other devices, 440–44, 538
section 303 redemption, 442–43
section 2032A: special use valuation, 443–
44
section 6166: FET in installments, 440–41
tax returns filed after death, 520–22
Pot trust, 487–88
Pour-over will, 307
Power of appointment
adverse power, 193
ascertainable standard, 193
defined, 38
estate taxation, 193–94
"5 and 5 power," 193
gift taxation, 222–23
Power of appointment trust, 342
Power of attorney, 493
Powers of executor, 72
Powers of trustee, 65, 68, 72–73
Present interest
defined, 39
requirement for gift tax annual exclusion,
220–21, 378–81
Present value of costs of probate, 312–14
Principal (of trust), 37, 60
Principal beneficiary, 61
Prior transfers credit; *see* Estate tax
Privacy (living trust), 308

Private annuity, 392–94
Probate
  administration, 111–22
    substantial formal supervision, 112–22
    summary probate in California, 127–28
    UPC states, 119 22
  alternatives to, 300–16
    joint tenancy, 300–6
      advantages, 301–3
        clear, undisputed disposition, 301–2
        convenience and privacy, 301
        income shifting, 302–3
        low administrative cost, 301
        reduced creditor's claims, 302
      disadvantages, 303–6
        basis problem, 304–5
        gift taxation, 305
        inflexible disposition, 303
        possible higher estate tax, 305
        surrender of ownership and control,
          304
    living trust, 306–12
      advantages, 307–10
        alternative to conservatorship, 309–10
        greater privacy, 308
        lower cost than probate, 307–8
        minimize litigation, 310
        opportunity to test the future, 309
        speed, 308–9
      disadvantages, 310–12
        funding burden, 310–11
        greater legal uncertainty, 311
        tax factors, 311–12
  ancillary administration, 299
  benefits, 295–98
    court supervision promotes fairness, 295–
      96
    income tax savings, 297–98
    greater protection from creditors, 296–97
    orderly administration of assets, 296
  decision to avoid probate, 294–316
    present value of costs, 312–14
    probate versus living trust, 312–14
    which alternative is best, 314–16
  defined, 26, 111, 294
  drawbacks, 298–300
    complexity, 298
    cost, 298–99
    danger of unintended disposition, 300
    delay, 300
    lack of privacy, 299
Probate estate, defined, 23
Prolonging estate life unduly, 531
Proof of subscribing witnesses, 114
Property, defined, 23
Property interests, 29–41
Property transfer documents, 47–73
  contracts, 49
    life insurance, 49
    pension and profit sharing plans, 49
  joint tenancy arrangements, 48
  trust, 59–73
    living trust, 61–68
      example, 62–66
    trust-will, 68–73

Property transfer documents, trust, trust-will—
    Cont.
    example, 69–73
  will, 50–61
    holographic will, 52–53
    simple will, 53–59
      example, 54–56
    who may execute a will, 50–52
    witnessed will, 52
Property transfer process, 96–122
  consanguinity, degrees of, 100–101
  intestate succession, state laws, 100–108
  legal rights of omitted and adopted children,
    108–9
  legal rights of omitted, divorced, and
      disinherited spouses, 109–11
  per stirpes versus per capita, 101–3
  probate administration, 111–22
    substantial (non-UPC) formal supervision,
      112–19
    summary probate in California, 127–28
    UPC states, 119–22

Qualified pension plan, estate taxation, 190
Qualified use valuation, 443–44
Quantitative comparison of costs of probate
    versus living trust, 312–14
Quasi-community property, 34
Questionnaire, sample client fact finding, 15–22
QTIP property, 207
QTIP election, 343, 535–38
QTIP trust, 343

Real property, defined, 31
Recap, 468–72
Reciprocal trusts doctrine, 199
Redemption agreement, 459
Redemption of decedent's stock, 442–43
Reducing the estate tax value, 282
Remainder, defined, 39
Remainderman, defined, 41
Requirements for a valid gift, 217–18
Residuary bequest, defined, 27
Residue, defined, 27
Restrictions against assignment, 65, 67–68, 71,
    358–59
Retained interests and controls; *see* Estate tax,
    federal
Retained life estate; *see* Estate tax, federal
Retirement Equity Act, 110
Revenue Act of 1987, 132, 197, 206, 375, 467–72
Reversion, defined, 39
Reviewing client facts and preparing a plan, 7
Revocable transfers; *see* Estate tax, federal
Revocable trust, 60
Revocable trust estate plan, 351
Right of election; *see* Spousal right of election
Right of representation; *see* Per stirpes
Rule against perpetuities, 77–81, 489

Sale
  defined, 24
  of a remainder interest, 394–96
Sale or exchange of property; *see* Income tax,
    individuals

Sample client fact-finding questionnaire, 15–22
S Corporation, 453, 456
Second death insurance, 431
Self-canceling installment note, 391
Self-proved will, 114
Separate property, defined, 34
Settlor; *see* Trustor
Shifting income to a lower-bracket taxpayer, 279–81
Short taxable year, 522, 527
Short-term trust, 415–18
Simple trust, income taxation, 256–57
Simple will, 53–59
Simultaneous death; *see* Uniform Simultaneous Death Act
Small estate, 53
Special use valuation, 443–44
Specific bequest, defined, 27
Spendthrift clause, 67–68, 71, 488–89
Split gift; *see* Gift tax
Split interest gifts to charity; *see* Lifetime transfers
Split purchase; *see* Joint purchase
Splitting income, 368, 527
Sponge tax; *see* Pickup tax
Spousal remainder trust; *see* Lifetime transfers
Spousal right of election, 110–11
Springing durable power of attorney, 497, 500
Standard deduction, 237–38
Standby trust, 497
State death tax, 349
Statement of witnesses, 56, 73
Statutory wills, California, 83–94
Step up in basis, 249, 279, 365
Subchapter S Corporation; *see* S Corporation
Summary probate in California, 127–28
Surrogate decision makers, 277, 348
Survival clause 58, 483–85
Survival period, 58, 483–85
Surviving spouse, legal rights, 109–11

Taker in default, 38
Tangible personal property, defined, 31
Taxable distribution, 228–29
Taxable estate, defined, 130
Taxable termination, 228
Tax clause, 482
Tax returns (federal)
  estate tax, 149–84
  gift tax, 145–48
  income tax, 267–69
Team, estate planning; *see* Estate planning team
Tentative tax, defined, 130
Terminal value, 195
Terminible interest rule, 206, 341–44
Term life insurance, 27, 424–25
Testamentary, 85
Testamentary capacity, 51–52
Testamentary trust, defined, 37
Testator, defined, 26
"Theoretical tax," 137
Three-year bringback rule, 201–3
Throwback rules, 260
Time value of money, 291, 312, 332
Totten trust, 201

TRA 76, 130, 204, 219
TRA 84, 132, 410, 414
TRA 86, 237, 239–40, 245, 260, 279, 370, 381, 389, 391, 400, 417, 419–20, 456, 460
Transfer, defined, 24
Transfer for value rule, 428–29
Transfer process; *see* Property transfer process
Transfer taxation; *see also* Estate tax, federal *and* Gift tax, federal
  estate tax; *see* Estate tax, federal
  gift tax; *see* Gift tax, federal
  introduction, 129–38
    annual exclusion, 134
    complete unified tax framework, 136–38
    cumulative gift doctrine, 135–36
    estate tax framework, 131
    gift tax framework, 130
    history, 129–30
    marital deduction, 134
    unified credit, 133
    unified rate schedule, 132
Trust; *see also* Living trust *and* Trust-will
  defined, 26
  in general, 59–61
Trust beneficiary, defined, 37
Trustee
  defined, 37
  powers, 65, 68, 72, 489–90
  selection, 485–86
Trustor, 37
Trust principal, defined, 37
Trust-will
  defined, 68
  example, 69–73

Undue influences, 1–2
Unduly prolonging estate life, 531
Unification, 286–91
  perfect unification, 286–88
  presently imperfectly unified system, 288–91
Unified credit, 133
Unified wealth transfer taxation; *see* Estate tax, federal; Gift tax, federal; *and* Transfer taxation
Uniform Gift to Minors Act, 376, 478–79
Uniform Probate Code
  intestate succession, 103–7
  probate administration, 119–22
Uniform Simultaneous Death Act, 58, 433
Uniform Statutory Rule Against Perpetuities, 80
Uniform Trustee Powers Act, 490
Universal life insurance, 427
Unlimited marital deduction; *see* Estate tax, federal *and* Gift tax, federal
Unused unified credit, 136, 142–44

Vested remainder, defined, 39

Wait and see statute, 80
Waiver of executor's commission, 526–27
Wealth transfer taxation; *see* Estate tax, federal; Gift tax, federal; *and* Transfer taxation

Will
  defined, 25
  holographic will, 52–53
  oral will, 50
  simple will, 53–59
    example, 54–56

Will—*Cont.*
  statutory format requirements, 52–53
  who may execute a will, 50–52
  witnessed will, 52
Witnesses, statement of, 56, 59, 73